European Legal History

EUROPEAN LEGAL HISTORY

Sources and Institutions

Third edition

OF Robinson, MA, PhD
Reader in Law, University of Glasgow

TD Fergus, MA, LLB, PhD
Senior Lecturer in Law, University of Glasgow

WM Gordon, MA, LLB, PhD, FRSE
Douglas Professor of Civil Law Emeritus, University of Glasgow

OXFORD
UNIVERSITY PRESS

OXFORD
UNIVERSITY PRESS

Great Clarendon Street, Oxford OX2 6DP

Oxford University Press is a department of the University of Oxford.
It furthers the University's objective of excellence in research, scholarship,
and education by publishing worldwide in

Oxford New York

Auckland   Cape Town Dar es Salaam   Hong Kong   Karachi
Kuala Lumpur Madrid Melbourne Mexico City   Nairobi
New Delhi Shanghai   Taipei   Toronto
With offices in
Argentina Austria Brazil Chile Czech Republic France Greece
Guatemala Hungary Italy Japan South Korea Poland Portugal
Singapore Switzerland Thailand Turkey Ukraine Vietnam

Oxford is a registered trade mark of Oxford University Press
in the UK and in certain other countries

Published in the United States
by Oxford University Press Inc., New York

ISBN 978-0-406-91360-9

Printed and bound in Great Britain by
CPI Antony Rowe, Chippenham and Eastbourne

PREFACE

Geographically, European legal history is primarily concerned with those countries of western Europe that share a common legal heritage, based on the mingling of Roman or civil and canon law – the learned law – with feudalism and customary law. It therefore excludes eastern Europe as defined by the one-time supremacy of Islamic rule or of the Orthodox rather than the Catholic Church, although there are of course elements common to east and west, such as the influence of Roman law. Again although, for example, Ireland and Scandinavia, Poland and Hungary, and in a different sense Spain, are part of western Christendom, these were not central areas of activity for the developments in legal thinking and legal practice which had such profound effects on most of the West, and so such countries are only lightly touched on. Nor did England share fully in these developments, but her close ties with France and with Scotland make the anomaly of her relative isolation worth investigating. Moreover, through her colonies overseas, England in many cases provided the image of Europe to other cultures. The focus, however, will be on the heart of Europe, the Italian peninsula, France and Germany (that is, the German-speaking lands of the Holy Roman Empire).

European legal history is more than the histories of the individual legal systems of the modern European states, although one could argue that the very existence of European legal history may be proved from these individual histories. Historical introductions to their own systems, whether written for Austrian or Spanish, French or German, or any other continental students, feature background chapters on Roman law and its reception and on the influence of the canon law, as well as on customary law and feudalism, before they describe the growth of a national system. Then, in their turn, Humanism, Natural Law and codification exercised a greater or lesser influence on the shape taken by the particular judicial institutions and procedures. For all the countries of the civilian tradition their classification as such is valid because much of their legal history concerns the interpretation and adaptation of the chief monument of Roman law, the *Corpus Iuris Civilis*, to fit new circumstances, to match local needs, to form new blends of law. This constant reinterpretation only ceased to be central to legal development after the codifications of the eighteenth and nineteenth centuries, which culminated in the German civil code, the BGB, which came into force in 1900, and the Swiss Civil Code, the ZGB, of 1911.

Our last chapter is an attempt to consider the main trends in the twentieth century and the beginning of the twenty-first, the last of the second millennium. It inevitably concentrates on the law of the European Union. Among lawyers we hope to interest not only legal historians but also those who are interested in comparative institutions and in the history of ideas; the community of background may surprise the English lawyer. It cannot be unprofitable, in the era of the European Union, to look behind the trivial details of the harmonization of noise levels on powered lawnmowers or of the permitted ingredients in beer, to the common traditions of the member states. Inevitably we deal mainly with judicial institutions, with the sources of law and with the interpretation of law rather than with the rules of substantive law.

It would be difficult to give an overall picture through substantive law, and the detail required would be a deterrent to all but the enthusiast. The published work on the history of some of these rules is mentioned in the Further Reading or the Select Bibliography. For the historian, law is one aspect of society and it is pervasive; indeed, for the mediaevalist it is unavoidable. Furthermore, although specific rules of law may be technical and seem dry, many great minds in the past have seen society in terms of its legal organization; much philosophy and political theory has only been conceivable in terms of law. While law may often be the means by which a ruling class can safeguard its position, law is also the means by which justice can be achieved, or at least sought; laws may be oppressive, but the absence of the rule of law is more so.

Our stage, then, is western Europe; our time-span extends from the Roman Empire to the European Union. Our perceptions, our prejudices and our approaches arise from our Scottish standpoint. This book had its origins in a course in European Legal History which we gave in the University of Glasgow for more than a decade, and so it was aimed at meeting the demands of our students. It is a textbook, not a work of original scholarship. We hope that it will provide a sketch for many, and for some an introduction from which they can proceed to more detailed studies. This is why at the end of every chapter there is Further Reading, which is limited to the English language, and to works which are explanatory rather than engaged in scholarly argument. There is also a Select Bibliography to ease the further investigation of any topic. This includes not only standard works of reference but also books in other languages which we have used in our teaching and research. It is obvious that, even for the three of us, many areas we have dealt with can be known to us only at second hand through the specialized work of scholars from many countries. We are conscious of our debt.

A subsidiary point arises: style of nomenclature. Since most mediaeval writing was in Latin, people were generally know by the Latin form of their names, but some mediaeval figures are to be identified in the language of the state from which they came, and others are so well known that their name is translated into the relevant modern usage. After much thought we have decided that we shall be inconsistent. Most names are given in their Latin forms, and those that are not are to be found by cross-reference in the Index. (Perhaps it is as well to point out here that mediaeval persons are normally known by their Christian names.) Where one form is more familiar, such as Azo, we have used that rather than the more correct Azzo; similarly we have referred to Peter Abelard and Thomas Aquinas. Other names seem to fall naturally into a vernacular: Jacques de Révigny and Pierre de Belleperche rather than Jacobus de Ravaniis and Petrus de Bellapertica. English historians customarily talk about William Longchamps although he would have been known as Guillaume de Longchamps or Guillelmus de Longo Campo. We have therefore translated common names like John or Peter into English, except where familiar usage is very strongly the other way, as with Johannes Andreae. We hope that double entries – or even treble – in the Index will ward off confusion; there is unfortunately no authoritative list of mediaeval jurists, or even of the relatively few we have mentioned in our text. The dates, as far as possible, of all individuals (whether of their life or their reign) are given in the Index.

The Select Bibliography explains the citations we have used for learned journals, etc, in our footnotes and in the Further Reading. Books and articles listed in the Further Reading are given simply under name of author (and date where necessary) when they occur in the footnotes of the relevant chapter. In spite of being able to provide a couple of maps, we nevertheless recommend the use of a good historical atlas.

Olivia F Robinson
T David Fergus
William M Gordon

ACKNOWLEDGMENTS

The other two authors owe much to Bill Gordon, who created the course in European Legal History at the University of Glasgow, and who persuaded his sometimes reluctant colleagues that the study of the later history of Roman law was as important as Roman law itself. Olivia took the initiative in finding a publisher for the book in prospect, and has effectively applied her enthusiasm to the arduous task of putting all the contributions into final shape. She appears deservedly as first author.

Among many others who have made comments or criticisms, and especially our students, we owe particular thanks to: JH Baker, E Bund, N Burrows, RC van Caenegem, MT Clanchy, IB Cowan, B Dietz, AAM Duncan, J Durkan, R Feenstra, J Gaudemet, RH Helmholz, F Hutchison, JP Larner, HL MacQueen, AH Manchester, AE Örücü, DJ Osler, AMV Robinson, S Robinson, D Sellar, JA Clarence Smith, P Stein, DM Walker, CP Wormald and J Wormald. We also thank our reviewers for the constructive suggestions they have made, which have helped us with this third edition.

Translations are by the authors, except where otherwise indicated.

CONTENTS

TABLE OF DATES

MAPS

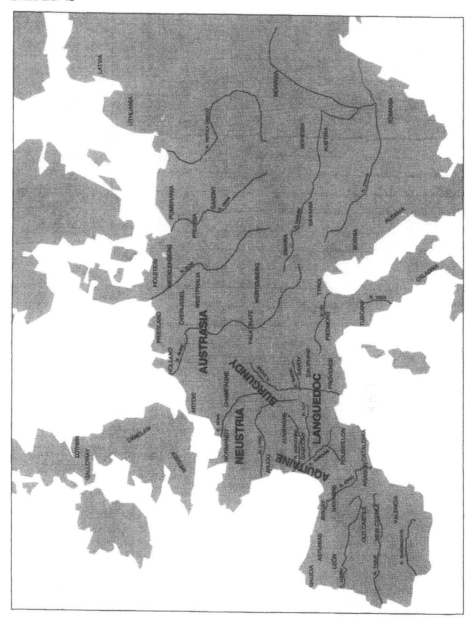

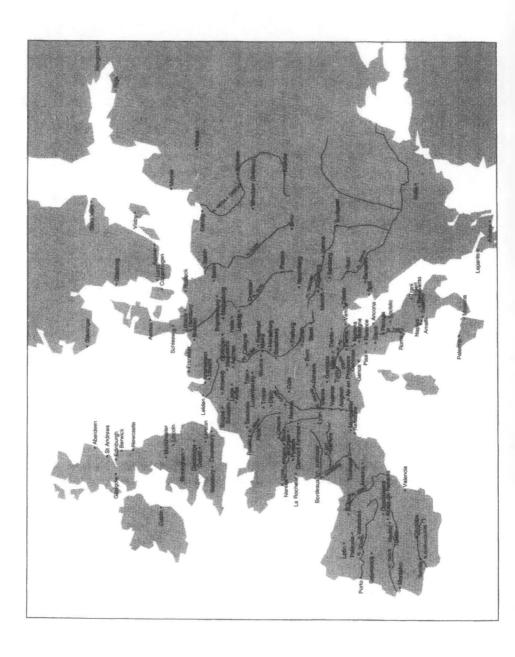

Chapter 1

THE BACKGROUND

1.0 This chapter is essentially introductory. Its main purpose is to indicate the extent of continuity between ancient and mediaeval worlds, particularly in the legal field but also in institutions of government and in the Church. Moreover, the events of these 'Dark Ages' affected deeply the structures and habits we find when we emerge into the enlightenment of the twelfth century, and therefore an attempt must be made to give a brief account of the confused history of these times. Nevertheless, legal history is our concern, and for Europe that really starts around 1050.

A. Roman law and the Roman Empire

1.1 ROMAN LAW AND THE JURISTS

1.1.1 In the Roman Republic, which is generally reckoned to have ended in 27 BC, there were men of the upper classes, known as jurists, who specialized not so much in acting on behalf of others in courts of law (as orators like Cicero did) as in giving advice on legal matters. Self-selected by their interest in the law and because this was an acceptable method of taking part in public life, the jurists discussed and, more importantly, wrote about legal problems. Jurists as a class continued to function in the Empire, although gradually the development of the law became integrated into the machinery of government. In the earlier Empire, the Principate, the period of classical law, jurists advised parties to litigation, they advised the lay judges who decided cases on the facts, and they advised the magistrates with jurisdictional competence, such as the Urban Praetor, who laid down the legal issues which went to the trial judges.

1.1.2 Legislation, in the strict sense of the passing of statutes by the Republican assemblies (and later by the Senate), was a relatively unimportant source of private law; more important were the formal edicts issued by the magistrates, in particular that of the Urban Praetor, which set out the legal remedies available to those appearing before him. The contents of these edicts seem to have been largely dictated by the jurists. Not surprisingly, as the emperors' role developed into that of chief magistrate, and as they acquired a jurisdiction both at first instance and on appeal, they too called on the legal expertise of the jurists, and included such men in their councils. Thus the jurists' role, although becoming institutionalized, was as important in the Principate as in the Republic. As late as the third century there were still individual jurists who were experts with identifiable habits of thought and with independence of mind, but all those of whom we know during this period were also functionaries in the imperial administration. The last major jurist, Ulpian, was killed (probably in AD 223) when holding the office of Praetorian Prefect, the highest office under the Emperor.

1.1.3   Juristic writings included general commentaries and monographs and also some elementary works, but their typical form was casuistic, collections of opinions or problems, in which the jurist argued his way to a particular solution. For example:

> 'A number of people were playing at ball, and one of them pushed a small slave-boy who was trying to pick the ball up, and the boy fell and broke his leg. The question was put whether the slave-boy's owner could raise an action under the *lex Aquilia* [on damage to property – a slave was property] against the man whose push had caused the fall. I gave the opinion that he could not, since the thing seemed to have happened more by mischance than through fault.'

This particular text (D 9.2.52.4, Alfenus, 2 *digestorum*) comes from the compilation of juristic writings known as the Digest, published in AD 533 on the orders of the Emperor Justinian. This casuistic approach leaves room for discussing what degree of roughness would take the incident out of the class of simple accident and make it culpable, whether the answer would have been different if the slave-boy had been forbidden to be near, and so on. It was later to provide scope for widespread development of the texts to fit very different circumstances.

1.1.4   The third century was a period of economic crisis and political turbulence – in the first 262 years of the Roman Empire there were some twenty-five emperors, and then in the next fifty years a further twenty-one. This ended the stability and self-assurance which had permitted individual jurists to have an authority of their own without casting any doubt on the reality of imperial power. The *Codex Gregorianus* and the *Codex Hermogenianus*, Diocletianic collections of imperial legislation, presumably reflect their compilers' names, and we also hear of a jurist called Innocentius working under Diocletian (AD 284-305), but thereafter, although there must have been individuals who were acknowledged experts, none are on record; they are veiled behind the various offices of the imperial administration. Stability was restored, but at the price of overtly autocratic government. Only under the Emperor Justinian (AD 527-65), the restorer of the ancient law, do we again learn something of the careers of certain major jurists of his time. (And by his time much of the West had fallen, and the Empire was centred on Constantinople, the Greek Byzantium, modern Istanbul.)

1.2   THE *CORPUS IURIS CIVILIS*

1.2.1   Justinian was determined to restore the former glory of the Empire by reconquering Africa from the Vandals and Italy from the Ostrogoths, and in particular by recovering the city of Rome, but his work in restoring Rome's legal glories was largely independent of these military ventures. Indeed, the lawyers he employed to compile the *Corpus Iuris Civilis*, as it came to be called, all came from the eastern half of the Empire and will have been Greek speakers; nevertheless Justinian clearly saw himself as in the tradition of his imperial predecessors, back to Hadrian and Augustus.

1.2.2   The contents of the *Corpus Iuris Civilis* are fourfold:[1] the Institutions (or Institutes), expressly issued as an elementary textbook for first-year students of law; the Digest, a compilation of edited juristic writings, dating from the very late Republic to the mid-third century; the Code (or *Codex*), a collection of imperial enactments, that is, general edicts, judicial decisions, and authoritative opinions, from the time of Hadrian (AD 117-38) on, although only a handful come from before Septimius Severus (AD 193-211); and the Novels, which were Justinian's own enactments subsequent to the publication, in AD 533-4, of the other three parts – of the Novels there was never an official, definitive collection. The continuing usefulness of the *Corpus* as a source of law lies not only in its rich store of ideas, but also in its bringing together different views and arguments, showing law as something dynamic, not as mere rules. The jurists frequently cited their predecessors, and the Code is arranged chronologically within each title (which deals with a particular topic), so that developing concepts can be traced as the facts in a particular case were distinguished from previous, apparently similar, circumstances. However, on the instructions of Justinian, the compilers edited both the juristic extracts in the Digest, and the imperial enactments in the Code; thus the law preserved in the *Corpus* is neither the authentic law of the classical period of Roman law, that is, of the Principate, nor a simple statement of the law of Justinian's own day, but a layered amalgam which ignored many of the immediately post-classical changes. (The alterations made are known generically as 'interpolations'.) The Institutions (or Institutes), the Digest, and the Code were officially brought into force in Italy by the Pragmatic Sanction of AD 554, when Italy rejoined the territories under Justinian's effective control.

1   Conventionally cited as Inst, D, and C (or CJ), followed by number of book, of title, and of juristic fragment or law – and often of sentence; hence the opening extract from the Digest is D 1.1.1*pr.* (The *pr[incipium]* is the first sentence in a fragment; s.1 is the second – just like a British 'first floor'.) The Novels are cited as Nov, by number and paragraph.

1.3   VULGAR ROMAN LAW IN THE WEST

1.3.1   Although the *Corpus* was authoritative within Justinian's realm and that of his successors, that is, within the Byzantine state (as it is known in the succeeding period), it was not the law that was known to and practised by most Romans in the western half of the Empire. In AD 212 an edict known as the *constitutio Antoniniana* had extended Roman citizenship to practically all free inhabitants of the Empire. There is no complete agreement on what its consequences were for the law. Theoretically, the existing principle of personality of law (that the law you use depends on your personal status) should have meant that everyone thereafter used Roman law, that is, the traditional law of the citizens of Rome, but probability and some positive evidence argue against this. An increase in the use of Roman law, even in the civilized urban centres of the East which had their own legal systems, can be postulated. In the western part of the Empire, where there was seldom a pre-existing legal system able to withstand Roman law, the latter seems to have become the sole regime, but it was undoubtedly modified by local custom.

1.3.2   The enormous expansion in the number of persons subject to Roman law, and the political upheavals of the third century, led to a widespread desire for simplification and certainty. Men thought it more important to get a decision that could be given effect at once than to seek the ideal solution. In the late third century, therefore, elementary legal books were published with this aim in mind; there survive epitomes of the *Institutes* of Gaius, the *Regulae* of Ulpian, the *Sententiae* of Paul (all jurists of the classical period) and then, a little later, in the early fourth century, selections from some of the leading jurists of the past, known as the *Vatican Fragments* (because found in a manuscript in the Vatican library) and the *Collatio legum Mosaicarum et Romanarum* (*Comparison of Mosaic and Roman laws*). Their acceptance as the working manuals of the courts is one aspect of what is described as the vulgarization – the over-simplification – of law, which also showed itself in such things as, for example, the blurring of the previously clear conceptual distinction between ownership and possession.

1.3.3   The Later Roman Empire may be said to have begun under the Emperor Constantine (306-37) a century after the *constitutio Antoniniana*. Thereafter the only active source of law was imperial legislation; all legal authority, whether making or applying the law, stemmed explicitly from the emperor. In the fifth century, Theodosius II, emperor in the East, had a project to codify the whole law; as far as juristic work was concerned it came to nothing, but a collection was made of imperial enactments issued since Constantine, the first Christian emperor. This was published in AD 438, in both East and West, as the Theodosian Code. Although it did not include much vulgarized substantive law, this Code is notable for its stress on status and its relative neglect of contract – foreshadowing the mediaeval world. Furthermore, custom was recognized as a source of law, provided that it was not in conflict with reason or with statute. This meant local custom rather than the *mos maiorum*, the ancestral custom of Rome; it meant, therefore, the usages of the Greek speakers of the East, and the traditions of the recently enfranchised tribesmen, perhaps even of barbarian *foederati* (allies).

1.3.4   The other new element in the fourth century was the introduction of Christianity as the official religion of the state. The early Church had been localized and predominantly Greek-speaking, with its leading centres in the Near East and Asia Minor. Now, despite – or perhaps because of – Constantine's shift of the administrative capital of the Empire away from Rome to his new eastern city of Constantinople, the Church in the West came rapidly to prominence. The foundation of a legal order for the government of the Church can conveniently be dated to AD 325, to the first General Council of Nicaea; the western Church in a sense came of age around AD 404 by which time, in the Vulgate of St Jerome, the whole Bible was translated into Latin from the original Hebrew and Greek. The fourth century was crucial in the establishment of a structured organization in the Church which enabled it not only to play a vital role in legal history in the distant future, but also to do so in the fifth century when the western provinces were invaded by German tribes from across the frontiers, settled by them, and step-by-step withdrawn from imperial control. These German peoples were all Christian, although some held views condemned by Rome and Constantinople as heretical, and so they conformed, at least in theory, to the laws of the Church; they also made use of Roman structures, including ecclesiastical ones, in their administration.

1.4 SOURCES OF CHURCH LAW

1.4.1 The sources of authority to which the Church looked at this stage were partly devotional and partly juridical or administrative. In the first group were the Bible itself, other works recording the apostolic tradition, the writings of the early Fathers of the Church, and the literature of the early saints and martyrs; to these were to be added the teachings of the Doctors of the Church. (The four great Latin Doctors are Saints Ambrose (c.334-97), Jerome (342-420), Augustine (354-430), and, much later, Gregory (540-604).)

1.4.2 Among the sources of a juridical or administrative nature were the conclusions, or canons, of church councils, the decisions of bishops, and on occasion the secular law, at that period Roman law. While all conciliar canons carried weight, the canons of General Councils of the whole Church, also known as Ecumenical Councils, had the greatest authority, as the public expression of the collective mind of the whole Church.[2] These early ones were backed by imperial authority, for the emperors viewed themselves as exercising a quasi-episcopal function. The Council of Nicaea of 325 was the first; its main business was the condemnation of the Arian heresy, which denied the true Godhead of Christ.[3] Second was the Council of Constantinople in 381, which confirmed the Nicene creed as defining the Catholic faith, and also gave the bishop of Constantinople primacy of honour after the bishop of Rome, 'because Constantinople is New Rome'. The third, the Council of Ephesus in 431, was largely engaged in condemning Nestorius, bishop of Constantinople, for his denial of the single personality of Christ; Nestorius was deposed by Cyril, bishop of Alexandria, with – significantly – the aid of Celestine, bishop of Rome. The Council of Chalcedon in 451 was the fourth; it was for this Council that one of the earliest collections of ecclesiastical law, the *Didascalia* (*Teachings*), was produced in a Latin version. As well as General Councils there were provincial councils, meetings of the bishops and clergy of one Roman province or of a group, for example Gaul (roughly modern France); their canons often referred only to events within the province, but some became accepted as of universal validity. Diocesan councils, more commonly called synods, were naturally of still less weight, being concerned usually only with local matters.

2 General, and other, Councils are referred to by the place of their meeting and a Roman numeral, eg Lateran IV of 1215 is the fourth held in the great basilica of St John Lateran, cf Vatican II of 1962–1965.
3 The Nicene creed is the product of this Council: 'And we believe in one Lord Jesus Christ, the only begotten Son of God, born of the Father before time began; God from God, light from light, true God from true God; begotten not made, one in essence with the Father, through whom all things were made.'

1.4.3   The decisions of bishops also varied in authority. Of most importance in the early Church were the five patriarchs, the bishops of Rome (the word 'pope' means only the late Latin *papa* or father), Constantinople, Alexandria, Antioch, and Jerusalem; each exercised a superior jurisdiction. In the West, Rome's formal primacy was unchallenged although, while St Ambrose was bishop of Milan, he was the effective leader of Christendom, partly because Milan was then the western imperial capital (since Rome's site was strategically unsuitable for countering the 'barbarian' invasions). During the fifth century Rome's primacy of honour became juridical supremacy in the West, a step made easier by the separation of eastern and western halves of the Empire even before the disintegration of the latter. Pope Celestine I (422-32) not only took part in the deposition of Nestorius, an eastern patriarch, but he also set up the principle of appeals to Rome from the western provinces; this appellate jurisdiction was confirmed in 445 by the Emperor Valentinian III (*Nov. Val.* 17). Pope Leo I (440-61), the Great, by his personal character and ability strengthened the position of Rome as the see of St Peter, the holder of the keys of Heaven and Hell. A year after playing a leading role at the Council of Chalcedon, he negotiated with the invading Huns led by Attila, and induced them to withdraw beyond the Danube. In 455, although he was unable to stop the Vandals occupying Rome, he was able to prevent any serious bloodshed. The Papacy was not yet exercising direct and active control over the (western) Church, but Leo could write in a letter (*Ep.* XII *altera* c.9 in Migne, *PL*) of AD 446 to certain African bishops that they should observe the apostolic constitutions and the decrees of the canons, and that Rome reserved the right to pardon or to punish. Nevertheless, there was as yet no clear hierarchy among the sources of the Church's law and, furthermore, the Western Empire, while it lasted, provided unquestioned secular jurisdiction in matters other than those of strictly ecclesiastical discipline, as is evidenced by the Theodosian Code – although a bishop might well be called upon to act as an arbiter.

1.5   THE GERMANIC CODES

1.5.1   The Germanic tribes, principally Ostrogoths, Visigoths, Franks and Burgundians, but also others, who came to settle in the territories of the Western Empire were not 'barbarians' in the sense of savages; they admired Roman traditions, and they were Christians. There were no invasions, in the usual dramatic sense, of Gaul after the defeat of Attila and the Huns in 451, just a steady, if forcible, advance by the Germanic peoples. Battles and sacks indeed took place in the migratory movements, but no attempt was made to destroy the Empire as such; the German peoples saw it as a necessary institution, in which they had a right to a place. The murder of Valentinian in 455, which led at once to the sack of Rome by Gaiseric and his Vandals (whence the pejorative use of the name), rather than the death of Romulus Augustulus in 476, is perhaps the best symbol of the downfall of the Empire in the West. It was somewhat unfortunate, from the point of view of smooth relations between Roman and German, that all the original settlers, except the Franks under Clovis, were Arian heretics. But despite a lack of support from the Church, the Germanic peoples were ready to adopt many of the institutions with which they had come into contact, and one which impressed them enormously was the existence of written law.

1.5.2 Hence we find appearing a number of legal codes, written in Latin, designed either for Romans living under Germanic rulers or, as in the case of the *Edictum Theodorici* (Edict of Theodoric), for the Germans as well. The *Edictum* seems to have been issued around 460 when the Visigoths were settled in south-west Gaul. It is heavily Roman in its content, and seems to have been necessary because of the absence of any clear political authority which could give a definitive legal ruling. It drew from the imperial enactments of the *Codex Gregorianus*, the *Codex Hermogenianus*, and the Theodosian Code, and from the *Sententiae* of Paul, but the wording is frequently a simplified paraphrase rather than the original; it is a characteristic product of the vulgarized western jurisprudence. Less controversial in its origins is the Code of Euric, published about 475, in which the Visigothic king was clearly assisted by Roman legal experts; it is more likely to be an application of the vulgar law than a statement of Germanic custom as modified by their contacts with the Romans. Thus it was probably of territorial application, governing all inhabitants of the regions ruled by Euric; the surviving fragments show undoubted Roman influence but do deal with areas of the law where such influence is most to be expected. Under Euric the Visigoths had extended their kingdom into Spain; save for the area round Narbonne, their settlement in Gaul was brought to an end by the Franks under Clovis in 507. In 506 King Alaric II had produced a code known as his Breviary, or as the *Lex Romana Visigothorum*; this consisted of a considerably abbreviated version of the Theodosian Code, together with some later imperial enactments, an abridged and modified version of Gaius' Institutes, and a few further juristic texts. The whole, except for Gaius, was accompanied by an 'interpretation', which usually summarized and sometimes paraphrased the contents and occasionally made references to other works. Alaric's and Euric's codes reflected the Visigothic view of their relations with the Empire.

1.5.3 Other Germanic codes were issued at about this time which also indicate the German view of their settlements as compatible with the Empire.[4] The Roman provincials did not really regard their new rulers as purely parasitical; they were often acceptable for bringing about the restoration of order, suppressing brigands or rebuilding bridges. The Code of Gundobad (474-518) of the Burgundians and the Law of the Bavarians are among the products of the vulgarized Roman law, codes which must have been produced by Romans serving the Germanic kings, although it remains unclear whether their application was territorial or personal. In northern Gaul the customary law of the Frankish settlers (or Salic law, under which name its later versions were known), was much more Germanic, reflecting a purely agricultural society, but from its beginnings it was drafted in Latin. The existence, the authority of the written Roman law influenced even those settlers who never came into direct contact with the Empire. The Franks on the Rhine who had invaded independently of the Salian Franks had their *Lex Ribuaria* (*Law of the Riparian [Franks]*) by the seventh century, and Roman law, transmitted through the Visigothic codes, was known to tribesmen in the Alps in the *Epitome* of St Gall, and in the *lex Alamannorum*.

4   Collins (1991) p 276, argues that the concept of 'personality of law' was largely an invention of the Carolingian Franks.

1.5.4   Of all these codes the Visigothic, whether Alaric's or Euric's as revised by King Leovigild, were the most influential, surviving particularly in Spain. The western provinces had been accustomed to the Theodosian Code, to epitomes and elementary law books, and to these Germanic codes for fifty or a hundred years before the Pragmatic Sanction of 554. This was why Justinian's 'correct' revival of the sophistication of classical law, well suited to Byzantines trained in theological niceties, fell flat with Romanized barbarian rulers and also with barbarized Roman subjects, even though some vestiges of legal science survived. After all, even before Justinian, students in the eastern law schools took a four- or five-year course to master the intricacies of Roman law; Justinian reformed the curriculum and laid down a five-year period of study at Constantinople and Beirut (and Rome presumably, after the recovery of Italy) before qualification as advocate or judge in the supreme courts. There was nothing really comparable in the barbarian West. Of the new sources of law only the Institutions seem to have been absorbed. The Digest was too difficult, too complex, too sophisticated – in a word unsuitable. The Code, although somewhat better attuned to the needs of the time, was nevertheless too lengthy, even when abbreviated, and it presupposed a political system that had ceased to exist. The Novels, while they were of importance where the Byzantine Empire continued to flourish, until modified or superseded by the legislation of later Byzantine rulers, were mostly very long, and usually in Greek; the *Epitome Juliani*, containing 122 of them in an abridged Latin version, was the edition best known in the West.

1.5.5   Furthermore, even apart from problems of doctrine, there was already coolness between the Church in the West and the Church in the East, between Pope and Patriarch. Naturally enough, the Church in the West continued to be influential in many aspects of administration. In the absence of effective imperial control, the Church, in particular the bishops in their cities, had acquired a greater jurisdictional role than that laid down in Justinian's compilation. When, in 568, the Lombards (see section 1.8) invaded Italy, ecclesiastical judges were fully accustomed to using the older Theodosian Code; Gaul, like Spain, had never felt Justinian's influence.

1.6   THE CHURCH OF GREGORY THE GREAT

1.6.1   Secular law in the West had thus become fragmented by the sixth century, but the Church continued to function as a supra-national institution. Councils, general, provincial, and diocesan, continued to meet. In Visigothic Spain the king came to conduct the business of his kingdom at provincial councils; they were the places for considering lay affairs as much as ecclesiastical. In sixth-century Gaul, as earlier in Visigothic Spain, there were still literate and legally trained laymen, competent to continue the modified practice of traditional Roman administration. This fact and a different, more popular, structure of government may explain why the business of provincial church councils under the Merovingian dynasty – the descendants of the Frankish King Clovis – was purely ecclesiastical; there were more than fifty of these councils in the sixth and seventh centuries. Such activity was one reason why, in the early years of the sixth century, Dionysius Exiguus, a Scythian monk working in Rome, made a collection of *Apostolic Canons*, based generally on the Latin version (the *Didascalia*) used at the Council of Chalcedon. (He was also the man who fixed the date of the Christian era as beginning 753 years after the founding of Rome.) This collection, in various editions, was to have considerable authority in the West under the name of the *Dionysiana*. In Spain it was superseded by a collection known as the *Hispana*, of which the first edition was compiled in 633. This made use of the *Dionysiana* but also included canons of Gallican (French) and Spanish councils of the sixth century and, in later editions, of the seventh. The *Hispana* is noteworthy for being arranged systematically, not chronologically. It was perhaps the most influential example of a local collection, but it was one of several, for there was as yet no clear and convincing authority in the whole Church, no efficient hierarchy.

1.6.2 It was also during this period that a new agency arose within the Church; monasticism appeared in a form acceptable to western notions, unlike the various asceticisms of the east. Saint Benedict established on an organized basis his Rule, a way of life that was out of the world but not hostile to it. Manual labour and intellectual work, as well as prayer, were parts of the Rule and so monastic houses could be both self-sufficient farms and centres of teaching and preaching. Monks of the Benedictine obedience, particularly St Boniface (c.680-754) from Devon, were the principal carriers of Christianity to the rural areas of Europe east of the Rhine and north of the Alps, although Irish monks, such as St Columban (c.540-614), had also played an important part in the mission field.

1.6.3 The last Latin Doctor among the Church Fathers, Pope Gregory the Great (born in 540), lived in the transitional period between the Roman and the mediaeval worlds. In his younger days, before he became a monk, Gregory held the office of Prefect of the City, the chief magistracy of Rome. Rome was no longer a great city since its desolation in Justinian's wars against the Ostrogoths, but by this time there were few cities at all in the West, and Rome still had the echo of former greatness. Pope Gregory, like Pope Leo before him, was clearly the moral leader of (western) Christendom; like Leo, he negotiated with an invading people, the Lombards, and in the absence of imperial aid his efforts held them back from Rome. As pope, Gregory was not uninterested in dogma, but the chaos caused in Italy by the Lombard invasion, the low moral quality of the Frankish royal court, and upheavals elsewhere, meant that the enforcement of discipline was of particular interest to him. A new category of devotional works, frequently of Irish origin, known as Penitentials, became popular. Their weakness was a tendency to codify the Church's procedures concerning sin and penance in a rather mechanical way, so that penance sometimes appeared as payment for sin rather than as an aspect of contrition. Nevertheless, they fitted with the movement for reform, and Gregory reinforced this movement from above: 'I know of no bishop who is not subject to the apostolic see, when a fault has been committed' (*Ep.* IX, 59 in Migne, *PL*). He also intervened of his own initiative in cases of oppression and public scandal.

1.6.4 His theological work, heavily indebted to St Augustine, remained a storehouse for later thinkers; his decretals, that is his judicial decisions and pastoral rulings, remained an important source of guidance to later bishops. In view of his international influence, it is hardly surprising that papal decretals became an increasingly important source of authority, particularly as no General Councils were held in the West until the twelfth century. Gregory's energy and perseverance, his benevolence and practicality, his administrative ability and monastic links, provided a programme for the Papacy, a Papacy which was to survive what were perhaps its unhappiest days in the hands of squabbling and self-seeking Roman families to emerge, in the eleventh century, as the mainspring of reform.

1.7   FROM THE ANCIENT TO THE MEDIAEVAL WORLD

1.7.1   At the end of the sixth century it was not clearly apparent to contemporaries that the ancient world, the Roman world, had ended in the West. The Senate, however attenuated, still met in Rome, where the Empire remained theoretically sovereign, although the Papacy in practice governed central Italy. The Empire, the Byzantine Empire, effectively controlled the Dalmatian coast and the Exarchate of Ravenna in north-eastern Italy, as is evidenced by surviving documents which duly reflect the law of Justinian and his successors. In the Mediterranean area west of Greece, the Byzantines still held the coastal area of southern Spain (until the 620s when they were pushed out by the Visigoths), Africa around Hippo and Carthage (until the Arab conquest at the end of the seventh century), as well as Sicily and Calabria or southern Italy, and also Corsica and Sardinia. It still seemed possible that the Lombards might be made to abandon Italy, as the Ostrogoths had before them. Frankish Gaul, henceforward more recognizable as France, like the Rhine provinces under the Burgundians, could be viewed as settled by allies, and Catholic allies in the case of the Merovingian Franks. Only the Anglo-Saxon settlement of England, an outpost of Empire where Roman law had probably never been truly absorbed, was outside the circle, and even there Christianity was to provide a link with the rest of civilized Europe.

1.7.2   In Spain the Visigoths in many ways seemed to have made a fruitful union between Roman and Germanic civilization; the ample surviving evidence in the fields of law and theology (they had been officially Catholic since 589) suggests a civilization inferior to none in the world of its time. King Leovigild had revised Euric's Code; using this as a base, King Reccesuinth produced a new code in 654, entitled the *Liber Iudiciorum* (*Book of Judgments*), divided into twelve books, sub-divided into titles, with the subject matter arranged systematically. This in its turn was revised by King Ervig and reissued in 681 as the *Forum Iudicum* (*Province of Judges*; *Fuero Juzgo* in Spanish); in this some subsequent legislation was inserted. Thus in the mid-seventh century Alaric's Breviary (see para 1.5.2) ceased to have any force in Spain, although it continued in use in France, especially in the Burgundian region of the south-east, as can be judged from the numerous surviving manuscripts. It was superseded in Spain, it would seem, because it became outdated in detail, not because the system failed; as a statement of law, indeed, it was comparable to the authoritarian edicts of Lombard as well as Roman law.

1.7.3   Among the Visigoths there were constitutional elements, specifically the Church, which tried to decree limits to the autonomy of the kings; we find, for example, a decree of the Eighth Council of Toledo which distinguished between property held by the king in trust for the people by virtue of his office and property pertaining to his family which could be disposed of as he wished. The *Liber Iudiciorum* similarly contained laws which restricted what the king could lawfully take from his subjects, and which repeated the distinction between property held for the people and property at his disposition, but it went further than its Roman model or the Lombard equivalent in holding the king subject to the law. In practice the king's power was great and often unchecked, but the codes were statements of principle as well as handbooks for administrators, and here the influence of the Church in Spain was centuries ahead of European political theory. In other respects, such as the development of the responsibilities of local communities to hand over runaway slaves and to check on unknown incomers, or the formalization of trial by ordeal, Visigothic Spain was simply evolving in a way that other western societies were, unconsciously, to follow.

1.7.4   The Arab conquest of 711 ended the political history and the creative law-making of Visigothic Spain; much survived, and was to re-emerge in the Christian kingdoms of the *Reconquista*, but its influence then was either internal or in the Spanish American colonies. In the Asturias, the Basques (rather like Asterix) held out against the Arabs as they had against the Visigoths, but the significant check to the Arab impetus was their defeat at the Battle of Poitiers in 732, by the Frankish Charles Martel, founder of the Carolingian line. Thus the new political map of Europe took shape under Frankish influence, and one may conveniently look to the Franks in order to measure the survival of Roman law amidst the growth of the new customary law. Lombard legislation and practice in Italy were significant for the future, but it was the military strength of the Franks which made them and their legal developments particularly important.

1.8   THE LOMBARDS (OR *LANGOBARDI*)

1.8.1   The Lombards, who invaded Italy in 568, differed from the majority of the Germanic peoples who had settled within the Empire before them in that they appeared, at least to contemporary sources, as an almost abstract force of pure destruction, but this picture must be exaggerated. The forty years of conquest that followed left them accepted rulers of some two-thirds of the Italian peninsula. Further, even after the Frankish conquest of Lombard Italy, the institutions of the Lombard kingdom persisted in a way that Ostrogothic institutions had not. Lombard institutions persisted partly because they had taken advantage of Roman or sub-Roman urbanized structures both in central administration and at the level of the cities and dioceses. The Roman population also survived, and continued to use Roman law, although this survival is not really evidenced until the eighth century when records become more abundant.

1.8.2   Indeed, the first Lombard code, the Edict of King Rothari, issued in 643, was intended to be valid for all his subjects, and it may well have been named after the edict of the Praetorian Prefect. It shows various signs of Roman influence, being written in Latin, comprehensive in character, and perhaps also in its assessment of all compensation for injuries in the Roman *solidus*. Rothari deliberately set out as much Lombard custom as he and his advisers could, but it seems certain that there were Roman functionaries to collect and write down its 388 titles. Its substance was rather like that of the contemporary Anglo-Saxon codes, with the stress on agriculture and matters such as *wergild* (feud compensation). Daughters had no claim on an estate if there was legitimate male issue, and in general a man could not disinherit his son either by legal act or by granting away his property; any grant of land had to be made in the popular assembly, and such a grant was only possible for men without legitimate sons. Women were in life-long subordination, to the king if there were no suitable male kin, and they could not dispose even of moveable property without their guardian's consent; there was a bride-price as well as a dowry, and the husband also had to make a substantial gift to his wife after the marriage.

1.8.3   The next major Lombard law-giver was King Liutprand; he extended women's rights of succession, and also allowed the alienation of land to the Church. Both these changes demonstrate Roman influence, as did Liutprand's circumscription of the use of trial by battle, explaining: 'for we are uncertain about God's judgment, and we have heard of many losing their cases in battle unjustly; but on account of the custom of our Lombard people we cannot ban the practice entirely.'[5] Specifically Christian influence appears in the ban on marriage between first cousins, which is ascribed to the injunction of the pope, 'the head of God's churches and priests throughout the world'. Liutprand added 152 titles to the Edict, a further pointer to the primacy of the written law; royal written law was increasingly acquiring supreme authority.

5   Cited by Wickham, p 44.

1.8.4   Legal change in the Lombard and its successor Frankish kingdom came explicitly from the top of the pyramid, from the king, whereas the other Germanic societies mostly illustrated an 'ascending theme of government', that is from the populace. This concept of legislation and jurisdiction as vested in the state, an entity to be succeeded in due course by the cities and communes, was unique in the West to Italy. It is not surprising, therefore, that it was in the north Italian cities that Roman law was to have its great revival. Indeed, this obedience to a sovereign, this 'descending theme of government' (as Ullmann calls it), explains why Lombard law could co-exist with traditional civil and canon law in the eleventh and twelfth centuries when other Germanic codes were ignored. A Germanic civil law imperceptibly succeeded in penetrating Italian life; men of Roman descent continued to use the Theodosian Code or perhaps, after the Frankish conquest, the Visigothic version, but they also found it necessary to follow Lombard law when the Roman law made no allowance for new relationships, or for new social, economic, or political structures. Administration continued to centre on the royal court, normally at Pavia, and local government was conducted from the cities, the ancient *civitates* which included the immediately dependent country areas; Lombard duchies and episcopal dioceses normally coincided. Little positive role was played by the people in Lombard government, although witnesses in large numbers might be required in dispute settlements, particularly in cases of reparation. Litigation took the form either of trial by battle (despite Liutprand), or of oath, taken by the defender and six of his kin, chosen by the pursuer, and five more free men, chosen by these seven. Written evidence was dominant in the spheres of property law and status, which reflected the very high level of literacy in Italy compared with the rest of Western Christendom

1.8.5 Although the Lombards did eventually blend in with the Roman population of Italy, as the dominance of the Latin element in the Italian language bears witness, their pressure on neighbouring but unconquered areas had political effects lasting over a period of at least two centuries. They played a significant part in the transfer of the internal organization of Byzantine and Roman Italy from a theoretically civil government to a military system of defence, a sort of feudalism; thus we find in Italy, as in France, the warrior class as one of the chief divisions of the free populace. Power and wealth necessarily continued to rest on land-holding; *tribuni*, who were usually major local landowners, ruled a city state and led it in war. These *tribuni* were nominated by the Byzantine viceroy, the Exarch of Ravenna, but in practice their office was largely hereditary. *Collegia*, corporate bodies in the cities which had performed some of the functions of local government in the Later Empire, sometimes survived in the towns; at Naples the *curiales*, the hereditary town councillors, became a guild of notaries. Bishops became public functionaries, and took over much of local government; the great estates of the Church gave them influence and resources. Spoleto and Benevento were Lombard duchies, but they were semi-independent from the beginning, and their special status survived the fall of the Lombard kingdom.

1.8.6 The Lombard kingdom fell, in essence, because Lombard ambitions threatened the papacy, for which the Franks, who at that time had the strongest army in Europe, were ready to fight. Hence, after campaigns in 754-56, King Pippin of the Franks was acknowledged by the Lombards as their overlord. He then granted the administration of the former Exarchate of Ravenna, from which the Byzantine authorities had been driven out in 751, to the papacy, but it was not until 774 that Charlemagne invaded Italy, captured Pavia, the Lombard capital, and finally made an end of the independent Lombard kingdom. Thus most of Italy was within the new Holy Roman Empire that was founded, or recognized, on Christmas Day, 800, when Charlemagne was crowned as Emperor by the Pope.

B. The formation of Europe

1.9 THE EARLY CAROLINGIANS AND CHARLEMAGNE

1.9.1 For two hundred years after the death of the Frankish King Clovis in 511 the Merovingian kings personally or through their lieutenants, the mayors of the palaces, fought and murdered each other for the three provinces of Austrasia (north-eastern France and the Rhineland), Neustria (north of the Loire and west of the Meuse), and Burgundy (which included the length of the Rhone) (see second map); the Frankish kingdom nevertheless remained a single realm, aided by the support of the Church. Then, out of the Austrasian mayors of the palace there emerged a new line; Pippin II of Heristal, already in effective control of Austrasia, subdued the Neustrian Franks and became their mayor of the palace too. He restored Frankish supremacy over the Alamanni and the Bavarians, among whom he encouraged missionaries, as he also did among the Frisians. His work nearly failed for, on his death, he divided his realm, as was the Frankish custom, granting it to his young grandsons, but his bastard son Charles seized power and became the first, the eponymous, Carolingian. Charles' greatest victory was at Poitiers, near Tours, when he defeated the Islamic invaders who had already overrun Spain. This was perhaps the decisive battle that ensured a Christian Europe, and with his victory he won for himself the name of Martel, the Hammer; however, his counter-attack, in temporary alliance with Liutprand of the Lombards, was ineffective. On his death in 741 the realm was divided between his two sons, Carloman who took Austrasia and the east, and Pippin (the Short) who took Neustria, Burgundy, and the west; both were still, in name, mayors of the palace.

1.9.2   On Carloman's retiral to a monastery in 746, Pippin took all, and in 751 he was elected king of the Franks and anointed to that office by St Boniface and other bishops. His coronation had a papal blessing; papal support was reinforced in 754 when, at the abbey of St Denis, Pope Stephen himself anointed Pippin and his two sons and created them patricians of the Romans. This was a result of Stephen's appeal to Pippin when the Lombards, after conquering Ravenna, threatened Rome. His appeal to the Franks, rather than to Byzantium, was natural since, in 727, the papacy had come to a final breach with the Empire in Byzantium,[6] although over three centuries were to pass before the schism with the Eastern, the Orthodox, Church became definite. The first campaign against the Lombards did not settle the matter, and the Pope appealed for help a second time; on this occasion Pippin acted decisively. A Byzantine request that Ravenna be restored to the Empire was turned down and, by the Donation of Pippin, the Exarchate was delivered to the government of the Pope.[7] Relations were for the present excellent, but the possibilities of future conflict between spiritual and secular power were there. Pippin went on to expel the Arabs from those parts of south-western France which they still held and to bring Aquitaine back to submission. By the time of his death in 768 France reached to the Pyrenees and the Rhine, as well as retaining nominal suzerainty over Bavaria; Pippin also took the first steps that led to the Carolingian renaissance in the fields of learning and culture.

6   Tierney, document no 5.
7   Tierney, no 7.

1.9.3   Charles, better known as Charlemagne, became sole king of the Franks on the death of his brother Carloman in 771. In 774, after a war with the Lombards, he captured Pavia and put an end to the independent Lombard kingdom. He then journeyed to Rome and confirmed, probably with some modifications, the Donation of Pippin. From this time Charlemagne styled himself 'King of the Franks and of the Lombards and Patrician of the Romans'. Lombardy, subject to increasing Frankish influence, nevertheless retained its separate character, but the pope and the Papal States also found

Charlemagne acting as overlord. Benevento, south of the Papal States, remained effectively independent; thenceforward the division of Italy into north and south remained unchallenged until the nineteenth century. On his eastern frontier Charlemagne subdued the Saxons, thus extending his Empire to the Baltic and the Elbe, and he strengthened his suzerainty over the duchy of Bavaria, which included what was later Austria – the East March of Bavaria. In the south-west he created the Spanish March on the southern side of the Pyrenees, roughly Andorra to Barcelona; thereafter Catalonia had an identifiable existence on both sides of the Pyrenees. Only in the north, on the Danish frontier, was Charlemagne content with a defensive role. The sole increase in this empire for his successors was Brittany, whose submission was due more to fear of seaborne enemies than to Frankish expansionism.

1.9.4 In secular law Charlemagne ordered the unwritten customary law of various tribes to be written down, and the Salic Law to be edited authoritatively. His own legislative acts, however, took their legal force from the words of the sovereign, of which the writing was merely evidence – such royal edicts were known as capitularies. In the sphere of canon law Pope Hadrian I presented Charlemagne in 786 with a version of the *Dionysiana*, supplemented by various decretals and some canons of Roman synods, which was thereafter known as the *Hadriana*. In 802 Charlemagne, two years after his coronation as Emperor by the Pope, laid down that the *Hadriana* was to be followed by the Church in all his dominions; in practice the *Hispana* or the *Vetus Gallica* (the pre-Dionysian collection used in Gaul) continued to be used alongside the newer version, as did various Penitentials. In the ecclesiastical field the Carolingian reform movement saw a joint attempt by secular and spiritual authorities to restore clerical, and lay, discipline, and to recover Church property and patronage from secular hands. But as the unity of the first establishment of the Holy Roman Empire crumbled, so did the reform movement. Simony, that is, the buying and selling of ecclesiastical offices, particularly bishoprics,[8] continued to be rife; many bishops were little more than feudal nobles in mitres; church benefices remained in lay hands; celibacy of the clergy remained largely an ideal.

8   Eg Tierney, no 13.

1.10   THE SUCCESSORS OF CHARLEMAGNE

1.10.1 The ninth century saw the steady growth of outside threats to the Carolingian Empire from Moslem pirates, Norse Vikings, and Magyar raiders; the impact of this on the movement known as feudalism will be considered in the next chapter. Within the Frankish realm dynastic struggles continued among the heirs of Charlemagne, aggravated by the Frankish custom of joint inheritance, even of kingdoms. A series of accidents made Charles the Fat sole emperor from 884 to his deposition in 887, and the division which then took place turned out to be permanent. Descendants of Charlemagne continued to rule the kingdoms of Germany, France, and Italy (as it is now convenient to call them), while semi-independent principalities flourished in Burgundy,

Provence, and Catalonia (Barcelona and south-west France); the Basques recovered their independence, and the counts of Brittany offered no more than nominal allegiance. Germany was most prone to attack, having a frontier at the North Sea and being relatively easy of access from the Mediterranean, as well as lying open in the east to the Magyars, who burst through the Moravians of Hungary in the early tenth century. Local separatism was also perhaps strongest in Germany, with Saxons, Bavarians, and Slavs all having their particular interests. In France things may have been a little easier. In 911 Charles the Simple ceded the duchy of Normandy to Rollo the Norseman, obtaining an oath of loyalty from him as count of Rouen; the creation of this buffer zone did in fact check Viking incursions into France. Lorraine was already embarked on its long alternation between French and German lordship.

1.10.2   Italy, too, was ravaged by Moslems and Magyars, and in addition there was civil strife, as the nobles fought each other for influence, for the royal title and for the papacy. The tenth century was the nadir of the papacy and the episcopate; in Rome we find John XII elected pope at the age of twenty at a time when a priest was supposed to be at least thirty-five years old and, similarly, in the 930s we find a five-year-old elected as archbishop of Reims to serve the ambitions of his father, the count of Vermandois. In general the papacy of this period was merely the tool of the factious Roman nobility, with the emperor intervening on occasion, in his own interests. But anarchy and corruption brought reaction. The Cluniacs, a strict monastic order, arose to spearhead the reform movement, and other groups of monks, following severe versions of the Benedictine Rule, helped to foster a spiritual revival.

1.10.3   In the secular sphere matters improved. Warfare became less endemic as the Norsemen made more or less permanent conquests at Novgorod and Kiev, and in the eastern districts of England – the Danelaw – as well as in Normandy. The Magyars were finally induced to settle in Hungary and their raids were limited, particularly after the decisive victory of the Emperor Otto the Great in 955 at the Lechfeld (just south of Augsburg). The Moslem invaders of the ninth and tenth centuries had, like the Norsemen, come by sea. Their colony at Fréjus in southern France was extirpated in 972 after lasting a century-and-a-half in that stronghold; it had been a base from which they commanded the Alpine passes as well as the coastal regions and the sea. A Byzantine-Frankish alliance had repelled them from the Italian mainland, though not from most of Sicily, by early in the tenth century. The Moslems ceased to exist as a serious threat to sea trade after the maritime victories of the increasingly powerful and effective commercial cities of Italy. Important victories were won by the Venetians off Bari in 1002 and by the Pisans off Reggio in 1005; in 1016 Genoa and Pisa united to clear Sardinia, although Sicily was not to be recovered until the Norman reconquest after 1060 – when the Normans also took over Calabria, the Byzantine province in southern Italy. Thus by the end of the tenth century conditions were such that men began to conduct their arguments and fight their quarrels with law-suits as well as the sword. And the rivalry of pope and emperor, to which we shall shortly come, positively encouraged the pursuit of learning, as each side sought for arguments against the other.

1.10.4 After the ninth century the centre of interest in the development of law in Europe turns away from France, where the kingship went into profound eclipse. The Carolingian line there died out in 987, and the Capetian dynasty, named after Hugh Capet, began the slow process of recovery, based on the lands they controlled directly in the Ile de France. South of the Loire there remained a different culture, less rebellious than the turbulence of the northern lords, but no more obedient. There were counts of Barcelona, counts of Toulouse, dukes of Gascony, dukes of Aquitaine, kings of Burgundy (which included Provence); all of them were content with effective independence, and so there was relative peace in the Languedoc. In the north the greater vassals often outshone their king, but the support of the bishops, and the fortunate survival of caution and common-sense as Capetian traits, enabled Hugh Capet's great-great-grandson, Louis VI (1108-37), the Fat, to create a relatively prosperous and peaceful order, at least within the Ile de France.

1.10.5 In Germany, recovery from the tribulations of the ninth and tenth centuries was quicker; there were fewer over-mighty vassals and a more stable society, with a limited degree of popular participation in public affairs. This last quality, however, also meant that there was more separatism, more stress on local or tribal distinctions, in particular between the four main races, Saxons, Bavarians, Swabians, and East Franks or Franconians. Thus the kings, or emperors as they more usually were, ruled a federal rather than a united realm. This particularism also helps to explain why such a diversity of custom survived in Germany – the *Lehnrecht* or feudal law, the *Stadtrecht* or town law, the *Hofrecht* or peasant law, etc. But at this period the emperors could rule, rather than merely reign, partly because there remained ample land for them to give away or to grant as beneficces – that is, land held in return for service – and partly because of the support of the Church which favoured unity.

1.10.6 In Italy, the descendants of Charlemagne continued to rule from the cities, as had the Lombards before them, until the mid-tenth century, when local power passed at much the same time almost everywhere to the city communes. The German-based emperors continued, however, to exercise a more or less effective overlordship in the north, as well as involving themselves in the affairs of the papacy.

1.11 EDUCATION, LAW AND TRADE

1.11.1 In the sixth century there had been higher education at Rome; Justinian had paid professors of grammar, oratory, medicine, and jurisprudence, but it seems unlikely that any such posts survived. Nor is there any evidence for a comparable survival at Ravenna where, if anywhere, one might expect it for, although the city fell to the Lombards in 751, it was under papal control by 774. One can, however, assume a certain continuity of administrative and legal skills, and the training to support them, at the papal *curia* or court. In and after the seventh century, Latin continued to be taught and used, for it remained the language of the Church, and the normal language of written documents. What education there was, in particular the learning of Latin, was mostly centred on the monasteries, but until perhaps the eleventh century it remained elementary.

1.11.2   The Carolingian renaissance brought into prominence the work of the Christian writers of the end of the Empire, such as Boëthius (480-524) and Cassiodorus (c.490-583); also read were the writings of Irish monks, such as St Columban (540-615), and of English scholars such as Aldhelm (c.640-709) or the Venerable Bede (673-735). There was a conscious attempt to revive the civilized past; there was a school at Charlemagne's palace, and others were founded, attached to cathedrals or monasteries. The Caroline minuscule style of handwriting made reading easier; it was used to copy the works of the Fathers and the heathen classics, which led to their widespread availability and contributed to a certain unity of culture. For example, Alcuin (735-804) came from York to be abbot of the monastery of St Martin of Tours; he taught extensively and wrote voluminously on grammar, history, and theology. Paul the Deacon (d. c.797), from Lombardy, wrote on grammar and a History of the Lombards; he referred in passing (*H.L.* 1,25) to Justinian's 'laws of individual magistrates and judges', which seems to mean the Digest. Einhardt (c.775-840), a Franconian, modelled his *Life of Charlemagne* on Suetonius' *Lives of the Emperors*. Churchmen produced the Forged Capitularies and the False Decretals, including the Donation of Constantine, by which that emperor purportedly handed over to Pope Sylvester considerable secular power. Such forgery was an exercise rather comparable to the putting by Greek and Roman historians of suitable speeches in the mouths of leading characters; it was not falsification in our modern sense, but a description of what might, and indeed what ought to, have happened. These forgeries made use of genuine material in a way that showed their authors to be learned and widely read. However, the military and political turmoil of the later ninth and earlier tenth centuries put learning into abeyance.

1.11.3   This is the intellectual background to the problem of the extent of continuity in the practice of law. Our evidence is plentiful for matters concerning land, for example charters granting benefices and laying down the counter-obligations of the grantee or vassal, but is much more sparse in the fields where Roman law had been most highly developed. Trade between different countries, regions and cities never entirely disappeared, particularly in Italy; in France, towns such as Marseille, Arles, Narbonne, Bordeaux, Cahors, Orléans, Autun, Laon, Trier and Metz remained trading centres of a sort. But in spite of the considerable increase in coined money during the eighth century and the revival of urban life in the Carolingian peace, the law of contracts unrelated to land remained a special area, an area for the custom of the merchants, as we shall see in a later chapter.

1.11.4   In Visigothic Spain we find that the (late) Roman element in contracts remained strong; for example, although writing was commonly required, it was still required essentially to prove, not to constitute, the contract. Sale, however, was seen as necessarily involving a transfer of title, and the document was the necessary proof that the price had been paid.[9] The *Forum Iudicum* seems to have remained influential even after the Arab conquests, perhaps because the surviving Christian kingdoms were relatively isolated; it is probable that its use remained open to the Christian subjects of the Arabs. There are, in any case, many manuscripts of the *Forum* surviving from ninth and tenth-century Catalonia and León, and also many bequests of copies. Court proceedings often cite specific texts or sometimes merely refer to them; from surviving court records it is clear that procedure followed the norms of the old law. Notaries flourished, and judges seem to have been at least semi-professional, although nothing is known about their training.

9   See King, pp 105ff.

1.11.5   In France the *Lex Romana Visigothorum* was the legal code for the clergy and the Gallo-Romans; in Aquitaine, in particular, people continued to describe themselves as Romans not Franks, but it is hard to tell how far they could avoid resorting to customary law and rules of feudal law as social facts changed around them, and there was no authoritative source to administer the old written law. In the Midi, where feudal institutions, creating formal ties of dependence, were not universal and many smaller landowners survived with only a loose attachment to a greater man, explicit sales, not grants, of land continued. However, in the Toulouse area, stipulations, warranties against eviction etc, all disappear from legal documents after 980, and the written evidence portrays a feudal society (where *traditio*, simple physical delivery, can convey an abstract thing like seisin – which will be further explained in the next chapter).

1.11.6   In a group of charters from what is now Belgium those from before 750 are very Roman in form, citing the Theodosian Code; gifts are made in accordance with the requirements of CTh 8.12.1 (of 316), save for the registration on the court register, which no longer existed; the term '*trado*' is used correctly to indicate the physical delivery of property, and not where it should not be; documents recording sales quite properly use the past tense because the writing is evidentiary, although the contract refers to a delivery for a price rather than the pure Roman agreement – but this is normal vulgar law; warranties against eviction are valid against the world. But in the later group, from the Carolingian period, a sale is delivery by charter for a return, in other words, it is not really a contract at all but a formal grant of land; the same terminology is used for gift and sale, even when the two transactions appear in the one charter; warranties against eviction are only effective against intrusion by the seller or granter or by his family.

1.11.7   In another group of charters (from the Dauphiné in eastern France), consisting of acts in expectation of death, the picture is similar. An eighth century will seems in good form, and indeed refers to Justinian's Code; during the ninth century gifts *pro anima*, that is, for the benefit of one's soul, in expectation of death, are often confused with gifts having present effect, which would require physical delivery. By the tenth century the concept of universal succession, of the heir succeeding to most of the rights and duties as well as the physical property of the testator, has disappeared completely, and the will itself has become rare. North of the Loire the will disappeared during the eighth century, and so did the very word 'sale' for transactions concerning land, which were all seen in terms of grant and service; estates were no longer disposable, and tenure had replaced ownership.

1.11.8 It is not entirely clear why the break with Roman traditions should occur where it does; perhaps Merovingian ineffectiveness left the *Lex Romana* to flourish, while the early Carolingians had a policy of centralization which was inevitably enforced in predominantly Frankish terms, so that when Charlemagne's empire broke up there was a vacuum for feudal institutions to fill. Although such a theory may explain the evidence from the north, it hardly fits with that from Toulouse. There it is more likely to be linked with the lack of an outside or objective set of standards; in the absence of an accepted governmental authority, the family had become the sole *'force sociale'*.

1.12   THE EMPIRE IN GERMANY

1.12.1 The reign of Henry the Fowler (919-36), duke of Saxony, marks the coming of the new, the post-Carolingian, order; as well as gaining the allegiance, at least nominal, of Thuringia, Swabia, and Bavaria, he recovered Lorraine for Germany, and he also maintained a steady push against the Slavs in the east. His son, Otto I, the Great, destroyed the Magyar threat at the battle of Lechfeld, and aimed at becoming a new Charlemagne. Since effective power rested on the extent of a lord's private domains rather than his titular territories, the hereditary aspect of feudalism was often in opposition to any efficient centralization. For if a vassal's lands and offices passed to his successor, usually his son, whether or not that successor was suitable from the king's point of view, it was difficult to put into effect any coherent policy. Otto therefore adopted widely the practice of endowing bishops and major abbots with large benefices; ecclesiastical magnates were in general more efficient and more trustworthy than lay ones, and they offered no hereditary threat, since there was real freedom to reappoint on their death.

1.12.2 In 951 at Pavia, Otto took the Italian crown, marrying the widow of the previous king; he returned to Italy in 962, and on this occasion achieved his ambition and was crowned Emperor, a title which is thereafter normally linked with the rulers of Germany. He then proceeded to intervene in the affairs of the papacy, imposing two popes in rapid succession. In northern Italy he strengthened his power as feudal overlord, although his attempts to extend his influence in the south were only moderately successful. Under his successors Calabria was lost to the Saracens; vain attempts were made to get Germans and Italians to mingle in northern Italy, and manipulation of the papacy in the effort to achieve this was frequent. The Italian cities were growing prosperous in the new era of relative peace, and their leading citizens, who were often also the local landowners, resented, both as merchants and as lords, the Ottonian policy of favouring ecclesiastical magnates and not granting hereditary fiefs.

1.12.3 The Emperor Conrad II put more reliance on hereditary vassals, although he wished to restrain the greater magnates; he did not, however, show any understanding of the (relatively democratic) 'commune' movement in the Italian cities. In 1037, saying 'If Italy hungers for law, I will satiate her', he called a diet (or assembly) at Pavia and regulated the position of the lesser fiefs, confirming their hereditary nature. The following year, at Rome, he laid down that within Roman territory Roman law should decide all cases, a decision clearly favouring the territoriality of law, not to say Roman law; it is, however, not quite clear what he understood by 'Roman law'. Conrad's son, Henry III, tried to end private wars by the Indulgence of 1043, whereby he and all those he could persuade or command solemnly forgave their enemies and renounced all feuds; this had even less effect than the Church's efforts in the Truce of God and the Peace of God (see para 5.6.1). In Rome itself, however, it was largely Henry's influence which brought about the election of the great reforming pope, Leo IX, which was to have incalculable influence on the role of the Church and on relations between Church and state.

1.13   THE INVESTITURE CONTEST

1.13.1   Pope Leo IX surrounded himself with a group of reformist cardinals, drawn from all over Europe, of whom the youngest, Hildebrand, was especially fierce in his belief in the supreme dignity of the papacy and in the need for the complete independence of the Church from secular domination. A number of councils were held,[10] and the search for the authentic rules of the Early Church, for the discipline of primitive Christianity before its corruption in the barbarian age, led to the further investigation of ancient writings; it seems likely that it was in the course of this search that the manuscript of the Digest – the one on which we mainly rely for its text – was recognized for what it was.

10   Tierney, nos 15 and 16.

1.13.2   Hildebrand became Pope Gregory VII; his aims were expressed in the so-called *Dictatus Papae* (*Papal Statements*) of 1075.[11] They set out a programme for a rebirth of spiritual guidance, with authority in matters of faith, morals and discipline coming from the Pope alone. In particular, however, Gregory's pontificate was marked by his struggle with the Emperor Henry IV. This is known as the Investiture Contest because the main issue was the lay claim to appoint bishops and to invest them with the ring and pastoral staff which symbolized their office, as well as with their fiefs; at a lower level there was the issue of lay appointment of priests to parishes. The practice had originated under the Carolingians, partly from the theocratic nature of the power they claimed, partly from ordinary feudal attitudes concerning public office and land-holding, and partly from the need of kings in difficult times to have loyal vassals and capable servants. The practice had 'provided a most effective counter to the disintegrative tendencies of early feudalism',[12] but it had also encouraged simony and a tendency for some sees to become hereditary. The reformers rightly saw lay investiture as, even at its best, aimed at serving secular not spiritual purposes but they, as much as emperors and kings, saw a bishopric's 'lands, rights, jurisdictions, and duties [as] one indissoluble juridical entity'.[13] The eventual solution lay in distinguishing separate functions, a solution which in essentials was first put forward by Ivo of Chartres, who realized that spiritual office and temporal jurisdiction were conceptually distinct.[14]

11   Tierney, no 26; cf RW Southern, *Western Society and the Church in the Middle Ages* (Penguin 1970), pp 102ff.
12   Tierney, p 25.
13   Tierney, pp 34ff.
14   Tierney, no 40.

1.13.3   Henry IV had received help from Gregory VII against a rebellious Saxony, but he now broke with the Pope. He discarded the (unconsecrated) archbishop of Milan whom he had already invested, disregarded the canonical election of one Atto, and invested a fresh nominee of his own with the see, which had become vital for the German control of Lombardy. Gregory issued threats against Henry. Henry called a synod of German bishops at Worms in 1076 and declared Gregory deposed; the Lombard bishops immediately followed suit. Thereupon Gregory, at the Lenten Synod in Rome, deposed the rebellious bishops, granting them a time for repentance, and excommunicated Henry, forbidding him to exercise his royal office. Gregory's estimate of his authority was better than Henry's. The German bishops and lay magnates forced Henry to submit by threatening to renounce their allegiance and elect another king; Henry made his submission as a penitent to Gregory at Canossa, a castle of the Countess Matilda of Tuscany.

1.13.4   Canossa was an immense surrender to the papal claims to supreme jurisdiction as God's vicar, but the Church needed the support of the secular power as much as the latter needed the support of the Church, and the struggle was not yet over. Pope Paschal II indeed made the radical proposal that the Church should abandon all lands and temporal powers and return to a primitive simplicity, thus logically achieving the total independence from the secular powers that the reformers sought.[15] But this proposal was too startling for Church to swallow or state to understand, and in view of the economy of the time it was probably impossible to separate spiritual office from material property. The English achieved a settlement in 1107, with the king receiving feudal homage for the temporalities of the bishopric, but only following on a canonical election; the Pope would then send the ring and staff. A compromise in similar terms was achieved for the Empire at the Concordat of Worms in 1122. Henry V guaranteed the canonical election of bishops and abbots, and renounced the imperial claim to investiture with ring and staff; Pope Calixtus, for his part, granted the emperor the right to be present at elections and to intervene if these were disputed. Lateran I of 1123, the ecumenical council called in the year after the settlement, was not only the first General Council for 250 years (since Constantinople IV in 869-70), it was also the first to be composed solely of clerics and free of direct imperial influence. The canons of this Council were aimed at reforming the ministry of the Church. For example, they prescribed the celibacy of the clergy, and they also created a stronger juridical structure to enforce these reforms. Lateran I marks the start of the heroic age of the mediaeval papacy and of canon law.

15   Tierney, no 42, and pp 85ff.

1.14 THE ELEVENTH-CENTURY RECOVERY

1.14.1   In the eleventh century there began to take place (most markedly in Italy, despite the internecine strife and the wars brought on by German ambitions) a renaissance, far outdistancing in importance, for the knight or the peasant or the merchant, those of the Carolingian court or of the fifteenth century. There was apparent an economic revival, of which one aspect was the increase in maritime and overland trade, and another the rise, even outside Italy, of the self-governing town. With a surplus in production, the population rose, and city life became much more widely possible; this was favourable to education and scholarship, as well as making life more pleasant, with little luxuries becoming available to a much larger proportion of the population.

1.14.2   In the early eleventh century we find Peter Damian at Ravenna, teaching law. For example, he taught the canon law practice on the prohibited degrees of kinship, within which no marriage could validly exist, and this was explicitly different from the Roman law. At Pavia both Roman law – mainly from the *Lex Romana Visigothorum* – and the customary and feudal law of the Lombard kingdom were being studied and developed by glossing the texts. Lanfranc was teaching there around 1042, and the jurists of Pavia were sufficiently sure of their discipline to be divided into *antiqui*, who held to the *Lex Romana* and other ancient sources, and *moderni*, who dealt with the blend between the *Lex Romana* and Lombard custom. The *Liber Papiensis* (*Book of Pavia*) contained material going back to the Edict of Rothari of 643; it was arranged chronologically. It was composed, probably in the early years of the eleventh century, with scholastic and practical comment by Walcausus, who was one of the judges of Henry III's imperial court at Verona. The contemporary *Lombarda* or *Lex Langobarda* contained much the same material, but arranged systematically in books and titles; it revealed some knowledge of Justinian's Institutions and of an epitomized Code but its main subject was Lombard custom. Around 1070 there was composed the *Expositio ad Librum Papiensem* (*Commentary on the Book of Pavia*), which cited various Roman jurists and quoted from Justinian's Novels in the edition known as the *Epitome* of Julian, who had been a Byzantine commentator thereon. The *Expositio* also quoted, although probably not at first hand, from the Digest; and it referred to certain rules of the canon law as in force at the time.

1.14.3   The Lombard capital of Pavia was not the only Italian city in which law books survived or were produced. From Perugia there is the *Adnotationes Codicum Domini Justiniani* (*Notes on the Codes of the Lord Justinian*), which probably dates from the seventh and eighth centuries. It was written in what has been described as horrible corrupt Latin, and it seems that this centre of study failed in the darkest centuries. Here the *Lectio Legum Brebiter* [sic] *Facta* (*A Brief Summary of the Laws*) of the ninth century was compiled mainly from the *Ecloga* (*Choice Selection*) of the Byzantine Emperor Leo III, the Isaurian, which it ascribed to Pope Leo the Great. The *Ecloga*, which had been in force in Byzantine Italy, was a codification based on the *Corpus Iuris Civilis* but much simplified and containing many subsequent changes in the law, such as the joint exercise by mother as well as father of *patria potestas* (paternal power), or the treatment, after the death of one spouse, of the property of the married couple as having been a joint estate. The *Lectio* suppressed the *Ecloga*'s references to the Digest, and it referred to the Code and Novels together as *ex libro Novelle*; it also contained material from the Edict of Theodoric and from Lombard law. At Pistoia a glossed version of the Code was extant in the tenth century.

1.14.4   There is thus no doubt that there survived in Italy the memory, and some knowledge, of Justinian's Code in an epitomized version, and of some of his Novels; the Institutions were also known. It must be remembered that the Byzantines had long held Ravenna and the Exarchate, that they held much of southern Italy (where pockets of Greek speakers long survived) until the coming of the Normans in the later eleventh century, and that communications between Rome and Constantinople never quite ceased. All Byzantine legislation descended from Justinian's *Corpus*, with simplifications and additions. Manuscripts of the codes of Leo III, of Basil I – the *Procheiros Nomos* (*Manual of Law*) – and of Leo VI, the Wise – the *Basilica* (*Imperial Books*) – all survive from Italy, and another code, specifically for the province, the *Procheiron Legum* (*Manual of Laws*) was composed there, probably in Calabria. The Normans took over the territorial law they found in force in the south, in itself a sign of continuity. Italian charters also frequently reflect this continuous if vulgarized relationship with Justinianic Roman law.

1.14.5   Notaries, public scribes, who had become very important in the Later Empire when so many transactions were required to be recorded in due form on the court registers, also survived the intervening centuries, at the papal *curia*, probably in some of the Italian cities and also at the imperial court. Notaries created by the Pope or the Emperor had authority to draw up public documents, acceptable in themselves as evidence of the transactions they recorded. Their continued use of forms simply because they were old, even if not well understood, was another factor making for continuity. Cartularies, like style books, were in widespread use, for teaching as well as practice. The profession flourished again in the new age of law.

1.14.6   Universities, let alone law faculties, were not yet institutionalized in the eleventh century. Eager students followed individual teachers of renown; thus Anselm attracted students to Bec and Canterbury in turn. But bishops or princes might encourage scholars by granting them, and even their students, privileges or immunities; guilds of students or of masters were in the making. By the eleventh century a curriculum had been established. The *trivium*, or the study of grammar (based on fourth- and sixth-century Latin authorities), of dialectic or logic (based on Aristotle in Boëthius' translation), and of rhetoric (based on Cicero), preceded the *quadrivium*, which was the study of geometry, arithmetic, astronomy or astrology (no distinction was yet drawn), and music. From Cicero's model, law was seen as a branch of rhetoric; thus there was some formal study of law even before it became a specialized topic. At certain centres more advanced studies were undertaken; men came to Salerno to study medicine, as they did in the twelfth century to Montpellier, and it was at Bologna that the serious study of the civil law, the Roman law as preserved in the *Corpus Iuris Civilis*, began. Medicine and law remained advanced studies, as did theology. The canonists had been searching the ancient authorities since at least the beginning of the eleventh century, and making use of what they found; the lawyers in Pavia and elsewhere were jurists reading their authorities critically and developing the law. When men came upon the Digest they knew what it was and, far more important, they had acquired the intellectual expertise to make use of it. The imperial jurists in particular must have welcomed the *Corpus* as ammunition against the papalists. With sufficient knowledge and adequate patronage available, the stage was now set for an explosive growth of legal studies.

FURTHER READING

H Chadwick	*The Early Church* (Penguin, 1967)
R Collins	*Early Mediaeval Spain* (London, 1983)
	Early Medieval Europe, 300–1000 (London, 2nd edn, 1999)
JM Wallace Hadrill	*The Barbarian West, 400–1000* (Oxford, rev edn, 1985)
E James	*The Franks* (Oxford, 1988)
JM Kelly	*A Short History of Western Legal Theory* (Oxford, 1992) chs 1–3
PD King	*Law and Society in the Visigothic Kingdom* (CUP, 1972)
FH Lawson	*The Roman Law Reader* (New York, 1969)
B Nicholas	*Introduction to Roman Law* (Oxford, 1962)
CM Radding	*The Origins of Medieval Jurisprudence* (Yale UP, 1988)
OF Robinson	*The Sources of Roman Law* (London, 1997)
RW Southern	*The Making of the Middle Ages* (London, 1953)
B Tierney	*The Crisis of Church and State 1050–1300* (Hall-Prentice Inc, USA, 1964)
A Watson	*Roman Law and Comparative Law* (Athens, Georgia 1991) Part I
C Wickham	*Early Mediaeval Italy* (London, 1981)
H-J Wolff	*Roman Law* (Oklahoma, 1951)

Chapter 2

FEUDAL LAW

2.1 DEFINITION OF FEUDALISM

2.1.1 Feudalism, in the context of legal developments in western Europe, is properly the grant of land, or, later, of office, by a king or other great man to a lesser man in return for military support, this land usually being reckoned an adequate economic unit to maintain the required number of soldiers. From a slightly different viewpoint, and if the initial conditions are varied a little, it is the system by which a lesser man commends himself and his land to a greater, offering military service in return for protection.[1] The terms used of this relationship are (feudal) superior and (feudal) tenant; those lower in the socio-legal hierarchy hold land from those higher in the hierarchy. This is a deliberately narrow definition, but for a book concerned with legal history it seems better to try to isolate the original and essential elements. The concepts, facts and relationships described are shadowy for the ninth and tenth centuries; most of our evidence comes from the twelfth century and later. Indeed, much of the impact of feudal law came in the latter period, but by then it was already mingled with civil law, the learned law.[2]

1   Eg, Herlihy, documents 9 and 10.
2   See Reynolds (1994).

2.1.2 The system of commendation by someone already in possession of land arose more naturally from the political, economic and legal framework of the Later Roman Empire; that of original grant was more fitted to the settlements of the various Germanic tribes. Feudalism was a military matter; as the importance of being able in person to fight diminished so feudalism in the narrow sense faded, although feudalistic legal and economic consequences long endured. And militarily it was linked with the central importance of the heavily armed cavalry-man, the knight. There has been much discussion about the origin of the knight's role: the invention of the stirrup; the example of Berber and other raiders; King Pippin's postponement, in 755, of the mustering of the Frankish army from March to May, with the consequent greater availability of forage; but it is worth remembering that the shift in tactical importance from infantry to cavalry had already taken place in the Later Roman Empire. From the fourth century to the eleventh, although there might well be danger from a neighbour, there was always danger from the migrant, the raider; mobile troops were required, and the frontier armies of the Later Roman Empire – the garrison troops – had become second-class soldiers. Military conditions thus explain the central role of the knight and the pre-eminent need for armed and mobile defence.

2.1.3 Along with the near-permanent state of war went the absence of an ordered political society, because a command from the capital would no longer reliably take effect at the frontier, the absence of constant and sure commerce, because a trader was too exposed to military danger, and the absence of civilization, in the sense that the pursuit of inessentials did not enhance life but threatened survival. Although not invariably, and not everywhere in equal degree, the characteristic need was for local self-sufficiency; hence the manorial economy is typical of feudalism, and towns, insofar as they survived, were by their nature non-feudal. This whole military system became most typical among the Carolingian Franks. In France before the Carolingians, custom was very strong in the Germanic north, whereas in the south the influence of Roman law survived; this division, which roughly followed the line of the Loire, persisted and later the northern area became known as the *pays de droit coutumier* or *pays de coutumes* and the southern as the *pays de droit écrit*. In France north of the Loire the situation was summed up as *'Nulle terre sans seigneur'*, but in the south there was *'Nul seigneur sans titre'*;[3] nevertheless, the subsequent growth of forces other than feudalism reduced the clarity of the picture.

3   'No land is without its overlord', and 'No man is lord unless he has some title'.

2.2   FEUDAL LAW AND CUSTOMARY LAW

2.2.1   Feudal law existed in the narrow sense of the law regulating the personal tie between lord and vassal and the tenure by which the vassal held his land of the lord, but it also had to exist as part of the whole legal framework of society, based on Germanic customary rules, usually unwritten, which were already in use when feudalism emerged. Feudalism blended so well with customary law that the two became interwoven or even confused, but they were not so blended originally. Anglo-Saxon law in England is sufficiently well evidenced to illustrate a customary society that was not yet feudal (in the narrow sense), but it did absorb or receive feudalism readily when the Norman Conquest introduced it in the form of knights and castles. The Anglo-Saxons used written law, but it was written in the vernacular and hence comprehensible to lay judges; feudal law operated in a culture where the written language was Latin and therefore inaccessible to the unlearned, and this helps to explain its reliance on its own local custom. Charters, that is documents (later sealed) laying down the terms agreed between lord and tenant,[4] were of very great importance because they gave the beneficiary a tangible symbol of his right and also because, in spite of the theory of an oral customary law, they were written.

4   Eg Herlihy, no 23.

2.2.2   Feudal law (in the narrow sense) dealt with land and succession to land, with some crimes, and with the knightly classes; there was virtually nothing on commercial contracts or even on moveables. It was also inextricably linked with jurisdiction, because its third highly characteristic feature, besides the personal tie and tenure, was the delegation, or rather dispersal, of governmental functions, such as defence, policing, justice, taxation, and general administration. The procedures by which disputes were settled came in part from the older tradition of life, in which the elders of the tribe defined what was the law and the king enforced sentence, but they were supplemented by the feudal practice of arms, whether in private war – which was seen as a legitimate way to pursue a claim – or in trial by battle. Compurgation, the practice by which a man's innocence or the truth of his claim was maintained, not on the basis of any objective evidence, but by summoning sufficient oath-helpers who would swear to his good character, was an element from customary Germanic law; it relied on the expectation that a man and his deeds would be known to his fellows, and seems not unreasonable in a closed society, provided that there was not too great a disparity of power between the parties. Trial by ordeal also had Germanic roots; it was based on the doubtful premise – doubtful in view of biblical and missionary history – that God would not allow the innocent to suffer and would therefore reveal the truth through the reaction to the ordeal.[5] But whichever of these three modes of trial was used, the judgment of the court was likely to be enforced by a feudal lord. Another customary element in feudal society was the institution of kingship; the king was certainly a feudal lord, at the apex of the pyramid, but he was more than a feudal lord; in the interest of public order, the Church reinforced his special role in the feudal age by anointing and other rites.[6]

5   Compare Liutprand's view on trial by battle; see 1.8.3.
6   Herlihy, no 30.

2.3   THE PERSONAL BOND

2.3.1   The basic tie in feudalism was the personal link created between the vassal and his lord. The vassal promised faithful service, or fealty, to his lord and did homage, a symbolic act of submission, for the fief, most commonly land, granted to him by the lord.[7] The lord invested his vassal with his fief, granting him the land and rights over it, and giving him lawful possession of it by delivery of seisin or sasine, another symbolic act such as the delivery of a clod of earth from the estate.

7   Herlihy, nos 11 and 15.

2.3.2   This personal tie was bilateral; both sides had duties as well as rights. The vassal owed his lord whatever good faith required, and, more specifically, aid and counsel (*auxilium* and *consilium*). Ward-holding or knight service was the basic type of aid, but aid might also include garrison duty, or the provision of a substitute in war when the vassal was personally incapacitated (or a sum of money in lieu – in English terminology called scutage); it included too the payment of certain regulated sums, known as feudal aids or casualties (see para 2.4.5) and probably the provision of hospitality. Counsel involved attendance on the lord, usually at the great feasts but also whenever he wanted to show his consequence, and in particular it involved attendance at his court, with the duty to advise there; this obligation became in the course of time a right. The lord in his turn must protect and maintain his vassal. Protection was by arms or in some other way such as acting as surety (in Normandy later the vassal would also have to be prepared to stand surety for his lord up to the equivalent of a year's rent, when the lord was sued in court for a personal injury).[8] Maintenance was by gifts, or by the provision of bed and board and other necessities, or, most commonly, by the grant of a fief or benefice.[9]

8   *Summa de legibus* 27.6 (Herlihy, no 32); the *Summa* is a compilation of Norman feudal custom, first put together about the middle of the thirteenth century.
9   Herlihy, no 23.

2.3.3   In theory the bond of fealty was supposed to be stronger than any other save a man's allegiance to God; after all, the fealty was enforced by an oath taken in the name of God. However, family ties and expediency operated, naturally enough, and kings strove to persuade their subjects to hold a higher loyalty to them than to their immediate lords.[10] There were, furthermore, circumstances in which a vassal could renounce his allegiance,[11] or be released from its normal operation.[12] Nevertheless, the concept of good faith between lord and vassal and, within the feudal classes, of the right of each man to due respect, were factors that could contribute to the amelioration of society.

> 'Between other lords and their vassals, faith ought so to be maintained that neither one of them ought to call for corporal violence or for violent blows against the person of the other party. If any of them should be accused of this in court and convicted, he is bound altogether to lose his fief for violating the faith he was obligated to observe. If this act should be discovered in a lord, homage should revert to his superior and dues should no longer be given, excepting what is owed the prince.'[13]

10   Eg *Summa de legibus* 12.1 and 13.1.
11   Herlihy, no 12, esp. items 77 and 104.
12   Eg according to the canon lawyers, in the event of an unjust war (see section 5.6).
13   *Summa de legibus* 13.2–13.3.

2.4   TENURE

2.4.1   Tenure is the term used to describe the grounds of a continuing possession of land, or of anything that could be equated with land. In a purely feudal society there was no ownership of land, except for the crown – which itself held under God; every man held of another, knight from lesser lord, lesser lord from magnate, magnate from the king. Tenancy too in the Roman sense of a contract of hiring and leasing gave way, as far as land was concerned, to fiefs, because men had commended themselves and this was the price they had to pay, or because the king had recovered the land and military service alone was of use to him in the face of crisis, or because money to pay a rent was undervalued because one could not eat it or ride it or wear it. Thus the link between vassalage and fief or benefice became normal, although vassalage remained possible without a benefice, as in the case of household knights, or a benefice might be something other than land, such as the right to hold a market, or to take rabbits and hares in a warren, or to exercise some particular jurisdiction or office.

2.4.2   Tenure could cover land granted for feudal services or in alms, or even land that had no lord – which is called allodial land (and did not exist in strict feudal theory). Lands granted to the Church were normally held in free alms (frankalmoign), which meant that the only return required was the saying of Masses and prayers for the granter and his family. Such piety had its disadvantages in that the Church never died, so that reliefs and aids such as wardship and marriage could never be demanded by the lord. Tenure also described those holdings for which military service was rendered but at a level below knight service (such as sergeantries – see para 2.7.1), or blench holding (the Scottish grant of land in return for nominal service), etc; these free tenures had many local variations. Indeed, tenure was also the proper term for servile and peasant holdings; naturally they too had many local variations. Feudal tenure, however, the concern of the law of fiefs, meant primarily ward-holding or knight service, or some equivalent.

2.4.3   There might be many steps in the chain of feudal tenure between king and knight; the king's direct vassals were tenants-in-chief, normally magnates but not always, for we hear of men holding by sergeantry direct from the king. The process of a tenant granting out part of his fief to another is known as subinfeudation, and in this way the feudal pyramid could become enormously complex since, for example, a tenant-in-chief might through a dowry or some such means become the vassal of a mere knight. The only inherent restriction on subinfeudation was that a man must still be able to perform the services due to his lord. Subinfeudation of other than the direct sort brought about the condition of multiple vassalage, in which a man might have done homage to several lords for several estates;[14] problems of fealty obviously arose, and so the personal nature of the feudal tie was weakened in that not every lord, but only the liege lord (the lord to whom a man promised personal allegiance in his homage, and who had the right to the indivisible profits of overlordship – that is, arising from personal relationships such as ward or marriage) was able to rely on his vassals.

14 Eg Herlihy, no 17.

2.4.4   In the pure, the military, model, land was granted in return for service and if, through death or incapacity, the service was no longer possible the land reverted – escheated – to the granter. This was neither a good way of ensuring loyal service from the vassal, nor an effective method for the lord of maintaining his military power. As early as 877, under the Carolingian emperor Charles II, the Bald, there is evidence for fiefs being treated as heritable,[15] although this ruling, the Quierzy capitulary, was not meant to set a precedent. However, it soon became normal to make a patrimonial claim; a man would expect the heirs-male of his body, or at least the eldest of them, to succeed to his lands, with the services attached to them, or even to some office. Primogeniture was a widespread rule because a normal knight's fief would not have the resources to support more than one knight, together with his men-at-arms; trained war horses in particular were very expensive. (Where, later, one does find fractions of a knight's service, this presumably was commuted into money.) The lord's right to recover his grant was given recognition in his right to claim a relief, a sum of money, from the heir before the latter could do homage and enter the fief. In Normandy in the thirteenth century we learn that the relief due on a knight's fief was £15, on a barony £100, 12d an acre on cultivated land, £3 on a mill which was not otherwise part of a fief, and so on.[16] With the development of the heritable principle the lord also acquired the right to appoint a guardian, or to act himself as guardian, if the heir were under age; such a guardian was entitled to enjoy the profits of the estate, although he must not waste its resources, but no relief was then due when the heir came of age. Similarly, when there was no male heir, the lord had the right to select the husband for a female heir, so that the fief she brought her spouse would be held by someone loyal to the lord. These rights are known as wardship, or ward, and marriage.

15 Herlihy, no 21.
16 *Summa de legibus* 32.3–32.4.

2.4.5 There were as well three (or four) feudal occasions, which became traditional, when the lord could demand money from his vassal. These were on the knighting of the lord's eldest son, on the marriage of his eldest daughter, and for the ransoming of the lord's person if he were captured in war; in some places an aid was also due to help with the lord's preparations for going on crusade. Feudal aids were normally levied in proportion to the relief due on an estate, and so both in quantity and in frequency the demands a lord might make were restricted, by custom which became law. Restrictions also came to operate on the length of military service which could be required; forty days was normal, and thereafter the vassal must be paid his expenses. Similarly, the lord's right to claim hospitality would be limited to so many nights a year, and the number of followers he could bring with him would be restricted.

2.4.6 Thus in the normal course of things there came to be security of tenure. Gradually everywhere the lord's right to recover a fief because of some abuse by his tenant became a matter for trial in the lord's court by the vassal's peers; this was laid down at least as early as 1037 in a constitution of the Emperor Conrad II,[17] and similarly in thirteenth-century Normandy we are told that for a vassal to be deprived of his land and right, he must be convicted in court, 'as the custom of Normandy requires'.[18] One form of misuse was the attempt to alienate the fief or some part of it without the lord's permission; the Emperor Frederick Barbarossa, at the Diet of Roncaglia in 1158, reserved the rights of lords in this matter.[19] The lord's permission, however, could normally be obtained for a payment.

17 Herlihy, no 22.
18 *Summa de legibus* 13.4.
19 Herlihy, no 38.

2.5 DELEGATION OF GOVERNMENTAL POWERS

2.5.1 The third element in feudalism was the dispersal of governmental powers. It is not clear how far this arose by conscious act and how far it was simply found to have happened. Merovingian and Carolingian kings granted immunities, that is freedom from the authority of royal officials, in matters of taxation or jurisdiction,[20] particularly to the Church; some magnates may have extorted such privileges from an unwilling king. On the other hand, powers of policing, judging and punishing as concomitants to the control of land may never really have been questioned in an era of crisis, and the *potentiores* of the Later Roman Empire had begun to exercise such powers, however unlawfully. In England, as we shall see, custom was decided in popular courts which were carefully controlled by the kings and so, after the Norman Conquest, royal justice was able fairly rapidly to supplant feudal justice. In France the resumption of justice by the Crown after the tenth century was a slow process; in the Empire it was even slower. In Scotland the establishment of royal power was only achieved over a long period.

20   Herlihy, nos 28 and 29.

2.5.2   Some fiefs were known (in Norman feudalism) as 'honours', because they were linked from their origins with public office. In thirteenth-century Normandy we are told that it was the duke, by now the French king, who was responsible for justice and peace, and so must search out and punish those who committed crimes of violence and those whose conduct led potentially to breach of the peace. In return for standing as liege lord to all free men he must 'rule, protect, defend, and treat them according to the rights, customs, and laws of the land'.[21] His feudal justice was still of more significance than royal justice, although the two gradually merged. This merger occurred partly because only the king had powers overtly to make new laws and a professional civil service to put these laws into practice, and partly because 'the lord has the right of judgment over all the fiefs which are held from him, whether they are held indirectly or directly'.[22]

21   *Summa de legibus* 11 and 12.2.
22   *Summa de legibus* 27.7.

2.5.3   It is clear that in the high Middle Ages, throughout the area of the Carolingian Empire although not outside it, there was a distinction between high justice and low. High justice gave power to punish with death crimes deserving of that penalty – although persons caught in the act of, say, highway robbery could be summarily hanged – and also, in civil disputes, to have jurisdiction in cases which were to be settled by trial by battle. Low justice covered petty crime, and other feudal and manorial disputes. In most areas high justice was restricted to princes, counts, and barons, and a simple knight would only exercise low justice within his fief. Whether high or low (or undivided as was the case in other areas), justice was essentially territorial, applying to all who lived within a particular fief. The powers to levy and lead troops, to raise certain taxes, to control various aspects of administration, were all important, but the power of justice gave a lord physical control over those within his jurisdiction. It was also a source of profit to him, for any fines he imposed went to him, and the parties to any settlement must normally pay him for the judgment.[23]

23   A 'fine' is literally a *'finis'*, a finish to a matter, but the word was early transferred to mean the payment to the court at the resolution of a case.

2.6 JUDICIAL PROCEEDINGS

2.6.1 The growth of feudal justice may be illustrated from France, where it absorbed most features of the older customary system. In the Merovingian kingdoms the customary form of judicial proceedings, except where the Church or some lord had been granted an immunity, was for the royal official, the count, who was under oath to know and to observe the law, to make a tour of the area of his authority. This area was divided into hundreds, a customary Germanic grouping, and in each hundred the count summoned all free men to his court, the *mallus*. There the assembly elected law-finders (doomsmen, *scabini*) to give their verdicts, under the presidency of the count. Their presence was the more essential while law remained personal rather than territorial; there is on record, for example, a case of 918 in the Languedoc when Roman, Salic, and Gothic *scabini* acted together. Charlemagne reformed this system. In order to ease the burden of attendance, he required the assembly of all free men in each hundred to meet only three times a year, for the consideration of major causes. Minor causes could be dealt with simply by the *scabini* (*échevins*) of whom thereafter there were usually seven for each hundred, elected for life, sitting most commonly under the presidency of the count's deputy; they continued to attend the *mallus* or *placita*. This was the origin of the formal distinction between high and low justice.

2.6.2 However, as effective government crumbled during the civil wars and the invasions of the ninth and tenth centuries, the popular element in the administration of justice diminished. Procedure became feudalized, either because lords took over, with or without a charter, the exercise of jurisdiction, or because the counts turned their tribunals and the land granted for their support into honours, or because the *scabini* took advantage of their position to strengthen their place in feudal society. By the eleventh century the hundred courts in France had virtually disappeared, and the *scabini* were normally within the feudal hierarchy, exercising the high or the low justice depending on their status as vassals. In the regions between the Seine and the Loire, high justice continued to be dispensed in general assemblies of the free population, under the presidency of a count or other magnate. The *scabini*, sometimes appearing as the lord's council, continued to give a collective judgment or declaration of the law; if necessary, inquiry could be made from such assemblies as to what was the law, the custom. Elsewhere north of the Loire, suit of court, the duty and right to attend a particular court, was attached to a particular tenement rather than to the status of free man, although the difference might not be very great in practice. Among the unfree or the very humble, it was normal for a superior to have jurisdiction over his tenants, not merely a knight over his villeins – seignorial justice – but even a villein over another villein, if the latter held land from the former; in such cases, jurisdiction would be restricted to the particular tenement, and would need the express permission of the overlord, whereas in the feudal ranks such permission was implicit.

2.6.3 In the German lands, in contrast to France, the law of fiefs (*Lehnrecht*) remained distinct from the law of the land (*Landrecht*), and so the feudal courts developed and remained side by side with the older courts, without absorbing them. Further, the idea, also found in England, that any free man could be a suitor to the king's court, helped to keep alive allodial holding, especially in the Swabian Alps and Saxony. However, the *scabini* (*Schöffen*) who met under a judge (*Richter*), who was usually a feudal lord, were normally required to hold land of a certain value, and there was also a tendency to regard their office as hereditary. Hence feudal attitudes, if not precisely feudalism, blended there too with customary law.

2.7   FEUDAL SOCIETY AND THE REST OF SOCIETY

2.7.1   There were, then, other classes in society than the feudal; this is to take a legal approach, viewing feudalism as a particular form of social mechanism. (It is quite possible to look at society as dominated by feudalism and thus feudal throughout, but that would be more a sociological or economic approach.) In this narrow sense, peasants or unfree tenants generally did not fall within the terms of feudal law. Furthermore, there were always, and nearly everywhere, some men who held land under a contract of lease or by customary right; they also are described as tenants, using the term in the modern (or Roman) sense. They paid rent in some form, rather than providing service. In feudalism proper there was no nationality, only hierarchy, but particular consequences were modified by local custom. And local variations considerably affected the distinction between the lesser gentry, the free peasant, and the sergeant. 'Sergeants' is a translation of the Latin term *servientes*, and they originated from the men, free or servile, who served in person on their lords. One group sprang from the major offices of a baronial or royal household, the butler, the steward, the seneschal, the marshal; great families were founded by many such servants (this was the origin of the Scottish royal house of Stewart) and fortunes were made even by the servants of lesser men. Other sergeants were soldiers, granted land to hold by a military tenure not amounting to knight service. In Germany, in particular, there was even a class of servile sergeants, *ministeriales*, who might achieve knighthood while still remaining unfree, and yet holding their lands by military service.

2.7.2   In some parts of Christendom, virtually all men were free; this was often the case in hill country, where the population was scattered, centred on a crossroads rather than a compact village, and occupied with raising sheep or with growing vines or olives. Where there was plentiful arable land, manors and nuclear villages were common. The usual model is of one manor to one village, but there might be two or more manors in a big village, and it was possible for one knight in his castle to dominate two or more villages.

2.7.3   The manor as an administrative and economic unit predated feudalism, but it adapted perfectly to it. The open-field system as a method of collective farming had customary roots, and the lord's share, the demesne, readily fitted into the scheme. Within the typical manor there would be some free peasants – some rich enough to own a plough team, others not – and more who were not free, but, in either case, the peasant would in many places make an act of homage to his lord for his tenement and be formally invested with it. A free man might hold by base tenure or an unfree man by free tenure, and both free and unfree would have suit of court at the manor, but the free man holding by free tenure might, in theory at least, have access to the king's courts. For free tenure payment would be in money or in kind; tenure for a money payment was described by the *Summa de legibus*[24] as 'voluntary', because it did not result 'from the necessity of inheritance'. Servile tenure involved week-work – the labour of a single man – for perhaps, three days a week. Free tenants as well might in some cases be called on for boon-work, for help with the harvest and at any other particularly busy time in the agricultural year. The villein would be subject at his death to the exaction of his best beast as heriot, the equivalent of the feudal relief, since this forfeit gave his sons the right to take over his (unfree) holding; the villein also had to pay a tax called merchet if his daughter married outside the manor (this is the basis for the fictional *droit de seigneur*). The village mill was often the lord's monopoly, as with the Scots thirlage, and so might be the village wine-press or brewery, and even the free peasant might be obliged to use it. The lord could also raise from the unfree a tax called tallage, originally arbitrary, but by the eleventh century usually fixed as to frequency and amount, often in writing, according to the custom of the manor; there might be other levies on special occasions, roughly comparable to the feudal aids. The lord's court would often be presided over, in the lord's absence, by his reeve or bailie; although the suitors spoke to the custom of the manor, trial by their peers was not a common right for those subject to seignorial courts. Such trial was rather more likely in the north, where Germanic customary law had stronger roots, and rather less so in the south, where men more often remembered that Roman magistrates had been the superiors, not the equals, of those whom they had judged.

24 *Summa de legibus* 26.8.

2.7.4   In the towns, the burgesses had their own courts based on mercantile custom, from which was to develop the law merchant (see chapter 6). They sometimes held their land freely, as allodial holding, or by some customary title, or by leasehold, or often from the king or prince by burgage tenure; such tenures could be bought and sold, just like moveable property, without any lord's consent and, usually, such sales could not be revoked by the seller's heirs or relatives. In burgage holding, sisters usually received an equal portion with brothers, and ward went normally to the next of kin, as was the old Germanic custom not dissimilar to Roman practice. Burgesses often put themselves under the direct protection of the king, for example, in London or at St Andrews; towns were in general, especially in the south of Europe, unfeudal in the narrow sense in which we use the term.

2.8   THE FORMALIZATION OF FEUDALISM

2.8.1   It is something of a paradox that one can see the end of feudalism, in the sense of the essentially simple system that has been described, as falling in the twelfth century, yet it is, in a different sense, just at this period that feudalism appears as something of which the men of the time were consciously aware. It is in the twelfth century that lawyers, known as feudists (so called because their basic subject matter was feus, as that of the canonists was the canon law), first appear in the Italian cities and comment on feudal law as a speciality, and that feudal law becomes a written law – and therefore able to blend with the civil or learned law, as we shall see in section 2.9. By the beginning of the thirteenth century, although private wars had not completely ceased, life in western Europe was reasonably peaceful; the 'heroic' age of feudal warfare had passed. Markets had grown as the population increased now that there was surplus production; towns and trade were flourishing. Feudal holdings were valued at least as much for their financial returns, such as judicial profits, as for their military strength. Kings and princes more commonly employed mercenary troops of soldiers than the feudal levy; such troops were paid from scutage (as a substitute for military service) or even by taxation raised for this particular purpose. Cross-bows and cannon came to devalue the old knightly skills and techniques; with developing technology, we find a weakening of the personal tie between lord and vassal.

2.8.2   The tendency to centralization on royal power made overt legislation possible; we shall see examples in England, and the same process was at work in France, in Scotland, and in the Empire. Moreover, professional civil services were also developing,[25] and their continuity strengthened royal at the expense of feudal justice. At the Fourth Lateran Council in 1215 the clergy were forbidden to take any part in trials by ordeal; although such trials did not at once disappear, their solemnity was much diminished and they began to fall into disuse.[26] Trial by battle also became less frequent, although it still had a long life (the last, and confessedly antiquarian, attempt to use it in England took place in 1818 – *Ashford v Thornton* (1818) 1 B & Ald 405); in the kingdom of Sicily, Frederick II was able to restrict it severely in 1231[27] on the grounds of its irrationality. The 'bad baron' had largely disappeared, although he had been a very real figure.[28] Lords, not yet in legal terms landlords under a contract, preferred other than military forms of service, and money ties were adequate between lord and vassal when there was little likelihood of their having to go into battle side by side. Money fiefs became common in England and France, as well as Scotland. From the thirteenth century, although feudal rules on property and succession had a long life ahead of them, the most active sphere of feudal thinking was probably in constitutional law.

25 Herlihy, no 45.
26 Herlihy, no 25.
27 Herlihy, no 26.
28 See the poem: *Raoul of Cambrai*, eg s 59 – Herlihy, no 31.

2.8.3   The court of the king, the prince, and in some cases of the great dukes and counts, as in Normandy and Flanders, always had a claim to an authority that was more than feudal. It was to such courts that cases concerning allodial estates must come, as also cases defining the boundary between secular and ecclesiastical jurisdiction. These are described as regalian rights; in the same category fell public highways and even markets, which also pertained by their nature to such sovereign courts, although jurisdiction over them was more likely to be granted away or usurped. The growth of the king's royal, insofar as distinguishable from his feudal, court was both to help and be helped by the growth in the knowledge and use of the civil law. It is a phenomenon, in France especially, of the thirteenth century and after; in France it was linked with the increasing political power of the Capetians. In Germany, the rival appeal of the imperial role, exercised especially in Italy, often distracted the prince from strengthening his kingly power; for example, the emperor Frederick III did not set foot in his German territories from 1444 to 1471. In Germany there was no network of itinerant justices or permanent representatives of the Crown, such as the Angevins developed in England and the Capetians copied as they could. Nevertheless, it was through the Crown that eventually, several centuries later than England and France, Germany was to acquire a degree of judicial centralization.

2.8.4 The other thing that strengthened the royal at the expense of the feudal courts was appeal. The concept of appeal linked the customary, sacred, role of the prince with the imperial supremacy of the civil law, in defiance of the feudal attitude that one's immediate lord was one's only natural judge and that to seek redress elsewhere was to weaken the tie of vassalage. But even in feudal custom the denial of justice to one's man was a breach of the duties of lordship. Hence, when a man was denied a hearing, or when false judgment was given, he could properly accuse his lord before that lord's lord. This was in theory an action for redress quite unrelated to the cause which lay behind the miscarriage of justice, but it is hardly surprising that the king's professional advisers turned such procedures into true appeal. The king's counsellors in such matters would be trained in the civil or the canon law, or both, wherein a hierarchy of courts was normal. The process fitted into the feudal pyramid, at the top of which stood the king's court, but it was not itself feudal. It was another step towards the unity of justice within a realm.

2.9 FEUDAL LAW AND ACADEMIC LAW: THE LITERATURE OF FEUDAL LAW

2.9.1 Even before the twelfth century and the explosive growth of interest in the civil law, the law of the *Corpus Iuris Civilis* (to which the next chapter is devoted, and where some of the technical terms used in the next few paragraphs will be more fully explained), legal scholars at Pavia had produced glosses and commentaries on the *Liber Papiensis* and the *Lombarda*; that is, they had explained particular words and phrases, and they had drawn out applications relevant to their own day. In the first flowering of the law school at Bologna, scholars were interested in the Lombard version of feudal customary law, for it was in force in much of Italy. Charles (Karolus) de Tocco from Benevento, who taught at Bologna, composed a gloss to the *Lombarda* which acquired considerable authority in both law schools and courts. But the tendency in the northern Italian cities during the twelfth century was to belittle the Germanic element in Italian law; in Naples and the south a more sustained interest was shown. However, even if the Glossators of Bologna were eager to stress the values of Roman law, they could not long exclude from their studies all aspects of feudal law. Moreover, there was a formal sense in which the modern, that is post-Lombard, developments of the feudal and customary law described in such works as the *Liber Papiensis* could not fail to be recognized, for they included the legislation of emperors such as Charlemagne, Otto the Great, Conrad II, and others, who claimed to be emperors in succession to Justinian.

2.9.2   In the 1150s one Obertus de Orto, a judge of the imperial court at Milan, and therefore aware of the traditions of the cities, made a collection best known as the *Libri Feudorum* (*Books of the Feus*). This was based mainly on imperial legislation in the kingdom of Italy but also included other materials such as decisions from various feudal courts, Lombard custom and some extracts from the writings of the school of Pavia. The story runs that Obertus' son went to study law at Bologna and was astonished to find no attention paid to the legal system to which his father devoted his life. Obertus replied to his son in two letters in which he laid out the basic elements of feudal law; the composition of the *Libri* was subsequent. Obertus had the weight of actual practice on his side; as was said: 'Roman law is of no weak authority, but its force does not extend to overthrowing custom'.[29]

29 *Books of the Feus* II.1.

2.9.3   Thus there developed among the jurists better known for their work as civilians (or specialists in the civil, the Roman, law) a degree of interest in feudal law (a specialist on which is known as a feudist). Pillius of Medicina (fl. 1169–1207), a pupil of the great Placentinus, commented on the *Libri Feudorum* when he was teaching at Modena, and he started on an *Apparatus*. Towards the middle of the thirteenth century the Bolognese jurist, James de Ardizzone, reorganized the material, with additions, into two books; he also wrote a *Summa* on feudal law. A third version of the collection divided the books into titles, on the model of the *Corpus*; an authoritative gloss to this, developing Pillius' *Apparatus*, was produced in the 1220s by Accursius and used in his Standard Gloss. It was in this form – the Vulgate version – that the *Libri* were eventually added to the final volume of the *Corpus* which contained Justinian's Novels. Thus the main collection of the sources of feudal law became classed among the *libri legales*, the legal books of the learned law. Thereafter, no longer despised as barbaric, it was studied as though an integral part of the *Corpus*. The glossed version of this enlarged *Corpus* was the edition in normal use by practitioners of law until the sixteenth century or even later. Scholars continued to use it until the critical editions of the nineteenth century were published.

2.9.4   Particular interest in the *Libri Feudorum* continued to be shown in southern Italy but, among other jurists whose main place is in later chapters, Jacques de Révigny (d.1296) commented on them, and James de Belvisio (1270–1335), sometime royal judge and councillor at Naples, later a lecturer at Perugia and Bologna, wrote on them and on the Novels (the *Authenticum* version). Baldus (c.1320–1400), a noted civilian and canonist (specialist on canon law) of the fourteenth century, wrote on the *Libri* and on the treaty of the Peace of Constance (1183), at which the emperor had conceded to the communes of northern Italy the use of their local customs. Antonio di Pratovecchio (c.1380–1468), while at Padua, recast the two *Libri* into six books, and edited their gloss; another teacher at Padua, Giacomo Alvarotto (c.1385–1453), introduced the non-specific use of the term feudal when he wrote a description of the basic and general principles governing the law of the feu or fief in a book entitled *De Feudis* (*Concerning Feus*).

2.9.5   While the academic lawyers were thus refining the concepts of feudal law in the universities, those who actually administered such law, whether on their own behalf or on their prince's, were blending into their practice the learning of the civilians. In England, shortly before 1190, a book known as *Glanvill*, after its supposed author, described the laws and customs of the realm, especially as administered by the royal courts; the main content is feudal and customary, but *Glanvill* quotes in certain areas from the Institutions of Justinian, and the shape and concept of the book derive from the learned law. (Glanvill was imported into Scotland somewhat later, with appropriate variations, and this version is known as *Regiam Majestatem*.) Nearly half a century after *Glanvill* a feudal lord called Eike von Repgow produced a similar work applicable to Saxony, the *Sachsenspiegel* (*Mirror of the Saxons*); it too was concerned with local custom, and it too could not have been written had not the study of feudal law become well established in the universities. It was an unofficial compilation, dealing mostly with matters of customary and feudal land law, but it was of great authority and was later adopted in other regions of Germany. We shall return to the influence of these works in later chapters.

2.9.6 The Customs of Beauvaisis, more properly the customs of the county of Clermont in Beauvaisis, were described in the 1280s by Philippe de Beaumanoir.[30] He also was not a jurist but a feudal lord with considerable experience of the administration of justice. The Customs reveal the blend that had come into being even in the *pays de droit coutumier* (region of customary law) in France north of the Loire, or, rather, they reveal one particular blend made up predominantly of feudal custom with a seasoning of the learned law. In his prologue Beaumanoir made a very significant point; he stated that he was led to write down these customs for their more secure maintenance, for he had observed that they prevailed over the ancient laws (that is, the Roman law) in practice but that, since memories are fallible, what is not written is soon forgotten. This need to put things into writing was one of the ways by which the learned law came to dominate custom, just as in the first reception of Roman law by the Germanic invaders of the Empire the existence of a written law had affected their customs and attitudes. Men's memories of an event which happened only days or weeks ago are unreliable; their memory of how their fathers dealt with some matter of moment is likely to be even less reliable, unless fortified by some record. It is the paradox of custom as a basis for law that one then looks to the record, and custom in the true sense ceases to be operative. The rules and attitudes which had grown up around tenure and services and traditional relationships remained the rules which governed these matters but, through writing, they lost flexibility while at the same time becoming open to reforms, such as the moves towards a more rational form of legal procedure.

30 Herlihy, no 33.

2.9.7 Beaumanoir limited himself formally to the customs of his region for 'we ought to have a better memory of that which we have seen practised and judged since our infancy in our district, rather than in another district of which we have not learned the customs or the usages'. He therefore based himself on the judgments made in the county in his own time, and the clear usages and clear customs long followed there. When there was doubt, he looked to judgments made in neighbouring jurisdictions; if those failed him, he then looked to the law common to the entire kingdom of France. This last might involve the law taught in the universities, the civil law, as well as the custom of the king's own court, but the ordering of priority in his sources is clearly feudal. He gave examples of custom and usage, which he distinguished by holding that custom was, within a jurisdiction, something universally observed, while usage was open to challenge. An example of a clear custom was the rule that a person who admitted a debt must pay up within seven days, unless he were of the nobility when he had fifteen days: 'This custom is so clear that I have never seen it challenged.' Only a usage, although it was widespread, was the rule that peaceful possession for a year and a day gave sasine or seisin, protected possession, although that sasine was still open to challenge on the question of title and right. He described as a second example of usage the peaceful tenure of a piece of property for ten years, in the view and with the knowledge of those who might have wished to prohibit it. This tenure, as long as there was a *causa* (apparent grounds for title) such as purchase, gift, legacy, forfeit or inheritance, and as long as the property was held from its lord by some rent that was due to him, gave the possessor sasine and full title. Peaceful possession for thirty years, even without a *causa*, as long as the lord received his dues, gave sasine and full title. These usages were of no effect where the land was held as dowry or for life or as leasehold or as a pledge, for no one could by his mere will change the grounds for his possession.[31] The year-and-a-day rule was indeed one of customary origin – for example, a serf who managed to support himself for so long in a town acquired freedom from his lord – but the other two usages are taken directly from the rules on acquisition through prescription laid down by Justinian.[32] The civil law is here apparent, but the context remains essentially feudal, as does the principle that no usage which diminished the normal value of an estate for its lord was valid against him unless he received some form of rent or return.

31   'Nemo sibi ipse causam possessionis mutare potest' (D 41.2.3.19).
32   Inst 2.6*pr*; CJ 7.39.8 (AD 528).

2.9.8   The academic development of feudal law thus came to be normal, normal in practice, normal in the schools, in the twelfth and thirteenth centuries. Men still stressed the importance of custom, partly for the secure feeling that they were following the habits of their ancestors. Yet writing allowed different types of changes to be made, which could accord with new notions of royal power or new demands of commerce. The blend of feudal and customary law with the civil law created its own new custom (which we shall look at in the later chapter on the *ius commune*) when the same general principles were applied, although still with local variations, throughout western Europe from the fourteenth to the sixteenth century. Even in the seventeenth century the same received ideas and accepted techniques were common practice throughout Europe. As an illustration, Sir Thomas Craig (1538–1608), a Scottish advocate who had studied in France and who became Sheriff of Edinburgh in 1573, produced a major work, entitled *Ius Feudale* (*Feudal Law*), around 1603. It was printed in 1655 and there were still sufficient traces of a European common law for it to be used as a textbook in German and Dutch universities. Feudal customary law is one of the major strands in European legal history; it is mildly ironic that its importance was enhanced by its confluence with the learned law.

FURTHER READING

JW Baldwin	'The intellectual preparations for the canon of 1215 against ordeals', *Speculum* 36 (1961) 613
R Bartlett	*Trial by Fire and Water* (Oxford, 1986)
M Bloch	*Feudal Society* (London, 2nd edn, 1962)
FL Ganshof	*Feudalism* (London, 3rd edn, 1964)
D Herlihy	*The History of Feudalism* (New York, 1970)
R McKitterick	*The Carolingians and the Written Word* (CUP, 1989)
S Reynolds	*Fiefs and Vassals* (OUP, 1994)
P Vinogradoff	'Customary Law' in *The Legacy of the Middle Ages*, eds CG Crump & EF Jacob (Oxford, 1926)

Chapter 3

THE GLOSSATORS

3.1 THE BACKGROUND TO THE REVIVAL OF THE STUDY OF ROMAN LAW

3.1.1 The ground was well prepared, but the arrival of the Glossators as a school of jurists on the European scene may appear as a sudden phenomenon. Traditionally the school was founded by one Irnerius, a grammarian of Bologna. The story goes that he turned to the study of law after having been consulted about the meaning of the word *as* (a Roman coin of small value) in the New Testament phrase: '*Nonne duo passeres asse veneunt*' ('Are not two sparrows sold for a farthing?' – Matt 10.29). His researches led to the discovery of the technical meaning of the term *as* in the Roman law of succession, where it is used as the duodecimal unit for dividing an inheritance up among more than one heir. From this he went on to the study and teaching of Roman law. Another tradition links him with the Countess Matilda of Tuscany, who is supposed to have encouraged him to set up a law school at Bologna. The suggestion that it was anti-imperial must be mythical since, as teachers (which is what the term 'doctor' means[1]) of the secular imperial law, the Bolognese civilians tended to support the Empire. All that can be said with certainty is that the study of Roman law was revived at Bologna towards the end of the eleventh and at the beginning of the twelfth centuries, and that Irnerius was an important figure in that revival. If he was not the first teacher there, for we do hear of a certain Pepo (Joseph), he was the first to leave any identifiable writings, and he was looked to in succeeding generations as the founder of the school.

1   'Master' was the normal title of the teacher in arts at a mediaeval university, but 'doctor' became the normal term for a law teacher in Italy from the mid-twelfth century; usage varied elsewhere.

3.1.2 As we have seen, the revival of Roman law was due to a number of causes: the superiority of the written law, the increase in leisure and commerce, the growth of towns, the intellectual battles of papalists and imperialists; but the single most significant factor, the *sine qua non*, was the recovery of the full text of the *Corpus Iuris Civilis*, and in particular of the Digest. For, while the Institutions and the Code were relatively familiar, the Digest was not known; a Tuscan judgment of 1076 certainly cites it, but without understanding, and a citation from Ravenna in 1084 ascribes to the Digest a text that is in fact from the Code. Two manuscripts seem to have appeared in the eleventh century; the one which survives to this day was written in the sixth century in southern Italy and was held at Pisa by the twelfth century. (It is known to us as the Florentine MS, because in a war between the two cities in 1406 Florence took it as booty and has possessed it ever since.) The other is the supposed ancestor of all the copies made at Bologna; it is known as the *Codex Secundus*. While we do not know precisely when or how they were discovered, it seems in the highest degree likely that it was by canonists engaged in the search for legal ammunition. It is evident that by the beginning of the twelfth century the capacity, the knowledge, and the techniques existed to master the complex and sophisticated Roman sources.

3.1.3 That Bologna became the first centre specifically concerned with Roman law may be partly a matter of chance, perhaps the chance that Irnerius was there and teaching in the school of arts. But Bologna was a crossing point for trade routes between various parts of the north of Italy and the south; it was also near the border between imperial and papal territory. Moreover, Pavia in Lombardy was not very far away and already a centre of study for Lombard law, and the Lombard lawyers had shown some familiarity with Roman sources.

3.2 THE IMPORTANCE OF THE GLOSSATORS

3.2.1 It is commonly said that Roman law was revived in the twelfth century – or sometimes, more accurately, that the study of Roman law was revived then – but this does not give a wholly correct impression. Certainly there was an enormous upsurge of interest in and study of the texts of Roman law, and particularly of Justinian's compilation, but what influenced the law from this time onwards was not necessarily what Justinian had intended to have effect as Roman law, far less what had been in force as Roman law in the classical period. What was important was the use made of the texts by the scholars who worked on them; this is why the term 'civil law' is often more apt for the mediaeval (and later) handling of the Roman law texts. There was room for creative activity because of the nature of Justinian's compilation, on which both study and teaching were based. As we saw in the first chapter (see para 1.1.3), arguments incorporated in the texts could be brought out and developed, or adapted to new circumstances.

3.2.2 The work of the Glossators is of fundamental importance in the long process of assimilation of elements of Roman law into European legal systems. First, the Glossators mastered the sources of Justinian's law and in particular the Digest, the least accessible by reason of its bulk and complexity. In effect, they produced a working edition of the *Corpus*, for the Standard Gloss of Accursius (to which we shall come) was the culmination of their control of the material. Second, they influenced legal practice and administration, for both of which they provided an education that was secular not ecclesiastical. It is false to suggest that the Glossators had no interest in law in practice; Irnerius himself acted as judicial assessor, and also as an envoy to the Emperor Henry V on the death of Countess Matilda, while in 1118 he was in Rome taking a prominent part in the election of an anti-pope in the imperial interest. Among others who played a significant part in public life were Bulgarus, Hugh of the Ravenna Gate (Ugo de Porta Ravennate), Placentinus, Pillius, Hugolinus,

James (Jacobus) Balduini, and Hubert of Bobbio (Ubertus Bobiensis), whose work we shall meet in due course (see 3.7.13-15). Third, the Glossators founded a science of law, in the sense of a framework of juridical concepts which made it possible to provide rational legal solutions to conflicts of interests in society in place of solutions based on custom or mere force. They offered law as a self-conscious structure, an ordering instrument for society, and this on a European scale.

3.3   APPROACHES TO HANDLING THE TEXTS

3.3.1   There has been much discussion of how far the Glossators were influenced by the prevailing Scholastic philosophy. Scholasticism may be described as a system of philosophy which sought to work out by dialectic the rational, harmonious and divine order which was believed to exist in the world and, indeed, in the universe. The name Scholasticism later became associated with hair-splitting distinctions and forced logic; some nineteenth-century scholars therefore attempted to clear the Glossators of any contamination by denying that there was any dependence. A better appreciation of Scholasticism, concentrating on its intellectually liberating initial effects rather than the somewhat exaggerated weaknesses of its later days, makes it clear that it would be extraordinary if there were no such influence. The Glossators were, after all, men of their time.

3.3.2   One must expect of the Glossators a knowledge of the subjects of the *trivium* and *quadrivium*; of these the most relevant to law were dialectic (or logic) and rhetoric. The arts of reasoning and argument are necessarily of some concern to lawyers. The foundations of both were laid in Greece, the most important contributions being the works of Aristotle known collectively as the *Organon* (*Tools*, ie of thought). But only the more elementary part of Aristotle's work, the *Old Logic* (*logica vetus*), was known before the mid-twelfth century; the remainder, the *New Logic* (*logica nova*), which forms the basis of the specifically Scholastic logic, came into use in the later twelfth and early thirteenth centuries. It can be demonstrated that the Glossators knew and used the *Old Logic* and rhetorical devices in their work. Irnerius, for example, used logical techniques to explain difficult texts; prefaces to works such as Azo's *Summa Codicis* follow the rhetoricians' advice on how to capture the reader's attention by tricks of the trade. There is, however, no reliable evidence of the use of the *New Logic*; it may have been known to the Glossators, but they had settled their techniques by the end of the twelfth century.

3.3.3   The more important point is that the whole attitude of the Glossators corresponded to the aims of Scholasticism – to harmonize and systematize, to use reason to explain and justify an authority which was at the centre of their studies as a guide to the harmonious order which they sought to discover (and, having discovered, to bring about). For the civilians the central authority was the *Corpus Iuris Civilis*, as the Bible and the Fathers of the Church were for the theologians, and Aristotle for the philosophers. The *Corpus* was the chief expression of Roman law, and Roman law held this central authority partly because of the idea of the continuity of Roman law under the Holy Roman Empire – the idea of *renovatio imperii* was a commonplace by the end of the eleventh century – and partly because of its place as part of the classical heritage. Certainly there was Scholastic influence, but dependence must not be pressed too hard, for there may have been reciprocal influence; the Glossators' *quaestiones disputatae* (*Questions for discussion* – almost comparable to modern moots; see 3.7.6-9) as a form of instruction seem to have been taken as a model by the theologians. In relation to *quaestiones* there is a significant difference between the lawyers and the philosophers in that the Glossators' aim seems to have been not so much to confute an opponent's line of argument as to present the arguments for decision by a judge. The solutions are not presented as absolutely correct; after giving arguments for and against a solution, they do not simply point out the faults in the other view but rather put forward a view as preferable, although still open to challenge, leaving the decision to someone else.

3.3.4 Moreover, the *Corpus Iuris Civilis* itself offered encouragement to harmonization and systematization because Justinian himself had claimed that it was a harmonious whole. There are also examples of the use of dialectic and rhetoric in the Roman texts, and whether they came from the classical jurists themselves or from interpolation by the compilers of the *Corpus* was not a matter which troubled the Glossators. In fact, the extent to which the Roman jurists used the techniques of rhetoric or were influenced by Greek philosophy is itself much discussed – again with a frequent tendency to claim independence for the jurists – but the Glossators simply looked at the texts as they had them. Furthermore, the Glossators clearly assumed that Roman law, as they understood it, was law to be applied. Although they could not fail to notice that not all its institutions, such as the Roman magistracies, were still in existence, and indeed they pointed out what was no longer used in practice, Roman law was discussed as a living system. For example, there is a text (D 9.2.7.4) which says that no action for wrongful damage would lie as a result of a wrestling or boxing match 'because the damage is held to have been done in the cause of fame and valour, not wrongdoing'; they applied this to tournaments among knights. This sort of updating was necessary because an important function of the Glossators was to teach the men who were intending a career as administrators, including forensic employment, in the service of princes and also of the Church; even though many ecclesiastics studied only the canon law, Roman law was a recognized, and indeed necessary, subsidiary source.

3.4 METHODS OF TEACHING

3.4.1 The name 'Glossators' is given to the jurists of this school because the characteristic product of their work on the texts was the gloss, marginal or interlinear, either in the sense of an explanatory comment on the individual word or phrase or text (ie, the whole passage), or in the sense of an *apparatus* (collection) of glosses to a part or the whole of the *Corpus*. The so-called Great Gloss of Accursius is the most famous and was the most widely used of such *apparatus*; it was the standard commentary on the text after its completion in the mid-thirteenth century, and its success helps to account for the name 'Glossators'. However, that name is somewhat misleading if it suggests that the gloss was their only literary product, and that the sole interest of the school lay in detailed comment on the Roman texts. What is true is that much of the literary production of the Glossators arose from their teaching, and that most forms of literature other than glosses can be traced back to comments made in the course of teaching. Because of this connection between their teaching and their writing it is illuminating to consider their teaching methods before dealing with the literature they produced.

3.4.2   For example, Odofredus (d. 1265) tells us that the lecturer would work his way through a particular section of the *Corpus*, such as the Institutions or the Old Digest,[2] following the order of the texts, which were known as *leges* (laws); hence the 'legal order' is the order which Justinian's compilers gave to the texts. The first step was to explain how the books and titles fitted together, that is, why one followed the other in the order that they did. In principle he would go on to discuss each text. First he would set out the factual case or cases dealt with. Then he would read the text through and deal with any grammatical or syntactical problems in interpreting it and any variant readings. He would refer to any parallel passages (*similia*), and also point out any texts which seemed to conflict (*contraria*). Where there were apparent conflicts he would resolve them, for example, by forming a distinction (*distinctio*) to show how one text applied in one situation and the other in one which was different in some way. He might even pick out pairs of arguments (*brocard(ic)a* or brocards) as commonplace examples of the arguments for and against a proposition – for example, silence means consent: silence is not consent – as rules to be applied in different contexts.[3] He would also point out any general applications of the text, showing how it could be used as an argument or 'proof' in forensic debate, that is, as authority for a legal proposition. Especially important texts or the principles contained in them would be picked out as noteworthy points (*notabilia*).

2   For the mediaeval division of the *Corpus*, see Appendix 1.
3   Tacitly allowing something to happen may operate as consent, as when you allow another to stand surety for you, but if someone sells your property your silence is to be interpreted as ignorance of the deed rather than consent to it.

3.4.3   At the end the lecturer would often raise questions (*quaestiones*) suggested by the text; he might discuss these in the lecture or, as did John (Johannes) Bassianus, master of Azo, at a separate time set apart for such discussion or disputation (often evenings or Saturday mornings). This last proceeding was very important because the questions discussed or disputed were usually points to which no text offered a clear solution, perhaps because they arose from contemporary practice, and the search for a solution allowed constructive use of the material in the *Corpus*. Ideas were taken from their original context and applied in new ways; a very famous example is the application of the phrase 'what touches all alike is to be approved by all' (C 5.59.5.2: '*quod omnes similiter tangit ab omnibus comprobetur*'), originally concerned with the liability of co-tutors, to insist on the need for consent, whether to certain steps in litigation or to taxation or to other matters, by the parties involved (see para 4.6.5).

3.4.4 Of course, not every text was necessarily dealt with in such detail. We hear criticisms of lecturers who pedantically did so, and we have reports of lectures where the students were told to go and read some texts for themselves because they presented no problems. On the other hand, some university statutes required lecturers to deal with all the texts and to omit none. But the approach described was the general scheme, which was still in use with only minor variations as late as the sixteenth century by those who followed the traditional methods.

3.5 FORMS OF LITERATURE: GLOSSES AND *APPARATUS* OF GLOSSES

3.5.1 These are the typical product of the activity of the Glossators as teachers. It is often suggested that they began by writing individual glosses and gradually progressed to writing *apparatus*. While it must be true that individual glosses came first, nevertheless *apparatus* are certainly older than Azo, who the nineteenth-century scholar Savigny[4] thought was the first to write an *apparatus* – at the end of the twelfth century. Whether they go back to Irnerius or his immediate followers, the Four Doctors (Bulgarus, Martin Gosia, Hugh of the Ravenna Gate, and Jacobus), as has been suggested, is more doubtful. Development before Azo is perfectly understandable when glosses and *apparatus* are seen as a product of teaching devoted to a particular part of the *Corpus*.

4   Savigny was very influential in the development of law in Germany during the nineteenth century; see Chapter 16.

3.5.2 Glosses which have survived from the earlier twelfth century reveal types of gloss corresponding to the various stages of discussion or exposition of the texts as described above, with the exception of *quaestiones*. These last appear as literature only towards the end of the century and seem to have originated as separate writings, in the form of collections recording disputations in which several lines of argument had been deployed. They then appear as explanatory glosses in the form of questions and suggested answers to questions which had not been settled by the texts, along with the other types of gloss. Insofar as they deal with points of difficulty which are not directly raised in the texts they are distinct from solutions (*solutiones*) of contrary texts.

3.5.3 One can thus identify forms of literature with methods of teaching. There are introductions to titles (*introductiones titulorum*) which usually appear as glosses to the rubrics – for Irnerius found the titles within the books which make up the Digest, Code and Institutions already named, as are the individual Novels. Introductions define the main concept or terms used in the rubric, and explain the context of the title and the division of the material within it. Sometimes such introductions led on to a more general discussion; for example, the discussion of the rubric to D 1.1 *On justice and law* was very fruitful for wide-ranging jurisprudential argument.[5] There are similar introductions to individual texts.

5   Appendix 1(A) gives an early example.

3.5.4   The basic explanatory gloss – naturally the most frequent of all – may even be fitted into the text, so that it makes sense only if read as a constituent part. For example, D 7.1.9.4 (a title on usufruct, or liferent) runs:

> 'There is a point *closely related to this* (*huic vicinus*) which is usually discussed in relation to the law on accession to land; it has been settled that the usufructuary is entitled to a usufruct of accessions by *alluvio* [land added by the gradual deposit of soil by a river].'

The gloss *Huic vicinus* runs:

> '*Closely related to this*, because other additions to something subject to a usufruct have been dealt with above and similarly are discussed below'

Glosses deal both with textual problems, such as variant readings or the explanation of difficult words, and with juristic matters, such as the reasons for decisions or the citation of other relevant material; in this way a thorough system of indexing was established. Many glosses are signed by a letter or symbol (*siglum*) indicating the author, but this is not a reliable form of ascription because of errors of attribution, and because each generation of the jurists built on the work of its predecessors.

3.5.5   Other forms of glosses were less closely attached to individual words or phrases and reach a more abstract level of interpretation, attempting to fit the text into the system of rules as a whole.[6] In early glosses particularly there are lists of parallel and conflicting passages (*similia* and *contraria*), giving cross-references throughout the great bulk of the *Corpus*. Parallel passages naturally reinforced the obvious interpretation of the basic text; for conflicting passages, solutions would be suggested which sprang from reading the material – whether within the title or even within the *Corpus* as a whole.[7] A special form of conflicting passages, known as *authenticae*, arose from the effect on the Roman texts of the Novels, including occasionally the legislation of the Holy Roman Emperors, especially in the Code (that is Books 1-9). For example, *Auth. Sacramenta puberum* provided that when a minor over the age of puberty incurred an obligation fortified by oath it could not be set aside on the grounds of his minority, which conflicted with the possibility of *restitutio in integrum* for minority offered by the Roman texts. Irnerius was responsible for many *authenticae*.

6   See Appendix 1(B), showing the modification of the Roman rules.
7   For example, Irnerius pointed out that Justinian claimed authorship of his Code. Yet many of its enactments were the work of other emperors; Justinian was not the sole author of the texts, although he was of the Code's compilation; see H Kantorowicz and W W Buckland *Studies in the Glossators of the Roman Law* (Cambridge, 1938, reprinted 1969 with addenda and corrigenda by P Weimar) p 233.

3.5.6   Distinctions are found in all types of gloss to explain doubtful or conflicting points, or to provide a guide through these. For example, the term 'will' (*voluntas*) we find categorized:[8]

Will [= intention]

sometimes	just	sometimes	unjust
	constant		inconstant
	of permanent effect		not of permanent effect
	granting to each his due		not granting to each his due

Will [= testament]

sometimes	last	sometimes	not
	in testamentary form		not
	concerning a patrimony		concerning a special fund
			a soldier's, or a rustic's

and so on. At this level a *distinctio* may seem elementary, but considerable confusion can arise from not first defining one's terms. Used in a general sense distinctions explained whole areas of law, as can be seen in the example, quoted from Irnerius by Roffredus, on the contract of leasing.[9]

8 Kantorowicz and Buckland, cited above, p 301.
9 Appendix 1(C).

3.5.7 Noteworthy points (*notabilia*) were particular or general thoughts or statements, apt for use as arguments in disputations on imagined cases or in solving actual problems of practice. For example, in the text (D 7.1.9.4) on the usufructuary and alluvial accessions the gloss on 'entitled' stressed the general rule: 'Note here that accessions follow the fate of the thing to which they accede', and went on to list other texts illustrating this rule. Such notable matters were often marked out physically in the manuscripts by pattern of writing or surrounding ornament.

3.5.8 *Quaestiones* as literature appeared later than other forms of glosses, as we have said; they involve the assembling of several arguments to find a solution. They will be considered in para 3.7.6.

3.5.9 *Apparatus* of glosses as a form of literature are distinct from reports of lectures. (The latter go back to John Bassianus and so are not as early as the earliest *apparatus*.) But only the earliest of them are individual works. Later ones built on earlier ones, the extent of the borrowing depending on the taste and degree of independence in thought of the later writer; some of the best known authors such as Azo and Accursius took over a great deal from previous writers, although they signed the whole *apparatus* as their own work – this was partly because the mediaeval (like the classical) mind had a much less severe view of what we would call plagiarism. We know that Azo in his apparatus to D 50.17 (the last title in the Digest, *de regulis iuris – On maxims of law*) derived much from Bulgarus (d. ?1166) and from John Bassianus, under whom he had studied, and that Accursius in his turn absorbed the bulk of Azo's work. Further, it is likely that later writers introduced into their *apparatus* without acknowledgment ideas from earlier jurists, whether these came from lectures or from any sort of gloss.

3.5.10   As glosses were expanded by the introduction of additional material, including previous work, a gradual change in the structure of *apparatus* becomes apparent. Glosses tended to become more discursive and to include in the one comment elements which had earlier been distinguishable as separate types. All glosses, not just the simple, explanatory ones, came to be attached to words in the text instead of being fitted in beside the passage without a specific link. This made it easier to find the relevant discussions. Azo seems to have been the first to do this in his major *apparatus* to the Old Digest and the Code, but for long the introductions and the citations of similar and conflicting passages remained separate. Hugolinus brought in the lists of citations, and this style was followed by Accursius, although he more commonly absorbed such lists in other glosses.

3.5.11   As time went by, there seem also to have been some formal changes in the style of lecturing which had their effects on the literature. Alexander de Sancto Egidio's reports of Azo's lectures on the Code suggest that explanations of difficult points were introduced at the point where the difficulty arose rather than at the end, as in the older order, but men such as Odofredus or James Balduini kept to the old order throughout the thirteenth century. A definite change occurred with the Commentators, the next main school of civilians, who laid more stress on the problems to be discussed, because they could discuss them while taking for granted the existence of the Gloss as a standard commentary. In their handling, the *apparatus* changed to a comment on the glossed text which dealt with connected extracts rather than individual passages, and concentrated on the more significant texts.

3.6   THE ACCURSIAN GLOSS AND ITS INFLUENCE

3.6.1   The Accursian Gloss, also known as the *Glossa Ordinaria* (Standard Gloss) or simply as 'the Gloss', is a huge compilation of glosses or *apparatus* of glosses to the whole *Corpus Iuris Civilis*. It totals nearly 97,000 items, and while the whole Digest (which is roughly one-and-a-half times as long as the Bible) is perhaps one-half of the complete mediaeval *Corpus*, it is significant of its special importance as a fruitful source of law that its glosses make up two-thirds of the total number of glosses. Much is still uncertain about the Standard Gloss, including the method and order of its compilation. We know that Accursius was born c.1184, taught from 1221, and died c.1263, aged 78. The composition of the Gloss was probably his life's work. He was young when he first glossed the Institutions, and he later produced a second edition of that *apparatus*, but there seems to have been no second edition of the *apparatus* to any other part. There was a gradual accretion of material but it seems mostly, if not entirely, by later hands. It is not easy to detect Accursius' personal contribution, although it is certain that he made some additions of his own as well as selecting from the work of others, such as Azo. Cross-references provide no real guide to the order of composition among or within the individual parts of the *Corpus*, because of constant revisions. But it is clear that he viewed his work as one single *apparatus* to the whole *Corpus*.

3.6.2 The status that Accursius intended for his Gloss is not entirely clear. If from the start he hoped to produce the definitive edition, he did this without imperial backing or any other authorization which could lay down the authentic interpretation of the texts; but then, Gratian's *Decretum* was equally unofficial. Moreover, he may have been mindful of the Emperor Hadrian's admonition (D 1.2.2.49) that authority stemmed from the intrinsic value of juristic work. He may well have hoped to provide a definitive selection of material, but his principle of collection is not clear because of the scale of the Gloss, the absence of detailed modern study, and our ignorance of the sources available to him.

3.6.3 What is certain is the success of the Gloss in its own time and afterwards. It gained rapid acceptance in Italy as the standard commentary on the *Corpus*. When produced in the mid-thirteenth century, it was accepted as the latest and most complete *apparatus*; thereafter, as the standard accepted commentary, it was regularly attached to the text for convenience of consultation. The Gloss is sometimes found without the texts, but for centuries it was rare to find the texts without the Gloss. In one sense it is the culmination of the work of the school of Glossators, that is insofar as it relates to the mastering of the content of the *Corpus*. In another sense one can say it is a sign of decay, in that it was never superseded, but the fact that it was never superseded more truly means that one approach to the texts had been followed up as far as was worthwhile. New lines were opening up.

3.6.4 Its acceptance can be explained not only by its merits as an *apparatus* of glosses, but also because it fulfilled the twin needs of practice and of legal science. For those concerned with the practice of law the Gloss provided a guide to the sources and their interpretation at a time when the statutes of many Italian city states were imposing liability on judges and legal assessors for fault in the performance of their duties; this was under the *podestà* constitution by which an outsider was brought in for a limited period as city manager, with special judicial responsibility. For legal science, whether as teaching or as scholarship, the Gloss provided a standard commentary as a basis for discussion and development. Development was possible because the texts were not viewed as a static body of material but as giving the solution to some problems and guidance on others. Thus, for example, the Glossators were able to develop the transfer of property by *constitutum possessorium*, that is in the form of a simple declaration by the transferor that he now held on behalf of the recipient.

3.6.5 The Gloss provided an indication of accepted usages, of answers to questions not settled by the texts, and of accepted interpretations of the texts. So on doubtful points the Gloss came to be given authority, although not usually binding authority. But on occasion it was made binding, as in fourteenth-century Verona where a statute of 1328 prescribed that the Gloss must be followed failing any higher authority: in the absence of statute or custom the judge must proceed in conformity with the Roman laws and the Standard Gloss of Accursius, as he himself had approved it. A statute of 1393 modified this by giving force to the Gloss as approved by Dinus (Dino) of Mugello, for Dinus had written a book on conflicting glosses (*De glossis contrariis*) and in it had indicated his preferences. Dinus is also notable for his possible share in the compilation of the final title (*On maxims of law*) in the Sext (one of the sources of canon law - see para 5.4.4), and for his great commentary thereon. But in general the authority of the Gloss, not as an independent work but as an interpretation of the texts, grew gradually, even in Italy where it was in immediate use. The Gloss was of support to judges under the *podestà* constitution, and their reliance on the Gloss gave it further authority. Sometimes the Gloss was too closely followed, and critics held that timid judges even followed the Gloss against the meaning of the actual texts whereas its proper function was as a guide to an understanding of the text. But such abuse sprang from the *podestà* system, not from the nature of the Gloss.

3.6.6   Apart from its use in helping judges to their decisions, the Gloss was also of practical help when jurists were called upon to give opinions on points of law submitted to them. In this field too, where several glosses put forward several views, the personal opinion of Accursius was of special importance. Where Accursius had not spoken, in principle the best opinion was to be followed; if this was not clear, the most recent interpretation was to be preferred. For although the Gloss of Accursius was the standard commentary, scholarship did not stand still, and men commented on the commentary.

3.7   OTHER FORMS OF LITERATURE

3.7.1   From the various types of gloss there emerged other literary styles which became independent of the gloss form, and the shaping of most of these is also due to the school we call the Glossators – hence the slightly misleading element in their title. Of these new styles there were some, variously entitled, such as *Summae* and *Casus*, *Commenta* and *Tractatus* which were essentially explanatory with a tendency towards generalization; many of these writings originated in the introductions to titles which had so often formed a part of the gloss proper. *Quaestiones* dealt with unresolved problems and had developed from the solution of conflicting texts; collections of Noteworthy Points and of Brocards were published independently of the texts; *Consilia* (Opinions) stemmed from actual cases, and formularies also grew from the needs of practice.

3.7.2   Notaries were mentioned in Chapter 1 as one of the factors making for a degree of intellectual continuity. In the new age they received at least some part of their training from the jurists; Accursius is recorded as an examiner of notarial candidates. And the notaries adapted their formularies to conform to Roman law; this is apparent from actual documents and from manuals such as the *Ars Notariatus* (*Notarial Art*) of Salatiele. So even at quite a humble level of legal practice the influence of the learned law was to be found, as it was also in the style books of feudal law.

3.7.3   *Summae* or *Summulae* were comprehensive commentaries on a whole title or group of titles, and then on a section or the whole of the *Corpus*. They were an early form of literature; *summulae* are known from three of the Four Doctors, from Bulgarus, Martin Gosia (Martinus) and Hugh of the Ravenna

Gate. For example, Bulgarus' *Summula* on ignorance of law and fact was based on one title from the Digest (D 22.6) and one from the Code (C 1.18). *Summae* of the Institutions served as general introductions to Roman law. *Summae* of the Code came to be what amounted to textbooks; from quite early days, although by definition based on the Code, they included material from the other parts of the *Corpus*, incorporated in the order of titles in the Code. The last and greatest example in this tradition was the *Summa Codicis* of Azo, also known as the *Summa Aurea* (*Golden Survey*).[10] Like the Standard Gloss, this was a work which owed much to Azo's predecessors, but the version he produced came to be widely accepted by practitioners and scholars. Its status as a comprehensive practitioners' textbook was shown by the saying: 'No one can go to court without Azo' ('*Chi non ha Azo, non vada a palazzo*'). At Cremona, and in some other cities, a statute required possession of a copy before a man could be admitted as an advocate.

10 Appendix 1(D).

3.7.4 *Casus* originally explained a whole text by means of a (usually imaginary) case, but they came to interpret a text as a whole, either by expounding the facts or summarizing the content. To explain several such passages which belonged together, and to generalize from the problems posed, there developed *Commenta*, which included explanatory paraphrases of the main texts. These came to be barely distinguishable from *Summulae*. John Bassianus and others wrote in this form on D 50.17, on maxims of law. The commentary was to give its name to the next major school of jurists.[11]

11 For an example from the stage intermediate between Glossators and Commentators, see Appendix 1(E).

3.7.5 Also springing from Introductions was another general form of literature, the *tractatus* (treatise). Treatises dealt with areas of law not confined to any particular title within any part of the *Corpus*. Martin's work on dotal law (*De iure dotium*) is sometimes called a treatise, but it was really a *summula*, being based on one title in the Digest and one in the Code; Bulgarus' *Civil Procedure* (*Ordo Iudiciorum*) is truly independent. Procedure was a favourite subject for the authors of treatises, but other areas were good subjects for systematization. For example, Pillius wrote *On the Violent Possessor* (*De violento possessore*), collecting together the various remedies against a person who has taken possession of another's property by some kind of force. This work deals firstly with civil actions – for theft, robbery, and force and fear – then with interdicts, possessory and other, then imperial constitutions which concerned forcible invasion or invasion of vacant property, and finally with the remedies of the criminal law. The texts cited are drawn from the Digest, the Code, the Institutions, and the Novels, including one enactment of the Emperor Frederick Barbarossa, and there is also a reference to Gratian's *Decretum*.

3.7.6 *Quaestiones* were, as we have said, usually treated independently of the normal lecture or gloss, although they clearly developed from the solution of conflicting passages. Some are little more than such solutions published separately; others are problems which were the subject of further exposition or disputation, arising either from the texts or from practice.[12] Then there are *quaestiones disputatae*, or moots, and dialogues between doctor and student; and perhaps one should include the *Dissensiones Dominorum*, which dealt with conflicting interpretations, frequently between the strict law view of Bulgarus and the equitable approach of Martin.

12 Appendix 1(F).

3.7.7   The simplest collections of *quaestiones* are those based on *quare* – why? The wider literary type is the *Sic et Non* (Yes and No) made famous by Peter Abelard in the field of theology, and shaping Scholastic philosophy. The aim was the harmonization of the sources, and the method was already to be found in the Digest. For example, D 45.1.56.8 runs:

> 'A slave promised to me by Titius is also promised to me, but conditionally, by Seius. If the slave dies after Titius is in arrears with performance but before the fulfilment of the condition, I can sue Titius, and Seius is not liable if the condition is subsequently realized. If I had released Titius from his obligation, Seius would be liable on the realization of the condition. The difference is that on the death of the slave there is no object for which Seius may be liable, but if there was a formal release and the slave survived it, then there is.'

Of the collections which have survived there is one, with twenty-eight examples, which perhaps dates from the Four Doctors, and another with 209 examples which comes from the school of John Bassianus.

3.7.8   *Quaestiones* which arose from the separate disputations held after the lectures allowed development of the law by applying the texts to new situations, real or imagined. Similar literature was produced by the theologians and philosophers, but the civilians again found a model in the Roman texts.

> 'A wild boar fell into a trap set by you for game, and while he was held there I took him out and carried him away; do you think the wild boar I carried away was yours? And if you think he was yours, suppose I had turned him loose into the woods, would he in that case have ceased to be or have remained yours? And, I ask, ought the action which you would have against me, supposing he had ceased to be yours, to be given as an action on analogous facts? The answer given was: Let us see if it makes any difference whether I have set the trap on public or private ground and, if on private land, whether on mine or someone else's, and, if on someone else's, whether with or without leave of the landowner; moreover, whether the boar has stuck so fast in the trap that he cannot get out by himself, or whether by further struggles he would have got loose. Still I think the governing principle to be this, that if he has come into my power he has become mine. But if you had released to his natural liberty a wild boar who had become mine and he had thereby ceased to be mine, then an action ought to be accorded me.' (D 41.1.55 – translation based on that of F de Zulueta.)

The Gloss raised the further question whether the captor must know of his success. There survive collections of this kind by Azo and others; Hugolinus' collection is somewhat gloomily entitled Insoluble Problems (*Insolubilia*).

3.7.9 Of the dialogues between doctor and student, the best known of this period (the type was to recur) is the work known as *Quaestiones de iuris subtilitatibus (Questions on the subtleties of law)*. The work is anonymous and has been ascribed to various of the Glossators. The student puts to the teacher the points which he finds puzzling, and these are explained to him.[13]

13 Appendix 1(G).

3.7.10 *Dissensiones dominorum* (Disputes among the masters) were collections revealing the differing opinions held by various Glossators. For example, Bulgarus held that a husband was bound to return a dowry to his father-in-law after the death of his wife even when there were children, but Martin disagreed. The story runs that Bulgarus' wife did indeed die and his father-in-law consulted Martin for his view on the return of the dowry. Martin said, 'I say he can keep it, but he holds he ought to give it back.' Bulgarus did give it back without argument, rather to Martin's disappointment. In general there was a conflict of jurisprudential principle between these two. Bulgarus was accustomed to hold to the strict law, and to view certainty of what the law was as most desirable for the parties concerned; Martin, more critical of the texts, preferred to strive for justice in the individual case even at the expense of predictability. This tension is ever-present in jurisprudence; later jurists giving more weight to equity than to strict law were often called Gosians, after Martin.[14]

14 Appendix 1(H).

3.7.11 Collections of Noteworthy Points (*notabilia*) were important for the growth of systematization and generalization. Some might be very simple, such as the maxim (Inst. 2.1.12) that things belonging to no one became the property of their occupant. Collections of brocards were often similar to the *Distinctiones* of the glosses proper, but in this form they were not tied to the texts. Pillius produced one such collection, published about 1185, called the *Libellus disputatorius (Book on the art of disputation)* which was comparable to Abelard's *Sic et Non*. It formed a kind of 'concordance of discordant texts', to borrow Gratian's alternative title for his *Decretum*. It is made up mostly of general rules, without exegesis, and it is interesting in particular because it is the first book to abandon the legal order. It is in three parts – one on presumptions, one on actions, and one on various heads of disputation; it is systematic within the first two, but lacks overall co-ordination. It did not have the same success as Azo's *Summa*, which proved easier to use as well as being more comprehensive; Azo also had produced a collection of brocards.

3.7.12 Apart from formularies, which we have mentioned briefly, there was another form of literature which arose from practice rather than teaching, the collections of *Consilia* (Opinions). Some of the problems in *Quaestiones* seem to have come from actual cases, and there was little intellectual difference between the two types of literature. Opinions, however, were responses to points of law put to jurists; therefore they were preserved for practical as well as doctrinal reasons.

3.7.13 Incidentally, they illustrate well the involvement of the Glossators with public life outside the universities. The Four Doctors at the Diet of

Roncaglia in 1158 all declared in favour of the Emperor Frederick Barbarossa, who was in dispute with the Italian cities over the extent of his imperial rights or regalia in such matters as taxation and control of the appointment of magistrates. However, they were not agreed on the limits of imperial authority, and the story goes that Bulgarus told the emperor that his title *dominus* meant that he was men's lord but not that he was their owner. Another version, variously ascribed to Bulgarus and Martin or to Azo and Lothar of Cremona, tells how Martin allowed a plenitude of power to the emperor and as a reward received a horse from him; whence it was said *'Bulgarus dixit (a)equum sed Martinus habuit equum'* ('Bulgarus said rightly, but Martin got the horse').

3.7.14 Accursius certainly gave opinions, and so did John Bassianus who gave them on points of feudal as well as civil law. Bulgarus, as we have seen, consorted with emperors, and his treatise on procedure was written at the request of the chancellor of the papal court for use therein. Hugh on at least one occasion was appointed as judge by Frederick Barbarossa. Placentinus favoured the Italian cities against the emperor, and this may partly explain his moves to Mantua and then Montpellier. His best known student, Pillius, practised as an advocate; it may have been his practical experience which led him to comment on feudal law. He also appeared on occasion in the ecclesiastical courts; on behalf of the monks of Canterbury he appeared against their archbishop in 1187 and against King John over a disputed election to the same archbishopric in 1205.

3.7.15 Hugolinus was a judge, and he also acted as Bologna's ambassador to Rome, Florence and Reggio. James Balduini was *podestà* of Genoa in 1229 and revised the laws of that city; he was also a member of the city council at Bologna. Hubert of Bobbio was consulted on behalf of the mother of Louis IX of France when she was regent; he also wrote a handbook on procedure for advocates. Roffredus of Benevento had a widespread practice as advocate at both imperial and papal bars; his treatise on procedure made use of his own pleadings as examples. Not all of these Glossators, of course, published opinions, although one may reasonably assume that they and others gave them.

3.8 LEGAL EDUCATION BECOMES FORMALIZED

3.8.1 While some law had been taught at Pavia, the concept of a university law school really begins at Irnerius' Bologna. He himself does not seem to have taught formally; the only pupils of his that we hear of are the Four Doctors. His teaching clearly did not stimulate the crowds in the way that his contemporary Abelard did in Paris. But the Four Doctors acknowledged him as their master, and so we get the start of the master–pupil relationships which often are still academically significant. Certainly at least one of the Four Doctors lectured to audiences of students; there is the anecdote of Bulgarus, the day after his marriage to a widow, reading out the text on which he proposed to comment and being greeted by a roar of laughter. The text began: 'It is no untouched field that we are entering'; it would be good to know if this was a deliberate choice or inadvertent.

3.8.2 During the earlier twelfth century law became established, along with theology and medicine, as a subject for study after the completion of a degree in arts. By 1158 there was a statute of Bologna which provided that no one might act as judge or legal consultant there without having studied law for five years. In the same year Frederick Barbarossa issued a constitution – the *Authentica Habita*, later inserted into the Code after 4.13.5 (in the older editions) – which gave specific protection to law students away from home, granting them the privilege of having any actions in which they were defenders tried in their university or by the bishop of their university town. How many there were at Bologna at this date (for there was as yet no other school of law firmly established) is not certain; Odofredus is alleged to have reckoned there were 10,000, but, assuming this is due to an error, even one tenth as many makes a sizeable group.

3.8.3 The major names of this period, Vacarius, Roger (Rogerius), Placentinus, John Bassianus, were all described as the pupils of Bulgarus; this may mean that he was seen as the head of the law school, for Vacarius, Roger and Placentinus were Gosians, interested in the development of equity. It was also the period when Roman law was taken abroad by masters, and taught in cities other than Bologna. Vacarius went to England and seems to have taught at Canterbury; his *Liber Pauperum (The Poor Men's Book)*, most likely produced during the 1170s, was the first to conflate texts from the Code and the Digest. Roger probably took the study of Roman law to Montpellier, and this explains why the first *Summa* on the Code, of which he may have been the author, was translated into Provençal around 1170. Known in this guise as *Lo Codi*, it had a long and influential life in southern France. Placentinus taught at Mantua for some years but he too went, about 1170, to Montpellier, which thus became an important centre of civilian study. John Bassianus stayed in Bologna; he was a conservative follower of Bulgarus' strict adherence to the plain meaning of the texts. Placentinus' student, Pillius, of Medicina, led a secession of scholars to Modena.

3.8.4 Azo, who died in 1220, was a pupil of John Bassianus; Charles de Tocco was a pupil of both John and Placentinus. He gave up teaching at Bologna to become a judge at Salerno, where he glossed the *Lombarda*. James Balduini was a pupil of Azo, but he preferred the Gosian approach; he died in 1235. By this time there were law schools at Mantua, Piacenza, Modena, Parma, Padua, Vercelli – where Hubert of Bobbio was teaching – as well as some short-lived ventures in other cities. Roman law was also taught at Montpellier, and perhaps at Valence, although it was forbidden at Paris in 1219, and in England in 1234. However, in 1224 Frederick II founded a university or *Studium Generale* (that is, a foundation for higher education, specifically with various faculties) at Naples, and in 1244 or 1245 Pope Innocent IV founded another in Rome. Roffredus may have taught at Naples from its beginning, but he spent the last thirty years of his life in his native Benevento.

3.8.5 Like the other supreme Glossator – and his master – Azo, Accursius despised places other than Bologna; he and James Balduini dominated the teaching there through the early thirteenth century. Since 1219, students at Bologna had had to be examined before proceeding to take a degree; this was laid down by Pope Honorius III and enforced through the Archdeacon of Bologna who actually awarded the degrees. There are stories of James Balduini and Accursius acting together as examiners, not always kindly; all examinations were oral – as, in general, Italian ones still are. At this period or somewhat later it became established that five years' study was required for a first degree in civil law (four years in canon law) and then a further three years for a doctorate – which only needed one additional year in canon law. The doctors were paid directly by the students for their teaching. Student nations, presided over by a Rector, negotiated with the doctors or the local bishop over the curriculum and timetable, and arranged such matters as lodgings and fair rents.

3.8.6 Thus, by the mid-thirteenth century there existed a standard gloss on the basic texts and a definitive and systematic textbook. The pattern of education was set. It was at this point that a historian of the past two centuries appeared in the person of Odofredus, a pupil of James Balduini, who taught at Bologna and wrote commentaries, in the legal order, on both Code and Digest. Although he was often critical of the conservative tradition enshrined within the Accursian Gloss, he naturally accepted the Gloss as the basis of his work. Later, after it was accepted as a work of authority, not just of scholarship, the maxim ran: 'What the Gloss does not acknowledge, the court does not acknowledge either' (*'Quidquid non agnoscit Glossa nec agnoscit curia'*).

FURTHER READING

RL Benson & G Constable (eds)	*Renaissance and Renewal in the Twelfth Century* (Oxford, 1982)
RC van Caenegem	'Law in the Medieval World', *TvR* 49 (1981) 13
	Legal History. A European Perspective (London, 1991)
R. Feenstra	'Roman law', in *The Legacy of Rome, A New Appraisal* (Oxford, 1992) ch 14
CH Haskins	*The Renaissance of the Twelfth Century* (Harvard UP, 1927)
HD Hazeltine	'Roman and canon law in mediaeval Europe', *Cambridge Mediaeval History*, vol V (CUP, 1927), ch xxi
E Meynial	'Roman Law', in *The Legacy of the Middle Ages* (Oxford, 1926)
S Reynolds	*Kingdoms and Communities in Western Europe, 900–1300* (Oxford, 2nd edn, 1997)
JA Clarence Smith	*Medieval Law Teachers and Writers* (Ottawa, 1975)
P Stein	Introduction to *The Teaching of Roman Law in England around 1200* (Selden Society, supp series 8, 1990)
	Roman Law in European History (CUP, 1999) ch 3
W Ullmann	*Medieval Political Thought* (Penguin, 1965)
P Vinogradoff	*Roman Law in Mediaeval Europe* (Oxford, 1929)
H Yntema	'Equity in the Civil Law and the Common law', *AmJCompL* 15 (1967) 60

Chapter 4

THE COMMENTATORS

4.1 THE PERIOD OF TRANSITION AND THE POST-GLOSSATORS

4.1.1 No exact date can be assigned for the completion of the Accursian Gloss, but it is clear that by the middle of the thirteenth century it was substantially in the form which has come down to us, and in the process of being accepted as the standard companion to the *Corpus Iuris Civilis*. Scholars used to refer, without differentiation, to all the writers who came after the Gloss, and whose work continued through to the sixteenth century (when the new school of Humanists appeared), as Post-Glossators, for the simple fact that their work assumes the existence of the Gloss. Modern usage, however, distinguishes among these writers, and the name Post-Glossators has come to be attached particularly to Italian writers of the later thirteenth century. The French jurists of the same period are known as the *Ultramontani* (men from beyond the mountains) because to an Italian they came from the far side of the Alps. The jurists of the fourteenth century onwards are usually called Commentators, to indicate that they were not simply the successors of the Glossators but had their own individuality and a positive contribution to make to legal development.

4.1.2 In Italy it has been argued that there was a period of decline, or at least stagnation, between the peaks reached by the Glossators and the great work of the Commentators. To distinguish, perhaps over-simply, the former school laid a foundation for the study of Roman law; the latter developed the application of Roman law in practical affairs. Indeed, the Commentators brought about the reception of Roman law into the legal systems of the greater part of western Europe. The theory of decline is open to question, because the Post-Glossators and their works have not been sufficiently studied to permit a well-informed judgment. Nor is it easy to draw a line between late Glossators (such as Odofredus), and early Commentators (such as Dinus of Mugello) on the basis of their method of instruction, for both founded on commentary rather than gloss. It is not that the former were more theoretical and the latter more practical for, as we have seen, the Glossators were often engaged in public affairs and took account of the developing canon law and of feudal customs. Moreover, there is theory as well as practice to be found in such Post-Glossatorial works as William (Guillelmus) Durantis' *Speculum Iudiciale* (*Mirror of Procedure*) or Albertus Gandinus' lucidly systematic *Tractatus Maleficiorum* (*Treatise on Crimes*); this dealt primarily with evidence and criminal procedure, but in the discussions of substantive law he drew on his own widespread experience as a judge. Again, it is untrue to say that there was excessive reliance on the Gloss in the later thirteenth century. Insofar as there came to be such excessive reliance, it was a later phenomenon; contemporaries or near contemporaries of Accursius, such as Odofredus or Dinus, were quite ready to be critical of him. Scholasticism doubtless encouraged the greater use of dialectic to solve difficulties in the texts, but this use was not new and was, indeed, the best tool available.

4.1.3 What is true is that, for a period at least, Bologna ceased to be the main centre of legal studies and had to recognize other law schools as equals. Odofredus taught at Padua before he went to Bologna; it was to the University of Padua, not Bologna, that the canons of the Council of Vienne were officially communicated, and both universities received from Pope Boniface VIII the compilation of papal decretals known as the Sext. Other influential jurists teaching at Padua were Guy of Suzzara (Guido de Suzaria) and James (Jacobus) of Arena; Albertus Gandinus had studied there, although his career was as judge not teacher. Naples was another centre of legal study. Dinus of Mugello seems to have taught there, and King Charles of Anjou, after his conquest of the Kingdom of Naples and Sicily, brought doctors and students from Orléans to help build up the university which he had reformed; James of Arena was teaching there at the end of the century. Reggio, Modena, Pistoia and Siena were probably the most prominent of the other law schools; for example, Guy of Suzzara taught successively at Mantua, Modena, Padua, Bologna, Reggio, and Bologna again.

4.1.4 Common to all these universities, including Bologna, was an intensified interest in the practical application of Roman law, and especially in its adaptation to the problems posed by new situations such as the existence of numerous independent jurisdictions and legal systems. Problems arising from the conflict of laws and from the reception of local laws into the Roman conceptual framework gave rise to new forms of literature. *Quaestiones Statutorum* (*Problems of Local Legislation* – for 'statute' at this period normally carries this meaning) were produced first by Guy of Suzzara and later by James of Arena and Albertus Gandinus. Both Naples and Orléans were situated in kingdoms independent of the Empire which were, compared with the communes of the cities of northern Italy, large and centralized. In Naples the central authority, the Crown, was strong, both willing and able to create new law, and also to continue in modified use the old law of the kingdom, the Lombard law. Not surprisingly Naples became famous for the work done there on public law; in the fourteenth century Lucas de Penna's great commentary on the *Tres Libri*, the last three books of the Code, which were concerned with administrative law, was produced there.

4.1.5 Thus in Italy there was a period of transition. The first great work of mastering the sources had been done, and new challenges had to be faced, in particular the development of legal rules from sources other than the *Corpus Iuris Civilis*. This in turn raised the question of the relationship of these rules to Roman law and to one another.

4.2 THE *ULTRAMONTANI*

4.2.1 It is clear that the Commentators of the fourteenth century onwards, who were predominantly Italians, made much use of the work of the French writers of the later thirteenth century, and particularly the work of the school of Orléans. Of the three writers most commonly cited by the Commentators two, Jacques de Révigny (Jacobus de Ravanis) and Pierre de Belleperche (Petrus de Bella Pertica), taught at Orléans, while the third, Guillaume de Cunh (Guillelmus de Cuneo), taught briefly at Toulouse; he died as bishop of Comminges in 1335. Orléans had a school of arts (and probably schools of theology and canon law) before 1200, but its school of civil law is known no earlier that 1235, when Pope Gregory IX declared that Pope Honorius III's prohibition on the teaching of the civil law at Paris (decreed in 1219 by the bull *Super Specula*) did not apply in Orléans and, further, affected only those clerics who had the cure of souls. Orléans thus became a seat of legal learning for clerics, who, except in Italy, far outnumbered laymen as students. The first known professor of civil law there was Guy of Como (Guido de Cumis), who had been a pupil of Hubert of Bobbio and James Balduini; he was teaching at Orléans by 1243 and, following his masters, was inclined to take a critical approach to the Gloss.

4.2.2 While it would be rash to carry the contrast too far, the universities of the northern Italian cities were modern, in the sense that many lay students came there, and to enjoy themselves as well as to qualify themselves for some career; north of the Alps students were almost invariably clerics who could expect to serve kings or princes in the administration of their territories, and to be paid for their services by clerical preferment. Thus Pierre d'Auxonne, one-time doctor at Orléans, went with Eleanor of Provence (bride of the future Edward I) to England in 1265 and became Official of the archbishop of Canterbury; his legacy of his books to the Sorbonne was the foundation of its library. This had the side effect, even more marked among teachers of canon law, of keeping down the average age of active scholars, since promotion usually took them away from their studies. Two popes (Clement V and John XXII), four cardinals, and several bishops taught civil law at Orléans at some stage in their careers, and other teachers went on to high office in the service of the king of France. Such service required the ability to accept local customs, often vigorously defended, and to blend them with Roman law, rather than simply to maintain the latter's superiority.[1] It also led to the introduction of elements of Roman law into the decisions given by the royal courts, since these were staffed by men trained in the learned law.

1 Appendix 2(A).

4.2.3 A contemporary colleague of Guy of Como at Orléans was Jean de Monchy who taught civil law there until 1263, when he went to Rome and acted for the pope in various matters, including the negotiations over the recognition of Charles of Anjou as king of Naples and Sicily. He was the master of Jacques de Révigny. Jacques acknowledged him as the source of various doctrines which he himself supported, such as the concept of a legal person as a *persona repraesentata* (a person given reality by the operation of law –

hence the fiction theory of the legal personality of corporations – whereas human beings have legal personality by the operation of nature). Jacques left commentaries on all parts of the *Corpus*. He taught until about 1280, and died as bishop of Verdun in 1296.

4.2.4   Pierre de Belleperche was the pupil of one Raoul d'Harcourt, who had studied under and later taught beside Jacques. Pierre began to teach at Orléans around 1280 and was there for some fifteen years. He was less original than Jacques but even more influential, perhaps for the very reason that he was less original and could be more readily accepted. After holding various offices he became bishop of Auxerre and, in 1306, chancellor of France; he died in 1308. His commentary on the Code was heavily used by Cino Sinibuldi of Pistoia (Cinus de Pistorio), the master of Bartolus; Pierre also wrote commentaries on the Institutions and the New Digest, and a collection of *Distinctiones*. But he was the last of the great names at Orléans; in the fourteenth century the jurists there tended simply to follow Italian doctrine.

4.3   THEIR APPROACH TO THE TEXTS

4.3.1   The name *Ultramontani* was given by the Italians to the French writers, and especially to those of Orléans, not merely as an indication of their geographical position but also with pejorative implication. Many harsh things were said by the Italians about them, for example, that they were airy-fairy philosophers and useless dialecticians, and that their arguments represented fantasy rather than reason. The *Ultramontani* in their turn criticized the Accursian Gloss with considerable freedom. We find particular glosses described by them as diabolical, or obscure, and as having more need of a gloss than the text itself, or even as being stupid or rubbish. As is very often the case in academic, and indeed other, controversy, there was a degree of exaggeration on both sides. Comments were needed on the Gloss, and a new form of literature much used by the *Ultramontani* was that of *Repetitiones* (*Studies*), which arose from their practice of delivering lectures in greater depth on certain selected texts. The French writers perhaps did not feel as closely bound to the texts as the Italian writers. The north of Italy was undoubtedly part of the Holy Roman Empire, and insofar as Roman law was studied and applied as the law of that empire, the texts had a strong claim to authority. The kings of France for their part resisted claims that France, because a thousand years ago it had been within the Roman Empire, was thereby subject to the jurisdiction of the Holy Roman Emperors. They claimed to be emperors within their own realm, following the partition of Charlemagne's empire; they rejected the suggestion that Roman law should automatically be applied in France – except in the south, the *pays de droit écrit*, where it was recognized as custom.

4.3.2   The willingness of the *Ultramontani* to argue independently of the texts may well owe something to the study of Aristotelian doctrine and to the work of St Thomas Aquinas. Aquinas reconciled Aristotelian and Christian thought and gave a new importance to the creative role of reason in establishing legal rules where no definite guidance existed from divine or Natural Law.

He thus gave reason a more positive role than had been allowed to it by St Augustine, whose approach had tended to dominate thinking up to the thirteenth century; St Augustine had minimized the role of legal rules in society and also the value of human reason in creating rules. But while the *Ultramontani* were often critical of the Gloss, they by no means rejected it, even in the more original work of Jacques de Révigny, and Guillaume de Cunh often supported the Gloss against Jacques.

4.3.3 The interest of the *Ultramontani* in practical questions was of special importance to the subsequent development of Roman law and the creation of the *ius commune*. In particular, their work on the conflict of laws was expanded by the Commentators. But Italian writers, such as Gandinus, had also been moving in this direction and were cited by Cinus, even while he was drawing on the work of Pierre de Belleperche as his main source. The Commentators are properly seen as a new school of jurists, but they built on the contributions, Italian as well as French, of the intervening period. Further, the more one investigates particular doctrines, the more one becomes aware of the extent to which the seed of the concept is likely to be found somewhere within the material collected by Accursius.

4.4   THE COMMENTATORS AND THEIR TEACHING METHODS

4.4.1   The Commentators have also been called – in German – *Konsiliatoren*, ie the writers of *consilia* or opinions (see para 4.5.7). While this is a useful name in that it indicates one of the important functions which these jurists performed, and gives due prominence to the immense number of opinions they produced, the term Commentators is just as apt if one looks at the type of literature published. Not surprisingly, they dealt with essentially the same material as the Glossators, that is, the *Corpus Iuris Civilis* in its mediaeval form which included the *Books of the Feus*, but they paid more attention to special legislation, such as that of the Italian city states. Again, it is not surprising that their teaching methods were similar to those of the Glossators. The emphasis was on lectures on a text or texts of the *Corpus* (or other book being read) including the gloss attached, and they published exegetical material based on this teaching. *Lecturae (Lectures)* were indeed often simply reports of actual lectures; it was quite common for these to be produced with the approval of the lecturer, and in these cases the text would probably be revised by the lecturer before publication. Sometimes, however, it is clear that there was no revision, as when the reporter says that he missed something because of the noise made by the students. In other cases what we have may be lecture notes prepared by the lecturer. Where lectures were delivered in more than one year, the version which has survived may contain additions and second thoughts.

4.4.2   The format of the lectures follows the same general pattern as is found among the Glossators. For example, Cinus, commenting on D 12.1.40, says:

'First I shall divide this fragment into its parts and set out the case, and I shall deal with textual questions. In the second place, I shall draw attention

> to contradictory passages and solve the contradictions. In the third place, I shall formulate certain questions and add the solutions to them. In the fourth and last place, I shall assemble certain arguments useful for this purpose.'

However, it was increasingly common to find that the regular lectures did not pay equal attention to all texts. The lecturer might even omit comment on some texts altogether, but this was not always allowed. The statutes of the University of Bologna of 1317 laid down that the doctors were not to pass over any decretal or fragment or paragraph. They also continued the system which required the lecturer to cover so much over each fortnight or month, under penalty of a fine – known as the *puncta* system. But even without any total omission, the concentration on some rather than others led to certain texts being used as the starting point for long treatises. For example, C 1.1.1 became the normal peg on which to hang discussions of the effect of local legislation and indeed to develop international private law.[2]

2   Appendix 2(B).

4.4.3   Where there were differences of opinion or apparent contradictions in the texts, the list of *oppositiones* became increasingly lengthy as the number of views to be explained and the list of supporters of each grew. When these lists are looked at carefully it becomes apparent that there was some tendency simply to lift the list from a predecessor and to add the latest views, without any weeding out of earlier ones or checking; one finds lists in which people are given as supporters of an opinion which it is certain they did not hold. Again, the list of questions dealt with tended to grow, whether they were related to interpretation or to doctrine or – as was increasingly common – to the actual application of the law. One can see the lecturer's abiding tendency to increase the syllabus for fear of discarding something of value.

4.4.4   In addition to the regular exegesis of the particular part of the *Corpus* on which the commentary was being given, there were special lectures on particular texts or particular problems; these, similar to the *quaestiones sabbatinae*, were now called *repetitiones*. In published form they were often collected separately from the regular lectures or commentaries, as they dealt much more fully with areas of particular difficulty and, for the same reason, they were given as special lectures.

4.5   THE LITERATURE OF THE COMMENTATORS

4.5.1   Generally the literature of the Commentators can be classified as first, monographs, second, exegetical material, arising out of teaching, and third, decisions and opinions, often arising out of practice; there were also other forms, such as encyclopaedias designed to be a plain man's guide to the law, or other works not of legal science but for practical use.

4.5.2   Monographs were not a new form of literature, but they were increasingly common, because the basic mastery of the sources had been established, and there was thus more scope for literature which systematized or developed particular topics. Monographs regularly departed from the order of the texts – the legal order – which continued to be used in commentaries; the subjects most often dealt with were feudal law, procedure, and questions of the interpretation of local legislation and of the relation between statutes and (Roman) law and, indeed, the *ius commune* (common law – the term will be retained in Latin to avoid confusion with the English Common Law). Among the earliest Commentators to write such a work was James of Belvisio (Jacobus de Bellovisu), who produced a treatise on criminal procedure (the *Practica Criminalis*) as well as commenting on the *Books of the Feus* and annotating the Gloss on the Old Digest. James started, and ended, his career at Bologna, but he also established between 1308 and 1321 the reputation of the law school at Perugia, where law had been taught since 1296. (Perugia had been a *studium generale* since 1308.) Other examples of monographs are Bartolus' *De alimentis* (*On Aliment* – or maintenance) and his *On presumptions of law*.

4.5.3 Much of the exegetical group was in the tradition of the Glossators, for the needs of students did not vary much and, although the Gloss now provided an adequate foundation, the techniques of problem solving must be learned, then as now. So, as well as *additiones* (additions) to the Gloss, which were an important production of the Naples school but which are not always readily distinguishable from lectures, collections of cases (*casus*) continued to be made, setting out factual situations extrapolated from the texts.

4.5.4 The typical Commentary that gave the school its name is illustrated by the work of Cinus of Pistoia. He had been a pupil of Dinus when a student at Bologna, where he probably also taught. He was a poet as well as a jurist, and a friend of Dante and Petrarch; he was an imperialist insofar as he sought an authority which could put an end to the constant and frequently bloody party strife endemic in the Italian communes. He began his teaching career at Siena, having been for some ten years active in practice, and moved to Perugia in 1326. There he wrote his great commentary – *Lectura super Codice* (*Lecture on the Code*) – which continued to be read as well as cited for more than a century. It was not systematic, but followed the legal order of those passages which provoked comment; the explanation of particular terms was taken quite for granted since it assumed knowledge of the Gloss, but otherwise it was closer to an *apparatus* than a *summa*. Cinus had heard Pierre de Belleperche on one occasion, when he came to give a visiting lecture in Bologna, and he made enormous – and acknowledged – use of Pierre's commentary; he also drew on the works of Dinus and James of Arena. He enjoyed the dialectical approach of the *Ultramontani* while remaining aware that the pursuit of logic could lead to arguments irrelevant to the actual application of law. At Perugia he was the master of Bartolus.

4.5.5 Bartolus of Sassoferrato took his doctorate at Bologna at the age of twenty, as pupil of James Buttrigar (Jacobus Buttrigarius) and of Rainer of Forlì (Ranierus de Forlivio); the former taught the *Code* and *Old Digest*, the latter the *New Digest* and *Infortiatum*. (James had practised as a notary when delayed by factional political intrigues in gaining his doctorate; he was, however, doctor at Bologna from 1309 until he succumbed to the Black Death in 1348; Rainer later taught at Pisa and then Padua.) All that is known of Bartolus' life between 1334 and 1339 is that during this time he served as judge in Todi and Pisa and engaged in private study; in 1339 he went to teach at Pisa, where he stayed four years, and then moved to Perugia, where he died in 1357 at the age of forty-three. He produced a monumental *Commentary* on the whole of the *Corpus* (filling nine folio printed volumes in some editions) which had an authority in succeeding generations unmatched even by the Gloss – '*nemo jurista nisi Bartolista*' (only a jurist if a Bartolist).

4.5.6 Bartolus' *Commentary* provided the most complete and richest discussion of the sources, a commentary on them which, like the Standard Gloss, was extensively used, frequently corrected, but never replaced as a whole. Bartolus also produced a number of opinions and many monographs. So extensively was he used that he is often treated as the author of doctrines which he had in fact borrowed from others but to which he gave currency by his support. Lectures on his work were established at Padua in 1544 and at Ferrara in 1613; the name Bartolo instantly conjured up for later generations the picture of a lawyer, as in Mozart's *The Marriage of Figaro*. Something of his approach, both practical and learned, can be seen from his treatment of C 1.1.1,[3] where he dealt with the application of a local statute to a non-citizen, a theme we have already seen handled by Pierre de Belleperche. His scheme was to investigate whether what was treated as punishable by local statute was punishable both under local statute and the *ius commune*; in that case it would apply to a stranger. If the matter were not punishable under common law, then a distinction should be made according to whether the stranger had stayed in the place long enough to know of the statute; if he had, then again it would apply. If he had not stayed long enough, then, in principle, he would not be punished, but a further distinction was made. If the matter were one which was generally forbidden, then he should be punished; if it were some peculiar provision, then he should not be, unless he happened to know of the statute. Bartolus' scheme was relatively straightforward in application and hence attractive to the practising lawyer who needed a clear and reliable guide; Bartolus also knew the texts and the work of earlier scholars.

> 'Not everyone agreed with all he said, but he could be called their spiritual domicile in the sense that it was from him that they set out on their journey, and to him that at the end of the day they returned. He expressed thoroughly and completely, with a touch as light as it was sure, the law as it had come to be lived, but in the terminology and according to the concepts which Justinian had caused to be written down.'[4]

3   Translated in Clarence Smith (1970).
4   Clarence Smith (1975) 82.

4.5.7   The other main type of literature of this period was the collection of *consilia* or opinions, and in this field Baldus de Ubaldis, a pupil of Bartolus, was pre-eminent; some 2,500 of his opinions survive. He taught briefly at Bologna and then returned to Perugia, where he spent most of his time until 1390, when he went to Pavia for the remaining ten years of his life. He was much involved in public life as well as teaching; he was a canonist and feudist as well as a civilian. Opinions were particularly required when there was a possible conflict between Roman law and local statute, or where it was not clear how far, if at all, Roman law applied to cases not specifically covered by its provisions. An opinion generally dealt with the whole case put before the jurist who was to give his opinion, but it might be restricted to a single point. The influence of the jurists on the application of the law was enormously important, and opinions continued to have this importance even after the Commentary had declined into practical insignificance, as is evident from the career of, for example, Jason de Mayno, master of Alciatus, who died in 1519.

4.5.8 Sometimes the opinion was given to one or other of the parties to the case, but more often it was given to the court itself. That is, a judge who wished to be informed on the law applicable to the case before him, or to some aspect of it, could put the relevant facts to a suitably qualified adviser, such as a doctor of civil law at one of the universities; indeed, he might sometimes be encouraged or even required to consult a doctor teaching at the local university. For example, the judge might put the case: a local citizen is suing a man from Paris in my court; have I jurisdiction? The answer might be a simple yes or no, or it might be explained with reference to appropriate texts; on difficult points the explanations became very elaborate. The practice of seeking advice in this way became regular in the thirteenth century, and it was provided for in the statutes of many Italian cities. William Durantis, in his *Speculum Iudiciale*, devoted a special section to the procedure for seeking an opinion, described technically as its requisition. The practice was particularly important in those cities which had a *podestà* constitution, and it was less important in those parts of Italy with a monarchic constitution, such as the kingdom of Naples or the Papal States.

4.5.9 While an opinion had distinct resemblances to a *quaestio*, it differed in that it did not always give much attention to opposing views but rather concentrated on the jurist's view or, as time went by, the views of the many scholars he cited to give weight to his opinion. For the authority of an opinion was persuasive (*probabilis*) rather than binding (*necessaria*), and the degree of authority was more or less persuasive, depending on the reputation of the person giving it. Sometimes opinions came to receive authority as custom if they were regularly followed and accepted but, in principle, an opinion, however buttressed with authorities, could always be refuted by the exercise of reason. Nevertheless, by the fifteenth century there had developed – at first among the canonists – a view that the common or generally accepted view was decisive unless it was demonstrably wrong. This is known as the doctrine of the *communis opinio* (received view). The rules which developed for the finding of the *communis opinio* bear a distinct resemblance to the rules governing judicial precedent, which is hardly surprising since opinions performed a function very similar to judicial decisions in case-law systems. As with the rules of judicial precedent, someone might reluctantly have to give an opinion with which he himself did not agree, and one finds this explicitly stated; in teaching, such divergence from the *communis opinio* could at least be argued rationally. To some extent the doctrine stifled original thought, but for the parties to a case it meant greater legal certainty; the problem of such balance is a perpetual one in the workings of the law, just as the citation of authority is itself a characteristic of lawyers' argumentation. The door to change was, however, always left open, in the sense that a contrary opinion might be argued and accepted to produce a new *communis opinio*.

4.6   ROMAN LAW IN USE BY THE COMMENTATORS

4.6.1   Opinions (*consilia*) are found in all areas of law, both private and public. They inevitably covered questions of feudal law, of custom, of local statute and of other local law, but all are seen as adhering to the framework of the civil law. Moreover, as leading teachers were consulted for their opinions, close contact was ensured between the teaching and the practice of the law, which was beneficial for both. Hence it is not surprising that the literature of the Commentators was not confined to works on Roman law. They were increasingly concerned with the relationship between Roman law and other sources of law, as Roman law spread throughout Europe and there was increasing contact between existing legal regimes and the new learning. One of the most important facets of this relationship was the influence of the civil and the canon law in the field of procedure, which we shall look at more closely in the chapter on the *ius commune*. Another product of this concern was a literature which compared and contrasted Roman law with an existing law, such as Blasius de Morcone's *De differentiis inter ius Romanorum et Langobardorum (On the differences between Roman and Lombard Law)*. Somewhat akin were the writings of the Neapolitan jurists, such as Andrew (Andreas) de Barulo, on the customs of the kingdom, which had been glossed in the thirteenth century. Andrew also produced a commentary on books 10–12 of the Code, although this was superseded by the work of Lucas de Penna; Andrew's *Summa* on intestate succession traced the history of the law of succession from the Twelve Tables to Justinian, and it took into account feudal claims and the Lombard custom of the widow's quarter. It must be remembered that, in Italy in particular, local statutes were often drawn up because of the existence of the learned law, and it certainly contributed elsewhere towards the increasing use of written law.

4.6.2   The Commentators' reconciliation of the learned law and local law produced what is known as the 'statute theory'. When dealing with actual practice the usual theory adopted was that the local statutes were the primary source and the civil (and sometimes the canon) law was supplementary. For example, Pisa adopted Roman law but retained certain elements of the Lombard codes. At Como in 1281 it was laid down that judgment was to be given: first in accordance with the city's written statutes; failing them, according to the approved customs of the city; and only failing them, according to the learned laws (*leges et iura*). In the fourteenth century at Casale Monferrato the primary source was again the written statutes of the city; failing them, the civil law (*iura romana*); and failing that, good custom. At Dervio, within the jurisdiction of the archbishop of Milan, men were ruled by a threefold law, canon, civil, and municipal. However, interpretation extended the use of Roman law and the range of its application in various ways. The words of the statute were to be applied in the first instance, as far as they were applicable; indeed, the sense of the provision might be applied even if the exact wording was not to the point. It was also possible to apply statutes by analogy, on grounds of equity (*ratio aequitatis*). For example, statutes dealing with succession and giving preference to agnates (a term which by this time meant relationships through males) were applied and extended in order to protect family property. They were not so extended when the result was clearly seen to be unjust, for example, if the result would be to allow an aunt on the father's side to exclude the mother from a child's succession – for the mother was only a cognate.

4.6.3 In spite of this primacy of the statutes, the civil law was the general subsidiary law and it could prevail in various ways. First, statutes might expressly incorporate the Roman law or *ius commune*, and to that extent the Roman law shared the primary authority. Second, statutes might use technical terms or concepts of Roman law, which would almost inevitably be interpreted in the civilian sense, as, for example, when referring to legal capacity or to pupils or minors. It was accepted that statutes were to be interpreted in such a way as to involve the least divergence from the civil law. For example, Dinus, in his *Consilia*, says: 'Doubtful words in statutes are brought within the interpretation and understanding they bear in the *ius commune*', and Baldus similarly held that statutes were to be interpreted so that they involved the least correction of the civil law. Even when statutes attempted to restrict this extension by requiring strict interpretation in the sense in which they had been passed, it could often be argued that they required declaratory interpretation in the light of other available sources of law.

4.6.4 Thus the giving of opinions by civilian doctors provided a *communis opinio* which ran far more widely than the particular jurisdictions, and so played a major part in the creation of the *ius commune*. In Italy the work of the doctors can be seen as a substitute for the court of appeal or legislative authority that made possible the existence of a common law in other countries. The opinions of men like Alexander Tartagni of Imola,[5] who himself selected the first four volumes of his *Consilia* for printing before his death in 1477, or Philip Decio,[6] who was also a canonist as well as a civilian, and for three years a judge of the *Parlement* of Grenoble, might properly be compared, in function, if not form, with the (contemporary) records of the decisions of the Lords of Council and Session in Scotland or of King's Bench or Common Pleas in England.

5 Doctor of civil and canon law at Bologna, and a teacher who kept his lectures for the evenings, since he had a lucrative practice at the bar.
6 Pupil of Jason de Mayno at Pavia, then doctor at Pisa, then at Padua, Pavia, and Valence, before his return to Pisa and final move to Siena, where he died in 1536 or soon after, at something over eighty.

4.6.5 The Commentators were remarkably free in their application of the texts regardless of the original context. For example, from the fact that in *Nov.* 105 the emperor was referred to as 'living law', it was argued that property could be transferred by the emperor without any physical delivery but by simple oral grant, because it is possible for a law to transfer property. We have mentioned (see para 3.4.3) the famous text: 'What touches all alike is to be approved by all', which was widely used as an argument for (relative) democracy in Church and state. The Commentators had no hesitation in applying a text to their own times, however anachronistic they might know its real meaning to be, if its use could be fruitful, as in equating an Italian city with a Roman *municipium*. Similarly, when they derived arguments from texts which had little or no relation to the current facts, they were not ignorantly distorting Roman law to fit their own times but deliberately adopting its principles as a source of ideas.

4.6.6   For example, in one of his opinions, Bartolus dealt with a case where a husband was seeking aliment (or maintenance) for his (second) wife from the children of the first marriage, to whom the property of his first wife had gone. The claim was denied on the basis of D 13.6.18.2 which, talking about a slave who has been lent, states that the expense of feeding him, etc, falls by natural reason on the person who makes use of him. Conversely, Bartolus argued from texts on dotal expenses that, where a tenant claimed from his landlord the cost of clearing ditches on the land which he had leased, if this was a regular job then the tenant must pay, but if the clearing was something which was necessary only at considerable intervals then the obligation fell on the landlord. In yet another opinion, a stamped notarial document had been destroyed; the question was, need the copy of the document be stamped? Bartolus held that it need not, because it was a matter of good faith that the same thing be not claimed twice – a principle which applies rather to the law of contract than to stamp duties.

4.6.7   Their use of the texts was partly due to a feeling that it was desirable to have some authority to quote, however reasonable in itself the conclusion. Bartolus once said: 'We lawyers blush to speak without reference to an authority', and the story is told that, on occasion, having given his opinion on a case put to him, he would go to a friend who had a better memory to provide him with the relevant texts to justify the opinion. This characteristic, however, is both a strength and a weakness in lawyers of any age.

4.6.8   By their work the Commentators developed whole new fields of law, and new doctrines to face new situations; for example, they worked out the distinction between *dominium directum* (superiority) and *dominium utile* (literally 'extended ownership' – in effect a share of ownership allowing use) to deal with such cases as the feudal superior and vassal both holding in the same land an interest which could be described as a right of ownership (*dominium*). It was really the Commentators who turned the Roman texts on criminal law into a legal science and who developed a general doctrine of criminal responsibility. It was they who produced the concept of international private law, who worked out the detailed rules of romano–canonical procedure based ultimately on the Roman *cognitio* procedure, who developed commercial law in such areas as negotiable instruments or partnership (as we shall see in the chapter on the law merchant), and who introduced doctrines of legal personality for entities other than human beings. With the assistance of the canonists they gave substance to the concept of the rights of a third party to a transaction and to the law of agency. It was the work of the Commentators that produced the *ius commune*, and then enabled the reception of Roman law in the countries of western Europe during the fifteenth and sixteenth centuries, although there is no doubt that the way for that reception was also paved by the canonists and the ecclesiastical courts.

FURTHER READING

HF Jolowicz   'The stone that the builders rejected' *Seminar* 12 (1954) 34

FH Lawson   *The Roman Law Reader* (New York, 1969), ch 7

JA Clarence Smith   'Bartolo on the Conflict of Laws' *AmJLegal Hist* 14 (1970) 157; 247

     Medieval Law Teachers and Writers (Ottawa, 1975)

P Stein   'The mutual agency of partners' *TulLR* 33 (1959) 595

W Ullmann   *The Mediaeval Idea of Law* (London, 1946)

     Jurisprudence in the Middle Ages (London, 1980)

Chapter 5

CANON LAW

5.1 THE IMPORTANCE OF CANON LAW

5.1.1 Canon law is the law of the Church, that is, of the western Church before (and particularly of the Roman Catholic Church after) the Reformation. ('Canon' in Greek means norm or rule.) In its developed form canon law can be said to start with Gratian and his *Concordia Discordantium Canonum* (*Harmonizing of Divergent Texts*), which is otherwise known as the *Decretum* – although it would more properly be the *Decreta* – and which saw the light of day around 1140. Gratian's work and that of his successors until the Council of Trent (1545–1563) is known as the *ius novum* (new law), while that which went before is described as the *ius antiquum* (ancient law); the period from Gratian onwards is the classical age of the canon law. The Council of Trent marks the de facto acceptance of a divided Christendom, divided that is within western Europe, since the schism between eastern Orthodox and western Catholic, after simmering for centuries, had become formal in the eleventh century. Canon law in the Roman Catholic Church since the Council of Trent is known as the *ius novissimum* (modern law). We have looked briefly at the period of ancient law in the Church as part of the formation of Europe (see section 1.4); this book is concerned with the *ius novum*, not with modern canon law, because the latter is itself a continuation of the system of the classical age; moreover, its subsequent influence in the general history of law is most marked in the development of Natural Law theories (see section 13.2).

5.1.2 Much of the development of the classical canon law stemmed from the struggle between Papacy and Empire but, despite the political tensions, it must be remembered that from the twelfth to the sixteenth century there was throughout western Europe a relatively uniform structure of ecclesiastical courts, administering a fairly regular system, and staffed by men who had undertaken a reasonably common education in canon, and frequently in civil, law. There were local variations; for example, in Spain the Church had a very limited jurisdiction over testamentary succession whereas in Scotland and England its jurisdiction was virtually total over succession to moveable property. Nevertheless, there was one international system. Moreover, canon law was more than a collection of technical rules; it was a force which shaped all society, lay and cleric alike; their membership of society made them members of the Church and subject to the rational ordering of a daily life that was seen *sub specie aeternitatis*.

'The fact that in its details canon law dealt with contingencies and practical necessities rather than with timeless truths must not blind us to the grandeur of its purpose, which is the ordering of those contingencies in a coherent whole.'[1]

1 S Kuttner, 'Harmony from Dissonance', repr *The History of Ideas and Doctrine in the Middle Ages* (London, 1980) 1–16, at p 2).

5.1.3 This universality of legal thinking and practice must have been an important factor in the creation of the *ius commune*, and in bringing such outlying areas of mediaeval Europe as Scotland within the framework of European legal civilization, but the extent of the influence of this factor remains somewhat unclear. For one thing, princely and feudal jurisdictions were generally administered by clerics but, in exercising that function, they would normally administer the royal or feudal law; for example, William Raleigh, bishop of Winchester, as a royal judge supported the English barons' refusal to recognize legitimation by subsequent marriage, a Roman institution which was taken into the canon law by Pope Alexander III. Thus in practice men might follow local custom rather than the learned law in which they had been trained. On the other hand, canon law made use of the Roman law as well as of its own proper sources, which were described in the first chapter (eg X 4.12.1 – see para 5.4.3 for the citation). Canon law procedure was based on the *cognitio* system of procedure of the Later Roman Empire (in which the whole case was heard by a magistrate), because that had been the living system when Christianity was adopted as the official religion of the Empire and institutionalized, and because the Roman texts continued to provide the only systematic guidance. Thus it is arguable how far the romano-canonical procedure, which (as we shall see in Chapter 7) penetrated to a greater or less extent every country in Europe, is the fruit of civilian or of canonist thinking. The influence of canon law is undeniable, but its very success makes the extent of this influence hard to measure.

5.2 CANON LAW IN THE ELEVENTH CENTURY

5.2.1 Around AD 1012 Burchardt, bishop of Worms, produced a collection of canon law in twenty books, his *Decretum*. He made use of the *Hadriana*, Penitentials, and other sources, some of them secular. He also made use of the False Decretals, a Frankish compilation of conciliar canons which, although mostly genuine, had been given a fictitious papal or imperial source for greater authority; they included the so-called Donation of Constantine, purporting to be an early fourth century grant of secular power to the papacy.[2] Burchardt's *Decretum* was used both by Pope Leo IX and by his cousin, the Emperor Henry III, but it was not adequate to satisfy the needs of the reforming party within the Church. It lacked a coherent system and suitably authoritative texts upon those subjects which were the reformers' chief concern: the primacy of Rome as the Apostolic See, authority within the Church to coerce the sinner, the investiture of bishops – and lesser clergy – by laymen, simony or trafficking in ecclesiastical appointments, and the validity of the sacraments.

2 Tierney, no 8; cf nos 80 and 82; and see Southern, pp 91ff.

5.2.2   At the end of the eleventh century rather the same failings still affected the works of Ivo of Chartres, who made much use of his predecessor. Ivo had pointed the way to the solution of the Investiture Contest as early as 1097; as a bishop as well as a canonist he was also concerned with the internal discipline of the Church. He wrote three major books: the *Tripertitum* (or *Three-part Book*) was a chronological collection from the Fathers, the Popes, and the Councils; his *Decretum* (to be distinguished from that of Gratian) was based largely on Burchardt, with additions from the Fathers and from Roman law; the *Panormia* (*Conspectus*) was a relatively short and systematic work, intended for everyday reference. The three formed a group of discrete items rather than one coherent whole. Nevertheless, Ivo gave sound advice on the interpretation of historical material, and he distinguished principles of eternal validity from the variable elements of legal discipline, such as the particular circumstances of time or place or person. When such work was combined with the Scholastic thought developed by the contemporary Peter Abelard, it was to prove capable of constructing the necessary blend of authority and argument that, in Gratian's *Concordia discordantium canonum*, founded the science of canon law.

5.2.3   The twelfth and thirteenth centuries were dominated, and not only in the field of the continuing tensions between papacy and empire, by law and lawyers. Intellectual argument took legal form, and,

> '. . . on the practical level too, in an age of rapidly advancing civilization and expanding economic activity, there was a widespread popular demand for rational and equitable legal procedures. In such circumstances any ruler whose courts could provide fair and enforceable judicial decisions found his status greatly enhanced, and kings who sought to increase their powers came to rely more on the efficiency of their judges and administrators than on the sanctity of their office or the personal devotion of their vassals. Moreover, the study of Roman law provided a very exalted theory of legislative sovereignty, together with a wholly non-papal account of the origins of imperial authority.'[3]

In the conflict between Emperor and Pope the Donation of Constantine could as well be interpreted to imply that imperial grant was the source of papal jurisdiction as to prove the latter's supremacy. On both sides the lawyers were hard at work. The canonists may have discerned the Digest for what it was, but it was in the light of the work of the Glossators that their scholarship flourished and made of canon law a system comparable to the civil law.

3   Tierney, p 97f.

5.3   GRATIAN AND THE DECRETISTS

5.3.1   Gratian is a man of whom we know very little – although Dante placed him in Paradise. Our only certainties are that he was working in Bologna in the 1130s and 1140s, and that he played a significant part in the production of the work which goes under his name. It remains convenient to talk in terms of 'Gratian' rather than of 'the compilers of the *Concordia discordantium canonum*' who are equally invisible in the mists of time. Gratian's work was produced in the same atmosphere as and not long after that of Irnerius, and it marked the creation of canon law as a science. It was also roughly contemporary with the publication around 1150 of Peter Lombard's *Sententiae* and thus signalled the separation of canon law and theology. Gratian's work was not commissioned, nor did he hold any significant official position (or surely we would know more of him), but through its own virtue it became accepted. Within fifteen years or so the *Decretum* was being analyzed and extended by the jurists who are known as the Decretists.

5.3.2 Gratian's ability to synthesize his sources was rendered effective in the practice of the courts by the existence of a new, efficient and centralized bureaucracy, based on the reformed and consolidated papacy – and about this we know much. The most influential popes of the next hundred years – Alexander III (1159–1181), Innocent III (1198–1216), Gregory IX (1227–1241), Innocent IV (1243–1254) – were all interested in the administration of the law.

'New legal procedures, often borrowed from Roman law, were adopted in order to facilitate appeals to Rome and, as the appeals flowed in by thousands from every corner of Christendom, the necessary apparatus of papal courts, bureaucratic administrators, and delegate judges was developed to cope with them. This great growth of administrative machinery in the twelfth century added flesh and bone and muscle to Gregory VII's abstract assertions of papal sovereignty.'[4]

It made effective in each country, in each diocese, the rules of the Church. These rules dealt with the obligations of her members, lay and clerical, with the procedures necessary for the maintenance of worship, with the administration of ecclesiastical properties and monies, and with matters of doctrine.

4   Tierney, p 98.

5.3.3 Gratian used ordinary Scholastic methods to order his existing materials: the canons of the apostles, liturgical and penitential books, conciliar canons from many sources, papal letters and decrees, the works of the Fathers, and some secular jurisprudence. The diversity of his sources can be illustrated from the First Part, *Distinctio* 12: it draws from a letter of Pope Calixtus I (218–223), the writings of Popes Gregory IV (827–844), Leo IX (1048–1054), and Nicholas I (858–867), a letter of St Jerome (d.410), Justinian's Institutions 1.2.9 (533), C 8.52(53).1 (224) – wrongly cited – three letters of Gregory the Great (590–604), two letters of St Augustine (d.430), a canon from the Eleventh Council of Toledo (675), and another from the First Council of Braga (561). More typical treatment of a topic might quote more from the Fathers, including biblical commentary, and rather less from any source later than Gregory I. Not all Gratian's sources seem to have been known to him at first hand, and he made very little use of the canons of the General Councils of Lateran I (1123) and Lateran II (1139); the secular references seem largely drawn from the collections of Ivo of Chartres.

5.3.4 The *Decretum* in its established form is divided into three parts. The first[5] deals with the nature and sources of law, and with ecclesiastical offices and conduct. The second part[6] deals further with clerical behaviour, with procedure and penal law, with church property, with religious orders, with marriage and, in a semi-independent treatise, with penance. The third part[7] deals with the sacraments and with doctrine; it is known as *De Consecratione (On Consecration)* from the opening rubric. Gratian applied to each topic the new dialectic. He put the arguments for and against each proposition, using the sources but aiding them with his own comments. Where there were divergent answers he sought to reconcile them by redefining the meaning of the words or by distinguishing the circumstances which governed a particular application of a principle. By linking them together in this way he aimed to give his authorities coherence, but the user must never take any one text in isolation because conflicting views are offered. It is to the overall resolution and conclusion that one must look and, even so, a complete answer is not always given. For example, C.29, q.2 has eight chapters on the problem of whether a free woman can put aside a man she had thought free if, after their marriage, she finds he is of servile status;[8] the conclusion is not very clear.

5   Consisting of 101 *Distinctiones*, each divided into chapters or canons, cited as, eg, D.10.1 – quoted in fn 38.
6   Consisting of 36 *Causae*, each divided into *quaestiones*, which are in turn divided into canons; thus *De poenitencia (On Penance)* is C.33, q.3.
7   Also consisting of *Distinctiones*, five of them, each divided into chapters.
8   Appendix 3(A).

5.3.5   The *Decretum* was a little like the Digest in drawing from a range of sometimes conflicting sources; thus it is not surprising that it gave rise to glosses and comments in much the same way. Moreover, since it was already an established principle of canon law that account must be taken of what the parties had understood, of the circumstances of time or place, of the need to balance two apparently contradictory rules in a particular instance, there was clearly room for further elaboration of the sources by the canonists. Very early some additional texts were included in the *Decretum*; these are known as *paleae*, and may come from one Paucapalea who had produced a short *summa* before 1148. The actual texts were often already part of the common currency of the canonists, and there was in the papacy a source of authoritative interpretation; thus the Decretists needed to spend somewhat less time on basic glossing and could move rather faster towards systematic development than the Glossators had been able to do with the Digest.

5.3.6   Rufinus, later bishop of Assisi and the man chosen to give the opening address at Lateran III in 1179, taught canon law at Bologna; around 1158 he published a *Summa* (of some 170,000 words) which was of great influence in Italy and beyond until its supersession by the work of Huguccio. One of Rufinus' pupils, Stephen of Tournai, who was also a pupil of Bulgarus, published a *Summa* soon after 1160; through him, and others, canonist learning spread to France. Bologna, however, remained the centre of the new studies; Huguccio, perhaps the greatest of the Decretists, both studied and taught there. His *Summa*, which appeared around 1188, continued to be cited until the fifteenth century; it was the first to make significant use of both Roman law and the decretals. His views on such matters as when a marriage was to be presumed, the force of a bare pact, the importance of *causa* in contract, shaped decisively those of his successors; he also laid particular stress on the importance of equity and the need to exercise mercy. Then too it was at Bologna around 1213 that the standard gloss for the *Decretum* was produced by Johannes Teutonicus (John the German); he made considerable use of the work of Laurentius Hispanus (Lawrence the Spaniard), who in his civil law studies had been a pupil of Azo.

5.4 THE DECRETALS

5.4.1 Meanwhile a series of efficient popes, imbued with the legal spirit of the age, were providing more material for the canonists. Alexander III summoned Lateran III; he also issued a number of decretals on matters of legal significance, such as those on legitimation through subsequent marriage. Innocent III summoned Lateran IV in 1215 and was thereby responsible for a very large number of canons. Innocent did indeed study at Bologna for a while in his youth, but recent scholarship has shown that neither of these popes was a doctor of canon law, although they were of great importance in its development. The canons of the two General Councils and the various decretals issued subsequently to the publication of the *Decretum* were at first simply known as canons *extra Decretum vagantes* (circulating – literally, wandering – outside the *Decretum*) but collections of them soon began to be made. The first was that of Bernard of Pavia (Bernardus Papiensis) who, soon after 1190, produced a *Breviarium Extravagantium* (*Brief Account of the Wanderers*) which included decretals of Clement III (1187–1191) as well as of Alexander III, and also some older material omitted by Gratian; he stressed the legal points by leaving out most of the usual narrative. The *Breviarium* was arranged in five books, concerned with ecclesiastical jurisdiction, with procedure, with the clergy and church property, with marriage, and with sins and their correction. This arrangement became standard in later, official collections.

5.4.2 Other collections were made by John of Wales (Johannes Galensis), Peter of Benevento (Petrus Beneventanus), John Teutonicus, and – probably – Tancred; these five collections are known as the *Compilationes Antiquae* (*Old Collections*). Tancred was a pupil in canon law of Lawrence and of John of Wales and, like the former, in civil law of Azo; he became archdeacon of Bologna and thus the channel through which degrees were granted there. Whether or not he compiled the collection of Honorius III's decretals ascribed to him, he certainly made use of them in his court and in his teaching. He also wrote a monograph on marriage, and an *Ordo Judiciarius* (*Judicial System*) on canonical procedure which remained the standard authority for more than fifty years. It was full but also lucid, and it was arranged conveniently, beginning with the persons concerned in an action, then the preparatory acts, then the stages of the process proper, then the judgment, and finally the execution of the judgment.

5.4.3 Although the *Compilationes Antiquae* and other less well-established collections had all been useful to administrators and teachers, they lacked authority. Gregory IX therefore commissioned Raymond of Peñaforte to produce an official collection. In terms very similar to Justinian's instructions to his compilers, Gregory told Raymond to edit the decretals, removing contradictions and repetitions; apart from citations from Gregory the Great, very little of the material predates Alexander III or Lateran III. The selection was organized in five books on the system of Bernard of Pavia, and divided into titles on the model of Justinian's Code; the titles in turn were divided into chapters, each with its source at its head, and, again like the Code, normally arranged chronologically within each title (see Appendix 3(B)). These Decretals were published in 1234 by the papal constitution or bull *Rex Pacificus* (A Peace-bringing King) as the first authorized, official source of canon law. The work (of more than 300,000 words – closer in length to the Digest than Justinian's Code) has always been known as the *Liber Extra* from the full title *Liber Extravagantium Decretalium.*[9]

9   It is often cited as *X* – for Extra – followed by the number of book, title, and chapter; eg Tierney, no 79.

5.4.4   Later papal decretals were at first known as Novels, in imitation of the Roman sources. Boniface VIII (1294–1303), however, ordered the consolidation of those which were suitable, together with select canons from the General Councils of Lyon I (1245) and Lyon II (1274); in 1298 this was published as the *Liber Sextus* (Sixth Book) because it followed on the five books of Extra. The title is a mild joke, for the Sext (as it is commonly known – sometimes thus cited, and sometimes as *VIto*) is in fact divided into five books, with the titles matching those of Extra; it finishes with a new title *de regulis iuris* (On maxims of law), composed on the model of the last title in the Digest and using much of its material. The Sext, which is only about one-fifth as long as Extra, like its predecessor was exclusive, that is, on its publication – when Boniface sent copies to Bologna, Padua, Orléans, Toulouse, and to the papal university in Rome – all material not included, apart from the *Decretum* and Extra, was to have no validity.

5.4.5   This did not hold for the next official compilation, the *Clementinae* (or Clementines), named after Clement V (1304–1314) who had proposed the publication of a *Liber Septimus* (Seventh Book) to include the canons of the Council of Vienne (1311); they were issued in 1317 by John XXII (1316–1334), who had himself studied law at Orléans. Subsequent collections, the *Extravagantes* of John XXII, and the *Extravagantes Communes* – selected decretals from Boniface VIII up to Sixtus IV (1471–1484) – were not official, still less exclusive. Their authority was only that of the individual chapters or canons, as remained true of the *Decretum*, until in 1582 the *Decretum*, Extra, the Sext, the Clementines, and these *Extravagantes* were all published together as the *Corpus Iuris Canonici*. Even then, although this *Corpus* was as a collection both official and exclusive, it was not to be interpreted as legislative in the manner of a modern code, but as providing authentic texts from which arguments could properly be drawn.

5.5   THE DECRETALISTS

5.5.1   Decretalist is the term given to those jurists who glossed and commented on the decretals, particularly Extra and the Sext. Decretists as such disappeared as the Decretalists incorporated the material of Gratian's book into their work. Tancred was one of the first to specialize in the study of the decretals, but by the end of the thirteenth century the distinction was otiose, and it is better to talk simply of canonists.

5.5.2 Geoffrey of Trani (Goffredus de Trano), a pupil of Azo and a doctor at Bologna, gave the *Liber Extra* an *apparatus* around 1240; shortly afterwards he wrote a brief but influential *Summa* (which was among the sources for the Scottish *Regiam Majestatem*). Sinibald of Fieschi, who became Pope Innocent IV, edited his own decretals and produced a commentary on Extra. Perhaps unsurprisingly, his work was pertinent rather than original, taking account of the other legal traditions of the period. It continued to be cited; indeed, it was printed, and it remained in print until the end of the sixteenth century. Extra had a standard gloss by about 1256 at the hands of Bernard of Parma, who drew from Lawrence the Spaniard and Tancred, among others. Other canonists were busy with *Quaestiones* and *Summae*; *Notabilia* and Brocards were also produced.

5.5.3 Perhaps the most famous canonist of his generation was Henry of Susa (d.1271), usually known as Hostiensis (because he became cardinal bishop of Ostia). He was a pupil of James Balduini in civil law; he taught only briefly, in Paris, but he wrote enormously. His *Summa Aurea* (*Golden Summary*) made use of the civil as well as the canon law – he seems to have known Azo's *Summa Codicis* well – and was important for the process of the formation of the *ius commune*. It brought together and systematized the law of the *Decretum* and of subsequent decretals; it followed the order of the texts, but where he found gaps in the scheme Hostiensis inserted new titles. He also produced a *Lectura*, a detailed commentary, on the decretals of Gregory IX and Innocent IV, which laid particular stress both on equity and the need to love the sinner while chastising the sin, and on the theological underpinnings of the canon law. The *Summa Aurea* became definitive and it, like Innocent's commentary, was re-edited even after the Council of Trent.

5.5.4 William Durantis, known as the Speculator from the title of his major work, the *Speculum Iudiciale* (*Mirror of Procedure*), was a pupil of Bernard of Parma; he taught canon law at Modena and perhaps also at Bologna. He later became a judge (*auditor generalis*) at the papal court for a dozen years, hearing appeals from all over Christendom. Innocent IV and Hostiensis had established a theoretical framework for canon law; the Speculator now laid down the principles of its practice so well that editions of his work were produced down to the seventeenth century, and such noted jurists as Johannes Andreae and Baldus commented on it. Although it followed the internal order of Extra, the *Speculum* was in four parts, dealing with the persons concerned in an action, with procedure in civil causes, with criminal procedure, and in the fourth part providing a formulary. It made much use of the work of Roffredus, Rolandino Passagieri, Tancred, and many others, but the Speculator emphasized the role of the papal court, making use of his own experience there. The *Speculum* replaced Tancred's *Ordo* as the standard work on procedure; it was not itself superseded until the age of the modern law.

5.5.5 Many canonists, having made their mark in academic law, went on to administrative careers in Church or state. The Speculator was papal governor of the Romagna for five years, until his death in 1296; a century earlier William of Longchamps had written a treatise on comparative procedure, both civil and canon, which seems to have been intended for the Plantagenet possessions in France, before he became Chancellor to Richard I of England as well as bishop of Ely. Some, however, remained as scholars, frequently combining civil and canon law. Johannes Andreae produced the standard gloss for the Sext in 1303 and for the Clementines in 1326. He also wrote a commentary on the Sext, a substantial book of *Problems* on the title *de regulis iuris* which completed the Sext, and a commentary on Extra called *Novella*, as well as two not very original monographs on marriage; he died from the Black Death in 1348. Baldus was primarily a civilian, but he left a notable commentary on the decretals, and to add to his accomplishments he was also a feudist of renown.

5.5.6 In the later fourteenth century the university of Bologna was in decline, partly because of local political turbulence, partly because of the rival attractions of other universities which were founded in considerable numbers in that century. The feudist Antonio di Pratovecchio, who was also something of a canonist, taught at Bologna, Padua, Florence and Siena. Nicholas Tedeschi, who is better known as Panormitanus (from Palermo, where he became archbishop; he is also sometimes cited as the Sicilian abbot – *abbas Siculus*) taught only briefly at Bologna before moving to Parma and then to Siena. He left a very influential commentary on Extra, numerous opinions, and a collection of leading points in canon law (*Thesaurus singularium in iure canonico decisivorum*). He was also an important figure in the Conciliar Movement, which tried to heal the Great Schism by arguing that the Church's plenitude of power resided in its whole body, as represented by a General Council in which the Pope participated, and stressing that the Pope was a member of the Church rather than its commander. The Great Schism had its origins in 1309, when Pope Clement V had fixed the seat of the papacy at Avignon (then in the County of Provence, which owed allegiance to the King of Naples) because he was French and wished to evade the worst of Italian factionalism. There it stayed until 1378 when the successive elections of Urban VI and Clement VII, representing the Italian and the French parties, brought scandal to the Church and revealed the deep political differences in Europe. A settlement was finally reached after the Council of Constance (1413–1417), a settlement brought about by legalistic compromise and political exhaustion.

5.6   THE CANONISTS AND THE THEORY OF THE 'JUST WAR'[10]

5.6.1 The moral and practical problem of whether war can be justified is not new. Roman philosophers had developed theories of the just war, and St Augustine had given lengthy consideration to the problem as posed for Christians. In the eleventh century the Peace of God and the Truce of God were attempts to modify the consequences of war.[11] The Peace was intended to protect the helpless, such as women, children, merchants, travellers, farmers with their animals and tools, and also clerics and religious, at least from direct attack. The Truce tried to impose temporal restrictions on the waging of war, forbidding it, for example, in Christmastide or in the ten weeks of Spring between Septuagesima and the octave of Easter. The Decretists attempted to define the just war. Rufinus laid down three requirements: the one who proclaimed the war should have due authority – that is, be a prince, not a mere lord; the adversary must be guilty of something which deserved measures of force; the actual fighters must be suitable and inspired by worthy motives. Stephen of Tournai pointed out that a war might be justified on the grounds both that the attacker was in the right, and that the defender was in the wrong, or on only one of these grounds. A war waged against a guilty party, but from malice, lacked justification in the initiator of the war; in that the defender deserved punishment it was unilaterally just, or justified. The war by Saul on David (I Sam 19, 23–26) had no ground of justification, because Saul was moved solely by envy and David (in this case) was undeserving of such persecution. In theory a war was possible in which both parties were in the right, as when a war was declared on false premises, but in general the Decretists insisted that in a just war one side only had a monopoly of justice.

10 This description of canonist discussion is deeply indebted to FH Russell *The Just War in the Middle Ages* (CUP, 1975).
11 Extra 1.34.1–1.34.2; see Herlihy, *Feudalism*, no 48; cf M Bloch, *Feudal Society*, pp 412ff.

5.6.2 Huguccio shifted the focus from the punishment of crime or sin in the wrongdoer to the maintenance of proper authority; those who avenged their own injuries were guilty of sin, unless they were acting on judicial authority. In his teaching a war of aggression, as distinct from one of self-defence, was unjustified, as was a war waged with direct clerical participation, or when the enemy did not deserve something so drastic as the affliction of war. But a city, unlike an individual, could defend itself on its own authority, and denial of free passage was held a just cause; this doctrine was applied to Jerusalem, as a ground to justify the Crusades. The Emperor was justified in making war on subjects who rebelled; he also could properly authorize war to recover lost property which was being withheld. The twelfth-century canonists stressed the necessity of a superior jurisdiction to give legitimate authority for the prosecution of a war. Although their definition of a prince as one entitled to wage war was somewhat self-referent, it was a limitation on the local and immediate violence of lords and knights.

5.6.3 The Decretalists tried to make more systematic the concept of the just war. Lawrence the Spaniard provided five criteria by which the justice of a war could be assessed: first, the person waging the war must be a layman; second, the object of the war must be defence of the *patria* (one's native country) or the recovery of stolen goods; third, only necessity made the war just; fourth, the desire to punish was not of itself justificatory; and, fifth, the war must be waged on princely authority. These five criteria are described as *persona*, *res*, *causa*, *animus*, and *auctoritas* respectively. Teutonicus adopted them; so did Raymond of Peñaforte who pointed out that all five must be met. Raymond also held that anyone, however just his cause, who intentionally exceeded the limit of minimum force should be excommunicated; he taught that this limit was lower in the defence of property than in the defence of the person. Hostiensis used the Roman law texts, amplifying the gospel command, to imply a cognatic relationship between all Christians, a family bond;[12] his view tended to restrict legitimate authority for a just war to the Emperor or the Pope.

12 The Poles in the fifteenth century were very indignant that the Teutonic Knights made attacks on Poland and Lithuania on the pretext of converting the pagans.

5.6.4 A problem linked with the notion of authority was that of obedience: was a subject bound to follow his lord in a war waged out of cupidity? Teutonicus required a vassal to refrain from giving aid to his lord's enemy, lest he render himself guilty of treason – a Roman concept – as well as of rupture of the feudal bond; he also prohibited a vassal from obeying his lord's command to commit atrocities.[13] The Speculator took a position helpful to the efficiency of royal power in France and England; where there was a war involving the *patria*, a vassal's allegiance to his king must take precedence over his obligation to his immediate lord. Innocent IV, speaking as canonist rather than as Pope, specifically denied to a vassal who obeyed the summons to fight in an unjust war, the action on mandate to recover his losses in the war from his lord. (Mandate in Roman law was a request by one party that another should do something for him, without payment, but with reimbursement of expenses.) Innocent thus equated the relationship of lord and vassal to that of mandator and mandatary. He reached his conclusion on the Roman ground that no contract could be enforced which had an immoral foundation. The corollary was that a vassal could not be forced to participate in an unjust war, and that any measure his lord took against him to this end would be in itself unjust. However, when a vassal followed his lord in a just war, he would normally be able to recover his expenses by an action on mandate.

13 Compare the treatment by Jacques de Révigny in Appendix 2(A).

5.6.5 The right of capture was another area of warfare given consideration by the canonists. There were considerable difficulties in trying to reconcile the feudal right to exact a ransom, as well as the pagan Roman law which held that prisoners of war were automatically slaves, with the Church's ban on Christians enslaving other Christians. Hence the canonists' treatment concentrated on how property rights were affected by war. Lawrence the Spaniard discussed whether a just party who had recovered his property by means of war could then make a claim before the courts or properly continue the war. Feudal custom allowed the pursuit of both courses, but Lawrence held that the principle of good faith, as expressed in Roman law, forbade the seeking of the same remedy twice; once satisfaction had been received, the just party must seek nothing further.

5.6.6 Innocent IV and Hostiensis systematically linked the limits on violence and on legitimate spoils to the theory of the just war itself, by specifying how property rights and personal status were affected by the various levels of licit violence. Innocent did not make use of Roman public law in his analysis, because that had predicated a centralized single state, but Roman private law was readily adapted to the feudal confusion of public office and private right. The rule that an illegal or immoral act could not ground a lawful obligation could be used to protect the just and penalize the unjust warrior. Innocent understood that it was unrealistic to try to prevent all acts of warfare between feudal lords, and so he stressed not so much the abstract justice of a war as its legally enforceable consequences. The just war, or any licit defence by force, was deemed to constitute an extraordinary legal procedure, to supplement the normal methods for settling disputes; this put some controls on the incidence of violence.

5.7 THE LOCAL APPLICATION OF CANON LAW

5.7.1 The description of just war theories has illustrated how, in this as in other fields, canon law developed concepts of lawful authority and due obedience, including the duties involved in the former and the rights implied in the latter. Despite some of the larger claims made for papal jurisdiction,[14] we find Innocent IV upholding the proper sphere of secular jurisdiction,[15] and even maintaining the reality of legitimate government among infidels.[16] The canonists' definitions of spheres of authority were helpful tools in the political theorizing which led to the creation of nation states in Europe.[17] At least until the sixteenth century canon law continued to be very influential in the growth of public law as a science and in practice; some doctrines of Natural Law also owed much to canon law. However, canon law was not only the concern of the papacy and the doctors, it also dealt with the daily needs of diocesan administration, and it was at this level that most people felt its effects. We shall therefore look at examples of the pastoral application of canon law, using the records of the diocese of Lincoln in the thirteenth and sixteenth centuries for our illustrations.[18]

14 Tierney, nos 87 and 88, quoting Hostiensis.
15 Tierney, nos 84 and 85; cf no 57.
16 Tierney, no 86.
17 Cf Tierney, nos 89-92; see generally the works of W Ullmann.
18 *The Rolls and Register of Bishop Oliver Sutton, 1280-1299*, ed RMT Hill for the Lincoln Record Society (vol I = LRS 39, 1948; vol II = LRS 43, 1950; vol III = LRS 48, 1954; vol IV = LRS 52, 1958; vol V = LRS 60, 1965; vol VI = LRS 64, 1969), cited as *Sutton* III,33 etc; *An Episcopal Court Book for the Diocese of Lincoln, 1514–1520*, ed M Bowker, Lincoln Record Society 61, 1967, cited as *Court Book*. Lincoln was in some ways an unusual diocese, but these examples of its bishop's jurisdiction can safely be taken as typical.

5.7.2 All Christendom was divided into dioceses, and the bishop of each diocese was the judge ordinary, the man with universal jurisdiction in that diocese, except where there was specific reservation to some other court. The bishop was the proper judge in both civil and criminal cases falling to the courts spiritual; from him there might be appeal to the metropolitan (from Lincoln to the archbishop of Canterbury with his Court of Arches) and also appeal either thence or directly to the pope. Appeals to the papacy might be heard in Rome or locally by judges delegate, appointed to hear cases on the spot.[19] The papacy, as well as providing an appellate court, reserved to itself certain great causes, such as claims against bishops, and also dispensations and absolutions of certain types.[20] The pope, as well as any other bishop, also had the power and the duty to intervene where morals or Christian discipline required it;[21] such intervention might be through judges delegate or by a decretal. The pope did not necessarily hear cases in person, although he might;

at Rome there were auditors (*auditores*) who, between the twelfth and fourteenth centuries, changed from mere assistants into full delegates. They heard cases individually, but each was bound to take advice from his colleagues. From 1331 there were three panels of judges, and from these there developed the court of the Sacred Roman Rota, whose reports survive partially from the sixteenth century. Religious orders (that is, of monks, nuns, and friars) were, in general, not directly subject to the bishop as ordinary but only, via their Superiors, to the Pope. However, they would owe some duty to the bishop in whose diocese their house was situated,[22] and they would also be subject to him in matters concerning the cure of souls.

19 *Sutton* III,33 – Sutton and the bishops of Winchester and Salisbury were appointed to hear the case of Edmund, Earl of Cornwall, and his wife, Margaret de Clare, in 1290.
20 Eg, dispensation to a cleric to hold more than one benefice, see *Sutton* I,105 or *Court Book* 103; a cleric who fornicated with a nun was sent to Rome to obtain absolution, *Sutton* IV,40.
21 We find Bishop Sutton in 1291 forbidding the letting of lodgings in Boston to harlots; the local clergy were to see that this was enforced – *Sutton* III,112.
22 See CR Cheney, *Episcopal Visitation of Monasteries in the Thirteenth Century* (Manchester UP, 2nd edn, 1983) for one aspect.

5.7.3 Within the diocese the canons of the cathedral chapter to some extent shared the bishop's power, in that they administered the see during a vacancy, came together to elect the new bishop, and acted as his council and as the reservoir from which he drew his senior staff. Subordinate to the bishop were his archdeacons (of whom there were eight in the large diocese of Lincoln, whereas in the diocese of Exeter there were four, one covering all Cornwall). Within his archdeaconry, a grouping of parishes, each archdeacon had a wide but inferior jurisdiction at first instance, covering laymen as well as clerics. From the archdeacon and his court, appeal lay to the bishop; major causes lay outside his jurisdiction. Rural deans, or deans of Christianity, had a similar but subordinate function. Also subordinate was the official, the bishop's official or the archdeacon's official, but in either case a delegate whose specific function was jurisdiction, since his superior might be occupied with other aspects of administration. The bishop's official – the one usually referred to when the term is used without qualification – normally had legal training. As he was a delegate, appeal from him lay to the metropolitan or directly to Rome (Sext 2.15.3). Vicars-general also emerged as members of a bishop's permanent staff, or household; in many dioceses their duties were administrative rather than judicial, or only exercised in the absence of the bishop. Commissaries might be permanent or ad hoc but, although they might well be used for judicial business, this was not their specific function. There were, however, no hard and fast rules; one man, Richard Roston, was official-principal, vicar-general, commissary-general and chancellor to the bishop of Lincoln between 1514 and 1520.

5.7.4 Civil jurisdiction in the spiritual courts covered Church property, including ecclesiastical benefices (that is, tenure of parishes, canonries, bishoprics, etc), wills and succession, status, marriage, dowry, obligations fortified by oath, and usury; all these were defined as 'spiritual causes' or annexed thereto. Other cases fell to the ecclesiastical courts by reason of the person involved, such as clerics,[23] or widows and orphans, or crusaders, or because some aspect of doctrine or morality was involved. This was the theory; in practice there were local variations – for example, in causes dependent on the person, ecclesiastical jurisdiction was much wider in Spain than in England.

23 Benefit of clergy, although subject to local variations, in general allowed a cleric, even one in minor orders, to choose as his forum, in criminal as well as civil matters, the relevant ecclesiastical court, to the exclusion of secular jurisdiction.

5.7.5 In Lincoln in 1294 we find the bishop appointing commissaries to hear a case concerning entitlement to the mortuary dues of the parish of Milcombe; in another parish one of the local gentry had refused to pay his tithes, and he was told to seek absolution or to come before the bishop for judgment.[24] In 1519 Merton College, Oxford, was cited to explain the decayed state of the parish church at Diddington, whose revenues were annexed to the college.[25] The bishop is regularly found discharging executors who have completed their duties, appointing commissaries to try disputes arising out of wills, asking the sheriff to hand over the goods of one who had died intestate to the sequestrator (so that the Church could make fair disposition of his moveable estate), and dealing with maladministration by executors.[26] The bishop informed the secular courts of people's status, and saw that a widow received her dower.[27] Marriage questions lay in the bishop's jurisdiction, whether for confirmation or dissolution.[28] We find, too, Bishop Sutton granting licences to hold in the seasons of Lent or Advent legal proceedings which required the taking of an oath. In 1298 he dispensed one Agnes Cross from a rash vow she had made concerning fasting, and he bade her do some good work instead.[29]

24 *Sutton* IV,182; III,26.
25 *Court Book* 90.
26 *Sutton* III,21; III,48; V,20; V,93.
27 *Sutton* V,20; IV,126.
28 *Sutton* IV,66; *Court Book* 10; see RH Helmholz, *Marriage Litigation in Mediaeval England* (CUP 1974).
29 *Sutton* III,81; III,169; VI,59.

5.7.6 The criminal jurisdiction of the bishop's court covered crimes against clerics or Church property, against the ministry of the Church – and this included crimes committed by clerics[30] – against doctrine (which included heresy, blasphemy and sacrilege, simony, witchcraft, and disobedience) and against morals. In England most criminal jurisdiction seems to have been concerned with fornication and other sexual offences; most of these cases were dealt with in the archdeacon's court. Assault on or brawling with clerics seems to have been quite common; the excommunication imposed on Robert of Bavert for this reason was lifted when he explained that he had not recognized as a cleric the noisy fellow in striped clothes.[31] Heresy is not common in episcopal records, perhaps because it was often dealt with by specially appointed inquisitors; in 1518 the vicar-general heard the case of Elizabeth Sculthorp who had lost her faith and ceased going to church. She was not accused of witchcraft, in spite of her confession that she had betaken herself and all her children to the devil, but was kindly treated.[32] In 1295 we find an unusual offence: two men, recently appointed as canons in the cathedral chapter of Ferns in Ireland, were to be absolved from the excommunication incurred for attending lectures on civil law at the University of Oxford, and other excesses – they should, of course, have had formal permission.[33]

30 Eg, the man appointed to a cure of souls who had failed to be ordained priest within the year; he was also charged with perjury and forging papal bulls – *Sutton* VI,146.
31 *Sutton* III,126; cf II,35; IV,15; V,113, or *Court Book* 32ff.
32 *Court Book* 84–85,and cf 33.
33 *Sutton* V,76.

5.7.7   The main penalties imposed were excommunication, greater or lesser, interdict, which was collective in that it was imposed on a community not an individual, beatings, fines, fasting, and public or private penance. On clerics alone might be imposed degradation from orders (which would make them susceptible to secular jurisdiction), deprivation of benefice, suspension from the exercise of office, and also imprisonment for obduracy, although the secular arm gaoled contumacious laymen on the Church's behalf. Excommunication was understood by the canonists as primarily a means to repentance and amendment; while it might well act as a deterrent, any retributive aim was subordinate to the bringing about of submission, to be followed by a suitable penance. Thus excommunication was pronounced against those who poached game in Spalding Priory's or the bishop's parks, until they made reparation; similarly it was pronounced against those who remained unrepentant in their adultery.[34]

34 *Sutton* IV,78; V,136; III,189.

5.7.8   To give other examples of penalties, when Nigel of Hargrave had sought sanctuary in St Giles', Oxford, but was dragged out and severely manhandled, the perpetrators of this violation were sentenced to six beatings, and to pay for his medical expenses, to visit him in prison, and to have three masses said. Robert of Grendon was to receive two beatings in the archdeacon's household for striking a cleric's servant in the face over a game of dice. A canon who struck another cleric was to receive five beatings and was suspended from his ministry for six weeks; the chaplain who struck a canon of Stonely Priory was suspended until he should receive a dispensation and for the rest was to fast for three Fridays on bread, beer – drunk then like tea or coffee now – and vegetable soup, and to pay three shillings to the Priory. John Fuller, a cleric, who shed the blood of another in a churchyard was to stand at the chancel steps on three successive Sundays singing psalms during Mass.[35] The publicity of such penances was quite often mitigated because humility rather than humiliation was the purpose; fines were on occasion imposed instead. Sometimes monetary penalties were intended as reparation, but sometimes they were simply fines, put to a good cause such as the rebuilding of the Fosse Dyke.[36]

35 *Sutton* V,1; III,27; VI,144; V,94, cf *Court Book* 138; *Sutton* VI,73, cf *Court Book* 32.
36 *Court Book* 109; 139.

5.8   CANON LAW PROCEDURE

5.8.1   Procedure in the ecclesiastical courts had a very considerable influence throughout Europe – except in England – on that of the secular courts, as, for example, on the Court of Session in Scotland. Canon law built on the *cognitio* procedure of Roman law, a rational system taking account of documentary evidence and witnesses' relation of events within their knowledge; this at a time when the feudal courts preferred trial by battle or by ordeal. In the ecclesiastical courts auditors were appointed to act as examining magistrates, and all the proceedings were recorded in writing (Extra 2.19.11), usually by qualified notaries.

5.8.2 By the thirteenth century, if not earlier, proceedings normally started with a written libel served with a summons. In the libel the pursuer had to state what he claimed, and on what grounds, and the nature of the action. The defender would normally appear to contest the claim; this stage was called *litis contestatio* (joinder of issue) as it had been in Justinian's law. The defender could put forward certain pleas in defence (*exceptiones*). Declinatory (for example, rejecting the jurisdiction of the court) and dilatory (denying that a claim had yet fallen due) defences must be pleaded before *litis contestatio*; peremptory defences (that is, those defences, such as duress, which would bar an action in perpetuity) came afterwards, and would usually be considered together with the matters of fact. After *litis contestatio* proceedings were oral. The pursuer set out his facts, his allegations, in articles or *positiones*; the defender then admitted or denied each, and set out his own *positiones*. The judge then investigated or tried the points not admitted by the defender, and found the facts on the evidence. The evidence might amount to full proof, that is, the testimony of two witnesses or a notarized document, or to half proof, that is, of one witness, or a private document, or general report, each of which could be rebutted. This was more reliable than compurgation which, however, was tolerated in many ecclesiastical courts, for, as has been remarked, as long as local reputation was important and social units were small enough, the oaths of neighbours as to a man's character were probably fairly trustworthy.

5.8.3 In canonical procedure, after proof of the facts, the judge heard the parties' arguments on points of law, including the legal effect of the facts proved; he gave his decision then or, more commonly, after an interval. All the proceedings, including the judgment, were put in writing. Appeal was possible on interlocutory matters as well as on the final decision; this gave considerable opportunity for delaying tactics. For this reason summary procedure was introduced; it was authorized and regulated in 1307 (Clem. 5.11.2), but it had clearly been practised for quite a while before.

5.8.4 Criminal proceedings began either with accusation by the injured party or someone on his behalf, or with denunciation in the public interest by someone with no personal *locus standi*, or through an official investigation by the court where there had been persistent rumour of wrongdoing. By the fifteenth century, inquiry by the court on its own initiative had become the most common start for a criminal action in the courts spiritual. The accused must receive due notice of the charge made against him and of the witnesses who would be called. Once begun, criminal trials in ecclesiastical courts differed little from civil actions.

5.8.5 Roman rules, including rules of evidence and procedure, were used where appropriate. For example, in marriage litigation they were applicable in questions of capacity or consent, or of certain impediments; Roman rules were not, however, used on presumption of marriage,[37] and the treatment of divorce was entirely different. Gratian, quoting Pope Nicholas I, expressed the general canonist attitude to Roman law.

> 'The imperial law is not to be used in every ecclesiastical dispute, especially where it conflicts with the rule of the gospels or the canons . . . Not that it is to be completely rejected, for example, against heretics and other wicked men.'

Indeed, 'the imperial law is to be used in ecclesiastical matters wherever it is found not to conflict with the sacred canons'.[38]

37   Cf D 23.2.4 with *Decretum Grat.* C.30, q.5, cc.1-2.
38   *Decretum Grat.* D.10.1; *dictum post* C.15, q.3, c.4. X 4.12.1 shows the straightforward following of a Roman rule on forbidden degrees.

5.9   SUBSTANTIVE CANON LAW

5.9.1   Canon law was primarily concerned with the administration of the Church and its rules; from consideration of the wider aspects of government within the Church much political theory applicable to the secular world was developed. Some elements of canon law, however, were related to, or contrasted with, the daily practice of the secular law. For example, canonical doctrine largely ignored the feudal distinction between moveable and immoveable property; the canonist attitude was adopted from the law of Justinian's time and was partly in the interests of the claims of women, who enjoyed inferior rights in feudal property.

5.9.2   Canonists naturally wished to maintain the rule of law, and to this end they stressed the importance of the protection of peaceful possession. The *actio spolii* first appeared around 1180;[39] by this action the victim of any unjustified loss of possession, indeed of any obstacle to the exercise of a right, could claim restitution. The action went beyond the protection of possession given by the interdicts of Roman law, and far beyond the assize of novel disseisin and other feudal remedies, in that it covered any subject of alleged benefit, including moveable property or an office or benefice. All the claimant had to do was to show that he had held this benefit peacefully before the present possessor; the question of right, of title, could be settled afterwards.

39   Extra 2.13.7; cf *Decretum Grat.* C.3, q.1, c.3; see le Bras, pp 350ff.

5.9.3   Another development that affected secular law in the sphere of possession was the canonists' restriction on the acquisition of title by prescription. In Roman law, initial good faith was required for such acquisition (*usucapio*), as well as a *iusta causa* (that is, apparent grounds for acquisition of title, such as sale or gift); supervening knowledge that there was a better claimant did not bar acquisition, provided that no challenge was made. The canonists, however, held that the absence of good faith was bad faith, and of its nature sinful, and so an acquisition where there was supervening knowledge of a better claimant was to be equated with theft. From the fifteenth century the requirement of continuous good faith became in many areas a principle of secular as well as of ecclesiastical law; it was received into French and into German law.

5.9.4   Good faith was stressed by the canonists in other ways. It was on the basis of general good faith that agreements, even without oath, were held to bind the parties, thus giving a *causa*, a ground of action, before an ecclesiastical court. *Pacta sunt servanda* (agreements are for keeping) was the canonist ruling, but performance could normally be required only if the first party had done or offered to do his part. A fair amount of argument was needed to reconcile this doctrine with the Roman view that bare pacts might only act as a defence to an action and did not give rise to an obligation. Hence there was considerable emphasis on the will, intention, as playing the fundamental part in grounding obligations, or at least contractual obligations. The doctrine of a *causa* as a requirement for a contract developed from this approach and became part of the *ius commune*. While the adoption of canonist procedure was of particular importance for the *ius commune*, the substance of canon law was influential in other fields, including the law merchant, and also, of course, in later consistorial jurisdiction.

FURTHER READING

G le Bras	'Canon law' in *The Legacy of the Middle Ages* (Oxford, 1926)
JA Brundage	*Medieval Canon Law* (London, 1995)
C Duggan	*Decretals and the Creation of the 'New Law' in the Twelfth Century* (Aldershot, 1998)
PC Ferguson	*Medieval Papal Representatives in Scotland* (Stair Society 45, Edinburgh, 1997)
RH Helmholz	'Excommunication as a legal sanction' *SZ* (*Kan*) 68 (1982) 202
	The Spirit of Classical Canon Law (U Georgia P, 1996)
JM Kelly	*A Short History of Western Legal Theory* (Oxford, 1992) ch 4
S Ollivant	*The Court of the Official in Pre-Reformation Scotland* (Stair Society 34, Edinburgh, 1982)
OF Robinson	'Canon law and marriage' *JurRev* (1984) 22
	'Canon law in theory and in practice', Index 22 (1994) 475
JD Scanlan	'The tribunal of the Sacred Roman Rota' *JurRev* (1969) 97
E Schrage	*'Descendit ad inferos*: And Belial sued Jesus Christ for trespass' in *Critical Studies in Ancient Law, Comparative Law and Legal History* ed JW Cairns and OF Robinson (Richard Hart, 2000) 353
RW Southern	*Western Society and the Church in the Middle Ages* (Penguin, 1970)
JR Sweeney & S Chodorow (eds)	*Popes, Teachers and Canon Law in the Middle Ages* (Cornell UP, 1989)
JAF Thomson	*The Western Church in the Middle Ages* (London, 1998)

B Tierney	*The Crisis of Church and State, 1050–1300* (Hall-Prentice Inc, USA, 1964)
W Ullmann	*The Growth of Papal Government* (London, 3rd edn, 1970); *The Church and the Law* (London, 1975)
E Vodola	*Excommunication in the Middle Ages* (Berkeley, 1986)

Chapter 6

THE LAW MERCHANT

6.1 PROBLEMS OF DEFINING THE LAW MERCHANT

6.1.1 The law merchant is comparable to feudal law in that its origins are customary. As had happened in earlier centuries with kinship or feudal groups, bodies of craftsmen or traders or seafarers formed associations for their own safety. A few of those in Italy may well go back to the Roman *collegia* (associations of men such as the bakers or the salt suppliers of Rome) but mostly they were of Germanic origin; a special peace was often granted – or sold – to groups of merchants by Carolingian or Anglo-Saxon rulers. Most of these associations were based on towns which, as we have seen, emerged in the eleventh century as instruments of the economic revival and as the markets which stimulated yet further growth. Just as feudal law everywhere involved the personal tie between man and lord, tenure, and delegation of governmental powers (but in different localities the means by which these were achieved and the implications varied), so everywhere the needs of trade were physical safety, financial security, and speedy settlement, and again the mechanisms for satisfying these needs varied. Different customs applied at sea or on land, between the north of Europe and the south, and even between neighbouring cities.

6.1.2 Common institutions were shared; for example, the use of negotiable instruments received general acceptance, but the precise enforceable rules for their use varied in different countries and in different jurisdictions. In some areas there developed a general mercantile jurisdiction; in others only certain classes of person or of transaction had their own courts. Some modern civilian systems, such as the German and the French, have separate commercial codes; others, such as the Italian or the Dutch, no longer do. In the Scottish and the English legal systems commercial law is not formally distinct from other areas, but manuals are written and courses taught on mercantile law in modern Britain. Certain transactions are more commonly entered into by merchants, others by consumers, and there may be special provision for commercial cases, or at least some difference in such matters as the standard of proof required to evidence a transaction. Problems raised by trade across national frontiers need special regulation and so do special customs in a commercial community, whether the members of the modern Stock Exchange or the underwriters of Antwerp in the seventeenth century. Such special treatment, however, is not peculiar to merchants even now, and in the mediaeval and early modern world there were many examples of a law which was restricted to a particular group within a body of citizens.

6.1.3　During the Middle Ages it was the international ramifications of trade and manufacturing which significantly marked out mercantile from other branches of law of more local application. Moreover, from the sixteenth century onwards when national systems are clearly developing, the Law Merchant continued readily to cross the boundaries between them and to preserve its international character. Its common feature was community of institutions rather than community of rules; there was no central legislature, no central court, through which uniformity of rules might be achieved. There continued to be a general tendency to follow accepted custom, and to accept foreign customs or authorities as highly persuasive in the decisions of national courts. Also discernible was an inclination to speed and informality of procedure (for example, arbitration), and to reliance on equity and good faith – although it is worth remembering that this meant equity and good faith as understood by merchants, which might involve strict compliance with accepted custom. It did not just mean fair play, or a moral philosopher's concept of good faith.

6.2　ROMAN ELEMENTS IN THE LAW MERCHANT

6.2.1　The interpretation of good faith in terms of conventional practice was very Roman, and Roman too were some of the widespread specific rules to be found in the more developed stages of the Law Merchant. The Romans had employed many contracts which were available to anyone suing in a Roman court; they described these as being of the *ius gentium*, the law of peoples generally. Thus it was possible to make a binding contract of sale or hire by simple, unwitnessed and informal agreement on the subject matter and the price; one could enter into any sort of obligation, simple or complex, by formally putting a question and replying with a promise (in the contract known as stipulation). Roman law had no technically distinct mercantile law but certain institutions, sometimes of Greek or other origin, were special to mercantile transactions. It is not clear that there was any continuity in these institutions between the ancient and the mediaeval worlds, though certainly the Law Merchant came in time to borrow from the learned law of the *Corpus Iuris Civilis*. However, continuity is not impossible, especially as most of these institutions were particularly concerned with maritime commerce, which had never ceased between the Italian peninsula and the Byzantine Empire, and which was the earliest field for the codification of custom in the history of the Law Merchant.

6.2.2　To give some examples: the *actio exercitoria* was an action given against a ship-owner in respect of contracts entered into by the master of the ship – the comparable *actio institoria* was given against the owner of a shop or business in respect of contracts entered into by the manager whom he employed. *Faenus nauticum* was a loan (at a high rate of interest) made for the purpose of a sea voyage, repayable only if the ship arrived safely. *Receptum nautarum* was the implied promise of a carrier by sea that he would deliver the goods entrusted to him, unless the goods were lost through circumstances beyond his control such as shipwreck or attack by pirates. The edict *nautae caupones stabularii* imposed double liability on the master of a ship (or on the keeper of an inn or stable) if goods were lost, damaged or stolen by his employees. The *lex Rhodia*, or Rhodian Sea Law, dealt with general average; it provided that where cargo was jettisoned in order to save a ship and the ship was saved, the loss was to be shared among all those who benefited including the owner of the ship, so that the whole loss did not fall on the party or parties whose cargo had been jettisoned. When the learned law came to be applied to comparable situations in the mediaeval world, reference was made to the Roman texts on these and similar matters.

6.3   MARITIME CODES

6.3.1   Even before the economic revival of the eleventh and twelfth centuries there was some long-distance sea-borne trade in luxuries through certain Italian ports, and when the revival came it was centred upon the Mediterranean; in consequence Italian practice influenced all aspects of commerce as trade spread outwards through Europe. (It should be remembered that even when trade became easier in later centuries, transport by water was cheaper and safer than by land right up until the nineteenth century.) Naples, Amalfi and Salerno aroused the admiration of one Ibn Hawqal,[1] a Saracen compiler of a handbook for merchants in the late tenth century, although Bari, Trani and the other Apulian ports confined themselves primarily to local trade. These cities were in the Byzantine sphere of influence as was Venice, founded among the marshes at the head of the Adriatic by refugees fleeing the Lombards; she was unique among cities in that her two main exports, salt and glass, owed nothing to the cultivation of the land. In the eleventh century Pisa and Genoa developed as maritime powers; in 1016 they united to clear Sardinia of Moslem control, and the Pisans had already won a sea battle against the Moslems in 1005 off Reggio (see para 1.10.3). The two cities acquired allies through the Norman conquest of southern Italy and of most of Sicily during the eleventh century. However, Norman encroachments in the Balkans, like the nomad invasions southward across the Danube, led to the hard-pressed Byzantine Empire appealing to the West for help against the even more threatening Seljuk Turks. In the wake of the ensuing First Crusade markets in the Levant which had hitherto been dominated by Byzantium's allies were opened to Pisa and Genoa. Venice survived the set-back, retained a near monopoly of trade with Constantinople, and established colonies at Tyre and Sidon, but she was no longer unrivalled.

1   Cited by Hyde, p 19f.

6.3.2   Nothing concerning maritime custom survives in written form from before the beginning of the thirteenth century, but clearly the earliest writings available to us were not the first of their kind. From Venice in 1205 came the *Capitulare navium (Shipping Rules)* which was reissued in a much fuller form in 1255 under the title *Statuta et Ordinamenta super Navibus (Statutes and Regulations on Shipping)*. This code was extremely influential in the other Adriatic ports, although Ancona had her own code of which a late fourteenth-century version survives. In Apulia at the very end of the twelfth century two judges independently put into writing the customs of Bari; one was more conscious of the Lombard element, the other of the *ius commune* of the northern cities but he included some maritime custom. At Trani the maritime code seems to date from the fourteenth century, although ascribed to the eleventh; it is in Italian not Latin which better fits the later date but it doubtless contains older elements. At Amalfi in the kingdom of Naples there was a code of which parts go back at least to the thirteenth century; it has twenty-one chapters in Latin and forty-five in Italian. The customs of the city of Pisa were first written down shortly after the Peace of Constance (1183), and it was in the early thirteenth century that a maritime court (the *ordo maris*) came into being there with its own proper code; the oldest surviving version of this *Breve curiae maris (Manual of the Court of the Sea)* dates from 1305. The consuls, or judges, of the *ordo maris* at first exercised a concurrent jurisdiction with the city's mercantile judges and were subject to appeal, to a Judge of Appeals. In the fourteenth century they acquired an exclusive and irrevocable jurisdiction in maritime matters, including shipyard contracts. Genoa's sea customs were of great importance in the Levant. It was Genoese and Pisan influence which led to the compilation in Barcelona of a code which was to become the most widely used of all codes of maritime law; it was originally entitled *Costumes de la Mar (Customs of the Sea)* but is most generally known as the *Consolato del Mare (Consulate of the Sea)*.

6.3.3   The term 'consul' had developed for judges in the cities' courts. Those who exercised a general jurisdiction came often to be replaced by a *podestà* (see para 3.6.4) but the name frequently survived for those who presided over guild or maritime courts. Those, too, who heard the disputes of their fellow guildsmen or fellow countrymen at fairs or in foreign ports were often called consuls. The term has survived into the modern world for persons appointed to represent the maritime and commercial interests of their country in a foreign state; in the Middle Ages they often exercised a general jurisdiction within a quarter of a town reserved to a particular group of foreigners. A consul might also be a national of the state in which the trading post was sited, who acted as host to a particular group. From Italy the institution spread to France and Spain as well as the Levant. The county of Barcelona and the kingdom of Aragon were the earliest parts of Spain to share in the economic revival; there the commercial courts were controlled by the Crown, unlike the communes of Italy but as in France and England. It was by royal ordinance in 1336 that summary procedure was introduced for the Sea Consulate of Valencia; it was a royal charter which in 1401 established the Barcelona consulate not simply as a maritime court but as one exercising general jurisdiction.

6.3.4   The *Consulate of the Sea*[2] begins with the procedure for the annual election of the judges by the senior members of the marine corporations and the sea guilds:

> 'Such is the custom. Although it has been stated [in the royal charter of 1284] that His Majesty the King or his procurator would designate annually the person who would exercise the office of judge, the elders of the sea guild enjoy this privilege because His Majesty the King and his procurator have never at any time since the inception of this privilege exercised their prerogative (art 3). . . . Consuls shall have jurisdiction in all matters relating to lading charges, damage suffered by the cargo once loaded aboard the

vessels, wages of sailors, shareholders of vessels, sale of vessels, throwing of cargo overboard, command of vessels entrusted to patrons or sailors, indebtedness of shipowners who took out loans to equip the vessels, obligations of the merchants to shipowners, obligations of shipowners to the merchants, all salvage found on the sea and on the sea shore, outfitting of vessels galleys barques, and all types of agreement which generally refer to the custom of the sea' (art 22).

In case of doubt the consuls were to consult the elders of the merchants' and sea guilds; if the advice differed the consuls were to follow that of the elders of the sea guild – not because they were forced to seek advice by royal or other provision, but because it was the ancient custom. The substantive provisions are described as the

> 'beneficial customs of marine intercourse which well-informed people, having journeyed throughout the world, imparted to our predecessors who wrote them down in learned volumes, all of them relating to the proper customs to be followed. In the material which follows one can learn in what way a patron of a vessel is obligated to the merchants, the sailors, the passengers, and other persons aboard his vessel; also, what are the responsibilities of merchants, sailors and passengers toward a patron of a large or a small vessel' (art 46).

Other provisions cover the initial construction of a vessel and taking shares in that venture (art 47–54), conditions in which there would be an obligation to aid another vessel in distress (art 94), general average (arts 95–99), the employment of a pilot (art 250), and there is a considerable section on privateering (arts 298–334).

2   *Consulate of the Sea*, tr SS Jados (Alabama, 1975).

6.3.5   The *Consulate* went through many editions; the repetition of various provisions in modified form indicates the accumulation of material, for example art 157 deals with desertion by crew members, art 158 is an amending article, and the matter is also the subject of art 268. The book was translated from the original Catalan into Latin, French and Italian; the Italian edition of 1519 was to be found all over Europe and was described as 'the custom commonly received in all provinces and lands'. It inspired or provided a model for other collections of maritime custom in the northern part of Europe. A collection called *Jugements de la Mer* (*Judgments of the Sea*) or *Rôles d'Oléron* (*Records of Oléron* – from near La Rochelle) goes back to the thirteenth or fourteenth century and, in the older parts, contains Gascon custom. Other additions were from Brittany or Normandy, and it was used also in Flanders, the Netherlands and England, where later the *Black Book of the Admiralty* was compiled. It directly provided the bulk of the material for the *Waterrecht* (*Sea Law*) of Damme (near Bruges) and then of Wisby (in the Baltic), and in this form was widely used in the Hanseatic towns such as Lübeck and Hamburg and in other northern ports. These substantial and widely accepted codes gradually superseded most of narrowly local customs.

6.3.6   In maritime law there were many institutions peculiar to the sea. Some were modifications of the Roman law, such as the rule of general average, or the form of loan called *faenus nauticum*. Bottomry bonds, giving security over a ship to a creditor, seem to have developed from *faenus nauticum*, being payable only if the ship came safely home. Sometimes new custom appears to have been influenced by the revived Roman law, for example, the owning of ships in shares or parts, and the rules of liability after a collision where there had been no fault. Insurance was a growing field of maritime law, and new legal documents appeared such as bills of lading or analogous documents in which the ship's writer or clerk listed the cargo and gave a copy of the connossement, as it is called, to the freighter as proof that the goods had been shipped. These and similar practices found an acceptance so widespread as reasonably to be called universal, and the needs of maritime commerce have changed little, although it is doubtful if in a modern container ship there is a legal requirement to carry a cat to deal with the rats (*Consulate*, art 68).

6.4   BURGH LAW AND GUILDS

6.4.1   In tenth-century Italy, Pavia (as the capital of the Lombard kingdom) was perhaps the only inland city apart from Rome to attract substantial groups of foreign merchants; it had also its own merchant guild, as well as various craft guilds exercising a monopoly in their respective trades. By the start of the thirteenth century Florence had separate guilds for textile importers and finishers and for textile retailers, as well as for bankers and money-lenders. The economic revival in the eleventh century sparked off a tremendous growth of city life in the twelfth; by the early thirteenth century Pisa had grown from some 30 to 114 walled hectares and Bologna from about 23 to around 100. New towns were founded in considerable numbers, for example, some twenty were established in the district of Vercelli alone. The Peace of Constance in effect gave the cities self-government, free from more than the shadow of imperial control. While the classes were certainly distinct, in practice the line of division between lords and merchants was blurred; land was best, but trade was not vulgar. Not surprisingly as the cities began to write down their customs in their statutes they included customs connected with trade.

6.4.2   The major social development of this period in the cities was the emergence of the guilds. While the guilds' first concern was to regulate themselves in the interests of their members, they were also fairly readily adaptable to the public welfare. City statutes therefore regulated the guilds, and thereafter we find guildmasters or consuls acquiring jurisdiction not only in those matters concerning the guilds but also in general commercial affairs. In some cities there was a clear distinction between the courts; for example, in twelfth-century Pisa there was a *curia legis* (court of law) for what was covered by the city's statutes and a *curia usus* (court of custom) for mercantile cases – and it was from the latter, as we have seen, that the *ordo maris* (maritime tribunal) developed. In Genoa on the other hand the consuls were tax collectors, and commercial cases were heard by the city's general court. In principle the guilds were concerned with their own members, and in this context developed written registers of membership, styles for articles of partnership, etc. However, in the majority of cities the guild courts became, expressly or tacitly, general commercial courts and even where they did not their members were likely to provide the judges when questions of commercial usage came before the regular courts. The same tendencies are observable in northern Europe in, for example, the Dean of Guild courts in Scotland (which survived until 1975, although they lost their mercantile jurisdiction during the eighteenth century).

6.4.3 It has been pointed out[3] that law and rhetoric had a vital role to play in enabling the new intense urban life to survive without political disaster and with adequate structures for the new scale of trade, both local and national, which was necessary. New structures and forms of association needed expert definition and regulation. Judges and notaries formed influential and sizeable professional groups (for example, 120 doctors of both laws and 1500 notaries, compared to 440 butchers, in Milan and its *contado* in 1288); they often stood closer to the governing class than to the ordinary guilds. The universities studied intensively the civil and the canon law but the legal expertise so gained was applied to political theory and to commercial needs. The law merchant was based on custom and the usages of trade but it was elaborated and refined by the learned lawyers, men who were living and working in the flourishing centres of commerce. Around 1300 the populations of Venice, Milan, Florence and Genoa were probably approaching 100,000 each, with some twenty-two other Italian cities having between 20,000 and 50,000 inhabitants; in northern Europe only Paris and Ghent were clearly over the 50,000 mark and only London, Cologne and Bruges over 20,000. In southern Italy Palermo, Naples and Messina owed their size and prosperity to their foreign connections; Rome suffered as a city from the temporary removal of the papacy to Avignon. Most cities, however, were primarily centres for the distribution and consumption of relatively local produce; of the inland cities only Florence would have listed banking, long-distance trade and industry as her predominant concerns. We shall look at banking and international trade in due course.

3   Hyde, Chapter 3.

6.4.4 The guilds, to resume, were primarily concerned with their own internal organization, with the interests of the masters in a monopoly – or near monopoly – in the control of the standards of the craft, and in relations between employers and employees. Their statutes, once their customs were written down, tended to follow the outlines of their city's statutes, at least in Italy. Sometimes one finds a 'reception', as when the goldsmiths of Brescia adopted as their own the statutes of the goldsmiths of Venice. Particularly in the textile industry traders often carried to their export markets the statutes of their native city. It seems likely that in the northern cities of Europe, of which the most flourishing were concerned with long-distance trade, the guilds were to some degree so influenced, although the very growth of towns will have been enough to call forth somewhat similar institutions. For example, in 1120 their feudal lord granted by charter to the burgesses of Freiburg (in the Black Forest) the right to settle disputes among themselves by the customary law of merchants, and in particular by the custom of Cologne.

6.4.5 In France Philip Augustus (1180–1223) granted rights including jurisdiction over the Seine and its banks to the guild of river merchants. In England we find the regulations of the guilds being proclaimed and put into effect in a general commercial court. For example, at the fair court held in March 1332 at Wye in Kent two girdlers of the City of London saw to the reading of King Edward III's confirmation of their statute that no girdler should garnish girdles of silk, wool, leather or linen with base metal, and that in each town two men of the craft should be elected to see that the statute was observed; two men of Wye were duly elected and went on to discover five makers of girdles in breach of the regulation whose work was thereupon burned.[4]

4   Selden Society, vol 23, p 110.

6.4.6 Burgh law could cover a wide range of concerns, some of them only loosely linked to commercial life and some of them merely the consequence of living in a built-up area. In May 1324 at the fair court of St Ives (in Huntingdonshire) accusations brought by neighbours included:

'that there is a deficiency of water in the row of William of Hurst; . . . that John Hering senior receives harlots in a house of his; . . . that Robert Woodward obstructs a certain road near the quay; . . . that Lawrence Pegg does not clean his road in Cross Lane to the nuisance [of passers-by]; . . . and that Richard Brewhouse receives the merry-andrews in the midst of the fair to the disturbance and peril of the merchants.'[5]

The safe organizing of trade needed more than credit facilities, and when a fair was being held the normal concerns of the town must be adjusted to take it into account.

5   Selden Society, vol 23, pp 106ff.

6.5   FAIR AND PIEPOWDER COURTS

6.5.1 The mediaeval law merchant, in the sense of the customary usages of traders, had roots in the fairs and markets held, although not always at regular intervals, throughout Europe even in the Dark Ages. Market is usually applied to a regular weekly or monthly gathering serving a smallish district, while a fair is usually an annual meeting, although it may be more or less frequent. We know of fairs in Merovingian Paris and elsewhere in France in the eighth and ninth centuries. From the tenth century on there were numerous royal grants of markets with rights of jurisdiction, and the holding of great fairs such as those of Champagne is well evidenced. Such fairs and markets would be under the special peace of the king. Fairs were by no means exclusively a phenomenon of the north, but they had more weight there, just as did maritime trade in the Mediterranean lands.

6.5.2 These early fairs had their own informal courts for dealing with trading disputes and for keeping the peace, the sort of courts which in England were later called courts of piepowder, that is, *pieds poudrés* – referring to the dusty feet of the merchants or pedlars who travelled from fair to fair. The courts sometimes acquired jurisdiction over persons coming to and going from the fair as well as in matters arising during the fair. The right to grant a market or fair was generally recognized as a regalian right – a right belonging to a prince

– and the authority which this indirectly gave to the fair court favoured the development of a special custom for merchants and its acceptance as legally enforceable; this included such measures as distraint against any fellow citizen of a defaulting party – the right of reprisal. In time, and the heyday of the fairs of Lyon and Champagne was during the fourteenth and fifteenth centuries, the fairs also became centres for raising capital, for settling obligations and for transferring credit.

6.5.3   Just as fairs were generally accommodated to the feudal law in that their jurisdiction sprang from a prince's grant (as burghs were granted charters by their feudal lords), so in the north especially the judges might be appointed by the prince. From 1174 the judges at Champagne were appointed by royal ordinances, and from them appeal lay to the *Grands Jours* (Great Sessions) of Troyes and the *Parlement* of Paris (of which more in the next chapter). Similarly at Lyon the fair court's jurisdiction was in the sixteenth century extended by royal ordinance to make it a general commercial court. In 1655 Lyon succeeded in following Toulouse, Paris, Nantes, Bordeaux, Poitiers and Tours in obtaining merchant judges selected by their fellows; this was roughly the time at which the Champagne fair disappeared after being for centuries an almost permanent institution, moving quarterly from one of four cities (Lagny, Bar, Provins, Troyes) to the next. At a much earlier stage of development Florentine consuls had been exercising jurisdiction over their countrymen at the Champagne fair under the somewhat misleading title (for Florence is in Tuscany) of the Captain of the Lombards.

6.5.4   By the thirteenth century the wool and cloth trade in the north had established itself in cities, especially Bruges, Ghent and Liège, and the fair courts were urban in flavour. In Germany it was the towns along the Rhine which played a leading commercial role, Basel, Mainz, Worms and Cologne. Lübeck, Hamburg and Bremen were the leading towns in the north; all were members of the Hanseatic League. Munich had received its charter in the mid-twelfth century from Henry the Lion of Saxony and Bavaria in order to encourage trade along the Danube and through the Alpine passes. In Germany generally before the fifteenth century procedure in mercantile courts seems to have been purely oral – there are no records and no records of records. In Frankfurt we know that commercial procedure started as arbitration with a special summary process, but it soon became the practice to refer to a carefully kept book of precedents. As early as 1508 there was imperial recognition of the merchant judges at Nuremberg, but as the reception of Roman law gathered pace, mixed courts of merchants and jurists became the rule, as at Leipzig by 1682.

6.5.5   English practice is interesting because written records of merely local commercial jurisdictions survive from the thirteenth century. There were special courts in the staple towns through which, for fiscal reasons, the foreign trade in wool and woollen goods was channelled; from them appeal lay to the Chancellor and the King's Council. There were guild courts, but these English ones were largely confined, even in London, to matters affecting their organization, which did not extend to settling disputes between individuals. There were also fair courts, where the mayor or the representative of the feudal lord might preside but judgment was given by the merchants or burgesses. Of the central courts, the Court of Admiralty claimed commercial as well as maritime causes, although it lost the former to the Common Law courts. In England, however, the term 'law merchant' seems to refer as much to a particularly speedy (cases were traditionally heard between successive tides) and summary form of procedure and to special rules of evidence as to any particular body of substantive law.

6.5.6   It has indeed been argued that there was no substantive law peculiar to fair and burgh courts, and that mercantile matters could as readily be brought before the Common Law courts. Any specific reception by the Common Law courts of a body of peculiarly mercantile law must remain highly problematic but, on the other hand, juries of burgesses and merchants would be likely to come to somewhat different conclusions from those of juries of knights and peasants. For example, when at St Ives a horse was arrested as a pledge and a third party claimed that the horse was his, in spite of a sworn verdict that the claim was collusive, 'the judgment was put into respite until it should be more fully discussed by the merchants. And the merchants of the various communities and others being convoked in full court' held that the third party's payment of earnest to the defender was sufficient according to the law merchant to give him title.[6]

6   Selden Society, vol 23, pp 44ff.

6.5.7   The lack of any commercial code in England means furthermore that records of English fair courts are not necessarily a safe guide to other local jurisdictions in Europe, but these records do offer useful illustrations of the peculiarities of mercantile cases and of the special interests of the mercantile community. For example, after the twelfth century, English procedure was predicated upon a shire-sized jurisdiction, yet the needs of merchants meant that they must travel abroad. In 1270 at the fair court of St Ives, Gottschalk of Almaine (that is, of Germany), burgess of King's Lynn, made a complaint against the communities of Ghent, Poperinge, Douai, Ypres and Lille concerning a consignment of wool to be exported from England to Flanders; he was claiming against the communities, rather than against any particular merchant, under the right of reprisal, and the communities claimed that they had charters from the English crown exempting them from reprisal.[7] In 1291 the records of the same court reveal a fairly widely established occupation, that of broker, which included an official responsibility for weights and measures.

> 'Alnagers of canvas . . . made oath that they will act honestly in their office, and that they will make honest measurement for both sellers and buyers, and that they will take nothing from the one party or the other whereby any harm may befall or accrue to the buyer or the seller.'[8]

7   Selden Society, vol 23, pp 9ff.
8   Selden Society, vol 23, p 41.

6.5.8   At the fair court of Wye of 1332 a pursuer craved execution of a debt found due to him five years previously in the same fair court; jurisdiction here would seem to have lain only in the fair court. However, frequent sittings for the speedy discharge of business among peripatetic disputants are also evidenced. At a fair court at West Malling, in Kent, in November 1364 we have an example of the defender's normal three opportunities to appear being compressed into one day when Alan Dyer of Maidstone claimed £25.10s. from John Stonehill; the parties were to appear at nine o'clock. John made no appearance and so a hearing was called for noon; again he made no appearance, and so the case was put down for the evening session. When John still did not appear all his property at the fair – which had already been attached in security – 'appraised by credible men at £27.4s.3d.' – was left in the custody of the bailiff of the fair until the next fair the following August.[9] Again, at the staple court of Westminster in June 1401 we find Hamond Eliot of London, grocer, being allowed to 'have his law single-handed', that is, he was allowed to swear without compurgators, as to the sum owed him by Martin Dyne of Heydon, chapman; such an oath was 'according to their usages and customs and according to the law merchant'.[10] On the other hand, sometimes men seem expected to travel with enough companions to warrant their credibility: Gerard of Cologne 'did not come sufficiently equipped according to the law merchant' to the fair at St Ives in 1270, and he was given two days to find the required five oath-helpers for his claim to a consignment of Rhenish wine which lay with a merchant of Lynn.[11]

  9 Selden Society, vol 23, p 112.
 10 Selden Society, vol 23, p 114.
 11 Selden Society, vol 23, p 5.

6.5.9 The importance of fairs declined from the late Middle Ages as steadier demand elicited a more evenly distributed supply. The need for special concessions to foreigners, that is, all men not of the immediate locality, diminished as local feudal jurisdictions gave way to central governmental powers. It was quite a common privilege of fairs that *aubaine* or *ius albanagii* – the right of the feudal lord to any property within his jurisdiction of a foreigner who died there, regardless of that foreigner's heirs or of his will – should not be enforced against those attending them; the privilege could be bought by other merchants. In France the Crown's general claim to *aubaine* was only abandoned at the Revolution. Tolls and taxes might occasionally be waived or more frequently be lowered for a fair; temporary concessions might be made which freed aliens from customary restrictions on residence or trade. Nevertheless the decline was a lingering one; the piepowder court at Eye in Suffolk kept its records open until 1813, and Bartholomew Fair in London had a court book until its demise in 1854, although this recorded payments from the stall-holders, not pleas.

6.6   THE FINANCIAL ORGANIZATION OF MEDIAEVAL BUSINESS

6.6.1 While in mercantile transactions relating to land-based commerce there was not the same acceptance of common rules as in maritime affairs, institutions did develop which received general or outline acceptance. A fair number of these related to money, the lubricant of commerce. Deposit banks were fairly common among the northern Italian cities, and in France there was at Cahors an internationally famous centre of deposit banking. But although the credit arrangements they offered were of great use to craftsmen and small-scale traders, such bankers were often restricted in the scope of their loans by their cities, which wished to protect their own currency. Further, simple loans were harder to make profitable when the Church frowned on usury. Merchant bankers, merchants lending and borrowing money in the furtherance of international trade, were of much greater significance in the development of commercial credit. They too accepted money on deposit and paid interest to the depositor; they too lent money so deposited at a higher rate of interest, often to prelates and nobles and above all to kings. Loans to princes could be very profitable, and also very risky; between 1290 and 1310 the Frescobaldi Bianchi of Florence lent the English Crown at least £122,000 sterling. The Bardi, bankers to Edward III, were even richer, until they failed in 1346, unable to recover credits of more than a million florins from the kings of England and Sicily.

6.6.2 The chief technique, other than the concessions granted by grateful princes, by which such merchant bankers could make their profits was the letter (or bill) of exchange. Money advanced in one currency in one place was repayable at a later date in another currency and in another place; high interest charges could be hidden in a carefully adjusted rate of exchange. Bills of exchange are one form of negotiable instrument; others (some of modern growth) are promissory notes, bank notes, cheques, dividend warrants, bearer bonds, etc. They are all documents containing an undertaking to pay money, which by mercantile custom do not need to state the grounds of or the consideration for the transaction. They are transferred by mere delivery (with endorsement where applicable) and the new holder in good faith has full title to any benefits or rights of action. By the end of the thirteenth century business by correspondence had become established practice and, for the great Italian firms at least, money had become a commodity.

6.6.3 The firms which dealt in money and in goods – such as spices and dyestuffs, skins, silk and wool – were normally no longer either associations for one voyage or lifelong partnerships based on community of family property. These kinds of partnership did indeed survive, fitting well into the Roman models of the *societas unius rei* (partnership for a single deal) and *societas omnium bonorum* (partnership in all property), but it became more common to arrange an association for a term of years, after which profits were distributed in proportion to the shares which members had contributed. This sort of partnership, with joint and unlimited liability for the partners, was known as the *compagnia*. Although it was not unlike the Roman *societas quaestus* (partnership for all business matters), it was more concerned with questions arising from relationships with third parties, in effect with agency; Roman law had been primarily concerned with the internal relationship between the partners. The *compagnia* was not incompatible with the contract of commission, whereby one merchant took care of another's business for a percentage or a fixed fee. In firms like the Bardi or the Peruzzi the family connection remained strong, and hence membership stayed fairly constant at each renewal of the partnership. Partners shared profits proportionately, but investments by outsiders usually drew only a fixed rate of interest. The number of investors nevertheless increased greatly in the early fourteenth century. Accounting methods improved; double-entry bookkeeping was introduced around the middle of the century. Although the Italian economy collapsed in the later fourteenth century when huge numbers of firms went bankrupt under the pressures of the Black Death, warfare, bad debts and other troubles, the skills acquired were not lost but were taken over by such firms as the Medici of Florence in the fifteenth century, and the Fuggers of Augsburg, and also the great banking houses of Bruges and Antwerp, in the sixteenth.

6.6.4 Since in a *compagnia* all partners were liable without limit it became necessary to discover who they were, for firms often traded simply under the family name 'and partners'. Originally the books of the firm were held sufficient for giving this information, but it became a normal requirement of city or guild statutes that the names of the partners be registered by public instrument. From the fourteenth century onwards such registers were widely kept by city authorities as part of their public records. Similarly there was need to record powers to act as procurator on the firm's behalf; such agency was by mercantile custom acceptable, but it only slowly penetrated the ordinary courts.

6.6.5 Maritime ventures were not suited to the *compagnia* because of the higher risks and because each voyage had its natural conclusion in the arrival of the cargo. Money for voyages, or for other single ventures, was usually raised by the *commenda*. Under this, money was lent for the duration of the venture, with the lender or investor incurring no liability to third parties. The lender usually put up the capital and was entitled normally to three-quarters of the profits, but it was a partnership not a loan. This was the source of the *societé en commandite* or *commenda* of the later civilian systems, in which one class of member has a responsibility limited to the sum contributed and the other class has an unlimited liability for the debts of the society but has sole control of its management. The lender in the *commenda*, however, could as readily be a small investor putting money into a great merchant's affairs as a rich capitalist using the labour of others to garner his profits. The risk was on the lender in that if the ship or goods were lost through accident or *vis maior* he had no claim for the recovery of his money.

6.6.6 Joint stock companies first appeared in fourteenth century Genoa. Public loans had earlier been raised to finance the expansion of Italian cities, with the loans divided into shares of which the owners were registered; these shares were heritable and, indeed, freely negotiable, that is, they could be bought and sold. Genoa raised such a loan in 1346 for the conquest of two Greek islands, and granted to shareholders a *dominium utile* in the common stock, the conquered lands. The scale of Genoese trading expanded in the fifteenth and sixteenth centuries by such means, although it was not until the era of exploration beyond Europe and colonial expansion that such companies became a feature of mercantile life in northern Europe.

6.6.7 Insurance contracts were important sooner in maritime than in land-based affairs, appearing early in the fourteenth century. They first took the form of a (feigned) interest-free loan from the ship-owner to the insurer to be returned unless the ship – or earlier the cargo – arrived safely; towards the end of the century they more often took the form of a feigned sale. This was accompanied by a real payment to the insurer, the premium. An interest of some kind in the safe arrival of the ship or cargo was required of the insurer, or underwriter; an insurance which was a mere wager was not enforceable. The ship in which the goods must be carried was likely to be named, and the period during which the insurer was responsible was usually fixed. Risk in the cargo was borne from when the ship set sail to the unloading of the goods, but in the case of the ship itself it normally also covered the first twenty-four hours in port. In early documents unauthorized change of route freed the insurers from risk but by the end of the fourteenth century it was usually only the destination which must not be altered. Reasonably enough, fraud by the ship's master always released the insurers. An opinion of the early fifteenth century runs:

'By the common unwritten custom of the country and by the general and tacit understanding of those concluding the contracts there is one exceptional case in which the risk pertains to the insured, to wit, when it is proved that the things were lost of set purpose by the fraud and contrivance of the captain.'[12]

Other risks might be excluded by clauses of exception, such as general average or action by a specified enemy. The premium was paid in advance, and it was only slowly that the contract became enforceable as such rather than disguised as a sale. As an institution, however, insurance rapidly became common; in 1393 one Genoan notary drew up eighty contracts within three weeks. Legislation, first in southern then in northern Europe, frequently confirmed custom, although in England there was no legislation before the eighteenth century; the London underwriters explicitly adopted 'the custom of Antwerp'.

12   Cited by Mitchell, p 149.

6.6.8   As well as dealing with money, negotiable instruments, forms of partnership and insurance, mercantile custom also had its own view of the contract of sale and its related agreements. Perhaps the most dramatic new usage introduced by the growth of trade was the rule that the buyer in good faith at a public market – market overt – immediately acquired title to the goods bought. This was at variance with both Roman and Germanic law. In the former the original owner never lost his title if the property had been stolen, and by Germanic law, while the owner could raise an action against someone who stole from him, if he had lent the property to a friend, that friend acquired the right of action for the stolen goods. It might well be hard for a merchant, constantly travelling, to produce the seller from whom he had bought goods, and he was not in a good position to know if the seller actually had the right to sell. It took time for this usage of merchants to be accepted by the ordinary courts but, provided such protection was firmly linked to market or fair, it was likely to be agreeable to the feudal lord as another inducement for men to frequent the market, from which he profited. The Church's stress on the value of good faith and the importance of supporting agreements, however informal, also worked to protect the merchant, although in general she preferred the interests of the producer to those of the trader. In a few areas, in the Netherlands and in certain German sea-ports, all possession in good faith was protected, but for the most part the rule was restricted to the open market, and in this form passed into later law.

6.6.9 Another tendency arising from mercantile custom was to give effect to formless contracts. Roman law had recognized only a limited number of contracts as created by consent alone, and it had not given effect to nude pacts as the basis of an action but only as a defence. Germanic law recognized only formal and real contracts. The Church's insistence on the honouring of any agreement slowly helped the custom enter the law, and it was accepted in fifteenth-century France, as it generally had been throughout northern Italy, on the grounds of equity. Nor was it mercantile custom to require grounds to be stated in any document recording an obligation; this applied particularly to negotiable instruments. Writing was, nevertheless, a normal feature of commercial usage. This was another area in which the influence of notaries was considerable in bringing about standard clauses to meet the standard situations encountered by merchants.

6.6.10 We shall look again at the commercial courts in the context of the states which gave them their powers, at later measures aimed at the harmonization of international trade, and also at the relationship of mercantile to other custom and to the learned law which shaped the *ius commune*. The law merchant has been aptly compared with public international law. It was

> 'the system of rules actually enforced in the commercial courts and actually observed by merchants in their dealings with one another, just as international law is the system actually observed by modern states in the relations of state to state. The treaties, the legislation, and the actions of individual states do not necessarily conform to the generally recognized rules of international law, but they may be and are used as evidence to establish what those rules really are. In the same way, the statute law of mediaeval states, the ordinances of mediaeval kings and the usages of mediaeval law need not conform in any particular case to the commercial regulations generally enforced among mediaeval merchants, but they may be used to establish the general usages of merchants in commercial cases. Both international law and the Law Merchant are from their very nature vague and uncertain.'[13]

13 Mitchell, pp 113ff.

FURTHER READING

JH Baker	'The Law Merchant and the Common Law before 1700' *CLJ* 38 (1979) 295
RH Bautier	*The Economic Development of Medieval Europe* (London, 1971)
WS Holdsworth	*A History of English Law*, Vol V, 60–154; Vol VIII, 99–300 (London, 1922–66)
JK Hyde	*Society and Politics in Medieval Italy* (London, 1973)

E Jenks	'The early history of negotiable instruments' *LQR* 9 (1893) 70
RS Lopez & IW Raymond	*Medieval Trade in the Mediterranean World* (New York, 1955)
W Mitchell	*Early History of the Law Merchant* (CUP, 1904)
R de Roover	*Money, Banking and Credit in Mediaeval Bruges* (Cambridge, Mass, 1948)
	Business, Banking and Economic Thought (Chicago, 1974)
Selden Society,	*Select Cases concerning the Law Merchant 1270–1638*, ed C Gross, vol 23 (London, 1908)
P Stein	'The mutual agency of partners' *TulLR* 33 (1959) 595

Chapter 7

THE *IUS COMMUNE*

7.1 THE DEFINITION OF THE *IUS COMMUNE*

7.1.1 The *ius commune* is not a simple concept. It is indeed the complex result of the coming together – in varying proportions from place to place and time to time – of local custom with feudal law, Roman law in modified and elaborated form, canon law and the law merchant. It is the culmination or climax of the new growth of law and jurisprudence which started in the twelfth-century renaissance. It is also the starting point or source from which developing municipal systems moved on during the sixteenth century when single legal regimes became dominant as part of the growth of the nation state. *Ius proprium*, the local law of territories and cities, is the foil to the *ius commune* in the narrower sense, the blending of the two learned laws. It was dominated by custom and feudal usages, and it was what the ordinary knight or burgess would think of as his law. But the advantages of a written law and the steady progress, on political as well as intellectual grounds, of canon and civilian influence modified the *ius proprium* throughout Europe.

7.1.2 In the further reaches of Europe the situation might be somewhat different. In England the *ius commune* seemed for a while to be acceptable, but the Common Lawyers then drew back from it (see paras 8.8.5-6). The main Scandinavian countries – Denmark, Norway and Sweden, united under the Danish crown from 1397 to 1532 by the Union of Kalmar – were Christian from the beginning of the eleventh century, and they naturally used Roman law as subsidiary to canon law. All three countries, however, already had strong traditions of written law, and, despite the foundation of the universities of Uppsala in 1477 and Copenhagen in 1479, do not seem to have been greatly affected by the *ius commune*. Such Roman influence as there has been came in the sixteenth and seventeenth centuries. In Poland the *ius civile* was rejected in the thirteenth and fourteenth centuries for political reasons springing from the constant conflicts with the Teutonic Knights, although the canon law was fully accepted. Despite the foundation of the university of Krakow in 1364, originally to teach civil as well as canon law, it was not until the sixteenth century, under the influence of Natural Law, that Poles could take a relaxed attitude to the system they associated with a hostile Holy Roman Empire. Bohemia, with its famous university at Prague (founded in 1348), was within the Empire and the mainstream of European legal thought, as was Hungary (Buda was the second university there, founded in 1395). So, of course, was Austria, where the duke of Bavaria and the archbishop of Salzburg had been formally seeking legal advice from Padua since the early thirteenth century, while in Vienna in 1284 a judicial decision might be given with the advice of the masters and doctors of both civil and canon law. Romania was somewhat isolated, but remained attached to the Latin or Romance world, whereas Russia, on the fringe of Europe, had a link to Byzantium through the Orthodox Church.

7.1.3 In a basic sense Roman and canon law, developed by the mediaeval jurists as the learned law, were common to the habits of thought and background knowledge of all educated lawyers in Europe (with the partial exception of England) from the thirteenth century onwards – many law graduates still receive the LLB (a degree in both laws, civil and canon). It was only in this sense that there was a *ius commune* in Germany between the collapse of imperial authority in the earlier thirteenth century and the deliberate and general adoption of romano-canonical procedure in the higher courts in the late fifteenth century. Among the cities of northern Italy, where too there was no effective superior authority to produce any regulated move towards uniformity, the *ius commune* was close to being the sum of the customs which were common, with relatively minor variations, to all. These customs were permeated by the learned law, which was the major cause of their publication in writing as statutes. In France, Spain, and other monarchic states the *ius commune* (like the English Common Law) means primarily the law common to the whole kingdom and in particular within the royal courts. In this sense *ius commune* naturally included the learned law, but the learned law blended with royal legislation as well as with customary practices, old and new.

7.1.4 Thus the particular relationship between the learned law and local usage was one aspect of the *ius commune*. The later mediaeval jurists were well aware of the problems involved. They wrote about 'special' and 'general' custom, and about the weight of private consent; they even attempted to define custom. Since, as we have seen, those who had the task of interpreting custom were trained more often than not in the learned law and understood rational interpretation in the light of the learned law, the more custom was overtly recognized and written down the more susceptible to civilian influence it became. Thus in Italy 'immemorial' custom came to be equated with the *longi temporis praescriptio* of Justinian's law and set at ten years' unchallenged usage. In another definition, found in Azo among others, which was influenced by the canonists' as well as the Roman rules of proof, two acts were held to make a custom; for this purpose decisions of a court came to be defined as acts. This was not a true doctrine of precedent, for it was not the decision itself that was persuasive or even binding, but decided cases were seen as proofs of custom – an attitude also found in Scotland, and which endured in legal practice within France into the middle of this century.

7.2 ACROSS THE FRONTIERS

7.2.1 Another aspect of the *ius commune* was the continuity and similarity of certain approaches to law throughout Europe. The universities of the Middle Ages were international.

'For three hundred years, from 1050 to 1350 . . . the whole of educated Europe formed a single undifferentiated cultural unit. In the lands between Edinburgh and Palermo, Mainz or Lund and Toledo, a man of any city or village might go for education to any school, and become a prelate or an official in any church, court, or university (when these existed) from north to south, from east to west. It is the age of . . . Vacarius of Lombardy, Canterbury, Oxford, and York; . . . of Nicholas Brakespear of St Albans, France, Scandinavia, and Rome (where he became Pope Hadrian IV); of Thomas of Aquina, Cologne, Paris, and Naples. . . . On the level of literature and thought there was one stock of words, forms, and thoughts from which all drew and in which all shared on an equality.'[1]

Latin was the common language. The Scholastic techniques of harmonizing contradictions were coupled with the belief that there was a rational and divine order. The mediaeval doctors played a role in their societies not so different from that of the Roman jurists, although they put much more stress on harmony and system – in itself a unifying factor. In the law schools there was teaching in canon and civil law, but not in local law, except insofar as it had been received by the learned law. Nevertheless, by the fourteenth century Roman law was only one piece of the cultural baggage of a jurist, although, in its glossed form, it was a large part of his professional tool-kit. The methods learned in the study of the Roman texts were applied in daily practice to a variety of rules, customary, feudal, statutory, imperial, royal. The actual rules of Roman law were frequently subsidiary but its principles, and increasingly its procedural characteristics, dominated the primary sources.

1   D Knowles, *The Evolution of Mediaeval Thought* (London, 1962) pp 80ff.

7.2.2   Academic literature included works on court procedure. Among the more influential were Roffredus of Benevento's *Libelli iuris civilis et canonici* (*Forms of Summons in Civil and Canon Law*), William Durantis' *Speculum Iudiciale* (*Mirror of Procedure*), and the *Practica aurea* (*Golden Manual of Procedure*) of Petrus Jacobus, which was produced in Montpellier at the beginning of the fourteenth century. The manuals of notarial practice, such as the works of Salatiele and Rolandino de Passagieri, were also linked with the law schools. Notaries were trained in the universities, and shared to some extent in the common culture of the doctors. Imperial and papal notaries knew no frontiers, although others had a more limited sphere of action,[2] but the tendency was undoubtedly towards harmonization, whether in the Italian communes or in princes' courts, and particularly in matters of commercial law. And the common approach to procedure survived even when intellectual fashions changed. The humanists and Natural Lawyers might reject as fustily mediaeval the work of the Glossators and Commentators on substantive law, but until the eighteenth century they took for granted romano-canonical procedure. And despite its use of canonist sources, this procedure survived in Protestant Europe after the unity of western Christendom dissolved in the Reformation and the Catholic (or Counter) Reformation.

2   Appendix 4.

7.2.3   There were also certain customs, or certain kinds of custom, which were of their nature transnational. We have already given some consideration to the law merchant; there were comparable, and even related, areas of law, such as the widely accepted rules on piracy, the dubious status of privateering, the whole business of imposing some mitigating rules on the conduct of war and of providing conventions for the easier making of peace. The work of Alberico Gentili, doctor of civil law at Perugia and later Regius Professor of Civil Law in the University of Oxford, was important in this field, although overshadowed half a century later by the more original work of Grotius; he was confessedly in the Bartolist tradition. He discussed the privileges granted to accredited envoys, the freedom of the seas and the limit to which territorial sovereignty extended over adjacent waters, the justification of war, the treatment of persons such as hostages[3] and non-combatants, safe conducts and prize law, and similar matters. His method was not the mediaeval one of elaboration on the Roman texts, but his reasoning was based on civilian and canonist arguments as well as on those of the humanists and other moderns; his writings were firmly in the tradition of the *ius commune*.

3   Hostages were not prisoners-of-war, but they were unable to make a will, because they were held to come under the Roman rule that a man in enemy hands had no power of testation.

7.3   ITALIAN PRACTICES

7.3.1   Feudal jurisdictions faded faster in northern Italy than elsewhere, owing to the greater development of trade and city-based life, but they did not totally disappear. In general, the private jurisdictions of lesser vassals gave way before those of the princes, which had a more public character. Different procedures often subsisted side by side. For example, at Pavia in 1112 the consuls exercised jurisdiction, but trial by battle was held before the local count. In 1181 at Verona a case was heard in the consuls' court-house by the consuls sitting together with the count and the bishop. In 1225 at Siena, where Roman law was the custom of the city, trial by battle was justified on the grounds that Otto I had made it part of the general law in the tenth century. The Peace of Constance weakened the jurisdiction of the bishops as feudal lords, and the communes generally took over lay jurisdiction within the area of the diocese.

7.3.2   The judges in eleventh-century cities were usually simply the civic magistrates; judicial business only gradually became a specialized activity, but by the thirteenth century a professional judiciary was frequently replacing magistrates with general powers. Sometimes consuls were specifically appointed *de placitis* (for pleas), but often an outsider was brought in for a term of six or twelve months as *podestà* (see para 3.6.4). Some men made the *podesteria* a career; Giuglielmo Pusterla, of Milan, had at least seventeen periods of office as *podestà*. Some families, such as the Rossi of Parma or the Visconti of Piacenza, made of the office a family tradition. It was normal, although not essential, for a *podestà* to be trained in the learned law. Nevertheless, as we have seen, the *podestà*'s liability to the losing party for giving a decision wrong in law, a liability based on incompetence or negligence, was a great encouragement to the seeking of opinions from noted jurists, and hence to the establishment of the *communis opinio*.

7.3.3 This liability was imposed on the basis of the Roman quasi-delict of the judge who makes the case his own (*iudex qui litem suam facere intellegitur*), although the precise meaning of the original Roman liability remains contested. In the Italian cities there were variations in how far the judge was required to pay attention to learned opinion. In many early statutes the judge was bound to take into account any opinion given, but he was not bound to follow it. Where no municipal statute governed the proceedings, this remained the general rule, with the proviso that the judge was himself entitled to seek advice. But in many cities, and particularly from the fourteenth century onwards, it was common to require him to follow any opinion he obtained, and sometimes, as in Benevento, he was required to obtain an opinion. Sometimes the obtaining of an opinion was at the discretion of the parties, but often, unless there was no serious doubt as to the point of law or the sum involved was trivial, there was no choice in the matter, despite the expense and time usually involved. Furthermore, the frequency of consultation inevitably led to a vast swelling of the legal literature; the bulk of doctrine made it unmanageable, as had been the case with Roman law before Justinian's compilation.

7.3.4 From the fifteenth century the system was widely extended to apply not only to the *podestà*, who usually no longer exercised any general administration but only simple jurisdiction with some police powers, but to most office holders, even those acting within their native city, who should therefore have been subject to ordinary forms of process. Inevitably, judgments tended to be cautious, adhering to the letter of the Gloss even when reason or changed conditions suggested that some other answer should be given. And few people were likely to act in a judicial capacity more efficiently with a permanent threat hanging over them. The system did, however, work for predictability in the law, and also enhanced the application of common rules.

7.3.5 As the *podestà* took an oath to give justice according to the city's statutes, he also needed local knowledge. *Giudici dell' uso*, lawyers specializing in local or some particular area of custom, were bound to make this available to him in the earlier period. As more city statutes were put into writing or revised, *emendatores statutorum*, officers specifically charged with the duty of revision in the light of felt needs and of the practice of neighbouring cities, came to the fore; thus they were another factor in the growth of the *ius commune* as common custom (and, because it was written custom, under the influence of the learned law). Nevertheless, particularly in the light of the 'statute theory', the doctors of civil law in the universities continued to exercise the greatest influence, even when lacking in originality; the writings of Baldus and above all Bartolus remained pre-eminent.

7.3.6 Not surprisingly, in northern Italy judicial decisions were rated low and academic opinions high. But only a court could give a judgment, and so the works on procedure of the civilians and the canonists were absorbed into court practice. The use of written pleadings developed, as did written records and written decisions. Preparatory and interlocutory stages in a process were recognized; rational rules of evidence became general. Summary proceedings for petty causes appeared in secular as well as ecclesiastical courts. However, attempts at further simplification of the complexity of procedural rules and at clearer statements of principles based on reason and good faith tended to be blocked by the continuing judicial liability for wrong judgment.

7.3.7   There was a limited role for appeal to a higher tribunal as a unifying factor. In the cities there was usually no appeal other than a claim against the *podestà*, although the emperor retained a theoretical supremacy of judicial as of other authority. However, as his political power waned, his superior jurisdiction might be ignored; furthermore, immunity had been purchased by many of the communes. His feudal jurisdiction survived in a limited way, providing a court for princes, or even cities, who owned no other lord and could find no other forum, as, for example, in litigation over a great fief like Montferrat. A few of the major cities had councils with judicial and sometimes appellate powers, as at Milan or Venice; in Bologna and some other places the supreme court was called the Rota, on the model of the Sacred Rota at Rome. The city of Rome, the capital of the Papal States, was still relatively backward economically and culturally, and in the secular field we hear of few notable judges and not many more scholars. Nevertheless, the Church's appellate procedure which centred on Rome gave to the ecclesiastical judiciary there an active role in the creation of law, and provided an example for all Europe.

7.3.8   The kingdom of the two Sicilies, with its capital at Naples, was a centralized state with a hierarchy of courts, more akin to France or Spain than to the rest of Italy. Romano-canonical procedure was put into practice there by royal authority, but men continued to live by Lombard, Frankish or even vulgar Roman law. Elsewhere in Italy, there was no effective ruler who could shape the development of civil procedure and civil law. Political structures, rather than litigants' needs, defined the status of the Italian courts, a fact which the men of the sixteenth-century Renaissance, who reacted against Bartolism and the *communis opinio*, rather failed to grasp.

7.3.9   Although the humanists and their new style of law were predominant in sixteenth-century legal studies, they did not affect the working of the courts, which maintained the traditional blending of the Gloss, canonical procedure, general and particular custom. In the Italian cities, where this was especially true, the primacy in legal matters remained that of the learned men, who had to resolve the tension between custom and the civil law, but legal literature grew ever more complex and less innovatory. The *ius commune* survived as a living relic of the past into the modern world and Italian jurisprudence became relatively as backward as it had been forward. There were, however, some Italians of the late fifteenth and early sixteenth centuries – such scholars as Jason de Mayno and Philip Decio – who combined the tradition of the *ius commune* with a degree of humanist insight. Elsewhere, the work of the Commentators was adapted to new customs, new structures, and men like Dumoulin in France and Carpzov in Saxony showed the continuing worth of the *mos italicus* (the Italian usage).

7.4   GERMAN CUSTOMS

7.4.1   After the reign of the Emperor Frederick II (1212-50), Germany, like Italy, had no effective centralized authority; unlike Italy, there was no primacy of the learned men but rather the guardians of the legal order were the law-finders, the *Schöffen*. The movement towards compliance with the mainstream of European development became strong in the later fifteenth century. In the city court of Frankfurt-am-Main written pleadings came into use in the 1480s, mostly in cases brought to arbitration rather than to trial; in the 1490s romano-canonical procedure was in use beside the oral forms, but by 1505 the latter had disappeared. The *Schöffen*, the (elected) members of the court, when faced with the nice distinctions and technicalities of the professional lawyers, had to fall back on the knowledge of the city's learned clerk. They abandoned their own statements of customary practice and issued judgments which had been drafted by him in conformity with the new procedures. Frankfurt was a major city and early among first instance courts in its conversion to the new forms, but at the appellate level, the princes had been taking advantage of the same movement. The learned law had sprung from a centralized Empire, and thus to adopt the new procedure tended to strengthen the princes' political authority; by offering more equitable and more subtle justice, they could strengthen their moral authority through their courts. The emperors had hastened the process with the replacement of the *Reichshofgericht* by the *Reichskammergericht* in 1495, but in the 1450s the dukes of Bavaria already had a superior court, or *Hofgericht*, on which doctors of law sat. There were law professors sitting on the Heidelberg *Hofgericht* from 1472, and doctors from Tübingen at Würtemberg from 1477. In Leipzig the Duke of Saxony's *Oberhofgericht* existed from 1483 in the new style, staffed by nobles, knights, and doctors of law. Thus the princes sought learned men to take over judicial functions, and professional judges replaced lay judges. The preference of litigants was also a factor in the growth of new procedures, which offered more subtle and rational solutions.

7.4.2 The major cities had been somewhat more open to legal influences from elsewhere; their *Schöffen* were sometimes great merchants who at least knew of other regimes. Further, these cities might themselves exercise a wide influence, for when new towns were founded on the frontier of the Wild East (or North) they might take their customs en bloc from older cities. Such daughter towns would, through their *Schöffen*, appeal to the mother town for advice. When the *Schöffen* court of a mother town replied with guidance (*responsa*), it can be described as an *Oberhof*, or appeal court. The issuing of guidance was to lead at the end of the fifteenth century to the *Aktenversendung* (despatch of record) to law faculties for the opinions of the professors, in an extension of private consultation. Some trace of the law merchant can be found in the decisions of the *Schöffen*, but not much; certainly there was nothing of the learned law, simply the custom of the place.

7.4.3 The courts spiritual naturally used canonical procedure, and it was predominantly canon rather than civil law that was taught in the German universities which began to be founded in the fourteenth century. Prague, the first within the Empire north of the Alps, was founded in 1348; it was followed by Vienna in 1363, Heidelberg in 1386, and Cologne in 1388; after Tübingen's establishment in 1477 there were thirteen. Germans who had trained in the learned law practised in the ecclesiastical courts or, more frequently, served the emperor, the princes or the cities in a general administrative capacity.

Although the *Sachsenspiegel* (*Mirror of the Saxons*), which we mentioned (para 2.9.5) along with feudal literature, was revised and glossed in the new German universities, very little learned law penetrated Saxon custom before the later fifteenth century, and even less into the customs of other regions. The reception of Roman law into Germany was both late and sudden, and for this reason Germany had no real part in the creation of the *ius commune*. When the learned law was received there, it had already been modified; it was the civil, rather than the original Roman, law that was blended with the customary laws which were codified in sixteenth-century Germany. It is indicative that the first great German jurist, that is, the first notable scholar working in his native land, was Zasius (1461–1535), and he became a leader of the humanist movement, interested in the historical Roman law, because the development of the *ius commune* was effectively over. It seems likely that the cultural movement we know as the Renaissance played a significant part in the speed and the thoroughness of the legal changes made in Germany at the reception.

7.5   FRENCH COURTS

7.5.1   In France the *ius commune* is far more apparent in the field of procedural than substantive law, because of the relative strength of custom, and because the French Crown had good political reasons for appearing independent of the Empire and imperial jurists. In the *pays de droit écrit*, that is, the lands south of the Loire, Roman civilization had been deeply embedded; Roman law continued to be used there, most frequently in the form of the *Lex Romana Visigothorum*. The area was not, however, immune to Germanic influences; the *Exceptiones legum romanarum Petri* (*Peter's Abridgments of Roman laws*), which was produced under this title in Provence in the early twelfth century,[4] explicitly took into account local custom when proffering generalizations from Roman law for modern use. The strength of customary usage is also suggested by the translation into Provençal – as *Lo Codi* – of Roger's *Summa* on Justinian's Code in the later twelfth century; it too mentioned local practices and made reference to a wide range of customs. There seem to have been at least three hundred identifiable jurisdictions in Provence at this period, each with its own custom.

4   Provence was a wider area in mediaeval than in the modern terminology, but Peter's sources were Italian and, it is now agreed, influenced by Irnerius.

7.5.2   Roman law, as shaped by the civilians, was undoubtedly strong in the *pays de droit écrit*, as the flourishing law schools at Montpellier and Toulouse indicate, but Roman law was still only a subsidiary source. It was accepted as the general custom of the area, which was looked to when particular custom failed. The legists, men with legal training whose careers lay entirely in the service of the French Crown, were careful to ascribe to it no more authority than that of a custom; King Louis IX stated that he was therefore not bound by it. The legists firmly maintained the doctrine that the king of France was emperor within his own realm, and this aided the introduction of the civil law; this was done, however, by royal decree, so that it was the Crown which was the source of law. Philip IV, the Fair, in a royal ordinance of 1312 stressed that his kingdom was governed primarily by custom; the extensive use of Roman law was dependent on royal permission, which was normally granted because of its wide acceptance as custom.

7.5.3 In the *pays de droit coutumier* or *pays de coutumes* Roman law never achieved the status of a general subsidiary source. Roman terminology and concepts did, however, provide a framework within which custom could be supplemented and system imposed. It was *ratio scripta*, written reason – no more – but by the same process as we have seen elsewhere the learned lawyers' reasonable interpretation of custom led to its modification. We have looked in some detail at the Customs of Beauvaisis; other works of the thirteenth century showing rather more civilian influence, although also primarily concerned with the law of their particular regions (Vermandois and Orléans), are Pierre de Fontaine's *Conseil à un ami* (*Advice to a friend*), and *Les Livres de Jostice et de Plet* (*The Books of Justice and Pleading*). During the later Middle Ages certain areas of law, such as obligations, about which the customs had comparatively little to say, emerged as essentially civilian; other fields too were developed with the aid of the learned law. It was possible by the sixteenth century for some jurists to hold that Roman law was the subsidiary common law of France, and that it should be recognized as such, but this was not the general opinion. In the event, the codification of the customs provided a different common law for the north, but this in its turn continued to be subject to the influence of civilian thought.

7.5.4 In twelfth-century France innumerable private jurisdictions had replaced the Frankish community courts, the kind of court on which the royal power in England was able to build. The Capetian dynasty's struggles to become kings of, rather than merely in, France were closely linked to increasing royal control of the courts. One of their methods was the adoption of the romano-canonical procedure for use in the royal courts. The adoption was not technically difficult because so many royal councillors and royal judges were trained in the learned law; many of them were clerics and so already accustomed to its use in some other aspect of their lives.

7.5.5 Philip II, Augustus, had made use of men trained in the learned law, the legists, but it was Louis IX, St Louis, who took the first decisive step towards the adoption of the new procedure. The ordeal had fallen out of use after the Fourth Lateran Council of 1215 had forbidden clerical participation; in 1258 Louis abolished trial by battle in royal courts. He further ordained that, in order to avoid threats or improper influences, his judges should use secret examination of individual witnesses under oath. In 1278 the *Parlement* of Paris was established in a permanent form. Royal ordinances thereafter governed the procedure of the *Parlement*, although it had a subsidiary power to regulate itself by decisions described as *arrêts de réglement*; these are comparable to the Acts of Sederunt of the Scottish Court of Session (see para 14.3.4). Royal ordinance also governed the Châtelet, the ordinary court for Paris and the surrounding area within the jurisdiction of the *prévôt* of Paris.

7.5.6 Among Louis' successors, important ordinances were issued by Philip IV and Philip V, and also Charles V, first as Dauphin and regent and then as king. In 1454 Charles VII issued the Ordinance of Montils-lès-Tours. Its 125 articles treated every major point of judicial practice; they extended the new procedures to royal jurisdictions within the provinces, governed the procedure in provincial *parlements*, provided for summary proceedings, and dealt with details of proofs and of appeals. They were effective over a wide area since the King of France had come to rule as well as reign over most of France. (At the end of the Albigensian Crusade in 1229, the Crown had acquired most of the Languedoc, although it was not until the seventeenth century that Perpignan and much of Roussillon became French; in the fourteenth century, Philip VI, of Valois, had brought Dauphiné into the royal domain, which thus at that time covered some three-fifths of modern France.) The establishment of the provincial *parlements* followed the king's gradual recovery of the supreme jurisdictions formerly exercised by the dukes of Normandy, Burgundy, Gascony, and other magnates.

7.5.7   In 1360 the Languedoc was divided into three *sénéchaussées*, Beaucaire (south of Avignon), Carcassonne, and Toulouse, where the earliest provincial *parlement* was first created in 1420 and firmly established in 1443. Rouen in Normandy acquired the next *parlement*, then Grenoble, Bordeaux and Dijon. It was also during the fifteenth century that further law schools were founded: Dôle in 1423, Louvain in 1426, Poitiers in 1432, Valence in 1452, Bourges in 1464, and so on. This made available sufficient trained lawyers for the multiplication of professional courts, a movement which was in itself a major factor in the foundation of the law schools.

7.5.8   The core of the development in civil procedure, including the creation of appeals and their centralization on the Crown, lay in the *Parlement* of Paris which had the widest territorial jurisdiction of all *parlements*; the provincial ones, however, remained sovereign within their spheres. By the mid-thirteenth century some specialization of function had become normal among royal advisers, and so it was primarily, although not exclusively, those of his tenants and officers who were trained in law whom the king appointed to sit in the *Parlement*. In the feudal structure, appeal in our juridical sense, appeal to get a judgment reversed or amended, was not possible; one could only complain that one's lord had not done right, and accuse him of false judgment before his lord. In the Languedoc, where custom retained some Roman roots and the learned law was taught, appeal for correction of error was known and practised from the late twelfth century. In the northern parts of France this form of appeal seems to have originated as special royal grants of a privilege. In 1258, Louis IX made the royal courts available to all who complained on grounds of false judgment; his Ordinance permitted the royal courts to approve or reverse the original decision, but they soon came to assert, without meeting any effective opposition, the power to modify it. The element of 'false' judgment remained, however, in that the inferior court might be subject to a fine or some other penalty.

7.5.9   At first it was predominantly from lesser royal courts that appeals came to the *Parlement*, in particular from the courts of the *baillis* and *sénéchaux*, whom Philip II had appointed to a function roughly comparable to that of the Anglo-Norman sheriff. But feudal lords learned to tolerate appeal from their courts directly to the royal courts, rather than up the feudal hierarchy to the same eventual end. A few great lords, such as the English king in his capacity as duke of Gascony, developed their own system of appeal based on Roman procedure, but the king of France had clearly become the ultimate source of justice within his kingdom.

7.5.10 The *Parlement* made some use of the group inquest (*enquête par turbe*) – the institution which in Britain seems to have developed into the jury – but the production of a suitable group required an effective central power that was by no means always available. It was simpler, as well as more in line with legal developments elsewhere, for the judges to interrogate under oath witnesses who were presented to them by the parties to a suit. In criminal cases accusations were normally matters of private initiative until the fourteenth century, when criminal investigation by a judge, acting *ex officio* on the canonical model and armed with powers to torture, became normal. Cases before the *Parlement* always began with oral pleadings, with spoken statements of claim and defence made before the *Grand' Chambre*, one of the three chambers into which the *Parlement* was divided at least as early as 1296. Usually the *Grand' Chambre* would be unable to settle the issue without investigation, and so it would order an inquiry or inquest to be made.

7.5.11 Such an inquiry was made by the *Chambre des Enquêtes*, which comprised half or rather more of all the judges of the *Parlement*. Here written statements were required, repeating the claims and allegations of the oral complaint. On this basis were drawn up the articles, the summary of the evidence – by witnesses or documents – which each party would proffer, and the questions that each party wanted asked of the other. Objections on points of law could be raised at this stage. Thereafter commissioners, who travelled if necessary, were appointed to examine the witnesses; the commissioners would include one or more judges from the *Chambre des Enquêtes* and might well also include other lawyers and local men of standing. The witnesses, under oath, were examined privately and separately, and their testimony written down. The whole written record was then brought back to the central court where a judge, acting as *rapporteur*, read through the whole, summarized the arguments, and recommended what facts should be found and the consequent ruling on points of law. The parties had received copies of the written statement of facts (the *procès-verbal*) and of any written evidence presented, but they had no opportunity to conduct any examination, let alone cross-examination, although a party's lawyer might appeal on the basis of this documentation.

7.5.12 The whole system was heavy on judicial manpower. In 1296, there were fifty-one judges of the *Parlement* of Paris and in 1319 there were sixty-seven; from 1345 onwards there were something over eighty, as compared with the nine or so judges of the contemporary English central courts, who had juries to find their facts for them. But the procedure of the *Parlement* was in accord with the learned law, and demanded a high level of legal skill from its practitioners; it is obvious that jurists' opinions had no significant part to play in French procedure.

7.5.13 The procedure of the provincial *parlements* followed that of Paris closely, and was similarly dependent on trained manpower. The *Parlement* of

Paris also influenced other, lower, courts. In the confusion of the Hundred Years' War and its aftermath the *Parlement*'s regulations for itself took on what was in effect some general legislative power. It issued *arrêts de règlement* (regulating decrees) which laid down lines of interpretation for the future, usually after consultation between the Chambers. These were not binding on other courts but inevitably they were persuasive, particularly where appeal might follow.

7.5.14 When appeal began to be taken direct from lesser feudal courts to the royal court, the vassals who were the judges in their lord's court might find themselves having to come to Paris to justify their verdict; they could be subject to fines if it were reversed. This was in some ways less onerous than the old liability, when they might have had to defend themselves by battle against an appeal of false judgment, but the fine might be heavy, and the proceedings both alarming and lengthy, as well as far from home. Therefore in feudal courts too the move towards specialization of function was apparent; by the sixteenth century, trained lawyers had largely replaced the lord's 'men' nearly everywhere. The process was speeded up by the general growth in judicial business; when private jurisdictions had to hold courts two or three times a week, attendance was burdensome for men who were called from other duties. Lay judges retreated before the learned men, although it was not until the Revolution that feudal jurisdictions were finally swept away. The increase in litigation was aided by the simplification of substantive law after the codification of the customs in the sixteenth century; this itself followed a degree of harmonization of custom arising from single *parlements* deciding cases from several areas. Fundamental to the increase in both specialization and business was the romano-canonical procedure of the *ius commune*.

7.6   SPAIN DURING THE *RECONQUISTA*

7.6.1 During the thirteenth to fifteenth centuries, as earlier, any consideration of law in Spain must take into account not merely the existence of different principalities but also their fluid relationships and changing fortunes as the Christian forces in the peninsula steadily pushed back those of Islam. In Castile-León, benefice and vassalage never completely fused to produce the fief proper; there was, consequently, no delegation of governmental powers through the instrumentality of the fief, and so feudal law did not develop fully. Catalonia was recovered by Louis the Pious, Charlemagne's son, less than a century after the Moslem conquest; therefore much of its history is more closely linked to the Languedoc than to the rest of Spain, although it was independent of the Frankish empire from 987. Old Castile – New Castile is the name for the areas later reconquered – broke away from León in the mid-tenth century, and in consequence rejected the *Fuero Juzgo* (*Province of Judges*, formerly known as the *Forum Iudicum*), which had been issued by the Visigothic King Ervig (see para 1.7.2), since it made provision for appeal to the king (of León) as supreme judge. All available copies are said to have been ceremonially burned, and the judges were ordered, in the absence of any acceptable law book, to base their decisions on equity. In the mid-eleventh century Castile and Aragon emerged as monarchies; the former, which included

Galicia and the Asturias, later reunited with León, while the latter came to include Valencia and Catalonia.

7.6.2 In Castile-León the king was the fount of justice, exercising jurisdiction as the natural lord of all his subjects in the royal courts. This political strength and the existence of appeals to the king's court diminished the importance of regional customs or *fueros*. As early as the twelfth century the *alcaldes de corte* (presidents of the court) were sophisticated professional judges, while in the course of that century the Roman law of the learned men became influential. *Letrados*, men of law trained in the universities, were high in the royal service. The earliest students attended Bologna but in 1239 the university of Salamanca was established (as a migration from Palencia – not far from Valladolid – founded in 1214); students continued, however, to study in Italy, for in 1346 a Spanish college was set up in Bologna. Ferdinand III (king of Castile 1217–1252 and of León from 1230) envisaged a kingdom with a single body of law. He commissioned the translation into the vernacular of the *Fuero Juzgo* – attractive as being written law – and he granted this to each newly reconquered town as its *fuero*, for example, to Cordoba in 1241 or Seville in 1248; succeeding kings followed the same policy. His son, Alfonso X, the Learned, was responsible for the publication of *Las Siete Partidas* (*The Seven Parts* [*of the Law*]), an encyclopaedic and comprehensive work based chiefly on Roman law. Alfonso's tutor, Jaime de las Leyes, who wrote several books on romano-canonical procedure, seems to have been influential in its production and also in the compilation of the *Fuero Real* (*Royal Custom*), a selective code which, among other things, regulated appeal to the *corte real* (king's court). Like the *Fuero Juzgo*, the *Fuero Real* was issued to individual cities as their *fuero*, but in its case to long-established places such as Burgos and Valladolid, which lacked a clear custom of their own because in Old Castile there had been no general written law for three hundred years. The *Fuero Real* was in four books as opposed to the *Fuero Juzgo*'s twelve; there was some debt to the earlier code and also to the work of the civilians, but it was mostly a compilation of customary law.

7.6.3 *Las Siete Partidas*, although rearranged at various times both in Spain and in the Americas, remained the foundation of Spanish law until its supersession by the *Codigo Civil* of 1889, and even that was not complete. It was firmly in the tradition of the received learned law, and had its own standard commentary, the *Leyes del Estilo*. The influence of the *Ultramontani* was strong in Spain; the development of constitutional history was affected by the work of the Commentators. Many thirteenth- and fourteenth-century Spanish manuscripts of the *Corpus Iuris Civilis* and of the work of the civilians have survived; the University of Salamanca was established to teach both canon and civil law.

7.6.4 *Las Siete Partidas* at first met political opposition to its enforcement in areas where custom was strong. Only in 1348, by the *Ordenamiento de Alcalá*, was it promulgated as general law by Alfonso XI; it was general law, but subordinate to particular custom. The *Fuero Juzgo* remained the custom of León, but it, like other customs, needed to be proved to a court as being still observed, whereas there was a presumption in favour of the *Fuero Real* and *Las Siete Partidas*. The learned law of the *ius commune* was clearly dominant in Castile-León; so much so that, to avoid confusion, in 1427 John II restricted the citation in court, as authorities, of canonists or civilians later than Johannes Andreae and Bartolus.

7.6.5 Within the territories of the Crown of Aragon the monarchy was explicitly constitutional; lordless land in Aragon, unlike Catalonia on the one hand or Castile on the other, was not automatically regarded as the Crown's. As we have seen, cities were influential within Valencia and Catalonia and commercial law important. The *Consulate of the Sea* was exported from Barcelona to Castile, among many other places; it was thereafter found in force at Burgos and at Seville, and from there it was taken to the New World. Roman law had been recognized as general subsidiary law in Catalonia since 1173. The *Usatges* (*Usages*) of Barcelona were produced in the mid-twelfth century by the civilian jurists at the court of Ramón Berenguer IV; the basic texts were from feudal and customary law, with some constitutional and criminal matters, but the whole was handled in the context of the learned law. In the thirteenth century King James I of Aragon attracted many jurists to his court, among them Raymond of Peñaforte, compiler of *Liber Extra*. In 1247 an authoritative collection was made of the customs of Aragon, but they were interpreted in the light of the civil law, and in the field of procedure romano-canonical rules were specifically adopted. Peter IV's *Ordinacions de Cort* of 1344 among other things created a new final court of appeal under the chancellor.

7.6.6 In Navarre the *Fuero Juzgo* was accepted as the custom of the kingdom, modified after 1234, when the French acquired control, by the *Fuero General*, which owed much to the Glossators. *Las Siete Partidas* came into force there when, in the early sixteenth century, Navarre was reincorporated into Spain by Ferdinand of Aragon, who married Isabella of Castile in 1469. In the united kingdom of Spain reforms in private law were made primarily in the *cortes* (parliament). The *Leyes de Toro* of 1505, building on the *Ordenanzas de Montalvo* of 1485 (collecting those laws still in force which had been passed since the death of Alfonso X), dealt with sources of law and their authority, and gave due weight to the *Fuero Juzgo*, the *Fuero Real*, and *Las Siete Partidas*. The *Leyes* were confirmed by Philip II, son of Charles I of Spain (who was also the Emperor Charles V), and husband of Mary Tudor of England, and given application in the New World; they continued in force for centuries and were reissued in 1805 by Charles IV.

7.6.7 Just as the various city statutes in Italy needed reconciling, so did the *fueros* of the cities and the principalities in the Iberian peninsula, and the methods used were similar in some ways. In Spain, court practice played a more important part than in Italy and less than in France, while legal science was respectively less and more important than in those countries, but law in Spain, both private and public, was an undoubted example of the *ius commune*.

7.7   SCOTLAND AND THE *IUS COMMUNE*

7.7.1 Scotland too was affected by the *ius commune*, and more particularly by the romano-canonical procedure. In the twelfth and thirteenth centuries the influence of Anglo-Norman administration and legal procedures was so strong that Scotland might possibly not have developed a legal system of its own. However, the Wars of Independence, although they by no means abolished Anglo-Norman institutions, reduced the influence from England, including the ecclesiastical authority of the archbishop of Canterbury. (Scotland, lacking an archbishop with metropolitan jurisdiction, was declared a 'special daughter' of Rome in 1192.) The most obvious external influence was that of the Church. We have records of cases heard by papal judges delegate from early in the thirteenth century; at local level, a bishop's official is recorded for the dioceses of Glasgow and of St Andrews before the end of the twelfth century. It seems reasonable to assume that Scotland conformed in the Middle Ages to the general European pattern in ecclesiastical jurisdiction, particularly as there was no royal attempt to block (or even control) direct appeals to the Roman *curia*. Furthermore, Scots students were attending Italian and French universities from at least the thirteenth century. In the fourteenth century law graduates seem mostly to have followed careers in the Church, but in the following century we find them busy in the courts temporal. Universities were founded at St Andrews in 1412 and at Glasgow in 1451, with chairs in canon and civil law. In the fifteenth and sixteenth centuries, however, Scottish students preferred to resort to universities in France or Germany and, particularly after the Reformation, in the northern Netherlands. In 1496 an Act of the Scottish Parliament required the nobility and gentry to educate their sons in schools of arts and law, so that they might have knowledge and understanding of the laws. The cultural background was thus favourable to the learned law; the reception of substantive Roman rules is harder to measure, but certainly custom was modified by learned interpretation.

7.7.2   In the field of procedure it is apparent that there was no deep division between the secular and the ecclesiastical courts. It has been said: 'there is no doubt that familiarity with the rules of an official's court procedure in the 1540s is as good an introduction as any to sixteenth century legal procedure in general'.[5] For example, procurators were much used in ecclesiastical business, and not merely as general representatives but also as advocates before a court; their employment is recorded in the early fourteenth century. The regular employment of advocates in the secular courts, which is evidenced by the early fifteenth century, was a practice alien to feudal procedure and it may well stem from ecclesiastical example. Similarly, the oath of calumny, a regular stage in canonist procedure, was enjoined upon advocates by Parliament in 1429. Lawyers in sixteenth-century Scotland seem to have felt no confinement to one jurisdiction, secular or spiritual; the same man might practise before the court of the official of Lothian, the High Court of Admiralty, and the Court of Session. This versatility suggests there was little to choose between the courts in terms of practice and procedure.

5   S Ollivant, *The Court of the Official in Pre-Reformation Scotland* (Stair Society, vol 34, Edinburgh, 1982) p 131.

7.7.3   Since 1424, after James I's return from exile, attempts had been made to provide Scotland with a supreme court. The *Acta* (Proceedings) of the Lords of Council (the forerunners of the Lords of Council and Session, and in turn of the Court of Session) of the early sixteenth century[6] suggest that the model of the courts spiritual was already well established in the higher temporal courts, and the movement between jurisdictions recorded later is unlikely to have been a novelty in the early sixteenth century. The refounded Court of Session of 1532 used a version of romano-canonical procedure; of its original membership (fifteen judges) the Lord President and seven others were clerics. And when the religious revolution came, the bishop's officials in Lothian and Glasgow, who were lawyers first and priests second, moved naturally to head the new commissary courts of their respective jurisdictions.

6   *Acta Dominorum Concilii 1501-03, 1532-33*, Stair Society, vols 8, 14.

7.7.4   Movement towards the romano-canonical procedure in the local secular courts is less clear. By the fifteenth century, brieves of summons to the sheriff court had become simply written citations to appear, not pleadable forms of action. By the end of the century a version of this modern procedure, if somewhat more oral and less technical than elsewhere in Europe, had become normal in the sheriff courts. Moreover, the status of bishops and abbots as feudal magnates meant that their regality and barony courts were as important, or almost, as their courts spiritual, and it is likely that there was some harmony of procedure and personnel. In the burghs the courts recognized other jurisdictions. At Selkirk, for example, we find a party claiming under a will being sent to 'ane sperituall judge', and when the assize found itself at a loss it had recourse to men of law. Particularly in the cities of the east coast, where trade with France, the Low Countries and other continental regions made most impact, the *ius commune* made some penetration through the law merchant.

7.7.5   Some such penetration may have been merely verbal, as when one finds consuls in Edinburgh in the fifteenth century. However, Welwod's treatise on *The Sea-Laws of Scotland* (of 1590) assumed that disputes arising out of a voyage would be settled by a judge of the burgh to which the ship was bound, 'a judge of many hundred years old in this land', who is to be identified with the Dean of Guild. The Guild Court had jurisdiction over admission to the privileges of a burgess or guild brother, over actions between merchant and merchant and between merchant and mariner, and also over the laws of neighbourhood. The Glasgow Dean of Guild Court was founded late, in 1605, but on the model of the much older Edinburgh court.

> 'The procedure of the court was uniform, whatever the nature of the action. Actions were begun by a bill, apparently always in writing. . . . The defender would then be summoned three times, lastly by the court officer, and in the event of his failing to appear, judgment would be given against him "as confessed". If the defender appeared, he might admit the libel, and possibly pay the sum claimed at the bar of the court; or simply deny; or plead one or more exceptions. . . . Exceptions were either peremptory or dilatory. Declinatory exceptions . . . are not recorded. After the bill and answers a verbal debate would follow, leading to the assignment of the method of proof. Proof would be by oath, witnesses, or writs.'[7]

In the course of the seventeenth century the court seems to have moved, in the case of proof by witnesses, from the mercantile custom of accepting one witness to demanding two or more, that is, corroboration, the canonist requirement for full proof. As the same author says: 'In the case of written evidence, there were certain common law restrictions on what constituted probative writs, but in merchant cases these did not apply.' In most of the cases recorded the pursuer was a Glasgow merchant, but he might be a merchant from outside the burgh, or a Glasgow notary suing as the assignee of a foreign merchant. Towards the end of the seventeenth century the Court of Admiralty developed as the principal mercantile court of Scotland, with exclusive first instance jurisdiction over maritime causes; it too had always used romano-canonical procedure.

7 AM Jackson, *Glasgow Dean of Guild Court: a History* (Glasgow, 1983) p 28.

7.7.6 It is impossible to read the chapter on civil procedure in Wilson's excellent *Introductory Essays*[8] without being struck by the resemblance between modern Scottish practice and the procedure of the developed *ius commune*, particularly when an action goes to proof rather than to jury trial; the main difference is in the publicity of the testimony. Also significant is a letter in the *Journal of the Law Society of Scotland*; the writer is encouraging his fellow Scots lawyers to point out to possible European clients the benefits of Scottish law. Scottish has over English law such advantages as

'enforcement of performance by specific implement; expedited enforcement of payment by extract-registered bond; clearly stated contracts enforceable in accordance with their terms; a coherent unitary system of law as opposed to a sprawling dichotomy of conflicting laws.'[9]

The contrast with England will be apparent from the next chapter. There the *ius commune* had little effect. It did influence the civilian courts, such as the English Admiralty, but they remained peripheral to the Common Law. As Chancery became more central to the English legal system, it grew closer in its attitudes to the Common Law. The Regius Chairs of Civil Law established by Henry VIII had no effect on practice. Individuals were aware of the *ius commune*, but from the fourteenth century onwards the dominant system was the Common Law, and the Common Lawyers denied any outside influence.

8 WA Wilson, *Introductory Essays on Scots Law* (Edinburgh, 2nd edn, 1984) pp 63ff.
9 *JLSS* 29 (1984) p 184.

FURTHER READING

RC van Caenegem 'History of European Civil Procedure' in *International Encyclopaedia of Comparative Law*, vol XVI, ch 2

C Calisse *History of Italian Law* (Continental Legal History vol VIII, Boston, 1928)

H Coing 'The Roman law as *ius commune* on the Continent' *LQR* 89 (1973) 505

JP Dawson *A History of Lay Judges* (Harvard, 1960)
The Oracles of the Law (Ann Arbor, 1968)

R Fawtier *The Capetian Kings of France* (London, 1960)

R Feenstra *Philip of Leyden* (Murray Lecture, Glasgow, 1970)

WM Gordon	'Roman law in Scotland' in *The Civil Law Tradition in Scotland*, ed R Evans-Jones (Stair Society, suppl vol 2, 1995)
EM Hallam	*Capetian France* (London, 1980)
EN van Kleffens	*Hispanic Law until the End of the Middle Ages* (Edinburgh, 1968)
W Kunkel	'The reception of Roman law in Germany: an interpretation' in *Pre-Reformation Germany*, ed G Strauss (London, 1972) 263
A MacKay	*Spain in the Middle Ages* (London, 1977)
P Stein	'The influence of Roman law on the law of Scotland' *JurRev* (1963) 205 [also reprinted in *The Character and Influence of the Roman Civil Law* (London, 1988) 319] *Roman Law in European History*, (CUP, 1999) ch 4
CC Turpin	'The Reception of Roman law' *IJ* 3 (1968) 162
F Wieacker, tr T Weir	*A History of Private Law in Europe* (OUP, 1995)

Chapter 8

THE COMMON LAW OF ENGLAND

8.1 THE SIGNIFICANCE OF ENGLISH LAW

8.1.1 English law is remarkable. It lies outside the central current of European legal development, and has been touched relatively lightly by juristic movements from the continent. Conversely, English jurisprudence probably had no influence on European legal thinking before the eighteenth century. So, in one sense, after Bracton (see para 8.8.2) it ceased to be fully part of European legal history. However, English law absorbed the legal systems first of Wales and then of Ireland, and it overshadows, although it has not succeeded in absorbing, Scots law. From the eleventh to the fourteenth centuries Anglo-Norman institutions were a major force in the development of Scots law, and so the two systems share some common roots. From the Union of the Crowns in 1603 the bigger country had the power to affect the Scottish system, and this power was enhanced after the Union of the Parliaments in 1707. The Industrial Revolution and the French Revolutionary and Napoleonic Wars put Scotland firmly within England's sphere of juridical influence. Thus the history of English law is a part of Scotland's legal history. Furthermore, English law has been the only rival to the civilian systems based on Roman law in creating a legal empire, in providing a model. Within Europe and in those areas colonized by Europeans one finds either a civil law or a Common Law system – or, in a few places, such as Scotland or South Africa, a mixed system where the Common Law has tended, for political or constitutional reasons, to dominate the civilian inspiration.

8.1.2 There was nothing extraordinary about Anglo-Saxon customary law; it was not particularly different from the customs of the Franks or, indeed, the Saxons in north Germany. However, the institutions of government for the whole realm which had developed by the eleventh century were unique, if only in the extent of their development. Public law played a far more important part in England than on the continent in the formation of the legal system. Feudal law, when established in England by the Normans, was not very different from feudal law in northern France but it developed in a different way. Again, for many centuries the Church's courts administered canon law, with substance and procedure virtually universal within Christendom, and yet English Common Law does not seem to have been much influenced. Roman law was hardly received in the twelfth and thirteenth centuries, and in the sixteenth it was definitely rejected by the legal profession, when the new kind of reception was widespread in Europe.

There were indeed areas of civilian influence, for example, in the court of the Admiralty, but they were marginal; the central core of the legal system remained uniquely English.

8.2   THE MAKING OF ENGLAND

8.2.1   The Romans abandoned Britain in the early fifth century; shortly after the middle of the century, Roman-British society seems to have collapsed, but not as a result of any single invasion. The various Germanic settlements were piecemeal; indeed, in Kent the settlement seems to have been of *foederati* (allies), although as allies of the Romano-Britons rather than of any central Roman authority. Furthermore, the pace of the Anglo-Saxon advance was slowed by British resistance, typified by the legendary, but not mythical, Arthur. However, during the mid-sixth century the advance quickened. By 613 the Anglo-Saxon conquest was virtually complete; it stretched from Kent to the Clyde, and from the Wash to the Severn.

8.2.2   There seems to have been some continuity of culture in Kent, because of its early settlement, observable in such institutions as gavelkind (the division of land among all the heirs), and the consolidated fields of the Kentish villages. Certainly the names themselves of Kent and Canterbury retained their Roman origins. Kent was the closest part of Britain to Gaul, where the Franks maintained some of the Roman heritage. In the north-west and in the south-west of Britain the Romano-Celtic peoples remained unconquered, although their territories were gradually encroached upon by the Anglo-Saxons during the succeeding centuries. In Wales the old ways survived, although there they had been more British than Roman anyway, and there was virtually no Anglo-Saxon presence. Christianity survived in these areas, as it did in Ireland and in Argyll.

8.2.3   In 597, the same year that St Columba died on Iona, Augustine of Canterbury, sent by Gregory the Great to evangelize the heathen English, landed in Kent. The wife of Ethelbert, king of Kent, was Bertha, a Frankish princess and a Christian. Within less than a century the various Germanic kingdoms in the island had achieved a sort of unity, not only among themselves but also with their Celtic fellow Christians, in their recognition of the leading role of the archbishop of Canterbury. Theodore (archbishop 668–690) established a permanent framework of diocesan government and held provincial synods. Thereafter English kings, like rulers elsewhere in Europe, were able to make use of trained clerics in their administration.

8.2.4   When King Alfred died in 899, although half of England was under Danish rule, the half that was English was strong and well-organized under the overlordship of Wessex, which even extended over Wales. In the face of the constant Norse attacks, royal authority was strengthened at the same time as elements akin to feudalism were grafted onto English customary law. The king's thegns, the landed nobility, would henceforward forfeit their estates if they failed to provide due military service, and this service was in many cases to be mounted, the better to deal with raiders. No tie of blood was to excuse treason to one's lord, but failure in military aid was seen as a crime rather than as a breach of tenure; there was no concept of all land being the king's to grant – the brute fact of conquest was to make this practicable under the Norman King William. Charters conferred not title or possession but the king's special peace; lords, whether thegns or bishops (or monasteries), might thus receive the privilege of taking fines for offences against the king's peace as well as against their own peace. In this way the personal tie, the link between land and military service, and private jurisdictions, all became part of the English social structure. But in other respects conditions were very different from those on the continent. The language of government was vernacular, Anglo Saxon, as well as Latin. Fortified boroughs, usually with a mint and a court as well as a market, were an integral part of Alfred's centralized plan of defence, rather than being seen as the property of a lord. The Crown's position was strong; the king's justice held sway over all men, and his peace ran everywhere. There was even relative uniformity of law; in broad outline the customs of Mercia and Kent became incorporated in those of Wessex, while the Danelaw was followed in eastern England.

8.2.5 During the tenth century, the administrative system of shires extended over all England as far as the Mersey–Humber line. Within the shires the smaller unit of the hundred was formalized, a dozen or so to each shire. Linked to the hundred was the tithing system under which every free man (beneath the rank of thegn) was enrolled in a group of ten (at least originally), who were permanent sureties for each other's good behaviour. By the reign of Edgar (959–975) the administrative and judicial structure is clear, although there was, of course, a multiplicity of particular local customs. The shire court, presided over by the ealdorman and the bishop, met twice a year, and, under the same two men, the borough courts met three times a year – there was normally only one borough in each shire. The hundred met every four weeks, to pursue thieves, to determine custom, to witness major transactions, and to hear the king's word. Appeal to the king's own justice was restricted to those cases where a man could not otherwise obtain redress. In the Danelaw the men of the Norse settlements acknowledged the Wessex dynasty as their overlords but kept to their own customs; there were considerable similarities and doubtless many cross-influences. The Danelaw knew more of commerce and had a uniform system of taxation and of coinage.

8.2.6 In the decades after the death of Edgar, Ethelred the Unready (978–1016) lost England to the Danish King Canute, or Cnut (1016–1035). At his coronation in 1016 Cnut swore to observe the laws of King Edgar within the English sphere, while maintaining the separate customs of the Danelaw; his laws show that he kept his word. Edward (1042–1066), known to us as the Confessor, had spent more than twenty years of exile in Normandy. Although of the line of Alfred he was accused of foreign habits, but his Chancery used Anglo-Saxon as well as Latin, and his relationship with the Church was in the old English tradition. William of Normandy came to England in 1066 not only as Edward's heir but also as the Church's champion against the forsworn Harold; he was recognized as king by the *witan*, or royal council, just fifty years after Cnut's acceptance.

8.3   ANGLO-SAXON INSTITUTIONS OF THE ELEVENTH CENTURY

8.3.1   The shire courts were the major forum for administrative and judicial business. The shires were entrusted by the Wessex kings to ealdormen or earls who, together with the local bishop, each led a group of shires. The shire courts therefore dealt with ecclesiastical business as well as lay, out of step with the Hildebrandine reform movement on the continent. The earl's deputy as president of the shire was the shire reeve or sheriff; the sheriff was the king's man, and so jurisdiction in the shire was a matter for the community under the protection of the king's peace. The sheriff's tourn to take 'view of frankpledge' may in this terminology be Norman, but the actual review of the tithings to make sure that every man was adequately accounted for by his fellows seems to date from Athelstan (927–939) or Edmund (939–946). As well as being the forum to which men came twice yearly, bringing their suits, the shire court might also receive jurisdiction in cases initially brought before the king and his *witan*;[1] it was also the body to which, through the earl or the sheriff, the king announced any grant he had made.[2]

1   Harding, no 3.
2   Harding, nos 4 and 5.

8.3.2   The hundreds were closer than the shires to the primitive Germanic tradition in that all free men had suit of court there. They were meetings for all matters requiring publicity, not just for the settlement of disputes. The courts of the hundred, or of the equivalent wapentake within the Danelaw, with their four-weekly sessions, seem to go back to Edward the Elder (899–925); they were already fairly sophisticated when Edgar issued his ordinance regulating their practice. Some of the hundreds were ancient divisions, others were created in the tenth century organization, but it is as jurisdictions and as fiscal units, not as territorial areas, that they are of significance. Hundred courts were presided over in the tenth century by a royal reeve, since they were a creation of the royal administration, although they fitted well with customary usage. Naturally enough those reeves who were not already lords had a tendency to improve their status; it was also natural to put someone already a lord into such a responsible office. Hence there was some movement towards a feudal model, a tendency enhanced by frequent royal grants of hundredal jurisdiction.

8.3.3   Grants of 'sake' (the right to hold a court) and 'soke' (the right to enforce attendance at it) were regularly made to lay and ecclesiastical magnates, particularly in the eleventh century. Grant of hundredal jurisdiction did not necessarily mean a grant covering the whole hundred; it often meant a grant of that level of jurisdiction within the lord's estates. Great sokes of several hundreds might be created, as for the monasteries of Peterborough or Bury St Edmunds, or the right might apply to just one manor.[3] Hundred courts were particularly important because of their link with the tithing system; Athelstan prescribed summary justice for the man out of tithing or without a lord to answer for him. Ethelred and his *witan* laid down for the whole nation that at each four-weekly meeting the twelve senior thegns and the reeve were to swear that they would accuse no innocent man nor conceal any guilty man. This implies a duty to produce the guilty for judgment, and is clearly a forerunner of the jury of presentment. Moreover, the thegns were to seize men frequently accused; this is another expression of the reliance on local knowledge and public opinion that justified compurgation.

3 Harding, no 5.

8.3.4 At the lowest level of jurisdiction was the hall-moot, or future manor court, the meeting of the village at which all free men must find sureties or 'borh' in case of some misconduct which would lead to appearance before a court. In practice the tithing, which lay somewhere between the hall and the hundred, came frequently to be identified with a vill or village rather than with a personal group. At the other end of the scale, by the eleventh century, the *witan* had, in general, ceased to act as a court; it had not, however, lost its judicial potential.

8.4 PROCEDURE IN SHIRE AND HUNDRED COURTS

8.4.1 The defender in any suit, and there was as yet no clear distinction between private and criminal law, normally had the right to clear himself by oath, that is by compurgation. He summoned oath-helpers, whose number would depend on the gravity of the charge and the status of the defender, to swear that his oath of denial was pure. If the defender had been caught in the act or in suspicious circumstances or was a man who had frequently been accused or had ever been convicted of perjury, then it was the accuser's right to bring oath-helpers to join with him in swearing to the defender's guilt; the accuser had normally to take a preliminary oath that his accusation was true. If the defender managed his oath he was absolved; if he was unable to provide it, or if the accuser had had the right to swear the oath, the defender would then go to trial by ordeal. The ordeal might be of cold water, of hot water, or of hot iron,[4] or, for the clergy, of consecrated bread.[5] Failure at the ordeal might result in a lesser penalty than when the culprit was caught red-handed, but it might not.

4 Herlihy, no 25.
5 A guilty man's mouth might well be so dry that he choked upon the bread.

8.4.2 There were fixed fines for many offences, and in other cases there was the *wergeld* (or *weregild*). The *wergeld* was a sum of money calculated according to rank, and was originally the redemption price for a murder, given to avoid a blood feud; it was extended to provide a useful valuation for other fines, for example, for adultery in the laws of Kent. Under the influence of the Church the death penalty was somewhat less common in Anglo-Saxon England than on the continent; mutilation was held to be a milder punishment. Slavery was also a customary penalty which could follow from inability to pay a fine; the kindred of the penal slave had a year in which they could redeem him, and after that year custom permitted his wife to marry again. Imprisonment was an occasional penalty, but money payments of some sort were far commoner, for reparation as well as retribution. Higher rank, while it entitled a man to higher compensation, also made him liable to higher fines. The court normally had no discretion save in its interpretation of fact, but simply published sentence according to law or custom.

8.4.3 A wide variety of offences were seen in terms of breaches of the peace. Every man of note had his peace; the King's peace was the greatest, but the king's cook had his peace which covered the royal kitchens and each lord had his peace and each free peasant his. Breach of the peace therefore often involved two payments, one to the actual victim and one to the owner of the peace. Breaches of a peace given by the king in person to a particular individual were reserved to the king for judgment, as were '*botlos*' or uncompensatable crimes; examples of these were arson, murder by poisoning, harbouring outlaws, violent obstruction of royal messengers, and treachery to a lord. In such cases the king alone had power to pardon and restore from automatic outlawry the man who had committed them. The eleventh century is still too early for one to talk about pleas of the Crown, but there was no doubt that the king's peace was specially hallowed by God and deserving of support by man.

8.4.4 In general the social status of women was high; royal women (and those from the old noble families which had once been royal) and abbesses are found sometimes as members of the *witan*. 'The freedom with which women could hold and dispose of land is in striking contrast to post-Conquest conditions'.[6] Women, however, only inherited land in the absence of male heirs of the same degree; it was normal for a man's sons to divide his land equally between them. Before alienating land out of the family, and this included gifts to the Church, it was advisable to obtain the consent of one's kin, who might otherwise have a claim on it. Land thus alienated from the family, 'bookland', could thereafter be alienated at will. The king retained ultimate jurisdiction over bookland and hence would be heir if the land were forfeit. Under Edward the Confessor written instruments became common as giving a grant greater security.

6   D Whitelock, *The Beginnings of English Society* (*The Anglo-Saxon Period*) (Penguin, 1952) pp 151ff; cf Harding, no 3.

8.5   1066

8.5.1 In 1066 the Normans came. William I, the Conqueror, swore at his coronation to observe the laws of England as they had been in Edward's day, but modifications, such as the general substitution of mutilation for the death penalty, were soon introduced. Slavery as such disappeared, with many slaves falling into the enlarged class of serfs, for the Normans were readier than the Anglo-Saxons to hold peasants unfree. Inevitably, the attitude of a king who was, even if only temporarily, a military despot was different from that of Cnut. He could make an *ab initio* distribution among his followers, first of the Wessex lands of the Godwin family and later, in 1071–1072 after the defeat of the earls of Mercia and Northumbria, of most of the rest of England. In this way the greater part of the country was divided into knights' fees, with a substantial number of manors reserved to the Crown.[7] With the exception of some of the wilder parts of the north-west, he gave effect to the feudal concept that all land was held of the king. Land-holding and military service had been linked since Alfred's day, but the tie was now made systematic and almost universal.

7 Tenants on royal manors had some special privileges; later we find them obtaining their own writ – the little writ of right close – to protect their holdings; see Harding, p 34.

8.5.2 Thus the king's court was now feudal, whereas the *witan* had adhered to a customary tradition; however, the king's court, the *curia regis*, did retain the royal omni-competent jurisdiction of the Anglo Saxon kings.[8] New, at least in their scale, were the honour courts, the courts of the great lords to which their tenants, the lesser lords or knights, came as suitors; these diminished the importance of the shire court. Manors, frequently being the products of the new distribution, were tidier units under the Normans; seignorial jurisdiction was that of a master, but manor courts continued to proceed by inquest in disputes about leasehold or descent. Hundred courts were very widely in private hands even before the Conquest; the process accelerated afterwards, but they continued to be centres of local knowledge.[9] Some remained as franchise jurisdictions, where being subject to the court was not dependent on being a tenant of the court's owner, but most were seignorial, where holding from a lord made a man subject to his court.

8 Harding, no 6.
9 Harding, no 7, third paragraph.

8.5.3 The Normans introduced trial by battle for both civil and criminal cases. It was even simpler than compurgation or the traditional ordeals, because there was no need to award the burden of proof to one side rather than the other. Another change made by William was his removal of clerics from the courts secular; in particular the bishop gave up his joint presidency of the shire court. Henceforward the line was drawn between spiritual and temporal causes much as in the rest of Europe, although in England, as elsewhere, clerics continued to serve the king in lay matters.

8.5.4 The Normans thus introduced some new things, in particular military feudalism with knight service and castles to overawe their surroundings, but their blending of old and new was a hopeful sign of the unity to come. This blending is well illustrated from the compilation known as the Domesday Book. In the eleventh century only in England was local government sufficiently organized and central government sufficiently strong for the success of such a project. A survey was made during 1085–1086 of the greater part of the realm in order to discover the annual value of all land in the kingdom, whether or not anything was owed directly to the king; it is fairly clear that the motives for the undertaking were fiscal rather than administrative. Men were sent out as commissioners to groups of counties; they made their enquiries in the shire courts. Questions were put to the sheriff, the barons and other Normans as to the greater tenements, and to the reeves, the priests and six peasants of each vill as to their knowledge of each hundred, and sometimes each village; these questions were to be answered on oath.[10]

10 Herlihy, no 37.

8.5.5   The commissioners must on occasion have decided disputes over tenure in order to make accurate returns. The sheriff was already accustomed to going on circuit (ayre in Scotland, eyre in England) to sit twice a year in each hundred of his shire to review the tithings, and so there was no novelty in travelling judges. Some use of a sworn jury of inquest to discover the truth through local knowledge was not new to either English or French tradition; the Anglo-Saxon kings had made judicial as well as administrative use of it, regularly in criminal, occasionally in civil procedure.[11]

11   Harding, no 7, first paragraph; RC van Caenegem, *Royal Writs in England from the Conquest to Glanvill* (Selden Society, vol 77, 1958–1959) pp 69ff.

8.5.6   The use of written instruments or writs to convey instructions, to make grants, and to publicize oral transactions had become regular under the Anglo-Saxons, and was readily adopted by William and his successors. Writs could be used to order a sheriff to discover something through inquiry from the men of the shire, or to command that right be done to someone by the sheriff if his lord would not, or to grant a privilege such as holding a market.[12] The use of writing was on the increase everywhere at this period, as we have seen; under Norman rule, however, Anglo-Saxon was ousted by Latin.

12   Harding, no 7, first, second and fifth paragraphs.

8.5.7   William II made no mark on English legal history, save in that his brother and successor, Henry I (1100–1135), was able to paint a picture of him as an unjust man, resorting to the feudal letter against the customary spirit of the law. By contrast Henry, so said Henry, would 'restore to you the law of King Edward, with the reforms made to it by my father with the counsel of his barons'. Henry ordered the shire and hundred courts to meet where and when they had met in Edward's time, but trial was to be by battle unless a settlement was reached.

8.5.8   Henry's frequent absences in Normandy led to some institutionalization of his household. The Exchequer was established for the keeping of the royal accounts, with records (known as the Pipe Rolls) of all moneys due and paid in; it also had jurisdiction in this field. It was during this period that writs issued by the royal chancery began to take set forms. Henry was personally active in judicial business, but even so he needed deputies whom he could send where they were needed; the first predominantly judicial eyres took place in his reign. At these eyres criminals were accused under oath by a jury of presentment in the hundreds, in a manner similar to Anglo-Saxon practice, although it was in the shire courts that the royal justices sat. As elsewhere in Europe, all feudal courts led eventually to the king, as feudal superior of every man; appeal from local courts led to the king as the source of the peace of the realm.

8.5.9   Around 1118 a work known as the *Leges Henrici Primi* (*Laws of Henry I*) was produced; its title is misleading in that it was a compilation of older material. Its purpose was to explain the customary and vernacular law of the local courts to the Norman sheriffs and lords in a language – Latin – that they could understand, in order to make the administration of justice more effective. It began by remarking that the Anglo-Saxon kingdom was divided between the customs of Wessex, Mercia, and the Danelaw. It described the shires, the hundreds and the tithings, and the sheriff's tourn for view of frankpledge, and it stressed the importance of the shire courts. Seignorial courts were also mentioned, together with the duty of suit of court and the importance of the fealty of vassal to his lord. The author, although overwhelmed by the diversity of custom in his attempt to clarify the law, saw that unity lay in the king's peace; he also tried to relate the rules of law he knew to contemporary continental practice. The Normans seem to have been following a sharpened Anglo-Saxon tradition, not abrogating but up-dating old custom. In Baker's words: 'The Common Law emerged in the twelfth century from the efficient and rapid expansion of institutions which existed in an undeveloped form before 1066'.[13] It is from the reign of Henry II, the first king since the Conquest to claim to be English (however much this claim was propaganda) that one can recognize the king's court, then and thereafter, playing the leading role in the creation of a single Common Law.

13 Baker (1990) p 14.

8.6   HENRY II: THE EYRE, THE JURY, AND THE WRIT

8.6.1 How far the reshaping of the law of England that took place under Henry II was his deliberate act is difficult to tell. Henry, after his coronation, stated explicitly his intention to revive the good laws of his grandfather, Henry I. It is certain that there were no comparable legal developments in Henry's other territories of Anjou and Aquitaine, although there were parallels in Normandy. Henry was described by contemporaries as dilatory in legal business. Yet the royal power was such that a Common Law could be effective for the whole kingdom, and the old institutions provided the instruments. The *Treatise on the Laws and Customs of the Realm of England*, which is commonly known as *Glanvill* after its supposed author, describes the remedies offered by the royal courts under Henry II; it is a work different in kind as well as in scale from the *Leges Henrici Primi*, and one which would have been impossible to produce in France where the king's political position was still weak outside his own domains. As an example, in 1176 in England the royal justices were to exact an oath of fealty to the king from all men, villeins as well as free.[14]

14 Harding, no 8.

8.6.2 Henry's first legislation, the Constitutions of Clarendon, was issued ten years after his accession as part of his struggle with the Church and in particular with Thomas Becket, formerly royal chancellor and then archbishop of Canterbury. Two years later in 1166 the Assize of Clarendon was enacted.[15] The Assize of Clarendon marked an innovation in the use of the eyre in that commissioners were sent out who were exclusively judicial. In each shire of the kingdom twelve 'lawful' men from each hundred and four from each township were, on oath, to present the names of those suspected of robbery or murder or theft, or of harbouring such persons, since the date of the king's accession. These suspects, of whatever status (so that serf as well as free man here became subject to royal justice), were to be arrested and put to the ordeal of water. The sheriff might receive the presentment but was to have no jurisdiction; he was simply to keep the accused safe until they could be tried before the commissioners. Nor was any other court to have jurisdiction over those accused by this sworn jury, although other criminals could be dealt with as was customary. All men, regardless of any private court they might have the right to hold, were to attend the shire court to be available to serve on a jury of presentment; no one – and this included boroughs – whatever jurisdiction he enjoyed was to deny the sheriff entry to enforce the frankpledges. Persons of really bad reputation, even if they succeeded in the ordeal, were outlawed and had to leave the kingdom within eight days.

15 'Assize' literally means being seated, usually therefore a session of a court, and thence it was extended to cover: something roughly equivalent to an Act of Parliament; the authorization of particular judicial proceedings; the proceedings themselves; the jurors who formed an essential part of these proceedings; and, finally, the sessions of the itinerant justices who were appointed to hear such proceedings.

8.6.3   The sending out of royal justices in eyre was not in itself a novelty, but the members of the royal court, the *curia regis*, who had been thus despatched had previously acted for the king in fiscal and administrative as well as judicial matters, as they did again in 1170 at the Inquest of Sheriffs, or the Assize of Arms in 1181. The Assize of Clarendon was general, in that it extended to all the shires, but it was also specifically judicial, and in this it set a pattern. There was another general eyre in 1173, with itinerant justices being sent to each of six circuits.

> 'The conduct of business at an eyre epitomized its historical role. The first part, the pleas of the Crown, represents the system of itinerant government, the first stage in institutional centralization . . . The other part of the eyre's business was the common pleas, ordinary litigation between ordinary people. And since almost all our evidence comes from a time when there existed also the central court which came to be known as the Court of Common Pleas, and since that court became the ordinary forum for such litigation, it is important to emphasize that it was in the eyre that such pleas could first come to royal justice as a matter of routine. It was the central court that was at first the exceptional thing, in that cases were begun there for special reason, sometimes for special payment by a litigant unwilling to wait for the next eyre; and it always needed the special authorization of a writ.'[16]

16 Milsom, pp 27–29.

8.6.4   As royal justice came to be more in demand, it was apparent that there was much that was too trivial for the solemnity of a general eyre, presided over by the greatest men in the kingdom. Elaboration of claims led to an institutionalization of the system and a division between civil and criminal causes. Eventually royal justices sat in the shires in five frequently overlapping capacities: permanently as justices of the peace; as judges sent out with commissions of *oyer et terminer* (to hear and determine specific offences); or of gaol delivery (to clear the prisons in a specific shire); or of assize (to hear possessory claims); or of *nisi prius*. To explain the last: when juries needed to be summoned before the king himself or before the royal courts which came to be fixed at Westminster, they were told to come 'unless before then – *nisi* *prius* – the king's justices shall have come' to the shire. Judges or commissioners were therefore sent out specifically to hear the testimony of a jury and to report back. They might be delegates without original jurisdiction in the matter, or they could include one or more of the judges hearing the suit in the *curia regis*; in the former case they were often judges with other commissions to which this task was added. Unlike the *enquête* of the *Parlement* of Paris, the judges did not interrogate individual witnesses but put questions which could be simply answered by a local jury. By the fourteenth century the general eyre had disappeared, although royal judges continued to visit a county at a time, and the central courts had become permanent and professional, but in the thirteenth century the eyre dominated the administration of justice and these circuit courts remained an integral part of the legal system for eight hundred years.

8.6.5 The jury of presentment, or Grand Jury, the sworn jury of accusers, survived in England until 1933 and still survives in the United States. Its roots went back to the Anglo-Saxon kingdom. Such presentment or indictment was only on suspicion and so it was followed by trial. Trial by battle could not be used because the king himself was viewed as prosecutor, and compurgation gave too much scope for local pressure; Henry therefore laid down the ordeal, but when the clergy were forbidden after 1215 to take part in trial by ordeal some other method of proof became necessary. During the thirteenth century it became the custom to put the facts to another jury of sworn neighbours, the petty jury. The accused must consent to this for, unlike God in the ordeal, the neighbours might be prejudiced – the more likely since it was not until 1352 that the two criminal juries were made fully distinct. If the accused did not consent, it was laid down in 1275 that while obdurate he could be kept in prison under harsh conditions; this turned into *peine forte et dure* which used torture to compel his consent to a jury.

8.6.6 The petty jury was a thirteenth-century creation, but the civil jury, like the jury of presentment, already had a long history. Athelstan had said that truthful men were to be named in each hundred to 'be for witness in every suit'. Nevertheless, swearing men to provide information which would settle private disputes rather than matters of public concern was a later use, perhaps first known under Edward the Confessor, perhaps not until the following century. In 1176, Henry II issued the Assize of Northampton, a revised version of the Assize of Clarendon which added arson and forgery to the pleas of the Crown. However, there is a clause referring to a possible abuse by lords:

> 'On the death of a free tenant his heirs shall have the seisin their father had on the day he died. . . . And if the lord denies the heirs the seisin of the deceased, the justices of the lord king shall make enquiry through twelve lawful men as to what seisin the deceased had on the day he died and in accordance with the finding shall restore the heirs.'

This is the assize of *mort d'ancestor* which clearly makes use of the civil jury and allows common pleas, that is the suits raised between one subject and another, to be heard by the king's judges.[17]

---

17 Harding, nos 8 and 9.

8.6.7   The importance of the jury in twelfth- and thirteenth-century England led to an emphasis on the techniques of pleading and also to a growth in the substantive law.

> 'The decision as to what were material questions of fact for the jury necessitated a decision as to what the law was. However, such questions of law were not in medieval times raised after the facts had been ascertained by trial, but in the course of deciding what the jury was to be asked to try.'[18]

18   Baker (1990) p 90.

8.6.8   The Assize of Windsor of 1179 allowed a tenant whose title was challenged to apply to the Chancery for a writ, the writ of right, which allowed him to submit his claim to a jury of twelve knights of the shire before the justices in eyre instead of having to undertake trial by battle in the court of his lord. This procedure, before a royal not a feudal court, was itself known as the Grand Assize, in contrast to the petty assizes such as *mort d'ancestor* which enquired into who had last had seisin as a matter of fact rather than of right. *Novel disseisin* was another of the petty assizes; there continues to be argument about its relationship to the interdicts of the civil law or to the *actio spolii* of the canon law. It dealt with who had had seisin before a recent dispossession. The two other petty assizes were *utrum*, whether land was held by lay or ecclesiastical tenure (which was extended to cover similar questions, such as whether it was freehold or leasehold, and whether an heir was of age or not, etc), and *darrein presentment*, or who had last exercised the right of patronage to a particular benefice; like the other two petty assizes these used a jury of twelve lawful men. A jury was also used in the investigation of encroachments upon royal property (*purprestures*) and at *nisi prius*. It was an excellent instrument in many ways for discovering local truth, even though a jury was limited to its own shire and could not speak as to occurrences elsewhere. Its firm establishment as an English legal institution must be credited to Henry II.

8.6.9   The writ was the third element in the pattern of countrywide royal justice. The eyre and the jury operated in the shires; the *curia regis* meant the king and his counsellors, including those whom he sent out as his justices in eyre, but it also had a more abstract definition as the home of the machinery necessary to co-ordinate the royal administration in the shires, although it was in theory attached to the person of the king. The Exchequer was probably the first branch of government to settle in a fixed place; after all, the financial records of the Exchequer dealt with the mainspring of government and in troubled times were safer in some secure castle such as Winchester. The Chancery, the writing office of the king, followed him for longer. Writing had long been used for communication between the king and his sheriffs but under Henry we find a new kind of judicial writ. These writs were close (sealed when folded) because they contained instructions for the sheriff's eyes only, and furthermore most of them were returnable, that is the sheriff must return the writ to the justices in eyre – or, later, to one of the king's courts at Westminster – with a note on it of what action he had taken in compliance with its instructions; that is why their normal ending is 'and have there the parties and this writ'.

8.6.10 So important were writs to the system of justice developed under Henry that Glanvill has been interpreted as simply a commentary upon them, although this is not a fair assessment. When the king's command still normally meant an oral command, it could hardly be viewed as a regular stage in procedure.

> 'The use of writs on the other hand meant that the king's authority extended as far and as fast as his chancery officials could write them out, as aggrieved litigants could fetch and carry them, and as sheriffs and bailiffs in the localities were willing and able to enforce them.'[19]

The quantitative change had qualitative effects. When writs became routine – standardized and repeatable – they became the normal, although never the only, method of exciting justice. Glanvill knew some thirty-six original writs (initiating litigation), roughly the same number, including many with but minor variations, for process in the course of litigation, and four for ordering execution of judgment. A century later, at the end of Henry III's reign, there were some 120 original writs; in 1320 there were about 890, and a *Register of Writs* printed in London in 1531 listed about 2,500. Most of these represent trivial modifications since the creation of fresh categories of writs had been restricted by the Statute of Westminster II of 1285 which, however, allowed the clerks to draw up new writs analogous to existing ones (*in consimili casu*). Hence new kinds of wrongs had to look in other directions for a remedy, but the writ remained fundamental for centuries. Not until the nineteenth century were its forms of action abolished in favour of – from 1875 – one single original writ, and this was little more than a direction to the parties to appear.

19 Clanchy, p 155.

8.6.11 There were writs for claims to title, writs of right, as well as writs for claims to seisin, or possession, and during the thirteenth century writs were introduced for real rights, such as a right of way, or hunting rights. There were also writs for the personal actions such as debt and covenant. The writs for trespass became routine under Henry III. Trespass covered various delicts, but always with a claim that injury had been done to the king's peace so that in this way the matter could properly be brought before the royal courts. Along with the increase in writs there were developments in other aspects of procedure, such as *essoins*, or excuses, for non-appearance. It was possible to send an attorney or procurator in one's place and this was soon encouraged, which benefited the growth of a legal profession. All writs presupposed a complaint to Chancery, and so there was an increase in personnel there. Naturally, it remained possible to make an oral complaint directly to the justices at the local eyre court; when this was put in writing it was known as a bill.

8.6.12 Many of Henry II's reforms were directed to safeguarding feudal jurisdictions and to trying to improve the working of the customary courts. In fact, these very safeguards and improvements weakened the old ways and replaced them with a dominant royal justice, but in view of the intention it is hardly surprising that the king did not concern himself much with canonist or civilian examples or comparisons. Although Glanvill's book was primarily concerned with writs dealing with common pleas it gave a reasonably coherent account of the Common Law of the realm. Partly because of his writing the workings of the royal courts could thereafter be equated with the *ius et consuetudo regni*, the law and custom of the kingdom.

8.6.13   Glanvill wrote some fifty years after the appearance of Gratian's *Decretum* and some sixty before the acceptance of the Accursian Gloss; he clearly knew something of the learned law. Book X in particular, which deals with contractual relationships, is influenced in arrangement, terminology and to some extent content by Justinian's Institutions; some knowledge is shown of romano-canonical procedure, as when the reader is assumed to know on what grounds a witness might be rejected in the courts spiritual. But the teaching of Roman law had been prohibited in 1149 by King Stephen. Vacarius (brought to England by Theobald, archbishop of Canterbury) probably published his *Liber Pauperum* in the 1170s, perhaps to make up for the lack of formal education. In spite of the likelihood that this ban was soon repealed, there was no lively centre of academic legal learning in England. Indeed, it was not to be very long before legal training became the prerogative of the practitioners, although Englishmen in fair numbers did go abroad to study canon and also civil law. Henry's reforms were possible in the context of the active intellectual society of the twelfth century renaissance, but the fact was that they were applied to a stable, well-organized and centralized kingdom; their efficiency was such that Englishmen saw no need to acquire the new learned law. Bracton, who flourished under Henry III, was, like Glanvill in the previous century, influenced by Justinian's codification and saw the magnitude of the learned law (although there continues to be scholarly debate as to the depth of his knowledge) but it was already too late for the learned law to play a significant part in English legal development. Bracton marks the end of a possible line of approach, not a springboard for the future.

8.7   THE *CURIA REGIS*: THE GROWTH OF THE CENTRAL COURTS

8.7.1   The chief innovation of the thirteenth century was the emergence of the *curia regis* as a professional court, or rather courts. The king's court was always supreme, and to the king's court, to his council, were summoned the wisest and most powerful men in the kingdom. The justices in eyre, when the eyre represented government itself, were normally members of the *curia regis*. The demand for justice stimulated by the eyres, which remained the usual forum for the ordinary man throughout the thirteenth century,[20] led to an increase in the judicial business of the *curia regis*. The Exchequer, because of the sheer weight of its records (and, one imagines, of its specie), was the first court to cease following a peripatetic king and to settle at Westminster. It continued to have a wide jurisdiction over any case where there was a revenue interest, and even in private causes, since debtors to the Crown might raise actions in this court as their success was in the king's interest. Since wager of law, compurgation, was not applicable in these proceedings, it was accepted as possible to raise an action against the executor of an estate after the death of the defending party.

20 Harding, nos 10, 12–14 and 16.

8.7.2 For tenants-in-chief, who owed suit of court to the king as their lord, and for those who wanted a remedy before the next visit of the eyre and were therefore prepared to pay for the privilege of using the king's court, it was burdensome to follow the king's person round England and Aquitaine and Normandy. Thus one of the clauses of *Magna Carta*, a statement of their feudal rights extorted from John by the barons in 1215, was that the common pleas should not follow the king but be heard in some certain place. After 1234 there were two sets of plea rolls, *coram rege*, where the judges sat in the (theoretical) presence of the king, hence King's Bench, and *de banco*, where the judges sat on the Bench at Westminster, the Common Bench or Court of Common Pleas. Further, the Chancery began to issue writs returnable to the Common Bench for actions raised in the shire courts. The King's Bench could not hear common pleas because it did not remain in a certain place; writs bringing causes before it were returnable 'wherever we may then be in England'. The Common Bench thus acquired an exclusive jurisdiction over causes in which the king had no kind of interest, which at this stage meant all the real actions and those personal actions which did not allege a breach of the king's peace. Because of their common origin in the *curia regis*, the Common Bench shared with the King's Bench jurisdiction over pleas of the Crown and cases involving trespass; however, by convention, appeals (accusations) of felony were not heard by the Common Bench after the later fourteenth century. There were normally four or five judges of the Common Pleas, also advocates called serjeants-at-law and a staff of clerks and other assistants. It was in the 'crib' or gallery in this court that pupils stood to learn their law; it was the debates there of judges and serjeants that made up most of the content of the Year Books, which are reports – in French, the language of the pleadings – of the arguments in selected cases before the Common Pleas or in eyre.[21]

21 Eg Harding, no 20.

8.7.3 By the end of the fourteenth century the King's Bench had also settled at Westminster, usually with three judges – the Lord Chief Justice and two puisne justices. Henceforward judicial business performed by the king in person or in his presence was described as 'before the king's council' rather than before the *curia regis*; somewhat strangely, it was not reckoned part of the Common Law. The King's Bench had a universal criminal jurisdiction, but after the fourteenth century it also functioned as something akin to a court of appeal, except for offences committed in Middlesex, the shire in which Westminster lay. Although barred from hearing common pleas it had a civil jurisdiction, in particular over actions of trespass and also to correct errors in the Common Pleas or in the courts of record, that is, the borough and palatine[22] courts. Since the bulk of criminal trials took place at the assizes held in the shires,[23] and since debt was a matter for Common Pleas, it is not surprising that it was predominantly the King's Bench which felt the loss of business during the fifteenth century to the conciliar and prerogative courts.[24]

22 The palatinates, Chester, Lancaster and Durham, had once been semi-independent frontier jurisdictions.
23 Harding, nos 21 and 23.
24 For the curious and elaborate fictions that the King's Bench adopted in order to stay competitive with the other central courts, in particular the Bill of Middlesex, see Baker (1990) pp 50–51.

8.7.4   When the King's Council became distinct from the King's Bench there remained people who wanted direct access to the king; the king still regarded active jurisdiction as one of his duties and prerogatives. Causes concerning the great could best be dealt with on such occasions as when the king was wearing his Crown in a parliament. The first adjournment of a case to Parliament – not yet an institution but a reasonably regular and formal gathering of the magnates, lay and ecclesiastical, to hear and petition the king – seems to date from 1236. By the later part of the century it was a normal court, at this stage not particularly different in its workings from the *Parlement* of Paris. Petitions, or bills, to Parliament might be made by any free man and the matter might receive judgment there, although it would more often be referred to one of the Common Law courts. Alternatively, a bill might lead to the issuing of a general edict on the subject, and so we find early parliamentary legislation; the shape of legislative procedure, however, was only settled under the earlier Tudors. It was through its function as a court that Parliament began to deal with legal affairs and so took from the judges the sole power of technical development of the law, a position they had still enjoyed in the time of Glanvill or even Bracton.

8.7.5   By Bracton's time judges had already become specialists, professionals rather than general servants of the king; generality remained useful for the business of the King's Council after it separated from the *curia regis*. Bracton wrote his treatise *On the Laws and Customs of England* so that judges could follow the wise decisions of their predecessors. By the 1280s these decisions were a matter of record in the plea rolls[25] and the year books, and by the following century they were being cited as evidence of law and practice – nothing peculiar to England here. Fourteenth-century judges were quite clear that they were creating law as well as enforcing it, but what was persuasive was the *communis opinio* of the judges and serjeants in Westminster Hall, not specific previous decisions. It was not until the later sixteenth century that weight was given to particular past decisions, and not until the nineteenth century that the full doctrine of *stare decisis* emerged as the peculiar characteristic of English law.

25 For an example of specimen pleadings, see Baker (1990), Appendix II at p 628.

8.8   THE CREATION OF THE COMMON LAW

8.8.1   The law of the Court of Common Pleas, the King's Bench and the Exchequer was by definition the Common Law. Common Law might be and often was used in other courts such as the Admiralty or Chancery, but the creation of Common Law was restricted to the three branches of the thirteenth century *curia regis*; in particular it was made between the thirteenth and sixteenth centuries in the Court of Common Pleas where the serjeants congregated. The divergence from the rest of Europe can be dated, since in the twelfth century England had been unusual only in its degree of centralized and effective royal power. In the earlier thirteenth century the clerical servants of the king who brought about the change from the jumble of the *Leges Henrici Primi* to the systematization of Glanvill and, half a century later, of Bracton, would have been at home throughout western Christendom, and the legal professionalism which emerged during this period can readily be paralleled elsewhere. But as early as the fourteenth century, English law could be distinguished from that of every other country in the civilized West because its lawyers were trained purely in the practice of the courts and at the Inns of Court, not at the universities. However, this very fact meant that the Inns to some extent functioned as a (collegiate) university from the late thirteenth century, using the normal techniques of lectures, *quaestiones*, etc (see para 3.4.2-3). The great difference is the total lack of references to Roman law, whereas everywhere in the universities the law taught was the civil and not the municipal law. The English legal profession refused to recognize the learned law as having any relevance to their practice.

8.8.2 Henry de Bracton (d. 1268) was a judge of the King's Bench in the 1240s and 1250s and wrote, or at least heavily revised, the great treatise which is known by his name. Bracton made much use of the plea rolls, going back to the 1220s; he described the customary laws of England as they had recently been developed for the use of judges. Although a much more substantial work, it is in the same tradition as that of Beaumanoir. There is scholarly argument about how well acquainted Bracton was with the civil law, but there is no doubt that it provided him with the concept of order, of a framework in which to handle English law.

8.8.3 The English legists of the later twelfth and thirteenth centuries were in perfect agreement with the notion that one must look first to one's own custom and then supplement it. William Raleigh, later bishop of Winchester, had been the champion of the traditional party in successfully opposing the introduction of legitimation by subsequent marriage into English law – 'nolumus leges Angliae mutari' (we do not wish the laws of England to be changed) (Statute of Merton 1236) – although, as a canon of St Paul's in London and then treasurer and canon of Exeter cathedral before his elevation to the episcopate, he must have known that canon law allowed it. But men like Raleigh and Bracton, who was archdeacon of Barnstaple and then chancellor of Exeter Cathedral, were in a somewhat invidious position as judges. As clerics they were unable to pass a death sentence, and in the thirteenth century the decisions of the earlier clerical reform movement were repeated, that clergy should not involve themselves in secular business (Extra 3,50). While clerics continued sometimes to serve the king in a judicial capacity, legal practice on behalf of clients other than the Church itself or the poor and unprotected was forbidden them; King's Bench was completely laicized by 1341.

8.8.4 The pleaders and attorneys (or procurators) doing regular business in the central courts came, in the fourteenth century, to be exclusively laymen; thus they would have had no reason to study canon law. The teaching of civil law at Oxford cannot have been strong; when Francis Accursius (son of the Glossator) was brought to England by Edward I, it was to serve in the royal household, and there is no trace of his teaching before his return to Bologna. Effective royal control (combined with the geographical fact of insularity) restricted study abroad (as it could appeals to Rome) and made it less attractive. Therefore, while law in England, as elsewhere, had become so technical that professional training was needed, there was no rival education that could offer an alternative approach in legal ideas. Moreover, because the Common Law lay outside the spheres of canon and civil law after the clerical withdrawal from the courts, the spoken language of the courts came to be French, still the language of the upper classes, rather than Latin, the language of scholars. This further intensified the isolation of English law, although much of the written formalities of litigation continued to be in Latin.

8.8.5   At roughly the same time as Bracton's treatise there appeared a formulary of writs known as the *Brevia Placitata* (*Pleaded Writs*); other similar works of the period were *Novae Narrationes* (*New Counts*)[26] and, more restricted in scope, *Placita Coronae* (*Pleas of the Crown*).[27] In *Brevia Placitata*, a conflation of writs and counts,

> 'the writs, which in real life were always in Latin, were translated into French, the language in which counts at any rate in the king's courts were actually spoken, the ordinary language of the upper classes. This collection was for the use, or more probably the instruction, of professional men, literate men, but men not at home in the Latin tongue and not interested in the riches to which it gave access. . . . It is one of the important facts in the history of western thought (or at least of legal influence beyond Europe) that the [*Brevia*] was to prove fruitful, [Bracton] sterile. . . . Just as the writs in *Brevia Placitata* show counters looking upward to learn the administrative and jurisdictional elements, so Bracton's book shows the administrator looking downward at what was happening in court. Many actual cases cited are taken from the plea rolls, mostly of the earlier thirteenth century. But the attempt is to make more than just administrative sense; it is to systematize in a substantive and not just a practical and procedural way. This is, as it were, a university law-book. When, in the half century after Bracton's death, his kind ceased to play any part in the Common Law and the bench came to be filled from below by counters, two qualities were lost. One was the administrative habit of seeing problems as a whole and making solutions work: the kind of man who had brought the Common Law into being would not have let it get into the state in which so many cases required the special treatment of the Chancellor's equitable jurisdiction. The other was a more specific quality . . . [Roman law] was no part of the counters' world. What centuries of development had made clear centuries earlier was to them alien learning in closed books; and they were starting again from the beginning. . . . They did not see the law as a system of substantive rules at all. They saw that their ancient pattern of claim and denial had been disturbed because jurymen were fallible, and that in some circumstances the defendant must be allowed a new kind of answer. Upon the infinite details of this problem they concentrated their great abilities; and they never looked up to consider as a whole the substantive system they did not know they were making.'[28]

26   A count was a formal statement of claim, declaring the cause of the action; it was very roughly comparable to the *libellus* (libel) of the Roman *cognitio* or the romano-canonical procedure.
27   Harding, no 15.
28   Milsom, pp 41ff.

8.8.6 The young man eager for a career in law therefore came to London. He could learn the rudiments of the writ system through a little tract called the *Old Natura Brevium* (*'Old' Nature of Writs*), the basic counts from *Novae Narrationes*, and an introduction to land law from a work known as the *Old Tenures*. 'The ultimate effect, certainly by the mid-fifteenth century, was to replace any coherent instruction in the Common Law.'[29] These manuals, with some similar works, such as Littleton's *Tenures* (1481), were virtually all there was of legal literature, apart from reports in various forms, particularly the Year Books. However, the 'readings', that is, courses of lectures given at the Inns (described below) on a selected statute, 'to some extent supplied the place of a doctrinal literature of English law'.[30] (The readings had to based on statute, for there were no other written sources on which to found an exposition of the law.) The would-be lawyer would also attend the courts themselves, particularly in the 'crib' at Westminster Hall to hear the judges and serjeants debate the cases before them. He would probably live with his fellows in one of the inns of chancery, as they came to be known. When or if he became a senior apprentice he would join one of the four inns (Inner and Middle Temple, Lincoln's Inn, Gray's Inn), known by Tudor times as the Inns of Court, which were established during the fourteenth century; here he would take part in moots – we know that some mootbooks had a life of up to 200 years. It usually took some seven years before the student was called to the bar by the senior members of his inn as an utter or outer barrister. From this status he might achieve that of bencher, normally by being a reader and giving a course of lectures upon some selected statute. Thus the Inns of Court provided, until the middle of the seventeenth century, some doctrine, which may have been almost as important as decided cases in creating the Common Law. But the instruction offered was at no time coherent or programmed, and even this mild form of education disappeared in 1642 with the outbreak of the First Civil War. There was no alternative, no legal education in England until the nineteenth century.

29 Baker (1990) p 214.
30 Baker (1990) p 215.

8.8.7 The senior branch of the legal profession was that of the serjeants, for, by the fourteenth century, it was exclusively from among them that judges were appointed to the King's Bench or Common Pleas; they had emerged in the thirteenth century as advocates specializing in making counts before the Common Bench. Since such counts became the terms of the issue which would be put to trial, these were central to litigation. By the end of the century serjeants had acquired, if they did not already by definition enjoy, exclusive rights to practise before the Common Bench, the most profitable of the Common Law courts, because its site was fixed, unlike the King's Bench, and its jurisdiction wider than the Exchequer's. The serjeants concentrated on elaborating their counts, which had necessarily become more complicated once the truth was not reached by an infallible, divinely backed ordeal but at the hands of the fallible but rational members of a jury. It was because the Common Law worked by producing a single issue for trial by a lay jury that the professionals could concentrate at Westminster and that their numbers were so few; there were fewer than a thousand members of the order of serjeants in all its history – the order faded away after 1875 when the last was created; similarly, there were at any one time only seven or eight judges for the two courts of Common Pleas and King's Bench. Most serjeants who lived long enough became judges; furthermore, promotion would not have been too startling a step, since it was usual for commissioners of assize to consist of a royal judge, a serjeant and a local man, and thus they would already have gained judicial experience.

8.8.8   The heyday of the serjeants, both in financial terms and for legal creativity, was the fourteenth and fifteenth centuries, when nearly all important civil causes were heard by the Court of Common Pleas. It was the pleadings put forward there by the serjeants and their debates with the judges, recorded in the year books and in the formularies of specimen counts, which applied the old formalities to new situations and adjusted, if hardly reformed, the law. In the *Humber Ferry Case* of 1348 (see para 8.11.5) trespass was the route by which contractual liability was achieved, a bizarre approach that still affects English views on contract. Their ingenuity found solutions to many problems, but they were forced into curious contortions in the process.

8.8.9   While the serjeants shared a collegiate life with the judges in the Serjeants' Inns, there were other practitioners at the bar, the barristers. Some would, after twenty or so years, themselves become serjeants, others would continue to practise before the royal courts, including those in eyre, while yet others seem to have returned to their own shires and practised in the local courts. Attorneys were procurators, whose actions in the courts bound their principals. They were clearly distinct from the serjeants at least by the early fourteenth century when the latter organized themselves into a guild. Solicitors appeared as an identifiable branch of the legal profession during the sixteenth century. Incidentally, not until the end of the seventeenth century was the independence of the judiciary finally established as a constitutional principle; furthermore, judges long expected their office to be profitable, from fees, patronage, and above all from gifts from hopeful litigants.

8.9   ENGLISH CIVILIAN AND PREROGATIVE COURTS; LOCAL COURTS

8.9.1   It was a curious feature of the early modern English Common lawyers that they tried, through statute and through pronouncements from the bench, to impose

> 'legal restraints on the power of the Crown to erect new jurisdictions, restraints on the very power which had earlier introduced the Common Law and its due process as an extraordinary alternative to regular local justice ... The notion that the king had exhausted his judicative powers by creating the Common Law courts was pressed to its limit by Coke CJ [Chief Justice] when in 1608 he told James [VI &] I that he had no authority to participate in the judicial decisions of his own courts.'[31]

But the king in his coronation oath swore to 'do equal right and justice', and he had a constitutional duty to furnish a remedy where the Common Law was deficient – although (probably) only where it was deficient. Since the Common

Lawyers were reluctant to recognize any deficiencies they fought against the prerogative courts, and these mostly failed to survive the struggle thus precipitated – which seemed to the Common lawyers proof enough of their wrongness.[32]

31 Baker (1990) pp 112-113.
32 Treason doth never prosper! What's the reason?
      Why, if it doth, then none dare call it treason.

8.9.2 In the fourteenth century, as we have seen, it was already common to petition the king for a remedy; the normal reply was to send the petitioner to the Common Law[33] but some bills were dealt with by the king and his council. By the end of the century only matters of the highest importance were dealt with by the great council as a body (a body which until mid-century had regularly included the judges of the King's Bench), and if bills were assented to they were then Acts of Parliament. Lesser matters were more often delegated to individual members of the council, such as the Chancellor or the Admiral; petitioners therefore took to addressing these officers directly in their several spheres of competence and in their several courts.

33 Harding, no 22.

8.9.3 The Chancery was originally simply the royal office; someone who wished to raise an action in the royal courts had to obtain a writ from the Chancery and pay a fine for it. But if he petitioned the king because he was too poor to buy a writ, or because his opponent was too powerful for the sheriff to do his duty or the jurors to tell the truth, then special treatment was needed. In hard cases the Chancellor provided a remedy other than through a writ, because he had the expertise both in framing writs and in finding other means to the same end. By the fifteenth century the Chancery had a clerical staff of some 120, of whom the senior twelve were known by Tudor times as the Masters in Chancery. These were usually doctors of law and able to act as the Chancellor's deputies; the chief of them was entitled Master of the Rolls, because he was responsible for the records. Even while the Common lawyers were losing all touch with the learned law, until the Reformation the Chancellor was usually a cleric – normally a bishop or even archbishop – and usually also a graduate in canon or in civil law.

8.9.4 The work of the Chancery was divided into two sides. On the Latin side were handled the king's interests as universal feudal superior. On the English side, where the petitions might be, and the pleadings were, in the vernacular (first French, then English), bills of complaint were received from individual petitioners. The Chancellor treated these ad hoc. His decrees were originally made by authority of the Council or with the advice of various judges and serjeants, but from at least 1473 he was issuing them in his own name. He was already accustomed to issuing injunctions (interdicts) to suspend a trial at Common Law while documents were discovered or witnesses examined; injunctions could also protect a tenant from interference until his case was decided at Common Law, and occasionally they came to be used to stay a Common Law judgment which enforced a contract formally good but brought about by fraud or with unintended evil consequences. Sometimes the

Chancellor could order specific performance of a contract, or enforce on grounds of conscience a bare pact not recognized by the Common Law. Relief was more usual than the award of damages, the only remedy available in Common Law. He also appointed commissioners to arbitrate in mercantile disputes or in cases with an international dimension.

8.9.5   Process in actions in Chancery was begun by subpoena which was not, like a writ, addressed to the sheriff of a specific shire but was directly binding (under penalty of a fine) on the party in whatever jurisdiction he might be. In the sixteenth century the threat of a fine was strengthened by the possibility of sequestration of the contumacious party's estate; the Chancellor could also hold men in prison for contempt of his decrees, although he had no power over life and limb. His cheap and rapid aiding, supplementing and correcting (as a romanist might say) of the Common Law made the Chancellor's jurisdiction popular; while John Stafford, bishop of Bath and Wells, was Chancellor (1432–1450) the annual number of petitions at least quadrupled.

8.9.6   This very volume of business helped to establish the Chancellor's jurisdiction on a more formal base, and it grew away from the general prerogative jurisdiction of the Council. It also came to specialize in a new area of land law, uses. A use was created when a man granted property to someone or to several people – feoffees to use – to hold in trust for himself or another – *cestui que use*. When the granter or feoffor died the feoffees were able, on his instructions, to hand the property over to another person. In this way a feudal tenant could grant away his tenement during his life, thus avoiding the incidents of relief or wardship at his death, but at the same time he could either preserve the normal succession by letting his heir on intestacy inherit the use from him, or sidestep feudal custom by leaving the use to someone else, such as a daughter.[34] Only the grant, not the trust, was recognized by the Common Law, to which the *cestui que use* was no more than a tenant on sufferance. Chancery, following the Church courts, established such a daughter's right in what came to be called the equitable estate; if the trustees alienated the land it was settled by 1465 that the purchaser acquired the duties of the trust. Where there was a use the legal owner had only bare title with, however, the reversion if the *cestui que use* died intestate and without heir. Because this conflicted with feudal rules on succession to land the Common Law never fully received the concept of the use into its courts, although the judges were obliged to take some account of its existence.

34   Harding, no 30.

8.9.7   Chancery jurisdiction was originally based on equity and good faith, and it continued to be described as Equity even after the Chancery had become as rigid and formal as any Common Law court.[35] It became formal partly as a natural result of the scale of the business concerning uses and partly because the Common lawyers disliked the subjective or arbitrary element in the Chancellor's judgments. During the later fifteenth and early sixteenth centuries, however, there was generally harmony between law and Equity, with judges of the two benches on occasion attending Chancery to give their advice.[36] It is clear that the ordering of the Chancellor's conscience (with one or two notable exceptions, such as Cardinal Wolsey and Lord Ellesmere) was normally in accord with the Common Law rather than with natural or civil law, even if aspects of Chancery procedure were more akin to that of the learned law. In 1675 it could be said without any irony that a contract without consideration was binding in conscience but not in Equity. By then Chancery cases were regularly reported, and Equity had become a known body of principles from which the court would not depart for fear of uncertainty.

35 See Charles Dickens, *Bleak House.*
36 Harding, no 29.

8.9.8 The Court of Chivalry, the Court of the Lord High Constable and Earl Marshal of England, and the Court of the Lord High Admiral of England also sprang from the general jurisdiction of the Council. Some of the matters they dealt with were outside the cognizance of the Common Law courts because they had occurred overseas or concerned persons not English subjects; due process in Common Law depended on the summoning of a jury from the shire in which the deed had been done. Fictions did occur; for example if a claimant alleged that wine had been loaded at Bordeaux in Kent and the defender denied only the substance of the claim, then a Kentish jury could be summoned. The Court of Chivalry dealt with the business side of warfare: ransoms for prisoners of war, the contracts between the captains of mercenary bands and those whom they hired, and appeals of treason or other felony committed overseas. For centuries accusations of even the most ordinary crimes in the Channel Isles or the Isle of Man could only (in English law) be heard in this court. Disputes about armorial bearings were not an important part of the court's work until its revival under James VI and I; they have become the sole business of the one English court still using civilian procedure.[37]

37 Eg, *Manchester Corpn v Manchester Palace of Varieties Ltd* [1955] P 133.

8.9.9 The High Court of Admiralty was much concerned with commercial affairs, for merchants could frequently find no other court willing to hear them. It also heard cases arising out of naval warfare and had a busy prize jurisdiction. It went back at least to the mid-fourteenth century and was only finally abolished in 1970; until 1875 it was a court using civil rather than Common Law.[38] Process could issue against ships and goods as well as persons, and it was familiar with the *lex Rhodia* and the customs of Oléron; its judges were frequently doctors of civil law.

38 Harding, no 26.

8.9.10 The later fifteenth century was a troubled period in English political history. In 1487 a special tribunal within the King's Council was set up to deal with particular problems of law and order; its business was fairly soon absorbed into that of the Council. Since the mid-fourteenth century the Council had often met for judicial sessions in a room in the Palace of Westminster known as Star Chamber, and this gave its name to the new jurisdiction.[39] From 1540 Star Chamber and the Council, now the Privy Council, were sufficiently distinct for each to have its own records and staff, but membership of the two bodies overlapped considerably. The law which Star Chamber applied was the Common Law but in exercising the royal prerogative it was not tied by the formalities of due process. It therefore attracted litigants by its speed, economy and efficiency. Business indeed grew too fast, particularly from men claiming they were too poor for the ordinary courts. At first a second clerk was appointed to handle such petitions, and in the 1540s this jurisdiction became that of the Court of Requests, as speedy as Star Chamber and even cheaper; it was immensely popular. Star Chamber was abolished in 1641 at the outbreak of the Civil Wars, and the Court of Requests disappeared with the disuse of the privy seal during the wars and the Commonwealth.

39   Harding, no 27.

8.9.11   The ecclesiastical courts had a wide jurisdiction in pre-Reformation England, although suits concerning advowsons (rights of presentation to benefices) were heard in the royal courts. They shared in the features common to all the western Church, such as the appointment of judges delegate with written instructions to take evidence, written interrogatories to be administered to the parties, and interdicts, ordering or prohibiting under penalty specific actions by persons subject to the court; juries did not normally feature in the Church's courts. After the English Reformation, which was doctrinally and institutionally less clear-cut than elsewhere in Europe, the *Corpus Iuris Canonici* remained in force, except where contrary to Common or statute law or to the royal prerogative. Canon law teaching was, however, suppressed by Henry VIII at Oxford and Cambridge, which therefore continued only with the civil law. The Court of Arches at Canterbury continued to be the normal superior court – the archbishop of Canterbury had always exercised a more effective jurisdiction than other metropolitans. The Court of High Commission was set up to replace the supreme personal jurisdiction of the pope, particularly in criminal matters; it disappeared in the 1640s. The Court of Delegates was established to hear such appeals as would previously have been heard by papal judges delegate; the new delegates included Common Law judges and doctors of civil law (or occasionally of canon law who had studied outside England). Civilian advocates had sole audience before these ecclesiastical courts; most were members of Doctors' Commons, which had its own library as well as a social life until its dissolution in 1858. The jurisdiction of the Court of Delegates was absorbed by the Judicial Committee of the Privy Council when that was set up in 1832 and 1833. But all this remained remote from the mainstream of the Common Law.

8.9.12   Manorial courts often continued to flourish, although their jurisdiction was largely confined to petty larcenies, the proper cultivation of the open fields and, most significantly, the conveying of copyhold property; thus copyhold, tenure by the custom of the manor, came in the later mediaeval period to be a true property right, a tenancy at Common Law. In the towns the borough courts (in London, hustings) dealt with commercial matters, and with the problems that arose within built-up areas, as well as with local civil and petty criminal causes.[40]

40   Harding, no 17.

8.9.13 The shire court remained the busiest forum, although there was relatively little litigation before an independent court presided over by the sheriff.[41] In many civil cases the sheriff was acting as a subordinate royal judge under a writ of *justicies*, and much other business was before the justices of assize[42] or at *nisi prius*. The provision of juries was one of the main functions of the sheriff in his court; it continued to be in the shire court that solemn proclamations were made and important dealings in land witnessed, and also that coroners were elected, as were knights of the shire to Parliament.

41 Harding, nos 18 and 19.
42 Harding, nos 21 and 23.

8.9.14 The local jurisdiction which was increasingly important was that of justices of the peace; many borough jurisdictions fell to them in the later Middle Ages. From 1361 their office carried with it the right to try all manner of criminals, whether accused of felony or of misdemeanour (as the lesser crimes came to be named in the sixteenth century), but excluding the pleas of the Crown. Although the royal justices continued to visit each shire twice a year on assize to hear these pleas, and in times of disquiet the King's Bench might come on circuit, the work of the quarter sessions before the justices of the peace became quantitatively the most important criminal forum, and until the eighteenth century some capital cases could be heard there. Monthly petty sessions, held within districts of the shire created for this purpose, dealt with minor business and such matters as enforcing wage regulations, and also with the summary trial – without a jury – of such offences as drinking out of the permitted hours and eavesdropping with a view to blackmail.[43] In the fifteenth century an unfortunate side effect of the wide powers of the local gentry as justices of the peace was that they abused the law for their own aggrandizement.[44] The known partiality of juries in this period was an element in the popularity of the prerogative courts.

43 Harding, no 25.
44 Harding, no 28.

8.10 JUDICIAL REVIEW OF DECISIONS AND APPEALS

8.10.1 On the continent the establishment of royal courts was closely linked with appeal and romano-canonical procedure, but in England the strength of the royal courts was such that there was no political need for a system of appeal. In feudal terms claims of false judgment could be made; this was extended to cover the verdict of a civil jury in an action called 'attaint'. This did not permit a review of the case; a motion for a new trial became a solution put forward in the later seventeenth century. Part of the problem in England was logical; so long as the *curia regis* was the king's own court there was no justification for allowing appeal from the king to anyone else, and the English *curia regis* had a jurisdiction at first instance far greater than that of any royal court elsewhere.

8.10.2 There were some checking mechanisms. Judges at *nisi prius* reported the jury's verdict back to the bench; the attention later given to appeals could be and was given to 'motions in banc' when, after the trial of the facts by the jury but before the judgment, further questions could be raised, originally procedural but from the sixteenth century onwards often dealing with substantive points of law. Moreover the Common Law courts were reluctant to enter judgment when there was any serious difference of opinion on the bench; adjournments were preferred until a consensus should be reached, and this consensus often included the opinions of the serjeants. Further, errors in the record could be corrected, but not until the sixteenth century could a writ of error lead to consideration of points of substance. Courts not 'of record', such as shire and feudal courts, could be required to submit to a review by the Court of Common Pleas; from the borough and the palatine courts and from the Common Pleas itself error lay to the King's Bench; from the King's Bench, from the Exchequer and from the Latin side of Chancery error lay to the king in Parliament. During the fifteenth and sixteenth centuries particularly important or difficult cases might be discussed by all the eight or nine judges of the Common Law, perhaps with the Chancellor, perhaps with the serjeants, either in the Exchequer Chamber or less formally at Serjeants' Inn; it is a little reminiscent of sittings of the whole Court of Session. Although they had no formal authority, the pronouncements which followed such consultations were reported as well as followed.

8.10.3   From the English side of Chancery there could not be error in the strict sense because there was no record. The Chancellor himself or his successor might review a judgment, or a commission might be appointed to this end; not until 1675 did judicial review of Chancery proceedings fall to the House of Lords. This was a true appeal – four centuries later than in France – for the absence of a definitive record allowed all facts to be taken into consideration, and the absence of a jury meant that a new trial was neither possible nor necessary. The creation of a Court of Appeal in Chancery in 1851 marked the introduction of a general appellate court into the English system.

8.10.4   The Privy Council's prerogative power to redress grievances which could not be remedied by the Common Law was also more than the correction of error; but it was not part of the Common Law. Furthermore, the Privy Council lost its jurisdiction in 1641 when the parliamentary party abolished the conciliar courts. For the formative period of the English Common Law the power of the royal courts and the importance of their procedure at first instance meant that appeal in the civilian, or the modern English, sense could not exist.

8.11   REMEDIES NOT RIGHTS

8.11.1   The stress hitherto has been on the procedural nature of the Common Law; this is largely due to its being a system which offered remedies not rights, just like classical Roman law. The outlines of a rational system of obligations were discernible in the work of Glanvill who, like Bracton, was in the tradition of those who wrote about customary law in the light of the learned law. The total disappearance of the latter element from the Common

Law before the fourteenth century meant that English law had to learn afresh how to move from formal *stricti iuris* contracts to ones based on good faith, that is, from the verbal and literal contracts to the real (except that these were never really understood) and consensual contracts. English lawyers had to tread this path as though for the first time, when men like Dumoulin in France (see para 12.3.2-3) had a body of principle and of rational discussion from which it was possible to draw when they were involved in the administration of their local law.

8.11.2 There were three early personal obligations enforced by writ: covenant, debt and account. Covenant, enforced by the writ *praecipe*, was formal, in that the agreement had to be contained in a written document under seal; oral agreements remained enforceable in local courts, but subject to the 40 shilling limit imposed there in the later thirteenth century by the Statute of Westminster II.

8.11.3 Debt was seen not as a real contract but as unjust detention. Only much later did lawyers find an implied promise to pay when a debt arose out of a transaction such as sale or loan; the writ said flatly that the debtor owed something to the pursuer and unjustly detained it from him (so early was the English habit of seeing a wrong to be remedied rather than a right to be enforced). A comparable action, called *detinue*, was available to recover personal property, often where there had been a deposit or a loan; where there had been no grant to the defender by the owner it was called *detinue sur trover*, or simply *trover*. Debt was a contract entirely *stricti iuris*; if a debtor had paid up but had not recovered his bond nor obtained a sealed document of receipt, he had no remedy in Common Law against another claim – hence one cause of Chancery's jurisdiction. In actual cases payment was made, but the creditor recovered the bond by force and raised his action again; he would be successful, but the debtor had an action in trespass for the seizure of the bond, and the damages he was awarded might cover the second payment he had made.[45] The contract of debt lacked inherently the element of good faith, although conditions could be endorsed on the bond. Moreover, because debt was a private matter in most cases and so unsuitable for putting to a jury, the defendant must deny it by compurgation (wager of law). One could not wage another's law and so when a debtor died his 'debts' died with him; his executors could not wage his law.

45 Baker (1990) p 369, fn 38.

8.11.4 The third personal action, account, was as much proprietary as contractual and primarily applied between bailiff and lord. All three actions were effectively dead by the seventeenth century, partly because of the equitable relief offered by Chancery and partly because of developments in the Common Law itself which, through the development of trespass, enlarged the scope of contractual liability.

8.11.5 A trespass is a wrongdoing, a delict; the writ *praecipe* ordered someone to do something in the future but the writ for trespass ordered the defender to show why – *ostensurus quare* – he had done something in the past. Any wrong which was a breach of the king's peace, actual or threatened, and in the end fictitious, could be brought before the royal courts. For example, in 1317 a plaintiff bought wine from the defendants which he left with them until he could arrange delivery; his count stated that the defendants had drawn off much of the wine with force and arms, to wit with swords, bows and arrows, and had topped up the cask with salt water so that the wine was totally spoilt, to the plaintiff's great damage and against the king's peace.[46] The King's Bench fairly soon found itself prepared to entertain claims even when no force of arms was alleged. The first known case in which the royal courts used trespass to impose contractual liability is the *Humber Ferry Case* of 1348. The plaintiff complained that the defendant, the ferryman, had undertaken to transport his mare across the Humber but had so overloaded his ferry that it sank, and the mare was drowned; King's Bench held that this was a trespass, rejecting defending counsel's plea that no action lay since there had been no covenant – covenant would not, anyway, have compensated the plaintiff for the loss of his mare. The second such case is *Waldron v Marshall* in 1369. A horse doctor had undertaken the care of a horse which had died through his neglect; he was held liable in trespass. In these early cases there was no doubt that the defendant had undertaken to do a thing and had then done it badly; there was a positive act which could be interpreted as falling within the terms of the writ of trespass. If the defendant's fault was that he had done nothing, it was much more necessary to stress that he had undertaken to act and was therefore in breach of his duty and so had committed a trespass. Thus *assumpsit* (he assumed [a duty]) came into being.

46 Milsom, p 289.

8.11.6 *Assumpsit* became a regular action for breach of contract during the sixteenth century. However, to ground the action it was originally necessary for there to be an element of wrongdoing, such as misfeasance or deceit, and it was not until around 1600 that this was regularly accepted as a fiction. Also it was required that the plaintiff had suffered real detriment, which was interpreted as meaning that there must have been consideration. The Common lawyers' first interpretation of consideration was not far from the civilian *causa*, the reason why the law should hold a promise to be a serious undertaking; in the later sixteenth century consideration was established as the immediate explanation for the promise, and it must be something financially measurable of fitting value and not already paid over.

8.11.7 The next move was to bring claims for money, for debt, under *assumpsit*; this was finally settled in 1602 by *Slade's Case*, when all the Common Law judges, with such noted figures as Coke and Bacon as counsel, argued over a period of five years a particular claim to payment for a crop of wheat and finally came to the decision that *assumpsit* to pay what was due was implicit in every executory contract. This for practical purposes put an end to the wager of law (compurgation) which was eventually abolished in 1833. Further, in 1612 all the judges came to agree that *assumpsit* was sufficiently contractual in nature for money debts as well as others to lie against executors. In spite of its delictual youth *assumpsit* had come to be reckoned as a contract – or an action for breach of contract – although it could still be brought as an action in tort for a malfeasance. There remained technical problems in the pleadings but thereafter there was a unified law of contract. This also covered obligations *quasi ex contractu* where there was no prior agreement; further, where money had been paid in error there was a variant of *assumpsit* called *indebitatus*. In the seventeenth century English lawyers imported a fictional promise to pay as well as a fictional tort. This was still a society where the Common Law courts would not hear the evidence of the parties even in civil matters because their testimony would be biased; this inability to question their intentions goes some way to explain the doctrine of consideration as indicating intent. Another English aberration was to insist on a sealed document rather than on the simpler formality of writing where there was no consideration to ground an *assumpsit*. Lord Mansfield (1705–1793) would have been quite happy to accept writing as a substitute for consideration in commercial cases, but the House of Lords held to the magic of the seal.

8.11.8 We may end this rapid sketch of the English lawyers' approach to obligations with a quotation. Baker could still write in 1990:

> 'Since 1833, for example, there had been an election between trespass and case, so long as the wrong complained of was not wilful. But what is the substantive distinction, if any, between trespass and case? The election between conversion and detinue remained important until a statute of 1977 declared curtly that "detinue is abolished". But what exactly was thereby abolished? . . . "The forms of action we have buried" said Maitland at the turn of the century, "but they still rule us from their graves". The passage of years has only gradually diminished their influence. . . . The categories of common-law thought were in a way closed in 1832.'[47]

Despite Bracton, despite Blackstone's timid references to Natural Law in the eighteenth century, English lawyers have looked largely to their own past, to the magic of the seal and the sacred cow of the jury; their skill and ingenuity have laboriously brought them to ends they could have reached centuries earlier if they had shared in the mainstream of European legal development.

---

47 Baker (1990) p 81; his language is modified from the first edition because 'in 1980 the immemorial writ formula itself was finally abandoned'.

FURTHER READING

JH Baker	*An Introduction to English Legal History* (London, 3rd edn, 1990)
	The Order of Serjeants at Law (London, 1984)
	'The third university of England: the inns of court and the common law tradition' (Selden Society Lecture, 1990)
	The Common Law Tradition: lawyers, books and the law (London, 1999)
RC van Caenegem	*The Birth of the English Common Law* (CUP, 2nd edn, 1988)
	Legal History: A European Perspective (London, 1991) ch 7

MT Clanchy   *England and its Rulers 1066–1272* (Fontana, 1983)
DR Coquillette   *The Civilian Writers of Doctors' Commons, London* (Berlin, 1988)
                        The Anglo-American Legal Heritage. Introductory Materials (Durham NC, 2000)
A Harding   *The Law Courts of Mediaeval England* (London, 1973)
D Herlihy   *The History of Feudalism* (New York, 1970)
D Ibbetson   *An Historical Introduction to the Law of Obligations* (OUP, 1999)
HR Loyn   *The Governance of Anglo-Saxon England 500–1087* (London, 1984)
SFC Milsom   *Historical Foundations of the Common Law* (London, 2nd edn, 1981)
Selden Society publications (London), particularly: vols 90, 96, and 97–98 on various eyres
P Wormald   *The Making of English Law*, vol I, *King Alfred to the Twelfth Century* (Blackwell, 1999)

Chapter 9

FEUDAL SCOTLAND

9.1 PRE-FEUDAL SCOTLAND

9.1.1 By the mid-eleventh century the Scottish kings ruled over an area roughly equivalent to modern mainland Scotland, although the Western Isles, and Orkney and Shetland were in Scandinavian hands; the former were added to the kingdom in the thirteenth century and the latter in the fifteenth. The people whom they ruled had various origins, the Picts of the North, the Scots of Dalriada or Argyll (like Galloway, not far across the sea from Celtic Ireland), the Britons of Galloway and Strathclyde and, in the south-east, men of Anglo-Saxon stock from what had been Northumbria north of the river Tweed.

9.1.2 Comparatively little is known of the law of Scotland in the pre-feudal era, although we may be certain that it was essentially tribal custom, varied and largely unwritten. The evidence of a later period suggests that until well into the eleventh century the laws (perhaps even in the south-east) were predominantly of the Celtic type; we assume that customs were broadly similar to those of Celtic Ireland, about which much more is known.

9.1.3 Celtic society was essentially kindred-based and the kin features prominently in the laws and customs of Celtic Scotland. The earliest evidence of land law is to be found in the *Book of Deer*, a ninth-century manuscript from a monastery in Aberdeenshire, to which were added Gaelic notes recording grants of land made to the monastery during the eleventh and twelfth centuries. These notes refer to various burdens on land. When feudal tenure was introduced these burdens were often turned into feudal incidents. Of the courts of Celtic Scotland and of their procedure there is little evidence. The *Book of Deer* makes reference to the brehon (or judge) but of his functions we know virtually nothing save that they were probably declarative, like those of the Irish brehons. Proof by compurgation was a feature of Celtic procedure generally and is likely to have been used in Scotland. There seems also to have been use of pledges or cautioners (sureties) for due appearance and the like; the Gaelic word for such a pledge is *culreach* and the word survived as a technical legal term – but requiring explanation – in the legal treatises of the feudal period.

9.1.4 The administration of justice in Celtic society reflects law at an early stage of development. The king's peace, together with penalties for its violation, seems to have been early recognized, but wrongs such as killing or

theft were primarily a matter for the individual concerned or for his kin.
The function of the court was not far from that of an arbiter, aiming to limit
the extent of private vengeance; retaliation was gradually replaced by an
elaborate system of pecuniary compensations with the amount payable
depending on the nature of the wrong and the rank of the party wronged.
Evidence of this system is to be found in an early collection known as the
Laws of the Bretts and Scots. Procedure on wrong also underlines the
importance of the kin in Celtic society; as well as the victim, the victim's
kin was entitled to compensation.

9.1.5   The extent of the survival of Celtic law is obscure. In the twelfth
century Anglo-Norman law was introduced into Lowland Scotland. Celtic
custom stayed in use in the Highlands, as it did in Galloway, a southern
province but remote and inaccessible. A statute of 1245 states that Galloway
'has its own special laws' (for making criminal accusations), and as late as
1385 a plea was made for the preservation of the custom of Galloway on all
points. In the Highlands the law of marriage shows the survival of Gaelic
custom. The marriage customs of Gaelic society differed greatly from the
canon law; divorce and re-marriage were permitted, and seemingly common,
while the canonical rules on the prohibited degrees were largely unknown.
There is some evidence to suggest that these customs were being followed
even in the seventeenth century; the Statutes of Iona of 1609, designed to
regulate the Highlands, declared, among other matters, that marriages
contracted for a term of years were to be illegal. Celtic law seems then to
have survived until at least the close of the Middle Ages in certain parts of
Scotland, but it is doubtful how far its rules made any contribution to Scots
law after the time of Stair. Further research may, however, show that Celtic
custom helped to mould the developing legal institutions of the modern
period.

9.2   THE CROWN AND THE INTRODUCTION OF FEUDALISM

9.2.1   In 1124 David I succeeded to the throne of Scotland; it was a time
when Scotland was growing in population and prosperity. The new king had
lived at the English court and married an English heiress and so was familiar
with the structure and institutions of the Anglo-Norman state. He took that
as his model when he determined that his kingdom must be improved as
part of the European-wide twelfth-century renaissance. Accordingly, under
David and his successors the government of Scotland was reformed on a
model similar to that of England, although in the course of time significant
differences emerged. Tenure of land was gradually transformed into feudal
tenure; prominent among the beneficiaries of the new feudal grants were
men of Anglo-Norman origin who had come north with David or who were
subsequently attracted to the opportunities which Scotland offered. The
country was thus provided – or at least the Lowlands were – with a new
style of aristocracy, but the older Celtic order was not entirely swamped by
the new regime. A native lord could protect his landownership by obtaining
a written title, a charter, and many of the feudal incidents found in the charters
are simply Celtic burdens and duties under the new French or Latin names.

9.2.2   Feudal law generally was the subject of Chapter 2. Perhaps it is worth restating that feudal and customary usage blend so well together that in many cases there is no point in distinguishing between them, but only in contrasting feudal custom with institutions derived from the civil law. 'Feudal' seems the more suitable term, however, where the language of modern law continues to speak of feus and feudal rights. In Scotland, as elsewhere, at the heart of the new structure was the fief, the lands held by a feudal tenant of his lord for a specified return. Charters recording rights in land seem to have become normal during the thirteenth century. The charter provided evidence of a tenant's right to his land and other rights as well, and sometimes also of what was due from him; it is therefore not surprising that they were carefully preserved and many still survive. The services owed by these tenants naturally varied. The classic form of Anglo-Norman feudal tenure was by the provision of one or more armed knights for so many days a year. Such military tenure, known as ward-holding, is found in Scotland as well as in England, but the burdens imposed in Scotland tended to be lighter; one example is the great Bruce fief of Annandale – one of the largest in the country – which appears to have been held for the services of only ten knights. Other forms of Scottish tenure also had their English counterparts. Lands granted to the Church were normally held in free alms, no return being required other than the saying of Masses for the granter and his family; burgh land was held in free burgage, owing a money rent and duties within the burgh, typically watching and warding. In Scotland subinfeudation was always possible, except in the burghs; Scotland never knew a statutory limitation, such as the English *Quia Emptores* (1290).

9.2.3   Characteristically Scottish was the tenure known as feu-ferme, because it does not seem reckoned as simply the commutation of knight-service. (In much of Scotland fighting remained a necessary aspect of life, regardless of formal obligation.) Its origins lay in the needs of the king when the old Celtic burdens were feudalized, or commuted into money; in its developed form it was the heritable holding of land in return for the annual payment of a fixed sum of money, the 'ferme' or feu-duty. Feu-ferme tenure became general as Scotland progressed towards a more money-based economy; it gave the feudal superior a guaranteed annual income and, of importance to an original granter, its creation was normally accompanied by the payment to the lord of a substantial lump sum, the *grassum*. The recording of landholding in this form is found in the twelfth century and was widespread from the later Middle Ages onwards; in the century or so before the Reformation the Church set much land in feu-ferme, and in the same period the feuing of its land was a policy actively pursued by the Crown. The older and more onerous feudal tenures declined from the fourteenth century onwards; new sub-grants on such tenure were not made and feu-ferme tenure emerged as the normal mode of landholding in Scotland.

9.2.4   Feudalism also involved the dispersal of governmental powers and in particular of the administration of justice. By the thirteenth century the king was seen as the fount of all secular justice; justice was administered by others – in feudal theory – only to the extent that the right to do so had been delegated to them by the Crown. However, the Scottish king, like other kings, could not be everywhere at once nor hope to deal with all judicial matters in person; delegation was necessary. It must also be remembered that the king's delegates

– justiciar, sheriff, chamberlain – performed a variety of general administrative tasks as well as their judicial duties. The king had his own court, the *curia regis*; it was the confluence of both his administrative and judicial functions and met indifferently for both purposes. Its composition was fluid because it was composed of those from whom the king sought aid and counsel; there was no inherent distinction between the smaller group of any king's regular advisers – what was to become the council proper – and any larger group called by the king and meeting *in parliamento*. (We shall consider the composition of parliament shortly; see para 9.7.2.) By the end of the thirteenth century the parliament functioned regularly as a court of law when it met, and had become the usual forum for the dispensing of royal justice by the king in person.

9.2.5   The office of justice appears in Scotland under David I, as an individual to whom specific cases (criminal or civil) were remitted by the king. By 1200 these cases were so many that the jurisdiction of the justiciar (for so he is called from c. 1210) could be defined as covering serious criminal cases and important pleas concerning land. By then he was a royal officer who provided a link between central government and the localities, travelling around the country on periodic ayres. He exercised some general governmental powers as well as hearing appeals from the shrieval and baronial courts. From the treatise compiled around 1292 and known as *The Scottish King's Household* it appears that the justice ayres were held twice a year. The justiciars were concerned with both criminal and civil jurisdiction. In the former sphere the justiciar could hear the pleas of the Crown, including murder, rape, robbery and arson, which were excluded from the jurisdiction of sheriffs and barons. His civil jurisdiction included the settlement of boundary disputes by the process of perambulation of marches, and also cases raised by pleadable brieves (comparable to the English writs); brieves will be discussed shortly. His court seems to have been expected to act as a filter; *The Scottish King's Household* says that the justiciar was to dispense justice in such a way that 'no plaints should be presented to the king save only those which, because the justices and sheriffs have failed to deal with them, cannot be remedied without the presence of the king himself'. There were normally several justiciars at any one time, and Scotland was divided into regions each of which was served by one or more of them. In the later thirteenth century there were three, for Lothian, Scotia (Scotland north of the Forth) and Galloway, but after 1305 there seem normally to have been two, one north and one south of the Forth. The king's chamberlain, his finance officer, also went on ayre to visit the royal burghs for the collection of dues, the supervision of their administration, and for hearing appeals from their courts.

9.3   SHERIFFS

9.3.1   Sheriffs and sheriffdoms were Anglo-Norman institutions, imported into Scotland from England. A sheriffdom was an administrative division of the country with at its centre (or *caput*) a castle, usually royal, or later a burgh which had grown up around such a castle; it was, however, some time before the whole country was thus provided. Only during the thirteenth century were sheriffdoms created in the northern and western parts of Scotland.

9.3.2 The sheriff was the king's officer, normally chosen from among the moderately great men of the realm. Initially, there appears to have been no established practice as to the term for which the office was held, but many sheriffdoms became hereditary; this was so at the beginning of the fourteenth century in Selkirk, Kinross and Cromarty, and the process continued, despite an attempt in 1455 by parliament to forbid any future gifts of office 'in fee and heritage'. The sheriff was permitted to appoint deputies and this soon became common practice; as time went on the heritable sheriff-principal became mainly a figure-head, leaving most of his duties to be performed by his deputies. These duties covered a wide range, administrative, judicial, financial and military, for the sheriff was the normal local agent of the Crown; many acts of parliament imposed on the sheriff the task of carrying out the measures they contained.

9.3.3 The principal judicial function of the sheriff by 1300 was to hold the sheriff court; in effect, within each sheriffdom it was the king's baron court. By the fourteenth century there were head, or full, courts three times a year at Yule (Christmas), Pasch (Easter) and Michaelmas (29 September) and these met at the *caput* of the sheriffdom. The sheriff usually presided in person, and all who owed suit of court (see para 2.3.2) were expected to attend. Here the more important cases were dealt with; if necessary, a case could be transferred to it from one of the intermediate (or lesser) sheriff courts, which could be held at other places within the sheriffdom. These intermediate courts dealt with the more routine or trivial matters; the presiding officer was usually a sheriff-depute, and not all who owed suit were called on to attend these lesser sessions. Suitors were nevertheless necessary because, by custom, the power of making decisions rested with them, not with the holder of the court. Suit of court was a feudal burden, but in the charters a distinction seems to be drawn between attendance at head courts, which was normally an absolute duty – although it could be performed by proxy – and at intermediate courts, which probably required due and specific notice. Not all tenants of the Crown within a sheriffdom were required to perform suit of court. Those who held their lands in blenche-ferme, that is, for a nominal return such as 'a rose in the season of roses', were generally exempt, as were church lands held in free alms, and exemption could be granted by the Crown as a special favour.

9.3.4 The sheriff had both a criminal and a civil jurisdiction, but these were subject to certain limitations. In the criminal field, he was not permitted to deal with the pleas of the Crown. The evidence of *Quoniam Attachiamenta*[1] suggests that the pleadable brieves of mortancestor, dissasine and breach of the king's protection (and possibly others) could normally only be pursued before the justiciar. Certain classes of person were not justiciable in the sheriff's court, most notably burgesses in matters of burgh law, and those living within a regality (where the lord exercised what was virtually the king's own jurisdiction and so excluded that of the sheriff). It was also possible to obtain exemption from the jurisdiction of a particular sheriff on the grounds of 'deadly enmity and feud' where there was an existing dispute or quarrel between an individual party and the sheriff.

---

1   A fourteenth-century treatise on procedure, which will be discussed in the next section; chapters 36-42 in the modern edition of the text printed in Stair Society, vol 44 (1996), deal with these pleadable brieves.

9.3.5   Nevertheless, the judicial powers of the sheriff were extensive. Provided that the culprit was caught red-handed the sheriff's criminal jurisdiction even extended in practice to murder and robbery as well as to all the lesser offences. As civil judge,

> 'the sheriff could decide actions of molestation, removing, ejection, spuilzie, and personal actions of all kinds; he could authorize poindings and apprisings; before him . . . brieves of inquest, terce, tutory and idiotry could be served.'[2]

In other words, the sheriff could hear actions dealing with such matters as dispossession from land and moveables, and distraint of lands and goods for debt, as well as brieves relating to a widow's claim to a liferent of a share of her husband's heritable property, and to the appointment of guardians for the incapable. The sheriff also had oversight of lesser courts within the sheriffdom and it was to his court that reference was made from these inferior jurisdictions. Moreover, in theory no baron could hold a court of 'life and limb' or resort to proof by ordeal unless the sheriff or his representative was present to see that justice was done and due process observed. And it was the sheriff who arranged the holding of the justiciar's court when he came on ayre, and who presented for indictment all persons charged with those crimes reserved to the Crown.

---

2   W Croft Dickinson, *The Sheriff Court Book of Fife, 1515–22* (Scottish History Society, 3rd series, vol 12, 1928), xxxviii and App. B. Brieves of right were also important in the shrieval administration of justice; see HL McQueen, 'The brieve of right in Scots law' *JLH* 3 (1982) 52.

9.4   FEUDAL COURTS AND BURGH COURTS

9.4.1   Built into the feudal structure was the right of a lord to hold a court for his tenants; it seems possible that in Scotland this right needed to be made explicit in each lord's charter. Like the sheriff, the lord normally held three head courts a year; at these the business of his free tenants was settled. His lesser courts were usually manorial courts for those who held by unfree or nonfeudal tenure. The lord or his bailie presided and his feudal tenants who owed suit of court attended the head courts to deliver their verdicts. Such courts dealt with matters related to feudal holdings and similar concerns, and with such crimes as assault, theft and riot, which were not reserved to the Crown.

9.4.2   As well as holding his feudal courts a lord might exercise a franchise jurisdiction (territorial rather than tenurial), just as in England grants were made of hundredal jurisdiction. The exact limits of such a grant would be defined in a charter, but they normally included sake and soke (as in England, see para 8.3.3) and also the power to hang persons living within the franchise. From the early fourteenth century such a lord is described as holding of the king *in liberam baroniam* (in free barony). Grants were also made *in liberam regalitatem* (in free regality), more extensive than free barony. Such franchises have been described as amounting to petty kingdoms, for the court of the regality might exercise a jurisdiction almost equal to that of the king and include the pleas of the Crown, save only treason. As a result, the king's writ did not run in a regality, which had its own chancery issuing its own brieves, and neither justiciar nor sheriff had jurisdiction over the lands of the regality or its inhabitants.

9.4.3 Burghs were towns which had been granted the special status of burgh by charter. When they first appeared in Scotland, during the twelfth century, they were always granted their status by the Crown; later we find burghs holding of other lords, lay and ecclesiastical. To encourage the growth of trade they were accorded various rights and privileges, administrative as well as judicial, including a monopoly of foreign trade which lasted until as late as 1672. By the later Middle Ages, Scottish burghs were largely self-governing communities, electing their own officers and employing their own seal in matters affecting the town. From the early fourteenth century they began to acquire feu-ferme status; the community would pay to its superior a fixed annual sum in place of the various negotiable individual burdens, of which the collection and payment remained the responsibility of the burgh officers.

9.4.4 Each burgh had its own court to which the burgesses owed suit; this burgh jurisdiction in many matters excluded that of the sheriff. The burgh administered its own law and customs, which might differ considerably from the general law of the land; for example, tenure of burgh land did not usually include feudal casualties of ward and relief. Burghs applied the common law too, hearing cases involving, for example, brieves of right and distress. From their very nature (see para 6.4) burgh courts were also concerned with matters of trade, such as settlement of disputes between merchants, the control of markets and the enforcement of standard weights and measures. From the burgh court appeals went to the king's chamberlain, who visited the burghs on periodic ayres. The chamberlain also presided over the Court of the Four Burghs which was composed of representatives from four towns, Berwick, Edinburgh, Roxburgh and Stirling; when Berwick and Roxburgh were occupied by the English after 1369, they were replaced by Lanark and Linlithgow. The *Leges Quattuor Burgorum* (*Laws of the Four Burghs*) is a collection of material, some probably going back to the twelfth century; much of it was derived from the customs of Newcastle and general mercantile usage. It may never have been applied directly as burgh law but provided a model for the particular customs of individual burghs. The Court of the Four Burghs heard falsing of dooms from the chamberlain's jurisdiction and also disputes between burghs; doubtful points of burgh law could be referred there for clarification. Membership of the court was gradually expanded to include representatives of most of the Scottish burghs, and during the fifteenth and sixteenth centuries it became more a convention and less a court of law. The term disappeared in the early sixteenth century and the institution was replaced in the 1550s by the Convention of Royal Burghs, which thereafter represented the interests of the burghs.

9.5   PROCEDURE IN FEUDAL SCOTLAND

9.5.1 There were considerable innovations in legal procedure in Anglo-Norman Scotland, in particular the introduction of the inquest (the jury of which facts were inquired) and the writ or brieve. It seems likely that, after the initial introduction of some English usages, for a time the two kingdoms followed a course of parallel development, with Scotland's borrowings from England (compare 8.6) being selective and adapted to its needs. The inquest was originally used solely on the Crown's authority and to ascertain the extent of royal rights, in much the same style as for the compilation of the Domesday Book. The judicial use of the jury of inquest remained a royal prerogative, and its employment by others needed a specific grant – usually for a price; this did, however, become a benefit as a matter of course for a litigant who initiated his action by the purchase of an initial brieve from the royal chancery.

9.5.2   The Scottish brieve of right was the equivalent of the English writ of right, being the brieve which initiated process over title to land. The English writ was only concerned with tenants-in-chief; there was an analogous writ for land held of some lesser lord. Scotland knew only the one form (as far as we can judge from the records) which seems to have applied to tenants-in-chief; perhaps the same procedure was used for settling other disputes as to title. The Scottish brieve of dissasine seems to have been a more general remedy than the English novel disseisin, since it did not incorporate a fixed term for the dispossession. Similarly, the Scottish brieve of mortancestor was a broader remedy than mort d'ancestor, not being limited by a fixed term and coming to cover a wider class of ancestor. The differences may be due partly to the utility of specifically Scottish brieves such as perambulation, and partly to the early technical development of English law with its professional bench and bar and highly skilled Chancery clerks. Scottish judges were largely untrained laymen, and the country lacked anything approaching an established central court until the fifteenth century. In other words, circumstances led to an increasing divergence.

9.5.3   Procedure by brieve remained normal throughout the Middle Ages and a number of fourteenth-century registers survive. Brieves were still important during the fifteenth century but after 1500 the system began to decline (compare para 8.6.9-11). An Act of 1491 restricted the categories of brieves to those then existing; no new forms were to be introduced. About the same time the brieve was beginning to be displaced by the summons as a means of initiating judicial process. In the courts based on the king's council, which were the ancestors of the Court of Session and which had in effect given Scotland a central court by the end of the fifteenth century, the brieve was never competent as a means of initiating an action. Even in those courts where the brieve was competent, it seems gradually to have given way to the summons via the brieve of citation; that is, a brieve which was initially designed to compel the attendance of witnesses gradually acquired the more substantive function of summoning the defender to court to answer the pursuer's allegations. The advantage of the summons was that the pursuer did not need to fit his case into the formula of an existing brieve; he need only state that he had been wronged, leaving the details of his claim until a later stage. Accordingly, the mediaeval pleadable brieves eventually disappeared.

9.6   EARLY LEGAL LITERATURE

9.6.1   It is clear that from at least the thirteenth century there began to appear in most European countries writings inspired by the learned law but dealing with local customs – the beginnings of national legal literature. Mediaeval Scotland shared in this movement, but scholarship has done less work to reveal the Scottish details than for the treatises of England or France or Germany. The two best known of the Scottish treatises, *Regiam Majestatem* and *Quoniam Attachiamenta*, are available in modern editions but the first is unsatisfactory, the text repeating Skene's edition of 1609 (see para 9.7.3); the new edition of *Quoniam* (by TD Fergus) supplants the older one (see para 9.3.4, fn 1). Other treatises, such as the *Liber de Iudicibus* (*Book of Judges*), remain unedited among the manuscript sources.

9.6.2 *Regiam Majestatem* (*Royal Majesty* – the opening words) is essentially a commentary on the procedures followed in the royal courts in both civil and criminal matters. It is heavily based on *Glanvill*, but it is nevertheless more than a reissue of the English book for Scottish use. A substantial section is direct citation, but other material from *Glanvill* was adapted to take account of Scottish conditions. There is also a significant proportion of the text which owes nothing to *Glanvill*; in particular, the first dozen or so chapters seem in essentials original. Much of Book IV, which deals with criminal law and procedure, appears to have been drawn from the statutes and assizes of the Scottish kings. At the end of Book I and the start of Book II comes a section dealing with pacts, arbiters and arbitration, serfs, and gifts between husband and wife; this section has a definite romano-canonical flavour and seems to have been drawn from the canonist Geoffrey (Goffredus) of Trano. The evidence for the direct influence of Roman law, the law of the *Corpus Iuris Civilis*, as opposed to a debt to other works which were influenced by civilian learning, is not strong. The opening words may reflect Justinian's opening of *Imperatoriam Maiestatem* (Imperial Majesty) for his Institutions, but it is more likely that they simply echo *Glanvill*. Again, the argument that the division into four books is a deliberate imitation of the structure of Justinian's Institutions is weakened by an examination of the manuscripts. The oldest manuscript tradition reveals a division into three not four parts; the fourfold division may well be due to civilian influence, but an influence exerted much later than the original composition of *Regiam Majestatem*. The date of the treatise is problematical. The better view is in favour of the early fourteenth century – fairly late in the European context – for in 1318 the Scottish parliament enacted a number of reforming statutes dealing with procedure by brieve. These seem to be reflected in the treatise's handling of the brieve of right in a way which suggests that the passage is an integral part of the text and not an intruding gloss.

9.6.3 Associated with *Regiam Majestatem* and sometimes overshadowed by it is the treatise known from its opening words as *Quoniam Attachiamenta* (*Since Attachments*). Along with the *Regiam* it is referred to in a statute of 1425 as one of 'the books of law of this realm', and it was still being so described in 1566. *Quoniam Attachiamenta* would appear to have been compiled somewhat later than *Regiam Majestatem*, probably at some time in the fourteenth century. *Quoniam* seems to have been an exclusively Scottish work, owing no obvious debt to any English treatise. Its subject matter is procedure but, unlike *Regiam*, the emphasis is on procedure in the baronial courts, and this presumably accounts for the alternative title found in some manuscripts, the *Leges Baronum* (*Laws of the Barons*). The compiler of

Quoniam, as of *Regiam*, is unknown, but seems likely to have been someone involved in the practice of the courts which he described.

9.6.4   During the Middle Ages, Scotland was to some degree affected by the revival of Roman law on the continent, but it was some time before its doctrines began to be of direct or substantial influence. The place of Roman law in *Regiam Majestatem* has already been dealt with. Some of the other mediaeval law tracts show their compilers' acquaintance with the learned law. The vocabulary used is often Roman – hardly surprising since Latin was the common language – and occasionally a distinction is drawn between the Roman and Scottish uses of a term; for example, *Regiam* notes that in Scotland the word *dos* (dowry) is normally used to mean 'that which a free man gives to his bride at the church on the occasion of their marriage', whereas in Roman law it signified what in Scotland was normally termed *maritagium* – 'the portion given to the husband along with the wife'. Further evidence of a knowledge of Roman law, or at least of its terminology, is to be found in several of the charters preserved by Scottish monasteries, in the form of renunciations of Roman remedies and of pleas in defence. Among those which have been noted are *restitutio in integrum*, the provisions of the *Senatusconsultum Velleianum*, which prohibited a married woman from standing as surety for others (including her husband), and the *beneficium divisionis*, which provided that when one of a number of co-cautioners (co-sureties in English terminology) was sued for the whole debt, he could insist on his liability being limited to his proportionate share.[3]

3   However, these seem to be inserted only in order to exhibit the drafter's knowledge, because the last two anyway could not have had any actual effect in mediaeval Scotland.

9.7   THE FIFTEENTH CENTURY

9.7.1   A crisis over the succession followed the death of King Alexander III in 1286, and this led to the Wars of Independence when the Scots resisted the attempts of Edward I of England to impose himself on Scotland as the feudal superior of the kingdom. For three hundred years England was the enemy, frequently at open war, and Scotland looked to the mainland of Europe for her political allies, and also for guidance on matters of law and legal doctrine. There appears to have been some degree of economic and administrative confusion in the aftermath of the Wars of Independence, and the machinery of justice probably did not work so well in the fourteenth as in the thirteenth century. The many statutes of the fifteenth century enjoining the regular holding of justice-ayres would suggest that the ayres, if held at all, had become by then more irregular; the repetition hints at non-observance. Similarly, the pressure of judicial business experienced by the Crown during the fifteenth century, when steadily more litigants sought a remedy in the king's court, may indicate that local justice was not being provided, or was being provided in less than an impartial way. On the other hand, the preference for royal (and for ecclesiastical) justice may be attributable to its superior quality, as it adopted romano-canonical procedure and administered an improved substantive law.

9.7.2 By the fifteenth century parliament, although still a fluid body, clearly had a structure, composed of the estates of the realm. The basis of the estates was that they were the different classes of tenants in chief. The great secular lords were expected to attend on the king in person; the lesser lords came sometimes as individuals, when they counted as one estate with the magnates, and sometimes as shire commissioners, when they formed a separate estate. The upper clergy, bishops and abbots, formed an estate of the clergy; burgesses, who came from the royal burghs which held collectively from the king, formed yet another estate. There were usually reckoned to be three estates – lords, clergy, and burgesses – but sometimes there were four when the shire commissioners formed a separate group. (Unlike in England, nobody had a hereditary right to a seat in parliament, although his hereditary right to his land would entitle him to attend.) In any event, during the fifteenth century, parliament began to show an interest in reform of the law, both in the administration of justice and in the substantive law. For example, in the law of leases at the beginning of the fifteenth century, a tenant holding under a contract of lease had a personal right only; if his landlord alienated the land, the tenant was without protection from eviction by the new owner. In 1429 a tenant was given security of tenure for one year, unless the landlord required the land for his own use. In 1450 a tenant was given security of tenure for the currency of his lease, even when ownership of the land changed hands during that period. In 1469 it was enacted that a creditor of the landlord was no longer to be permitted to recover the debt by distraint of the tenant's goods or the tenancy itself. It looks as though the men who came to parliament were consciously pursuing a policy of reform in this field.

9.7.3 Parliament was also concerned to settle authentic and accurate texts of the law in force – both recent statute and the 'auld lawes', that is, the various treatises and statutes of the fourteenth century or earlier. In 1425 a parliamentary commission was appointed to 'see and examine the books of law of this realm, that is to say *Regiam Majestatem* and *Quoniam Attachiamenta*, and mend the laws that need amendment'. In 1469 another commission was appointed to reduce 'the king's laws, *Regiam Majestatem*, acts, statutes and other books' which were 'to be put in a volume and to be authorized and the rest to be destroyed'. Nothing concrete appears to have resulted, and other similar commissions appointed during the next century seem to have been little more successful. In the later 1500s various collections of post-1424 statute law were published, but it was not until 1609 that an authoritative and enduring compilation of the 'auld lawes' was published by Sir John Skene, and a useful handbook for practice was thus provided.

9.7.4 The fifteenth century in Scotland, as on the continent, was a period when changes were taking place not only in the substantive law but also in the structure of the courts. The king's council in parliament, when sitting as the supreme feudal court, was competent to deal with questions of fee and heritage, whereas the king's council in the narrower sense was not. It has been remarked (see para 9.2.4) that by the end of the thirteenth century parliament sat as a court of law, and in 1399 it was enacted that the king was to hold annual parliaments 'so that his subjects be served of the law'. During the fourteenth century delegation from the full parliament to auditors became regular practice in dealing with judicial business which was too lengthy or too trivial for the full parliament. By 1466 (when the surviving regular and official records of parliament begin) it was normal for parliament to appoint two judicial committees of auditors, one *ad iudicia contradicta* (for the falsing of dooms, or challenges to the decisions of lower courts) and one *ad causas et querelas* (for disputes and complaints – cases at first instance). However, the competence of these committees lasted no longer than the sitting of the parliament which appointed them.

9.7.5   Matters which needed judicial redress when parliament was not sitting could not be ignored, and so the king's more permanent council had to deal with them. But it was concerned with the general business of government and had neither time nor established machinery for regular judicial sittings. James I, in his personal reign (1424–1437), tried to deal with the problem by sending litigants back to the ordinary courts and making the council a tribunal of last resort. The pressure, however, continued and in 1426 parliament enacted that the chamberlain (or perhaps chancellor), and with him certain discreet persons of the three estates chosen by the king were to 'sit henceforth three times in the year to examine and finally determine all and sundry complaints, causes and quarrels that may be determined before the king's council'. In other words, a group of men was appointed to sit – or to hold sessions – to dispose of judicial business on behalf of the council; its jurisdiction was not as great as that of parliament.

9.7.6   There were modifications to the scheme in 1439 and 1456. There were to be three groups, each consisting of nine members; each group was to sit for a month, at first in Edinburgh and thereafter wherever it seemed most expedient; the judgment of such a session was exempt from appeal to king or parliament. Parliament continued to appoint sessions during the 1460s, but thereafter we hear no more of these particular judicial bodies. The repeated statutory appointment of sessions suggests that they were not intended to be permanent institutions. Even though they exercised a very wide jurisdiction, their existence did not mean the cessation of the work of the parliamentary auditors and of the council itself.

9.7.7   However, the jurisdiction of the parliamentary auditors did fade away in the later fifteenth century. The committee which dealt with appeals under the feudal process of the falsing of dooms gradually became redundant, as less cumbersome procedures developed which made it simpler for an appellant to bring his case directly to the council. The jurisdiction of the committee which heard cases at first instance was replaced by that of specialist lords of council whose availability to administer justice did not depend on the sitting of parliament. By the 1460s the practice had grown up whereby actions started before the auditors which had not been brought to a conclusion before parliament rose were transferred to the council. In the 1490s the lords of council often joined the auditors towards the end of their sessions, with the result that the jurisdiction of the latter almost imperceptibly merged into that of the former. When parliament appointed auditors in 1496 it was clear that they were simply those lords of council who dealt with judicial business under another name. Although auditors continued to be appointed until 1544, it appears that their appointment was purely formal and that no judicial business was conducted before them in this capacity.

9.7.8 The council itself never ceased to hear civil causes, and in the later fifteenth century its judicial business seems to have been increasing steadily. Under James IV (1488–1513) attempts were therefore made to improve the administration of conciliar justice. In 1491 the chancellor, along with certain lords of council, was to dispense justice at three terms in the year; in 1495 a system was established whereby the council was to hear cases in rotation, according to their place of origin. By the early sixteenth century there were clearer signs of the later division of the council into the group forming the king's secret or privy council and the group composed of the lords of council and session. There was a tendency for some members of the council to hold sessions at fixed terms in Edinburgh for the disposal of judicial business, while the king and other members of the council moved around the country, also hearing cases as required but concerned too with general administration. In 1526, after the set-backs of the politically troubled early years of James V (1513–1542) when he was still a minor, certain lords of council were again appointed whose only function was to 'sit continually upon the sessions', that is, to deal with judicial business; in 1528 it was laid down that members of the council not so appointed were to be excluded from these sessions. Thus the 1520s saw the emergence of a specialized group from within the council whose sole and exclusive remit was to hear and dispose of civil causes. It was this group which in 1532 was transformed into the College of Justice and whose members, as lords of council and session, formed the nucleus of the 'new' Court of Session (see para 14.3.1).

FURTHER READING

DL Carey Miller & R Zimmermann (eds)	*The Civilian Tradition and Scots Law: Aberdeen Quincentenary Essays* (Berlin, 1997)
W Croft Dickinson	'The administration of justice in mediaeval Scotland', *Aberdeen U Rev* 34 (1951–1952) 338
	Scotland from the Earliest Times to 1603 (Oxford, 3rd edn revised by AAM Duncan, 1977)
C Jones (ed)	*The Scots and Parliament* (Edinburgh UP, 1996)
WE Levie	'Celtic tribal law and custom in Scotland' *JurRev* 39 (1927) 191
H McKechnie	*Judicial Process upon Brieves 1219–1532* (Murray Lecture, Glasgow, 1956)
HL MacQueen	*Common Law and Feudal Society in Medieval Scotland* (Edinburgh, 1993)
JJ Robertson	'The development of the law' in *Scottish Society in the Fifteenth Century*, ed J Brown (London, 1977) 136
P Stein	'The source of the romano-canonical part of *Regiam Majestatem*' *ScHR* 48 (1969) 107
	'Roman Law in Scotland' in *Ius Romanum Medii Aevi*, vol V 13b (Milan, 1968) (also reprinted in *The Character and Influence of the Roman Civil Law* (London, 1988))

Stair Society publications (Edinburgh), particularly

> vol 1 (1936) – *An Introductory Survey of the Sources and Literature of Scots Law*
> vol 1A (1939) *An Index to vol 1*
> vol 10 (1946) – *The Register of Brieves, 1286–1386*, ed Lord Cooper
> vol 11 (1947) – *Regiam Maiestatem* and *Quoniam Attachiamenta*, ed Lord Cooper
> vol 20 (1958) – *An Introduction to Scottish Legal History*
> vol 23 (1966) – *The Origins and Development of the Jury in Scotland*, ID Willock
> vol 44 (1996) – *Quoniam Attachiamenta*, ed TD Fergus

Chapter 10

HUMANISM AND REFORMATION

10.1 AN OUTLINE OF THE SIXTEENTH CENTURY

10.1.1   The sixteenth century was marked by a ferment of ideas, religious, political, cultural and commercial. Of considerable significance were the growth of the nation state and the consequent rivalries between nation states, and the appearance of the policy of the balance of power. The ideal of European unity disappeared, which is why subsequent chapters will look at the development of national law within France, Germany and Scotland. Moreover, the nation state was built up around a strong central government (save in the Netherlands) and, while powerful families of course survived, the independent feudal nobility faded before the concept of national sovereignty – although 'absolute' governments did not appear until the following century. Italy, whose cities had been the commercial, intellectual and artistic centres of Europe, declined. Humanism, as the new intellectual tool for legal study, was a French and not an Italian phenomenon; hence we hear of the new *mos gallicus* (French usage) in contrast to the traditional *mos italicus* (Italian usage). Italy's decline was also linked with the shift in trading interests from the city to the state and from the Mediterranean to the wider world of the Atlantic and beyond.

10.1.2   The expansion of Europe was in progress. Vasco da Gama returned from his voyage to India in 1499, and Portuguese supremacy in the Indian Ocean was soon established. In 1492 Christopher Columbus arrived in America, thinking that he had reached the Indies; Magellan's expedition circumnavigated the globe in 1519–1522. In 1519 Cortes conquered Mexico and in 1533 Pizarro conquered Peru. The Spaniards viewed central and southern America as their preserve, but in 1539–1543 a French expedition under De Soto explored the lower course of the Mississippi; Cartier had sailed up the St Lawrence in 1534. English seamen searched for the North-West and North-East Passages to the East and in so doing helped bring the Russian Empire, under the rule of Ivan the Terrible (1530–1584), into the reckoning of western European states; however, western influences scarcely penetrated before the end of the following century. From the East, the Moslem Ottoman Empire under Suleiman the Magnificent menaced Christendom until the failure of the siege of Vienna in 1529; it remained a serious threat until the crushing sea victory by the combined Spanish, Venetian and papal fleets off Lepanto in 1571, six years after the Turks had failed to win Malta from the Knights of St John.

10.1.3   In 1494 the French invaded Italy and for the next half century or so the French and the Spaniards fought for domination there; in the course of these wars Rome was sacked by a mutinous imperial army. Charles I of Spain, elected Holy Roman Emperor as Charles V in 1519, succeeded to Ferdinand and Isabella (who had united the houses of Aragon and Castile – see para 7.6.6) and thus to the kingdom of Naples as well as the Spanish American empire; he also succeeded to Maximilian (see para 11.3.1) and Mary who had united Austria and Burgundy. He was lord of nearly all western Europe, save for the Papal States, France, and the British and Scandinavian kingdoms. (In Sweden Gustavus Vasa founded a new dynasty, independent of the Danish Crown, in 1523.) Within Germany, however, Luther distracted Charles from other concerns.

10.1.4   The Lutheran Reformation can probably be said to have started with the publication in 1517 of Martin Luther's ninety-five theses against indulgences. A number of his points were acceptable to the reforming party within the Church but their sum led to his excommunication in 1520; this was confirmed at Worms in 1521, at Charles V's first Imperial Diet. Thereafter Luther was protected by Frederick, Elector of Saxony, not so much for his principles as because the Elector wished to remain supreme within his own territories. Wars and compromises followed each other in rapid succession until in 1555 the Peace of Augsburg settled the religious problem for Germany on the basis of *cuius regio eius religio* (whoever rules, let his be the religious faith) – orthodoxy was to be laid down by the ruler of each state. No account was taken of imperial institutions. This was not a triumph for toleration; each ruler could choose to stay Catholic or to become Lutheran, and his subjects must conform, although the Peace granted them the right – for a period – of unhindered migration if they preferred to live under the other faith. No third possibility was envisaged; this failed to take account of the religious movements in Switzerland, which was technically within the Empire but was, in practice (since the Peace of Basel in 1499), an independent federation.

10.1.5   Ulrich Zwingli of Zürich was a friend of Erasmus and a humane man, but he developed views on doctrine which were beyond compromise, in abolishing the Mass and holding that Christ's Real Presence was diffused among all believers in their corporate act of worship at the Communion service. Within Switzerland the Zwinglian reform movement led to a polarization of attitudes and eventually war. Zwingli was killed in 1531 when serving as chaplain at the Battle of Kappel between Zürich and the other Swiss cantons. Thereafter each canton agreed to decide on its own faith. Zwingli's successor, Heinrich Bullinger, was a man of some influence, particularly in England but also in Geneva.

10.1.6   It was thus to an already Protestant Geneva that Calvin came in 1536. Calvin was a Frenchman who had studied law at Orléans and at Bourges; his legal training marked his subsequent thought, in particular in his stress on the ruler as sole legislator. His studies had been Humanistic, as the lucidity of his Latin (and his French) showed; in 1532 he produced an edition of Seneca's *De Clementia (On Clemency)*. Forced to flee from France when Francis I turned to a policy of persecution, Calvin found himself in Geneva where the Zwinglian reform movement was under way, supported by Berne. After a false start, he returned in 1540 and took control. From Geneva, 'pastors' were sent out, first to other parts of French-speaking Switzerland, then to France and then further afield; John Knox of Scotland was one. Refugees came to Switzerland, and Calvinist communities came to exist in France, Scotland, and the Netherlands; in France, Calvinists were known as Huguenots. Luther and Calvin held very different views, and the breach between the two churches was complete from 1566, after the *Confessio Helvetica* (Swiss Confession).

10.1.7 The Catholic Reformation started simultaneously with the Protestant Reformation; materialism in high places within the Church and a decrease in vocations to the priesthood were clear signs of spiritual decline which brought forth counter-measures, in particular the foundation of the Jesuit Order in 1534, officially recognized in 1540 by Pope Paul III. Christ had told his followers to be one, and nobody who held a position of religious leadership could surely feel that it was right for secular governments to decide the faith of their subjects. Many therefore felt that a General Council might be able to reconcile western Christendom and, despite some papal reluctance, in 1542 a Council was called at Trent (Trento in northern Italy) to define dogma and to promote reform within the Church. It met in several sessions between 1545 and 1563. The main outcome was much greater centralization and uniformity within the Church, and a strengthening in particular of the position of the bishops, who thereafter exercised much greater authority over the clergy and the liturgy.

10.1.8 Francis I of France had deliberately turned to persecution to suppress the Protestants, but one of the reasons for the difficulties (difficulties which proved insuperable) in reaching reconciliation through the Council was the continuation of the wars between France and the Empire or, after Philip II's succession to Charles V, between France and Spain. The Peace of Cateau-Cambrésis in 1559 finally brought these to an end, but during the celebrations Henry II of France died from a jousting accident. His widow, Catherine de Medici, dominated the reigns of her sons Francis II (1559–1560), Charles IX (1560–1574) and Henry III (1574–1589); she tried to preserve the power of the monarchy by balancing the various factions, in particular the Huguenots and the extreme Catholic party led by the Guise family. For thirty years France suffered from intermittent civil war, until a rather more stable society emerged after 1589 with the accession of Henry IV of Navarre, who became a Catholic soon after his accession; in 1598 the Edict of Nantes formally granted a limited religious toleration. Henry, however, was assassinated in 1610, a year after the de facto recognition of the independent Netherlands.

10.1.9 The Netherlands had long been famous as an artistic and mercantile centre; their position as feudal inferiors of the dukes of Burgundy brought them under the rule first of Charles V and then of Philip II of Spain. Philip's attempts to suppress the spread of Protestantism there led to the wars of independence, which began in 1566. William of Orange, the greatest landowner in the Netherlands, emerged as the Dutch leader until his assassination in 1584. Thereafter English aid supported the Dutch cause; the failure of the Spanish Armada in 1588 was a victory for both of them. The death of Philip II in 1598 allowed a subsidence from open war to uneasy peace.

10.2   HUMANISM AND ITS FIFTEENTH-CENTURY ORIGINS

10.2.1   Humanism as a new way of thinking became widely important in the sixteenth century, particularly in the field of law. Humanism marks the change from constructing law as a supportive framework for society, as the mediaeval scholars had done, to using law as a glass through which to view society. Once the development of law had reached a certain stage the Humanists could invent jurisprudence, the critical examination of different ideals of law. Humanism was not, however, the only intellectual movement of the period relevant to the history of law; the Protestant Reformation, with which Humanism in France had some links, also brought about considerable changes in the legal institutions of those countries which it affected.

10.2.2   Like the Renaissance in literature and the fine arts, the roots of Humanism were firmly in the fifteenth century. Both sprang from the new interest in classical and especially Greek culture. The fall of Constantinople in 1453 led to numerous Greek scholars seeking refuge in the West and to a heightening of interest in and a search for Greek manuscripts. The Greek fragments and constitutions in the Digest and the Code were restored, and the Novels could be looked at afresh. Important technical developments assisting scholarship were the invention of printing with moveable type and improvements in the supply and quality of paper.

10.2.3   Humanism was a whole style of thought, in effect replacing Scholasticism as the normal method of analysis and argument, whether in the field of Biblical studies (where important figures were Valla – to whom we shall shortly come – and Erasmus) or Greek literature (notable were Aldus Manutius, the publisher, and Marsilio Ficini) or politics (Macchiavelli and Thomas More) or Latin philology (where Valla and perhaps Politian were the leading figures). As a tool, Humanism was well adapted to these areas of study because it approached them by the study of language and the history of words. This antiquarian and philological approach is the essence of Humanism. It involved a new way of looking at law because one of its most marked characteristics was its historicism, its awareness that anachronisms existed, that evidence must be weighed critically, and that social changes were complex. This sense of history contributed to the new attitudes; so did the technological advances of the past century or so, such as the mechanical clock, small arms, the quadrant in navigation and the combination of square and lateen rig on ships. These discoveries and inventions encouraged the individual to make changes in his environment and fostered a new belief in the power of the human mind, a feeling that progress was possible by purely human means.

10.2.4   The Humanists did not despise the past; indeed, they were fascinated by classical antiquity which they saw as representing their ideals. However, the reverse of this fascination was a lack of sympathy with the men of the Middle Ages who, in their view, had distorted the surviving classical material for expediency's sake. By the fifteenth century Scholastic thinking was very prone to the citation of vast numbers of authorities, and little else; the Humanists rejected the piling up of authorities because it tended to stifle original thought. The new emphasis on individualism and on history was linked with the growth of the vernacular, of the Italian or French or German languages, whereas Latin (like Greek) was studied more and used less. This was both an outcome of increasing nationalist feeling and a factor which enhanced it.

10.2.5 Humanism was a style rather than a school; it did not immediately supersede traditional methods, and this was particularly true in the field of law. In Italy its intellectual implications had for centuries very little effect on practice; in Germany too, and elsewhere, the recently 'received' Roman law took root in its glossed form and survived as the *usus modernus Pandectarum* (modern application of the Pandects, or Digest). It was in France that the new Humanist influence was most strongly felt (although only slowly in the courts), and it was from France that the new ideas spread within northern Europe.

10.2.6 The first legal Humanist to achieve prominence was Alciatus, but he had forerunners. Indeed Petrarch (1304–1374), the friend of Cinus, is often held to have been the signpost to the future. But the story so far as law is concerned really begins with Lorenzo Valla (1405–1457), a rhetorician whose philological studies led him to an investigation of Roman law (as had happened with Irnerius). Valla stressed elegance – lucidity – not merely as an aesthetic ideal but as an essential ingredient of understanding. Thus the Humanist approach to Roman – and other – law came to be known as the elegant jurisprudence; the lawyers of the new style were also sometimes known as *I Culti* (Italian for 'the cultivated' [lawyers]), which referred to the knowledge of classical civilization which they used in interpreting Roman law.

10.2.7 The concept of elegance was by no means incompatible with an interest in the application of law, but Valla's approach was a deliberate attempt to set Roman law in its historical context. He tried to uncover the words of the classical jurists whose work had been distorted by the compilers of the Digest; he rejected much that was the basis of the daily practice of the courts because it was Justinianic. Even more strongly did he reject the bulky mediaeval commentaries on and accretions to the *Corpus Iuris*. The mediaeval jurists had liked to comment on D 50.17 *de regulis iuris* (On maxims of law), which could provide handy catch-phrases for practitioners; Valla, with his philological interests, set a fashion in writing on D 50.16 *de verborum significatione* (on the meaning of terms). Valla's rejection of Scholasticism in favour of a strictly historical approach marked the first step in the revolution of the study of Roman law. In particular there was a growing interest in obtaining accurate texts of the legal as well as the literary sources. Good texts could by this period be printed, and readily disseminated; textual criticism in the modern sense began to appear.

10.2.8 Angelo Poliziano or Politian (1454–1494) followed in this field. He was interested in the *Paraphrasis* of Theophilus, the earliest and much enlarged version – in Greek – of Justinian's Institutions by one of the compilers, but his greatest fame is that he was the first man who studied the Florentine manuscript of the Digest in order to correct a printed edition. Not entirely surprisingly this manuscript had been regarded as something almost sacred, kept under guard and only brought out with special ceremony; thereafter it was also viewed more literally as a historical document.

10.3   THE FRENCH RENAISSANCE

10.3.1   Andrea Alciato or Alciatus (1492–1550) went in 1508 to study law at Pavia and there attended the lectures of Jason de Mayno and Philip Decio. In 1511 he moved to Bologna where five years later he took his doctorate. He learned to admire the clarity of Justinian's Institutions isolated from the crabbed and complex mass of glosses and commentaries adhering to the *Corpus Iuris*; turning his back on these, he reverted to the texts themselves and wrote *Adnotationes in Tres Libros* (*Annotations on the Three Books* [Code books 10–12]). He returned to Milan, where he practised as an advocate and continued writing. His writings led to his being called to a chair of civil law at the university of Avignon in 1518. There he introduced the historical method into the teaching of law, stressing the need for reconciliation between the two disciplines of history and law. The economy and elegance of his methods, without the customary interminable recitation of older opinions, attracted students and created the *mos gallicus* as a way of teaching law. At Avignon Alciatus began his commentary on D 50.16 (on the meaning of terms), and he continued publishing works on a variety of topics. He also gave numerous *consilia* or opinions, of which some 800 have survived; they dealt with municipal, canon, feudal and criminal law, with wills, contracts, privileges and civil procedure. Apart from his interest in literary history he saw the importance of inscriptions as evidence of Roman life and law, so that Mommsen, the great nineteenth-century legal historian, described him as having laid the foundations for the science of epigraphy.

10.3.2   While he was at Avignon, Alciatus met Guillaume Budé or Budaeus (1467–1540). Budé came from a legal family and had been sent to Orléans to study law but, unlike Alciatus who always gave credit to Jason among his teachers (while revering Politian and Erasmus as his masters), Budé held that his teachers had given him only a distaste for the subject. Nevertheless he recognized that the most impressive monument of the Romans was their law, and he agreed with Valla's views on the need to achieve accurate texts, particularly on material held to be so near to wisdom itself. In 1508 he produced *Adnotationes ad Pandectas* (*Annotations on the Pandects*) in which he attempted to recover the original texts; this work was much plundered by Alciatus. He was also interested in such topics as the extent of Greek influence on Roman law, the social and linguistic changes which had affected the law, and the question of interpolations. The notes and commentary of Politian on the Florentine manuscript were necessarily the foundation of Budé's method, since the Florentine itself had not yet been published; for the rest, he resorted to intelligent guesswork. He was confident, if not always right, in his emendations since he relied heavily on his knowledge of classical culture, of the poets and historians, some of whom were mentioned in the Digest. Like Alciatus he made much use of the work of less famous predecessors, but between them they made certain of the triumph of the new ways of thought. Budé was sophisticated enough to point out that Roman historians could be wrong, and that they relied upon each other and so could perpetuate fictions. His Humanist style of thinking saw contradictions not as dissonances to be harmonized – in the Scholastic fashion – but as historical evidence of conflict and change; he also frequently made comparisons between ancient and modern

(French) institutions and practice. He was better able to do this because for much of his life he was in the royal service as a diplomat, as *maître des requêtes* (dealing with the petitions of persons privileged to be exempt from suit in the ordinary courts) and as hereditary royal archivist. It was probably due to Budé, who saw Alciatus as his successor in the task of purifying the Digest of its corrupt passages, that Alciatus became professor at the university of Bourges in 1528 some six years after he had returned to practise in Milan.

10.3.3 At Bourges, Alciatus continued his policy of going back to the sources and of clarifying the texts. He set a style which meant that for the rest of the century Bourges remained the most exciting institution for legal study not only in France but in all Europe. Nevertheless, in 1532 Alciatus returned to Italy; he had found the political atmosphere in France uncongenial, for he was an avowed supporter of the Empire against Gallican claims, and of papal supremacy in a city where Protestant reforming ideas were freely circulating. He spent the rest of his life in Bologna, Ferrara and Pavia, but his influence and that of others among the Humanists was minimal in Italy. There the Bartolist tradition survived almost unscathed in the field of private law – Gentili stoutly defended the *mos italicus* as superior to the *mos gallicus* – although attitudes to the criminal law showed some awareness of Humanism.

10.3.4 North of the Alps, however, Alciatus' inspiration was prolific. His mind was analytical rather than systematic, exploratory rather than dogmatic, seeing the *Corpus Iuris* in its historical setting but accepting that it had a place in modern law for its equity and technical skill. The old tradition had been very much one of working with static material; in their search for the historical origins of laws the Humanists made legal study more dynamic. Pomponius' fragment on the development of the Roman legal system (D 1.2.2) made a useful starting point. Zasius, the earliest German scholar to take an interest in the Humanist approach, who was very impressed by Alciatus' work and corresponded lengthily with him, wrote on this fragment. Zasius was a professional jurist who also wrote on feudal law, but he too denounced mediaeval and Tribonianic barbarisms; he saw law as springing from custom rather than from pure reason, and so he falls within the historical school of law. However, Humanist scholarship was not sufficiently advanced for either Alciatus or Zasius to take a very critical view of the Pomponius fragment.

10.4 THE ELEGANT JURISPRUDENCE OF CUJAS, BAUDOUIN, HOTMAN, DONEAU

10.4.1 Jacques Cujas or Cuiacius (1522–1590) was probably the leading figure of his generation, although both Hotman and Doneau condemned him for being too idealistic. Cujas studied law at Toulouse under Ferrier, a former pupil of Alciatus who became president of the *Parlement* of Paris and chancellor to the King of Navarre. Cujas began his teaching career at Toulouse, although without a chair; his deep interest in pre-Justinianic sources of law was already apparent, and he produced a book on Ulpian. He moved in 1554 to a chair at Cahors and two years later he was called to Bourges to fill the chair left vacant by Baudouin's departure to Germany for religious reasons. He was not, however, happy in Bourges and soon moved to Valence. He spent a year based in Turin during which he visited other Italian cities to see their methods of teaching and to examine the manuscripts in their libraries, although he did not actually see the Florentine. He returned to Valence and then, disturbed by the troubles consequent on the Wars of Religion, went to teach at Lyon, Bourges again, Paris, and back to Bourges.

10.4.2 Cujas devoted himself primarily to the exegesis of the sources; he was helped by being able to use the published text of the Florentine Digest which had appeared in 1553. He wrote commentaries on Papinian and worked on other individual jurists such as Africanus; he also wrote on the *Pauli Sententiae*. He published editions of other western pre-Justinianic lawbooks and began on the Theodosian Code. He produced an improved version of the Institutions after collation of the manuscripts, restored (along with Antonio Agustín) the Greek constitutions to the Code, revised the Novels and discovered more of the *Basilica*. He was of some note as a feudal lawyer and wrote a little on canon law, but French national law was not of intellectual interest to him in its own right, although he made some comparisons between it and other legal systems; naturally he had to take it into account when, as any law professor might, he gave consultations. Cujas never lost touch with the need for law to be tailored to fit the exigencies of practice; he is said to have recommended that students beginning their legal studies should learn to use the Gloss. His published work, however, was almost entirely concerned with the historical approach to the texts. He held that commentaries were often otiose and court decisions frequently biased for expediency's sake, but that rigorous textual criticism could reveal the true basis of the law. His search for interpolations revealed such substitutions as *traditio* (simple delivery) for *mancipatio* (formal conveyance), already obsolete when abolished by Justinian. He did not attempt, as did some of his contemporaries, to rewrite the *Corpus Iuris* as it should have been done – in the eyes of the Humanists – but he helped bring into favour the Institutions; this was to have great effect on those who tried to systematize the law in the light of Humanist (and later) learning.

10.4.3 François Baudouin or Balduinus (1520–1573) was a disciple of Alciatus. Early in his career he practised law in Arras and wrote on the custom of Artois; in the last five years of his life he was *maître des requêtes* to the duke of Anjou, the future Henry III of France. He taught canon law at Paris and then civil law at Bourges, Strasbourg, Heidelberg and Angers (as he moved from orthodoxy to Calvinism, then Lutheranism and back to a resigned Catholicism), but it was specifically as a legal historian that he was most influential. In 1545 he produced the first history of Roman legal science, not just discussing the changes within the law of antiquity but taking the story down to his own day. His most important work was his *Institution of Universal History*. He wrote: 'I have become aware that law books are the product of history and that historical monuments evolve from the books of law.'[1] He emphasized that law was of merely antiquarian interest when it pertained only to the facts of a particular time or place, but that ancient law could retain legal authority if it was still relevant to modern social facts. Baudouin nevertheless spoke of the importance of legal records, equating public documents with eye-witness accounts as superior to any other written evidence; he distinguished primary from secondary sources. He was a model of the Humanist interest in legal institutions, which led to the study of the public as well as the private law of Rome. His work, however, was soon followed and somewhat overshadowed by that of Jean Bodin, who is better known for his political philosophy.

1   Cited by Kelley (1970) p 131.

10.4.4   François Hotman (1524–1590) studied law at Orléans and then became an advocate and lecturer in Paris; his Calvinism led to his spending his later life in Switzerland. He took the historical Humanist approach and found that it led him to reject the Roman law in its entirety as having no legal authority in France. He saw civil and canon law as the source of the chicaneries of the law courts, and he developed a myth of the pure and simple golden age of French law before the coming of writing. He therefore approved the mandatory use of the vernacular in civil law suits, which had been introduced in 1539 by Francis I. He was important, along with other Humanists such as Dumoulin and Brisson, in the development of French national law.

10.4.5   Hugues Doneau or Donellus (1527–1591) also became a Protestant and therefore had to leave France; he taught at Heidelberg, Leiden and Altdorf (the university of the territory of Nuremberg). He had a particular interest in the systematic application of the law, and was more concerned than other Humanists with the meaning of the texts in their legal context within the *Corpus Iuris*. He saw the *Corpus* less as a precious fragment of antiquity suitable for historical study than as a body of law which could be made the basis for a systematic modern legal regime. He was thus closer to the *mos italicus* than were most of his contemporaries, although with no hint of being subject to the legal order of the texts. His method was to follow the order prescribed by nature; he said that he put first that which naturally came first and continued in an orderly fashion thereafter. He began his great *Commentaries on the Civil Law* (*Commentarii iuris civilis*) with a definition of his subject matter and then proceeded in roughly the order of the Institutions, although with much greater elaboration. Perhaps because he was inclined to be dogmatic, he had a great influence on later writers.

10.5   THE TECHNIQUES OF LEGAL HUMANISM

10.5.1   An important aspect of the Humanist revolution in law was its approach to education. One factor which profoundly affected this was the existence of printing and therefore the existence of relatively cheap multiple copies of published works. The Humanists wrote to be read privately, and in their lecturing they could refer students to the books, whereas the Commentators had had to rely primarily upon oral transmission of their ideas and had, so to speak, included their footnotes in their lectures. The availability of printed books was another reason why the Humanists could lay less stress on the memory work of mastering the material in the *Corpus Iuris* and more on developing ideas on the nature of law and its place in society. Elegance of expression in teacher and student was viewed as essential in aiding clarity of thought and ease of understanding. The Humanists looked back to a lost work of Cicero of which only the title has survived – *De iure civili in artem redigendo* (*On reducing the civil law to a practical science*) – as an exemplar of their task.

10.5.2   Many followed Doneau in criticizing the order of treatment in the *Corpus Iuris*; one writer said: 'Although in terms of content there is nothing more perfect than it, in terms of arrangement of the content there is nothing more perverse.' There were some Humanists, including Cujas, who defended the traditional order of the material and explained the historical reasons why one topic followed another; nevertheless, it was increasingly clear that the aspect most widely accepted as requiring renewal in the treatment of Roman law was the presentation of its content. Many of those who suggested improvement were in favour of the order in Justinian's Institutions, that is Persons, Things, and Actions; Duarenus (Douaren), to whom Stair refers (in his own *Institutions* 1.1.17), recommended starting the study of law with a thorough grounding in the Institutions. The institutional order was influential with the Natural Lawyers of the seventeenth century and the codifiers of the eighteenth because it seemed rational to treat legal problems by considering first the persons involved, then the substance of the legal relationship between them, and finally the means of enforcing rights and duties.

10.5.3   Another attempt at a fresh start was made by the German scholar Johannes Althaus or Althusius (1557–1638) who presented the law in a series of dichotomies; for example, he divided individual things into corporeal and incorporeal, and corporeal into moveable and immoveable, and so on. At the end of each chapter he listed the Roman sources from which he had drawn his material and in the body of the work he referred to other texts and other authors. He inspired no followers, however, and was much more influential as a political theorist (see para 13.2.6).

10.5.4   Humanism implied a great admiration for classical antiquity – and its languages – and also the desire to recover as much as possible of the surviving evidence for that civilization. In the legal sphere this meant recovering not only the correct text of the *Corpus Iuris* but also all legal material that dated from before Justinian, whether in the West or the East, and also using Byzantine texts to increase knowledge of Roman law. Unfortunately, some Humanists were prepared to invent sources to justify their hypotheses. Alciatus, for example, gave no provenance for the manuscripts he alleged he had seen; such men

> 'carried on introducing into the classical texts, under the banner of manuscript readings, the wilful, violent and arbitrary alterations which were the product of their conjectural fantasies. In so doing they succeeded in corrupting the texts to a degree far beyond the imagination of the most wooden-headed mediaeval scribe.'[2]

Others, such as Politian and Agustín, were conscientious, and so was Gregor Haloander (1501–1531) who produced the first new edition of the *Corpus*

Iuris. He did not have access to the Florentine Digest (first published in 1553); nevertheless his suggested emendations are much cited, as are those of Cujas, in the Mommsen edition which remains the standard version of the Digest. However, the edition of the whole *Corpus* of Dionysius Gothofredus or Godefroy (1549–1622) was such an advance as to provide, until the later nineteenth century, the standard working text. Some versions were produced with the text alone, others with Gothofredus' own notes, and yet others with the Standard Gloss attached; the last were most useful for practitioners because of the continued importance of the Gloss in the courts. His son, Jacobus Gothofredus (1578–1652), produced a learned commentary on and a critical edition of the Theodosian Code. Modern scholars must still take into account the work of the sixteenth-century French Humanists, particularly as regards the surviving pre-Justinianic sources.

2   DJ Osler 'Graecum legitur', *Rechtshistorisches Journal* 2 (1983) at p 195.

10.5.5   A related area which the Humanists began to investigate was the problem of interpolations, alterations to the classical jurists' texts introduced by the compilers of the *Corpus Iuris*. Various indications of 'interpolation' were recognized: changes in terminology and style, illogical arrangement, the abolition of previous law or the retention of anachronisms, and abridgment. Some of the criticisms addressed to Tribonian and his colleagues were on the grounds that they had not been thorough enough in their updating of the law. The Humanists assumed less often than do most modern scholars that pre-Justinianic law was necessarily better than that of Justinian's time. Their desire to uncover the different historical layers was often linked with the historicist view, which we have seen exemplified in Hotman, that law must be relative, itself changing with changing social and economic circumstances. Others held that the confusion caused by interpolations was the root cause for what they described as the barbarous and obscure attempts at explanation of the sources by the mediaeval writers.

10.5.6   Whereas Hotman took the down-to-earth line that where law no longer fitted the facts it was useless, others were more concerned to enhance the practical application of the texts by interpreting them with as full a knowledge as possible of the context in which they had been written. Thus scholars like Budé saw it as an essential part of the interpreter's task to bring to bear on the texts all one's knowledge of classical literature and civilization; to them it was a mark of barbarous ignorance to use the texts simply as they stood. This fault, along with an utter inelegance of Latin style, the Humanists saw as the greatest failing of the mediaeval jurists. It was even worse in the case of those of their contemporaries who persisted in error when they could rejoice in the light of modern scholarship; Accursius and Bartolus might be forgiven something for being men of their time and erring out of ignorance.

10.5.7   The desire to apply the texts without misunderstanding was only possible after the correct text had been established and its context revealed. A few Humanists were led by their classical studies to take a disparaging view of law as compared with other preoccupations such as the pursuit of literature or the exercise of military skill; Cicero had often been very rude about lawyers – particularly in *pro Murena*. Others, as we have remarked, came to see law as relative; this may be some explanation of why legal Humanism flourished in France, where the balance between the sources tilted less to the Roman and more to the home-grown than in Italy. There was considerable nationalist feeling in France, in legal and ecclesiastical as well as political matters. Humanist techniques were readily applicable to the development out of – and therefore away from – the *ius commune* towards national systems of law. Although the popular image of the Humanist is of a literary figure, many of the legal Humanists were lawyers concerned with practical affairs, trying to use the lessons of history to solve current disputes. Cujas' famous reply, when asked to make a definitive statement of his position in the religious strife of the day, that there was nothing relevant in the praetor's edict ('*Nihil hoc ad edictum praetoris*'), was not a widely found reaction; Cujas himself had views, even if he concealed them, but most of his contemporaries were prepared to express theirs publicly, and often.

10.5.8   To sum up, the Humanists were an important new influence on the study of Roman law partly because they saw that the term 'law' did not necessarily mean Roman law; many challenged the authority of Roman law as the unique guide to the solution of a legal problem. At the same time, they expanded knowledge of what Roman law had actually been. By rejecting it as the sole source (almost) of legal thinking, they opened a new way to seeing in it a source of principle. The wider scope which they gave to reason as a basis for criticizing authority was also important in the growth of Natural Law thinking in its particular seventeenth-century manifestation. Their discussion of educational method, including the order of treatment of legal material, led to substantial changes in the form of legal instruction and to a rational shaping of national law. Their nationalist feelings led them to encourage the use of native law for its relevance, and also the use of native languages in place of Latin – a change less happy from the point of view of communication between scholars. In all these ways they had a profound influence on succeeding generations.

10.6   THE REFORMATION IN GERMANY AND SWITZERLAND

10.6.1   The Reformation also had profound effects in changing the way people thought. In mediaeval theory Church and state had been complementary, even if in practice pope and emperor had frequently disagreed about the proper boundary between matters temporal and matters spiritual. Other rulers too had within their own territories rejected the more extensive papal claims, but a widespread ecclesiastical jurisdiction, centred on the papacy, had been universally accepted. The Protestant Reformation changed all this. Where the authority of the papacy had been abrogated, what was to take its place? Where in the Reformed churches did authority lie? What was to be their relationship with the secular powers? The answers varied between Lutheranism and Calvinism and also more locally.

10.6.2   In Lutheran Germany the gap created by the repudiation of Rome was largely filled by the lay powers, whether princes or cities. In Nuremberg, for example, the Reformation was accomplished by the city council; the local magistrates introduced the necessary doctrinal changes, and the consistorial jurisdiction formerly exercised by the bishop was taken over by the council. This was quite in accord with the thinking of Luther himself. He disapproved of democratic church government and considered it to be the duty of the prince to oversee reform, if only because of the extensive changes required in legislation and court structures. He did not envisage that the lay powers would inherit all the duties of the Catholic hierarchy but only the administrative and judicial functions, leaving matters of doctrine to be determined and controlled by Scripture. Since someone had to interpret Scripture, there was a tendency for the beliefs of particular Lutheran rulers to assume a greater influence than Luther himself might have wished. The princes for their part were not reluctant to take charge of ecclesiastical affairs; quite apart from their individual religious sentiments, this was another way to consolidate their authority and possibly to enrich their treasuries from the revenues of the old Church.

10.6.3   In the Lutheran states, secular control of the church was achieved by means of the consistory, although the establishment of a consistorial system did not always immediately follow the Reformation; in some places it was not set up until the later seventeenth century. The consistory was a church court under the control of the secular ruler. Its members – lawyers and ministers of the church – were appointed by the prince; it met under his presidency, or more usually that of his deputy. (In the cities the municipal authorities took the place of the prince.) The business was essentially that of the former diocesan court. Thus the Lutheran Reformation did not produce a fixed frontier between Church and state; men still did not make a clear distinction between the spiritual and the secular aspects of daily life. In the Lutheran states the Reformation simply transferred many of the powers of the Catholic hierarchy to the lay authorities.

10.6.4   Matters were different in Calvin's Geneva. Calvin pursued an altogether more theocratic line than the German reformers. Aiming to imitate the early Church, he advocated independence from the state and at the same time emphasized the divine authority of the church's ministers. He opposed the exercise of ecclesiastical power by the lay authorities, holding that the spiritual jurisdiction must be independent of the lay power and that its authority was superior. Since concern for faith and morals could legitimize the church's intervention in virtually every aspect of civic life, the city council was slow to accept the full consequences of Calvin's doctrine. In 1541 Calvin persuaded the city of Geneva to establish a body of regulations known as the *Ecclesiastical Ordinances*; these outlined his scheme of church government. In the parishes laymen were to be elected as elders, disciplinary and pastoral office-holders whose duty it was to supervise the morals of their congregation. The main instrument of church government was again to be the consistory; this was to comprise the pastors of the city, together with representatives of the elders and the city council. Calvin envisaged that the consistory would act as an independent court; the city council, however, sought to limit its powers. To the text of the *Ecclesiastical Ordinances* the council added a clause:

'These arrangements do not mean that the pastors have any civil jurisdiction, nor that the authority of the consistory may interfere in any way with the authority of the magistrates and the civil courts.'[3]

Only in 1555 did the consistory at Geneva acquire an unfettered right of excommunication and until 1561 the council managed to maintain the symbolic presence in the consistory of a magistrate acting in his civic capacity.

3   Chadwick, p 84.

10.6.5   The difficulty was that of determining the scope of civil jurisdiction; we find the Geneva consistory giving

> 'its opinions on the bank rate, on the level of interest for a war loan, on exports and imports, on speeding the law courts, on the cost of living and the shortage of candles. On the other hand the council [sometimes] . . . may be found supervising the clergy and performing other functions which logic would have allotted to the consistory.'[4]

The dichotomy between church and city council was not absolute; if all matters seemed grist to the consistory's mill, the magistrates were members of the Calvinist church, perhaps even elders.

4   Chadwick, p 86.

10.6.6   It is therefore possible to argue that the Protestant Reformation did not reject the mediaeval notion of the oneness of life; it only removed the control of Rome. As in earlier times, the problem was one of drawing a boundary between the spiritual and the secular spheres. It was in these terms that there was a problem over the control of the Reformed churches – and of Reformed society.

10.7   THE REFORMATION IN SCOTLAND

10.7.1   In 1560 the Scottish Parliament enacted that 'the bishop of Rome have no jurisdiction nor authority within this realm in times coming' and that 'no bishop nor other prelate of this realm use any jurisdiction in times to come by the said bishop of Rome's authority'. While it was clear that papal authority was abolished for the future, the Parliament did not say what was to take its place. Nor did the Act seem to strike at the consistorial jurisdiction exercised up to then by the Scottish bishops. In the decade which followed we find a number of individuals and groups acting in a consistorial capacity, and so by implication laying claim to the old jurisdiction.

10.7.2   The Reformation did not mean the immediate abolition of the episcopate, and the Scottish bishops therefore continued to deal with the same types of business as before in their courts. During the 1560s Archbishop Hamilton of St Andrews dealt with matrimonial causes, as the records show; in 1566 Queen Mary formally 'restored' to him his consistorial jurisdiction. The Protestant party was indignant, not so much at his continuing to act, as because he had not accepted the Reformation and might therefore seem to be still acting under the authority of the pope. The exercise of similar jurisdiction by bishops such as Alexander Gordon of Galloway and Adam Bothwell of Orkney, who had accepted the Reformation, did not lead to similar objections.

Indeed, the General Assembly, the supreme court and governing body of the Church of Scotland, is found hearing appeals from their decisions without any hint that there was any doubt over their right to hear such cases.

10.7.3 The Court of Session (see paras 9.7.8; 14.3.7) also dealt with consistorial matters in the years immediately following the Reformation. Its intervention was partly due to its desire to extend its existing jurisdiction but was also a response to the prevailing uncertainty as to where such cases should be heard. Kirk Sessions, as they were established, acquired a minor moral jurisdiction over their congregations, but this was no more than a replacement for the archidiaconal courts. A scheme to establish Superintendents to inherit episcopal jurisdiction at diocesan level was abortive. The General Assembly therefore petitioned the Privy Council to resolve the issue.

10.7.4 In 1564 the Commissary Court of Edinburgh was created with exclusive jurisdiction throughout Scotland in causes involving benefices, marriage and status. In lesser consistorial matters, such as defamation, the confirmation of testaments, and disputes arising out of agreements fortified by oath, jurisdiction was to be exercised in local commissary courts, of which the geographical spheres approximated to those of the bishops' officials. Existing commissaries and officials seem to have been empowered to continue in office; in 1566 it was enacted that vacancies were to be filled by the Crown on recommendation from the Lords of Council and Session. Appeal from the local courts lay to Edinburgh, and thence to the Court of Session. However, the concentration, especially of marriage business, on Edinburgh was disliked by many. The Presbyterian faction was unprepared to allow the state to have jurisdiction over questions pertaining to religion; they wished the church authorities alone to deal with marriage causes, and they also resented the commissaries because they did not owe their office to the Kirk. Furthermore, until 1690 when episcopacy was abolished, the bishops were intermittently given the right to appoint commissaries, which the Presbyterian faction liked no better.

10.7.5 The later history of the Edinburgh and local commissary courts can be briefly stated. In 1609 an Act of Parliament permitted appeal from the local commissary courts direct to the Court of Session; as a result the Edinburgh court ceased to exercise its appellate powers, although they were not formally abolished until 1830, when divorce jurisdiction too was transferred to the Court of Session. In 1823 the functions of the local commissaries were taken over by the appropriate sheriffs, and in 1836 the local jurisdiction of the Edinburgh court was transferred to the Sheriff of Edinburgh. In 1876 commissary courts were abolished, as their jurisdiction had been absorbed by the sheriff courts.

10.7.6 The commissary courts had not, however, inherited all the consistorial jurisdiction of the pre-Reformation church courts. The Presbyterian Church which was ultimately established in Scotland had its own courts. At parish level the Kirk Sessions to some degree overlapped with the local commissary courts, for we find them issuing decrees of adherence (an essential preliminary for divorce on the ground of desertion) and dealing with defamation and minor assault. In addition their moral supervision allowed them to impose suitable penalties for sexual misdemeanours, blasphemy, Sabbath-breaking and the like. If their investigations brought to light matters which were in any way criminal, prosecution in the lay courts normally followed; the ultimate penalty at the disposal of the Kirk Session was excommunication. So long as excommunication was accompanied by civil penalties such as forfeiture of goods and revenues, their coercive powers were significant. However, by the end of the seventeenth century the civil authorities less commonly backed ecclesiastical censure with secular sanction, and the Toleration Act of 1712 (otherwise the Scottish Episcopalians Act 1711), despite opposition, removed the power to impose civil penalties. The established Church could no longer discipline non-members, and thereafter the judicial and disciplinary role of the Kirk Sessions gradually declined. Above the Kirk Sessions were the Presbytery, the Synod (now abolished), and the General Assembly. These bodies were the governing organs of the Presbyterian Church and so had (and to some extent still have) a judicial function. The General Assembly heard appeals from lesser courts; it was also a tribunal where ministers of the Church could themselves be tried and, if found erring, deprived of their benefices or charges.

10.8   THE SURVIVAL OF THE CANON LAW

10.8.1   The Protestant Reformation affected the jurisdiction of the Church rather than its rules. Although there were major changes in doctrine, the only really notable change in areas where the average layman might expect to find himself in an ecclesiastical court was in the law of marriage. In England in particular the institutional changes after 1534 were small – partly in reflection of the limited doctrinal changes (see para 8.9.11). There the structure of the Church continued functioning almost exactly as before, with the bishop as judge ordinary, his official deputizing for him in the actual conduct of legal business, and the archdeacons remaining as inferior judges. The archbishop of Canterbury's metropolitan Court of Arches survived. However, the former supreme personal jurisdiction of the Pope was given to the specially established Court of High Commission, and the Court of Delegates was set up to replace papal judges delegate. Modified romano-canonical procedure continued to be used in these courts as long as they endured (see para 8.9.11).

10.8.2   The Catholic Reformation sprang from the same roots as Protestantism when, by the close of the fifteenth century, entirely loyal and orthodox men within the Church were rejecting the prevalent abuses. The effect of the Protestant Reformation was to harden attitudes on both sides, in spite of the attempts to reach an accommodation made by some leading churchmen, such as Antonio Agustín, and some rulers, such as the Emperor Charles V and Henry IV of France. One lasting result of the reform movement within the Church was the compilation of an authoritative text of canon law. In 1563 a commission was appointed to review the existing sources, whether or not they had been printed, and to produce a definitive edition, free from error and omission. The influence of the Humanist way of thinking and the echo of Justinian's instructions to the compilers of the *Corpus Iuris Civilis* seem both to be present. The commission worked at Rome between 1563 and 1580 and in 1582 the results of its labours, the *Corpus Iuris Canonici*, appeared. The new text, composed of Gratian's *Decretum*, the *Decretals* (*Liber Extra*) of Gregory IX, the *Liber Sextus*, the *Clementines*, the *Extravagantes* of John XXII and the *Extravagantes Communes*, was sanctioned as the official text of the recognized sources by Pope Gregory XIII; it thus became the authorized version of the law of the Church, to be used in Church courts and in the universities alike.

10.8.3   The *Corpus Iuris Canonici* formalized canon law within the Roman Catholic Church; the rules were more definite thereafter, just as authority – of the bishops, and above all of the pope – was stricter, but the substance was much the same. Furthermore, it retained the formal status of its constitutent parts (see para 5.4.5); despite its enhanced authority, it was a quarry for argument rather than a regulatory code. The same was true generally in the Protestant states. In most of these, only that part of the existing canon law which ran counter to the Reformed religion was abrogated; not until the seventeenth or eighteenth centuries had most such states built up a body of native case or statute law on wills, marriage and status. Overt secularization was also a later phenomenon.

10.8.4   In Scotland, for example, some forty years after the Reformation, Sir Thomas Craig, the feudist and forerunner of the institutional writers, wrote:

> 'Notwithstanding that we have thrown off the papal yoke, the authority of canon law endures . . . provided always that the rule of the canon law is consistent with the principles of sound religion' (*Ius Feudale*, tr. Lord Clyde, 1.3.24).

More than a hundred years after the Reformation Lord Stair wrote:

> 'And so deep hath this canon law been rooted that, even where the Pope's authority is rejected, yet consideration must be had to these laws, not only as to these by which church benefices have been erected and ordered, but as likewise containing many equitable and profitable laws which, because of their weighty matter and their being once received, may more fitly be retained than rejected' (*Institutions* 1.1.14).

The Scottish institutional writers recognized canon law, like Roman law and feudal law, as having greatly influenced the development of Scots law, and many of its principles and rules were applied as part of that law. But canon law was received for its equity and expediency; it was not in itself authoritative.

10.8.5   In the field of marriage, for instance, the traditional rule of the Church, based partly on Roman law, was that the only prerequisite for a valid union was the consent of the parties – parties, that is, for whom there was no impediment. The Council of Trent required that valid marriage, in all normal circumstances, must be celebrated before the parish priest of one of the parties in the presence of at least two witnesses. This was, however, subsequent to the Reformation in Scotland; in Scots law consent continued to be 'the one thing sufficient and indispensable' to the valid constitution of a marriage, as

Baron Hume explained.[5] Although there was a distinction between regular and irregular or clandestine marriage, as there had been in traditional canon law, the efficacy of irregular marriage was in no doubt, until the position was somewhat modified by the Marriage (Scotland) Act of 1939 which abolished two of the forms of contracting an irregular marriage, leaving only marriage by cohabitation with habit and repute (where a man and woman hold themselves out and are generally reputed to be married) as a form recognized along with regular marriage by the secular power. The canonical rules barring marriage on grounds of consanguinity or affinity up to the fourth degree of relationship could be inconvenient; in 1554 we find Archbishop Hamilton of St Andrews complaining to the Pope of the great difficulty experienced by those of good family in finding partners who were not related to them within the forbidden degrees. The point was taken up by the Reformers, and in an Act of 1567 a less restrictive law was put in force, based on Leviticus, chapter 18. However, the canonical view of affinity as equivalent to consanguinity was retained, and only in the twentieth century were the rules concerning the former somewhat relaxed.

5   Hume, *Lectures* I in Stair Society, vol 5 (1939) p 22. This is why eloping young couples from England fled to Scotland, particularly Gretna Green, to be married.

10.8.6   Some abuses that the Reformers had condemned, such as abuses of the right of sanctuary or of benefit of clergy, were suppressed by Protestant governments; however, they were also largely curtailed by the Church itself and, after the sixteenth century, governments in Catholic countries had much less hesitation in legislating on matters once falling within the sphere of the courts spiritual. Inadvertently, but undoubtedly, the labours of the proponents of the Protestant and Catholic Reformations led, not to the godly rule that they had hoped for, but to the secularization of the institutions of government.

FURTHER READING

O Chadwick	*The Reformation* (Penguin, 1972)
J Durkan	'Henry Scrimgeour, Renaissance bookman', *Edinburgh Bibl Soc Tr* 5(1) (1971–1974) 1
MP Gilmore	*The World of Humanism* (New York, 1952)
	Humanists and Jurists (Harvard UP, 1963)
HD Hazeltine	'The Renaissance and the laws of Europe', in *Cambridge Legal Essays* (Cambridge, 1926) 139
RH Helmholz (ed)	*Canon Law in Protestant Lands* (Berlin, 1992)
Lord Hermand	*Consistorial Decisions*, ed FP Walton (Stair Society vol 6, Edinburgh, 1940)
DR Kelley	*Foundations of Modern Historical Scholarship* (Columbia UP, 1970)
	History, Law and the Human Sciences (London, 1984)
JM Kelly	*A Short History of Western Legal Theory* (Oxford, 1992) ch 5
Stair Society	*Introduction to Scottish Legal History* (Stair Society, vol 20, Edinburgh, 1958), chs 6, 7, 8 and 27

P Stein   'Elegance in law', *LQR* 77 (1961) 242
                    Roman Law in European History (CUP, 1999) ch 4
F de Zulueta   *Don Antonio Agustín* (Murray Lecture, Glasgow, 1939)

Chapter 11

LAW IN GERMANY

11.1 LAW IN GERMANY BEFORE THE RECEPTION (OF ROMAN LAW)

11.1.1 The struggle between the papacy and the Emperor Frederick II destroyed, as events were to prove, the effective power of the Empire. The later middle ages in Germany were marked by an accelerated political fragmentation into principalities, semi-independent states, free cities and the territories of the lesser nobility. The imperial dignity remained elective not hereditary, and the emperors, therefore, during their tenure of office, were more interested in advancing their own dynastic interests than in establishing a genuine imperial government. The *Reichstag*, or imperial diet, had no power to enforce any Acts it passed; the mediaeval *Reichshofgericht*, or imperial court of justice, known since 1415 as the *Kammergericht*, was rendered impotent by the widely granted privilege of exemption from its jurisdiction. It was in the principalities that the future of effective government lay.

11.1.2 The privileges of the princes largely originated in the emperors' need to obtain support for their ambitious policies in Italy and elsewhere beyond the German frontiers. The Emperor Frederick Barbarossa had confirmed the status of his greater feudal magnates as a distinct, and closed, estate of princes. Frederick II accorded to the ecclesiastical princes extensive rights within their lands; in 1232 he extended these rights to the lay rulers by the *statutum in favorem principum* (statute in favour of the princes). In 1356 the Emperor Charles IV issued the Golden Bull, ostensibly to regulate imperial elections, in practice recognizing the de facto independent authority in all matters of the seven imperial electors;[1] these privileges were later extended to all the German princes. The grant *de non appellando* meant that no subject of an elector could appeal to, and the grant *de non evocando* meant that no such subject could be called upon to answer before, any court outside his lord's territory. Furthermore, conspiracy against an elector was to be rated as treason; the electors thus enjoyed sovereign rights.

1 The prince-archbishops of Mainz, Trier and Cologne, the count palatine of the Rhine, the duke of Saxony, the margrave of Brandenburg and the king of Bohemia. (The duke of Bavaria became an elector after the acquisition of the Palatinate in 1648.)

11.1.3 When Charles V was elected emperor in 1519 it seemed that he might be able to restore the imperial authority because his many other territories did not leave him dependent on the princes. However, his lands were too vast; the problems they posed were too numerous and too pressing for any one of them to be dealt with effectively. In Germany, the Reformation brought about uneasy compromise. The outcome of the Peace of Augsburg in 1555 was the addition of religious division to an already divided Germany. The fundamental problem of the relations between emperor and princes was left in abeyance, and the Empire remained a loose confederation of autonomous states. Thus, although there were probably no more different customs in relation to every ten thousand people in mediaeval Germany than there were in France, these customs could not readily be collected into family groups, whereas the French Crown worked steadily towards uniformity. Imperial law-making and justice hardly existed in later mediaeval Germany. Such legislation as there was dealt with the preservation of public peace and the suppression of private warfare; in the *Reichshofgericht* justice was available but little wanted.

11.1.4 In this patchwork of localized and diverse bodies of custom, uncoordinated by any judicial hierarchy, the court of each community developed and applied its own customary usages, without any concern for a broader systematic whole. The situation was further complicated by the fact that 'community' in this context was not necessarily geographical but covered a community of interest. Thus alongside the local territorial law, the *Landrecht*, there existed other bodies of law applicable on the principle of personality of law to various social groups which were united by status rather than physical proximity. The feudal law, the *Lehnrecht*, remained distinct from the territorial law; feudal tenants owed suit to their lords, to the extent of the latter's jurisdiction. Similarly, unfree tenants were subject to the jurisdiction of their lord's manorial court, which applied the *Dienstrecht*. There had been nothing unusual about this in the thirteenth century, but (of mainstream Europe) only in Germany was this state of affairs permitted, by default, to survive unchecked into the fifteenth century.

11.1.5 In most jurisdictions there were *Schöffen* courts, courts presided over by a judge, usually the lord, but in which decisions were given by a panel of law-finders (*Schöffen*), laymen of the district or suitors to the court who normally enjoyed appointment for life. The law applied was usually unwritten, and the findings of the *Schöffen* were based on their collective memory modified by considerations of practical common sense. Their justice was thus flexible but unrelated to the growth of written law elsewhere. They had not developed skills in interpreting previously established objective criteria nor in understanding the systematic implications of each decision. The *Stadtrecht* (town law) worked with similar courts, although the positive law administered there was sometimes influenced by mercantile custom. Urban jurisdictions started as privileges granted by feudal lords, but the major cities acquired practical autonomy both in their courts and in their right to legislate for themselves. Among the cities there was, as we have seen, more extensive grouping than in the territories of the princes and lesser lords; the existence of leagues, such as that of the Hanse in north Germany (see para 6.5.4), and the development of 'daughters', taking their law from a mother city such as Magdeburg or Lübeck, led to some degree, if not of uniformity then of compatibility of law, and written law at that.

11.1.6   In Germany, therefore, law was fragmented and uncoordinated, but this was not of itself discouraging for the future of the indigenous law; in France both Roman law and native customs made their own contribution to the emerging national law in the early modern period. The extent of the eventual reception of Roman law into German practice at the expense of the native Germanic law is difficult to explain – after all, in England it was the other way round. The superior attraction of written as against largely unwritten law is certainly relevant, but some written law emerged throughout all Europe in the thirteenth century, even in Germany. The most famous and influential of the privately compiled treatises which appeared in Germany was the *Sachsenspiegel (Mirror of the Saxons)*, composed in the first half of the century by one Eike von Repgow. Eike's experience of law was as a *Schöffe*; his purpose was to expound the traditional law of Saxony as handed down through successive generations. The treatise therefore deals generally with Saxon law but more particularly with those areas within Saxony with which Eike was most familiar. He wrote of both territorial and feudal law, each treated separately in its own book, as was fitting for the subject matter of separate courts. Eike originally wrote in Latin, but later produced a vernacular version of the treatise; it was subsequently translated into a number of other German dialects.

11.1.7   In the courts of Saxony the *Sachsenspiegel* soon came to be treated almost as if it were an authoritative text; like the *Leges Henrici Primi* in England it acquired the myth of a royal and legislative origin. Throughout Saxony it provided a basis for development and gave life to the law of the whole region. During the fourteenth century it was glossed on a number of occasions, either in whole or in part, and supplements to it, especially in the form of manuals of court procedure, were produced. It provided a focus for all the courts of Saxony, so that there was a counter to legal particularism; its existence and use probably explain why Saxony was one of the areas in Germany least affected by the Reception of Roman law.

11.1.8   The *Sachsenspiegel*'s influence in other parts of Germany is evidence of the widely felt desire for written law and also for the synthesis of such law into more than localized usage. The *Spiegel der deutschen Leute* (or *Deutschenspiegel – Mirror of the German People*) of the mid-thirteenth century relied heavily on the *Sachsenspiegel*; as its title suggests, it attempted a synthesis of German common law which was doomed without an effective superior court. Towards the end of the century there appeared the *Kaiserliches Land-und-Lehnrecht (Imperial Territorial and Feudal Law* – also known as the *Schwabenspiegel, Mirror of the Swabians*) which also was heavily based on the *Sachsenspiegel* but again had a synthetic intention. This compilation and the *Sachsenspiegel* itself were revised and adapted on a number of occasions for use in particular areas.

11.1.9   In many parts of Germany the desire for the certainty of written law was met by the *Weistum*, an authoritative ruling, which declared the existing local custom, usually by means of a sworn inquest. The procedure was well suited to such matters as establishing the feudal and customary usages of a particular manorial court, and so mostly dealt with law at a very local level. It ameliorated rather than cured the problems created by the fragmentation of jurisdictions, but the *Weistümer* were useful if only because they were in writing. They recorded usages well enough established to have achieved the status of legal rules and gave for the future an objective statement on matters potentially productive of dispute. They remained, however, little collections of laws, not of law, and were unstructured and unsystematic. To blend them with the learned law, as feudal law had been, and as was done with native law in France, the application of trained juristic skills was necessary, and these were never brought to bear.

11.1.10 In the towns too, the inquest was often used in the process of reducing custom to writing; sometimes a town might order its officials to compile a law-book which would then be ratified by the oath of the citizens. When the greater cities acquired the 'elective right' to legislate for themselves they could proceed without reference to their overlord and could also introduce new custom when they codified their law. A legal literature devoted to town law appeared, comparable to that dealing with territorial and feudal law. In Saxony, perhaps because of the *Sachsenspiegel*, such treatises were produced early, and they also aimed at a certain generality. The *Sächsische Weichbild* (*Saxon Precinct*) and the *Rechtsbuch nach Distinktionen* (*Law Book according to Distinctions*) were not limited to the law of one city alone but attempted to give a review of town law throughout Saxony.

11.1.11 As mentioned in the chapter on the *ius commune* (see para 7.4.2), within a family of town law, the court of a daughter town, faced with a new or difficult problem, might refer it to the court of the mother town where the *Schöffen* would hear the case sitting as an appeal court, an *Oberhof*. In the early fourteenth century it was only function which distinguished these sessions of the court from its regular sessions but, as the practice developed, it became common for the *Schöffen* to divide into two bodies, one dealing with local disputes, the other appellate. The business of the *Oberhof* was not the retrial of questions of fact but guidance on points of law. Written summaries were sent to it, and its answers were given on the assumption that the allegations were correct. Furthermore, because the duty of the *Schöffen* was to find the law not make it, their answers were usually terse, without a statement of how they had reasoned to their conclusions. Nevertheless, the existence of precedent books in various cities implies a concern for certainty and for a degree of systematic consistency.

11.1.12 Although the *Oberhöfe* were able to transcend merely local jurisdictions, they were not really in a position to provide for Germany the nucleus of a system of indigenous law. They were concerned only with town law and their activities had no effect upon the law administered in the territorial and feudal courts. Moreover, the very fact that families of town law crossed territorial and regional boundaries within Germany and even extended across frontiers into Polish, Swedish and other Baltic territories, meant that they would be unacceptable to princes who were trying to consolidate their rule within their own territories. Indeed, as the princes strengthened their courts they came to regard references from cities within to cities outside their lands as derogating from their authority. Accordingly they tried to limit the practice;

as early as 1432 the Elector of Saxony forbade any subject to seek legal advice from outside the duchy. Similar provisions were enacted elsewhere in local as well as princely courts, but such restrictions did not become very effective or widespread until the emergence of absolutist government after the Thirty Years War (1618–1648). By then the *Oberhöfe* were in decline both for political reasons and because of the economic devastation of the War, and the restrictions were chiefly aimed at the *Aktenversendung* procedure – to which we shall shortly come. Nevertheless, the process of limitation had started in the fifteenth century and in the event made the way clearer for the reception of Roman law.

11.2 THE RECEPTION OF ROMAN LAW

11.2.1 We have considered in the context of the *ius commune* how Roman law, as modified by the Glossators and Commentators and blended with the canon law, was absorbed into the legal systems of Europe in the later middle ages, except in England and, in a different way, in Germany. In Germany, men had for centuries been studying law at university, and from the middle of the fourteenth century they had been able to do this within the Empire. But these men had gone on to serve in the government of Church or state, not to become a professional judiciary. When Roman law was finally received into the practice of the secular courts it was as a flood, overwhelming what was previously there, not the persistent trickle we find in France or the constant stream in Italy. It caused a break in the potential legal development of German common law (*Gemeines Recht*), and so aroused passionate responses, even into modern times. That is why, although the term can be used for the adoption of Roman law by the Visigoths or the Burgundians in the fifth and sixth centuries and for the influence exercised by Roman law after the rediscovery of the Digest, the Reception most usually refers to the authority given to Roman law by the German princes when it was accepted in its entirety as a common, if subsidiary, source of law.

11.2.2 To some extent there had been a much earlier Reception of Roman law, in the deliberately fostered notion that the Holy Roman Empire was the continuation of the Roman Empire and that its emperors ruled in succession to those of Rome. As we saw (para 7.3.1), at Siena where Roman law was the custom of the city, Otto the Great was held to have added trial by battle to the general law in the tenth century; Otto III and Conrad II had both encouraged the concept of continuation. Frederick Barbarossa had not merely approved the revival of the study of Roman law at Bologna but had added some of his own enactments to the Novels of Justinian. In the sixteenth century the myth was created that Lothar III had prescribed the teaching and application of Roman law within the Empire at the request of Irnerius (or of the Countess Matilda of Tuscany). This theoretical reception was argued as immensely important by the proponents of the Roman as opposed to the German party when the codification of German law was under consideration, but it had no real basis in practice; the emperors in their struggles with the papacy or the princes or the king of France had sought support from the texts on the powers of the ruler, but they had shown little concern for the private law as it affected disputes between citizens. Far more important in actuality for preparing the intellectual climate were the pervasive influence of the canon law and the ecclesiastical courts, and also the revival of interest in all aspects of antiquity which is associated with the Renaissance.

11.2.3 There were already some traces of Roman law thinking in Germany. Johann von Buch's gloss on the *Sachsenspiegel* compared Saxon rules with those of Roman and canon law. Both the *Deutschenspiegel* and the *Schwabenspiegel* showed signs of a knowledge of Roman law on the part of their compilers, together with a willingness to make some use of it; they were in the same tradition as Beaumanoir in France or *Regiam Majestatem* in Scotland. In the *Klagenspiegel (Mirror of Actions)* of the early fifteenth century considerable use was made of Roman law; its terminology was used to describe Germanic institutions and particular attention was given to the rules of Roman procedure. Even apart from the major works on romano-canonical procedure there were manuals specifically adapted for use in Germany, such as the *Speculum Abbreviatum (Mirror Abbreviated* – a fourteenth-century précis of Durantis' *Speculum Iudiciale*) or the mid-fifteenth-century *Vocabulary* of Jodocus, which gave a simple explanation of Roman and canonical terminology.

11.2.4 The German universities, or rather, the universities within the Empire, were originally created as centres of theological studies. The emphasis in their law schools was on canon law and on the needs of the Church; the Protestant Reformation destroyed the career prospects of many such graduates. Some of the more recent universities, such as Basel (1460) or Tübingen (1477), had chairs of Roman law from their foundation, and similar chairs came to be established at other universities, sometimes for political reasons, sometimes because of the religious troubles. Yet until the princes created the courts for these graduates to staff, the academic contribution to the application of Roman law seems more passive than active – responding to a growing preference rather than seeking to impose the learned law.

11.2.5 Canon law procedure had long been established in the ecclesiastical courts. This procedure relied on written pleadings and rational methods of proving disputed facts; its appellate process involved a reasoned and wide-ranging review of the issues in contrast to the 'false judgment' procedure of the essentially feudal lay courts. It required skill and learning in the framing of its processes and the disposal of its business; precision both of thought and of expression was necessary to clarify and distinguish the legal rules and concepts of which it made use. The terminology of the canonical system was, naturally, Roman and when further definition or elaboration was needed it was simple to resort to Roman doctrines. While delays might result from the attempt to balance all possible interests of the parties, the courts spiritual offered in general a more attractive justice than the less articulate or subtle *Schöffen*. We have seen that romano-canonical procedure began to be adopted by the princes for their superior courts in the latter half of the fifteenth century. If the preferences of litigants were leading them to the ecclesiastical courts because of the efficiency of the procedure, the princes could only recover the business they were losing by offering equally attractive justice. The increased availability of the new procedures in its turn served to confirm litigants in their preferences. Cities like Frankfurt-am-Main soon followed the example of the princes; most others took longer to respond to the pressures. Gradually, however, legally trained men serving as town clerks or civic notaries were called in as assessors or advisers to the lay tribunals, and steadily the effective power of issuing judicial decisions passed to them.

11.3   THE *REICHSKAMMERGERICHT*

11.3.1   Although the *Reichshofgericht* (and then the *Kammergericht*) was a court of very limited effectiveness because of the many privileges of exemption from its jurisdiction, it was nevertheless the supreme court within the Empire; it was important as a symbol or model even when it lacked the power to entertain cases or to enforce its decrees. The compiler of the *Klagenspiegel*, for example, lamented the troubled state of Germany and saw the remedy as lying in the provision of a certain and uniform law, adequately enforced. His concern was fairly typical, and under the Emperor Maximilian I (1493–1519) attempts were made to strengthen the imperial position. In the legal sphere the principal act to this end was the establishment in 1495 of a refurbished imperial court of justice, the *Reichskammergericht*. This court sat first in Nuremberg, then Esslingen, and then in Speyer from 1527; later, 1693–1806, it sat in Wetzlau, not far from Frankfurt.

11.3.2   The new court consisted of sixteen voting members under the presidency of a single director. Initially it was laid down that half of the sixteen were to be drawn from those of knightly or higher status and the remaining half from those 'learned in the laws'. In 1521 the representatives of the nobler classes were required, if possible, to have received a legal education; in 1548 legal training became a mandatory qualification for all members. In 1530 the court was divided into three divisions or senates (this number varied from time to time thereafter) in order to deal more promptly with the cases coming before the court. The sixteenth and seventeenth centuries saw further changes in the composition of the court, mainly occasioned by a considerable increase in business. The presidency was ultimately shared by four directors, and the membership of the court reached fifty in the mid-seventeenth century. It proved difficult, however, to attract suitably qualified men because the imperial treasury was constantly short of funds; the number of judges was usually below the full strength. The court's business was mainly appellate but it remained the tribunal of first instance for tenants-in-chief of the emperor.

11.3.3   From the beginning the *Reichskammergericht* was instructed to use a written procedure. This did not necessarily mean romano-canonical procedure but, in view of the composition of the court, it was the obvious way to develop. An elaborate and written mode of process, based on the ecclesiastical system, soon came into use. Further, the court was also instructed to judge in accordance with the 'common law of the Empire' as well as with such 'righteous, honourable and practised ordinances, statutes and customs of the principalities, seignories and courts' as might be brought before it. Here the 'common law of the Empire' meant Roman law, which thus received formal recognition as, at the very least, a general subsidiary source of law. In practice the place of Roman law was more central; an imperial appellate court could not be expected to have judicial knowledge of the law and customs of each dispute's place of origin. If local law was to be taken into account, it had to be specifically drawn to the attention of the court and the judges had to be satisfied that the particular provision was indeed as alleged. Roman law required no such proof; it was by definition within the knowledge of the court and so was normally applied unless displaced. Even when a local rule was established the learned judges were likely to interpret it in the light of Roman law, as had happened during previous centuries in Italy.

11.3.4 The *Reichskammergericht* was thus very much a court of the civil law, but it was much less effective than the *Parlement* of Paris, let alone the English central courts. It was expensive and inclined to be slow, and it lacked the power to enforce its decrees. Furthermore, as had happened with the mediaeval *Reichshofgericht*, privileges of exemption ate at its jurisdiction. The Reformation brought problems of distrust or enmity between Catholic and Protestant members of the court, as well as for parties before it. The ultimate control of the court established by the pro-imperial Catholic faction made Protestants less ready to resort to it. Then again, most of its business was of a public nature, dealing with keeping the peace and the like, and relatively little concerned the potentially receptive field of private law. Thus the immediate importance of the *Reichskammergericht* did not lie in the direct impact of its jurisprudence on German law, but in its provision of a model to the princes.

11.3 5 As we have seen, some appellate courts staffed by doctors of law had been established in the half-century preceding 1495 by such great princes as the dukes of Bavaria and Saxony. The era of the Reception in Germany was also the era in which the territorial rulers within Germany were trying to expand their powers and to consolidate their government; an increasing control of the administration of justice was simply one aspect of this particularist centralization. One approach was to limit resort to foreign *Oberhöfe* or to restrict the *Aktenversendung* procedure; another was to set up their own appellate courts. As yet the princes as a class were not strong enough to gain control of the lesser territorial and feudal courts within their realms. The new imperial court provided a stimulus and an example. The princely high courts adopted romano-canonical procedure in both imitation of and rivalry to the *Reichskammergericht*. As had happened earlier and elsewhere the procedure was attractive to litigants, and the princes were usually in a position to enforce their decrees. The attraction of the new courts led to an increase in business, and this led to a need for more skilled men to staff them – and to a closer link between the courts and the law faculties of the German universities. The superior technique and professional training of such men reinforced the Roman element in the law administered by these courts, although local custom had more weight at princely than imperial level.

11.3.6 In Saxony in particular the tradition of the *Sachsenspiegel* prevented a complete romanization of the courts and the law they dispensed. The Leipzig court was certainly staffed by men trained in the learned law but they used a simpler written procedure than that of the *Reichskammergericht* and they had judicial knowledge of Saxon custom. In Saxony they borrowed from Roman law but they were able to blend it with indigenous law. Collections of decisions in the Saxon courts were published; for example, Benedikt Carpzov (1595–1666) in 1642 produced *Responsa iuris electoralis* (*Answers on the Law of the Electorate*). Nevertheless, at one tier below the imperial government, the princely courts of appeal were also a force for the reception of Roman law.

11.3.7 The influence of the *Reichskammergericht* became more widespread as lawyers throughout Germany came to a fuller knowledge of its proceedings; during the sixteenth century reports of the work of the court began to appear in print. The court had early realized the desirability of keeping some sort of written record of its activities, although this was as much to safeguard the position of the judges as to develop legal thinking. The court was subject to visitation by imperial commissions with power to review its decisions and, if necessary, to remove judges; the latter was a power seldom exercised, but it lent considerable weight to the commissioners' enquiries. Furthermore, in 1532 the judges were made personally liable to litigants for bad decisions, defined as arising from judicial corruption or partiality. Thus the early records were intended to protect judicial interests, not designed to publicize their decision-making. Indeed, originally, like the judges of the French *parlements*, the judges of the *Reichskammergericht* were required to swear an oath that their reasoning, their 'mystery', should be kept secret. However, as in France (see para 12.4.2), the pressures towards publication were stronger than those towards concealment.

11.3.8 In 1563 Joachim Mynsinger von Frundeck, a judge of the court between 1548 and 1555, published a volume of reports, entitled *Observations*. He was a doctor of law of noble birth, a former professor of Roman and canon law at Freiburg and before that a student of Zasius. He himself had participated in some of the decisions which he reported; others he took from the court's records. There was alarm that public confidence in the court might be destroyed, but his reports reflected well on proceedings there, and the volume proved very popular; it ran to twenty-one editions and was in print for 150 years. Another former member of the court, and a graduate of Bologna, Andreas Gail, in 1578 published his own *Observations*, based on his experiences; this publication was welcomed, due to Mynsinger's work. Although the two books had the same purpose, the earlier volume was condensed and analytical, whereas Gail's was Bartolist in approach and, despite its lengthiness, it proved more popular.

11.3.9 The publication of these and similar works did much to restore a degree of prestige to the *Reichskammergericht* by organizing the mass of civilian learning for that court to use and others to copy. After about 1600, however, a new form of report began to appear, produced not by former judges but by lawyers practising before the court; these contained much more detail on the procedural stages of the cases reported, although many of these will have been conducted in private. Clearly, many persons had access to the official records. Moreover, after 1654 each judge in a case was required to furnish for the record a written statement of the reasons for his decision, and these too were added to the reports. The *Reichskammergericht*, although still slow and ineffective,

> 'acquired a kind of leadership in the development of law through legal decision. . . . the court had become a source of applied legal doctrine that was at least thought worthy of study by lawyers.'[2]

2   Dawson, p 226.

11.4 *AKTENVERSENDUNG* AND THE UNIVERSITIES

11.4.1   The universities played a very important part in the development of law in Germany after the Reception. In a manner similar to the obtaining of opinions from the Italian doctors, judicial consultation of the legal experts led to further interpretation of the civil law for the needs of practice. Such consultation was encouraged by an imperial statute, the *Carolina*, of 1532, to which we shall return in the next section. It contained in more than thirty of its clauses the instruction that in cases of doubt advice was to be sought by the courts from 'those who know the law'. The *Carolina* dealt with criminal law and it did not prescribe the consultation of civilians alone, but it gave imperial sanction to the usage.

11.4.2   For much of the sixteenth century, the consultation was of individual jurists; for example, in 1538 there was published posthumously a volume of the *consilia* of Zasius, who had died three years before. There developed, however, the practice of submitting an issue for the collective response of a university law faculty, and this became the normal form. Often it resulted in the virtual abdication by the courts of their power to make decisions. Rather than deliberate an issue and seek an opinion only on the particularly thorny points, the courts began simply to send all the written documents relating to the cause to the advising law faculty. The courts which were still staffed, at least in part, by lay judges found this an attractive way round the technicalities of the romano-canonical procedure and in effect they surrendered their judicial function. The faculties which had been consulted came to send back their answer in the form of a draft decree. Of course steps to enforce decisions could only come from the courts, but their legal dealings were often limited to the 'despatching of the documents of the case' (*Aktenversendung*). The faculties remained in theory advisory bodies only, but their decisions were rarely questioned; if they were, the invariable course adopted by the transmitting court was to refer the matter to a different law faculty. The system had various advantages. Litigants received learned and impartial justice. The ordinary courts, anxious to preserve their independence from the centralizing tendencies of the princes, were able to offer justice comparable to that of the new princely appellate courts. The faculty doctors saw the triumph of the rational learned law.

11.4.3   Furthermore, the law faculties were no longer simply producing graduates for legal and administrative posts and studying Roman law in academic isolation. They were using the Roman law they were working on, that is, both the historical pursuit of classical Roman law in the Humanist tradition and the accumulated interpretative knowledge of the Gloss, to solve actual disputes, in a sense repeating the work of the Commentators. But the new external circumstances meant that Germanic local law and custom were pushed firmly into the background, not blended in. The preponderance of Roman over Germanic solutions was encouraged by the frequency with which an advising faculty might lie in a different territory from the consulting court. Unless a local provision was convincingly argued, the faculty members would inevitably turn to the civil law in reasoning their way to a solution. A party relying on the civil law came to have a presumption in his favour and the onus was on the other party to prove that the Roman law on this point had not been received or, once received, had since been rejected. This was why the seeking of legal advice across territorial frontiers had been forbidden in Saxony as early as the fifteenth century, and in Brandenburg and a few other precociously centralized states during the sixteenth century; such prohibitions only became widespread in the eighteenth century.

11.4.4   The faculties themselves might sometimes consult with other faculties; faculty decisions were collected and published. In this way there was a growing body of common doctrine which transcended state boundaries within Germany. The general doctrinal approach, which was not confined to Germany, is well described as the *usus modernus Pandectarum* (modern application of the Pandects – literally the Digest, in practice the whole *Corpus Iuris Civilis*), although this phrase may not have been coined until the seventeenth century when Samuel Stryk (1640–1710) wrote a book with that title. Carpzov's influential *Jurisprudentia forensis romano-saxonica* (*Romano-Saxon Law as Applied in the Courts*) of 1638 was in this practical tradition which the German law faculties had established, an approach akin to the *mos italicus*. The *usus modernus*, however, differed from the *mos italicus* in that it was inclined to give imperial authority rather than the self-evident reason of the texts as the basis for the acceptance of Roman law; it also gave authority to the local sources, rather than interpreting them strictly in order to bring them within the scope of the Roman sources. In 1643, however, H Conring (1606–1681) wrote a book *De origine iuris germanici* (*On the origin of German law*) which argued that Roman law had in fact been received by a gradual process of assimilation, not by a supposed ordinance of Lothar or of any other mediaeval emperor, and that it should be applied only insofar as it had been positively accepted. This work had a fruitful future but little immediate impact. Practising lawyers continued to accept Roman law as binding, and simply, as a matter of convenience, put the burden of proof on a party who wished to found his case on Germanic law.

11.4.5   The universities were not exclusively oriented towards Roman law; chairs of private law were until the eighteenth century concerned with the civil law, but there were also chairs of feudal law, public law, and civil procedure – although the last remained based on the romano-canonical process. Within the teaching of the civil law the 'legal order' was no longer followed in German universities of the seventeenth century, and professors ceased to be appointed to teach the different parts of the *Corpus Iuris*. Moreover, private sessions of teaching were added to the public lectures and these could deal with any material the teacher thought appropriate. In this modern atmosphere there were complaints from students that professors neglected their teaching in order to concentrate on the more lucrative business of composing draft decrees in response to *Aktenversendungen*, or else to act as judges or as members of the council of the local ruler. Another innovation (not in Germany only) in legal education was the habit of requiring a student to defend a thesis or theses as evidence of his knowledge of the sources and his ability to handle legal materials. The thesis to be defended was a more or less controversial statement of law – for example, that delivery is always required in order to transfer property – and the candidate had to produce arguments in favour of it and refute contrary opinions. Such disputations were also collected and published, often by the professor who had presided.

11.5 THE USE OF LEGISLATION IN GERMANY

11.5.1 The sixteenth century saw a considerable enactment of imperial legislation, but most of this had to do with public matters; hardly any of it dealt with private law. The most important and influential of these statutes was the *Constitutio criminalis Carolina* (Charles V's statute on criminal law), commonly known as the *Carolina*, published in 1532. The *Carolina* was based on an earlier criminal code, the *Bambergensis* of 1507, compiled for the lands ruled by the bishop of Bamberg; this had blended existing German criminal law with the doctrines of the Italian jurists. The *Carolina* hence preserved the German classification of crimes but interpreted this in the light of the learned law. It thus proceeded on the assumption that crime was a matter of concern for the state as well as for the victim and his family; the preservation of law and order was justification for the imposition of punishments by the public authorities. Fault was held to be an essential element of liability, and civilian teaching on the distinction between *dolus* (malice or fraud) and *culpa* (fault, including negligence) was taken up.

11.5.2 The *Carolina* was a comprehensive code of criminal law and procedure; it was the first code of any branch of law designed to be applicable throughout the Empire. This attempt at universal application met with considerable hostility from among the German princes; the Imperial Diet only passed the statute after it had been agreed that its provisions would not derogate from the 'ancient, just and lawful usages' of the various territories. The princes had in effect maintained their position at the expense of the emperor, and within Germany the *Carolina* took second place to the territorial laws. For example, in Saxony legislation was passed in the early seventeenth century requiring jurisdiction in all but the most minor of crimes to be surrendered by the lower courts to the duke's court in Leipzig. The result, as the records show, was that a huge amount of criminal business came before that court, which was thus able to mould the development of Saxon criminal law; for example, an elaborate system of safeguards for an accused person was introduced. Through the writings of Carpzov Saxon practice also influenced other German jurisdictions. Saxon decisions, together with the *Carolina*, provided the basis for most future thinking on criminal law throughout the whole of Germany.

11.5.3 The sixteenth century also saw many 'reformations' of the town and territorial laws, that is, a putting into writing of local customs with those modifications which were thought necessary. The cities were first in the field, with codification in Nuremberg and Worms, for example, taking place in the later fifteenth century. During the course of the following century a substantial majority of the cities and princely states had reformed their laws. This was partly in response to the romano-canonical procedures in, and the recognition of Roman law by, the *Reichskammergericht* and the princes' appellate courts; it was clearly expedient to clarify whether the rules on a particular issue were to be derived from customary or from learned law. In general clarity meant Roman clarity, partly because the men most likely to be commissioned to systematize local usage in the light of the Reception were those who had been trained in the learned law.

11.5.4 In Frankfurt, for example, the city's court received romano-canonical procedure at the close of the fifteenth century. At the time this produced a degree of confusion as the customary and the new systems for a while existed side by side. The city's court was not yet fully romanized and the lay officials who served there found considerable difficulty in understanding the technicalities of the new procedure and in dealing with the substantive Roman law that it brought in its wake. In consequence Frankfurt codified its law in 1509. The reformed law sanctioned the new procedure but attempted to make it somewhat simpler for the lay judge; the old oral procedure was thereafter limited to certain minor causes, such as small debt. The code also settled the substantive law that the city would use; the Roman did not entirely override the indigenous law, because one result of the review of the local customs was their systematization, which made them easier to blend. In general, the law of persons and of succession remained rooted in custom, but in areas where there had been conflict between the two traditions Roman law was normally preferred. This is the less surprising in that the 'reformation' in Frankfurt was largely the work of the city's advocate, Schönwetter, a man trained in the learned law.

11.5.5 By the seventeenth century it was clear that all Germany had received Roman law, although not always to the same extent; in Saxony especially the Reception was discriminating rather than general, while in some states it was thoroughgoing. As in Italy centuries earlier, the putting into writing of the local laws of the cities and territories had opened the way to civilian influence. The fact that the texts of the new codes were often terse and incomplete and that some topics might be omitted altogether – in particular those concerned with obligations, and especially contracts – left considerable scope for judicial interpretation. Interpretation by the appellate courts meant virtually automatic use of the learned law; interpretation by lesser courts carried a strong likelihood of reference to the learned law through *Aktenversendung*.

11.5.6 The universities had always produced trained men, suitable for government posts; indeed, in late mediaeval and early modern Germany, to be a law graduate was the surest route to gainful and probably influential employment. After the establishment of courts with romano-canonical procedure there was great demand for trained men to staff them, which encouraged the growth of law faculties. The existence of the law faculties in itself led to a more scientific attitude to law within Germany. Over and above accepting individual doctrines of Roman law, scholars took a structured and analytical approach to the whole discipline; they distinguished between laws and law. Humanism had some impact in Germany; Zasius was much respected and Doneau, in exile from France because of his Protestantism, first found a home in Heidelberg. But in spite of the intellectual challenge of Humanism, the tradition of the universities was close to the *mos italicus*; the universities' intimate contact with the courts through their consultations meant that the purely Roman influence was strong, and thus there developed the *usus modernus Pandectarum*. In the specific field of legal education, German universities were responsible for innovations which were to affect university teaching throughout the western world, but that was for the future. Meanwhile, through the Reception, with each factor – the political ambitions of emperor and princes, the desire of litigants, the urge towards system whether in general or local legislation, the growth of professional courts, the work of the law faculties – enhancing the effects of the others, Germany had acquired a kind of common law.

FURTHER READING

H Coing — 'Roman law as the *ius commune* of the continent', *LQR* 89 (1973) 505

JP Dawson — *The Oracles of the Law* (Ann Arbor, 1968) ch 3

R Hübner — *History of Germanic Private Law* (Continental Legal History series, vol IV, Boston, 1918)

W Kunkel — 'The reception of Roman law in Germany: an interpretation', in *Pre-Reformation Germany*, ed G Strauss (London, 1972)

Various European Authors — *A General Survey of Events, Sources, Persons and Movements in Continental Legal History* (Continental Legal History series, vol I, Boston, 1912) Part IV

P Vinogradoff — *Roman Law in Mediaeval Europe* (Oxford, 1929) ch 5

A Wacke — 'The Reception of Roman law in Germany', *Lesotho Law Journal* 1 (1985) 165

G Wesener — 'Kaspar Manz, a German jurist in the seventeenth century' in *Critical Studies in Ancient Law, Comparative Law and Legal History*, ed JW Cairns & OF Robinson (Richard Hart, 2000) 399

F Wieacker, tr T Weir — *A History of Private Law in Europe* (OUP, 1995)

Chapter 12

THE DEVELOPMENT OF FRENCH LAW

12.1 THE MOVEMENT TOWARDS CODIFICATION

12.1.1 Although the adoption of romano-canonical procedure in the *Parlement* of Paris and the other *parlements* – of which there were eventually twelve in the provinces,[1] each formally independent within the boundaries of its territorial jurisdiction – had brought about a degree of unity in the administration of the law, the multiplicity of existing custom continued to make for diversity. In the Midi, the *pays de droit écrit*, the problem was less acute in that Roman law was recognized as general subsidiary custom, but in the *pays de coutumes* there was no such unifying factor, although the predominant position of Paris gave its custom great influence. In the North customs were strictly territorial; this meant that a man might find his personal status changed as he crossed into the area of some other custom, or that a document which was valid in one region was without effect in another through some lack of formality in its execution. Moreover, there were no official collections defining local custom in the North until the sixteenth century. There were, indeed, important unofficial compilations, such as Beaumanoir's *Coutumes de Beauvaisis* or *Les Livres de Jostice et de Plet* from Orléans; in Normandy the *Grand Coutumier* and in Brittany the *Très Ancienne Coutume* had a semi-official status and could be led as proof of custom, but these provinces were unusual.

1 Of these, Bordeaux, Toulouse, Aix and Grenoble lay in the *pays de droit écrit.*

12.1.2 The first serious attempt to solve the problem of how to define one's status was made by the Breton jurist, Bertrand d'Argentré, in the sixteenth century, in the course of his commentary on the custom of Brittany. His solution, the doctrine of *statut personnel*, was derived from the writings of the Commentators who had had to solve similar problems in connection with the different laws of the city states of northern Italy. This doctrine held that certain aspects of custom, in particular those attaching to personal status and capacity, must be viewed in relation to the person rather than the territory; a man acquired them by birth or domicile and carried them with him as he moved from region to region. This at least eased the problems of merchants and of the growing number who travelled to find employment, but it was still a long way from any concept of Frenchness.

12.1.3 There was also a tendency to group customs into provincial families; this was encouraged by the existence of the *parlements*, each of which had jurisdiction over a region which included many customs. As a *parlement* heard the results of various inquests into the range of local customs within its jurisdiction, it tended to assimilate comparable usages. Although its decrees concerned the present case and were not binding for the future, a consistent run of decisions would clearly be of weight in redefining custom. Local custom normally needed to be proved before the court. Some usages were held notorious, that is, so well known as not to require proof, and others would have been incorporated in a local charter or clearly been previously accepted by the court, but if there was any uncertainty a party must be prepared to lead proof of the custom on which he was relying. From the late thirteenth century onwards this was most commonly accomplished through the *turba* or group inquest. The number required to constitute a *turba* was finally fixed at ten; their verdict on whether or not an alleged usage amounted to custom had to be unanimous. A complication arose in consequence of a royal ordinance of 1499 which laid down that the verdict of a *turba* was to rank as the equivalent of the testimony of one witness; the generally accepted canonical rule of evidence required two witnesses for full proof, and hence corroboration of the verdict came to be required. Thereafter it was necessary to put the matter to two inquests, which inevitably made the process slower and more expensive; it remained, however, the usual method of settling disputed custom until the abolition of the *turba* in 1667, when local judges, after appropriate consultations, certified local usage.

12.1.4 The drawbacks of uncertainty of particular usage, doubts about the territorial extent of a custom, lack of customary law in areas such as contracts, and absence of system or principle on which to found a developed law were already recognized in the fifteenth century. To deal with these problems men such as Jean Masuer, advocate and later chancellor in the *sénéchaussée* of Riom in the Auvergne, tried to blend together the customs of a whole province; he also linked his work with the practice of the *parlement*. Masuer's *Practica senescalliae Alverniae* (*Practice of the Sénéchaussée of the Auvergne*) was published in mid-century; it was published bilingually and it is noticeable that the Latin editions of the work make more direct use of Roman law than do the French. In the 1540s Jean Imbert produced his *Institutionum forensium Galliae pene totius quae moribus regitur communium libri iv* (*Four Books of Institutions of the Court Practice of Almost All Customary France*). Imbert discussed both civil and criminal procedure; he made use of many *arrêts de règlement* (decrees – the term covers rulings for the future as well as decisions in particular cases) of the *parlements* as well as of Roman law in his interpretation of custom. He also wrote a book which discussed what written law was actually observed and what abrogated; this too was very popular.

12.1.5 The Estates-General, that is the three estates of nobility, clergy and commons, on various occasions in the sixteenth century demanded a clarification and simplification of the law. At Orléans in 1560 the Third Estate petitioned for a summary of what law was in force between the king's subjects, for the removal of what was unnecessary, and also for reforms in procedure. In 1576 at Blois there was a request for the consolidation of edicts, royal ordinances and custom by learned men and experienced persons appointed for this purpose; again, what was wanted was a compilation of those customs which were actually in force and the abrogation of others. The response was the Ordinance (*Ordonnance*) of Blois in which, among other matters, the king promised to codify the ordinances. We shall return to the theme of royal legislation in section 5.

12.2   THE CODIFICATION OF THE CUSTOMS

12.2.1   The petitions of the Estates-General at Orléans and Blois were only possible because a significant codification of the customs had already taken place in the earlier part of the sixteenth century. In 1498 the Crown had ordered that the customs and usages of the various regions in the North be codified, and official texts produced. Local assemblies, after consultation with knowledgeable parties, produced draft texts defining their region's customs; many of those immediately concerned in this work were local lawyers. Royal commissioners attended the final stages of the assemblies' meetings to approve the agreed drafts; these were then promulgated by the commissioners in the name of the king. Thus each written collection of customs amounted to a royal enactment, binding and authoritative for the future, and capable of being cited in the courts. The customs of Melun, Ponthieu and Sens were promulgated in 1506, and the Custom of Paris in 1510, a year after that of Orléans. In the 1580s revised versions of some of these codes were issued, improved after being tested by use; by then the overall work had been completed in the North. There were left in force some sixty-five separate general customs, applicable to a considerable area, but several hundred purely local customs remained as well. Some codification had also taken place in the Midi.

12.2.2   While the process of codification was primarily designed to provide a statement of those customs actually in force, the opportunity was also taken to reform existing law where this was thought desirable. The distinction between the two aims was not always clear because to establish the correct custom was almost the same as to choose the better one. The purpose was not in general to innovate, but the need to reduce customs to writing produced a new precision in the existing law and revealed areas where legal guidance was lacking. The form of words adopted was often affected by Roman law, and this could of itself bring about changes in institutions such as tutory or gift. Although the men chiefly concerned with the work of codification were predominantly interested in the practice of the customary courts, they were often graduates in law and not untouched by Humanist thinking. They had a sense of history and readily distinguished between ancient custom and custom to be observed in the future; in the 1530s the procedure of codification was modified to allow an official record to be kept of such innovations. The influence of the royal commissioners also sometimes worked towards a greater uniformity, tinged with the learned law, where they suggested reforms that would be acceptable on grounds of equity.

12.2.3   By the end of the sixteenth century the process of codification in the *pays de coutumes* was complete in the sense that all officially recognized customs had been reduced to writing and carried the royal authority. On the other hand, uniformity was still a long way off. On the eve of the Revolution of 1789 it is easily possible to count more than three hundred customary jurisdictions. However, the compilation of settled written texts meant that for the first time the material existed for a thorough juristic treatment of the customary law. The sixteenth and early seventeenth centuries saw a wealth of commentary on the customs that, in effect, created a French national law, which in due course was to become fully codified.

12.2.4 It is significant that although such men (with whom we shall shortly deal) as Dumoulin, Coquille and Loysel were neither ignorant of nor uninfluenced by Roman law, they were not Romanists. The specifically Roman studies of the legal Humanists had little influence on French practice; in general the professors of civil law in the French universities were not in the leading rank of scholars. Furthermore, because the clearest way to fame and success lay in the service of the king, the more able or ambitious of these professors sought to enter his service, and few taught for more than a decade or so – a pattern we observed earlier among teachers of canon law. Thus it was the advocates and judges who created French law, just as in England the bench and bar created English law, but in France these men had academic as well as practical legal training.

12.2.5 In the Midi, Roman law retained its status as a general subsidiary source; in the North arguments based on it were frequently accepted, but on grounds of reasonableness and not authority. It had a considerable role to play, however, because the subject matter of the customs was restricted. Since the customs were based on feudal law or Frankish usage they dealt above all with land law, including leases, with inheritance and with family relationships, but they had little to say about obligations, whether contractual or delictual, and they were not normally concerned with criminal law or procedure; civil procedure had long been dominated by romano-canonical notions. In the field of obligations therefore, within a framework made possible by the mediaeval influence of the learned law, the French jurists introduced civilian ideas while formally addressing themselves to the customs. Procedure and the criminal law were spheres of interest to the crown, and royal legislation became pre-eminent there, as it did also in the field of mercantile law, as economic policy came to be one of the more central concerns of government.

12.3 LEGAL LITERATURE IN THE SIXTEENTH AND SEVENTEENTH CENTURIES

12.3.1 We have remarked that the major French jurists of the sixteenth and seventeenth centuries were not academics – although French lawyers did train for the law at universities – but practising lawyers. They were all, however, familiar with Roman law, on which they drew for particular solutions and comparisons. They steadily built towards a private law common to all (northern) France, but the absence of a single central court and the persistence of local variations meant that a systematic and national French law was not achieved until the nineteenth century.

12.3.2 The most famous of these jurists, Charles Dumoulin, or Molinaeus, (1500–1566) started his career as an advocate before the *Parlement* of Paris but, according to one story, a speech defect led him to consultancy and writing rather than speaking. Dumoulin felt himself to be within the Humanist tradition, particularly the nationalist tradition of Hotman. While hardly a Protestant in doctrine, he too suffered a period of exile in consequence of his unbridled attacks on ecclesiastical jurisdictions, his rejection of papal authority within France, and his opposition to the work of the Council of Trent. In 1539 he published, as the first title of a work *On fiefs*, the major part of his enormously influential commentary on the Custom of Paris, which he called 'the chief of the customs of this realm and of all France'. In this he made a vigorous attack on the feudal courts and their bad customs; strict interpretation should be used to minimize feudal rights and to stress those of the Crown. In this d'Argentré opposed him, holding that feudal rights were important for the good ordering of society.

12.3.3 Dumoulin also wrote more generally on the customs; he wanted to find a general custom common to all France which could be used in preference to Roman law as a supplementary general source, and he proposed that the Custom of Paris should be used to achieve this degree of uniformity. The reformed Custom of Paris, issued in 1580, relied heavily on Dumoulin's observations on the 1510 version; it was also in essence the law provided for the French colonies established before the Revolution. He was not concerned with the *pays de droit écrit* but wanted for the *pays de coutumes* one short, clear and equitable code; he firmly linked equity and royal power. His style was Bartolist, setting out the full arguments of various authors for and against the proposition he was maintaining, and his learning was immense; he was well acquainted with the *Corpus Iuris* and the work of the Glossators, Commentators and canonists. He wrote commentaries on various titles of the *Corpus* and also on contemporary problems of canon law. His views, however, were independent and original. He had no hesitation in rejecting doctrines he thought unsuitable to the needs of contemporary France or in adapting others in accordance with his own views. His conviction of the rightness of these views was given strength by his regular attendance at the sessions of the *Parlement* and his close relationships with bench and bar in Paris; conversely, the decrees of the *Parlement* were influenced by his published works. He more than anyone else was the creator of French law.

12.3.4 Guy Coquille (1523–1603) studied law at Padua and at Orléans, where he also came to the practice of law; he then attended the bar in Paris and returned to Nevers as an advocate. He later became *échevin* and then procurator-general to the duke of Nevers, and he was a deputy of the Third Estate at three meetings of the Estates-General, at Orléans in 1560 and at Blois in 1576–1577 and 1588. He too was noted for his Gallican sympathies, but his attacks on the papal jurisdiction were more discreet than those of Dumoulin. He was interested in public law, including the popular element in the creation and acceptance of custom, and in royal legislation as well as in the customs. His major work, the *Institution au droit français* (*Institute of French Law*), was published as the possible basis for fulfilling his dream of legislative unity. For current needs he also produced a clear and simple commentary on the Custom of the Nivernois.

12.3.5 Antoine Loysel (or Loisel) (1536–1617) was a poet and scholar, a legal historian as well as a legal practitioner. This may partly explain why he was more willing to combine Roman with French law. He was educated at Toulouse where he studied under Cujas, whose disciple he always held himself to be, and whom he followed to Cahors, Bourges, Paris, and Valence. In 1560 he became an advocate in Paris; some twenty years later he was for three years the king's advocate in the Protestant court permitted in Guyenne. He wrote on the Custom of Beauvais, his native town, and also on the *Parlement* of Paris, but he was most influential through his *Institutes Coutumières* (*Institutes of the Customs*), published in 1607. His style was brief and axiomatic, not explanatory. He saw future progress in terms of the 'conformity, equity and reason of a single law, custom, and weight and measure under the king'. When in 1679 the first professor of French Law was appointed in Paris, he gave lectures on Loysel's *Institutes*, which thus acquired an unofficial but significant authority as a source of law.

12.3.6 Jean Domat (1625–1696) was to some extent an exception to all the jurists already mentioned. He dealt with Roman law but, like Doneau, he claimed to present it in its natural order in *Les lois civiles dans leur ordre naturel* of 1694. Although dealing with Roman law, he was working towards a new planned society; he wanted to integrate Natural Law and secular justice. He anticipated much of Montesquieu, and he is generally held to be a direct ancestor of the *Code Civil*, although his work was perhaps more widely admired than read. He was a graduate and indeed a doctor of law of Bourges, and a contemporary and close friend of his fellow citizen, the great philosopher Pascal. He spent most of his life in his native Clermont, practising at the bar there and being much involved in the affairs of the province; his interests extended to public as well as private law.

12.3.7 Under Louis XIV (1643–1715) those jurists who had the king's ear or lawyers who became royal servants had more chance of having their doctrines put into practice, but we shall refer to Lamoignon and Colbert in the context of royal legislation. Natural Law was the intellectual fashion of the seventeenth century – we shall consider it in the next chapter. Its influence is discernible in the *Institutions du droit français*, published in 1665, of Clément Fleury, who was a tutor to the royal children, and also in Domat's work; nevertheless it did not really have much impact in France until the eighteenth century.

12.4 THE *PARLEMENTS* AND OTHER COURTS

12.4.1 The *Parlement* of Paris had played a crucial role in the success story of the French Crown; the existence by the end of the fifteenth century of a strong centralized monarchy (at least by comparison with the Empire) was very largely due to the royal control of the administration of justice. In the difficulties of the Hundred Years War the *Parlement* had acquired a policy-making role; during the Wars of Religion, when the kingdom was divided and the members of the *Parlement* with it, it had become something of a check upon the absolute or arbitrary power of the Crown. For a law to be held valid and applied it must have been registered with a *parlement*, most frequently the *Parlement* of Paris. In 1566 the right of remonstration, of telling the king to think again, was formally recognized in the Ordinance of Moulins, although in 1563 Michel l'Hospital (d. 1573), the chancellor of France since 1560, rebuked the *Parlement* of Paris for respecting some and not other royal ordinances. Louis XI (1471–1483) had made the judges of a *parlement* – and some other officers – irremovable; this together with the perquisites of office helped create from the upper levels of the legal profession a *noblesse de robe* to rival the old nobility. Thus the *parlements* were important on political and social grounds as well as for their primary judicial function.

12.4.2   Since the *Parlement* of Paris held that it was exercising by delegation the judicial powers of the Crown, it felt free to depart from existing law when justice and equity demanded. The exercise of this discretion was for long shrouded in mystery owing to the scarcity of reports of decided cases prior to 1600, although the records themselves are voluminous. From early times there seems to have been a reluctance to allow the court's reasons for its decisions to be revealed; this may partly be explained by the *Parlement*'s early role as the king's council when there were such awkward vassals of the French Crown as the king of England, who spent much of the later Middle Ages at war with his feudal superior. The confirmation as late as 1550 of this secrecy, when it was decreed that the mystery of the court should be inviolate, was probably due to the religious tensions and conflicts of the period; certainly secrecy was not inherent in the canonical system, where it was normal to publish the evidence and the full judgment. It is clear, however, that in some form adequate records were kept because the *Parlement* was concerned with consistency; as early as the later fourteenth century we know that it was prepared to consider its own prior decisions in coming to judgment.

12.4.3   Some reports of cases in the *Parlement* did survive from the fourteenth century. Du Breuil, an advocate, wrote a manual on procedure which referred to numerous cases, in most of which he himself had participated; among other reporters another advocate, Jean Le Coq, produced widely circulated notes of decisions covering fifteen years at the end of the century. In the fifteenth century there were some reported decrees from Paris which Dumoulin was able to use; for the first fifty years of the *Parlement* at Toulouse there were digests of its sentences. In the *Parlement* of the Dauphiné, established at Grenoble in 1451, *Decisions* were recorded by one of the judges, Gui-Pape; since the Dauphiné lay in the *pays de droit écrit* the arguments reflected were mainly from Roman and canon law and the learned doctors. In the second half of the sixteenth century one Jean Papon, a judge in a lower court – a royal *bailliage* – published his *Arrêts Notables* (*Notable Rulings*) which referred to decisions of all the *parlements* and ranged over three centuries; his arrangement was systematic, by topic rather than chronological.

12.4.4   The demand which Papon had done something to satisfy was even better served by the publication in 1609 – a year after the author's death – of the *Arrêts Notables* of George Louet, for twenty-four years a judge of the *Parlement* of Paris. The publication was arranged by the first or senior president of the *Parlement* and was given formal approval by that body. The cases reported were from Louet's own experience, in particular when he had been acting as rapporteur (see para 7.5.11) for one of the *Chambres des*

Enquêtes (of which there were by that time five). He gave the arguments (which included civilian as well as customary references, and citations from Dumoulin), an outline of the facts, the decision and the reasons for that decision. In 1629 another judge of the *Parlement* called Bouguier published his *Arrêts de la Court Decisifs (Decisive Rulings of the Court)*, and in 1645 a further series came from another judge, Claude Le Prestre, who quoted extensively from the private but official record kept for the court's own use.

12.4.5 Whether because of the secrecy rule or because the Crown was again seeking to control the courts, no more case reports emerged from the bench of the *Parlement* of Paris until Grainville's in 1750. However, in the provincial *parlements*, particularly at Toulouse, some judges continued to publish decisions of their courts. The bulk, and it was a very considerable bulk, of seventeenth century reports were, however, made by practitioners at the bar. These reporters tended to concentrate on the pleadings rather than the decisions but some, like de Montholon, also reported the decrees 'in red robes'. On these occasions, after a solemn procession, the whole bar was assembled together and the judges, splendidly dressed in their red robes of office, issued decrees which were intended to instruct the legal profession on the future treatment the courts would give to the matter in question.

12.4.6 Despite the growing power of the Crown, the rule-making powers of the *parlements* as subordinate legislatures continued to be exercised freely throughout the seventeenth century. Many such *arrêts de règlement* concerned the procedure of the *parlements* themselves and of the lower courts, but others applied to public order and the general population, such as the prohibitions of blasphemy by the *Parlement* of Paris. But it was in the development of private law that the *parlements'* decrees far outweighed royal legislation, at least until Colbert's time (see para 12.5.3ff). For the *parlements* interpreted the customs and supplemented existing law, and ruled authoritatively in disputes over the law merchant.

12.4.7 In spite of the buying and selling of judicial office, corruption, at least corruption as recognized by contemporaries, seems to have been rare in the seventeenth century *parlements*; in the sixteenth century their reputation had been lower when religious conflicts had confused justice. It was largely because of the political role of the *parlements*, which led the opposition to authoritarian government and provided a check on royal power, that new courts were created, rather than further powers being granted to the *parlements*.

12.4.8 In 1551, to avoid flooding the *parlements* with business and to give litigants a more convenient forum, *présidiaux* were set up as appellate courts from the *baillis* and *sénéchaussées*; each was based upon a strictly geographical area with no regard to the boundaries of ancient provinces and regions. Many litigants, however, preferred the greater security of a judgment from a *parlement*, and the maximum sum over which the *présidiaux* had jurisdiction meant that inflation diminished their competence. Some attempt was made to give them an appellate jurisdiction from customary and seignorial courts but this was resisted, by the arguments of Coquille among others. *Tribunaux consulaires* were specifically commercial courts; the first was created in 1549 for Toulouse, and L'Hospital established another in Paris in 1563. They were courts for specific classes of person, for *négociants*, *marchands* and *navigateurs*, and not for the ordinary citizen; they were staffed by men of the merchant class and they used summary procedure. The *tribunaux* survived the Revolution without serious modification. Although the *parlements* disliked this further invasion of their jurisdiction, the courts were very popular with their users; the problem was that not enough were set up. There was, however, an intellectual and emotional argument against such special courts based on the rational desire, linked with the movement towards codification, for a single hierarchy of courts, competent to hear all kinds of suit. Thus it was on the *parlements* as much as any other single issue that the Revolution ultimately hinged.

12.5 ROYAL LEGISLATION

12.5.1   In the Middle Ages legislation was on the face of it a matter of declaring what was the law, of restoring good custom; this had been as true of Henry II of England as it still was for Charles VII in the Ordinance of Montils-les-Tours in the mid-fifteenth century. But the movement towards codification of the customs, which specifically included the establishment of new practices, was echoed in the movement, seen at Orléans and Blois, towards the consolidation of the edicts and ordinances. In 1539 Francis I issued the celebrated Ordinance of Villers-Cotterêts which substituted romano-canonical for feudal procedure in criminal trials, required the registration of gifts (on the pattern of the later Roman law), regulated the function of notaries, and provided for registration of civil status. In 1566 the Ordinance of Moulins substituted written proof for oral witnesses in civil procedure.

12.5.2   The constitutional theory of a sovereign king, developed by men like Bodin and Dumoulin, placed on the Crown the duty to be active. In the seventeenth century economic planning was to appear as part of the attempt at the rational ordering of society. The first serious step towards a code of law based on royal legislation was made by Barnabé Brisson (c.1530–1591), consequent upon the Ordinance of Blois of 1577. It was no coincidence that Guy Coquille had been a deputy at the Estates-General whose petition had led to this edict and that he also had attended the meeting in 1566 at Orléans. Brisson, who had already issued a popular dictionary of law, produced a collection of all the royal ordinances then in force, arranged on a systematic basis; it was to be known as the '*Code Henry III, Basilica*'. It included the Ordinance of Villers-Cotterêts, which was linked with the introduction of the official use of the French (as opposed to the Latin) language for private law suits, and the Ordinance of Moulins on the reform of judicial procedure. However, because it appeared just after the king's death it was never made official; indeed, the insertion of forged ordinances led to further confusion. In 1614 the Estates-General (in its last meeting before the Revolution) repeated the request for a codification of the ordinances; the Third Estate also petitioned for the *parlements* to reveal the reasoning behind judicial decrees where these depended on rules of law or custom. The need for the imposition of uniformity through royal edicts became more necessary in the seventeenth century in that the division between the *pays de droit écrit* and the *pays de coutumes* became more marked as each became more unified within itself.

12.5.3 The two major legal figures of the reign of Louis XIV (1643–1715), after his emergence from regency in 1661, were Jean Baptiste Colbert (1619–1683) and Guillaume de Lamoignon (1617–1677); the one was Louis' chief minister from 1661, the other, first president of the *Parlement* of Paris. Advised by Colbert, in 1665 Louis set up a special commission, the *Conseil de Justice*, composed of eminent jurists and members of the King's Council; its function was to act as a kind of law commission, proposing reform in the law. The coming into being of such a body, individually appointed by the king, meant the exclusion from the reform process both of the *Parlement* of Paris as an entity and also of members of the legal profession collectively. From the provincial *parlements* and from various legal experts, memoranda were requested which would detail what was in need of reform and suggest remedies. *Maîtres des requêtes* were sent out to discuss these and to forward them to Paris. The *Parlement* became involved, through its own initiative, a mere three months before the publication of the Ordinance of 1667 on civil procedure, when the bulk of the preparatory work had already been completed. The influence of Lamoignon himself was significant because the jurists on the commission knew and appreciated his outlines for a code. The Ordinance aimed to provide a complete and detailed systematic codification of this branch of the law; despite this, supplementary edicts were found to be necessary. It regulated the authority of edicts, ordinances and judicial decrees; it prescribed limits on adjournments and appeals; it abolished the *enquête par turbe*; it distinguished diligence – rights of enforcement – arising from commercial and from civil debts. In 1670, but this time with the co-operation of the *Parlement* throughout the preparatory sessions, an Ordinance on criminal law and procedure (of which the drafting owed much to Lamoignon) was published; it defined crimes more precisely, settled criminal procedure and the spheres of the various jurisdictions, and sanctioned penalties.

12.5.4 Lamoignon had meditated on a reformation of the Custom of Paris as the basis of a renewed and unified French law well before Colbert's rise to power. He and the jurist Barthelémi Auzanet had circulated working papers and held discussions on the project with advocates and magistrates. Colbert, however, had the ear of the king and Lamoignon was left outside the inner circle of reformers. Indeed, many of his comments on the draft Ordinances were without effect, such as his protests at the refusal to allow accused persons legal advice. Nevertheless his book, *Arrêtés ou Lois Projetées*, in which he laid out his scheme for a single code based on the customary law, was immensely influential. It was much more used by jurists of the eighteenth century than was Domat's work, and in particular it was drawn on by the chancellor, Henri-François Daguesseau (1668–1751), in the composition of the mini-codes on donations (1731), wills (1735), and substitutions – entails – (1747), which were issued as royal ordinances under Louis XV.

12.5.5 Undoubtedly Colbert's inspiration lay behind the Ordinance of Commerce (or *Code Marchand*) of 1673; it only concerned merchants, who were still a legally identifiable class, grouped in guilds, not ordinary citizens.

Mercantile interests were widely consulted in its drafting; it was designed to free commercial law from local custom and, in thus providing a uniform law merchant within France, to diminish the length and cost of litigation. It also regulated commercial accounts and laid down rules for companies and partnerships. In 1681 a maritime code (*Ordonnance de la Marine*) was issued, dealing with admiralty jurisdiction and procedure as well as the rights of consuls in foreign countries and the duties of ships' masters. These statutes were to provide much of the material for the *Code de Commerce* of 1808, and exercised considerable influence on mercantile law generally.

FURTHER READING

J Brissaud	*History of French Private Law* (Continental Legal History series, vol III, Boston, 1912)
	History of French Public Law (Continental Legal History series, vol IX, Boston, 1915)
JP Dawson	'The codification of the French customs', *MichLR* 38 (1940) 765
	The Oracles of the Law (Ann Arbor, 1968) ch 4
JH Shennan	*The Parlement of Paris* (London, 1968)

Chapter 13

THE SEVENTEENTH CENTURY

13.1 THE MAIN THEMES OF THE CENTURY

13.1.1   In many matters, as we have observed in both Germany and France, the seventeenth century saw the continuation of trends established in the sixteenth. The conscious continuation of these trends was in itself significant but there were new ideas as well.

13.1.2   From a point of view centred on Europe the world was still expanding; journeys of exploration continued side by side with the settlement of newly discovered areas. Religion was still a fertile source of dispute both within and between the states of Europe. These nation states were consolidating their frontiers and establishing their spheres of influence; many political changes of this nature, such as Sweden's acquisition of western Pomerania, Brandenburg's of Magdeburg, and France's of Alsace, or the recognition of the independence of Switzerland and the Netherlands, resulted from the Treaty of Westphalia which, in 1648, ended the Thirty Years War. The Scandinavian kingdoms of Denmark and Sweden became more a part of the European scene, as did Russia at the end of the century, under Peter the Great (1672–1725). The Holy Roman Empire was diminished and set on the path towards its decline into the Austrian Empire. Spain began to decline, and the Netherlands to take a leading role, in both economic expansion and legal creativity. Within states, political power was mainly in the hands of monarchies whose pretensions to absolute authority were justified by the writings of political theorists such as Hobbes. Not all monarchies were absolute and power might be shared even in those that were, but popular democracy was still far away. The economy was still predominantly agricultural; land was – as always – important for status as well as being the major source of wealth. Commerce, however, was expanding especially in the field of colonial trade; industrial production was becoming increasingly significant, along with the necessary developments in technology, although the Industrial Revolution was a century or more away. Mercantilist theory encouraged governments to intervene to protect and increase their state's share of international commerce in order to increase its wealth and power. The scientific revolution was in the offing; observation and experiment led to new understanding of the physical world.

13.1.3   In terms of legal history the century is remarkable for the development of a new concept of Natural Law, first by Grotius following the Christian tradition and then by the German rationalist lawyers, and for the growth of the Dutch Elegant Jurisprudence. The other new factor was that English jurisprudence began to share more fully in the European tradition, although its own influence was not to become widespread until the later eighteenth and nineteenth centuries. We shall look at these movements in turn. It is also noteworthy that in dealing with legal thought in the seventeenth century it becomes convenient to use current jurisprudential terms.

13.2 NATURAL LAW AS DEVELOPED BY GROTIUS

13.2.1   The roots of Natural Law theory (that certain legal rules are in some sense 'natural' and not purely arbitrary creations) lie in Plato and Aristotle, the great philosophers of ancient Greece. For Plato, the idea of justice was the pattern to which law ought to conform; in his thinking, however, justice was a virtue accessible only to the philosopher-kings who were to rule his ideal society and to legislate as far as possible in conformity with justice. This view, that law should conform to an ideal of justice but that knowledge of what justice demands is not granted to everyone, was transmitted to the early mediaeval world by St Augustine. Aristotle had taken a more practical approach to Natural Law. He made a clear distinction between morality and law, and he introduced the concepts of distributive and commutative justice. The former requires that we should give to each his due; the latter requires that we should make up inequalities brought about by our actions, and give due return for what we have received. To determine what is due, Aristotle relied on observation of nature, since he held that the natural world was created with a discoverable purpose; for example, observation shows that reason is what distinguishes men from other animals and consequently men should act rationally.

13.2.2   Aristotle's ideas were taken up in the thirteenth century by St Thomas Aquinas, who amplified them in his *Summa Theologica*. The Stoic philosophers, whose ideas were reflected by Cicero, had applied the idea of Natural Law to a wider world than Plato's city state of Athens; the world was of its nature orderly, but Natural Law was a moral rather than a legal order and justice was a private virtue. Both Aristotle and the Stoics believed in versions of the 'social contract' as an explanation of the existence of a legal order within any particular state; the state itself was seen as formed by agreement among the members (at the relevant time) of the society constituting the state. The 'social contract' was a concept much used in political and legal theories of the seventeenth and eighteenth centuries.

13.2.3   Aquinas was philosophically an idealist, believing that values such as justice have a real existence; he also believed that human reason, being the creation of a rational God who is the source of Natural Law, could discern justice. Positive law created by human authority could and should try to conform to divine justice. In the sixteenth century Calvin held to a version of this Christian Natural Law tradition. He held that God has the sovereign power of making law, and that human authority has a duty to give effect to God's law, which can be known partly through revelation in Scripture and partly through reason. The most influential Natural Law thinkers of the sixteenth century, however, were the Spanish scholars – canonists and theologians –

whose works were among the most important of Grotius' sources. Their leading figure – in that he was the master of several of the others – was Francisco de Vitoria (c.1483–1546), professor at Salamanca.

13.2.4 Vitoria departed most clearly from Aquinas' thought in being a voluntarist in the tradition of William of Ockham, the fourteenth-century philosopher; that is, he held that the only ground of an obligation was an act of will of a superior directed to moving the will of an inferior. For him *ius* had ceased to mean what was the due, the right balance, as between the parties to any situation, and had become a right capable of exercise by the beneficiary. It was with this view of rights that he argued that the native Indians of the Americas, being peaceful possessors, must be treated as owners of their property, despite their being in mortal sin as pagans. Furthermore, since they were rational and not of unsound mind, they could not be forcibly converted to Christianity, and their refusal to be converted was not a just ground for making war on them.

13.2.5 Among other influential Spanish legal thinkers were Agustín, whom we have mentioned as a Humanist, and Domingo de Soto (1494–1560) who also championed the Indians and opposed the trade in slaves; he developed the notion of the *ius gentium* as positive law, able to bind princes – Vitoria had held princes to be bound by their own stipulations at least. De Soto also wrote on the criminal law, opposing all 'purely' penal law theories which asserted that law imposed not an obligation as to conduct but simply, or purely (as in Kelsen's theory) an obligation to undergo a penalty, the performance or non-performance of the action being the condition of the penalty. Luis de Molina y Morales in the later sixteenth century discussed political authority in the light of Natural Law; he was also the author of an authoritative treatise on the law of entail in Castile. The civilian and canonist Diego Covarruvias (1512–1577) was influenced by Natural Law theories in his application of law to contemporary problems; he was the leading jurist who set out to justify the Spanish conquests in the Americas. Francisco Suarez (1548–1617) continued Vitoria's interpretation of Natural Law, being both a voluntarist and a rationalist, and like him criticized much Spanish conduct towards the Indians, arguing for their right to life, liberty and property. Like de Soto, he wrote on the criminal law, and also on the problems of the will of the law-giver and the need to be able to depose a wicked ruler.

13.2.6 Another important thinker of the late sixteenth century was Althusius whom we have mentioned as a Humanist (see para 10.5.3). In his *Politica*, first published in 1603, he propounded a doctrine of popular sovereignty; some of its roots lay in the Conciliar Movement of the fifteenth century but it owed more to the Calvinist view of an ideal human community. In a very different juristic tradition was Alberico Gentili, whose work we have already discussed (see para 7.2.3). When Grotius appeared, his importance lay not in the novelty of any particular idea in his work but in his expansion of Natural Law into something separate from the civilian or canonist tradition; he laid the foundations of the Natural Law of the Enlightenment. He did not, however, use to the full the enormous potential of the new theory; in his own writings Natural Law remained essentially explanatory, providing a rational background for existing law, whereas for the German rationalists who followed him Natural Law was the justification for and guide to reform and change.

13.2.7   Hugo de Groot (1583–1645), better known as Grotius, studied at the University of Leiden, acquired a law degree from Orléans, engaged in practice at the bar and at the age of twenty-four was appointed Advocate-General of Holland, Zeeland and West Friesland. His religious and political views eventually brought him into conflict with the government of Holland, and he was charged with treason and with disturbing the established religion of the United Provinces; after serving nearly two years (1619–20) of a life sentence of imprisonment he escaped and left the Netherlands for France. Some ten years later he returned briefly to Holland but was forced into exile again and spent the last ten years of his life in the service of Queen Christina of Sweden. It was while in prison that he drafted the *Introduction to the Jurisprudence of Holland* to which we shall return later (para 13.4.4). It was in France that he wrote his treatise, seminal for the development of Natural Law, *De Jure Belli ac Pacis* (*On the Law of War and Peace*), published in 1625, which built on an early work of his, *De Jure Praedae* (*On Prize Law*), and in which, so the title page says, the law of nature and of peoples and likewise the chief elements of public law are explained (*'in quibus jus naturae et gentium, item juris publici praecipua explicantur'*).

13.2.8   The practical problem Grotius was trying to meet in this treatise was that of providing a law which would be binding on all nations without necessarily having its basis in any particular legal tradition. The difficulty was that there was no longer – even in theory – any universally accepted authority, such as Pope or Emperor, as a result of the Reformation and the growth of national sovereign states. Grotius tried to provide an international law by the application of Natural Law, which he based on human experience as testified by tradition. He explains his approach in an introductory chapter (*Prolegomena*). Warfare was prevalent – the Thirty Years War distressed all central Europe between 1618 and 1648 – and in the noise of conflict the law could not be heard, yet

'among the characteristics of mankind is the craving for society, that is for a communal life not just of any sort but peaceful and ordered in accordance with reason' (para 6).

Animals instinctively seek their own good and so, although lacking intellect, do infants.

'The maintenance, in a form suitable to human reason, of society is the source of that law which deserves the name, from which result: abstention from what belongs to another, making restitution of anything of another's we have obtained together with its increment, the obligation to fulfil promises, reparation for loss caused by fault, and the deserved infliction of penalties among men' (para 8).

He observes that it is in the nature of man to follow, in accordance with reason, a rightly formed judgment; that his system of Natural Law is not logically dependent on the existence of God or of a god concerned with the affairs of men, although both reason and tradition, confirmed by many proofs and miracles, support Christianity. Law comes from instinct and from the will of God which we must discern by the exercise of reason. Roman law recognized the social nature of man, and Grotius cites the Digest as declaring that a cognatic relationship between us has been created by nature. Civil laws flow from the fact that it is of the nature of law to stand by one's agreements.

'Human nature, giving us the craving to live a social life, is the mother of Natural Law; the mother of civil law is obligation springing from agreement and, since it takes its force from Natural Law, nature can also be said to be a great-grandmother of this law' (para 16)

13.2.9 He cites approvingly Aristotle's condemnation of those who want only lawful rulers among themselves but have no care for justice among other nations. Some Christian thinkers, such as Erasmus, would solve the problem of war by forbidding all exercise of arms, but Grotius fears that this is impossible. Books on the laws of war have been written by Vitoria and Alberico Gentili, among many others, but he proposes to improve on them.

'It has been my first concern to relate the proofs of those things touching the law of nature to concepts so unquestionable that no one can deny them without doing violence to his own nature. For the principles of that law, if you direct your attention rightly, are in themselves clear and self-evident, almost in the way of those things which we perceive with the external senses; and the senses do not err if their organs are well formed and if other necessary conditions are present' (para 39).

13.2.10 For proof of this Natural Law Grotius explains that he has made use of philosophers, above all Aristotle (and also Cicero and Seneca who were much influenced by Stoicism), of historians, poets and orators, both Greek and Roman, of Scripture, of the canons of the Councils, of the Church Fathers and of the Scholastic thinkers, such as Vitoria and de Soto, also of the Roman law of the *Corpus Iuris* and the Theodosian Code, of the Glossators and Commentators – he cites Accursius and Bartolus – and of the Humanists as well as of the works of recent jurists such as Covarruvias, Bodin and Hotman. He is not aiming to deal with the art of politics; Aristotle had seen the distinction between politics and law, although Bodin did not.

13.2.11 Grotius was deliberately trying to deal in abstractions and to avoid being tied to particular times or places; although inspired to write by the misery of contemporary warfare, he claimed that his theories were not related to current events. The system he proposed could apply in any time or circumstance, and indeed his system of rules was capable of being drawn on not only in relation to disputes in international affairs but also in matters of private law. Through Pufendorf, Christian Wolff and Thomasius his work had immense influence on the development of both private and public law, particularly in Germany; in Scotland too Stair claimed direct inspiration from Grotius. His influence on these and other later writers appears both in the arrangement of materials, as in the treatment of property and obligations, and in specific rules, such as the transfer of property by consent. Accordingly, although he is most commonly known as the father of modern public international law (and he was the institutional founder of Dutch law), Grotius was also a starting point for the codifying lawyers of the Enlightenment and a support for an increasingly mercantile society, in which good order and a clearly defined system of rules of property and obligations were seen as highly desirable. He provided an overall scheme, not merely a set of rules for particular application. It is somewhat ironic that, in basing the law on the subjective rights of the members of a community, that is such rights as the right to property or to reparation for injury, his approach to the presentation of law could be taken up by the legal positivists – a strange fate for the originator of a system of Natural Law.

13.3 THE GERMAN SCHOOL OF NATURAL LAWYERS

13.3.1 Whereas Grotius was to a large extent within the Humanist tradition, the German Natural Lawyers based, or tried to base, their approach on the scientific method of Galileo or Descartes. The method aimed at building up a system deduced logically from axioms, worked out by experiment and observation, which in their turn corrected the results achieved by logic. In theory this made it possible to free Natural Law from any particular authority or presuppositions; Natural Law thereafter was based on the consideration of man as part of a natural world which followed natural laws discernible by observation and reason.

13.3.2 Thomas Hobbes (1588–1679; see also para 13.5.4), the English political theorist, was the first to apply the method in jurisprudential writing in his book *De Cive* (*On the Citizen*, published in Paris in 1642) and again in his more famous work, *Leviathan*. He was widely read and his political philosophy was found attractive by absolute rulers and their supporters, but his general views on Natural Law were not accepted. Individual points, however, were taken over by other writers; for example, his view that a contract is a declaration of will by the parties and involves either the transfer of right by one party to another or the giving up of rights by one party in favour of another. This required that the will of a party to a contract must be expressed in such a way as to be known to the other party, and that the transfer or cession of rights must be accepted by the beneficiary in order to complete the contract. Hobbes also argued that later agreements cannot be effective against earlier ones because the right would already have been transferred; therefore the first buyer in a double sale (where the same thing is sold twice to different people) is preferred to the second.

13.3.3 Hobbes was an influence on Samuel Pufendorf (1632–1694), who is best known for his textbook, *De Jure Naturae et Gentium* (*On the Law of Nature and Nations*, 1672); a summary of this was published the following year under the title *De Officio Hominis et Civis iuxta Legem Naturalem* (*On the Duty of Man and Citizen according to Natural Law*). Pufendorf also made the social life of man the basis of his scheme of Natural Law but, unlike Hobbes, he argued that the natural state of man was one of peace and that the maintenance of peace was instituted and sanctioned by nature herself without any human intervention; men were therefore obliged to recognize Natural

Law insofar as they were endowed with reason. He distinguished divine law, Natural Law and positive law, but he treated divine law, which is based on God's revelation, as being in a separate sphere from the others because it goes beyond the concerns of this life. Natural Law was law which so harmonized with the intrinsic and social nature of man that the human race could have no wholesome and peaceful social organization without it. Positive law was that law which proceeded entirely from the will of the legislator, although it should not lack reason and usefulness, at least for the particular society of men for which it had been promulgated.

13.3.4 Founding on the sociable nature and individual weakness of man as a species, Pufendorf worked out a general system of rules for social living in a way which Hobbes had not. Hobbes had not felt any such need, since for him the content of the law was determined by the will of the legislator, which must be accepted for the sake of peace. Pufendorf followed the method of Hobbes and of Descartes, basing his system partly on deduction and partly on observation of man's conduct. Although his conclusions were closer to those of Grotius than of Hobbes, he used different methods from Grotius. He did not rely on the examples used by Grotius to find authority for his assertions but instead used both these examples and modern authors as material for observation, and from this he justified the premises on which he worked. He set out his principles in the first two of the eight books of *De Jure Naturae*; thereafter he applied them to the law of obligations (especially contracts), to property, to the law of persons and to public law, which was used in the sense both of law concerning the structure of the state and also of criminal law and law relating to international transactions.

13.3.5 Pufendorf was greatly respected by most jurists of his day and his subsequent influence was very considerable. His first book, *Elementa jurisprudentiae universalis* (*Elements of a Universal Jurisprudence*, 1660), led to his being appointed by the Elector Palatine to a chair in Law of Nature and Nations expressly created for him at Heidelberg; in this book he used the mathematical method, with axiomatic and observational deductions. While at Heidelberg he wrote a book vigorously attacking the Holy Roman Empire as then constituted, denying its descent from the ancient Roman empire and deploring the conduct of the ecclesiastical princes and of the Habsburgs. This led to his spending some years at Lund in Sweden where, after the publication of *De Jure Naturae*, he was appointed historiographer-royal. Shortly after the publication of *De Habitu Religionis* (*On the Usage of Religion*), which argued that the church was only a voluntary union of men, a corporation subject to the general rules affecting corporations and legally no more, he was invited to Berlin and became historiographer to the Elector of Brandenburg.

13.3.6 Pufendorf's work was influential for the structure of later codifications of law; it particularly affected the 'general part' which is commonly found at the beginning of codes and in which the principles of law are dealt with. Natural Law thinking also helped to systematize the Roman law material which was to be widely incorporated into codifications. (The work of Leibnitz (1646–1716), however – who thought little of Pufendorf – was also important in the movement towards radical legal reform and codification. He used a revised assembly of the Roman material; he also made clear the distinction between logical and empirical knowledge.) Pufendorf's legal theory gave a central place to contract, which he ordered into a general plan more systematically than ever before. The methods of ending obligations were also set out systematically; furthermore, obligation itself, along with succession, was seen as being a means of acquiring ownership. In the content of the rules which he sets out Pufendorf relied quite heavily on Grotius, and also on Hobbes in the case of contract, but he worked out more fully the consequences of the rules. For example, in the case of risk in sale – which according to Roman law passed to the buyer as soon as the contract was completed even if ownership had not yet passed – he went beyond Grotius when he argued that the passing of risk was dependent on whether the postponement of delivery was necessary, on whether the seller delayed in making delivery and on whether there was any fault in the buyer; Grotius had merely said that the seller should bear the loss if ownership did not immediately pass, thus disagreeing with the Roman rule. Again, on frustration of contract Pufendorf argued that only a change of circumstances making it actually impossible to fulfil the obligation released the party under obligation.

13.3.7   Christian Wolff (1679–1754) was a later member of the German Natural Law school who claimed to improve on Pufendorf's analysis. He argued that detailed rules of law were not immediately deducible from nature but that they could be worked out by proceeding from those of more general application which were immediately deducible, and thus to a detailed system. He proposed a more precise specification of the Natural Law rules which were appropriate for enactment as positive law. He alleged that his system was based solely on rational arguments, but one finds within it value judgments, such as a belief in the preferability of individual to common ownership. He was of considerable importance for the eighteenth-century German codifiers and for the nineteenth-century Pandectists. He also influenced writers on the *Gemeines Recht*, the German common law, and legal education in the German universities.

13.3.8   Christian Thomasius (1655–1728) began as a follower of Pufendorf but moved away from the older man's ideas when he applied the logic of the rational method to remove all necessary ethical content from Natural Law. Law was for him simply a compulsory duty imposed on the individual; there were therefore no eternal natural rules of law but only rules historically variable according to time and place. His interest in the development of German law followed naturally from this attitude, as did his interest in German language and history. His particular views were rational and humane; for example, he argued against the use of torture in obtaining evidence, and against the treatment of witchcraft as a crime – views which many states did put into effect in the century of the Enlightenment.

13.4 DUTCH ELEGANT JURISPRUDENCE AND DUTCH NATIONAL LAW

13.4.1   The rise of the Dutch Elegant Jurisprudence is connected in part with the Wars of Religion in France; many of the leading Humanists were Huguenots who fled from persecution to the Netherlands or Germany. Doneau, for example, left France for Geneva and was then in Heidelberg from 1573 to 1579, in Leiden from 1579 to 1587, and in Altdorf until his death in 1591. But such distinguished foreign visitors would not have been so influential if other factors favouring Humanist jurisprudence had not been present.

13.4.2 Towns had been important in the Netherlands from relatively early in the feudal period, and town law had close links with the general law merchant. Ecclesiastical courts had, as elsewhere in Europe, introduced romano-canonical procedure to a wide range of litigants; among the canonists the work of Johannes Andreae was particularly authoritative. There was no formal reception of Roman law but, in the fifteenth and early sixteenth centuries, there was a general acceptance of Roman law as a subsidiary source, especially in Friesland. Under Charles the Bold of Burgundy a central supreme court or *Parlement* had been established in 1473; this had only a brief life, and not until 1504 was the court re-established to become the Great Council of Malines (also known as Mechelen). It had an appellate jurisdiction from most of the provinces making up the Netherlands, northern and southern. Of the provincial supreme courts, the Court of Holland was founded in 1428 and throughout the rest of the century it increasingly came to be manned by judges trained in the learned law. Although there was no university in the northern provinces until the later sixteenth century, Louvain had been founded in 1425 and students from the Netherlands also studied law in Italy, France and Germany. In 1575 Leiden was established; other universities followed, such as Groningen in 1614, Amsterdam in 1631 and Utrecht in 1634.

13.4.3 During the sixteenth century there was a movement towards the collection and codification of customs within the provinces; Charles V ordered the provincial courts to undertake this work. A degree of codification was achieved in Friesland and Overijssel; Zeeland had already codified its feudal customs, but Holland was somewhat backward in this respect.[1] There was also some general legislation covering all the provinces in this period. Charles V in 1529 promulgated a general law on transfer of and charges on land, and the *constitutio Carolina* (see paras 11.5.1-2) was published in 1532; in 1570 Philip II issued an edict on criminal procedure. As a result of its wealth and of its leadership in the Wars of Independence, Holland[2] emerged as the most influential of the provinces; the wide acceptance of Roman law as a subsidiary source was strengthened by its use in Holland's supreme court at The Hague which also had jurisdiction over Zeeland. Nevertheless it may be reckoned that Roman-Dutch law, as it was named by the seventeenth century jurist van Leeuwen, began to emerge considerably earlier. The history of the late sixteenth and early seventeenth centuries not only encouraged the ever-present tendencies towards particularism but also pointed to the need for harmonization between the provinces. It is said that as late as the eighteenth century there could be doubt whether a crime should be tried by the Roman law, the Mosaic law, the *Carolina*, or a local statute of 1342.

---

1 Holland, Zeeland, Friesland, Overijssel, Utrecht, Groningen and Gelderland became the United Provinces of the Northern Netherlands; the Southern Netherlands were, broadly, modern Belgium.
2 The importance of Holland is indicated by the fact that in English its name is commonly given to the whole country.

13.4.4 This was the background to the work of Grotius. His *Introduction to the Jurisprudence of Holland* (*Inleidinge tot de Hollandsche Rechtsgeleerdheid*), first published in 1631, of which the first draft was written in prison with only limited access to other literature, provided the outline of a unified legal system, built on a combination of feudal and customary with Roman and Natural Law. It was thus in the same tradition as the work of Hotman and with the same purpose as that of Dumoulin and Coquille. Grotius was already developing his theory of Natural Law, but in the *Introduction* he was also concerned with the growth of legal institutions and with producing solutions to particular problems. It was with this latter intention that he dealt with the law of husband and wife, or classified delict as being directed against life, against the person, against freedom, against honour, and against property; it is also noticeable that he treated wrongs from the point of view of crime as well as delict. He established Roman-Dutch law as a practical system open to rational juristic development; in essence this was the law taken by the Dutch to their colonies in South Africa and the Dutch East and West Indies and Guyana. In South Africa, Ceylon and Guyana, subsequently ruled by the British until the coming of independence, it still, in part, survives, although being pushed into the background by the stress on customary, indigenous law.

13.4.5 The leading jurists who succeeded Grotius in the Netherlands continued to be inspired by the more practical aspects of Humanism and those methods of Natural Law of the less purely theoretical kind. Arnold Vinnius (1588–1657), professor of law at Leiden, wrote a commentary from the viewpoint of his own time on the Institutions of Justinian which was used for centuries, also *Jurisprudentia Contracta* (*The Law Abridged*), a textbook of Roman law which drew on Doneau, and a book of *Select Questions on Law* which dealt with contemporary problems of private and constitutional law in a style essentially traditional but not unaffected by the latest thinking. Simon van Leeuwen (1625–1682) practised law in Leiden for most of his life; the book which created the term Roman-Dutch law, *Het Roomsch-Hollandsch Recht*, was published in 1664, and has remained in use in South Africa as a work of authority. He naturally paid more attention to the decisions of the courts and the law of procedure than had Grotius, on whom he depended; his historical sources, however, were almost entirely Roman to the exclusion of custom. Ulrik Huber (1636–1694) was professor at Franeker in Friesland and for three years a judge in the Frisian supreme court; he wrote commentaries on the Institutions and the Digest, and a treatise on Roman law as applied in Friesland. Johannes Voet (1647–1713) wrote a major commentary on the Digest, *Commentarius ad Pandectas*, which has had great authority in the Netherlands and South Africa and has also been much cited in Scotland – even in the last decade. Professor successively at Utrecht and Leiden, his work was in the Humanist tradition but was also affected by rationalist theory. Unlike his more 'Elegant' contemporary, Gerhardt Noodt (1647–1725), who also taught at Utrecht and Leiden, his method was to consider Roman law not as an abstract legal complex but as the product of a changing human society, but the teaching of both men emphasized clarity of thought and expression.

13.4.6 The major figure of the early eighteenth century in Holland was Cornelius van Bynkershoek (1673–1745) who was from 1704 a member and from 1724 President of the Supreme Court of Holland, Zeeland and West Friesland. Four volumes have been published of the daily notes he made on the cases before the court, his *Observationes Tumultuariae* (*Observations in the Throes of Practice*), but they were designed for his own use rather than for publication. He wrote on Roman and municipal law and also on public international law; he is perhaps most deserving of fame for having produced a workable solution to the problem of claims to sovereignty over the sea. Bynkershoek, following the Roman doctrine of acquisition by possession, pointed out that continuous possession of the sea was not possible and denied English claims on the legal effect of maritime superiority; he acknowledged, however, that maritime nations might have special rights over certain parts even of the high seas, although not complete sovereignty. Effective protection, based on the force of arms, was made the criterion of sovereignty, and the marine league of some three miles, itself defined as the distance of a cannon shot, was accepted as fixing the limit of territorial waters. Bynkershoek's opinions were also influential in such areas of the law as the status of ambassadors, the taking of prizes in war, neutrality, blockade and contraband.

13.4.7 The Elegant Jurisprudence, the Humanist tradition, was, in the seventeenth century, best exemplified in the writings of the Dutch jurists, but there were Humanists elsewhere. We have already mentioned, in the context of the Humanists, the work of the two Gothofredi, Dionysius and Jacobus, who died in 1622 and 1652 respectively. Antoine Favre (1557–1624) wrote much on the civil law and also published decisions of the court of Savoy; he too was an adherent of the Humanist style. In Germany, although the *usus modernus Pandectarum* was dominant, there were some Humanists; JG Heineccius (1681–1741) was the most important of them. He was a pupil of Thomasius and, inspired by his master's ideas, wrote on Germanic law and its history; he also wrote a book entitled *Syntagma Antiquitatum Romanarum Jurisprudentiam Illustrantium* (*Collection of Roman Antiquities Illustrating Jurisprudence*), which was based largely on the order of the Institutions and was a typical work of Humanist learning, and also some smaller works on Roman legal history. His elementary textbook of Roman law was much used in Scotland as well as in the Netherlands and Germany. He also wrote a manual on Natural Law which did not, as so many others had done, overtly reject the value of the civil law; nevertheless he pointed out, for example, that the principle of reparation for wrong, commonly called Aquilian liability after the Roman *lex Aquilia*, was also to be found among the Turks or the Chinese, while the details of the *lex* had not been received.[3]

3   Cited by Alan Watson, *Legal Transplants* (Edinburgh, 1974) p 80.

13.5 ENGLISH JURISPRUDENCE

13.5.1 The final strand in seventeenth-century legal history is the appearance on the European scene of English jurisprudence. England had felt the Humanist movement in the sixteenth century but not in such a way as to affect the Common Law. In the fifteenth century two enduring legal works had been produced. Littleton's *Tenures*, first printed in 1481, was primarily concerned with feudal land law, but Littleton dealt sufficiently thoroughly with (Equitable) uses (see para 8.9.6) for the book to stay in print in student editions until the mid-nineteenth century. Fortescue's *De Laudibus Legum Angliae* (*In Praise of the Laws of England*, c.1470) was concerned with praising the English legal system as opposed to that of France; it was important in English constitutional development but had little impact in the wider world. The most original legal work of the sixteenth century in England was Christopher St German's *Doctor and Student* (published in 1523 and 1530), framed as a debate between a doctor of divinity and a student of the Common Law. At the time, it was relevant to the arguments about the extent of chancery jurisdiction and that of the ecclesiastical courts generally, but it put into popular form the Natural Law thinking of the canonists on the tensions between law and conscience; it remained much used as a textbook for some two centuries. It reflected European thinking but did not influence it.

13.5.2   A decade or so later Henry VIII, with political rather than jurisprudential motives, created Regius Chairs of Civil Law at Oxford and Cambridge; academic lawyers showed that they were well aware of intellectual movements on the continent, although practising Common Lawyers remained unmoved. William Fulbeck (1560–c.1603) wrote on the parallels between the civil, the canon and the Common laws; John Cowell (1554–1611), professor of civil law at Cambridge, wrote a description of the law of England organized on the model of Justinian's Institutions. John Selden (1584–1654) was interested in legal history and, for example, proved that trial by battle had been introduced by the Normans, whereas Sir Matthew Hale (1609–1676), whose *History of the Common Law* was published posthumously in 1713, was inclined to believe that all institutions of English law dated back to the Saxon period, if not earlier. Selden, however, did appear on the European stage when in 1618, consequent upon an international incident, he composed a reply to Grotius' *Mare Liberum* (*The Free Sea*) which had defended the freedom of the seas; *Mare Clausum* (*The Closed Sea* – only published in 1632) was unsuccessful as an argument, but Selden's skill as a disputant was recognized by Grotius himself.

13.5.3   The seventeenth century conveniently marks the passage from a degree of English receptiveness towards the influence of the Humanists and the Christian Natural Lawyers to the recognition on the continent of some English jurists as worthy of remark. Alberico Gentili, although brought up in Italy, spent the second half of his life in England and is remembered as Regius Professor at Oxford from 1587; he was widely influential, although his fame was somewhat overshadowed by that of Grotius. Richard Zouche (1590–1661), also Regius Professor at Oxford, was much read for his blending of Natural Law with a strongly Roman base in his *Elementa Jurisprudentiae* (*Elements of Jurisprudence*, 1629), which adopted a systematic division between rights (*ius*) and remedies (*iudicium*) in a general survey of the whole field of law. He also was prominent in international law, particularly with his *Jus Fetiale sive Jus inter Gentes* (*Ambassadorial Law or Law between Nations*, 1650). He himself was influenced by such writers as Fulbeck, Welwood and Selden as well as by Grotius. The influence he enjoyed on the continent is indicated by the frequent publication of his works; *De Jure inter Gentes*, for example, was printed at Leiden in 1651, at The Hague in 1659 and at Mainz in 1661, and a German translation was published in Frankfurt in 1666. Zouche invented the expressive term, law between nations, which more accurately indicated the difficulties implicit in the phrase than did the term law of nations; he also put stress on the importance of law based on agreement rather than on nature, although accepting that in international affairs the problem of enforcement diminished the force of positive law.

13.5.4 Another English thinker of great importance was Hobbes. As a firm believer in positive law – law is 'the command of him or them that have coercive power' – he was the intellectual ancestor of John Austin; he was himself influenced by the thought of Sir Francis Bacon. He is best known for his political theory, supporting, in the interests of peace, the absolute power of the ruler, but he also wrote on Natural Law. He founded human society on a form of social contract, and in his system the law of nature was an ordering which restricted natural rights.

> 'If a covenant be made wherein neither of the parties perform presently but trust one another: in the condition of mere nature, which is a condition of war of every man against every man upon any reasonable suspicion, it is void; but if there be a common power set over them both, with right and force sufficient to compel performance, it is not void.'[4]

He described the laws of nature as 'the dictate of right reason', and gave examples such as that one must relinquish some of one's rights, that one must perform contracts and keep trust, and, foreshadowing Bentham, that where one is in reasonable doubt one is to prefer that which promises the greater sum of good. Hobbes also held that the degree of punishment for an offence should be related to the effect of the punishment rather than to the nature of the offence.

4   Hobbes, *Leviathan*, I, ch 14.

13.5.5 Natural Law in Hobbes was more a context, an explanation of origins, than a system to be applied. This rather weak acceptance of Natural Law is also apparent in the work of Blackstone in the eighteenth century. Both the nature and the influence of Blackstone's work are such that it is more suitably described in the context of the seventeenth than the eighteenth century. Sir William Blackstone (1723–1780) was the first man to produce on the English Common Law something approaching an institutional description, in the tradition of Coquille, Grotius or Stair, although it is weak in the field of obligations. The *Institutes* of Edward Coke (1552–1634) may perhaps have owed their title to contemporary intellectual fashion but the content reveals only a traditional view of the Common Law. The *First Institute* is a commentary on Littleton, showing much learning but little system; the *Second, Third* and *Fourth Institutes* concerned the older statutes, the pleas of the Crown and the jurisdiction of the courts. Blackstone's *Commentaries on the Laws of England* were based on the lectures he gave as Vinerian Professor at Oxford, where he was the first occupant of this chair (founded in 1758). However, it is significant that the students to whom his lectures were addressed were far more likely to become parsons or squires than lawyers, since the notion of academic education for lawyers hardly existed in England[5] and legal training remained firmly in the hands of the profession. The move towards the teaching of municipal law in English universities was not so very much later than in other universities of Europe, but the available legal literature on the Common Law was centuries behind.

5   In 1846 the House of Commons Select Committee on Legal Education reported that 'no legal education, worthy of the name, of a public nature is at this moment to be had [in England]'. Cited by P Stein, *Legal Evolution* (CUP, 1980) p 78.

13.5.6   The structure of Blackstone's *Commentaries* was derived eventually from the civilian division of law into that relating to persons, to things and to actions. Book I of the Commentaries deals with the rights of persons; Book II with rights concerning things; Book III, on private wrongs, is primarily concerned with civil procedure although there are some chapters on delict; and Book IV, on public wrongs, deals more with the substantive criminal law, perhaps on the analogy of the last title in Justinian's Institutions. Blackstone's structure was sufficiently logical for the work to be adapted to new conditions; this happened particularly in the United States of America. For example, the Louisiana civil code of 1808 owed a considerable debt to Blackstone in its treatment of persons, and his work was not incompatible with the earlier civilian system found there. By the time of the American Revolution Blackstone's *Commentaries* were already well known in America. As American legal institutions increasingly grew away from their roots in the English legal system of the colonies, they found in Blackstone an institutional base on which to found a specifically American common law, the more attractive for its departures from the English tradition.

FURTHER READING

JW Cairns	'Blackstone, an English Institutist: legal literature and the rise of the nation state', *Oxford J Legal St* 4 (1984) 318
AP D'Entrèves	*Natural Law* (London, 1951)
R Feenstra and CJD Waal	*Seventeenth Century Leyden Law Professors and their Influence on the Development of the Civil Law* (Amsterdam, 1975)
J Finnis	*Natural Law and Natural Rights* (Oxford, 1980)
G Gorla and L Moccia	'A "revisiting" of the comparison between "continental" law and English law', *JLH* 2 (1981) 143
K Haakonssen	*Grotius, Pufendorf and Modern Natural Law* (Aldershot, 1999)
JM Kelly	*A Short History of Western Legal Theory* (Oxford, 1992) ch 6
Lord Lloyd and MDA Freeman	*An Introduction to Jurisprudence* (London, 5th edn, 1985)
K Luig	'Institutes of national law in the seventeenth and eighteenth centuries', *JurRev* (1972) 193
C Peterson	*Peter the Great's Administrative and Judicial Reforms: Swedish Antecedents and the Process of Reception* (Stockholm, 1979)

D Seipp   'The structure of English Common Law in the seventeenth century' in *Legal History in the Making*, eds WM Gordon and TD Fergus (London, 1991) 61

P Stein   'The attraction of the civil law in post-revolutionary America', *Virginia LR* 52 (1966) 403 (also reprinted in *The Character and Influence of the Roman Civil Law* (London and Ronceverte, 1988)

CC Turpin   'The antecedents of Roman-Dutch law', *Acta Juridica* 2 (1963) 1

Chapter 14

THE MAKING OF SCOTS LAW

14.1 THE RECEPTION OF ROMAN LAW

14.1.1 Although Scots law is not, as is sometimes popularly believed, based entirely on Roman law, one of the major influences in its formative years, along with feudal and canon law, was the Roman system in the shape of its revived civilian tradition. Much of the modern Scots law of moveable property and contract is undoubtedly civilian, while it still occasionally happens that argument adduced in court is backed by direct reference to Roman law.[1] Yet important though Roman law in its developed mediaeval form undoubtedly was, its influence can be exaggerated. The use of Roman terminology does not necessarily indicate the adoption of a Roman institution; Scots law, for example, borrowed the Roman term 'interdict', but the remedy is different in the two systems. Again, Scots law adopted the provisions of the *Lex Rhodia* (Rhodian Sea Law) not directly from Rome but from the general mercantile custom of Europe. Roman law has never been of itself authoritative in Scotland. Rather, as in the *pays de coutumes*, the civil law was received because of its rational character and as a source of equitable principle when the native law was silent or obscure. This is made plain in the work of the early Scottish institutional writers who were the first to reflect on the content of Scots law. Sir Thomas Craig wrote that 'we in this kingdom are bound by the laws of the Romans insofar as they are in harmony with the laws of nature and right reason' (*Ius feudale* I,2,14). Lord Stair said that, although Roman law '[has] great weight with us, namely in cases where a custom is not yet formed,' nevertheless it does not have 'with us the authority of law; and therefore [is] only received according to [its] equity and expediency' (*Institutions* I,1,16). However, considerable sections of his *Institutions* are really an annotated paraphrase of the Roman sources, for example, on possession, or *negotiorum gestio*.

1   Eg, *Sloans Dairies Ltd v Glasgow Corpn* 1977 SC 223; 1979 SLT 17; *Morgan Guaranty Trust Co of New York v Lothian Regional Council* 1995 SC 151; 1995 SLT 299.

14.1.2 In the Middle Ages there was some influence from the learned law but not even the beginning of a true reception of substantive Roman law. The contents of the mediaeval law books were primarily feudal and customary; there was no systematic civilian influence on the substantive law or the procedures of the lay courts. Admittedly civil (or Roman) law was not considered as an alien discipline but as part of the common intellectual inheritance of Europe; it was frequently used by notaries, for example, but not always with real understanding. This is definitely suggested by the evidence from charters, for the renunciations mentioned in the previous chapter on Scotland (see para 9.6.4) often seem to be included more to parade the learning of the scribe than to serve any real need; for example, there was little point in renouncing Hadrian's *beneficium divisionis* (which restricted the liability of a co-surety to his proportionate share) when it was not known in Scots law.

14.1.3 The first serious civilian influence on Scottish legal development was through canon law. The jurisdiction of the mediaeval Scottish church courts was similar to that elsewhere, but it seems that the activities of the canon lawyers were not limited to the strictly ecclesiastical sphere. Unlike England, Scotland did not have an established and powerful central court, and those who administered justice in the localities were largely untrained laymen. In contrast the Church offered justice that was both learned and sophisticated; and Church courts could claim a wide jurisdiction, for example, where a breach of good faith was alleged or a claim was based on a notarial document. It seems likely that many cases which in England would have gone to the secular courts were in Scotland disposed of through the courts spiritual, or through the offices of an ecclesiastical arbiter. Canon lawyers formed the only established legal profession until the fifteenth or even sixteenth century.

14.1.4 Canon law and the ecclesiastical courts brought civil law to Scotland in two ways. First, there is evidence of argument taken from Roman law being used as the basis of pleadings in the church courts. Examples include claims based on prescription and the use of *restitutio in integrum* (restoration to the original state of affairs) to set aside a sale alleged to be at an unjustly high price. The law used in the ecclesiastical courts did not necessarily affect the secular law, but litigants became accustomed to using civil law in one forum, and to the notion that it had much to offer that was profitable. Moreover, in Scotland the Church followed the general canon law more closely than, for example, it did in England; rules not given effect in England were in Scotland ultimately absorbed into the secular law, as happened with legitimation by subsequent marriage – which the Church had taken over from Roman law.

14.1.5 Second, and more important, the church courts introduced romano-canonical procedure into Scotland and thus were responsible for its ultimate reception into the lay courts. Churchmen played an important part in the jurisdiction of the Council in the fifteenth century, and it seems likely that their presence resulted in the use of procedures based on those of the ecclesiastical courts. When the College of Justice was founded in 1532 the Lord President and seven of the fourteen judges were clerics, and the records show that the 'new' court from the beginning employed a procedure similar to that of the church courts.

14.1.6 By the later fifteenth century there were signs that civil law was beginning to have a direct, even if generalized, influence on the law of Scotland. In 1469, for example, parliament introduced the (Roman) rule that when a child needed a tutor the nearest male agnate over the age of twenty-five was to act – although in this context 'agnate' was used to mean any male relative and not in its specialized Roman sense of one related exclusively through the male line. But it was not until the sixteenth century that the reception proper can be said to have begun. As elsewhere in Europe the agents of the reception were those who had received a university education in law.

14.1.7   Since Scotland had no universities of her own until the fifteenth century, Scots in the mediaeval and early modern periods who wished to study law had necessarily to go abroad. Scottish students in substantial numbers were to be found at the universities of Italy, France, Germany and the southern Netherlands. Paris and Cologne were always popular, while at Orléans, famous for its law school, the Scots even formed a separate student nation. Initially many of these students concentrated on canon law with a view to ecclesiastical preferment, and on their return to Scotland pursued careers in the Church and her courts, perhaps moving into the service of the Crown. During the fifteenth century something of a change took place and university-trained lawyers began to consider a career in the secular courts; at first their numbers seem to have been small, but they were important for the future.

14.1.8   In 1412 a university was founded at St Andrews and in 1451 another at Glasgow; Aberdeen's foundation dates from 1495, Edinburgh's from 1556. From the beginning it was intended that each should offer instruction in the civil and the canon law; indeed, this was one of the purposes behind their erection. If a legal education were available in Scotland it would be easier to produce adequate numbers of legally trained men to staff the courts – the pattern was the same as in Germany or France. Further, a statute of 1496 laid on barons and free-holders of substance the duty to ensure that their heirs attended for 'three years at the schools of arts and law so that they may have knowledge and understanding of the laws'; that is, all those who were expected to succeed to heritable jurisdictions were to be trained to discharge their duties in a competent professional manner, relieving the king's council of some of the business pressing on it at this time. However, many of the hopes placed in the new universities were frustrated, partly because of inadequate financial endowment, and perhaps partly because of student preference for foreign travel. The teaching of canon law at St Andrews seems never to have begun, and at the end of the sixteenth century it is not certain that any law at all was being taught at Glasgow. Scots students continued to go abroad in considerable numbers for their legal education, at first to France and to universities within the Empire and, after the Reformation, to the Protestant German states and the northern Netherlands. Leiden, founded in 1575, was particularly attractive to foreign students, and among them was a sizeable proportion of Scots. Only during the eighteenth century did the teaching of law in Scottish universities begin to revive and the practice of seeking legal education abroad to decline the Napoleonic Wars.[2] There was a substantial fall in the numbers going to the Netherlands, and the Revolutionary and Napoleonic Wars made a break.[2] However, a new interest in law and legal education in Germany developed in the nineteenth century.[3]

2   Cairns (1991).
3   Cairns, *Syracuse J of Int Law & Commerce* (1994); Rodger.

14.1.9   The facts of Scottish legal education had important consequences for the reception of the civil law. On the one hand, unlike the countries of the continent, Scotland did not develop in its own schools a strong tradition of civilian study. There were certainly Scottish civilians of note, but they mostly made their academic careers in Europe. Of this number were Henry Scrimgeour (1506–1572), who became professor of civil law at Geneva and produced an edition of the Novels, Edward Henryson, another sixteenth-century scholar, who became professor of civil law at Bourges, and William Barclay (1547–1608), professor at Angers. On the other hand, unlike the English, Scots who returned home to practise law after a legal education at a continental university were armed with some knowledge of up-to-date civilian scholarship as well as with some first-hand experience of other legal systems. Both factors had an effect on the development of Scots law.

14.1.10 Much of the Roman law that was received was the civil law of the *ius commune*, and in the sixteenth and seventeenth centuries this was hardly surprising. Even Germany, with its much more thorough reception of Roman law and the scholarly traditions of its universities, absorbed a Roman law that had for the most part been adapted to new circumstances. The Scots knew the Dutch civilian writers well and made much use of them, while references to the French jurists and the decisions of the French courts are to be found in Scottish works such as, for example, Spottiswoode's *Practicks*. Also instructive in this context is the first catalogue of the Library of the Faculty of Advocates, published in 1692; this gives a good indication of the kinds of material consulted and used by lawyers and thus helping to shape Scots law. The Library included

> 'the Bartolists, the French customary lawyers and the Dutch civilians and customary lawyers . . . the texts of the *Coutumes* of Paris, Bourges, Burgundy, Brittany, Troyes and Orléans, the decisions of the French *parlements*, and the works of Charles Dumoulin . . . and of Guy Pape. . . . [There were] treatises by Van Leeuwen, Matthaeus, . . . Voet, Grotius, Huber, Noodt, Vinnius, and many others.'[4]

4   Stair Society, vol 1, 177.

14.1.11 The Scottish reception of Roman, or civil, law seems to have been accomplished largely through the practice of the courts, and in particular of the Court of Session, or the Session, as it was generally called in its early years. By the mid-fifteenth century there appears to have been a well-established, if as yet small, body of professional pleaders regularly appearing in the lay courts. The foundation of the College of Justice in the following century established the Session, or Court of Session, on a firmer footing, and served to increase the attractions of such a career; the Reformation effectively closed the door on the alternative of ecclesiastical preferment. Not surprisingly the civil law was more explicitly used by advocates in the presentation of their arguments than by the judges in reaching their decisions, but this did not mean that the latter were ill-disposed towards civil law. The judiciary was bound to administer the law of Scotland as found in the statutes of the Scottish parliament, and in the various treatises devoted to the customary and feudal law. However, in the sixteenth century it became apparent that much of this indigenous law was uncertain; it did not exist in any authoritative form comparable to the codified customs of France. Moreover it was not a particularly mature or sophisticated law; with the exception of fields dealt with by some recent statutes. In default of other guidance the judiciary naturally turned to the *ratio scripta* (written reason) of Roman law and the writings of the civilians; one sixteenth-century Lord of Session commented:

> 'Thus far to the laws of the realm we are restricted, if any cumbersome or troublesome cause fall out, as often chances, which can not be agreed by our country's laws, incontinently whatever is thought necessary to pacify this controversy is cited out of the Roman laws.'[5]

The *Practicks* of Sinclair (see para 14.2.1) provide ample evidence of resort to the civil (and canon) law and doctrine.

5   Quoted by Stein (1963) p 216.

14.1.12   Such ready resort to the Roman or civil law did not please everyone. In 1609, reflecting Humanist attitudes, Sir John Skene (in the preface to his edition of the 'auld lawes') complained of those who spent all their time on the study of Roman law at the expense of the laws of Scotland which, he considered, ought to have been their primary concern. Indeed, part of his purpose in producing an edition of the 'auld lawes' was probably to counter this trend and to provide for Scotland a clear and definitive statement of at least part of its native law for use in the practice of the courts. But Skene's work was not adequate for this purpose, and the reception of civil law continued. The legal literature reflects its importance. In 1590 William Welwod, professor of civil law at St Andrews, produced *The Sea Laws of Scotland*, perhaps the first modern treatise on an area of Scots law. Welwod's own sources included the law merchant and appropriate Scottish material, but his greatest debt was to the learned law. Somewhat later the institutional writers, who are considered in the next section, inevitably placed Roman law among their sources, and, particularly in the field of obligations, a great deal of what they have to say is shot through with civilian doctrines as well as with those of Natural Law.

14.1.13   From the eighteenth century the direct impact of civil law in Scotland began to decline. This was partly because by then Scots law was emerging as a coherent national system; much of what the learned law had to offer had already been absorbed, and it was more practical to refer directly to the institutional writers or to the body of case law. Moreover, after the Act of Union in 1707 English law began to influence Scots law, partly because of the appellate jurisdiction of the House of Lords and, more generally, because with the expansion of Scottish industry and trade at that period a greater interest was taken in the commercial law of England. This is particularly evident in the later eighteenth century (see para 14.2.9). At that period mercantile law in England was being brilliantly developed in the judgments of Lord Mansfield; 'to him in particular can be attributed the creation of a modern system of commercial law'.[6] Further, some mercantile statutes of the Parliament of Great Britain applied to both countries, and they tended to be weighted in favour of the larger country's law.

6   AH Manchester, *A Modern Legal History of England and Wales 1750–1950* (Butterworths, 1980) p 28.

14.1.14 The Union of the Crowns of Scotland and England (and Wales) in 1603 was essentially a normal early-modern dynastic settlement, a result of the death without children of Elizabeth of England. James VI and I had plans to unify his two kingdoms, but there was not enough community of interest, let alone of institution, for this to be a realistic prospect. The languages were close but far from identical; both kingdoms had Reformed churches, but with very different doctrinal and disciplinary attitudes. Further, the move south to London of James, and of his son (Charles I) and grandson (Charles II) after him, led to a remote and absolutist governance of Scotland, which indirectly led to the Kirk's willingness to support the supplanting of the Stuarts in the revolution of 1688–1689. In effect, the civil wars of the 1640s and 1650s had been fought in England on grounds of constitutionality, that the king was only supreme within parliament, whereas in Scotland it had been religion that was the issue, the rejection of episcopalianism, Catholic or Anglican. However, the outcome of the Act of Settlement of 1688 and the revolution settlement in Scotland in 1689–1690 was a constitutional monarchy, which could not be responsible to two very different parliaments, potentially following very different policies. Fission or fusion were the choices, and fusion gratified many more interests, particularly in the economic field. Hence the Treaty of Union, and the Acts of Union of 1706, taking effect in 1707 (see Appendix 5). In theory the two parliaments, of Scotland and of England and Wales were abolished, and a new Parliament of Great Britain created. However, it was not merely the roughly ten to one ratio of population and (non-popular) representation which ensured English dominance, but also the survival in the new parliament of all the distinguishing features of the English parliament, such as separate Houses of Lords and Commons and deeply entrenched procedures (compare para 9.7.2). Reading any English textbook on constitutional or parliamentary history would never suggest that there was any break in parliamentary continuity. This is some explanation for the movement, devolutionary as well as Scottish Nationalist, which has led to the Scotland Act of 1998 and the meeting of a Scottish Parliament in May 1999. Future relations between Edinburgh and Westminster remain less clear than even the terms of the convoluted Act, but interesting. The Westminster Parliament retains substantial powers, for example, in the area of commercial law, and the authority to legislate even on devolved matters (1998 Act, s 28(7)). The acts of the Scottish parliament are valid only within its restricted competence (s 29).

14.2 LEGAL LITERATURE

14.2.1 We shall consider reports of decisions in the Court of Session in more detail when we come to look at that court in the next section. The earliest collections, described as *Practicks*, were compiled for private use by members of the court, not for publication; they were notes by judges (usually) of decisions at which they had been present. An example, indeed the earliest known collection, is the *Practicks* of Sinclair (see para 14.1.11), one of the Lords Ordinary and later Lord President of the Session (see para 14.3.1). Towards the end of the sixteenth century *Practicks* of a new kind began to appear, which are sometimes known as 'digest' *Practicks*. Instead of simply containing notes of decisions, they tried to offer a digest of the law, subject by subject, with all the material relevant to each topic being drawn together under the one heading – rather similar to the English *Abridgements* (or Papon's *Arrêts*). Their authors drew not only on the decisions of the Court of Session, and of the Lords of Council who operated in a judicial capacity before its foundation, but also on statute and the 'auld lawes' as found in such treatises as *Regiam Majestatem*. The first of these digest *Practicks* to be compiled was that of Sir James Balfour (Stair Society vols 21–22), completed in the 1570s, and possibly connected with one or both of the commissions appointed to revise the laws, of which Balfour was a member. Other examples in the seventeenth century include the *Major Practicks* of Sir Thomas Hope (Stair Society vols 3–4) and the *Practicks* of Sir Robert Spottiswoode. They were the forerunners of the institutional works, and Stair for one made much use of them in writing his *Institutions*.

14.2.2 While the phrase 'institutional writer' has become a term of art in modern Scots law, used to signify a small group of writers whose works – or at least some of whose works – are regarded as formal sources of Scots law, originally the term did no more than describe someone who wrote a particular type of book. Institutional writings in this sense were common throughout seventeenth-century Europe as the various nations began to break with the traditions of the *ius commune* and to create self-contained national legal systems. In each country the blend of indigenous law and elements taken from Roman, canon and feudal law varied, but in all we find a literature, usually in the vernacular, setting out the native law in a comprehensive and systematic way on the analogy of Justinian's Institutions. Often these works were intended to be used as textbooks, as local and sometimes even national law began to be taught in the universities of Europe. We have mentioned Carpzov and Stryk in Germany (see para 11.4.4) or Coquille and Loysel in France (see paras 12.3.4–5); Blackstone in eighteenth-century England (see paras 13.5.5–6) was belatedly in the same tradition.

14.2.3 Sir Thomas Craig owes his place as the first of the Scottish institutional writers to the purely Scottish usage of the term, for his *Ius Feudale* (*Feudal Law*) was not institutional in the European sense. Craig's book was written in Latin, not English or Scots, and it dealt only with feudal law, in which context we have considered its European influence (see para 2.9.8). Nor did Craig confine himself to the feudal law of Scotland; he produced what can better be described as a general work on the feudal law of the *ius commune* with special reference to Scotland. However, it was important for the future of Scottish legal writing; its systematic approach looked forward rather than backward and placed it in a different world from the relatively crude assembly of source material found in the digest *Practicks*.

14.2.4 Of fundamental importance for the future of Scots law and its development as a national system was Sir James Dalrymple, Viscount Stair (1619–1695). Born in Ayrshire, Stair studied and then taught in the University of Glasgow before turning to the law; in 1648 he became an advocate and in 1657 he was appointed to the bench. From 1671 until his death he was Lord President of the Court of Session, save for the years 1681–1688 which he spent in exile in Holland, returning with William of Orange. Stair's contribution to Scots law lies above all in his *Institutions of the Law of Scotland*, first published in 1681. The work was a landmark. First, Stair's approach was that of the early Natural Lawyers; he held to the view – not, he thought, shared by most lawyers – that law 'should be handled as a rational discipline, having principles whence its conclusions may be deduced'. In his introductory title on Common Principles of Law (1,1) he gave a primary definition of law as 'the dictate of reason' and he thought that the law of Scotland 'could be no other than *aequum et bonum* (equitable and good)'. In short, Stair offered a reasoned and systematic approach to the science of law: reasoned because he took equity as his overriding principle, and systematic because he attempted to expound the law in a logical and structured way.

14.2.5 Second, the *Institutions* are important as the first work of their kind to be devoted to the municipal law of Scotland. As Stair tells us in his opening words, his design was to

'give a description of the law and customs of Scotland, such as might not only be profitable for judges and lawyers, but might be pleasant and useful to all persons of honour and discretion.'

Native sources, particularly in the form of decisions of the Court of Session, have a prominent place in the exposition. The elements of the *ius commune*, Roman, canon and feudal law, are not – indeed, could not be – neglected, but 'none of these have with us the authority of law', having place only where native custom was silent, and then only on the grounds of their innate equity and expediency. Stair also made use of the continental, particularly the Dutch, civilian writers. But unlike that of Craig, Stair's work was not based on the *ius commune* with Scottish annotations but was rather an exposition of Scots law in the light of all the sources available; in particular, it was composed as a deliberate construct, founded on the principles of Natural Law, against which he measured Roman law (and other sources). It was an institutional work in the European sense; its appearance both marked the emergence and aided the further development of Scots law as a self-contained system of national law. It also set a pattern for the legal literature which came after it, in the sense that it provided a systematic exposition of the law. In looking at this we shall deal first with those writers who acquired the technical status of institutional writers.

14.2.6 On the margins of technical institutional status, but nevertheless an important influence, was Sir George Mackenzie. In 1684 the first edition of his *Institutions of the Law of Scotland* was published. This was very much shorter than Stair's book, although it also offered a comprehensive survey of the civil law of Scotland. Legislation is given a far more prominent place among the sources of the law, where Stair had emphasised the role of the courts. It was probably designed, on the model of Justinian's own Institutions, which it closely follows in arrangement and scale, to provide an elementary introduction to Scots law. It fulfilled this function in successive annotated editions for well over half a century after the author's death, until it was replaced by Erskine's *Principles* (see para 14.2.8). Mackenzie had been a student in France before becoming an advocate in 1659; he later held the office of Lord Advocate, adviser to the Crown and chief public prosecutor. His experience in dealing with the criminal law at the bar and in office was reflected in his treatise on criminal law (see para 14.2.11), which is a far more substantial work than the slender *Institutions*. As Dean of Faculty he played a leading part in the foundation (in 1682) of the Advocates Library – a scheme proposed by his predecessor, Sir John Dalrymple, Stair's son.

14.2.7   The eighteenth century saw two institutional writers of note: Andrew McDouall, Lord Bankton (1685–1760); and John Erskine (1695–1768). Bankton became an advocate in 1708 and a Lord of Session in 1755. His massive *An Institute of the Laws of Scotland* was published in three volumes between 1751 and 1753. In scale it was far closer to Stair's, whose arrangement it expressly followed (with some modification) than to Mackenzie's. It was an institutional work in the general sense, dealing with all of Scottish private law; it makes extensive reference to the Roman civil law as well as to court decisions and legislation. Most of the titles are followed by a comparative exposition of the relevant English law. Among other things, his book was intended to protect the integrity of the Scottish legal system by comparing and contrasting it with English law; it also shows the increased interest in English law which followed the Union of 1707.

14.2.8   Erskine entered the Faculty of Advocates in 1719 and was professor of Scots law at Edinburgh from 1737 to 1765. He is remembered for two books, *The Principles of the Law of Scotland* (1754) and *An Institute of the Law of Scotland*, published posthumously in 1773. The former, which is not usually counted as a formal source of law, is nevertheless an institutional work in the general sense, for it is an elementary introduction on the model of Mackenzie's, which it rapidly replaced as a textbook. Like Mackenzie, Erskine follows the arrangement of Justinian's Institutes; like Bankton he makes extensive reference to the civil law while emphasising that the civil law is not to be followed slavishly.The *Institute* is a more ambitious text; its scale is similar to the works of Stair and Bankton, and so is the range of material covered and the degree of detail.

14.2.9   Last among the institutional writers was George Joseph Bell (1770–1843). Advocate from 1791, in 1822 he accepted the chair of Scots law at Edinburgh in succession to David Hume, nephew and namesake of the philosopher, who had been appointed to judicial office as a Baron of the Court of Exchequer (see para 14.2.11). In 1829 he published his *Principles of the Law of Scotland* which, in the tradition of Erskine's *Principles*, was designed as an introductory student textbook, as well as a handy first reference book for practice. Of greater importance was his *Commentaries on the Law of Scotland and the Principles of Mercantile Jurisprudence*, which was an expanded version of his *Treatise on the Law of Bankruptcy in Scotland*, first published in 1800. The *Commentaries* mark a break with the institutional tradition which had formed and developed Scots law during the seventeenth and eighteenth centuries. Bell's point of departure was bankruptcy and, more broadly, mercantile law; the exposition is impressive but it does not offer the clear system and breadth of coverage which is an essential characteristic of the institutional approach. There is also considerable use of and reliance on

English authorities, partly because of the topic itself, partly because of the virtual cessation of Scottish lawyers' regular contacts with the universities of the continent, and partly because in the wake of the Industrial Revolution the links between Scotland and England were inevitably closer. Perhaps Bell's work was also a sign of maturity of the legal system; the time had come when Scotland needed detailed treatises on particular aspects of the law.

14.2.10 These institutional writers were not the only jurists who produced works of note, even institutional ones, during these centuries. There was, for example, *The Institutions of the Law of Scotland* by William Forbes (d.1745), whose other major work, *The Great Body of the Law of Scotland* (c.1720) remains unpublished. Son of a professor in Padua, he became an advocate in 1696 and in 1714 was appointed the first Regius Professor of Law at Glasgow. Forbes was responsible, as official reporter, for the first volume of Session case reports (see para 14.3.6); he also wrote treatises on various fields of law within Scotland. Another important book was the *Principles of Equity* of Henry Home, Lord Kames (1696–1782), who also published several volumes of *Decisions of the Court of Session*. Some authorities would hold that Kames is institutional (in the technical sense) and would exclude Mackenzie. Then there are Hume's *Lectures*, unpublished in his lifetime, which were delivered while he held the chair of Scots law in Edinburgh (Stair Society vols 5, 13, 15, 17–19). Although hardly original, they provide a wide-ranging description of Scots law, with many references to decisions reported and unreported. They were valued by the students who attended them, and are useful still for their description of the law at the turn of the eighteenth and nineteenth centuries.

14.2.11 In the sphere of criminal law there are two important works which are generally regarded as institutional in the sense of carrying authority. The first is Mackenzie's *The Laws and Customs of Scotland in Matters Criminal* (1678), which is also the first major treatise on Scots criminal law. Important in its day, and for basic principles, it is no longer regularly consulted since, for example, treason is largely described in straightforwardly Roman terms, and witchcraft was then still a crime. The second is Baron Hume's *Commentaries on the Law of Scotland respecting Crimes* (1797). It is based on extensive research into the records of the practice of the courts but, significantly, he states that in the absence of native authority he has looked to England rather than to Rome, in that English society offers a better model in an area of law where social habits have an important influence. Hume is still of considerable authority, being regularly cited both in court and in the literature. Other works, such as those of Sir Archibald Alison (1792–1867) on the *Principles* (1832) and the *Practice* (1833) *of the Criminal Law of Scotland*, remain on the margin of formal acceptance. The division between institutional and non-institutional seems largely to be due to the practice of the nineteenth-century Scottish judges; certain works passed from being frequent sources of reference to possessing a definite authority as the bench found itself increasingly reluctant to depart from the views they contained. This problem of the definition of books of authority was not unique to Scotland; it can be discerned in other European countries, such as France or the Netherlands.

14.3 THE COURT OF SESSION

14.3.1 In 1532 the bench of the Court of Session, or Session, consisted of the Chancellor of Scotland, the Lord President of the Court, fourteen Lords Ordinary and a number of Extraordinary Lords. The size of the court is indicative of a procedure more demanding of judicial manpower than the English but less so than the French. It was envisaged that when he sat the Chancellor would preside, but in practice his attendances were infrequent with the result that the Lord President effectively became the senior judge; this position was confirmed by default when after 1707 the office of Chancellor lapsed. Hardly surprisingly, as the Church through taxation had helped to finance the new College of Justice, the Lord President and seven of the Lords Ordinary were to be clerics. Apart from the Church's financial interest, it had been generally the case in the King's Council of the fifteenth and early sixteenth centuries that the members who had received a formal legal training in the continental universities were clerics; the evidence of the sederunts from the pre-1532 Council suggests that such men formed the nucleus of those who sat in session to administer justice. In accordance with the constitution of the College of Justice the first four Lords President were all churchmen, but its provisions on clerics as necessarily members of the Court could not survive the Reformation; new provision was made on qualification for judicial office, emphasising both legal knowledge and good reputation. Nevertheless, some clerical participation in the Court of Session continued until the mid-seventeenth century; the last churchman to hold judicial office was Archbishop Burnet of Glasgow, who was appointed an Extraordinary Lord in 1664 – he died in 1668.

14.3.2 The Extraordinary Lords were Crown nominees; they were entitled to sit or not as they pleased, and they were not affected by the rules on qualification for judicial office. Appointments were made on purely political grounds and many of those appointed were without any formal legal training. In 1553 when the number reached eight the Court felt moved to protest and the number was then reduced to four; in 1723, when the whole system of appointment of judges was revised, it was enacted that no further such appointments were to be made, but the last holder did not die until 1762.

14.3.3 Until 1808 the structure of the Court of Session remained virtually unchanged. It was essentially a unitary court, whose members gave one collective judgment, although up to three judges might be absent, supervising the preparatory stages of the cases coming before the court, and the junior Lord Ordinary might be sitting in the Bill Chamber, which was originally a vacation court but acquired a special jurisdiction involving a bill or petition to the court. Pressure of business and time-consuming reliance on written pleadings led in the nineteenth century to reforms by statute. The Court was divided into two Houses, Inner and Outer. The Inner House, whose jurisdiction was to be mainly appellate, was itself divided into the First Division headed by the Lord President and the Second Division headed by the Lord Justice-Clerk, who had come to be vice-president of the Court, as also of the High Court of Justiciary (see para 14.4.1). The new Outer House consisted of a number of Lords Ordinary sitting singly to exercise a jurisdiction at first instance. At first judges in the Outer House were drawn from the Divisions, but this arrangement was soon changed and the Outer House came to be staffed, as it still is, by judges appointed for that function. Such 'permanent' Lords Ordinary may, in due course, be promoted to one of the Divisions.

14.3.4 From the beginning the Court of Session had the power to regulate its own proceedings, a power confirmed in 1541 by a statute which gave the Court the right to make such 'acts, statutes and ordinances as [it] shall think expedient for ordering of process and hasty expedition of justice'. This rule-making power resulted in a vast number of enactments known as Acts of Sederunt. The power itself was akin to that of the *Parlement* of Paris to make *arrêts de règlement*; like that *Parlement* the Court did not always restrict itself to governing its own procedure and sometimes introduced what amounted to new rules of substantive law, for example, new rules concerning bankruptcy. By the end of the eighteenth century, however, the Court was required to confine its enactments to the administration of justice in the strict sense.

14.3.5 Initially the court conducted its business *in camera* (secretly) but by the close of the seventeenth century, under the Court of Session Act 1693, this policy had been abandoned in favour of open hearings. The first reports which survive are Sinclair's *Practicks*, compiled by an judge who became Lord President in 1565 and covering the years 1540–1549. Like so many others, such as Haddington's – much cited by Stair – they have never been printed, but an edition is in course of preparation (and a provisional text is available through the Stair Society). Other examples – one of them already mentioned among the digest *Practicks* – include Maitland's *Practicks* which dealt with the years between 1550 and 1580 and Hope's (*Major*) *Practicks* covering the period 1608–1633. *Practicks* remained the only form of regular law reports until the early eighteenth century, although Stair himself published *Decisions* to show that like cases were treated alike.

14.3.6 In 1705 William Forbes was appointed by the Faculty of Advocates to report the decisions of the Court of Session, and with his appointment the history of the modern Scottish law reports begins. Forbes was succeeded by other Faculty reporters, but it was only in the early years of the nineteenth century that the reports began to carry the opinions of individual judges. As on the continent the bench appears to have been reluctant to allow its reasoning to be made widely known. The *Practicks* had offered little more than terse statements of what the Court had decided, but gradually the reports became more elaborate until by the mid-nineteenth century they had substantially assumed their modern form. The aim of the earlier compilations was simply to promote consistency in judicial decision-making; there was no doctrine of precedent, in the sense of the binding force of a single decision. Only a uniform course of decisions was regarded as creating law, and this doctrine applied even to the decisions of the House of Lords on appeal (see para 14.3.12). In the nineteenth century, however, something akin to the English doctrine of *stare decisis*, but considerably less rigid, was gradually absorbed into Scots law. It is difficult to account completely for this development, but it seems that the appellate jurisdiction of the House of Lords, inevitably steeped in English habits, and the creation of an appellate house within the Court of

Session itself contributed; so probably did improved standards of law reporting, and it was, moreover, a period when English economic strength – with all the consequences – was predominant.

14.3.7 Although the Court of Session was already Scotland's supreme civil court in 1532, its jurisdiction was for a while limited. At first it was not even quite clear that the Session had jurisdiction in matters of fee and heritage – that is, title to land – as these were traditionally the province of the feudal courts or the full parliament. However, whatever the position at strict law, practice (probably in the shape of the preference of litigants) rapidly proved otherwise and the Session's jurisdiction in this area expanded during the 1530s and 1540s. The principal restraints which remained lay in the existence of other courts whose jurisdiction was both specialized and exclusive. Such courts were the Commissary Courts (dealt with in the context of the Reformation; see para 10.7.4–5), the Court of Exchequer (reconstituted in 1707) and the Teind Court (dealing with the post-Reformation fate of teinds or tithes, and the allocation of ministers' stipends), which survived until its absorption into the Court of Session in the nineteenth century.

14.3.8 The Admiralty Court also disappeared in the nineteenth century as its jurisdiction was dispersed among the Courts of Session and Justiciary, the sheriff courts, and the English Court of Admiralty, which was now given all prize jurisdiction. Maritime matters in Scotland were originally dealt with by the magistrates of the seaward burghs but, particularly where foreign merchants or questions of trading policy were involved, these matters might be of more than local concern. The Crown's interest led to the establishment towards the end of the fifteenth century of the jurisdiction of the Court of Admiralty under the High Admiral of Scotland. The court sat at Edinburgh and had competence throughout Scotland but, at least in the early years, acted through deputes sitting in the ports. It had both a civil and a criminal jurisdiction, including questions of prize, and its procedure was swift and summary – as was characteristic of a court dealing with the law merchant and foreign litigants. Its jurisdiction was not always welcomed by other courts; comparatively their procedures were slow, and in the area of mercantile contracts in particular there was some suspicion that the Admiralty Court would attract increasingly more business away from the Session. It was unable to resist these pressures and from the eighteenth century onwards it began to decline.

14.3.9 Another limitation on the Court of Session appeared in the eighteenth century as a consequence of the Union of the Parliaments in 1707. Article 18 of the Treaty (see Appendix 5) provided that, with the exception of revenue law and the regulation of trade, Scots law was to remain as it was, although subject to alteration, particularly in matters of public law, by the new Parliament of Great Britain. The legal systems of the two countries thus remained distinct, but subject to the one legislative body. This has sometimes led to the imposition of English usages on the Scottish tradition, but more significant has been the matter of appeal.

14.3.10 Prior to the Treaty of Union, appeal by protestation lay from the Court of Session to (the Scottish) parliament, but the parliament's right was challenged. In 1674 the Session's decision in *Earl of Callendar v Earl of Dunfermline* was appealed to parliament; this move was opposed by the court. The judges contended that they had supreme jurisdiction in civil matters in Scotland and they invoked the aid of the king, Charles II. The Crown was inclined to side with the judges but support for the right of appeal came from within the College of Justice itself; a substantial number of advocates withdrew their services, thus bringing the business of the court to a virtual standstill. Then, during the political revolution of 1689, the Scottish Convention of Estates included in their Claim of Right a clause securing the right of appeal from Session to parliament. The right of protestation thus confirmed, however, does not seem to have been much used.

14.3.11   Article 19 of the Treaty of Union laid down that

> 'no causes in Scotland be cognizable by . . . any . . . court in Westminster Hall; and that the said courts . . . shall have no power to cognosce, review, or alter the Acts or Sentences of the Judicature of Scotland or to stop the execution of the same.'

This left unclear the question of appeals from the Court of Session. The judicial powers of the English parliament had been exercised by the House of Lords; absence of express provision in the Treaty meant that it was open to question whether the new parliament, acting through the Lords, was entitled to consider itself as heir to the judicial powers of the Scottish parliament and so entertain Scottish appeals. After all, the House of Lords did not sit in Westminster Hall.

14.3.12   Practice, if not constitutional theory, settled the matter. In 1708, shortly after the Union, the 1695 decision of the Court of Session in *The Earl of Rosebery v Sir John Inglis* was appealed to the Lords; the appeal was accepted, although never actually concluded. Then, in 1710, came another appeal;[7] this time it ran its course and resulted in the Lords overturning the decision of the Session. (The point at issue here was the right of episcopalians to worship according to their own forms.) The right of appeal to the Lords thus established by practice was happily used by Scottish litigants, to whom it offered opportunities of delay as well as the hope of reversal of decisions against them, but the Scottish legal profession was less satisfied. As an English court, the House of Lords did not necessarily contain a Scottish judge or anyone acquainted with Scots law. Consequently the Lords tended to think and speak in terms of English law, and on occasion gave decisions based on English rules unknown to Scots law and out of line with its principles; an English Law Lord is on record as having remarked: 'If such be the law of England, on what ground can it be argued not to be the law of Scotland?'[8] However, the contribution of the Lords has not always lain on the debit side. There has become evident a somewhat more sympathetic attitude towards Scots law, and some English judges there have tried to learn and apply Scots law,[9] and of course some appeals have referred to law common to both countries. Only since 1876 has it been required that there be at least one Scottish Law Lord; usually there are two. The Scottish judges normally sit on Scottish appeals and tend to give the leading opinions, but they have no formal claim to authority, and indeed do not necessarily sit at all. Scottish judges involved in a Scottish appeal may still have to work hard to convince their English brethren that Scots law is and shall remain different. This is one aspect of an ongoing debate over the survival and continuing value of the civilian tradition in Scots law.

7   *Greenshields' Case* (1710–1711) Rob 12.
8   *Bartonshill Coal Co v Reid* (1858) 3 Macq 266, 285 (per Lord Cranworth).
9   *Wills' Trs v Cairngorm Canoeing and Sailing School Ltd* 1976 SC (HL) 30; 1976 SLT 162.

14.4 OTHER COURTS

14.4.1   In mediaeval times royal justice was administered locally by the justiciars and their deputes – and to a lesser extent by the sheriffs – and, with the growing importance of Council and Session in the fifteenth and sixteenth centuries, this local jurisdiction became almost exclusively criminal. In 1514 the Earl of Argyll was appointed Lord Justice-General (that is Justiciar) of Scotland, and the office remained heritably in his family until 1628, when it was surrendered, and the Justiciarship of Argyll and the Isles was granted in its place. In 1524 the Lord Justice-General was instructed to remain continually at Edinburgh or with the king in order to deal with criminal business. In practice most of the work was done by his deputes; by the 1660s it was accepted that the Lord Justice-Clerk – an officer risen to the bench from relatively humble beginnings as clerk of the court – presided in the absence of his superior.

14.4.2   In the localities the ayre system had been decaying from the fifteenth century onwards; attempts then and in the following century to provide regular and efficient criminal justice other than in Edinburgh were unsuccessful. In the 1660s the inefficiencies and abuses within the system led to the appointment of a committee of investigation. The result was the creation in 1672 of a new criminal court, the High Court of Justiciary, consisting of the Lord Justice-General, the Lord Justice-Clerk and five Lords of Session. The court was based in Edinburgh, but provision was made for the holding of circuit courts throughout the country; in actual practice it seems that no circuits were held until the early eighteenth century. At first the position of Lord Justice-General was usually bestowed on members of the nobility, and not for their legal qualifications, until in 1830 the office was combined with the Presidency of the Court of Session; from 1887 all the judges of the Court of Session were also made Lords Commissioners of Justiciary. There was (and is) no appeal from the High Court of Justiciary to the House of Lords although, since 1926, the High Court itself also sits, with a quorum of three, as a court of appeal.

14.4.3   In 1540 parliament enacted that the sheriff courts were to follow the same procedure as was used in the Court of Session. The Act probably confirmed a change that was already taking place rather than making any positive innovation. By the mid-sixteenth century the feudal jury of suitors had disappeared, save in criminal cases and in those matters which still proceeded by brieve; with the disappearance of the jury of suitors the sheriff became a judge who acted on his own initiative in place of being merely the executive president of his court. This did not necessarily improve justice in the shrieval courts; complaints were common in the sixteenth century and later that sheriff courts were held irregularly or not at all, that the required records were not always kept, and that shrieval justice was often dilatory and sometimes less than impartial. Under James VI, for example, four sheriffs were summoned to explain why, among other lapses, they had not held their head courts for fourteen years, and why known criminals within their sheriffdoms had been allowed to remain there undisturbed.

14.4.4 Part of the problem was lack of training. The heritable sheriff was part of a system which made no provision for inquiring into the fitness or even the willingness of such men to discharge their duties. Certainly sheriffs could appoint deputes, who could in turn appoint substitutes, and an Act of 1540 specifically instructed the sheriffs to appoint 'men of best fame, knowledge, understanding and experience'. However, it appears that some deputes were no better qualified than their principals. Later in the seventeenth century the Privy Council tried the experiment of examining candidates for shrieval office, but this was more to discover their religious and political convictions than their legal knowledge. When after 1708 there was no longer a Scottish Privy Council, the official duty of supervising the sheriffs fell on the senators (the judges) of the College of Justice; when on circuit as Lords of Justiciary these judges invited and heard complaints against the sheriffs.

14.4.5 Major reform came in 1747 in the aftermath of the Jacobite risings of 1715 and 1745. In that year the Heritable Jurisdictions (Scotland) Act (technically of 1746) was passed which abolished most heritable jurisdictions as from 1748. The heritable sheriffs were to be replaced by advocates of at least three years' standing. The purpose of the Act was to reduce the risk that holders of heritable jurisdictions with Jacobite sympathies might not enforce penalties on Jacobites, but the step taken was an important one in the gradual professionalization of the sheriff courts, which led to an extension of their jurisdiction in the nineteenth century. Under the sheriffs were the sheriffs substitute, initially appointed by the sheriffs to whom they were responsible; in 1825 it was enacted that they too should be advocates or solicitors of three (later five) years' standing. Since 1787 their salaries had been paid by the Crown, but not until 1877 was the power of appointing them vested in the Crown.

14.4.6 The importance of the franchise courts also began to diminish in the early modern period, and with the exception of the more important regalities, they gradually gave way to the Courts of Session and Justiciary. By the early seventeenth century (and sooner in the Lowlands) the baronial courts were dealing mainly with minor disputes and the maintenance of 'good neighbourhood', that is, the supervision of the communal well-being, enforcing by-laws and dealing with cases relating to such matters as common pasturage, the upkeep of boundary walls and similar domestic matters. By the Heritable Jurisdictions (Scotland) Act most of the franchise courts formally lost their powers to the courts of Session, Justiciary and sheriff, as appropriate; the baron courts alone survived, with a much attenuated jurisdiction.In the nineteenth century they ceased to be held, and they are being formally abolished in the context of the abolition of the remnants of the feudal system of landholding.

14.4.7   The Privy Council, the king's inner council, existed from mediaeval times and fulfilled a variety of functions. It was the principal executive arm of the Crown and, especially after the Union of the Crowns in 1603, it played a leading role in the government of Scotland. It also exercised a judicial function; although the emergence from it of the Court of Session substantially reduced the amount of business with which it had to deal, its jurisdiction did not cease. Rather, the Session was subordinate to it and subject to its supervision. The Council also exercised the equitable jurisdiction of the Crown, dealing with those matters which lacked a remedy in any other forum. The Council's jurisdiction did not long survive the Union of the Parliaments. An Act of 1708 created a new Privy Council for Great Britain, and so ended the separate existence of the Scottish body. Moreover, the new Council was to have the same powers as, and no more than, the former English Privy Council, which had lost all jurisdiction within England and Wales with the general abolition of the conciliar courts in 1641. The jurisdiction of the Scottish Council therefore disappeared; the result was that 'many matters were, by the abolition of the Council, left without a remedy'.[10] No arrangements were made to confer it on other courts, and when the Court of Session stepped in by default it was only in a limited way. Kames in his *Historical Law Tracts* urged the Session to take up the noble office of the Council, the extraordinary jurisdiction to step outside or modify strict law in the interests of justice. However, the Court of Session's exercise of this *nobile officium* was always cautious, and gradually became restricted to established precedents, or situations closely analogous thereto.

10   PGB McNeill 'The passing of the Scottish Privy Council', *JurRev* (1965) 263.

14.5   THE LEGAL PROFESSION AND LEGAL EDUCATION

14.5.1   We have sufficiently discussed the emergence of a professional judiciary. The origins of the other two branches of the profession, of advocates and solicitors, are rather more obscure, although it is clear that they are mediaeval. Representation in litigation was first accepted in the romano-canonical procedure of the ecclesiastical courts. Feudal mediaeval courts were generally reluctant to deal with litigants who did not plead in person, and strict rules governed the appointment of representatives. *Regiam Majestatem*, for example, tells us that 'no person should be admitted to act as attorney unless he has been so constituted by his client [who is] personally present in court'. This rule survived into the sixteenth century, and is repeated by Balfour, who also adds that the powers of the representative are strictly limited and confined to the terms of the mandate given to him by his principal.

14.5.2   Nevertheless, it is possible to trace the emergence during the fifteenth century of a small but clearly identifiable body of men practising as professional pleaders in the higher courts. The evidence is somewhat scanty but adequate for us to see the origins of what became known as the Faculty of Advocates. In 1424, for example, statutory provision was made for the appointment of a faithful and wise advocate to act for poor litigants unable to arrange their own representation; in 1455 it was laid down that all men of law who were paid to appear in court on others' behalf should wear a special dress when before parliament. The position is clearer in the sixteenth century. A decision of 1530 determined that no one could be compelled to answer a summons without the assistance of an advocate. When the College of Justice was founded, provision was made for the licensing of ten advocates to appear before the court – although only eight were actually appointed. At first advocates were confined to civil suits, but in 1587 they were empowered to act in criminal matters.

14.5.3 By the end of the sixteenth century there were about fifty advocates in practice. Although it is impossible to point to the first appearance of this group as a corporate body, as opposed to a set of men with professional interests in common, it is from this time that the Faculty began to take shape. We hear of a Dean of the advocates of Session in 1582, but nothing of his powers or duties at this stage. By the middle of the next century, however, it is clear that the Lords of Session looked to the Dean for the maintenance of discipline at the bar. More telling in the evolution of the Faculty is the acquisition by the advocates of control over admission to their number. Initially scrutiny of would-be advocates lay with the judges, who seem not to have been very demanding of legal qualification. This led to complaints from the established advocates that their profession was being held in contempt; in 1610, at their suggestion, reforms were introduced. The chief article of reform was the examination of intrants – or some of them – by the advocates themselves; in this examination Roman, or civil, law played a prominent part. It remained possible to obtain extraordinary admission by bill and thus to escape the Faculty's examinations, but in 1688 it was provided that such intrants should be examined by the judges; in 1692 the advocates acquired the right to scrutinize these men. The retention of entry by bill was probably to allow those who had had no opportunity to study Roman law to practise at the bar, for they were examined only in municipal law and procedure; nevertheless, entry by examination in civil law was always considered the more honourable. Only in 1750 did examination in Scots law become compulsory for all intrants; an examination on Roman law has remained so to this day.

14.5.4 We know less of representation in the lower courts. Clerical pleaders or procurators were to be found in the later mediaeval church courts of Scotland, but in the secular courts, with their lay judges and juries, litigants normally appeared in person, perhaps with the assistance of family or friends. Representation, however, was not forbidden and from the sixteenth century the practice of using procurators in the lower courts was beginning to establish itself. Often local notaries combined their forensic duties with those of procurator; by the seventeenth century such law agents become well enough established to form local professional associations, for example, the Society of Advocates in Aberdeen (at least from 1633) and the Faculty of Procurators in Glasgow (at least from 1668).

14.5.5 There were many notaries in mediaeval Europe and they made an important contribution to the *ius commune*. While papal or imperial licence permitted a notary to practise anywhere, it was also competent for a prince (or a city) to grant a licence valid within his jurisdiction (see Appendix 4). An

Act of 1469 confirmed the Scottish king's right to create notaries and forbade imperial notaries to act within the realm without royal approval, but apostolic or imperial notaries were always much the most common. After the Reformation apostolic notaries as such had no standing and royal licence became normal. There were, however, very many notaries, not all properly qualified, and in the sixteenth century a number of statutes imposed severe penalties on the 'false notary' (one acting without licence). Attempts were also made to regulate admission; a number of statutes prescribed examination and registration of intrants. These culminated in the Act of 1587 which laid down that a new register was to be drawn up, that intrants were to have a knowledge of Latin, to have served an apprenticeship, and to undergo examination before admission.

14.5.6   The notary was important because he provided what was in effect a register for deeds and transactions of all kinds; documents could be authenticated in his presence and a formal record of them entered in what was known as his protocol book. Later the practice of registering deeds in the books of a court of record made this function increasingly redundant, but the notary was also important in connection with documents concerning the completion of title to land. Particularly significant was the instrument of sasine, the notarial document formally recording the delivery of possession of land. The need for such instruments lasted for this purpose until 1858; they had, and still have, other uses, such as protesting bills of exchange, and authenticating legal acts.

14.5.7   Procurators and notaries thus practised law – although not before the supreme courts – well before the establishment of the College of Justice; from the late sixteenth century onwards there were other associations of practitioners, most notably the Writers to the Signet. The Writers to the Signet developed from the office of the King's Secretary; they were closely associated with the College of Justice because of their duty to draw up official documents and adhibit the royal signet to them. By 1594 they had formed their own society and were beginning, like the procurators, notaries and other, local, writers to act as law agents – 'solicitor' has come to be the more usual designation. Until the nineteenth century, however, the requirements for entry to this branch of the legal profession were not uniform. This only came to pass in 1873, under the general supervision of the Court of Session, to which petitions for admission as a solicitor are addressed. Solicitors may also petition for admission as notaries, and many do so; there is no longer a separate profession. In 1933 the General Council of Solicitors was formed, to control entrance to and the conduct of the profession of solicitor; it was succeeded in 1949 by the Law Society of Scotland.

14.5.8   As we have seen, the foundation of Scotland's three senior universities did not result in the growth of a strong native tradition of law-teaching and, despite attempts by James VI to establish a chair of law at Edinburgh, it was not until the eighteenth century that any real progress was made. The bias in favour of the learned law is indicated by the fact that until 1727 lectures were given in Latin, not the most suitable language for modern Scots law. At Edinburgh what law-teaching there was had traditionally been conducted in private by individual advocates, but during the early 1700s three chairs were founded at the university – Public Law and the Law of Nature and Nations in 1707, Civil Law in 1709, and Scots Law in 1722. At Glasgow during the same period the teaching of law was revived; in 1714 William Forbes (see para 14.2.10) was appointed to the chair of Civil Law. Between 1761 and 1801 this chair was held by John Millar, a close friend and colleague of Adam Smith and important also in the history of sociology; Millar was also a friend of Kames, in whose house he spent two years just before passing advocate. Millar's primary duty was to teach civil law but he also offered lectures on public law, Scots law and, latterly, even English law; his reputation was immense and his gifts as a teacher attracted many students, including the future Baron Hume. The increasing importance of Scots law was recognized during the nineteenth century. In 1861 a chair of Conveyancing (which in Scotland includes land law) was established at Glasgow under the patronage of the Faculty of Procurators; the Writers to the Signet had already endowed one in Edinburgh. New degrees in law widened the intellectual scope of legal education later in the century while still maintaining a close connection with the needs of practice, because most students were also training for entry to the profession. More radical changes in the later twentieth century made law degrees full-time, and attractive to students thinking of other occupations. Entrants to the legal profession take law degrees followed by professional training in which the universities play a part. Thus the tradition of a university training in law has been maintained by the legal profession of modern Scotland. (Even those who intend to qualify only as licensed conveyancers or executry practitioners – dealing with the winding up of people's property after death – take university courses relevant to their specializations.)

FURTHER READING (and see Select Bibliography D (i))

JW Cairns	'Institutional writings in Scotland reconsidered', *JLH* 4 (1983) 76
	'Rhetoric, language and Roman law: legal education and improvement in eighteenth-century Scotland' *Law & History Review* 9 (1991) 31
	'The influence of the German Historical School in early nineteenth century Edinburgh', *Syracuse J of Int Law & Commerce* 20 (1994) 191
	'From "speculative" to "practical" legal education: the decline of the Glasgow law school, 1801–30', *TR* 62 (1994) 331
	'"As famous as a school of law as Edinburgh for medicine": the Glasgow law school, 1761–1801' in *The Glasgow Enlightenment*, ed A Hook and R Sher (East Linton, 1995)
	'Scottish law, Scottish lawyers and the status of the Union' in *A Union for Empire. Political Thought and the British Union of 1707*, ed J Robertson (CUP, 1995) 243
JW Cairns, TD Fergus and HL MacQueen	'Legal Humanism in Renaissance Scotland', *JLH* 11 (1990) 40

DL Carey Miller and   *The Civilian Tradition and Scots Law: Aberdeen*
R Zimmermann (eds)   *Quincentenary Essays* (Berlin, 1997)
J Durkan   'The early Scottish notary', in *The Renaissance and Reformation in Scotland. Essays in honour of G Donaldson*, ed IB Cowan and D Shaw (Edinburgh, 1983) 22
R Evans-Jones (ed)   *The Civil Law Tradition in Scotland* (Stair Society, supp vol 2, 1995)
K Luig   'The institutes of national law in the seventeenth and eighteenth centuries', *JurRev* (1972) 193
HL MacQueen (ed)   *Scots Law into the Twenty-first Century. Essays in Honour of WA Wilson* (Edinburgh, 1996)
NT Phillipson   *The Scottish Whigs and the Court of Session 1785–1830* (Stair Society, Edinburgh, 1990)
A Rodger, Lord   'Scottish advocates in the nineteenth century: the German
Rodger of Earlsferry   "connection"' *LQR* 110 (1994) 563
TB Smith   *Studies Critical and Comparative* (Edinburgh, 1962), esp chs 3 and 7
P Stein   'The influence of Roman law on the law of Scotland', *JurRev* (1963) 205 – reprinted in *The Character and Influence of the Roman Civil Law* (London & Ronceverte, 1988) 319
R Sutherland   *Lord Stair and the Law of Scotland* (Glasgow, 1981)
Stair Society publications (Edinburgh), especially vols 1 and 20 (see ch 9), vols 29, 32 and 36 – *The Minute Book of the Faculty of Advocates, 1661–1783*, and vol 33, *Stair Tercentenary Studies*

Chapter 15

ENLIGHTENMENT AND CODIFICATION

15.1 THE AGE OF THE ENLIGHTENMENT

15.1.1 The intellectual movements of the eighteenth century are described in the major European languages as being of the Enlightenment.[1] These movements which, in the field of law, were frequently directed towards reform or codification, or sometimes reform by means of codification, were based on a belief in the liberating influence of reason both in intellectual life and in the organization of society; this belief itself had grown out of Natural Law. Enlightened men were inclined to be critical of received thought, but they claimed to be able to provide a rational and therefore sound treatment of all problems, social and economic, political and legal. In France these attitudes were to culminate in the Revolution and in the *Code Civil*.

1 In German *die Aufklärung*, in Italian *l'Illuminismo*, in French *le siècle des lumières*.

15.1.2 Meanwhile, changes in agricultural practices were enabling a much larger population to be supported, and the beginnings of the Industrial Revolution were becoming apparent in both England and Scotland; improvements in transport were to allow the building of large cities. These changes and an expanding commercial life were to lead in the nineteenth century to new tasks for the law. In the economic sphere Adam Smith argued for the rationality of free competition in promoting the most efficient use of resources, as against the mercantilist view that the state should intervene to protect and encourage the growth of wealth for its citizens. This laissez-faire doctrine became dominant, in a form taken beyond Smith's conception, where it was tempered by other, social, concerns.

15.1.3 Natural law and rationalist thinking had created the Enlightenment; indeed, it was during this period that legal philosophy became a subject which could be divorced, or at least separated, from the practical needs of law because Natural Law was inevitably linked with 'philosophy' in the sense of overall views of the origins and good working of human society. Not all legal ideas of the Enlightenment, however, sprang from rationalism or tended towards codification. A society which well exemplified the Enlightenment in its blending of legal and philosophic thinking, and also in its combination of those areas with history, politics and economics, was to be found in eighteenth-century Scotland. Its roots lay in the Natural Law of Grotius and in the institutional approach of Stair, but it developed its own doctrines.

15.1.4   Great names of this period in Scotland are Francis Hutcheson, Lord Kames, David Hume, Adam Smith and John Millar. Hutcheson, professor of Moral Philosophy at Glasgow 1730–1746, was Adam Smith's teacher as well as his predecessor; he also exercised a profound influence on the thinking of David Hume. Moreover, Hutcheson was important in that his political and legal ideas were widely disseminated in the emergent United States of America; he held liberty an indispensable pre-condition for individual happiness. Lord Kames, like John Millar, we have considered in the specifically Scottish context. David Hume (uncle of Baron Hume) was for many years Librarian of the Faculty of Advocates. His various philosophical works, especially his *Enquiry Concerning Human Understanding*, strongly influenced Bentham and John Stuart Mill, and also Auguste Comte. His 'sentimental', that is, psychological, approach to explaining law and society was innovatory – but also a far cry from Natural Law thinking. He held that law was an historical phenomenon to be explained, rather than a tool for reform. Adam Smith, professor of Moral Philosophy at Glasgow 1752–1763, although best known for his economic theories, also held that jurisprudence, the study of law, was fundamental to any discussion of social relations. His belief in the empirical approach meant that he opposed codification as too idealistic and likely to be ineffective, if not pernicious, insofar as it tried deliberately to alter social attitudes.

15.2 CRIMINAL LAW AND THE ENLIGHTENMENT

15.2.1   Legal philosophy and law reform came together in an exemplary manner in the case of criminal law. As central governments had become stronger in the fifteenth and sixteenth centuries, crime had become an increasing object of their concern. Penalties had multiplied and sharpened, but crimes had diminished neither in number nor gravity; laws were constantly revised and re-enacted but the desired reform of morals was not achieved. The general tendency was towards harsh repression. Political crimes were created and punished as especially heinous, yet it was an age when the modern distinction between legal and moral wrongdoing was in the process of being created by the proponents of rationalism. (Just as the mediaeval world had seen no real division between the temporal and spiritual authorities, so too had men, as members of the one society, properly incurred public punishment for sin which was not seen as private.) While the commonest Christian theory of punishment held that it should aim at the correction of the criminal – and Roman law could be cited to support this – the weight of the Roman texts centred on deterrence, to preserve the tranquillity of the state. This was welcome to the growing number of absolute monarchies. Farinacius, an Italian jurist of the late sixteenth century, after demonstrating by citations from many authorities that the insane should be totally exempt from punishment since they were incapable of any wrongful intent, then limited his rule by declaring that, however, in the interests of the state they could be punished.

15.2.2 Penalties included fines and confiscation, death, mutilation and flogging, prison and outlawry; in general torture was, as it had been in Roman law, an instrument of criminal procedure for the discovery of crime or a means of obtaining proof, not a penalty. The death penalty was widely imposed for treason, *lèse-majesté*, sacrilege, heresy, rebellion, homicide, and robbery. It was also, at least for those who repeated their crime, likely to be imposed on smugglers, forgers, false witnesses, those who broke regulations governing the food supply or public hygiene, those who committed sexual crimes (which included adultery) – even without violence – attempted suicides, blasphemers and many others. In England in 1776 there were reckoned to be 166 capital offences; generally there was no crime which might not be punished with death if the ruler saw fit. A deserter might have his foot amputated, a pick-pocket his hand, while a slanderer might have his tongue slit, although the two latter might get away with a flogging. Because they were designed to be deterrent, such penalties were almost invariably inflicted in public and with minatory ceremony. In contrast to the publicity of the penalties, criminal procedure frequently permitted secret accusation; vague suspicion was enough to ground a prosecution, informers were encouraged, and torture regularly employed to obtain a confession. These conditions did of course vary; where government was not absolute there were likely to be procedural safeguards as, for example, in England and Scotland, but grave penalties for minor offences were virtually universal.

15.2.3 It is hardly surprising then that men influenced by Natural Law and a belief in the power of reason should expose the defects of such practices and propose reforms. Part of the problem sprang from the continuing willingness of so many lawyers to rely on the Roman criminal law, which was much less developed than had been its private law. Natural law had led, as we have seen, to a recognition of the fundamental equality of men as rational beings, and this attitude was bound to be opposed to the brutalization inherent in the usual punishments. Moreover, while the social theories of the legal philosophers were necessarily concerned to some degree with the criminal law as the guardian of social values, they were also bound to hold that the law, being based on human nature, should be rational and the same for all. The natural behaviour of the individual should not be restricted except where harm was caused to another; crime must then be punished as a violation of the social contract. However, since a crime was defined as an act which directly injured the civil community, scope for deeming an act criminal was much reduced. Furthermore, any penalty which exceeded the level needed for the defence of civil society was unjust and indeed tyrannical.

15.2.4 In eighteenth-century France men such as Montesquieu, Voltaire and Rousseau were also including the penal law in their analyses of society, analyses undertaken in the rational philosophic mood. South of the Alps, Giambattista Vico (1668–1744) held that the sanction provided by nature for wrongdoing was the remorse of a guilty conscience; since habitual depravity weakened the conscience, it could become necessary to supplement the sanction of remorse. If this stress on conscience was accepted, it was clearly wrong to punish acts which were harmful to the wrongdoer alone – what Bentham was to call 'reflective justice'. The first duty of the legislator was to bring about amendment, the second, and only if necessary, was to safeguard society. Cesare Bonesana, Marchese de Beccaria (1738–1794), the most notable Enlightenment figure in penal reform, produced his ideas under the influence of such thinkers; on the practical side, one of his friends, Alessandro Verri, was an inspector of prisons in Milan, the capital of Austrian Italy. In 1764 Beccaria published his *Dei Delitti e delle Pene (On Crimes and Punishments)*.

15.2.5   This book attacked the Roman basis underlying criminal law, the contemporary approach to which had jumbled and made obscure what was already antique and alien. Beccaria accepted the theory of the social contract, and consequently the need to defend the social order thus established. He followed Vico in holding that crime only existed insofar as there was injury to some right which society was bound to defend for its own preservation, which included the rights of individual members of that society. Other acts, even if generally accepted as bad, should not be punished but left to the forum of conscience; the Church could deal with sins, but they were no concern of temporal courts and temporal penalties. The duty of the ruler was to prevent violations of the social contract; to this end he should ensure that laws were clear and simple, that all citizens had an interest in their enforcement, that all men were treated alike, and that education was made widely available. Before any punishment was inflicted there must be certainty that a crime had been committed, and committed by the accused. Secret accusations and the use of informers should be forbidden, and so too should the arbitrary exercise of a judge's discretion. In a trial there should be no leading questions or oaths intended to prejudice the accused; above all, torture must not be used, as it exonerated the hardy criminal and condemned the weak and innocent – indeed, the Roman emperors had wished to restrict its use for the same reasons (D 48.18.1.23). Credible witnesses and sure facts must establish the crime, and punishment must be limited to what was necessary to prevent the criminal further harming his fellow-citizens. All beyond was abuse and injustice; penalties that went beyond the preservation of society's safety were of their nature unjust. Penalties therefore should not be inhumane; confiscation was unjust because it affected the victim's family and, above all, the death penalty was unjust and ineffective – life imprisonment, being continuing and visible, was also more of a deterrent.

15.2.6   Beccaria's book caused a tremendous stir, and not only in Italy. In 1766 it was translated into French, and there soon followed translations into other languages, including English and Spanish. It was admired by Catherine II of Russia and by Frederick the Great of Prussia; perhaps to keep him in the country, a chair in the political sciences was set up for Beccaria in Milan. In 1791 Beccaria was appointed to the commission established by the Austrian government to reform criminal and civil procedure in Lombardy, a part of Italy then within the (Habsburg) Holy Roman Empire, but he died before this could bear fruit. Some Italian jurists opposed him vigorously, maintaining the advantages of secret justice in Venice or holding that Roman law, if purified, did provide a sound foundation for criminal procedure, but in general his ideas were rapidly accepted and sometimes rapidly put into practice. Both Catherine II and Frederick of Prussia ordered the abolition of torture within their realms. In England Bentham was much impressed with Beccaria's work, in which he saw implicit his own Utilitarian principle of the greatest happiness of the greatest number; John Howard, the notable champion of prison reform who travelled widely on the continent, must also have been acquainted with his theories.

15.2.7 The Grand Duke of Tuscany (the future Emperor Leopold II) in 1786 issued a code of criminal law under the influence of the reform movement. This abolished the crimes of suicide, duelling and *lèse-majesté*, although it retained offences against religion and morality; it also abolished the death penalty, mutilation, torture and confiscation. However, perhaps through alarm at the French Revolution, there was a reaction within a few years and the death penalty was re-introduced. In Lombardy itself the Habsburg emperor Joseph II in 1787 published a code which to some extent reformed the substantive criminal law. Further reforms, proposed by the commission of which Beccaria was a member, were frustrated by the outbreak of the French Revolution. In France, the Declaration of the Rights of Man (see Appendix 6), which in 1791 preceded the first revolutionary constitution, had stated the principle that law should prohibit only actions harmful to society and should establish only those penalties strictly and clearly necessary; political factors, however, made sure that the death penalty was not abolished there. In the Kingdom of Italy, which as created by Napoleon consisted of Romagna, Lombardy, Venetia and the Marches, the more conservative French penal code was put into effect in 1810. In 1808 in the Kingdom of Naples there were promulgated a reforming code of criminal procedure and a penal code, based in part on the work of Beccaria and his followers; in 1812 these too, however, were superseded by the French penal code.

15.3 THE CODIFICATION MOVEMENT

15.3.1 The new alliance of legal and social philosophy inevitably stimulated many projects of law reform. Natural law had encouraged new systems of arranging legal topics, first in treatises and then in codes. Justinian's Institutions provided a systematic foundation but, after the seventeenth century, many jurists felt that they could improve upon Justinian's method. The Institutions remained, however, a starting point, partly because it dealt with actual law in force and Natural Law had to come to terms with the practical needs of law, and partly because, conversely, it provided an example of a coherent outline of law which nevertheless had had legislative authority. The inherent weight of legal tradition[2] also favoured the continued use of the Institutions as a model.

2   Watson, ch 6.

15.3.2 Natural law also led, if one accepted the logical consequence of the essential equality of man as a rational animal, to a desire to overthrow legal institutions based on privilege. Legal thinking of the new kind was therefore often characterized by the desire to abolish 'feudalism', which by this time had become a much wider and more complex concept than in the days of its creation; along with feudalism were classed primogeniture, entails, the absolute power of princes, and ecclesiastical interference in secular matters. The desire

of some thinkers for radical reform was ~entually revolutionary; others held
that if the new method was to be embodied in an effective code it must be
official, and that the legislator must be educated to understand his duty. In all
cases there was a desire for law to be simplified and to be made easy to discover
by any citizen who wished to know his rights and the limitations on them. All
these factors are present to a greater or lesser extent in the codes of the
eighteenth century, some of which we shall shortly describe. (There were
other codes beside these four, for example in Sweden, and in some Italian
states where there were civil as well as criminal codes.)

15.3.3   Towards the end of the century a new variant of rationalist ideas in
legal philosophy appeared with Bentham. Jeremy Bentham (1748–1832) was
the acknowledged founder of Utilitarianism, the philosophy which holds that
the purpose of society is to arrange for the greatest happiness of the greatest
number of its citizens. He graduated from Oxford and was subsequently called
to the bar at Lincoln's Inn, but had no success in practice – not that he took
any serious steps to achieve it. In 1776 he published anonymously a vehement
attack upon the *Commentaries* of Blackstone and on their author's
interpretation of Natural Law. He then wrote a book on criminal law under
the influence of Beccaria; this was published in French at Paris in 1811 but
not in English until 1825. He was sufficiently admired in France to be created
an honorary French citizen in 1792, and in 1793 he addressed to the National
Convention a pamphlet advocating the abjuration of colonies. In 1789 he
brought out his major published work, *The Principles of Morals and
Legislation*, which soon appeared in French, German and Spanish editions.

15.3.4   Law, which Bentham saw as the command of the ruler in statute form
– a positivist approach which the rationalist development of Natural Law had
already reached – should be used to reinforce Utilitarian ends. Bentham was
led to his position on the role of law partly through his utter rejection of the
approach taken to law by Blackstone, and indeed all other Common lawyers,
who saw law as custom, created through its declaration by the judges, and
developed only as changing needs brought particular customs to the fore or
made them obsolete. In particular, Bentham favoured the abolition of the rule
of evidence that an interested party was not competent to testify; he also favoured
the registration of all conveyances, the paying of salaries, not fees, to court and
other officials, and in general cheaper and swifter justice. He wished too to
bring about the easing of the harsh penalties of the criminal law, and to relate
penalties to the nature of the offence. All government and all laws were in his
view to some extent evil as an infraction of the liberty of the individual, but
they were necessary, particularly because fundamental improvements could not
otherwise be made. He advocated universal suffrage and the secret ballot, and
some of his ideas led on to protective legislation such as the Factory Acts,
which will be treated in the next chapter. He firmly maintained the desirability
of the codification of the law in England, to help it escape from the arbitrariness
of the judiciary, to clarify what law was, and to make it enforceable justly, in
the sense that all men could know what its provisions were.

15.3.5   Bentham had considerable influence in both England and Scotland,
although not so much in his lifetime. Certainly such diverse persons as Lord

Brougham and Sir Henry Maine held that Bentham was the father of virtually all English legal reform in the nineteenth century; this description would seem to exaggerate Bentham's detailed influence and give insufficient credit to the many empirical reformers of the period, but it does reflect Bentham's part in changing the climate of opinion. He numbered among his followers John Austin, professor of jurisprudence at University College, London, who had studied in Germany and had there been much impressed by the early Pandectists (to be met in Chapter 16). Austin developed further the concept of legal positivism, and was himself of great influence in Britain, America and Europe. Bentham was also influential abroad, particularly in France, Spain and the Spanish Americas. He seems to have invented the very term 'codification' to describe the process of issuing a code.

15.3.6 Codification as restatement of the law, or of custom, had been, as we have seen, a common feature of the sixteenth century, whether in France, Germany, or the Netherlands, and at this period there had been recommendations, for example by Hotman or Dumoulin, for more thoroughgoing treatment. We have discussed the growth of institutional writings which in fact made the legislative codes possible, but codification in the sense of a rationally organized statement of the whole field of law (or of all private law) was only possible after the work of the Natural Lawyers. In the seventeenth century some schemes were produced, such as the proposed code for Mecklenburg of 1658. Scandinavia had a long tradition of written law, and in 1683 Christian V of Denmark promulgated a comprehensive restatement of private law, criminal law, and the law of procedure for Denmark, the *Danske Lov* (Danish Law), which was applied to Norway in 1688 as the *Norske Lov* (Norwegian Law). A Swedish Code (*Sveriges rikes lag* – Law of the Swedish Kingdom) followed in 1734, but none of them was strongly in the rational Natural Law mould.

15.3.7 The consequences of the work of the Natural Lawyers are to be seen rather in the codes of the eighteenth and early nineteenth centuries, which are dealt with in the following sections. In the first three of these the political factor which made them practicable was the existence of the 'benevolent despot', the absolute ruler who had accepted the new thinking of his (or her) day, at least where it did not touch his power, and who was prepared to put these ideas into practice. The French Revolution appeared to herald a radical upsetting of previously established ideas, but Napoleon's emergence led to the publication of a code which, taken overall, was the product of lawyers who had lived, worked and been generally respected under Louis XV and Louis XVI. It did, however, pay something more than lip-service to the ideals of the Revolution, and this was to affect its subsequent influence during the nineteenth century when democracy became respectable, at least in Europe, itself influenced politically by the United States of America.

15.4 BAVARIA

15.4.1 The Bavarian Code is the first to be considered. This is partly because, although the codification movement began to take shape in Prussia, it was in Bavaria that it first achieved substantial results. Further, Bavaria was one of the greater German states and, as a southern state, it was subject to rather different influences from those on Prussia. Saxony, in the north, was less affected by the trend towards codification because of the greater sophistication of Saxon law, traceable ultimately to the *Sachsenspiegel* but recently developed by Carpzov and other leading figures of the *usus modernus*; there was also the strong position of the supreme court at Leipzig.

15.4.2   In effect the Bavarian codification was the work of the Elector Max Joseph III and of Wiguläus Aloysius, Freiherr von Kreittmayr (1704–1790), successively his vice-chancellor and chancellor. As a young man Max Joseph had as tutor one Ickstatt who had been a pupil of Christian Wolff; not entirely surprisingly, Max Joseph was sympathetic to Wolff's ideas, in particular, that a benevolent ruler could specify in positive law, to the common advantage of ruler and subjects, the rights and duties arising by Natural Law. Wolff's doctrines were one source of the move to codify Bavarian law, but the direct impulse to action seems to have come from the contemporary Prussian work towards the same end. In Prussia in 1746 Frederick II (1740–1786), the Great, had issued his chancellor with instructions to codify the law, but the bulk of the project was postponed, first by the chancellor's death and then by the outbreak of the Seven Years War in 1756; we shall return to this in the next section.

15.4.3   Max Joseph aimed at achieving a rationalized and uniform law within his territories, a law which would settle disputed points in the *Gemeines Recht* (the German common law). The commission which he issued to von Kreittmayr ordered him to improve the arrangement of the law, to settle controversies and to suit the law to contemporary needs. The first step was the production in 1751 of a criminal code, the *Codex iuris Bavarici criminalis*. This did make clear what was and what was not criminal, but it was not in the spirit of the Enlightenment: for example, witchcraft was retained as a crime, the torture of witnesses was continued and so was mutilation as a punishment. Similarly, the 1753 code of civil procedure was a reforming measure in that it introduced uniformity, but it remained based on the traditional romano-canonical forms.

15.4.4   In 1756 came the last part of von Kreittmayr's commission, the civil code itself, named after Max Joseph the *Codex Maximilianeus Bavaricus civilis*. Unlike the later codes, the Bavarian civil code did not supersede all existing law and make a completely fresh start as the foundation of a new legal order. In fact, it gave primacy among the sources of law to certain statutes, while the code itself only took second place; the *Gemeines Recht* was retained as a subsidiary source since Bavaria was still part of the Holy Roman Empire and had no competence to discard the common law completely. Furthermore, to a large extent the code simply restated the rules of the *usus modernus Pandectarum* rather than showing allegiance to any particular theory of Natural Law. The arrangement largely followed that of the Institutions. Part I dealt with the law in general, its application and interpretation and its classification; it also dealt with persons according to their status, including such matters as when a person comes into being, degrees of relationship, marriage, paternal power and serfdom. Part II dealt with the law of things, covering ownership and its acquisition, prescriptive periods, pledge, servitudes, both personal and real, and compulsory services. Part III dealt with succession, covering wills, codicils, legacies, gifts in expectation of death and trusts, and also including intestate succession. Part IV dealt with contracts and other personal obligations. It classified contracts on the Roman pattern as real, consensual, verbal, literal and innominate; there were also chapters on quasi-contract, payment and other modes of release from obligation, delicts, and one on feudal law.

15.4.5 In spite of its widespread and heavy dependence on Roman law the code did show in content and arrangement some influence of Natural Law. This influence had led to the actual planning of the enterprise, to the clarity with which the law was expressed, to the use of German for the text – although the title was in Latin – and to the settlement of disputed points explicitly by the light of reason. For example, I.1.6 states that the law must be made known publicly so that everyone may know and learn about it; in II.2.4 the law of nature is described as being understandable by the exercise of reason, and as allowing men to know their obligations towards God, themselves and other men, whether as fellow citizens or as individuals. In III.1.3 it is stated that all agreements are in principle enforceable. Damage done to another is said to give rise to a claim for reparation by both natural and Roman law, but the subtleties of the *lex Aquilia* on damage to property are rejected (III.16.6). Although much of the content was little more than a statement of Roman law as then accepted, it must be recalled that many Natural Lawyers accepted the rules of Roman private law as rational, and thus suitable for adoption into their own schemes of law.

15.5 THE PRUSSIAN CODE

15.5.1 The first steps towards codification in Prussia (as the Brandenburg lands came to be best known) were taken in 1713 at the beginning of the reign of Frederick William I. His primary aim was to simplify and unify the administration of the various disparate territories which he ruled – the March of Brandenburg, Further Pomerania, the Duchy of Prussia, the bishoprics of Magdeburg and Halberstadt, Westphalia and the lands of the Lower Rhine. In 1714 he ordered the law faculty of Halle University to carry out a programme of rationalization of law under the leadership of Thomasius (whom he described as well known for his skill and learning). This was to settle doubtful cases, taking account of sound reason and the situation of the country. Only three months, however, were allowed for the enterprise and so its value would have been doubtful even had it been accomplished.

15.5.2 In 1738 Frederick William proposed a further and more extensive reform; a general law was to be published, based on the *usus modernus*, but also incorporating special laws which were to be gathered together separately, but under the same rubrics as in the general law; in this way both certainty and easy opportunity for reform of law could be provided. Within his territories he ended the practice of *Aktenversendung* (see paras 11.4.1–5); he also obtained a privilege barring appeal from his courts to the imperial supreme court. He died before the proposals for a restatement of law could be carried through, but Frederick the Great picked up his father's plans and modified them, partly in the light of the doctrines of Montesquieu.

15.5.3 In 1746 Frederick ordered his chancellor, Samuel von Cocceji, to produce a uniform law 'based purely on reason and on the constitution of the territory; [it] was to be in character German and in application general'. The provisions were to include a prohibition of any commentary on the law 'in order to prevent the citizens being taken in by the subtleties of professors and advocates'. This uniform law was still envisaged as supplementary to the laws of the individual provinces, but their laws were to be set out in its order. Von Cocceji did produce a part of the work. In 1748 the section dealing with the law of persons was issued, and that dealing with the law of things in 1751; both were intended as drafts for a *Corpus Iuris Fridericiani* (Frederick's Code of Law) in which Roman law would be reduced to 'a natural order and a correct system'. The draft for the section on obligations was completed in 1753, but Cocceji's death in 1755 effectively brought this stage of the work to an end.

15.5.4 The project for reform of the law was taken up again in 1780 when Frederick gave fresh instructions to the chancellor, von Carmer, who had been involved in law reform in his native province of Silesia. Von Carmer was to be assisted by Carl Gottlieb Schwarz, also known as Suarez, who in fact did most of the work. In these new instructions Frederick showed his continued distrust of lawyers; he expressed his dissatisfaction with the administration of justice in Prussia and the way lawyers procrastinated. He hoped to make the whole body of advocates redundant, and thus to free his subjects from a not inconsiderable burden while at the same time allowing the training of a greater number of skilled merchants, industrialists and artists, who would be of more value to the state. On a more positive note, he ordered that effect was to be given to Natural Law; the law should be expressed both clearly and simply and at the same time in a detailed and complete fashion so that all citizens might know what the law was without recourse to lawyers. The work was to be done by a legislative commission; this was to remain in being after the completion of the initial codification in order to set right any possible defects, errors or obscurities. No right of interpretation was to be allowed to judges or any other group of lawyers, or indeed to ministers of state; there was to be no expansion or restriction of the meaning of the written law. Any difficulties or deficiencies which might appear were to be reported to the legislative commission, which was to consider what was required and to report to the king for action. Frederick's ideas were clearly in accord with one aspect of the Enlightenment, the educative role of the benevolent ruler. Separate instructions were given for the publication of a code of civil procedure; this was completed in 1793.

15.5.5 The main work of codification took some time to complete. A provisional draft was published in 1784, based on the *usus modernus Pandectarum* and on the customary laws and the judicial decisions of the various territories under Prussian control. A revised draft was presented to Frederick shortly before his death in 1786; his comment was: 'But it is very thick, and laws must be short and not wordy' – in which he was (probably intentionally) echoing Montesquieu. Further consultations took place and further drafts were produced; most of the editorial work continued to be done by Suarez, but he had experts to assist him in the fields of criminal, commercial and maritime law. Finally Frederick William II in 1794 ordered its publication as the *Allgemeines Landrecht für die preussischen Staaten* (Universal Territorial Law for the Prussian States), commonly abbreviated to ALR. It replaced all other laws, positive or subsidiary, whether Roman, Saxon or otherwise, which had been applied within Prussian territory; it remained in force in the lands for which it had been issued (including Westphalia after 1815) until it was superseded in 1900 by the civil code applying to all Germany.

15.5.6 The ALR covered the whole field of law, both private – civil law in the sense inherited from the Roman sources, and also commercial law – and public, which included constitutional and criminal law, and also that relating both to the Church and to feudal privileges. A general introduction set out the basic principles and doctrines of the law relating to legal personality; the code was then divided into two parts. The first part dealt with law relating to the individual, the second with the individual in his social relationships, from the family through corporate bodies, local communities and the like up to the state itself. The system went back to Christian Wolff who had taken it from Pufendorf. Within the first part falls what may be described as the law of patrimony, although there was a preliminary exposition of the general principles which defined the relationship between citizen and state, and the ways in which rights came into being, were exercised, were adjusted in case of conflict, and were transferred and lost. The first part further dealt with ownership and possession and their acquisition, retention and loss, with real and personal rights over things and with contractual obligations. The second part dealt with marriage, parent and child, master and servant, societies and corporations (including charities), the rights and duties of peasantry, nobility and other citizens and also of soldiers and civil servants, with schools and universities and with the Church; it also covered constitutional, administrative and criminal law.

15.5.7 One feature of the ALR was the immense detail in which each topic was treated, far too great for a satisfactory code since it left no room for development or adjustment. In some cases it was the nature as well as the degree of detail which was unworkable; a remarkable example is the provision that a healthy mother must suckle her own child and that the father is to decide how long this is to continue before the child is weaned (ALR II.2.67–68). The attempt to avoid leaving anything to chance was due to the influence of Wolff, while from Thomasius came the idea of a Natural Law which was nevertheless peculiar to Prussia (in the sense of local law not in conflict with Natural Law), but the ideas of Frederick himself were obviously decisive. His views were clearly reflected in the prohibition on judges applying the opinions of the learned or the decisions of other judges, which arose from his distrust of lawyers. It was his paternalism which led to the efforts in the code to regulate the conduct of the citizenry in areas which might seem to be a matter for their own personal decision. It was characteristic of his approach that the citizens were legally obliged to support the common weal, and that their individual rights might require to be sacrificed for the public good; but in such cases the state was bound to give compensation to those whose rights had been sacrificed.

15.5.8 Natural law rules permeated the code. The idea was accepted that ownership could be transferred by consent; this led, for example, to the concept of a proprietorial right arising after a contract of purchase by X; even if the object of the purchase was transferred to Y, Y could not acquire a proprietorial right himself if he knew of X's right. Marriage and divorce were held to be in principle a matter of agreement between the parties, but there were requirements of form, and the existence of children in a marriage prevented divorce by mutual agreement. The ALR was a product of its time, too specifically so to have the lasting influence achieved by the Austrian or French codes. It was, however, the first complete product of Natural Law attitudes – even if adjusted to Prussian conditions – with the logical consequence that all previous legislation was superseded and all previous jurisprudence was in principle irrelevant; these features were to be found in its successors.

15.6 THE AUSTRIAN CODE

15.6.1 The process of codification in Austria followed a similar course to that in Prussia. It began under the Empress Maria Theresa (1740—1780) when in 1753 she set up a commission to produce for the hereditary Habsburg possessions (including Austria, the Tyrol and Bohemia) a law which would be certain, which would apply equally in all the territories to all the citizens, and which would be enforced by the same procedure in all courts. However, the new law was to be based on the *usus modernus*, although Natural Law was to supplement and correct the predominantly Roman rules. The first draft was in German, not Latin as had been planned; it followed the order of Justinian's Institutions but was in general simply a restatement of the *Gemeines Recht* of the hereditary lands. It was rejected as a draft by the Empress and her Council because of its great bulk and lack of clarity but was agreed on as providing the raw material for a codification.

15.6.2 A new commission was set up in 1772 with instructions to make the law short and clear, to aim at simplicity and natural equity. A draft was published in 1786 by Joseph II but further work was needed; this was continued by Leopold II (1790–1792) who succeeded to his brother, after having already been engaged in the work of codification in the duchy of Tuscany. Under his command opinions were sought from the governments of the various provinces, from university law faculties and from commissions of the judiciary; these submissions were made public. The new draft continued, however, to be essentially a code of the *usus modernus*. Under Francis II (1792–1835) a legislative board was set up of which the most active member was Franz von Zeiller, a judge and professor of Natural Law at the university of Vienna. While he was aware of the recent philosophic challenges to the school of Natural Law by Kant (who interpreted rights as the area of an individual's voluntary actions which did not conflict but harmonized with the voluntary actions of others), he relied largely on the Natural Law tradition and the spirit of the Enlightenment. In 1811 the Austrian Code was published as the *Allgemeines Bürgerliches Gesetzbuch für die deutschen Erbländer* (General Citizens' Code for the German Hereditary Territories [of the Habsburgs]), commonly known as the ABGB; it is still in force in modern Austria, although parts of it, especially those dealing with contracts, have undergone considerable revision.

15.6.3 The ABGB is confined to private law on the Institutional pattern, excluding specifically commercial law; it contains no public law because of the disparate constitutional arrangements in the various hereditary territories. The arrangement follows the typical Natural Law system with a division into three main parts: the first devoted to persons, the second to property and the third to provisions of more general application, including the constitution and alteration of rights and obligations. There is also a short introduction which deals with the application and interpretation of law. Under persons come legal personality, husband and wife, parent and child, and guardianship. Under property come both real and personal rights; real rights include possession and ownership, pledge, real and personal servitudes and succession, while both contractual and delictual obligations are included under personal rights. The third part, dealing with provisions of general application, is in later codes the 'General Part' normally found at the beginning.

15.6.4 The content of the ABGB is neither purely Roman nor purely Natural Law but a mixture of their rules. It does not accept the Natural Law rule that consent is sufficient to transfer ownership but requires some external form of conveyance, distinguishing between title, which justifies the acquisition of ownership, and the delivery which is necessary to its acquisition, as did Roman law. However, it excludes any future creation of customary rules other than those specifically recognized by statute, since Natural Law held that rules should be laid down and interpreted by the legislator alone; it takes a generous approach to Natural Law when the judge is told to supply deficiencies by analogy, failing which he must decide in accordance with the precepts of Natural Law. Again, every human being is said to have inborn rights which reason shows to be self-evident and which entitle him to be regarded as a person by the law; hence, slavery and serfdom are not permitted. In general the law was and is stated broadly enough to allow for its development, whether by judicial decisions or by doctrine, but specific provisions of the Code have been supplemented by later legislation. The ABGB has also been influenced by the work of the Pandectists in nineteenth-century Germany and then by the German civil code; certain areas have been modified and others, such as marriage law, superseded.

15.6.5 The Austrian code, although accepting the doctrine of the equality of the rights of men, was little influenced by political democracy or notions of the sovereignty of the people. Its equality is, moreover, legal equality, assuming that all citizens have roughly equal economic bargaining power in such contracts as hire and lease – an assumption now recognized as unrealistic. However, it is comparable to the French civil code in the uncluttered expression of its provisions and in the simplicity of its style. It has not had the same influence as the French code; where German is spoken the later German civil code has carried more weight, and for political as much as legal reasons the French code was normally taken as a model for nineteenth-century codifications. Nevertheless, the power of the Austrian Empire (as it became after 1804, or Austro-Hungarian Empire after 1867) extended the ABGB to Liechtenstein, Croatia, Slovenia, Dalmatia, the area which later became Romania (until a code largely based on the *Code Civil* was introduced there in 1865) and, after 1852, to the Hungarian possessions and temporarily to

Hungary itself. When the Empire was broken up after the First World War, the ABGB continued to apply in the successor states (or parts of them) – Yugoslavia (which incorporated Croatia, Slovenia and Dalmatia), Hungary, and Czechoslovakia; it also applied in parts of Poland to which territory was ceded. Its influence thus endured until after the Second World War. When these countries adopted Socialist (ie Communist) forms of government, the ABGB was either formally abrogated, as in Yugoslavia and the parts of Hungary to which it applied in 1945, or at least was set to be replaced in due course by a national law based – more or less closely – on Socialist principles. In Hungary, for example, a civil code was introduced in 1959, omitting family and employment law which were separately regulated. Czechoslovakia followed suit in 1964, while Yugoslavia (then still united) produced a new law of obligations in 1978. However, despite the adoption of Socialist principles, Roman law retained a place in legal education in these countries, and indeed has had some surviving influence on their substantive law.

15.7 THE *CODE CIVIL*

15.7.1 The process of codification in France took a somewhat different course. The idea of unity went back to Dumoulin, Coquille and Loysel in the sixteenth century. It had been continued in the seventeenth century by Domat, Fleury and his friend and close collaborator, Gabriel Argou,[3] and Lamoignon. In the eighteenth century the most notable figures are three near contemporaries – Daguesseau (1668–1751), Louis XV's chancellor, François Bourjon (d.1751), an advocate before the *Parlement* of Paris, and Robert Joseph Pothier (1699–1772) who held hereditary judicial office in Orléans, where he also studied, was admitted to the bar and, in 1749, became professor of French Law. Daguesseau was, as chancellor, responsible for three codifying ordinances on gifts, wills, and substitutions, which were incorporated largely intact into the *Code Civil*. He was influenced particularly by Domat but also by the Natural Lawyers including, somewhat unusually for a Frenchman, Christian Wolff. Bourjon, to whom the compilers of the Code acknowledged their considerable debt, was interested in the customary law, particularly the *Coutume de Paris*, in which area he drew on Dumoulin. However, he followed Domat's example in method and applied rationalist principles to the *Coutume*, which he held to be as worthy as Roman law of such treatment; in this sense he may be said to have provided a climax to the work of Loysel. In his *Le Droit commun de la France et la Coutume de Paris réduits en principes*, Bourjon drew on royal legislation, the *arrêts* of the *parlements*, the decisions of the Châtelet (the ordinary court for Paris and its surrounding area) and French legal literature of all schools. His arrangement of his material may have been somewhat, if indirectly, influenced by Natural Law through the work of Fleury and Argou, but it also owed a debt to the approach to Roman law which took the Institutions as the model of a systematic order.

---

3   Each was responsible for an *Institution au droit français* but the authorship was frequently confused. Argou seems to have borrowed much from his friend (who was pre-occupied with public life) but it was his book, first published in 1692, which was issued in its eleventh edition in 1787.

15.7.2 Pothier was not a particularly original thinker but he had an immense knowledge and tremendous organizing ability; he showed himself thoroughly familiar with Commentators such as Bartolus, Humanists such as Cujas and le Douaren, and Natural Lawyers such as Vinnius – much read in France – and Pufendorf. His first major work was his *Pandects of Justinian in a New Order* (Paris, 1748); for this he had mastered the whole Roman law which he then rearranged, but only within each title of the Digest. He then wrote a treatise on the Custom of Orléans; in the general introduction to this he laid stress on the division of the subject into persons, things and actions, very much in the Roman institutional mould. In 1761 he published what was perhaps his most influential work, the *Traité des Obligations*; this was followed by a dozen or so books on specific contracts. In 1768 he published a book on marriage which was followed by various other works treating all aspects of marital relationships. In the last two years of his life he wrote on ownership and possession. Pothier's monumental energy had led him to describe minutely French law as it was in the decade or so before the outbreak of the Revolution. He did indeed do more than describe; his work gave new proportions to French law, providing it with a clear exposition of both property and obligations.

15.7.3 In the field of obligations it was inevitable, and in the field of property likely, that the superior method of Roman law, with which Pothier was so well acquainted, should dominate the lack of organization in the customs. How far Pothier deliberately chose the Roman law tradition is difficult to tell. There is no doubt, however, that his is the last expression of doctrine concerning French law before the Revolution; for that reason alone, apart from the admiration in which he was held, it was bound to affect the compilers of the Code. Pothier seems in the mainstream of the civilian tradition, although he accepted much from the customary law. He saw Natural Law as the cause of obligations since it was Natural Law which held each man to his promise and obliged him to make good the loss incurred through his fault; this is not, however, the Natural Law as it had been developed by eighteenth-century philosophers but a version much closer to the sixteenth-century Spanish thinkers or to Grotius. Nevertheless, he rejected the Roman bases of the various contracts on the ground that they were all ultimately founded on agreement – convention, as both he and Stair called it; for legal enforceability he demanded not a mere pact but that a party must promise and engage himself to the performance of his promise.

15.7.4 This was the state of the law at the outbreak of the Revolution in 1789, and it seems clear that nothing less than a revolution would have sufficed to sweep away the traditional rights of the ancient provinces and the customs of their *parlements*. Not only law reform but codification was a demand of the Constituent Assembly in 1790; the first written constitution, that of September 1791 which was preceded by the Declaration of the Rights of Man (see Appendix 6), envisaged the preparation and promulgation of a civil code. Sufficient time, however, was not allowed for any serious draft, and the legislation which was actually passed in the next decade was concerned with particular reforms. The ancient provinces together with the *bailliages* and *sénéchaussées* were abolished; the modern *départements* were introduced as administrative units. The *parlements* were sent on indefinite vacation – from which they never returned. All Frenchmen became citizens, without differentiation of status, where formerly there had been the nobility and the commoners (*roturiers*), and the latter had themselves been classed by legal prescription into bourgeois or serf. All feudal burdens on land were abolished, as were all feudal privileges, such as the right of hunting over another's land and primogeniture; substitutions by means of trusts were set aside. Civil marriage and divorce were introduced. During the 1790s three draft codes were put forward by Cambacérès (1753–1824), but they were all rejected, usually as being insufficiently revolutionary; these outline codes were very brief because Cambacérès recognized that it would be impossible to have a code which could provide for all cases, and he also accepted that bulky laws were useless for informing the populace of their legal rights.

15.7.5   The actual achievement of codification only became possible after 1800 when Napoleon Bonaparte became First and Cambacérès Second Consul. In August 1800 a commission of four senior practitioners of law – Tronchet, Bigot-Préameneau, Portalis and Maleville – was appointed to produce a suitable code. Their records reveal that all these men were politically moderate, preferring Napoleon's rule to the uncertainties of Revolutionary fervour, but able to adjust to the restoration of the Bourbons in 1815. They had all studied Roman law at university in the normal way before going on to qualify for practice.[4] As their libraries reveal, all four were cultivated jurists, acquainted with Grotius, Vinnius, Pufendorf, Thomasius and Heineccius among foreign writers, and with French legal literature from Domat to Pothier and Olivier, a professor of law and judge in the appeal court at Nîmes. It was the authority of Napoleon himself (who admired Montesquieu's writings) which made possible the production of an enduring code, enduring because it had adequate links with the legal past.

4   French and canon law were usually third-year options, and French law was not taught in every law faculty; where it was, it was taught in French, not Latin, and by practitioners.

15.7.6   An outline of the proposed code was rapidly produced and published for comment from various courts and from the public. The commission then settled to the detailed discussions. Napoleon took a great interest in the scheme and presided over 57 of the 102 sessions which were devoted to the draft; he is recorded as having intervened frequently and effectively in the debates. Adoption in the full sense, divorce by consent, a general hypothec over the property of guardians as security for the proper performance of their duties, and unfavourable treatment of foreigners all seem due to Napoleon's own views. It was certainly because of his energy and his ambition to be remembered as much as a law-giver as a general that the code was pushed through the reluctant legislative body and issued in March 1804 as the *Code Civil des Français* in three books with 2281 articles. (It was re-issued as the *Code Napoléon* in 1807, became again the *Code Civil* after Napoleon's fall, was re-entitled the *Code Napoléon* between 1852 and 1870 under Napoleon III and after the latter's fall reverted to its original and present title.)

15.7.7   The arrangement of the *Code Civil* is firmly in the French Natural Law tradition of the previous half-century as compared with the rationalist and scientific approach of the Prussian code. The model is essentially the Institutions of Justinian, as interpreted in the light of reason. Domat had adopted this pattern in his systematization of the *Corpus Iuris*. Vinnius, the Humanist and moderate Natural Lawyer who was most influential in France, had earlier stayed close to it, simply dividing rights over things into either ownership and possession or obligations. This structure was used by Bourjon, whose first three books correspond closely to those of the *Code Civil*, although (since he wrote in six books) most of the subject matter of his last three must then be distributed within the Code. His chapter on feudal law was omitted from the Code (for, after all, it had been abolished) and the general title on obligations was indebted to Pothier since Bourjon had found no such treatment in the Custom of Paris. Olivier was probably one of the more influential and constructive critics of the draft code after its publication for comment; his *Principes de droit civil romain* (1776), after a brief preliminary on the nature of law and its object, had dealt with persons, their status and capacity, with things, seen as the objects of individual rights, with obligations, both the general theory and the special contracts, and with actions. Pothier too had dealt with the last title in the Digest (D 50.17 *de regulis iuris*) in a comprehensive way, dividing his treatment into a general part and then into persons, things and actions; he had stressed the same division in his introduction to the Custom of Orléans. He has frequently been described as the father of the Code and this is true as to content; there is relatively little in the Code that was not acceptable to or even drawn from Pothier. The arrangement of the Code, however, owes more to Bourjon. Moreover, when there was conflict between Roman and customary rules, it is clear that the compilers did not aim at producing a compromise solution but rather, in the spirit of the age, sought to take whichever was closer to reason and to the law of nature. It is probably because the *Code Civil* was not affected by any highly conceptualized theory of Natural Law but was simply designed to conform with the Declaration of the Rights of Man that it was found suitable in the individualistic, utilitarian, bourgeois, nineteenth century. It was also possibly advantageous that the model of the Institutions meant that commercial law was excluded from the *Code Civil*; although a commercial code was produced under Napoleon this did not attract the same emotional loyalty among Frenchmen and so it could more readily be adjusted to the new economic world.

15.7.8 Book I opens with six articles – the Code is normally cited by article alone, consecutive articles from the start of Book I to the end of Book III – on the publication, effects and application of the law; for example, laws are not to have retrospective effect. The main part of the Code then begins, dealing with persons; it includes titles (subdivided into chapters) on civil rights and the formalities of status, on marriage, divorce and paternal power. Book II, that is, articles 516–710, deals with property, both moveable and immoveable, with ownership and with lesser real rights. Book III, which is more than twice as long as the other two together, deals with modes of acquisition of ownership, starting with succession and proceeding to obligations. Ownership is acquired immediately on perfection of the contract in the case of sale, without need for delivery or payment of the price (article 1483). The law of obligations covers both the generalities applicable to obligations, and specific contracts, quasi-contract and delict. Security rights and prescription also occur in Book III, as does the property regime of marriage, since it is viewed as a matter of acquisition of property.

15.7.9   The style of the Code is very clear; the compilers sought for a simplicity of statement which would make the law accessible to everyone. At one level this was achieved; nevertheless the apparent simplicity has often led to the need for explanatory case law. For example, article 1382 which provides that everyone is obliged to make reparation for the damage caused by his fault[5] has given rise to an enormous quantity of case law on the law of reparation.[6] The Code itself has been much amended and supplemented by later legislation, as is inevitably necessary with all codes, but it has never been subject to a full revision, despite discussion.

5   'Tout fait quelconque de l'homme, qui cause à autrui un dommage, oblige celui par la faute duquel il est arrivé, à le réparer.'
6   See FH Lawson and BS Markesinis, *Tortious Liability for Unintentional Harm in the Common Law and the Civil Law* (CUP, 1982).

15.7.10   The *Code Civil* dealt only with that part of private law which was considered in Justinian's Institutions, excluding the final titles on procedure and the criminal law. The *Code de Procédure Civile* came into effect on 1 January 1807; it dealt with procedure before the courts, execution of judgment, and also with the formalities necessary for proving and giving effect to wills, and with arbitration. It embodied such revolutionary ideas as the freedom of the parties to determine the scope of the case, the right of immediate access by the parties to the judge, oral pleading and an independent judiciary. The *Code de Commerce* came into force the following year; its four books dealt with commerce in general, with maritime law, with bankruptcy and with mercantile jurisdiction. It drew heavily on the royal ordinances which had been the work of Colbert, the *Code Marchand* of 1673 and the *Ordonnance de la Marine* of 1681. It defined the status of merchant and dealt, for example, with the duty to keep books, with companies and partnerships and with bills of exchange. It did not innovate, but produced a clear and rational statement of the existing law merchant. The *Code d'Instruction Criminelle* or code of criminal procedure and the *Code Pénal* both came into force on 1 January 1811; the *Code Pénal* was a revision of an earlier code of 1791, dealing with serious crimes and dominated by the idea that both crimes and penalties should be precisely defined by law without room for any judicial discretion. The code promulgated in 1810 was rather more flexible but retained the principle that crimes and punishments must be clearly defined in advance; its penalties, however, were severe as well as inflexible.

15.7.11   The influence of the *Code Civil* and of the accompanying codes was enormous. This was partly due to its introduction into much of Europe as a consequence of Napoleon's conquests, and partly to its use in the French colonial empire. It was also widely imitated or borrowed, because of its quality as a piece of legislation, because it was accessible and because it expressed more generally, and therefore more attractively than its rivals, the ideals of the codification movement which continued in civil law countries throughout the nineteenth century. It was imposed on Belgium and the Netherlands, on those Italian states which fell to the French, on Baden and the Rhineland. Belgium kept it (as did the Rhineland until 1900); the Dutch code of 1838 drew much from it; the Italian codification movement, which was finally successful after the creation of a united Italy, was based on it. In Egypt, Syria and the Lebanon, in Algeria, Tunisia and Morocco, and in Indo-China it was the law of the colonial settlers and affected, profoundly in most cases, the law that followed the end of colonialism. In Louisiana and Quebec the direct impact was of the French law of Pothier's time, but the *Code Civil* had indirect influence. In Spain and the Spanish Americas, in Portugal and most of the Portuguese colonies and in the Balkans the *Code Civil* was admired and largely absorbed. Its dominance has lessened in this century for ideological or political reasons, and because some countries, like Brazil or Turkey, preferred to take the more modern German or Swiss code as a model, while others, like Italy and the Netherlands, have felt the need to produce a new code. Napoleon, however, was right to think he had produced an enduring monument.

FURTHER READING

A Broadie (ed)	*The Scottish Enlightenment. An Anthology* (Canongate Classics vol 80, Edinburgh, 1997)
P Jones and AS Skinner (eds)	*Adam Smith Reviewed* (Edinburgh, 1992)
JM Kelly	*A Short History of Western Legal Theory* (Oxford, 1992) ch 7
AJ MacLean	'Jeremy Bentham and the Scottish legal system', *JurRev* (1979) 21
J Maillet	'The historical significance of the French codifications', *TulLR* 44 (1970) 681
H Strakosch	*State Absolutism and the Rule of Law* (Sydney, 1967)
A Watson	*The Making of the Civil Law* (Harvard UP, 1981)
D Williams (ed)	*The Enlightenment* (CUP, 1999)
K Zweigert and H Kötz, tr T Weir	*An Introduction to Comparative Law* (Amsterdam-Oxford, 3rd edn, 1998)

Chapter 16

CODIFICATION IN THE NINETEENTH CENTURY

16.1 CODIFICATION IN ITALY

16.1.1   Codification was both a consequence of and a factor in the unification of Germany and of Italy in the nineteenth century. Italy's codes owed much to the French codification, and therefore they will be described before we turn to the nineteenth-century intellectual movements in Germany, from whose fruitful conflict there emerged the German civil code, the BGB (*Bürgerliches Gesetzbuch*). Italy's debt was more directly to the past.

16.1.2   The chapter on the Enlightenment and codification mentioned that some Italian states issued codes of various sorts, particularly criminal, in the eighteenth century. For example, by 1790 Venice had produced codes of criminal, feudal and maritime law. Under Napoleon the *Code Civil* was gradually extended throughout the peninsula as the various states fell to France; in this way Italy experienced a brief spell of legal unity for the first time since the Gothic invasions. The defeat of Napoleon saw a return to the earlier political fragmentation of Italy, but many rulers wished to maintain the legal benefits of the French occupation. Moreover, the *Code Civil* had introduced irreversibly the concept of the equal rights of man before the law.

16.1.3   Over the next half-century we must look again at separate developments in the individual states. By the time unification was achieved most Italian states had achieved systematic, codified statements of their law; to these codes French law had made a significant contribution. The code promulgated in 1819 for the Kingdom of Naples and Sicily was modelled fairly closely on the French codes; it was divided into five books, covering the fields of civil and criminal law, civil procedure, criminal procedure and commercial law. It did, however, contain a number of reactionary elements, such as restoring the religious effects of marriage – among them, indissolubility – to the secular law, and including ecclesiastical offences along with lay crimes. In the Papal States the codes of civil procedure (1817) and of commerce (1821) were little more than copies of their French equivalents, but the codes of criminal law and procedure which were issued in the 1830s were untouched by any spirit of the Enlightenment. In Modena the resumption of independence meant a return to previous law, but the process of reform was at work and resulted in 1852 in codes of civil law and civil procedure and in 1855 in a criminal code. Parma preserved the *Code Civil* until the work of a commission for reform of the law produced in 1820 a civil code and a code of civil procedure; the civil code was a blend of French style and enlightened current thinking on local law. Codes of criminal law and procedure followed. In Lombardy and Venice, which had been returned to the rule of the Austrian emperors, the Austrian Code of 1811 was put into force, although the French commercial code was retained with some modifications. The reactionary Austrian criminal code of 1804 was only replaced by a more liberal work in 1852.

16.1.4 It was, however, what happened in the Kingdom of Sardinia – which included Genoa and Piedmont and came to centre on the latter – that was most significant for the future of Italian law since unification (save for Rome itself) was finally achieved in 1861 under the leadership of Victor Emmanuel II of Piedmont. In the years immediately following the defeat of Napoleon the old law had been restored but, under Charles Albert (1831–1849), a comprehensive codification was planned which owed much to the French model. Five codes were produced – a civil code (1837), a criminal code (1839), a commercial code (1842) and codes of criminal and civil procedure (1848 and 1854). For political reasons these codes were inevitably the most influential in the production of a law for all Italy. Meanwhile, in some territories, such as Modena and Parma, the Piedmontese civil and commercial codes were introduced; Piedmontese criminal law was made applicable in northern Italy. The commissions which were to produce the new Italian codes actually began their work in 1860. In 1865 were issued a *Codice Civile*, a commercial code (replaced in 1882 and abolished as a separate field of law in 1942), and codes of civil and criminal procedure. There were greater difficulties in reconciling different penal traditions, and it was only in 1890 that a criminal code was promulgated. The commissioners who worked on this great project were influenced not only by the Natural Law tradition which was an element in the French codes but also by the thinking of the Historical School, of which the leading scholars were to be found in the German states. It is to their thought that we shall now turn.

16.2 THE GERMAN HISTORICAL SCHOOL

16.2.1 The general principles of the Historical School were not new; indeed, they bear marked similarities to many of the notions put forward by the Humanists. Essentially, its followers maintained that law evolved and was continually modified by conditions of time and place. What made their thinking important in European jurisprudence was its rejection of the schematic, universal approach of the Natural Lawyers who had dominated the previous two centuries. The men of the Historical School were interested in legal history in order that contemporary law could be firmly rooted in its historical past. On the other hand, Natural Law thinkers in Germany such as Thomasius and Wolff had argued that the principles of Natural Law could only be discovered by rational deduction from the nature of man. Their theories had been extremely abstract; the study of what was actually followed as law in any particular society was of less importance to men like Wolff than the logic of the system. This extreme approach was not adopted universally by Natural

Lawyers – we have seen a much more comparatist method in France, for example – but it had been predominant in much of Germany. The other main reason for support for the historical approach was political, and again in contrast with that of the Natural Lawyers. They had been inclined to support absolute rulers who would impose on their subjects the law which jurists and rulers knew was good; furthermore, in this kind of Natural Law theory any controversy or doubt must be settled by reference to the ruler as law-giver and final arbiter on the dictates of reason. In a more liberal society such reliance on a single source of authority was not generally acceptable.

16.2.2   There were other factors which explain the jurisprudential importance of the Historical School. There was an increasing interest, admittedly often antiquarian, in the study of history; we have mentioned the origins of historical sociology in the work of men like John Millar (see para 14.5.8). This was linked with the developing organization of universities, particularly in Germany, as centres of study in the arts as well as the sciences, but Montesquieu in France and Edmund Burke in Britain had already fervently held that a people's past was vitally important in determining its future. Among lawyers concerned with the practice of the law it was widely, if not always explicitly, recognized that law must be in sympathy with the spirit of the people for whom it was framed, and that penal sanctions could only work where the law was habitually and willingly obeyed. Then, too, there was widespread nationalist feeling in Germany; more people than ever before were interested in what made them different from the French or the English. This nationalism was associated with the Romantic Movement in Germany but also with law as embodying the spirit of the people.

16.2.3   The name most closely associated with the Historical School is that of Friedrich Carl von Savigny but, naturally, he built on the work of his predecessors and in particular that of Gustav Hugo who was appointed to a chair at Göttingen in 1792. Hugo was a Roman lawyer but one, like the Humanists, who believed that the internal development of Roman law must be studied against the background of its social context. He was particularly influenced by his reading of the chapter sketching the history of law in Gibbon's *Decline and Fall of the Roman Empire* (published 1776–1788). Hugo shared Gibbon's admiration for the lawyers of the classical period and their creative role; this was reflected in his opposition to codification which he saw as stifling the creativity of judge and jurist.

16.2.4   Savigny was instrumental in the founding of the university of Berlin, where he held a chair from 1810 to 1842; he came of a landed family and was for many years a member of the Prussian *Staatsrat* (the legislative body) and for some seven years Prussian minister for legislation. In 1803 he produced his first major work, *Das Recht des Besitzes (The Law of Possession)*. The treatise made a considerable impact; it drew from the Roman sources the Roman principles of possession but it also aimed to show how these principles had been modified during the Middle Ages and that the original Roman principles were superior to the civilians' modifications. His next major work was his *Geschichte des römischen Rechts im Mittelalter (History of Roman Law in the Middle Ages)*, which is still worth consulting. In 1815 he was instrumental in founding a periodical called the *Zeitschrift für Geschichtliche Rechtswissenschaft* (*Journal of Historical Legal Science*), and this marks a convenient point for the coming into existence of the Historical School.

16.2.5 When those German states which had been subject to French rule during the Napoleonic Wars regained their independence, the *Code Civil* was in general rejected along with most other reminders of French domination, although the *Landrecht* of Baden, for example, was little more than a translation of the *Code Civil*. There was hot debate on whether the gap should be filled by new local codes or whether there should be a return to the *Gemeines Recht* (common law) which was based on modified Roman law. Anton FJ Thibaut, a professor at Heidelberg, published a pamphlet calling for a general civil code for all Germany to replace the existing divisive chaos of contradictory provisions, which was impossible even for lawyers to know thoroughly. The Roman law of the *Corpus Iuris* he held to be inadequate for the modern world; further, it was obscure and ill-arranged. What was needed was a simple code in German, which would make the law accessible to all; this would be a symbol of unity and the first step towards unification.

16.2.6 Savigny responded in 1815 with a pamphlet which conceded the ills and the need for a remedy, but argued that codification was not the right remedy, certainly not at that particular time. Rather, jurists should examine what was good and what was bad in the German legal tradition and develop the law accordingly. A code was not a suitable tool for development because it was by nature static and, even if a code were one day to be desirable, it must be built on a sound historical understanding of Germany's legal past and no proper study of this had yet been attempted. Law, like language, was largely a product of unconscious growth, reflecting the spirit of the people or *Volksgeist* – a term coined by Puchta, although the concept is largely due to Montesquieu. A nation's law was the product of its *Volksgeist* and reflected the different influences which composed its history. Lawyers might have a special task in the development of the law and in giving it the necessary technical expression, but their work must go with, not against, the grain of the *Volksgeist*. This last point explained why Savigny held, contrary to the Natural Lawyers, that no system of law could be of universal application. Finally, Savigny argued, the only suitable time for the preparation of a code was when a nation had reached maturity, and then it would be superfluous. His opposition to the project undoubtedly played a large part in postponing codification for Germany as a whole.

16.2.7 Savigny as a Romanist argued that the great age of Roman law was the classical period, and that this greatness was due to the work of the jurists. However, Roman law had undoubtedly been extensively received in Germany during the sixteenth century and developed as the basis of the *Gemeines Recht*, and this Roman law was developed out of the law of Justinian. While Roman law could hardly be described as the product of the German *Volksgeist*, Savigny argued that in the period of the Reception the lawyers, as the trained representatives of the people, had fulfilled a need of the *Volksgeist* when they received Roman law; the Roman law of the *mos italicus* had thus become part of German law and the German legal tradition. Roman law still had much to offer, if only in the application of the principles of classical law; further development of German law should be founded on the Roman law of the great age. Later accretions to the classical law could be discarded if they were not worthy of use in the creation of an improved modern system; it was one of the tasks of historical legal science to determine what was and what was not of value in the legal tradition. Savigny did not, indeed, reject specifically Germanic law as unworthy of study; one of the achievements of the Historical School was to make German law a discipline in its own right, and the basis for further scientific development. The first comprehensive account of the development of Germanic law, based on original sources, was Karl Friedrich Eichhorn's *Deutsche Staats-und Rechtsgeschichte* (*German Constitutional and Legal History*, published 1808–1823).

16.2.8   Savigny intended that Roman and Germanic law together should provide the foundations of a new German legal science, but to some younger, Germanist members of the school, Savigny and his Romanist followers were champions of Roman law at the expense of the native tradition. By the middle of the century a split had developed between the Romanists and Germanists. Some of the latter argued that the Reception had been nothing short of a national disaster, others merely that it had been unnecessary; Otto von Gierke (1841–1921), for example, in his *Genossenschaftsrecht* (*Law of Associations*), held that a satisfactory system of partnership and company law could be built on the customs of the Germanic guilds without any recourse to Roman doctrines.

16.2.9   Nevertheless, the work of the Romanists and the Germanists represents two sides of the same coin; both engaged in an historical investigation of the evolution of law in order to advance the law in nineteenth-century Germany. The Germanists were breaking new ground. The Romanists were bringing new techniques of scholarship to bear on their study of sources which were for the most part well known; some new sources, however, were revealed. In 1816 Niebuhr discovered the Veronese palimpsest of Gaius' *Institutes* and thus brought to light the only largely complete classical work to survive untouched by Justinian's compilers; other pre-Justinianic fragments of legal writings were also found during this period, such as the *Vatican Fragments*. Bluhme's investigations resulted in his (generally accepted) theory of how the Digest had been compiled by three committees, each going through a different block of material.

16.2.10   Later in the century, when the eventual production of a code had become a certainty, Romanists were freed from the need always to think in terms of Roman law as a system for current application. In the later years of the century Lenel's *Edictum Perpetuum* and *Palingenesia Iuris Civilis* were published; in the former he reconstructed the Edict of the Urban Praetor, in the latter he re-assembled the writings of the individual classical jurists, which the compilers had scattered in their arrangement by subject, so that, for example, one may read what survives of Ulpian's 31st book *On the Praetor's Edict* and then go on to the 32nd – a Roman book was about the length of a short modern chapter. Other works appearing in this period which are still fundamental to scholarship were CG Bruns' collection of legal sources other than the legal literature, and Theodor Mommsen's surveys of Roman public and Roman criminal law, his (by now standard) edition of the Digest, and his foundation of the great collection known as the *Corpus Inscriptionum Latinarum* in which are edited and arranged by geographical source all surviving inscriptions in the Latin of antiquity.

16.2.11 Savigny's reputation was outstanding, but he had his critics. Hugo thought his theory of the *Volksgeist* too abstract and out of step with a reliance on empirically ascertainable historical fact. German commercial lawyers were satisfied with the Roman law developed by the Commentators as relevant to their needs; they did not want to regress to doctrines taken from the less developed classical Roman law. Rudolph von Jhering (1818–1892) was also a Romanist; his thinking about legal evolution, as expressed in *Der Geist des römischen Rechts* (*The Spirit of Roman Law*), differed from Savigny's in stressing the similarities between legal systems. He was not prepared to accept the strongly nationalistic approach of the Historical School, but thought that the ability to borrow wisely was one of the glories of a legal system. The comparative method of studying other systems as well as one's own enabled the absorption of those foreign doctrines and institutions which were most profitable.

16.3 THE PANDECTISTS

16.3.1 The Pandectists originated as an off-shoot of the Historical School, and their main concern was the scientific application of the Roman texts. Like the Historical School, their methods prompted discussion and imitation throughout Europe – including England – and also in America. The Pandectists took their name from the Pandects (ie the Digest) of Justinian and their scholarship was essentially concerned with the systematization of Roman law for contemporary use, with the emphasis on the jurists of the classical age.

16.3.2 The Pandectists were to some extent influenced by the rationalist Natural Lawyers, back to Pufendorf, in that they aspired to a rigidly schematic approach. They too tried to create an interlocking system of legal rules and concepts, from which solutions to new legal problems could logically be drawn; this was undoubtedly due to the particular influence of Wolff. Like the later Natural Lawyers, the Pandectists were influenced by the natural scientists of their time; they aimed to identify a new kind of truth, the positive or scientific truth, by observation and experiment. They were thus legal positivists, in that they expounded the principles of observed law as something without any logical link to moral justice. Once data had been collected, analysis could determine what was cause and what effect; classification and definition were also essential parts of the scientific method. It was possible, if not common, for a Pandectist to compare the discovery of legal principles with the analytic methods of chemistry.

16.3.3 The school was founded by Georg Friedrich Puchta (1798–1846), a pupil of Savigny who succeeded his master in the Berlin chair in 1842. Puchta himself was indebted to Savigny, particularly for the latter's theory of the jurist as representative of the *Volksgeist*, and in his turn he influenced his master. Puchta believed that the jurist, as representative of the people, was responsible for both the theory and the practice of the law and must use his skills to express rules and concepts hidden from the untrained mind. This special position meant that the rules elucidated by the jurist should ipso facto have the force of law – legal science therefore joined custom and legislation as a source of law. Moreover, it was the jurist's duty to guide both legislator and people and guard the law from any rash or ignorant interference. The jurist must also place legal rules in their systematic context, recognizing their effect upon one another, and acknowledging their lines of derivation, so that each rule could be traced back to its underlying principle; thus he could demonstrate the internal harmony of the legal system. This method, which is known as *Begriffsjurisprudenz (jurisprudence of concepts)*, aimed at creating a hierarchy from the very concept of law itself down to each particular rule, the validity of an individual rule being dependent on its logical place in this hierarchical pyramid.

16.3.4 The construction of such a systematic hierarchy of concepts clearly demanded definition of all the concepts involved. As time went by, these definitions tended to become more and more abstract and to lead their framers into language more familiar to legal philosophers than to practitioners. For example, a legal right was defined as 'a power of volition', a legal act as 'a definition of will', while the protection of peaceful possession was justified on the grounds that 'the law respects the realized will'.

16.3.5 Savigny, under the influence of Puchta, moved in his later years more strongly towards the systematic and away from the empirical in his study of Roman law. Even in his treatise on possession, some of his deductions had more in common with mathematical formulas than with the social realities of Roman law. His (unfinished) *System des heutigen römischen Rechts (System of Modern Roman Law)* well typifies Pandectist legal science (*Pandektenrecht*). The material was to be arranged under obligations, property, family law, and succession, with further sub-headings as appropriate. Certain basic concepts which applied throughout the system, such as status and juristic personality, he treated separately in the General Part with which he opened. He followed the same method within his treatment of obligations, explaining the generally applicable concepts before dealing with particular fields and their rules. The other major work of the Pandectists was Windscheid's *Lehrbuch der Pandekten (Textbook on the Pandects*, first published in 1862) which went through seven editions in the author's lifetime and became the standard manual of Pandectist doctrine. It was arranged according to the system outlined by Savigny. Unlike that of most of his fellows, Windscheid's work was of use to practitioners because he made frequent reference to court decisions.

16.3.6 Although some Pandectists became as rigidly schematic as any of the more extreme rationalist Natural Lawyers, their roots in the Historical School meant that they preferred the Roman law of the classical period to Justinianic law, let alone the modifications of the mediaeval civilians. This caused a degree of conflict with the majority of lawyers actually practising law, who adhered to the *Gemeines Recht* in the tradition of the *usus modernus Pandectarum*. Of the supporters of the latter approach, Bruns, for example, in his treatise on possession examined both the original Roman law and its evolution and the changes the concepts and rules had undergone since the twelfth century. He justified these changes on the grounds of their expediency and thus implicitly approved their continued application.

16.3.7 The Pandectists were a strong force in German legal thinking in the nineteenth century. Greater systematization than the *Gemeines Recht* offered was certainly desirable for the exposition of the law, whether to students or to the public, and also for its application. Again, although the Pandectists claimed to be politically neutral and concerned only with private law, their values were those of the dominant prosperous middle class which believed in the theory of laissez-faire; they stressed freedom of contract and the protection of private property – as indeed the Romans had. Finally, Pandectist legal science was attractive because it represented unity and not diversity; it offered a common juristic culture which took no account of regional variations, and it was therefore of appeal to the forces of nationalism. Their Romanism, however, was disliked, particularly by the Germanists of the Historical School. Many others, like Jhering, came to find their methods far too abstract and doctrinaire, and quite neglectful of the realities of social life.

16.3.8 In his *Geist des römischen Rechts*, Jhering moved away from Pandectist legal science and attempted to provide a sociological explanation for the evolution of the rules of Roman law. He laid the foundations of what was to become known as the jurisprudence of interests: that is, the approach which argues that the duty of a judge, especially when faced with a doubtful decision on a matter for which there is no explicit legislative provision, is to settle the case according to that estimate of the correct balance between the competing interests of the parties concerned which was to be found in the work of the legislator. The judge is not free to follow his discretion but must always look within the written law for this balance; nevertheless, he should concern himself with the legislator's social aims rather than with the ordering of concepts. Jhering stressed that legal science was concerned with social relations in general and business purposes in particular, and that the ideas of justice, law and the state were interdependent. There could be no clear and permanent line drawn between private and public law since the state must be interested in the pursuit of activities desirable for the community. Historical evolution and present needs defined justice for the particular place and time. Legal concepts had no meaning apart from the activities of human life.

16.4 THE BGB AND ITS BACKGROUND

16.4.1 Even after the creation of the German Empire in 1871, Germany remained a legally divided country. The states of which the new Empire was composed still retained a measure of autonomy, and the creation did not immediately affect the legal systems of its members. These legal systems continued to be various blends of codified law – Saxony acquired a code as late as 1863 – *Gemeines Recht* and local custom, while Schleswig-Holstein was under Danish law and much of the Rhineland adhered to the *Code Civil*.

There was also variation among the states over which of the three elements took precedence. Under the North German Confederation, created in 1866 as a step towards unification, the *Reichstag* and *Bundesrat* (lower and upper houses of a federal governing body, under the King of Prussia) were established; they made possible direct federal legislation in the specific areas of criminal and commercial law. In 1869 a supreme federal court was set up with jurisdiction in these two fields; in 1877, under the German Empire, this court was re-established at Leipzig with no restrictions on its jurisdiction. Since 1873 legislation too had been competent in any area of civil law. From 1877 therefore there was the machinery for a unified German law.

16.4.2   In the next chapter the process of harmonization, especially in the field of commercial law, will be described. In 1861 the German Commercial Code was issued. This was introduced by local legislation into the various member states of the North German Confederation in the following years. In 1871 it was re-issued as an imperial law. This Code expanded the scope of commercial law beyond that of the French code; in the latter, a matter was commercial only if both the parties could be described as merchants, but in the German code it was the commercial nature of the transaction which was stressed, even if only one party was engaged in pursuing his business. When the Commercial Code was revised and re-issued in 1897 it reverted to the more usual narrower sphere, limiting its authority to cases where the transactions involved business interests on both sides; this was possible because the Civil Code had already been passed as statute – although it was not yet in force.

16.4.3   In 1871 there was enacted an imperial German Penal Code, which largely repeated the penal code of the North German Confederation, itself based on the Prussian penal code of 1851. However, it was Prussia which had opposed a scheme, known as the Dresden Draft, put forward in 1865 in an attempt to reach uniformity in the law of obligations. There was no government-inspired attempt to unify the civil law until after the extension in 1873 of the imperial legislature's powers. The following year a single clause statute authorized the codification of German civil law and a commission was appointed to consider ways and means. The recommendations of this commission, although not given binding force, were followed in substance by the commission which was then appointed to produce a draft code.

16.4.4   The drafting commission consisted of eleven men under the chairmanship of the president of the imperial commercial court; it included Bernhard Windscheid, the Pandectist, who left the commission before the work was completed, but who, nevertheless, had a very considerable influence on the final draft. The commission included other academics and also practitioners, as well as officials regularly employed in the drafting of legislation. At the outset it was agreed to omit commercial law and certain aspects of land law from the code. After thirteen years of work a draft was completed in 1887 and published the next year, together with explanatory notes, to receive comments and criticisms.

16.4.5   Much comment was received, and a considerable proportion was unfavourable. Only one critic objected to codification in principle, and he was a member of the imperial supreme court, but there were two main lines of attack adopted by others. Some thought that the draft was excessively reliant on Roman as opposed to German law. To some extent this was only to be expected, in view of the membership of the commission; this included Windscheid and others trained in Pandectist legal science. Both the structure and the substance of the draft revealed the Pandectist approach. Others criticized both the language and the matter of the draft as too abstract and doctrinaire; insofar as one purpose of a code was to make the law readily known, it was a failure. As one wit remarked: 'Before it can be understood, it must be translated into German.'

16.4.6 A second drafting commission was appointed in 1890, but with the task of working on a revision of the original in the light of the comments received. This was a larger commission, and it included, as well as a range of lawyers, interested parties such as commercial experts, landowners, economists and representatives of other special interests. This commission kept consultations going while it worked, and it made some effort to simplify the condensed language of the code. The revised draft was finished in 1895 and was approved by the imperial council with relatively few amendments; it was given statutory force in 1896 with effect from 1 January 1900. A supplementary codifying statute on international private law was issued at the same time. The new civil code (the BGB) and the commercial code were comprehensive within the fields they covered, but other areas of the law were left to be dealt with by separate legislation; for example, insurance and copyright.

16.4.7 The BGB is divided into five books, but the articles are consecutive throughout. The first book contains the General Part; it covers persons – both natural and juristic – the definition of things, the classification of legal acts, prescriptive periods and so on. The second book deals with obligations, with the creation and discharge of voluntary obligations, with the individual contracts and delicts. The third book is on things, dealing with possession, then ownership of immoveable and moveable property, with servitudes and real security. The fourth book is on family law, which includes marriage, other relationships within the family and tutelage. The fifth book deals with succession, starting with the concept of hereditary succession and then going on to the rights of heirs, rules concerning wills, settlements and technical details of proof in connection with inheritance.

16.4.8 In its final form the BGB still owes a considerable debt to Roman law but it also takes account of German tradition. The arrangement conforms to the Pandectist system but the substance within each section is based on predominantly Roman or German rules according to the particular history of the relevant branch of law. The Roman contribution is dominant in the field of obligations, while in family law and succession the bulk of the material comes from the German tradition. Moreover, the opportunity was taken in producing the BGB to reform various areas of law; the law of husband and wife was brought up to date, for example. The language remains technical, rigorously consistent and not easy for a layman to use. Ready comprehension of the law is further hampered by the need to read different parts of the Code in the light of each other in order to obtain a complete picture. For example, to settle a problem on sale, the judge might well have to look first to the General Part, then to the generalities about obligations, thence to the general law of contract and finally to the particular rules affecting the specific contract of sale; cross-reference to the commercial code may become necessary.

16.4.9   Despite these drawbacks the BGB has had considerable influence outside Germany. In Greece the Pandectist approach dominated academic law, and when a Greek Civil Code was finally produced in 1946 its structure and content both owed much to the German model. The Austrian code was revised in the early twentieth century in the light of what the BGB had to say about obligations. In Switzerland and in Hungary it was influential; with the exception of family law and succession it was the basis of the Japanese Civil Code of 1898, and it was noted in China. Brazil too preferred the BGB to the *Code Civil* as the main source for its codification. In Britain it was the German experience as much as the process of harmonization in the commercial field which aroused in many a desire for at least limited codification. Such views did not in general owe much to the radical proposals of Bentham or Austin, and the British government gave no encouragement to anything more than revision and consolidation, as in the Sale of Goods Act 1893. This English approach was similar to that most commonly taken in the USA, but there were some, such as Sir Henry Maine and Sir James Stephen, who, after experience in codifying the Common Law for Indian use, saw the benefits of a more fundamental undertaking.

16.5 THE FRENCH REACTION TO CODIFICATION

16.5.1   French legal thought in the nineteenth century, while in some ways parallel to that in Germany, is most obviously different in that the Germans were working towards – or against – codification while the French were trying to come to terms with their existing codes, particularly the *Code Civil*. It had been a deliberate aim of the Revolution to subordinate the judges to 'the legislator' and to abolish their law-making powers. Distrust of the judiciary and of judicial discretion had been marked in the moderate reformers as well as the radicals; it was therefore not surprising that it was given effect in the *Code Civil*. It lay behind the requirement that judges should cite the articles of the *Code* on which they relied and explain their reasoning rather than rely on their own intrinsic authority; this requirement led to the extremely terse style adopted by the judges of all courts for their decisions, since too much explanation gives more room for argument. Thus the main problem that faced French lawyers was that legislation was in their theory the only source of law, and yet the law must be applied and understood.

16.5.2   The strong feeling which had imbued the *Code* that judges should limit themselves to the administration of its provisions, and not usurp the place of the legislator, was expressed in Article 5, which forbids any judicial pronouncement on a matter before the court by way of a general disposition having effect for the future. This became a fundamental tenet of French legal thought. How far it could be enforced in actuality was a problem ignored by the legislature. Academic lawyers held grimly to the theory and proceeded therefore to elaborate on the actual contents of the *Code* in an attempt to provide the judges with something to administer in every conceivable situation. The judges themselves observed the forms but soon, inevitably, began to interpret, and the accumulated effect of their decisions is what is meant by the French term *jurisprudence* – as opposed to the *doctrine* of the academic lawyers. Nevertheless, even the *Cour de Cassation*, the supreme court administering the *Code Civil* (in contrast to the *Conseil d'État* which is the supreme tribunal in matters of public law), has been carefully restricted so that it should not to appear to make law. Decisions appealed to it may be quashed (*cassé*) but they are then sent to a second lower court, equivalent to the first, for a fresh trial. Not until 1837, and then only when all the chambers of the court sat together, was the *Cour de Cassation* able to give a final decision, and the effect of this is still, supposedly, restricted to the case before the court. However, although the theory of the subordination of the judiciary means that there can be no doctrine of precedent, there has been a natural tendency in the courts towards consistency, aided by the reports of decided cases.

16.5.3 Every judgment must by law be constructed from the main relevant facts and the statutory provisions which apply to them in a series of logical steps leading inexorably to the conclusion of the particular issue; this is described as a *jugement motivé*. To avoid any appearance of discretionary interpretation such judgments are laconic. The case report may give the arguments of the advocates in some detail but the stated reasoning of the judges remains terse. However, such reports – the most notable surviving series are those of Dalloz and Sirey – have traditionally been accompanied by analytical notes and comments which can reveal the influence of sources older than the *Code* or of previous decisions of the court. These comments can be collected into *répertoires* or encyclopaedias, commonly arranged by topic, which fill the silences in the judicial decrees. The tradition of producing such works was established early, despite Napoleon's dislike of legal commentaries. Merlin, *procureur-général*[1] of the *Cour de Cassation*, was immensely learned in the old law and well placed to analyze the decisions of the new regime; the ample material he provided in his books during the 1810s and the 1820s was in itself an encouragement to the *Cour de Cassation* to supplement what was lacking in the *Code*.

1   The responsibility of the *procureur-général* was and is to state to the court a reasoned and objective view of the law, with proposals for the action to be taken on the appeal before it; a similar function is performed by the advocates-general of the Court of Justice of the European Union.

16.5.4 Partly through Merlin's influence, and partly through that of Savigny and the Historical School, many lawyers became involved during the earlier years of the century in the effort to describe the working law of France and to classify and analyse its development. The German scholars were interested in the *Code Civil* both as a product of legal science and as the law in force in the German Rhineland until the coming of the BGB. During the 1840s, however, academic interest in *répertoires* and case law waned, and the field was almost wholly occupied by practitioners. Their work was sufficiently thorough and critical for the courts to be secure in developing a *jurisprudence constante* which, in some areas, has achieved major changes in the law. For example, Articles 1119 and 1121 forbid entering into a stipulation on behalf of another, except in very narrowly defined circumstances; because these rules are most inconvenient in the context of life assurance – an institution which had not been imagined by the drafters of the *Code* – the courts have in effect put them into abeyance.[2] In connection with gifts the courts have also departed from the obvious meaning of the *Code* and have introduced new rules.[3] The means by which the courts achieved these changes have often been tortuous, but this has been because of the deliberate constraints on judicial power established by the framers of the *Code*. For practitioners, coming to terms with the *Code* meant accepting a gap between theory and practice; the theory so restrictive of judicial development is impossible to apply, but practical interpretation must always be achieved by using, or quite often distorting, some provision of the *Code*.

2   CK Allen, *Law in the Making* (Oxford, 7th edn, 1964) p 182.
3   JP Dawson, *Gifts and Promises* (Yale, 1980) gives a good picture of the different treatment of the topic in the French and German systems.

16.5.5   French academic lawyers played a small part compared with their German colleagues in the development of their legal regime, and their status was much lower. They had a bad start; as a direct consequence of the Revolution the law schools were defunct by 1793 and they were actually abolished in 1795. They were revived in 1804 by Napoleon but with the specific intention that their professors should be obedient exponents of the *Code* and nothing more. Even when men of more originality came to be appointed their focus was on the *Code Civil* and the other codes. Although some jurists in the 1820s were influenced by the Historical School, the dominant approach from the 1830s on was analytical and dogmatic, following the lead of Jean Proudhon, who held a chair of law at Dijon.

16.5.6   Thus for decades the great majority of academic lawyers concentrated on the texts of the codes and their interpretation, and on the relationships between the individual provisions and their possible interpretation. They assumed that legislation was the only source of law, that the coverage of the codes (and of the laws passed in the new fields of law which appeared during the nineteenth century) was complete and that there were no inconsistencies and contradictions. Careful analysis, they thought, could fill every apparent gap in the provisions of the law and supply an answer to any conceivable legal problem. Like the Pandectists, whom they much admired, they built up a structure based on logical deduction, but it was sterile because it ignored what was happening in the courts. Moreover, Pandectist legal science, because of its wider range of materials, had more hope of covering all possibilities than the French. French jurists restricted themselves almost entirely to the codes, occasionally looking back behind them to Pothier, but recognizing virtually no other source, while the Pandectists, although they concentrated on the classical Roman law, did acknowledge its Justinianic and mediaeval developments as well as the fact of the Reception, even if they tried to minimize the importance of these aspects of the law.

16.5.7   For half a century an immensely learned and ingenious flood of literature was produced in France, of considerable value as far as it went, but not fertile in new ideas. The exponents of *doctrine* despised the exponents of *jurisprudence* and their scorn was returned; it was only towards the end of the century that they began to see how their skills and their subject matter could be complementary. Some academic journals began to take notice of judicial decisions; some of the analytical notes in the case reports came to be written by academics. The natural exhaustion of the restrictive approach to the codes meant that the leading intellectual figures in the 1890s readily took a more historical or sociological approach to the study of law, including the study of its application. The distinguished romanist Esmein remarked that *jurisprudence*, 'just as much as the *Code* itself, must be studied directly and scientifically'. An exponent of the historical approach appeared at the end of the century who did much to reconcile the theory of the supremacy of the Code and of the inability of judges to make law with the actual reality of practice; this was François Gény.

16.5.8 Gény raised the question of whether a merely logical interpretation of the *Code* was desirable, or even possible. He held in his *Méthode d'interprétation et sources en droit privé positif* (1899) that it was necessary to investigate the realities of social life; from such researches he argued that custom, judicial authority and juristic tradition should be added to the effective sources of law, looking to the *Volksgeist* of French law, and 'free scientific research', which must take into account concepts like equity – hitherto rigorously rejected – the demands of public order and interest, and the just balance between conflicting private interests. While defining the function of judicial decisions as 'propelling' the formation of custom, he held that the operation of the courts was to look at the interests of the parties,

> 'estimate their respective force, weigh them in the scales of justice so as to give preponderance to the most important of them, tested by some social standard, and finally bring about an equilibrium.'

If the judge had no other guidance, he should apply the same principles as would a legislator. Gény's theories were not new, even in France, but the way he put them forward made a great impact. Because he still could not openly acknowledge explicit judicial rule-making, he had to complicate his discussion of custom with problems considered long before by the Commentators, such as: Who are the necessary users of a custom? How can one tell if they do consent to the formation of a custom? Are they 'represented' by jurists and judges? It was, however, on foundations laid by Gény that Planiol could say: '*Jurisprudence* is a customary law of recent creation.'

16.5.9 In his other major work, *Science et technique en droit privé positif* (1914–1924), Gény developed the more sociological aspects of his legal philosophy. He was part of the same intellectual movement as found its German expression in the *Freirechtsschule* (Free Law School). This movement opposed legal positivism and the jurisprudence of concepts and looked to men like Jhering who had advocated the jurisprudence of interests. (In some cases the doctrine that the judge should be quite free to choose his interpretation of the most suitable rule led to a cavalier disregard for statute and considerable unpredictability in the application of law, but mostly it was enlivening.) Gény defined Natural Law as the limits within which any legal system must work.

There are four premises: *le donné réel*; *le donné historique*; *le donné rationnel* and *le donné idéal*. *Le donné réel* covers physical and psychological facts, such as sex, or climate or religious traditions; *le donné historique* covers the historical facts and traditions which mould *le donné réel*; *le donné rationnel* (which includes much of the classic doctrine of Natural Law) states such things as the sanctity of human life, the right to property, the inviolability of the person and freedom of thought; and *le donné idéal* describes how society understands the facts and how it wishes changes to take place. Thus, to apply Gény's terms to marriage, its first basis is the sexual instinct of man and woman, its second the historical institution in any society, its third the need for a relatively permanent – although not necessarily monogamous – relationship for the secure life of the family, and its fourth comprises current ideas in any society on the proper relations between husband and wife, even if not yet embodied in the law. Gény provided a realistic foundation for the continuing relationship between *jurisprudence* and *doctrine* and in this way his work was immensely valuable, even if his more purely philosophical notions were not able to withstand much criticism.

16.6   THE SWISS CODE

16.6.1   In 1815 Switzerland was still a loose confederation of twenty-two virtually independent cantons; in 1848 the modern federal state was created, with a federal legislature whose powers were extended in 1874 and 1898 by constitutional amendments. In 1874 the private law of the several cantons was diverse; in the French-speaking cantons it was profoundly influenced by the *Code Civil*, in other cantons, such as Berne and Lucerne, it was based on the Austrian code, while in some cantons it was largely original, as in Zürich where, however, Pandectist influence was apparent. After 1874 the legislature was competent to issue general legislation in the fields of personal status and obligations as well as certain aspects of commercial law; this led to a Code of Obligations, promulgated in 1881, which drew from the German Commercial Code and the discarded Dresden Draft (see para 16.4.3). After 1898 the legislature had an unrestricted competence in all aspects of civil and criminal (but not public) law. Eugen Huber, a professor at Berne, had already been asked to prepare the draft of a civil code and this was published for comment in 1900. A commission of jurists and other experts was then appointed to amend the draft in the light of the criticisms. The final draft was submitted to select committees of both houses of the Swiss legislature in 1904; in 1907 it was enacted, with effect from 1 January 1912 as the *Schweizerisches Zivilgesetzbuch* (ZGB – Swiss Civil Code); the old Code of Obligations was revised and attached as, in effect, a fifth book.

16.6.2   The Swiss Code begins with a preliminary title on general matters and then has four books dealing respectively with persons, family law, succession and property; finally there follows the book on obligations. While the book on obligations is very clearly indebted to Pandectist thinking in its method, proceeding from the general to the particular, those who framed it did not allow system to dominate at the expense of clarity and accessibility. Nor was the rest of the Swiss Code framed in highly technical language. As with the *Code Civil*, it was deliberately kept as simple as possible in style so that it would be comprehensible to the intelligent layman as well as the lawyer. Furthermore, it is in the French creative tradition in that it does not purport to provide a complete and detailed statement of the law from which the solution to every legal problem may be deduced. (The framers of the *Code Civil* had consciously argued that a code could do no more than lay down general principles for guiding future legal developments; it was only Proudhon and his followers who had held that a code must itself be the logical source of all legal solutions.) Instead, the ZGB offers a statement of general principle, deliberately leaving scope for further development by judicial interpretation, as indeed is expressly ordained in art 1. Certain areas of commercial law which were in a state of flux at the time of the promulgation of the Swiss Code, such as insurance and copyright, were left to be dealt with by future legislation – which could also be adapted to the harmonization process within European legal systems.

16.6.3 In spite of both German and French influences, the Swiss Code is a distinctively Swiss product, firmly rooted in the existing cantonal law. The blending of disparate influences in the legal code was a reflection of the similar political, linguistic and cultural blending in the Confederation itself. This sympathetic relation to juridical history owed much to Huber, the drafter of the Code. Before starting on the work of preparing a draft, he had established himself as an authority on Swiss law and produced the fundamental *System und Geschichte des schweizerischen Privatrechts* (*System and History of Swiss Private Law*). This book has much in common with the work of men such as Dumoulin in the aftermath of the codification of the French customs, for it is a comprehensive and comparative account of the customary laws of the cantons. Huber described both differences and similarities and, on the basis of common underlying jurisprudential principles, attempted to distil a common customary law for Switzerland, using the knowledge and techniques developed by civilians and by Natural Lawyers to produce a balanced portrait.

16.6.4 Like the *Code Civil* and the BGB, the Swiss Code has been of influence beyond its own frontiers. It was much admired in Germany, where some even favoured its adoption. It influenced French juristic thinking, in particular in the French law of adoption of 1927. In 1926 it was imported virtually without alteration into Turkey when Kemal Ataturk decided on enforcing immediate westernization. It was also an influence in the production of the Polish, Russian, Czech and Hungarian codes.

FURTHER READING

A Alvarez et al	*The Progress of Continental Law in the Nineteenth Century* (Continental Legal History series vol XI, Boston, 1918)
M Berger	'Codification' in *Perspectives in Jurisprudence*, ed EMM Attwooll (Glasgow, 1977) 142
F Dahn	'The new code for the German Empire', *JurRev* (1890) 15
JP Dawson	*The Oracles of the Law* (Ann Arbor, 1968) ch 6
W Friedmann	*Legal Theory* (London, 5th edn, 1967)

M John   *Politics and the Law in late Nineteenth-Century Germany*
                        (Oxford, 1989)
H Kantorowicz   'Savigny and the Historical School of Law', *LQR* 53
                        (1937) 326
JM Kelly   *A Short History of Western Legal Theory* (Oxford, 1992)
                        chs 8 and 9
Lord Lloyd and   *An Introduction to Jurisprudence* (London, 5th edn,
MDA Freeman   1985)
P Stein   *Legal Evolution* (CUP, 1980)
                        Roman Law in European History (CUP, 1999) ch 5
I Williams   *The Sources of Law in the Swiss Civil Code* (Oxford,
                        1923)
JQ Whitman   *The Legacy of Roman Law in the German Romantic Era*
                        (Princeton NJ, 1990)
R Zimmermann   *The Law of Obligations: Roman Foundations of the
                        Civilian Tradition* (Capetown, 1990)

Chapter 17

NEW TRENDS IN LAW, 1815–1914

17.1 PUBLIC LAW AND LIBERAL DEMOCRACY

17.1.1 The wider consequences of the Industrial Revolution include the growth in population, the invention of mechanized transport, and developments in medicine and public hygiene, as well as the more strictly commercial and manufacturing changes. All of these were important in the daily lives of ordinary men and women, even if it was the direct economic developments which had more impact on the growth of new or significantly changed areas of law. Furthermore, this Revolution also affected political society, which itself was subject to the social and technological developments – an active spiral of change.

17.1.2 Nationalism as such was not a new factor in Europe; it went back to the sixteenth century at least. Nationalism in the nineteenth century, however, was something new. It was often based on a common language, and it arose out of the ashes of institutions which could be traced back to the beginnings of mediaeval Europe. The most important of these was the Holy Roman Empire, of which the death under Napoleon was recognized by the Treaty of Vienna in 1815, when Europe tried to settle down after the French Revolution and the Napoleonic Wars. It was also in this period that the greater part of the present map of western Europe was defined, although in the eastern parts, where the Austro-Hungarian Empire lingered as part-heir to the old Empire, significant changes were to follow at Versailles after the First World War, from the next great attempt at a peace settlement. The unification of Italy and of Germany are important parts of nineteenth-century political history. A major consequence in both cases was the movement towards producing a unified law that would replace the legal systems of all the smaller states which were being absorbed into the new nations. We followed the history of these national codifications in the previous chapter, but legal thinking was everywhere affected. The idea of the nationhood of a people, bound together by ties of race, language and culture, found its clearest expression in Savigny's theory of the origin and development of law, and in the work of those members of the Historical School who attempted to shed light upon Germany's legal past. But it was not only in Germany and Italy but also in the Netherlands and Switzerland, and to a lesser degree in other countries, that codification was seen as part of a wider process aimed at creating a sense of national identity and, where necessary, providing new national institutions.

17.1.3   Another aspect of nationalism in the nineteenth century was the growth of an active citizenship. Political theories were based on liberal reform or radical democracy; the latter was not to have much practical effect until the twentieth century. The new concept of citizenship was inspired by the creation of the United States of America and by the enduring consequences of the French Revolution (see Appendix 6). The notion was generally accepted that all men should have equal citizenship before the law, although this was not yet applied to a share in governmental powers. Explicitly in the United States, but to the same effect elsewhere, the idea was accepted that if the new large states were to have a soul they must bind individuals into a patriotic union: if men were required to participate in the common cause, they must be able to feel that this was in their own interests. Universal adult male suffrage was not by any means immediately achieved in most nations of Europe but such ideas were ripe for consideration; by the end of the century the extension of the vote to women was taken seriously. The economic changes, of course, also played a part in the growth of active citizenship; it was not so much that there was a new middle class, but that the existing prosperous middle class grew to huge proportions, and this inevitably upset the balance of internal power.

17.1.4   Although the Congress of Vienna tried in general to restore hereditary and absolutist monarchy, the new political factors which we have mentioned and the new spread of economic power made the consent, if not yet the participation, of the governed inevitable. Nineteenth-century liberalism, to put it simply, aimed at extending the politically privileged classes to include professional and commercial men; it favoured constitutional monarchy and a parliament in which property, and not people as such, was represented. Democracy was a more radical idea, locating sovereignty in the whole body of the people. Because of the excesses of the French Revolution democracy was for a long time widely feared, a fear enhanced by the events of 1848, the year in which the Communist Manifesto was issued. 1848 is sometimes known as the Year of Revolutions; in that year there were liberal or radical uprisings in France, Italy, Austria, Hungary, Prussia, Ireland and Romania, and unrest was felt in many other countries such as Switzerland, Denmark and England. Democracy entailed equal civil and political rights; it meant universal (male, still) suffrage and, in contrast to liberalism, held that the elected representative assembly should be guided by the will of the electorate.

17.1.5   For the legal historian the influence of liberalism and of democracy is apparent in the public law concerning parliamentary representation and the franchise. The processes of change naturally varied from country to country; moreover, the boundary between liberal and democratic motives for reform was seldom clear. Nevertheless, all the various states of western Europe experienced and responded to the same pressures. By the mid-1870s both France and Switzerland had adopted universal male suffrage. After 1871 the *Reichstag* (the representative assembly of the German Empire) was elected by universal male suffrage using a secret ballot, but Prussia retained a three-class franchise – the reality of power, however, remained with the Emperor and with his chancellor. In Belgium the right to vote remained based on a property qualification until 1893, and even after that date the claims of property continued to be favoured, in that those who satisfied a prescribed qualification enjoyed a plurality of votes. In Italy universal male suffrage was achieved early in the twentieth century. In Norway universal male suffrage was granted in 1898, while in 1906 Finland, after its revolt from Russia, extended the vote to all adults, male and also female.

17.1.6   The electoral law of Great Britain underwent a series of alterations during the nineteenth and twentieth centuries. In the early years of the nineteenth century, largely as a result of the Industrial Revolution, it became clear that the existing allocation of parliamentary seats throughout the country was out of step with the demographic changes that were taking place. Many of the new and expanding industrial towns were without any representation, while others (some of which, like the notorious Old Sarum, had virtually ceased to exist) were grossly over-represented. The new balance of economic strength also led to a shift away from the idea that Parliament should represent landed property above all other interests.

17.1.7   The first steps in the direction of parliamentary reform were the Reform Acts of 1832, extending the franchise.[1] The English Act granted the vote to the occupier of every house with an annual rental value of £10 or more in the boroughs and to leaseholders with property worth £50 in the shires; this measure increased the electorate from some 435,000 to over 650,000, but some men lost their votes. The Act also gave parliamentary representation for the first time to forty-two boroughs, including Manchester and Birmingham, while fifty-six lost all representation. The Scottish Act similarly gave the vote to the occupiers of premises with an annual value of £10 or more in the burghs – moreover, election was to be directly by the voters and not indirectly through the burgh councils – and to leaseholders in the shires with property of £10 or £50 worth, depending on the length of lease. It too revised representation in the shires, and revised and added to burgh representation. The Scottish Act raised the number of voters from about 4,500 to some 65,000 – a huge leap. The Acts failed, however, to introduce the secret ballot, with the result that undue influence at elections remained a problem.[2]

1   More properly, the Representation of the People and Representation of the People (Scotland) Acts, 2 & 3 Will 4, cc 45 and 65.
2   See Charles Dickens, *The Pickwick Papers*, ch xiii.

17.1.8   The secret ballot was introduced by the Ballot Act of 1872, by which time the Reform Acts of 1867 and 1868[3] had roughly doubled the electorate, granting the vote to all ratepayers. The Reform Act of 1884[4] brought some five million voters onto the electoral rolls, approximately one-sixth of the population; only in 1918 was universal adult male suffrage introduced, and it was not for another ten years that women acquired the same voting rights as men (see paras 18.3.2–3). Furthermore, the relative constitutional positions of Lords and Commons shifted in the decade before the 1914–1918 War, culminating in the Parliament Act of 1911, which laid down that Bills certified as money Bills by the Speaker of the Commons could not be touched by the Lords, that other Bills passed by the Commons in three successive sessions should become law two years after their introduction despite the Lords' rejection, and that the maximum life of a parliament should be reduced from seven to five years.

3   Representation of the People Act, 30 & 31 Vict c 102 and Representation of the People (Scotland) Act, 31 & 32 Vict c 48.
4   The Representation of the People Act, 48 & 49 Vict c 3; it marked the introduction of a uniform system of eligibility in the United Kingdom; it was complemented by the Redistribution of Seats Act of 1885.

17.2 THE ORGANIZATION OF BUSINESS

17.2.1   The Industrial Revolution slowly but fundamentally altered the economic base of Europe. Before 1800 most European manufacturing industry had been very local; it depended on workers who laboured individually or in small groups with the aid of simple tools and unsophisticated machinery. With unimportant exceptions, any power other than that of men and animals was that of wind or water. The refinement of the steam engine and its application to industrial machinery changed all this. The new machinery was expensive, requiring a considerable initial capital outlay. It therefore made economic sense to concentrate manufacturing industry and the necessary workers. The result was that mass-production and the factory began to replace small-scale domestic production; this was achieved first in the textile, pottery and iron industries. The advent of more sophisticated steam-powered industrial plant in its turn stimulated the mining of coal to run it, and the production of iron and steel from which to make it.

17.2.2   The revolution in industry was accompanied by a revolution in transport. Communications had indeed been improving during the eighteenth century with the development of better techniques of road building and with the construction of canal networks which could provide a cheap and relatively efficient means of transport. The real change, however, was brought about by the use of the steam engine in locomotives and the creation of the railways. In 1830 there were only two public railway lines in Europe, the English Stockton–Darlington and Liverpool–Manchester lines, but by 1840 there were some 1800 miles of track in Europe; by 1870 there were approximately 65,000 track miles. Journeys which had taken days could now be accomplished in a matter of hours, and goods could be transported more speedily and more efficiently than ever before. This was clearly a major factor in the growth of the urban population. Prior to 1800 the population of Europe seems to have been around 180 million following a long, slow climb; by 1900 the figure had more than doubled to something like 400 million. The relationship of the factors behind this increase remains somewhat obscure; improved agricultural techniques and the ability to transport fresh food into large cities were certainly important, but so were the improvements in medical science and the decline in serious epidemics.

17.2.3   The Industrial Revolution affected the organization of business in two ways. First, the advent of mass-production and the large industrial complex meant that those industries involved were now organized on a larger scale than ever before. In the second place, new ways of financing industry were needed. While any business needs steady capital investment if it is to succeed and create further wealth, the nature of these changes was such as to require financing on a scale which it was increasingly beyond the capacity of one individual or family to provide. Funding by the public thus became widely necessary; that is, contributions were needed from members of the public with capital to invest, who would take shares in an industrial concern and in return receive a proportionate share of the profits. This posed problems for, as had been the case with the *compagnia*, the purchase of a share was in law the purchase of a share in the ownership of the firm; as well as carrying an entitlement to a share of the profits, it also rendered the investor liable – potentially without limit – to contribute to any losses incurred.

17.2.4 The eighteenth century had seen the bursting of many 'bubbles', as speculative ventures were called; this had rendered investors more cautious and indeed brought the very concept of the joint stock organization into disrepute. In the early nineteenth century the risks involved in investment were often found unacceptably high. When a firm was small enough for all who contributed funds and took profits to be actively involved in its management, or at least to have an effective voice in determining company policy, the liability of co-owners was not unreasonable. When, however, large enterprises emerged with which the individual investor had no real contact, but only a certificate evidencing his fractional share in its ownership, the investment of even a few pounds (or other currency) carried with it, in the event of the company's bankruptcy, a liability quite beyond the investor's control and potentially far exceeding the amount invested. The problem was economic, in that capital investment was needed and had to be made attractive, and legal, in that a device must be found to make safe investment practicable. The solution lay in the intelligent development of the joint stock company and in the concept of limited liability. We shall look at the developments in commercial law in Britain and France.

17.2.5 The joint stock company is an incorporated body, a legal person in its own right, distinct from its shareholders and directors. This eases the path for those having commercial dealings with it; unlike an unincorporated body such as a partnership (put on a sound statutory footing in England by the Partnership Act of 1890), a company does not need to be reconstituted every time its membership changes. Moreover, it can sue and be sued in its own name – unlike a partnership in England. The participation of all its members is not required to validate conveyances of property and the like; such documents are executed on the company's behalf by signatures of appropriate officers, possibly with adhibition of the company seal. Then too, the liability of shareholders in a joint stock company is usually limited, which solves the problems we have mentioned concerning investment. Further, the shares in such a company are usually transferable, which facilitates the movement of capital and attracts the individual investor. Its advantages for the running of business on a large scale are considerable.

17.2.6 The development of the joint stock company in Britain was a slow process and not without opposition. Prior to the nineteenth century, incorporation was a privilege rather than a right, and it was granted only by royal charter or private Act of Parliament, for example to the East India Company (1600) or the Bank of England (1694) or, in 1766, to the Grand Trunk (or Trent and Mersey) Canal Company. The Bank of Scotland was incorporated in 1695 by an Act of the Scots Parliament; the British Linen Company seems to have been operating as a joint stock company well before it received Letters Patent in 1746, which were replaced by a royal charter in 1819 when its business had become clearly that of a bank. Judging from the remarks of both Adam Smith and George Joseph Bell, it seems likely that by the eighteenth century in Scots common law limited liability was already treated as characteristic of a joint stock company.

17.2.7   As business developed the need for incorporation became seen as more a matter of course; at the same time a simpler process was clearly becoming increasingly desirable. In 1841 a parliamentary committee was appointed to 'inquire into the state of the laws respecting joint stock companies, with a view to the greater security of the public'. The result of this inquiry was the companies legislation of 1844 and 1845. An Act of 1844, applying in the case of Scottish companies only to those having an office or place of business in some other part of the United Kingdom, created an office for the registration of joint stock companies; it also laid down regulations for such companies' formation, including the duty to provide information about the company's promoters and about the nature of the intended business. Further Acts of the same year dealt with the liquidation of English and Irish companies. In 1845 separate Companies Clauses Consolidation Acts for Scotland and England and Ireland eased further the process of registration by setting out standard provisions which individual companies, if they were 'undertakings of a public nature', were permitted to adopt by reference. The combined effect of this and other legislation was, as the remit of the 1841 committee had instructed, to provide for the greater security of the investing public, and to establish the Registrars of Companies as watchdogs. The principal drawback was that there was no general provision for limited liability.

17.2.8   In 1852 a mercantile law commission was appointed to investigate the consequences of limited liability and whether such an alteration of the law would be of general benefit to trade. The majority on the commission were against change, but it was admitted that in very large undertakings, such as railway and shipping companies, or in very humble ones, such as washhouses and reading rooms, the proposed reform might be advantageous. In spite of the majority view, in 1855 Parliament passed for England the Limited Liability Act which limited the liability of shareholders to the amount of their unpaid share capital, provided that the company had the word 'Limited' after its name and that at the registration of the company this intention had been stated. This Act was replaced a year later by a more comprehensive measure, the Joint Stock Companies Act, which applied to the whole United Kingdom but provided separate Registrars for England, Scotland and Ireland. Then in 1862 the Companies Act consolidated all previous legislation and established the company in something like its modern form.

17.2.9   As an indication of the pace of development, for much of the eighteenth century the principal English work on commercial law was Beawes'

Lex Mercatoria Rediviva (*Law Merchant Renovated*), published in 1758, and still including descriptions of the chief commodities of various countries and of the weights and measures to be found in different parts of Europe, as well as matters of legal interest. Only in the last years of the century did published books show a clear division between commercial law and the practice and theory of trade; Park on *Marine Insurance* was published in 1787 and Bayley on *Bills of Exchange* in 1789 and in the 1840s the American jurist Joseph Story wrote on *Partnership*, *Bills of Exchange* and *Promissory Notes*. Bell's *Treatise* and *Commentaries* (see para 14.2.9) show by contrast a much readier access to commercial aspects of the common law of Scotland, where Welwod had written on maritime law in the sixteenth century. Stair, Bankton and Erskine, who had dealt with the law coherently and systematically in their institutional writings, had provided the fundamental material needed for the creation of mercantile law.

17.2.10 By the beginning of the nineteenth century the concept of the *société en commandite* had been developed in France. This had its origins in the mediaeval *commenda*. Such a *société* retained the unlimited liability of those actively involved in running the business, but it limited the liability of the individual whose only connection with the firm was an investment of capital to the amount of that investment. It is essentially a limited partnership, and is usually restricted in size. During the course of the century there appeared the *société anonyme*, a form of company in which all the shareholders enjoy limited liability. Before 1867 such a company could only be created by government licence, but a law of that year laid down the fundamental rules concerning the formation and running of public companies. There are legally prescribed formalities for registration, designed to protect the interests of shareholders, before entry on the national Commercial Register. The law of 1867 also laid down the obligations of directors to shareholders and provided safeguards for the company's creditors. From the nature of the business, such transactions are regulated in French law by the *Code de Commerce* rather than the civil law.

17.3 THE REGULATION OF EMPLOYMENT

17.3.1 The industrialization of Europe brought with it changes in the nature and conditions of employment. Much of the new industrial machinery could be operated by unskilled or semi-skilled labour, displacing the craftsman. The increase in population meant that there was a ready pool of such labour. Moreover, the late eighteenth and early nineteenth centuries were the age of individualism and laissez-faire. The attitudes implicit in these theories discounted the value of protecting the weak and relied on market forces to settle relationships; nor did they encourage interference by the state in the life or business interests of the individual. Further, the scale of the new industries meant that there was a marked remoteness in many cases between employer and employee. Competition demanded that production costs be kept as low as possible; there was nothing to prevent an employer from paying only starvation wages, nor from employing women and children in preference to more costly adult male labour. While the nineteenth-century capitalist entrepreneur by no means always corresponded to his caricature, grinding the faces of the poor, there was no general concern on the part of employers for the conditions in which their employees worked.

17.3.2   However, as the century passed, the conditions of 'the labouring classes' began to attract the attention of humanitarians but, because of widespread non-interventionist attitudes even among those of a liberal persuasion, it was not easy to get governments to act. The first pressure to do something came not from the established political parties but from concerned individuals and groups, such as – in Britain – Lord Shaftesbury (the seventh earl) and the Benthamites. Legislation was slowly forthcoming to deal with the worst of the abuses, and so the foundations of modern labour law were laid.

17.3.3   In August 1834 all slaves within the British Empire became free, and in the previous year the first Factory Act to set up an inspectorate was passed. This Act covered the textile industry and forbade absolutely the employment of children under nine, and night-work for all under eighteen; a nine-hour day was laid down for those under thirteen and a twelve-hour day for those between fourteen and eighteen. In spite of the salaried inspectors appointed under the Act, its enforcement was probably not very effective. Another Act tried to stop the oppression of chimney sweeps' boys,[5] and another to check the old abuse of paying wages in 'truck', that is, in goods necessarily acquired from premises owned by the employer or in tokens only exchangeable at his shop.

5   See Charles Kingsley, *The Water Babies* (1863).

17.3.4   In 1842 there appeared the disturbing *Report on the Employment of Children in Mines* which gave a shocking picture of life underground, recording that the conditions experienced there anticipated 'the period of old age, decrepitude and death'. The result was the Coal Mines Act of the same year; the employment underground of boys below ten and of women was forbidden altogether and, again, inspectors were to be appointed to enforce this. The Factory Act of 1844 fixed a maximum working day of six-and-a-half hours for children under thirteen and of twelve hours for women; further, machinery was to be fenced. In 1847 Lord Shaftesbury – and the unions – finally succeeded in having the ten-hour day and the six-day week recognized by the law. The Factory Act of 1874 assumed the fifty-six-hour week; the Employers and Workmen Act of 1875 gave the Sheriff Court in Scotland (the county court and courts of summary jurisdiction in England) cognizance of claims by employees against their employers as well as vice versa.

17.3.5   A Public Health Act, also of 1875, created a sanitary authority in every English district; a similarly named Scottish Act of 1867 had made provision for local authorities to put into force measures safeguarding the public health. There had been some earlier legislation in this field in both countries, for example, the Nuisances Removal Act of 1848, but it was only in the later part of the century that advantage could be taken of the developments in medical and engineering science. These and other legislative acts did much to ameliorate conditions of employment in industry and the life of the urban poor. Adequate enforcement, however, remained a huge problem and the related problems of unemployment, loss of earnings through illness and the like were left untouched.

17.3.6   These problems were tackled by the Liberal Government which came to power in 1905. Economic and political factors weighed in favour of reform and the Elementary Education Acts of 1876 and 1902 had laid a foundation of compulsory universal education in England; in Scotland the Education (Scotland) Act of 1872 had extended earlier legislation already providing such measures. (Acts of 1616 and 1633, reinforced in 1696, had imposed on landowners the duty of establishing or supporting a parish school, but such schools were almost entirely confined to the Lowlands, and they were not free.) In 1908 non-contributory old-age pensions were introduced, and an eight-hour day for miners; in 1909 came labour exchanges, and minimum wage rates in some industries. The National Health Insurance Act of 1911, borrowed from a German example, laid down that all manual workers (further defined by maximum earnings) between the ages of sixteen and seventy were to share in a compulsory national insurance scheme, to which contributions would be made by the state, the employers and the workers; its benefits were to be administered either by approved societies (friendly or assurance societies and the trade unions) or by the Post Office. Thus there was protection from the consequences of unemployment or absence from work through illness, and also provision of medical assistance; from this Act, indeed, dates the framework of a national health service. But child labour in industry was not prohibited until after the 1914–1918 War.

17.3.7   Legislation of a similar kind was passed during the nineteenth century in many other of the industrialized countries of Europe. In Prussia the employment of children was limited in 1839 and 1853, and in the latter year a factory inspectorate was introduced. After the establishment of the German Empire, centred on Prussia, in 1871, the twelve-hour working day became the legally permitted maximum. Legislation between 1883 and 1889 introduced and extended a general contributory insurance scheme against sickness and accidents at work; provision was also made for financial support in old age. Germany was in general ahead of her neighbours in this field. Although the government's motive was to take the sting out of labour agitation, German workers, before World War I, were better protected against the hazards of industrial society than those of any other nation.

17.3.8   In France too there was some legislation in this sphere. It tended to lag a little behind, probably because French industrialization was a somewhat slower process than that of Britain and Germany. Legislation governing conditions of work and the length of the working day was passed during the 1890s; in 1900 a maximum working day of ten hours was introduced, and in 1906 a six-day working week. In Austria a factory inspectorate and also national insurance against sickness and accident were introduced during the 1890s. An Austrian industrial code of 1907 consolidated and improved on earlier regulations concerning the employment of children, the length of the working day and safety at work. By the outbreak of the First World War practically all the countries of Europe had found solutions – if only partial – to some, at least, of the problems produced by the industrialization of society.

17.4 TRADE UNIONS

17.4.1   The nineteenth century also witnessed the rise of the modern trade union movement. The concentration of workers in larger units than ever before provided a new kind of opportunity for associations; the stimulus came from the conditions in which they worked. This development of organized labour was something of which the law in all European countries had to take account, but this was done reluctantly. Quite apart from the vested interests of those represented in even the more liberal governments, there was among all governments (as there had been in ancient Rome) an ingrained suspicion of associations of any kind. Whatever its origin or apparent purpose, an association could too easily be turned to political ends. At best this represented a threat to law and order (as with the Chartist movement in Britain in the 1830s and 1840s), at worst it raised the spectre of incipient revolution (as among the United Irishmen of the 1790s). Furthermore, the nascent labour movement found its ideological backing in the writings of the early socialists who attacked the whole capitalist system.

17.4.2   Louis Blanc, who knew and influenced Karl Marx, believed that the capitalist system was essentially evil because it was based on competition. Competition divided rather than united the working class, as its members competed for employment; it even prejudiced the small manufacturer in that he had to compete for markets against the already advantaged entrepreneur. The solution advocated by Blanc was the elimination of private enterprise and its replacement with state-financed and state-run industries. Similarly, Karl Marx's doctrine of the class struggle laid stress on the enslavement of the proletariat – 'physically broken, spiritually bestialized' – and approved revolution as a means of attaining a just society. It is hardly surprising that the legal recognition of trade unionism had to evolve from an attitude of outright hostility to a gradual and usually grudging acceptance of such organizations.

17.4.3   In France the *Code Civil* rejected the concept of organized labour. In 1791 associations both of workers and of employers had been declared illegal; the *Code* reiterated this, forbidding the formation of groups of twenty or more people and outlawing both striking and picketing. It also provided that in any dispute between employer and employee over pay the final decision lay with the former; this remained a legal requirement until the reign of Napoleon III (1852–1870). The potential dangers of organized labour were made clear in 1831 when the silk-workers of Lyon, in an attempt to secure a minimum wage, revolted and seized control of the city; order was only restored by the intervention of the army. As a result, a law of 1834 closed a loop-hole by banning associations even of less than twenty persons when they were linked with a larger body. However, in 1839 the print-workers of Paris, without any overt interference from the government, formed a union for the purpose of collective bargaining; in the years following other groups of workers formed similar organizations. By the 1850s it was apparent that the total repression of organized labour and its demands was politically – and economically – unacceptable. Under Napoleon III conciliation boards, composed of employers and workers, were re-established as a procedure for dealing with industrial disputes. In 1864 the *Code*'s prohibition of strikes was repealed; labour associations became legal, and they obtained specific recognition in a law of 1884.

17.4.4 In Germany unions of skilled workers became widely established during the nineteenth century, although they only received legal recognition in 1869. In 1878, however, Bismarck, the German chancellor, obtained the passage of a series of repressive laws as part of a more general campaign against German socialism. Among other things, these laws forbade meetings by any unauthorized labour organizations and gave the government power to suppress such unions. This legislation remained in force until 1890, when the German trade unions finally won full legal recognition.

17.4.5 The British trade union movement also experienced a gradual recognition of its existence and its rights against a background of general suspicion, and of some hostility from the courts. Repression was formalized in the Combination Act of 1800 (itself a replacement for the Combination Act of 1799) which made it illegal for men to form combinations to negotiate wages or working conditions, or even to arrange preliminary meetings to this end. Also, any attempt to persuade others not to work for a master was an offence. The crime of conspiracy in this context was abolished by the Combination Act of 1824 which, however, forbade intimidation and acts of violence as breaches of the perfect liberty which ought to be allowed to parties to any contract. In 1825 another Combination Act repealed that of the previous year; it permitted the existence of associations which aimed at improving wages or conditions of work, provided that violence and intimidation were not used to advance these objectives, but incidentally revived the crime of conspiracy. With a limited right to collective bargaining thus established, the British trade union movement expanded and even began to attract a degree of public sympathy. Nevertheless, the attitude of the judiciary towards organized labour was slow to change; the inclination of the bench was to interpret the rights of the unions in as strict and limiting a way as possible (as being in conflict with the principle of free competition) and to impose severe penalties for conduct deemed criminal. For example, in 1834 a group of agricultural labourers from Tolpuddle, Dorset, were sentenced to seven years' transportation on the grounds that they had administered an illegal oath to the members of their association, although its aims were to further their interests by peaceful negotiation.

17.4.6 In 1867 a royal commission was appointed to inquire into the unions and their activities. Its report was favourable and resulted in the Trade Union and the Criminal Law Amendment Acts of 1871. The combined effect of these statutes was to establish that the activities of a union would not be held unlawful, and so in breach of the criminal law, merely because they tended to restrain trade, unless they were accompanied by aggravating factors such as violence or intimidation. In effect, the right to take action in support of legitimate claims had been acknowledged. Moreover, unions had acquired a degree of protection for their funds; a registered trade union was permitted to vest its property in trustees who had powers of administration. Further legislation in 1875 (the Conspiracy and Protection of Property Act) established the right of peaceful picketing. Boycotting was held not to amount to intimidation in *Curran v Treleaven*[6] but the courts interpreted the right of picketing narrowly. They found no difficulty in condemning trade unionists on the grounds that they were 'besetting' a place of work, and not just 'attending' to give information (*Lyons & Sons v Wilkins*[7]).

6   [1891] 2 QB 545.
7   [1899] 1 Ch 255.

17.4.7   In addition to the courts' restrictive interpretation of the legislation passed for the benefit of trade unions, there was an increase in the use of civil actions for damages by those whose business interests had suffered as a result of union activities. These civil actions were at first raised against individual union members, but in 1901 there came the decision in *Taff Vale Railway Co v The Amalgamated Society of Railway Servants*.[8] The House of Lords decided that a registered trade union could be sued in its registered name (for a strike which it had not specifically authorized); this overturned the previous assumption of immunity and threatened the effective existence of the unions. A union could now be sued and its funds attached whenever the activities of its members caused loss to any person. The Trade Disputes Act of 1906 reversed the decision in *Taff Vale* and cut away the grounds on which the courts had previously entertained civil actions against unions or their members. It lifted from the unions all liability to actions for conspiracy for acts done in furtherance of a trade dispute, and it re-defined peaceful picketing, specifically allowing the peaceful communication of information and the peaceful persuasion of others to refrain from work, even if this induced the breach of a contract of employment.

8   [1901] AC 426.

17.4.8   A further challenge to the unions came with the case of *Osborne v The Amalgamated Society of Railway Servants*,[9] when the House of Lords decided that the unions were not entitled to levy from their members a contribution for political purposes. Public opinion and the majority in Parliament, however, supported unions, their aims and methods. The Trade Union Act of 1913 permitted the political levy, although it made provision for those who wished to 'contract out' of payment. The Act made clear that a union, provided that its objectives were those defined in the Act, could pursue aims and use methods of any lawful kind. It confirmed the provision of the 1906 Act that:

> 'An act done in pursuance of an agreement by two or more persons shall, if done in contemplation or furtherance of a trade dispute, not be actionable, unless the act, if done without any such agreement or combination, would be actionable.'

9   [1910] AC 87.

17.4.9   After the First World War a period of poor labour relations led to the General Strike of 3 May to 12 May, 1926. This was a failure, and it led to the Trade Disputes and Trade Unions Act of 1927. The chief feature of this measure was the requirement that individual union members 'contract in' to payment of the political levy. It was repealed by the Labour Government of 1945 and not restored by the Conservatives in 1951. Nevertheless, the courts have continued to interpret strictly legislation concerning organized labour. Conservative legislation in the 1980s and 1990s imposed considerable restrictions on trade union activities and powers, and New Labour has not been disposed to reverse the trend with any vigour.

17.5 HARMONIZATION OF LAWS

17.5.1 The increased commercial intercourse between the countries of Europe consequent upon the Industrial Revolution, and the new speed with which goods could be moved from place to place, brought their own problems. There were many economic benefits, but divergences of law among the nations were highlighted as never before. Accordingly, from the middle of the nineteenth century onwards, attempts were made to harmonize at least the commercial aspects of the various legal regimes. The Scandinavian countries gave a lead in seeking harmonization over a wider field of law and, aided by a certain community of language and tradition, achieved considerable success from the latter part of the century onwards. Both the concept of harmonization and discussions on particular problems were promoted by several governments, and by such interested bodies as the Association for the Reform and Codification of the Law of Nations. Success, when it came, was reached by a variety of routes. Sometimes harmonization was achieved by incorporation into national legislation of the terms of a previously agreed convention. Sometimes voluntary agreement without the backing of legislation was found sufficient, as with the York–Antwerp rules, which will shortly be described. On other occasions harmonization was attained by the development of uniform rules in areas where there had been conflicts of law, or by the international recognition of institutions such as the International Postal Union and their regulations.

17.5.2 Commercial law, as well as being the field most affected by the new pressures, was also that in which the resolution of the problems was least difficult. The commercial law of all the European states had to a varying degree a common foundation in the mediaeval law merchant and there were no major local idiosyncrasies – even in England, after Lord Mansfield had done his work. There was therefore less nationalistic opposition to foreign influences and the adoption of foreign rules. As examples of these trends we can look briefly at the maritime law of general average (previously discussed in the chapter on the law merchant, para 6.2.2), the law of railway freight, and the law of negotiable instruments (see section 6.6).

17.5.3 Maritime law displayed a general similarity in principle, but much variation in detail. Attempts were made, by means of international conferences and discussions, to promote uniformity. In 1876, for example, the Bremen meeting of the Association for the Reform and Codification of the Law of Nations appointed a committee to look into the law of general average. At its Antwerp meeting in the following year the Association produced a set of regulations, known as the York–Antwerp Rules. These were based on the regulations drawn up in 1864 at an earlier international conference at York, held under the auspices of the British National Association for the Promotion of Social Science, but as amended in 1877 by resolution of the Antwerp conference. The York–Antwerp rules went a long way towards achieving an assimilation of the law of general average; despite some opposition from Lloyd's of London, they found general favour in the maritime world. These rules were nowhere given statutory force, although they did help to shape later Belgian, Spanish and Italian legislation on the subject, and also the Marine Insurance Act of 1906 in Britain. The implementation of their provisions, and of later modifications, rested solely on voluntary agreement and commercial practice; for example, it was agreed by most of the maritime trading nations that the rules would be adopted into the terms of all bills of lading and contracts of marine insurance as from 1 January 1879.

17.5.4   Unlike carriage by sea, railway freight was a new mode of transport. As we have mentioned, the railway network grew enormously after the middle of the century, and travel became both reliable and reasonably speedy. In the course of a single journey and in a comparatively short space of time, goods might well cross several frontiers. It was therefore clearly desirable to have a uniform set of rules governing disputes over carriage by rail rather than to leave their resolution to the chance application of the law of one particular country, whether the country of origin or that where some accident occurred. The impetus for assimilation came from Switzerland, since her small size and position at the heart of Europe inevitably meant that many international consignments passed through her territory. In 1874 the Swiss government issued a set of draft proposals to the governments of all countries having direct railway links with Switzerland. These were then discussed and amended as appropriate at a number of international conferences. The result was the Berne Convention of 1886 by which the participating states agreed to accept into their systems a uniform set of rules to govern the international carriage of railway freight through their respective territories.

17.5.5   Negotiable instruments had, like general average, a long history. The reasons for attempting harmonization in this field were also obvious. During its lifetime a negotiable instrument (of which the bill of exchange is typical) might well travel through a number of countries. Although there was an underlying similarity of principle in the treatment of this area of law throughout Europe, based again on the law merchant, there was much variation in detail. Prior to 1857 in Germany, for example, there were some sixty different sets of statutory rules governing bills of exchange. In that year the Diet of the German Confederation passed the Bills of Exchange Act, which was then given legislative force in all the member states of the Confederation.

17.5.6   A wider approach to international harmonization was taken in the later nineteenth century. The subject of bills of exchange was taken up in the 1870s by the Association for the Reform and Codification of the Law of Nations. It appointed a committee of experts who, between 1876 and 1878, produced what are known as the Bremen Rules, a body of proposals (largely based on Germanic law) which was designed to regulate the international use of bills of exchange. The proposals were readily taken up by the Scandinavian countries and formed the basis of new legislation there. They were also taken into account in both Italy and the Netherlands during the compilation of their commercial codes. In France their reception was less cordial; since they were based principally on Germanic law they were not readily accepted into the French legal system. Cheques, however, had been introduced into France in 1865 in imitation of British practice. In Britain itself a Bills of Exchange Act of 1882, covering Scotland as well as England, had codified a limited area of law; business interests favoured further codification and a wider degree of harmonization, but the government was not enthusiastic.

17.5.7 Various other associations and interested bodies continued to promote assimilation in the field of negotiable instruments, calling further conferences and producing further draft proposals. At the Hague Conference of 1910, at which thirty-five countries were represented, a set of draft regulations was produced which was submitted to the governments of the member states for consideration. The Conference reassembled in 1912 and amendments were made in the light of criticisms received; nevertheless, disagreement remained on some matters – particularly those on which there was a marked divergence between French and German law. Further, it was thought best to postpone detailed discussions on the assimilation of the law of cheques until a later meeting. It also became apparent at an early stage that neither Britain nor the United States would associate itself with any agreement reached. The Conference did, however, produce a convention for the unification of the law of bills of exchange which the participating states undertook to observe as their national law; departure from the terms of the convention was restricted to where it was in those terms specifically allowed. A greater degree of uniformity on both bills of exchange and cheques came at the Geneva Convention of 1930 and 1931.

17.5.8 The close relationship of law with matters of economic and social policy was not precisely new to the nineteenth century; what was novel was the degree to which law became used as an instrument of policy, and also the extent to which state intervention in the lives of citizens became normal. We shall turn in Chapter 18 to the institutions of the mid-twentieth century, including the welfare state, which clearly have their roots in this period of change brought on by the industrialization of western society.

FURTHER READING

A Alvarez et al	*The Progress of Continental Law in the Nineteenth Century* (Continental Legal History series, vol XI, Boston, 1918)
J Roberton Christie	'Joint stock enterprise in Scotland before the Companies Acts (1909–10)', *JurRev* 21 (1909–1910) 128
WR Cornish and G de N Clark	*Law and Society in England, 1750–1950* (London, 1989)
TD Fergus	'Women and the parliamentary franchise in Great Britain' in *The Legal Relevance of Gender*, ed S McLean and N Burrows (London, 1988)

WM Gordon   'Property and Succession Rights' in *The Legal Relevance of Gender*, ed S McLean and N Burrows (London, 1988)

HR Hahlo   'Early progenitors of the modern company', *JurRev* (1982) 139

N Horn and   *Law and the Formation of the Big Enterprises in the*
J Kocka (eds)   *Nineteenth and early Twentieth Centuries* (Holland, 1979)

BC Hunt   *The Development of the Business Corporation in England* (USA, 1936)

AH Manchester   *A Modern Legal History of England and Wales, 1750–1950* (London, 1980)

JV Orth   *Combination and Conspiracy: A Legal History of Trade Unionism 1721–1906* (Oxford, 1991)

PL Payne   *Entrepreneurship in the Nineteenth Century* (London, 1974)

H Pelling   *A History of British Trade Unionism* (Penguin, 2nd edn, 1976)

AF Rodger   'The codification of commercial law in Victorian Britain' *LQR* 108 (1992) 570

GR Rubin and   *Law, Economy and Society* (London, 1984)
D Sugarman (eds)

D Thomson   *Europe since Napoleon* (Penguin, 2nd edn, 1966)

Chapter 18

THE TWENTIETH CENTURY AND ON

18.0 In many ways, legal development during the twentieth century represents a continuation and fulfilment of what was begun by the social and economic changes of the nineteenth. But before the century was fifty years old, Europe had twice witnessed warfare on an unprecedented scale. Her struggles to recover from these cataclysmic experiences and to prevent their recurrence form a significant part of the history of more recent years, and they have had a marked effect on the development of law and legal structures. In this chapter, therefore, the focus will be more on what is new than on the continuation of the familiar.

A. The old and the new

18.1 CONTINUING INTERESTS

18.1.1 Liberal democracy seems to have survived. The welfare state staggers along, although the increase in the scale and complexity of taxation is one legal consequence of its continued existence, as all Europe has suffered the problems of economic recession, and everywhere the age profile has risen. Law has continued to be concerned (in certain respects) with the human condition and the removal of the injustices caused by poverty. Another legal consequence of the growth of government intervention in the twentieth century has been the perceived need to defend the individual against the tyranny of the state; this has led to the growth of administrative law. In Britain, for example, tribunals have come into existence in an attempt to provide less technical remedies for such ills as unfair dismissal or excessive rents and, in some countries, parliamentary, local and other commissioners (the ombudsmen) have been created to deal with failings in officialdom. The European Convention on Human Rights, incorporated into Scots and English law (on 2 October 2000) (see para 18.3.8), has attempted to lay down a standard to which each nation should conform, enforceable ultimately at the European Court of Human Rights in Strasbourg.

18.1.2 Business has been affected by the technological revolution, in particular that part of it brought about by the computer and the micro-chip. One problem that has been raised concerns the law of contract:

'Has a contract been concluded when the letter of acceptance has been transmitted by electronic mail but has not been seen by anybody at the receiving end other than the computer? Is a printout of what is now in the computer – which is, as I say, susceptible to interference and manipulation – sufficient evidence that the contract was made? And where was it made – in Edinburgh or London, where the sending and receiving terminals are, or in Washington (in a different time zone) where the text is processed and stored? And how is a court to verify, by any normal process to which we are accustomed, whether, when and where a contract has been made?'[1]

But the legal issues arising from this seem less of a problem than they did even a few years ago. There is, indeed, 'hacking', and there are difficulties over intellectual property rights, and electronic signatures, but computer viruses seem more of a threat to the conduct of business. Economic changes continue to have legal consequences; the existence of state enterprise and of multinational corporations needs to be reconciled with the human scale of values. The market economy as a concept has recently recovered a central position in the economic thinking of most governments, and organized labour has generally lost ground. Harmonization has become ever more important, and we shall deal with its mechanisms in the second part of this chapter.

1   DAO Edward, 'A little cloud like a man's hand', *JLSS* 30 (1985) 10.

18.1.3   There are, of course, many other legal issues which, while not new, have come to the fore in recent times. Partly as a consequence of former colonialism, partly because of new wealth based on oil, people following Islamic and other legal regimes have become involved in western legal systems, and the clash of cultures in a pluralistic society is not always easy to resolve. On the intellectual side there has been a revival of Natural Law in reaction to legal positivism and the 'pure' theory of law. In jurisprudence generally American thinking has been of considerable influence in Europe as well as Britain, both through the legal science of academics and through the deliberations of the courts. The Commonwealth, moreover, has enriched the Common Law tradition. American, English, and civilian lines of legal thought have been following similar paths because of the many common political, social and economic factors. Codification has remained a tool of legal progress. The denial of the parliamentary franchise to women is now seen as an aspect of legal discrimination. New in the twentieth century was the maturation of Communism as a political system, and the establishment of Marxist-Leninist Socialist legal regimes, now challenged by vigorous but sometimes ill-considered attempts to impose market-led economies in subversion of economies dominated by state enterprise.

18.2   CODIFICATION

18.2.1   Codification has been important in the twentieth century, even if the nineteenth was its great age. First, existing codes have inspired and been drawn on as models for new codifications by states within Europe and beyond. Indeed, in the case of Turkey, the codification of 1926 represented virtually a wholesale reception of the Swiss Code of 1912. Second, the twentieth century has also witnessed recodification – the revision and modernization of codes promulgated in the nineteenth century. Clearly, no code, however comprehensive its scope and however much framed (like the French Code) in terms of general principle, can be considered as immutable. Times change, and new social aspirations and economic structures emerge requiring regulation by the law. A code which cannot cater for such changes not only fails in its purpose but may also impede the very process of change itself. However, recodification is not easy. It is therefore not surprising to find that, in existing codified legal systems, much of the necessary work of development and updating has been accomplished either by judicial interpretation (however strained) of an existing code, or by means of special legislation devoted to a particular topic. Thus, for example, what has been in effect judicial law-making has been significant in the development of French law, although some matters, such as long leases and intellectual property, were first regulated by means of special legislation.

18.2.2 There have, however, been several successful re-codifications in this century; for instance, Quebec produced a revised draft code in 1977 which is now in force. In the Netherlands the task of recodification was begun in 1947; the work was produced in stages – in fact, it is not yet fully completed. Nevertheless, the result in 1992 was a new Civil Code which not only replaced the former Civil Code of 1838 but, by including commercial law, also rendered obsolete the Commercial Code of the same year. It thus drew these two formerly distinct spheres of law together.

18.2.3 By the start of the twentieth century it was becoming clear that the Italian Civil Code of 1865 – itself closely modelled on the French Code – was out of step with modern Italian society. Changes in Italian commerce and industry were creating new demands, while the individualism of the Code, its emphasis on private property and freedom of contract, demanded modification in the light of growing calls for social justice. Matters were assisted – but not resolved – by some special legislation and by the 1882 revision of the Commercial Code of 1865. In 1923 a royal commission was appointed to reform the codes; its work was to lead to the promulgation of a revised Civil Code, which came into force on 21 April 1942. That year also saw the disappearance, as a separate entity, of the Commercial Code of 1882, whose contents for the most part appeared within the new *Codice Civile*. Thus, in common with the Netherlands but unlike France and Germany, Italy did not preserve the formal distinction between civil and commercial law, even if in practice the latter survived as a separate topic of study.

18.2.4 The new Italian Civil Code was not a particularly revolutionary document. Drafted by members of the Italian legal establishment, the Code was grounded firmly in the jurisprudence of the nineteenth century even if, in accordance with its rationale, it took account of the economic and social developments of the twentieth. Certainly, when Mussolini came to power, pressure was brought to bear so that some of what were referred to as 'the general principles of the fascist legal order' were incorporated into the draft Code, reflecting the prevailing political ideology. But these modifications were mostly ill-defined; they did not permeate the draft Code that had already taken shape, and accordingly they were removed without any great difficulty in the post-fascist era. Modern attitudes and the requirements of the European Convention on Human Rights led to a new Italian Code of Criminal Procedure in 1988.

18.2.5   Finally, there have recently been proposals for the 'codification' of the secondary law of the European Community, particularly directives and regulations. Their sheer volume has been found overwhelming, and even if one can hardly expect another *Corpus Iuris Civilis*, it is clear that the same forces as motivated Justinian are nowadays present. The European Parliament has also called for a code of European private law as an aspect of unification, and progress has been made on a code of contract law. The idea that a unity might be achieved by legal science, creating a new *ius commune*, has been received by some with enthusiasm, by others with scepticism.[2] Reconciliation of the Common Law and civilian traditions clearly causes problems.[3]

2   D Osler, 'The myth of European legal history' *RHJ* 16 (1997) 393; see also J Blackie and N Whitty, 'Scots law and the new *ius commune*' in HL MacQueen (ed) *Scots Law into the Twenty-first Century* (Edinburgh, 1996) 65.
3   R Zimmermann (1998) and DJ Ibbetson (1998).

18.3   DISCRIMINATION

18.3.1   We have already written of how law in Europe responded to the advent of the industrial society and to the changes, social, economic and political, that came in its wake. One feature of the nineteenth century was the improvement throughout Europe of the lot of women; in Britain the most obvious realizations of this were the various Married Women's Property Acts, which gave married women control of their own property and independence from their husbands.[4] Another good example concerns the right of women to vote in parliamentary elections.

4   Largely achieved in England by the 1882 and 1893 Married Women's Property Acts, 45 & 46 Vict c 75 and 56 & 57 Vict c 63, and in Scotland by parallel legislation, culminating in the Married Women's Property (S) Act 1920 (c 64).

18.3.2   In both Scotland and England and Wales prior to the great Reform Acts of 1832 (see para 17.1.7), the franchise was limited to a very small number of males who satisfied a prescribed property qualification. Women were altogether excluded. The 1832 Acts and their successors gradually extended the right of men to vote, and the Reform Act of 1884 (which created a uniform franchise for Great Britain) could be said to represent 'the first clear recognition of the radical principle that the individual, regardless of property qualification, was entitled to vote', but nothing was done for women. A married woman's legal incapacity to own property, or to own it meaningfully, represented a logical barrier in a system in which the franchise rested on property ownership. Yet, although the proprietary disabilities of the married woman were gradually alleviated by Married Women's Property Acts, her exclusion from the franchise persisted. In the 1872 case of *R v Harrald*[5] it was argued successfully that a married woman 'is not a person in the eyes of the law. She is not *sui iuris*', because her status was so entirely merged in that of her husband. The argument from property was not, of course, relevant to the single woman who had full proprietary capacity. Indeed, unmarried women, or women living separately from their husbands, who fulfilled the requisite property qualification were able to vote, and also to hold office, in local government in the last third of the nineteenth century.[6] The justification for women's continued exclusion from the parliamentary franchise was by then to be found in simple conservatism, in the notion of 'separate spheres' – ie women's confinement to domestic matters, while politics and government ought to be the exclusive preserve of men.

5   *R v Harrald* (1872) 7 QB 361.
6   See, for example, the 1869 Municipal Franchise Act, 32 & 33 Vict c 55, the 1881 Municipal Elections Amendment (S) Act, 44 & 45 Vict c 13, the 1888 County Electors Act, 51 & 52 Vict c 10, and the 1894 Local Government (S) Act, 56 & 57 Vict c 73, which allowed even married women to vote provided they did it by right of property distinct from that of their husbands.

18.3.3   By the start of the twentieth century attitudes were changing. The more moderate sections of the women's movement were winning allies, while the more extreme kept their cause in the public eye. In the First World War many women successfully undertook the work, in the factories and on the land, driving as well as nursing, previously performed by the men who were now serving in the Armed Forces. The Representation of the People Act of 1918, which introduced universal male suffrage, also gave the parliamentary franchise to women for the first time – but not to all. Only women over thirty were granted the vote, and then only if they, or their husbands, were householders occupying property of a prescribed rateable value. Not until 1928 was the final step taken, giving women the franchise on the same terms as men. Elsewhere, the enfranchisement of women took place somewhat – although not significantly – earlier. Women first got the vote in New Zealand in 1893, while in Europe Finland led the way in 1906, closely followed by Norway; Switzerland long lagged behind.

18.3.4   The history of the female franchise both foreshadows and illustrates the concern in twentieth-century law to counter discrimination, by the removal of barriers deemed to keep an identifiable group in a disadvantaged position in comparison with society as a whole. For women the matter of public rights and full proprietary capacity was only part of the story. For example, in England there were no female legal practitioners until after the Sex Disqualification (Removal) Act of 1919; the English Court of Appeal had previously held that a woman was in the Common Law under a general disability by reason of her sex. Questions of equal access to, and equal treatment in, employment, have since been of much significance – and have been a matter of importance in European Community law.

18.3.5   Other groups in the labour market have also benefited from this anti-discriminatory trend. In the United Kingdom the Race Relations Act of 1976 has made it unlawful for an employer to treat disadvantageously an employee, or an applicant for a job, on the grounds of race. Legislation has also tried to assist physically and mentally disabled people in finding employment by imposing on employers a duty to take on a specified quota of such persons. Legal provision against discrimination has probably been most marked in the context of the workplace, but it is by no means limited to there. It now extends to sexual preference, and the discrimination to which homosexual men and women may be subject. In a number of European states, but not as yet the United Kingdom, same-sex couples may now by law register their partnership, thereby attracting some of the beneficial legal consequences of heterosexual marriage. The distinction between legitimate and illegitimate children has been (almost entirely) abolished. Children born out of wedlock are assimilated to those born within a marriage, so long as their paternity has been recognized.

18.3.6   Concern for human rights and civil liberties was a feature of the latter half of the twentieth century. The reasons are many, but in Europe a catalyst undoubtedly was reaction against the atrocities perpetrated during the years surrounding the Second World War against those deemed suspect on the grounds of race, creed, or simple unacceptability to the regime in power. Human rights consequently became part of the legal culture of Europe. The 'language of rights' took root amongst jurists and, today, non-lawyers are aware that they may lay claim to such rights, even if often vague about their precise extent. Modern constitutions, such as those of France and Germany, contain a commitment to the equality before the law of all human beings. In 1971, for example, the German Constitutional Court refused to apply certain rules of German private international law because, in their reference to the national law of the husband, they violated the principle of equality between the sexes given force by art 117 of the Fundamental Law.[7]

7   David and Brierley, p 138.

18.3.7   The European Convention on Human Rights and Fundamental Freedoms, drawn up under the auspices of the Council of Europe and ratified by its member states in 1951, has been of prime importance. The Convention came into force in 1953. It took account of the more notorious assaults on the dignity and integrity of the human being identified in Europe's recent past. Article 2 guarantees to the individual that his/her 'right to life shall be protected by law'. Further, 'no-one shall be deprived of his life intentionally save in the execution of a sentence following his conviction for a crime for which the penalty is provided by law'. Admittedly this does not exclude capital punishment (now abhorrent to most civilised societies), but it is nonetheless a clear statement that due process – and not arbitrary prejudice – must be observed before the individual is deprived of life. Article 3 states that 'no-one shall be subject to torture or inhuman or degrading treatment', while art 4 requires that no-one shall be held in slavery or servitude' or 'be required to perform compulsory labour'. But the Convention went further, and created rights that were not perhaps so obvious; thus, for example, there are provisions concerning respect for individual privacy, the privacy of the family, and private sexual life.

18.3.8   It was intended that the Convention should become part of the domestic law of its signatories. It would thus be enforceable by the individual against the state in the national courts, with ultimate appeal lying to the Council's Commission and Court of Human Rights in Strasbourg. (These two organs have now merged into the one body.) In the UK, despite her participation in the drafting of the Convention, this did not happen at once. The Convention could indeed be used in the courts as an aid to interpretation and, as from 1965, individuals have been able to take Convention matters to Strasbourg – but only if all domestic remedies have been exhausted, a requirement both time-consuming and expensive. Matters were rectified after the Labour government of 1997 fulfilled its manifesto commitment and passed the Human Rights Act 1998. As from 2000, public authorities in the UK exercising executive authority are required to comply with the Convention, or run the risk of proceedings raised by an aggrieved individual in the national courts. Parliament's doings are excluded from this requirement, but the courts may warn it of a discrepancy between national legislation and the Convention so that remedial action may be taken. Scotland was ahead of England here. Section 29 of the Scotland Act 1998 (which established the Scottish Parliament) provided that an apparent Act of the Parliament will not be law if it is found to be incompatible with Convention rights. Machinery was put in place to deal with such infringements.

18.4 SOCIALIST LAW

18.4.1 The origins of Socialist law are to be found in the doctrines of Marxism as developed principally by Karl Marx (1818–1883) and Friedrich Engels (1820–1895). Marxism postulates a symbiotic relationship between law and state; essentially, one is an expression of the other. Moreover, neither is inherent in human society; rather, they spring from capitalism, appearing only when one section of society seizes control of the means of production and establishes an economic dominance. When this happens, a class structure forms, and law and state are brought in by the dominant class as a means of protecting and perpetuating its superiority. Marxism sought a return to the classless society of economic equality which, it held, predated capitalism. Implicit in the achievement of this ultimate goal was a withering away of law and of the state itself.

18.4.2 Socialist law grew up in Russia after the Revolution of 1917 as part of the regime which triumphed there under Lenin (1870–1924). It was clear that the restoration (or creation) of a classless, communist society could not be achieved immediately. As Marx himself had admitted, 'between capitalist and communist society lies a period of the revolutionary transformation of the one into the other, to which there corresponds a period of political transition in which the state can be nothing but the revolutionary dictatorship of the proletariat'. In short, in the process of transition between the old and the new order, the state – and thus by implication law – must continue. What was different were the functions that each would perform during this Marxist-Leninist transitional phase.

18.4.3 Law, therefore, was not swept away by the Bolshevik revolution. What changed was the conception of its function and its use as a tool of control. No longer could law be regarded a means of dispute resolution; its role was to become an instrument in the policy of re-educating society. Not surprisingly, Socialist law also has a strong economic preoccupation, but then so do contemporary and long-established western legal systems. It is in the translation of this preoccupation into concrete legal rules that the differences are most easily seen.

18.4.4 Ownership will serve as an example. In the classic traditions of western legal systems, private ownership is fundamental. An identifiable legal person – the owner – is accorded legal sovereignty over the object of his ownership. So far as the law permits, he may use and exploit that object as he pleases, and it is he, to the exclusion of all others, who takes the economic benefits accruing to it. The emphasis is on the rights of the individual, regardless of his economic standing vis-à-vis other citizens. Further, few restrictions are placed on the nature of the property which may be owned. In Socialist law, the principal distinction in the law of property is that between the means of production and goods for consumption. The primary concern is not to identify legal sovereignty but to determine by whom the property is or ought to be exploited. Socialist law knows differing regimes of ownership. Personal ownership is restricted to such goods as the individual may require for his own use; it does not permit exploitation of goods for profit. Ownership of the means of production, agricultural and industrial, is vested in a socially responsible body, a co-operative, or the state.

18.4.5 Socialist law and legal thinking have had a profound influence on those countries which have found themselves members of the Soviet bloc. Since 1989, however, we have seen the disintegration of this bloc and the liberation of states hitherto subject to it and thus to Socialist-inspired legal systems. To what extent Socialist law will survive is an open question. In Germany, unification has meant the abrogation of the East German Code, the *Zivilgesetzbuch* (ZGB), brought into force in 1976, and the application of West German law to the whole reunited Germany. Elsewhere the change has been less dramatic but it is clear that liberation has often been accompanied by a desire for appropriate legal reforms, and that the West has been looked to as a source of inspiration. In this context, the new Dutch Civil Code (see para 18.2.2) has proved attractive.

B.   European integration

18.5 THE BACKGROUND

18.5.1 The aftermath of the Great War of 1914–1918 saw the creation of the League of Nations, the brain-child of the American president, Woodrow Wilson. Following the Second World War, the League gave place to the United Nations, whose forum is the International Court of Justice at The Hague. Despite these efforts at community on a global scale, which nowadays include the General Agreement on Tariffs and Trade (GATT) and the World Trade Organization (WTO), the countries of western Europe wished for ties of a closer kind among themselves. This aspiration found expression in several ventures. Among the organizations which have endured have been the original European Communities of the 1950s which, since the 1992 Treaty on European

Union, form the nucleus of the European Union. This legal development is at the heart of this chapter for two reasons. The first is because the European Community has had a profound effect on the legal systems of its member states. The second reason is more general. The import of this book has been to show how the disintegration of law and legal culture, which accompanied the disintegration of the Roman Empire in the West, found its corrective in the mediaeval revival of legal studies and the creation of the *ius commune*, that supranational body of law that could be – and was – drawn on to the profit of almost all Europe. The paradoxical result was renewed fragmentation; nation states emerged and fashioned their own distinct legal systems, even if the common origins were apparent. Now, with the advent of the European Community, the pendulum is starting to swing the other way again and, within its (ever-growing) sphere, the law of the European Community is overriding, binding on its member states and taking precedence over domestic law.

18.5.2   In the aftermath of the Second World War, at a conference held at The Hague in 1948, a call was made for economic and political union in western Europe. This was at least partially prompted by the fear of the military power of the Soviet Union and the perceived threat it posed to a disunited and weakened West. The post-war years saw the establishment of communist regimes in several east European states and it was not at all clear what the limits of Soviet ambition would prove to be. Western Europe reacted to this situation in various ways. First, as was perhaps to be expected, it looked beyond its immediate frontiers to its relatively unscathed allies across the Atlantic. The post-war settlement had seen the establishment of the Marshall Plan, by which the USA undertook to provide financial assistance towards the post-war reconstruction of Europe, and the Organization for European Economic Co-operation. In 1949, these trans-Atlantic ties were strengthened by the creation of the North Atlantic Treaty Organization (NATO), a military alliance of a primarily defensive nature between the USA, Canada and western Europe.

18.5.3   Within Europe itself, the establishment of the Council of Europe in 1949 must be accounted a success. The aim of the Council is the promotion of closer co-operation in economic, social and cultural matters among its member states. But the Council has no powers of legislation and if its resolutions are to be binding, further action is necessary. Yet the Council has made its mark, most notably, as we have seen, in the 1951 European Convention for the Protection of Human Rights and Fundamental Freedoms.

18.5.4   Two further initiatives of the early 1950s, for a European Defence Community and a European Political Community, failed, but the hopes survived to prompt further negotiations.

18.6 THE FOUNDATION OF THE EUROPEAN COMMUNITIES

18.6.1   The Communities have had from their very foundation the express aim of European integration, as can be illustrated by reference to art 2^8 of the Treaty of Rome which founded the European Economic Community. There we read:

'The Community shall have as its task, by establishing a common market and progressively approximating the economic policies of Member States, to promote . . . a harmonious development of economic activities, a continuous and balanced expansion, an increase in stability, an accelerated raising of the standard of living, and closer relations between the States belonging to it.'

8   A problem with the EC Treaty is that the Treaty of Amsterdam has renumbered most of the articles of the Treaty of Rome with effect from May 1999; the convention now seems to be to cite them as, eg, 'art 249 (ex art 189)', as in para 18.9.2.

18.6.2 The history of the European Communities begins in 1950 when the French foreign minister, Robert Schuman, proposed the merger of the coal and steel industries of France and Germany. There were two reasons. It was hoped that such a pooling of resources under the control of a supranational authority would both make impossible future conflict between France and Germany, and would also provide a firm basis for integrated economic growth between the two countries – and any others which cared to join them. Schuman's suggestions were enthusiastically received, not only by France and Germany, but also in Italy and the Benelux countries – the Netherlands, Belgium and Luxembourg. The result was the coming into being, in July 1952, of the European Coal and Steel Community (ECSC), consisting of these six countries. There was clearly a political agenda behind the economic objectives, and the UK declined to participate, on grounds of both national sovereignty and current economic policy.

18.6.3 In 1955, the foreign ministers of the ECSC member states met in the Sicilian town of Messina. Their deliberations made it clear that, as with Schuman before them, their principal aspiration was political integration, even if in the immediate future the way towards the achievement of this goal lay in the field of economic approximation. The following year, 1956, saw the publication of the Spaak Report, the work of the Belgian foreign minister, Paul-Henri Spaak, recommending further integration of the economies of the ECSC member states as the best way forward. The result was the creation, in 1957, by two treaties signed at Rome (the Treaties of Rome) of two further Communities – the European Economic Community (EEC) and the European Atomic Energy Community (Euratom). Both treaties came into force on the first day of January 1958; each of the new Communities so created consisted of the six states which had originally joined together to form the ECSC. Again, the UK declined to participate.

18.6.4 Of the three Communities which existed by 1958, two – the ECSC and Euratom – were subject-specific. The EEC, on the other hand, was not; its remit was broad enough to cover any economic activity not included in that of the other two. The result is that the EEC became by far the most important of the three Communities. Article 2 of the EEC treaty (quoted above) stated that the EEC should achieve its goals by means of the establishment of a common market among its member states. The remainder of the treaty furnishes the detail necessary to make this aspiration a reality, and so informs us of what its framers understood by the term, 'common market'. To this end, the treaty established four fundamental freedoms, which together represent the foundations of its economic order; their purpose is the removal of artificial restraints on trade, and the promotion of a common policy in such areas as competition law and the vital field of agriculture. First, the treaty provides that goods moving from member state to member state are not to be subject to customs duties or other restraints. Second, workers are given the right to move without restriction within the Community. Third, there is provision for the free movement of capital, and fourth, for the providers of services to be free to do so wherever in the Community they wish.

18.6.5 The ECSC had from the start an institutional structure consisting of four principal organs, which discharged legislative, executive, judicial and consultative functions. When the EEC and Euratom were founded, it was intended that they should each have a similar framework. However, it was realized that, although each Community was theoretically independent of the others, their identity of membership, coupled with the economic remit of each, would make superfluous the provision of completely separate sets of institutions. Accordingly, at the same time as the Treaties of Rome were signed, a Convention – the Convention on Certain Institutions Common to the European Communities – was also agreed. The Convention provided for a single consultative Assembly and a single Court of Justice for the three Communities. It did not touch the legislative and executive arms of the three Communities; for these there remained separate provision until a treaty, commonly referred to as the Merger Treaty, came into force in July 1967, providing for a single legislative arm, the Council of Ministers, and a single executive, the Brussels-based Commission; thus institutional unity has been achieved.

18.7 EXPANSION

18.7.1 At first the UK was too committed to her imperial past to believe that her future lay with the EEC. When the government changed its mind, the UK met with rebuffs in 1961 and 1967, but finally became a member of the Communities on 1 January 1973. This membership was confirmed in 1975 when a domestic referendum overwhelmingly endorsed British membership as renegotiated by the Labour government of the day. Ireland and Denmark became members on the same day as the UK. Greece joined in 1981, while 1986 saw the accession of Spain and Portugal. The six had become the twelve.

18.7.2 In 1960, seven European states – Portugal, the UK, Denmark, Norway, Sweden, Austria and Switzerland – which were not at that stage prepared to surrender national autonomy to the extent required for membership of the Communities, had joined together to form the European Free Trade Association (EFTA). The motivation was economic, not political. When the UK and Denmark became members of the Communities in 1973, the remaining EFTA states, augmented by the accession of Iceland and Liechtenstein, individually negotiated free trade arrangements with the EEC. Then, in 1992, the European Economic Area (EEA) was instituted. By the agreement creating it, all remaining barriers to trade between the Community and the EFTA states are removed. The four basic freedoms (see para 18.6.4) of the EEC Treaty (and Community law relating to them) are extended to embrace these states, as are

Community competition law and participation in a variety of other policy areas. The EFTA states were not, however, to be party to Community decision-making processes. The agreement came into effect on 1 January 1994 – a year later than originally planned because the Swiss, following rejection of the agreement in a national referendum, were unable to ratify it. However, for most of the EFTA states membership of the EEA really only made sense if it represented a stepping stone to full membership of the European Community. In January 1995, Austria, Finland and Sweden acceded to the European Community . They were originally to have been joined by Norway, but there too a national referendum produced a negative result, as had happened following a bid for membership in the early 1970s.

18.7.3 Enlargement still features prominently on the agenda. The success of the Community, particularly since the passing of the Single European Act of 1986 (see para 18.8.2) emphasized the attractions of membership, and underlined the dangers of less than full participation in the European club. Of particular significance, too, has been the break-up of the Communist world of Russia and Eastern Europe. Interest in membership amongst the emerging eastern democracies is high as they seek to orientate themselves towards the West and her economic ways. Commitment in principle to enlargement was given at the European Council held in Copenhagen 1993, which set out the criteria that applicant states would have to satisfy before membership was granted: these were both political (basically, a commitment to western-style democracy) and economic (the demonstration of a degree of economic health). The publication of the Agenda 2000 programme in July 1997 enabled the beginning of movement towards full membership for the states which were deemed most nearly to meet these criteria. Accordingly, in the following year negotiations with the first group of applicants began – Cyprus, the Czech Republic, Estonia, Hungary, Poland and Slovenia. Another seven applications are under active review as the process of enlargement gains momentum. All applicant states already have a history of relations with the European Union, in the form of Association Agreements.

18.7.4 Enlargement is not without its problems. An institutional structure which was originally designed for a membership of six will not necessarily suit an enlarged Europe which could conceivably have a membership in the high twenties. Already, divergences are apparent and remedial action is pressingly urgent; this point is covered in the discussion of the Treaty of Amsterdam (see para 18.8.8). Although applicant states have to satisfy minimum economic requirements before full membership is offered, some new states, certainly those of the eastern bloc, will, in the short term at least, need to be net recipients of European funding. This may well cause tensions with their longer established partners, who are themselves not always agreed on such matters as the common agricultural policy.

18.8 RECENT DEVELOPMENTS

18.8.1   The preamble to the EEC treaty makes it clear that it was designed to 'lay the foundations of an ever closer union among the peoples of Europe' and that it contemplated further action designed to promote closer integration among the member states. This aspiration has been given concrete expression, but progress in the face of national self-interest has often been slow.

18.8.2 During the 1970s and early 1980s, the quest for closer integration led to no practical result. Then in 1984 there appeared a draft treaty on European union, designed to replace the Treaty of Rome. The draft was far-reaching, envisaging a marked increase in the power of Community institutions at the expense of member states. It provided that a number of areas, for example economic and monetary policy, which are at present the preserve of national governments, should be brought within the competence of the Treaty. Not surprisingly the draft proved too radical for the governments of most member states. The outcome of an inter-governmental conference, called to consider the matter in December 1985, was therefore not approval of the proposed Treaty on European Union, but the Single European Act, which was signed in 1986 and came into force the following year. This, unlike the original draft, merely amends rather than replaces the founding Treaty of Rome. Nonetheless, the Single European Act is not anodyne. In the first place, it committed its signatories to the completion of the single market by the end of 1992; by and large this commitment has been honoured. Second, the Act brought new policy areas within the competence of the Treaty; among these were the environment and economic and social cohesion. Provision was also made for increased co-operation among member states in the field of foreign policy. Further, the Act gave formal recognition – for the practice was already well established – to the European Council, that is, to the regular meetings of the heads of state or government of member states, who, since 1975, have come together to deliberate on matters of Community policy and, generally, to provide the Community with the necessary impetus for its development.

18.8.3 The Act also enhanced the standing of the European Parliament, which had started out as the Assembly of the Communities. Official recognition of the title by which it is now known only came with the Single European Act itself, even if, unofficially, the usage had been current for some time. The original assembly was a nominated rather than an elected body, whose function was purely advisory. However, as required by the Treaty of Rome, nomination of delegates by member governments was replaced by direct election; the first such elections were held in July 1979. From that date, the European Parliament could – and did – claim democratically to represent the peoples of Europe, and it sought to increase its powers accordingly. These claims were acknowledged in the Single Act, when it permitted the European Parliament a more active and interventionist role in the legislative process.

18.8.4 In December 1990, the twelve member states of the Communities embarked on the ratification and implementation of a new Treaty on European Union, which, in the UK at least, has become known as the Maastricht Treaty. The first obstacle to be overcome was the stance of the UK government, which refused to agree to the finalization of the text of a treaty containing social provisions which went a good deal further than those in the Treaty of Rome, and which also reflected the European Social Charter of 1989 (from which the UK had also stood aloof). A compromise was reached, and in February

1992 the Treaty of European Union was signed at the Dutch town of Maastricht by all twelve member states; the Treaty incorporated an 'opt out' provision, freeing the UK from any obligation in respect of the disputed social provisions. Despite this concession, ratification of the Treaty still raised problems, especially in Denmark and the UK, while it was also challenged on constitutional grounds in the courts of four other member states. However, it was finally ratified by all the member states and came into force on 1 November 1993.

18.8.5   The European Union created by the Treaty of Maastricht is not the easiest of concepts to explain. But (to borrow the much-used but still useful analogy) it may be likened to a roof supported by three pillars. The most substantial of these pillars consisted of the existing three European Communities. The over-arching role of the EEC was, however, recognised: henceforth, it was to be known simply as the European Community (EC). As with the Single European Act, amendments were necessarily made to the founding treaties. Many of these broke new ground. For example, each national of each member state is accorded citizenship of the Union, a citizenship which, among other things, entitles him or her to vote and to stand for office in local and European elections wherever within the Union he or she may be resident. While this is new, it is hardly startling; Irish citizens in the UK have always been able to vote in local elections. Nonetheless, the concept of European citizenship did cause some unease concerning its relation to national identity: was the latter to be subsumed in the former? The answer was 'no' – but the ambiguities of the situation do help to explain the cool reception the Treaty met with during the process of its ratification by national governments.

18.8.6   More significantly, the role in the legislative process of the democratically elected European Parliament was once again strengthened. Furthermore, provision was made for an Ombudsman, to whom citizens of the Union could bring allegations of maladministration by Community institutions. The principle of subsidiarity was endorsed, a principle which allows action at the most local level of government able to achieve the desired result. This principle, drawn from modern Church law, does indeed fit with a concept of federalism, but it can also be called on by those who fear that the treaty marks a further inroad on national sovereignty. The difficulty lies in determining precisely when action at local or national, rather than Community, level will be more effective. The Treaty also underlined the importance of economic and monetary union for the European future; a common European currency (the ecu) is now in the course of introduction.

18.8.7   The second pillar upon which the Union was to rest was a common foreign and defence policy; the third a common approach to justice and home affairs. These were sensitive areas, raising – again – questions concerning the erosion of national sovereignty. Accordingly, and unlike decision-making in the context of the first Community pillar (where the emphasis has been increasingly on the will of the majority), unanimity was required for measures to be taken under these heads. Moreover, (and again unlike the first pillar) no real power was given to the Court of Justice to review action taken.

18.8.8   The late 1990s saw further developments which came to fruition in the Treaty of Amsterdam, effective as from May 1999. The treaty was not as comprehensive as many had hoped. It seems generally agreed that it ducked the question of institutional reform – a question made all the more pressing by the prospect of the imminent enlargement of membership of the Union. This matter has been put off until another day. Nonetheless, the Treaty has made its contribution. The role of the European Parliament in European affairs was again strengthened, while the use of majority voting (as opposed to unanimity) was extended in the legislative procedures of the Council, thus making swifter progress possible. The Treaty also registered a commitment within the Union – how practicable remains to be seen – to the elimination of discrimination on the grounds of sex, sexual orientation, race, age, disability or religion. It also revised the tripartite structure established by the previous Treaty on European Union. Certain aspects of matters relating to justice and home affairs have now been brought within the remit of the central, the Community, pillar of the Union: they are thus subject to the regime of majority (rather than unanimous) approval, and also amenable to review by the European Court of Justice. The commitment to a 'frontier free' Europe – a Europe characterized by the abolition of all frontier controls between its Member States – was given effect by the incorporation of the Schengen Agreement into the Treaty. The Agreement had, in fact, been in existence since 1990, but only as an agreement between some (not all) of the EU member states. It now acquired the status of European law proper, but not before 'opt-outs' had been agreed for the UK and Ireland, neither of which were prepared to accept the lack of frontier control involved. Finally, the Treaty made provision for what may be termed a 'two-speed' Europe. This means that, provided certain conditions are satisfied, it is possible within the regime of the Treaty for some, but not all, member states to proceed with initiatives. The rationale is, of course, the very different levels of economic, social and cultural development as between established and soon-to-be member states. It remains to be seen how these provisions will work, and with what success.

18.9 THE SOURCES OF COMMUNITY LAW

18.9.1 The principal sources of European Community law are the Community treaties, the secondary legislation of the Community, and the jurisprudence of the European Court of Justice. The first of these sources, Community treaties, consists of the treaties founding the three Communities, and subsequent amendments of them, as represented, for example, by the Single European Act and the Treaty on European Union. The Community legal order was created by, and takes its being from, these treaties. In terms of a hierarchy of sources they are therefore supreme; nothing can be done unless it is sanctioned by them. On the other hand, in the style of the classic continental code rather than the British statute, the treaties are, and were intended to be, no more than skeleton treaties. It was envisaged from the beginning that their provisions would require to be fleshed out; hence the importance of the other sources of Community law.

18.9.2 Article 249 (ex art 189) of the EEC Treaty (the Treaty of Rome) makes provision for secondary legislation. Under its terms, in order to carry out the tasks assigned to them by the Treaty, the Council and Commission are empowered to 'make Regulations, issue Directives, take Decisions, make Recommendations or deliver Opinions'. The most important of these are Regulations and Directives. A Regulation may be likened to a legislative act; as explained in art 249 (ex art 189) itself, it is of general application, being binding in its entirety throughout the Community. A Directive is also binding, but although a Directive, like a Regulation, is addressed to member states, art 249 (ex art 189) clearly envisages that a Directive addressed only to one or more individual states is as valid as one addressed to all. Further, while a Directive lays down an objective which its addressees are bound to achieve, it leaves those addressees to choose how best to achieve that objective. The nature of a Directive is best understood if it is recognized that it was primarily designed as an instrument of harmonization. If it is wished to standardize the regulation of a particular matter throughout the Community, the Community secondary legislation on the matter will normally take the form of a Directive. If the law of a particular member state already corresponds with the Community's desideratum, that state may be omitted from the ambit of the Directive. A Directive therefore binds each member state to which it is addressed to review its own law and to make whatever change, large or small, may be thought necessary to ensure correspondence with the aims of the Directive.

18.9.3   Regulations and Directives are formally enacted by the Council. But the Council may only act on a proposal framed by, and put to it by, the Commission; this body has the power of initiation. The original EEC Treaty provided that, on many issues, unanimity was required in the Council if legislation was to be enacted; this often meant that the Community could only move forward at the pace of its most reluctant member. However, change came with the Single European Act and, perhaps more tellingly, with the Treaty on European Union. Much can now go through on a majority vote. These enactments have also increased the role of the European Parliament in the legislative process. The term 'secondary legislation' is perhaps not entirely suitable as a description of Decisions, Recommendations and Opinions. Although Decisions may be addressed to member states, they can be, and more usually are, addressed to legal or natural persons. While Decisions are binding on those to whom they are addressed, this is not true of Recommendations or Opinions; in the words of art 249 (ex art 189), these have 'no binding force'. These types of Community act are administrative rather than norm-creating devices. They are not subject to the same legislative process as Regulations and Directives, but are often issued by the Commission on its own authority.

18.9.4   The Court of Justice of the European Communities sits in Luxembourg; in terms of the EEC Treaty, its remit is to ensure that 'in the interpretation and application of this Treaty the law is observed'. The structure and the procedure of the Court are in the civilian mould – unsurprisingly in the light of the traditions of the original six member states of the Communities. Nevertheless, its reliance on written procedures which do not require the presence of parties is to be explained just as much in terms of the extent of its territorial jurisdiction, and the expense that would be occasioned if representation in person was required at every stage of process. From its beginnings in 1958 the workload of the Court has grown considerably, with the result that unacceptable delays in the dispatch of its business began to occur. Accordingly, the Single European Act made provision for the creation of a second court, the Court of First Instance. This court began work on 1 September 1989. It is inferior to the Court of Justice. Its jurisdiction is confined to certain specified matters, eg competition law; appeal on points of law lies to its senior partner.

18.9.5 The Court of Justice has three principal functions. In the first place, it can entertain actions for judicial review of the acts of Community institutions. Second, it has jurisdiction in enforcement actions brought (in most cases by the Commission) to secure the observance of a Community obligation by a member state. Third, it entertains preliminary references. The preliminary reference procedure is provided for in art 234 (ex art 177) of the EEC Treaty; references under that article form a high percentage of the Court's work. Broadly, the article permits a court of a member state, faced with a question concerning the validity or interpretation of a point of Community law, to refer the matter to Luxembourg for a ruling. The action in the domestic court is sisted until the opinion of the Court of Justice is received; when it is received, it is applied in the light of the facts established in the referring court. Article 234 (ex art 177) thus provides the courts of member states with a point of reference. More importantly, it also helps to secure a uniform interpretation and application of Community law. Without it, there could theoretically be as many interpretations of Community law as there were legal systems within the Community. With it, particularly as in some cases (detailed in the article) the referral is not optional but compulsory, a single Community body defines the law.

18.9.6 The Court of Justice has had an important influence on the development of Community law. Indeed, without its particular approach the Community legal order, and thus the Community itself, would have developed in a very different way. The Court, regardless of its membership at any one time, has always championed the Community rather than any national interest, and it has done so by adopting a style of interpretation of Community law which has allowed it the greatest freedom in achieving its perceived task. Two examples will illustrate this point.

18.9.7 The first is the 1962 case of *Van Gend en Loos*.[9] The government of the Netherlands increased the customs duty on the import of certain chemicals. The pursuer, a Dutch firm, had imported into the Netherlands chemicals of the type affected. It raised an action in the Dutch courts for the recovery of the increased sums so paid on the grounds that the increase in the duty contravened the provisions of the Treaty of Rome. The importance of the case lay in the fundamental question of whether or not a private litigant had standing to found in his national courts on the provisions of the Community treaties. Reference was made, under art 234 (ex art 177), to the European Court of Justice. Here the Dutch government argued that such a litigant did not have the necessary standing; if a member state was in breach of its Community obligations, then the appropriate, and indeed the only, remedy was an enforcement action at Community level at the instigation of the Commission or another member state. The Court of Justice disagreed, and in doing so created the doctrine of direct effect: the doctrine which permits (subject to certain qualifications) a national of a member state of the Community to found in his national courts on a provision of Community law. It is no exaggeration to say that the enunciation of this doctrine has been fundamental to the creation of the Community legal order. Without it, the Community would have functioned effectively at an international level only; with it, its impact on domestic legal systems, and its relevance for those who are subject to such systems, was assured. There have been further developments, but this case marks the first, and the most fundamental, step towards the integration of Community with national law.

9   *Van Gend en Loos v Nederlandse Administratie der Belastingen* Case 26/62 [1963] ECR 1.

18.9.8   Moreover, in its judgment in *Van Gend en Loos*, the Court made a pronouncement which had even more profound implications for the future. It stated: '. . . the Community constitutes a new legal order of international law for the benefit of which the [member] states have limited their sovereign rights . . .' This dictum found concrete expression in our second example, the case of *Costa v ENEL*.[10] Here, the issue was a conflict between the provisions of the Treaty of Rome and of Italian legislation of a later date. Which should take precedence? The Treaty did not cater specifically for such an eventuality; the resolution of the matter therefore lay with the European Court of Justice. The Court looked to the objective of the Treaty – the establishment of the Community order – and held that any provision of national law which conflicted with the fulfilment of this purpose must be disregarded. In short, it enunciated the doctrine of the supremacy of Community law over the domestic law of member states. This doctrine has prevailed. For example, in the British case of *Factortame*,[11] it demanded that interim relief should be made available against the Crown, notwithstanding the long-established rule of English law to the contrary.

10   *Costa v ENEL* Case 6/64 [1964] ECR 585.
11   *R v Secretary of State for Transport, ex p Factortame* Case C-213/89 [1990] ECR I-2433.

18.10   COMMUNITY LAW AND THE INDIVIDUAL

18.10.1   It seems appropriate to close this chapter – and this book – with a brief examination of the way in which Community law has benefited the individual. We shall take as our example the law relating to sex discrimination. Article 141 (ex art 119) of the EEC Treaty lays down the principle that 'men and women should receive equal pay for equal work'. The rationale is primarily economic; in the absence of such a principle, member states who were prepared to countenance cheap female labour would have an economic advantage over those who were not, in that the costs of production would be lower. Clearly, this would offend against what the Community order is designed to achieve. However, in 1976, in its judgment in the case of *Defrenne v Sabena (No 2)*[12] the Court of Justice declared that art 141 (ex art 119) also had a social purpose, the improvement of living and working conditions, in the light of which it was also to be interpreted.

12   *Defrenne v Sabena (No 2)* Case 43/75 [1976] ECR 455.

18.10.2 Article 141 (ex art 119) is cast in general terms. Secondary Community legislation in the form of Directives has therefore been required to provide the necessary detail. These Directives have had the effect, among other things, of extending the notion of equal work to include work of equal value; of providing for equal treatment for men and women in the whole context of employment; and of providing for equality of treatment in respect of occupational pensions. Member states, naturally, have been required to implement these Directives. In the United Kingdom, it was originally thought that existing law, as contained in the 1970 Equal Pay Act and the 1975 Sex Discrimination Act, would suffice. The Commission, however, thought otherwise, and two further statutes – the Sex Discrimination Act of 1986 and the Employment Act of 1989 – were passed to remedy the omissions and to discharge fully the UK's Community obligations under the Directives. In this area, as in so many, the Court of Justice has done much to develop the law and, in doing so, to assist the individual litigant. For example, the European Court of Justice has found that refusal to employ a woman because she is pregnant is discrimination on the grounds of sex which cannot be justified; that equal pay includes benefits (such as travel concessions) granted on retirement; and that in respect of discrimination (as, indeed, of other areas) national courts are bound to ensure that real and effective provision is made available to the individual in the context of a breach of his or her Community rights. Behind the bureaucracy, there lies a commitment, not just to economic man but to the whole person; our interdependence within the nation, within Europe, within the world, has become both more obvious and more urgently in need of recognition.

FURTHER READING

M Cappelletti et al	*The Italian Legal System: an Introduction* (Stanford UP, 1967)
D Chalmers	*European Union Law*, I & II (Aldershot, 1998)
WR Cornish and G de N Clark	*Law and Society in England, 1750–1950* (London, 1989)
R David and JEC Brierley	*Major Legal Systems in the World Today* (London, 2nd edn, 1978)
N Foster (ed)	*Blackstone's EEC Legislation 1999–2000* (Blackstone Press, 10th edn, 1999)
DJ Ibbetson	'A reply to Professor Zimmermann' in *The Europeanisation of Law*, ed TG Watkin, 224
J Joll	*Europe Since 1870* (Penguin, 4th edn, 1990)
HL MacQueen (ed)	*Scots Law into the Twenty-first Century: Essays in honour of WA Wilson* (Edinburgh, 1996)
AH Manchester	*A Modern Legal History of England and Wales 1750–1950* (London, 1980)
TG Watkin (ed)	*The Europeanisation of Law* (UK National Committee of Comparative Law, 1998)
R Zimmermann	'Savigny's legacy – legal history, comparative law, and the emergence of a European legal science' in *The Europeanisation of Law*, ed TG Watkin, 1

Appendix 1

THE GLOSSATORS – EXTRACTS

Although the Glossators and the Commentators knew Justinian's divisions into books, titles, and fragments or laws, and they dealt separately with individual sentences (also known as paragraphs), there was no accepted system of numbering. For us C 8.55.8, working from book (the largest unit) through title to law (the second smallest unit) provides easily the simplest form of reference, but the mediaeval jurists referred to Code *de revocandis donationibus* – the rubric of the title, law *Si umquam* – the opening words of the particular imperial enactment. Similarly, when Azo referred to D 9.2.27.3 he said '*ff* (= Digest) *ad legem Aquiliam*, law *si servus*, paragraph *Iulianus*'. Later scholars, right up to this century, often used the order *lex* 8, *C de rev.don.* (ie 8.55), or *l.*27,3, D *ad l.Aquil.* (ie 9.2). In the extracts we have used in this and the other appendices, we have replaced the mediaeval references with modern numerical ones.

Similarly, the mediaeval division of the *Corpus Iuris Civilis*, and particularly the Digest, was different from Justinian's, or our own, and different even from Justinian's division into sections for teaching purposes in *constitutio Omnem*, one of the introductory enactments to the Digest. As the mediaeval lawyers reckoned it, it was made up of the Old Digest (*Digestum Vetus*), ie D 1.1 to D 24.2; the *Infortiatum*, ie D 24.3 to 38.17; the New Digest (*Digestum Novum*), ie D 39.1 to the end; the *Code*, meaning Books 1–9 thereof; and the *Volumen*, which comprised the Institutes, the *Tres Libri* (or last three books of the Code), the *Authenticum* (one version of Justinian's Novels), the *Books of the Feus*, and the *Extravagantes*, other legislation of the Holy Roman Emperors, including the terms of the Peace of Constance of 1183. This division of the Digest is slightly baffling, but may have been made for ease of handling the actual manuscripts, and also as a convenient division for teaching purposes, or even because of the order in which the manuscripts came to light. Further, the mediaeval writers generally knew no Greek, and so the passages in that language were often omitted, or else translated. Where no part of the *Corpus* is specified the Digest should be understood.

(A) A GLOSS OF IRNERIUS ON THE RUBRIC TO D 1.1 – ON JUSTICE AND LAW

(Printed in P Vinogradoff, *Roman Law in Mediaeval Europe* (Oxford, 1929) 148.) See para 3.5.3.

> While equity and law deal with the same matters, yet they differ. For it is a property of equity simply to lay down what is lawful. But it is the property

of law to lay down the same thing by an act of will, namely vested with some form of authority. On account of the fallen nature of mankind this may differ very much from equity, partly by containing less than equity would demand, partly by laying down more than ought to be laid down. Equity and law also differ from each other in many ways, and the interpretation of any discrepancy with a view to making general law is a matter reserved to rulers alone.

(B) A GLOSS FROM THE STANDARD GLOSS OF ACCURSIUS ON C 8.55(56).8 – ON THE REVOCATION OF GIFTS

See para 3.5.5.

If at any time a patron, having no children, has gifted to his freedmen his whole property or any part thereof, and afterwards has children, **all** that he gifted shall **revert** to remain within the power and disposal of the donor. Gloss on **all**: No; it seems to be a share of the property only, as in C 3.29.5 which is a conflicting text. Solution: this is a special case when there is a gift to freedmen; it is otherwise if the gift is to another class of person. Perhaps it is better to say that C 3.29.5 applies when he had given to other [emancipated] children, who should not be deprived of the whole property; this text applies where the gift is to a stranger. For I would give the same decision if he made the gift to any class of stranger, because it is improbable that he would prefer succession by an outsider to succession by his own children. See also C 6.42.30. Gloss on **revert**: Ipso iure, and so he has the kind of action a man uses to recover what is his own.

(C) A DISTINCTION OF IRNERIUS QUOTED BY ROFFREDUS, ON THE TOPIC OF *LOCATIO CONDUCTIO* – LEASING AND HIRING

(Printed in FC von Savigny, *Geschichte des römischen Rechts* (2nd edn, 1850) vol IV, App II, p 469.) See para 3.5.6.

Sometimes one lets one's property, sometimes one's services, sometimes one's property and services. When someone lets his property and the lessee is unable to use the thing which he has leased, either by reason of the acts of the landlord or by some accidental occurrence affecting him, then the landlord is liable to an action on the lease. But in the former case, namely when it is because of his act, the landlord is liable for damages, which includes gains lost, or for any penalty which he promised, provided that the tenant has paid his rent and cultivated the property as he ought and not misused the thing which he has leased. See C 4.65.3 & 15; D 19.2.15 & 54 & 33 & 24. In the second case, namely where it was by accident, the action lies for a proportionate remission of rent or for the return of the rent, eg if a house or land is destroyed by earthquake. See D 19.2.9 & 15 & 19 & 30. If, however, it was by the act of the tenant, or by an accidental occurrence affecting him, that he was prevented from using the thing leased, then he is required to pay the whole rent. See D 19.2.61. Where, however, someone lets his services or his property and services, and it is not by his act that he is prevented from rendering these services but it is by the act of the hirer, even if the hirer is prevented from claiming the services by some accidental happening, the one who lets his services will recover the fee for the whole time, as for example in the case of someone who undertook to transport slaves. See D 50.13.1; D 19.2.19 & 38 & 33; D 14.2.10. If, however, it was through the act of the one letting his services that he was unable to provide those services, or if he was prevented by an accidental happening affecting him, in the first case he is liable for damages and for the restoration of the fee, even for the period during which he rendered the services. See C 4.65.14; D 19.2.13.4; C 4.6.11.

(D)   FROM AZO'S *SUMMA CODICIS* ON C 8.53 – ON GIFT

See para 3.7.3. [(i) What a gift is. (ii) Gift is derived from the giving of a gift. (iii) The kinds of gifts.]

(i) Let us see then what a gift is. Gift is a pure liberality which is conferred without any legal compulsion (cf D 39.5.29; D 50.17.82), whether the compulsion be from civil law or from natural law. But I do not mean that the mere existence of an obligation by civil law which is unenforceable because there is a defence to the claim makes a gift impossible, for such an obligation gives no right of retention, but this is not so in the case of a natural obligation (cf D 13.5.1 & 3; D 39.5.19). It is called pure because there is no gift when something is done out of necessity (cf D 34.4.18). Nevertheless, in these cases one sometimes speaks improperly of a gift, that is, a giving which is irrevocable (cf D 9.2.27).

(ii) The derivation of the name. It is, as it were, a giving of a gift (cf D 39.6.35), but one must note that, unless there is the intention to transfer ownership, the ownership does not pass (D 39.5.9; D 6.2.13). It is not necessary, however, that there should be a transfer of ownership in order to constitute a gift.

(iii) What are the kinds of gifts? One is simple, another is where there is a *causa* – specific grounds. It is simple when the donor does not wish what he has given, or what he has promised to give, to be returned to him in any circumstances, and this applies whether the gift is unconditional or postponed or conditional. A gift is for a *causa* when it is given in order that something be done or be not done, and I hold that there fall into this class *donationes propter nuptias* [gifts on account of marriage] or *mortis causa* [in expectation of death] and dowry. But it may be otherwise in the case of an engagement gift, because that is made unconditionally and is a simple gift although there is a tacit condition in it by force of law (see D 39.5.1 & 19; Inst 2.7*pr* & 2).

(E)   CINUS' COMMENTARY ON C 8.55.8

This deals with the same passage as in (b). See para 3.7.4.

Note that a gift made to freedmen of all one's property, or of part thereof, is revoked if children are born afterwards. And there are two reasons for this: one is because a freedman must act dutifully towards his patron (see D 37.14.17). The second reason is that it is improbable etc [ie that a person

would prefer an outsider to his own progeny], as can be argued from
C 6.42.30. But a question is raised with regard to the present text: what if
the gift has been made to an outsider? The same rule seems to apply, as can
be argued from the said C 6.42.30. But on this branch of the discussion you
should take the view which I have set out fully in my commentary on
C 3.29.1 (on invalid gifts). The text we are dealing with here leads to the
following question: A certain man legitimated his natural son because he
had no legitimate children; he afterwards had legitimate children. Will the
legitimation be revoked? It seems from what we are saying that it will, but
appears in fact that it will not, see D 43.19.2; C 5.27.10.

(F)   *QUAESTIO* WITH SOLUTION ATTRIBUTED TO BULGARUS

(Printed in E Genzmer, 'Die Justinianische Kodifikation und die Glossatoren'
in *Atti Congresso internazionale di diritto romano* (Bologna, 1934) vol I,
347–430.) See para 3.7.6.

> The following is the statement of the facts in this affair, arising between
> Stichus and Titius: Stichus theftuously took away a horse of Titius, which
> he afterwards returned to a slave of Titius, unknown to Titius. The horse
> then perished in the hands of the slave (through accident) before it had
> come to his master.
>
> *Pro*: Stichus says that he is released by the death of the horse after returning
> the horse, for when he returned it to the slave he is regarded as having
> returned it to the slave's master, since what is acquired by a slave is acquired
> for the master. Therefore possession is regarded as having returned to the
> master and the horse is capable of being usucaped [which a stolen object
> could not be], in as much as the vice of the thing has been purged.
>
> *Contra*: Titius says that the horse is not regarded as having returned to his
> power, even if it was returned to the slave, because someone who pays to
> someone other than the person to whom he owes does not release himself.
>
> Solution: Bulgarus said that the thief was still liable for the value of the
> horse under an action called the *condictio furtiva*, and cited D 41.3.4.7.

(G)   DIALOGUE BETWEEN DOCTOR AND STUDENT FROM THE *QUAESTIONES DE IURIS SUBTILITATIBUS* DEALING WITH THE INTERPRETATION OF LAWS, AND CONSTITUTIONS

(Ed G Zanetti (1958), p 18.) See para 3.7.9.

> Student: Interpretation involving a decision between law and equity and
> also all interpretation of statute is a matter for the emperor alone. However,
> against this it is said (in D 1.3.12 and C 1.14.1) that a judge may interpret
> laws, namely, by applying them to similar cases. Others also may interpret
> the law in teaching or in disputation. Custom also is said (in D 1.3.37) to be
> an interpreter of laws.

Doctor: There is a form of interpretation which, although it is rightly called interpretation, has no necessary force, eg an interpretation by disputants or teachers. There is another form of interpretation which has necessary force, but only in relation to a particular case, for the interpretation of a judge is binding in the matter which he decides, but other judges are not to give judgment in accordance with this as precedent. For any interpretation which is to have general force is a matter for the emperor alone. That interpretation which is accepted by the force of custom is of the same kind, but with this restriction, that an interpretation arising from an error is not to be sustained.

(H)   HUGOLINUS' *DISSENSIONES DOMINORUM*

(Ed G Hänel (1834) p 330, para 91, on C 3.1.8.) See para 3.7.10.

Whether unwritten equity should be preferred to the strict letter of the law?

There is disagreement on this text: 'It is established that in all matters arguments of justice and equity are superior to those of strict law.' There are some who say that where it speaks of justice, this means as laid down by law and not justice as understood by someone from his own talents; for they prefer the strict law, as in Nov 18.8. The other view is that in all matters justice, whether written or not, is to be preferred to strict law, since, even if it is not written, it ought to be pursued as a good, as in D 1.3.32 & 33 and C 1.14.1.

Appendix 2

THE *ULTRAMONTANI* – EXTRACTS

(A)   A *QUAESTIO* OF JACQUES DE RÉVIGNY ON INST 4.6.13

(Ed R Feenstra, *Studi Senesi* 84 (1972), 379 = *Fata Iuris Romani*, 298.)

The Roman law on *emphyteusis*, the hereditary and alienable perpetual lease of land, is here applied by analogy to tenure in feudal law; see para 4.2.2 and cf para 5.6.4.

> A vassal cannot alienate his feu against the will of his feudal superior, on the argument of C 4.66.3. But I ask: if the superior will not consent to the alienation, and does not himself wish to buy, can the vassal sell after he has once asked the superior and the superior wishes neither to buy nor to consent to the alienation? It appears that the answer is yes – an *emphyteuta* [hereditary tenant] can, see C 4.66.3. Therefore the same applies in the case of a vassal on the argument of D 45.1.122. In this question the doctors admit as a matter of equity that a vassal can alienate in favour of someone like himself, so that the position of his superior is not prejudiced. For example, suppose the vassal is a knight, and he has alienated in favour of a knight, but not in favour of a cleric nor in mortmain, on the argument of C 4.66.3 and on the argument that one may proceed from one case to another similar case, as in D 45.2.5, I say that I see no reason why it can be alienated against the wishes of the superior, and that the case of the *emphyteuta* is not the same, because he holds by virtue of a contract and the superior receives money from him and it does not matter from whom he receives the money.
> In this context the following question arises. A certain person is a count in the kingdom of France; he rebels against the king; he wishes to gather an army against his superior, the king; he orders all his vassals to help him. The question is whether they ought to help him against his superior. Supposing the answer is no; if they in fact obey him are they excused because they are following his orders? To the first question the answer indeed is that they ought not to obey him; in the oath of fealty the person of the superior is excepted. In the oath of fealty illicit acts are not covered, because an oath simply given does not extend to illicit acts. A man who rebels against his superior acts in breach of the law, see D 12.6.6 and D 42.8.12. And that they offend against the *lex Julia maiestatis* [the statute on treason] is proved by the argument that the king is an emperor because he does not recognize any superior. I, however, say that this is an act against the emperor, not, as they say, because the king is emperor, but because the act is committed against a magistrate of the emperor, see D 48.4.1, because France and Spain were at one time part of the Empire, see C 1.27.2, and therefore will always be so, as I have shewn elsewhere from C 7.39.6. So far as the second question

is concerned, it would seem that the order of their superior would excuse his vassals, on the argument of D 3.2.6. But the orders of a master do not excuse in the case of atrocious acts. This is an atrocious act, namely offending against the statute on treason. It follows that the orders given do not excuse, see D 50.17.157.

(B) COMMENTARY OF PIERRE DE BELLEPERCHE ON C 1.1.1 – *CUNCTOS POPULOS*

(Ed EM Meijers, *Études d'Histoire du Droit* III (1959) 141ff) See para 4.4.2. The text of the Code reads: 'We wish all peoples whom the sovereign power of our clemency rules to follow the religious belief . . . that there is one Deity of Father, Son, and Holy Spirit.' The Accursian Gloss already made the point on this text that legislation, any legislation, applies only to the subjects of the legislator,

> The present fragment is used as a basis for questions. If it were at the end of the book, it would not have led to a single question, but because it is the first fragment it is given special attention. The modern writers put it as an actual case. There is a statute in a city that if someone draws his sword [within the city] he is to lose his hand. Suppose that some stranger from another city draws his sword, is he affected by the statute? The Doctors say that this fragment is an argument that he is not affected, because the emperor's order is binding only on the emperor's subjects. Therefore, a fortiori a statute of a city will not be binding on strangers. This is the first line of argument, and to support it there are D 2.1.20 and D 42.5.12,1 [which both talk about the limits of a judge's jurisdiction]. What, then, are we to say? The modern Doctors distinguish as follows – (a) the matter which falls under the statute is a wrong quite apart from the statute, or (b) it is not a wrong apart from the statute. (a) If it is a wrong quite apart from the statute, eg drawing a sword for the purpose of murder is a wrong quite apart from the statute (as in C 9.16.7), then strangers from another city are bound by this statute ... (b) Or the matter on which the statute was passed would not be a wrong in the absence of a statute, eg there is a statute that anyone who crosses the bridge into the city after a certain hour should pay a fine, then if a stranger crosses the bridge after the certain hour he is not liable to the statutory penalty. This is what the old Doctors say.
>
> Some newer writings [of Jacques de Révigny] make a fuller distinction, and it is a good one. If you ask whether a stranger is bound by a statute of a city it is important (a) whether the matter is a wrong quite apart from the statute, or (b) the matter would not be a wrong apart from the statute, and (c) the matter on which the statute was passed relates to the public interest, eg one must not sell dead fish [which might go off in the days before refrigeration] under penalty of a fine; in this case the statute will bind strangers, on the argument of D 1.12.1.11 & 12 [which say that the Prefect of the City is responsible for keeping order at the public games and for the control of the meat market], or (d) that the matter does not affect the public interest, eg where no one must cross the bridge after the curfew bell under penalty of a fine, and then the statute will not bind a stranger. I accept this distinction.
>
> However, there is one point on which I am in doubt. The Doctors say that if there is a statute on a matter which would in any case amount to a wrong, for example, drawing a sword with intention to kill, then if a stranger

draws his sword he, in effect, chooses to be tried in this jurisdiction. But I think there is a doubt whether he chooses this jurisdiction in the sense that he will be subject to the relevant punishment laid down in the [Roman] law or will be subject to the penalty laid down in the city's statute. It may be that the penalty in the law is not as great as the penalty in the statute. I accept that he is liable to a penalty, but I wonder whether he can be punished with the [harsher] penalty of the statute. On this point I think it should probably be said that if some stranger has committed a wrong here, and thus becomes liable here, he is not only liable to be punished with the penalty in the law but with the penalty in the statute, and the modern authors thought this but did not venture to say so.

My argument is this: the texts say that where someone proposes to commit one delict and commits a greater delict – which he did not realise he was committing – he is punished in accordance with the delict which he committed, and his intentions are not taken into account. Now the person who draws his sword ought to know that he is committing a wrong, and although he did not think he would be punished with so great a penalty nevertheless he will be punished according to the statute. In favour of this solution I cite: someone thought that he was stealing from me a block of brass and so should not be punished beyond double the value of the brass in an action for theft, but the block was of gold and he is therefore liable to double the value of the gold. The text (D 47.2.21.2) says that, insofar as he intended to commit a delict, he will be punished to the extent to which he in fact committed a delict.

Moreover, I am moved by other arguments in this direction. You must know that, just as someone in effect chooses the jurisdiction by committing a wrong, so he does by entering into a contract (as stated in D 5.1.19). From this I argue: as the text says that if a stranger makes a contract here he chooses the jurisdiction here, not only insofar as he is bound by any penalty in the [Roman] law but also in accordance with the statutes and customs of the place, therefore it will be the same in the case before us, namely that a wrongdoer is punished not only by the penalty of the law but according to the statutes and customs of the place. A further argument may be adduced from D 21.2.6, which holds that a seller of land must guarantee the buyer against eviction from that land in accordance with the custom of the region. This is what I think should be said on the present matter.

The commentary then goes on to discuss other questions, such as what law applies where a citizen of Orléans sues a Parisian in Chartres; the rule is that matters of procedure are ruled by the customs of Chartres but matters of substance by the customs of the place where the contract was made. Again, if a will in England requires ten witnesses and a will in Orléans requires seven, and a testator who has property both in England and Orléans leaves a will with seven witnesses, then, if English law specifically requires ten witnesses for the will to be valid, the heir will get only the property in Orléans. Pierre rejects the view taken by some that the will made in Orléans can in no circumstances affect the devolution of property in England; he would allow such a will to carry the property in England if there be no specific prohibition in English law depriving it of effect.

Appendix 3

THE CANONISTS – EXTRACTS

(A) GRATIAN'S *DECRETUM, CAUSA* 29, *QUAESTIO* 2

(*Corpus Iuris Canonici*, vol I, ed. E Friedberg (Leipzig 1879–1881).) See para 1.4.2; 5.3.4.

First Part [by Gratian himself]:

A second question concerning status is put: can a woman put away a man she had thought free if, after [marriage], she found he was a slave? From many arguments it seems that it can be proved that a woman is not allowed to divorce a slave. For in Christ Jesus there is neither Jew nor Greek, there is neither bond nor free [Gal 3,28], therefore neither is there in marriage of Christians. For each is ruled by the same law, in the faith of Christ. For the apostle said at large to all: 'Who wishes to marry, let him marry in the Lord'; and again: 'A woman is at liberty to marry whom she will, only in the Lord' [1 Cor 7,39]. He did not command that a freeborn woman marry a freeborn man, or a slave a slave, but each may marry as she wishes, but only in the Lord.

c.1 A slave is allowed to marry (Pope Julius, 337-52).

For all of us there is one Father in Heaven, and each of us, rich or poor, free or slave, shall, on equal footing, render account of our souls to Him. We cannot, therefore, doubt that all men, of whatever condition, have only one law before God. But if all have only the one law, therefore, just as a free man cannot be put aside, nor can a slave, once married, be put aside thereafter.

c.2 A man may not put away a slave girl he has taken to wife (Pope Zacharias, 741-52).

If a free man shall take a slave girl to wife, he has no power to put her away, provided they were married with the consent of both parties, except for fornication; but there shall be one law hereafter in all matters, for both men and women.

c.3 Marriage between patron and freedwoman is held legitimate (Pope Julius).

If someone shall have given his slave girl her freedom and joined her to himself in marriage, certain persons have doubted whether this is lawful marriage (*nuptiae legitimae*) or not. But we, settling this ancient uncertainty, hold that such marriage is lawful. For if all marriage springs from intention [*affectio maritalis*, the freely consenting intention to be married, which had been all that was required to constitute a marriage under Roman law (D 23.2.1)], and if there is no possibility of something impious or contrary to law in such a union, what would lead us to prohibit the aforesaid nuptials?

Second Part [Gratian]:

To these it can be replied: it is not denied that a freeborn woman can marry a slave, but the point is, what if she does not know his servile status? Can she be free to put him aside when his servility is made known? For the apostle [Paul] and Pope Julius are to be understood as speaking to those whose status was known to each other. But the man's status was not known to the woman; she is not, therefore, by the aforesaid authorities bound to remain with him, but is shown to be free to stay or to put him aside.

c.4 On him who marries a slave girl, thinking her free (canon 6 of the Council at Verberie [in the modern *département* of Oise] at which King Pippin was present, 753).

If a free man should take another's slave girl to wife, thinking that she is free, and if she is afterwards found to be servile, he should redeem her from slavery if he can; if he cannot release her, he may take another wife, if he wishes. But if he knew she was a slave girl and yet acknowledged her, he shall hold her as his lawful wife. Similarly, a free woman ought to behave in the same way with a man who is another's slave.

c.5 A woman may not put aside a man she married knowing he was a slave (c. 8 of the same Council).

If a freeborn woman marries a slave, knowing that he is a slave, she must keep him, because we all have one Father in Heaven. The law is the same for men and women.

c.6 There is no valid putting away on the grounds of servile status if there is subsequently a successful claim to liberty (Pope Gregory I, 590–604).

[This is a judgment given in 596 on a particular case where a man had discarded his wife; she proved herself free; he must therefore take her back.]

dictum post c.6 [Gratian].
When it is said [in c.5] 'knowing him to be a slave', it is implied that if she had not known that he was a slave, she is not bound to stay with him.

Because, therefore, she was deceived both as to his person and as to his status she is not bound to stay with a man by whose deceit she was misled. If, however, she took him when he was a free man and he, to provide grounds for divorce, becomes the slave of a third party, he cannot put her away, nor can she be reduced to servile status because of the marriage tie.

c.7 Having changed his status by fraud, a man cannot divorce her whom he took when he was free (at the Council of Tribur [not very far from Koblenz] in 895).

To this synod was brought a case in which a free man married a free woman and, after the birth of children to them, as an occasion of divorce made himself slave to a third party; it was asked whether she must abide with him? And, if she does, whether she too should become servile according to secular law? Judgment was given that she ought in no way to cease to be his wife, but neither, because of the law of Christ, ought she to be reduced to servile status, provided that he had not made himself a slave with the consent of the wife, who herself had married a free husband.

dictum post c.7 [Gratian].
It is also asked, if the slave of one person marries the slave girl of another, whether there may be marriage between them?

c.8 Masters may not on their own authority undo the legitimate marriages of their slaves (as was laid down at the Council of Chalons-sur-Saône, 813).
   It is told us that certain persons, presuming on their right of ownership, are parting lawfully wedded slaves, not heeding the evangelist: 'What God hath joined together, let not man put asunder' [Matt 19,6]. Whence it seems to us that the marriage of slaves may not be dissolved, even if they have different masters, but let them serve their masters while remaining in the one marriage. And this is to be observed where the union was legal and permitted by the masters.

(B)   *LIBER EXTRA* BOOK 4 TITLE 9 ON THE MARRIAGE OF SLAVES

(*Corpus Iuris Canonici*, vol II, ed. E.Friedberg, Leipzig 1879-81) See para 5.4.3.

c.1 A slave can contract marriage even against the will of his owner, but he is not thereby freed from the services due to his owner (Pope Hadrian to the Archbishop of Salzburg)
   It is proper and in accordance with with the path of reason that those matters which appear to contain the slightest doubt should be referred to the judgment of the Apostolic See, so that the faithful people of Christ may rejoice to find in the midst of doubts certainty from that source from which they are assured of having received the authority of faith. You, my brother, have, as we recall, sought guidance from the Apostolic See about what should become of the marriages of slaves which are contracted against their owners' wishes and forbidden: on which this is our considered reply. Indeed, according to the word of the apostle, and as your discernment recognizes, just as in Jesus Christ no-one whether slave or free is to be refused the sacraments of the Church, so also marriages between slaves are nowise to be prohibited; and even if they are contracted against their owners' wishes and forbidden, there is no ground for them to be dissolved by the Church courts on that account. But due and customary services must nonetheless [continue to] be rendered to their owners.

c.2 A marriage is dissolved when a free man contracts [marriage] with a slave woman in ignorance [of her status] unless he subsequently has carnal knowledge of her while knowing the fact. (Pope Alexander III to the Provost and Prior of Morter [in the South Tirol])
   The woman M, bringer of this present action, submitted to us that, after her husband had remained with her for a substantial length of time, he

brought up her servile status against her, alleging that she, whom he believed to be free when he took her to wife, was [in fact] a slave. However, when the case was being heard before the Bishop of Asti, the woman, fearing prejudice to herself there, appealed to our court. Because therefore, with both of them still living, after some little delay the husband withdrew from the as yet unsettled action, We order you, when approached on this matter, to summon the parties to appear before you and, having diligently inquired into the truth of the matter, if it be established that the husband had carnal knowledge of the aforesaid woman after he heard that she was a slave, you are to require him, after due warning, to accept her as his wife and treat her with marital intention. If however it should be otherwise, and a decree of divorce be pronounced, you are to ensure that the money which she gave to the husband by way of dowry is returned to her, as is just.

c.3 If the local custom is that the progeny follow the status of the father, then the child of a free man and a slave woman is free and contracts marriage as a free person. (Pope Urbanus III to the Archbishop of Rimini)
    Although we judge you competent in respect of those matters on which you desired to consult us, yet because you are asking for our judgment to ensure greater certainty in your pastoral care, we are replying to your enquiries in accordance with the duty of our office. As regards the question proposed on your part – whether a woman can sue for a divorce on the ground that her husband, with whom she contracted marriage in ignorance of his status, was a slave of the monastery – since on the other hand the same husband consistently affirms that his father (whose status he follows according to the laws of the province) was at the time of his death conducting himself as a free man, and that in the ten years which have elapsed since then there has been no challenge to his father's status or his own: it seems to us that, by reason of the time that has elapsed and the [presumption in] favour of free status, judgment should more properly be given for the husband.

c.4 If a free man contracted marriage with a slave woman in ignorance and, as from the time he knew this, withdrew his consent, the marriage is dissolved and he will be able to contract with some other. (Pope Innocent III to Bishop H. [of Ratzeburg, in Schleswig-Holstein])
    You are to know that a case has come before us after our beloved son Cardinal G., as papal legate, granted a separation to our beloved son the noble L., knight, from a certain woman on account of an error in [her] status. We therefore order you to inquire diligently into the truth of these matters and, if it be established to your satisfaction that the knight contracted marriage with a slave woman in ignorance, then, provided that after he learned of her status he did not consent, either in word or in deed, to [hold himself as married] to the same woman – for which reason he was separated by the same Cardinal from cohabitation with her – you are to grant him, by apostolic authority, free power to contract marriage with another.

Appendix 4

THE COMMENTATORS – EXTRACT

BARTOLUS ON NOTARIES

(Translation by JA Clarence Smith in *American Journal of Legal History* 14 (1970), at p 247.)

Bartolus, in his commentary on *Cunctos populos* – the same title as was the subject of Pierre de Belleperche in Appendix 2(B) – at one point discusses the position of notaries; here local legislation or custom is distinguished from general law, that is, matters pertaining to imperial (or papal) jurisdiction. It was important that the status of notaries was clear because, as we have seen, their forms and styles were in use throughout Europe, and were one of the unifying factors in the *ius commune*. There were also a great many of them; in thirteenth-century Bologna there are said to have been some 2,000, and in Padua 600.

> My seventh point concerns permissive local legislation; and in this connection there are two matters to be examined, namely, whether the act permitted may be performed outside the territory of the permitting authority, and again, if it is performed in that place or in a permitted place, whether it has any effect outside the territory. We shall deal with the two side by side.
>
> Sometimes then local legislation grants and permits something which in nature could be within no one's power, but only by franchise particularly granted, and in matters to which it extends. For instance, under a city's legislation someone is appointed notary: may he draw up deeds outside the territory of that city? This is a point discussed by Speculator. In my own view he may not draw up deeds outside the territory; and the rule is the same for similar matters which may be performed only within the territory.
>
> For acts of non-contentious jurisdiction, under power granted by authorities inferior to the Emperor, may not be performed outside the territory. D 50.16.2: 'Every provincial governor has jurisdiction immediately on leaving the capital, but only in non-contentious, not in contentious, proceedings'; which is a leading authority on this point. Sext 2.2.1.4: 'Nor should they send their clerks into the dioceses of their suffragans for contracts to be entered into or acknowledged before them, nor compel the subjects of the same suffragans to submit their differences to them for decision on such an occasion'. Pope Innocent IV on the limits of an archbishop's jurisdiction is also helpful, and is cited by Speculator as illustrative.
>
> But in my view deeds drawn up by such a notary within the territory should have full faith and credit anywhere outside the territory. So also an emancipation before the authority having jurisdiction by the law of any one

borough is treated everywhere as confirmed – C 8.48.1: 'If a law of the borough (*municipium*) in which your father emancipated you gave power to the co-mayors (*duumviri*) to allow even outsiders to emancipate their children, then your father's proceedings must be treated as confirmed'; and for this reason, that it goes more to the formalities than to the dealing itself, as we shall see below.

Appendix 5

THE UNION WITH ENGLAND ACT 1707 [1707 cap.7] – EXTRACTS

ACT Ratifying and Approving the Treaty of Union of the Two Kingdoms of Scotland and England

The Estates of Parliament Considering that Articles of Union of the Kingdoms of Scotland and England were agreed on the twenty second of July One thousand seven hundred and six years ...

Which Articles were in all humility presented to Her Majesty upon the twenty third of the said month of July and were Recommended to this Parliament by Her Majesties Royal Letter of the date the thirty one day of July One thousand seven hundred and six And that the said Estates of Parliament have agreed to and approven of the saids Articles of Union with some Additions and Explanations as is contained in the Articles hereafter insert And sicklyke Her Majesty with advice and consent of the Estates of Parliament Resolving to Establish the Protestant Religion and Presbyterian Church Government within this Kingdom has past in this Session of Parliament an Act entituled Act for secureing of the Protestant Religion and Presbyterian Church Government which by the Tenor thereof is appointed to be insert in any Act ratifying the Treaty and expressly declared to be a fundamentall and essentiall Condition of the said Treaty or Union in all time coming Therefore Her Majesty with advice and consent of the Estates of Parliament ... Doth ratify Approve and Confirm the same with the Additions and Explanations contained in the saids Articles in manner and under the provision aftermentioned whereof the Tenor follows

I. THAT the Two Kingdoms of Scotland and England shall upon the first day of May next ensuing the date hereof and forever after be United into One Kingdom by the Name of GREAT BRITAIN And that the Ensigns Armorial of the said United Kingdom be such as Her Majesty shall appoint and the Crosses of St Andrew and St George be conjoined in such manner as Her Majesty shall think fit and used in all Flags Banners Standards and Ensigns both at Sea and Land

II. THAT the Succession to the Monarchy of the United Kingdom of Great Britain and of the Dominions thereunto belonging after Her Most Sacred Majesty and in default of Issue of Her Majesty be remain and continue to the Most Excellent Princess Sophia Electoress and Dutchess Dowager of Hanover and the Heirs of her body being Protestants ...

III. THAT the United Kingdom of Great Britain be Represented by one and the same Parliament to be stiled the Parliament of Great Britain

IV. THAT all the Subjects of the United Kingdom of Great Britain shall from and after the Union have full Freedom and Intercourse of Trade and Navigation to and from any port or place within the said United Kingdom and the Dominions and Plantations thereunto belonging And that there be a Communication of all other Rights Privileges and Advantages which do or may belong to the Subjects of either Kingdom except where it is otherwayes expressly agreed in these Articles

XVI. THAT from and after the Union the Coin shall be of the same standard and value throughout the United Kingdom as now in England ...

XVIII. THAT the Laws concerning Regulation of Trade Customs and such Excises to which Scotland is by virtue of this Treaty to be lyable be the same in Scotland from and after the Union as in England and that all other Lawes in use within the Kingdom of Scotland do after the Union and notwithstanding thereof remain in the same force as before (except such as are contrary to or inconsistent with this Treaty) but alterable by the Parliament of Great Britain With this difference betwixt the Laws concerning Publick Right Policy and Civil Government and those which concern private Right That the Laws which concern publick Right policy and Civil Government may be made the same throughout the whole United Kingdom but that no alteration be made in Laws which concern private Right except for evident utility of the subjects within Scotland

XIX. THAT the Court of Session or Colledge of Justice do after the Union and notwithstanding thereof remain in all time coming within Scotland as it is now constituted by the Laws of that Kingdom and with the same Authority and Priviledges as before the Union subject nevertheless to such Regulations for the better Administration of Justice as shall be made by the Parliament of Great Britain And that hereafter none shall be named by Her Majesty or Her Royal Successors to be Ordinary Lords of Session but such who have served in the Colledge of Justice as Advocats or Principal Clerks of Session for the space of five years or as Writers to the Signet for the space of ten years With this provision That no Writer to the Signet be capable to be admitted a Lord of the Session unless he undergo a private and publick Tryal on the Civil Law before the Faculty of Advocates and be found by them qualified for the said Office two years before he be named to be a Lord of the Session yet so as the Qualifications made or to be made for capacitating persons to be named Ordinary Lords of Session may be altered by the Parliament of Great Britain And that the Court of Justiciary do also after the Union and notwithstanding thereof remain in all time coming within Scotland as it is now constituted by the Laws of that Kingdom and with the same Authority and Priviledges as before the Union subject nevertheless to such Regulations as shall be made by the Parliament of Great Britain and without prejudice of other Rights of Justiciary ... And that all other Courts now in being within the Kingdom of Scotland do remain but subject to Alterations by the Parliament of Great Britain And that all Inferior Courts within the said Limits do remain subordinate as they are now to the Supream Courts of Justice within the same in all time coming And that no causes in Scotland be cognoscible by the Courts of Chancery Queens Bench Common Pleas or any other Court in Westminster hall And that the said Courts or any other of the like nature after the Union shall have no power to Cognosce Review or Alter the Acts or Sentences of the Judicatures within Scotland or stop the Execution of the same And that there be a Court of Exchequer in Scotland after the Union for deciding Questions concerning the Revenues of Customs and Excises there having the same power and authority in such cases as the Court of Exchequer has in England And that the said Court of Exchequer in Scotland have power of passing Signatures Gifts Tutories and in other things as the Court of Exchequer at present in Scotland hath And that the Court of Exchequer that now is in Scotland do remain until a new Court of Exchequer be settled by the Parliament of Great Britain in Scotland after the Union ...

XXII. THAT by virtue of this Treaty Of the Peers of Scotland at the time of the Union Sixteen shall be the number to Sit and Vote in the House of Lords and Forty five the number of the Representatives of Scotland in the House of Commons of the Parliament of Great Britain ...

And Her Majesty with advice and consent foresaid expressly Provides and Declares that the foresaid True Protestant Religion contained in the above-mentioned Confession of Faith with the form and purity of Worship presently in use within this Church and its Presbyterian Church Government and Discipline that is to say the Government of the Church by Kirk Sessions Presbytries Provincial Synods and Generall Assemblies all established by the forsaid Acts of Parliament pursuant to the Claim of Right shall Remain and Continue unalterable and that the said Presbyterian Government shall be the only Government of the Church within the Kingdom of Scotland And further for the greater security of the foresaid Protestant Religion and of the Worship Discipline and Government of this Church as above established Her Majesty with advice and consent foresaid Statutes and Ordains That the Universities and Colledges of Saint Andrews Glasgow Aberdeen and Edinburgh as now Established by Law shall Continue within this Kingdom for ever ... And it is hereby Statute and Ordained That this Act of Parliament with the Establishment therein contained shall be held and observed in all time coming as a fundamentall and essentiall Condition of any Treaty or Union to be Concluded betwixt the Two Kingdoms without any Alteration thereof or Derogation thereto in any sort for ever ...

WHICH ARTICLES OF UNION and Act immediately above written Her Majesty with advice and consent foresaid Statutes Enacts and Ordains to be and Continue in all time coming the sure and perpetuall foundation of ane compleat and intire Union of the Two Kingdoms of Scotland and England ...

Appendix 6

DÉCLARATION DES DROITS DE L'HOMME ET DU CITOYEN

(Translation by Ian Brownlie, *Basic Documents on Human Rights* (Oxford, 1971) p 8.)

The French Declaration of the Rights of Man and Citizen, issued in 1789, was confirmed in the preambles to the French constitutions of 1946 and 1958. After the preamble:

Article 1: Men are born and remain free and equal in respect of rights. Social distinctions shall be based solely upon public utility.

Article 2: The purpose of all civil associations is the preservation of the natural and imprescriptible rights of man. These rights are liberty, property and resistance to oppression.

Article 3: The nation is essentially the source of all sovereignty, nor shall any body of men or any individual exercise authority which is not expressly derived from it.

Article 4: Liberty consists in the power of doing whatever does not injure another. Accordingly the exercise of the natural rights of every man has not other limits than those which are necessary to secure to every other man the free exercise of the same rights; and these limits are determinable only by the law.

Article 5: The law ought to prohibit only actions hurtful to society. What is not prohibited by the law should not be hindered; nor should any one be compelled to do that which the law does not require.

Article 6: The law is an expression of the common will. All citizens have a right to concur, either personally or by their representatives in its formation. It should be the same for all, whether it protects or punishes; and all being equal in its sight, are equally eligible to all honours, places and employments, according to their different abilities, without any other distinction than that of their virtues and talents.

Article 7: No one shall be accused, arrested or imprisoned, save in the cases determined by law, and according to the forms which it has prescribed. All who solicit, promote, execute, or cause to be executed, arbitrary orders, ought to be punished, and every citizen summoned or apprehended by virtue of the law, ought immediately to obey, and becomes culpable if he resists.

Article 8: The law should impose only such penalties as are absolutely and evidently necessary; and no one ought to be punished but by virtue of a law promulgated before the offence, and legally applied.

Article 9: Every man being counted innocent until he has been convicted, whenever his arrest becomes indispensable, all vigour more than is necessary to secure his person ought to be provided against by law.

Article 10: No man is to be interfered with because of his opinions, not even because of religious opinions, provided his avowal of them does not disturb public order as established by law.

Article 11: The unrestrained communication of thoughts or opinions being one of the most precious rights of man, every citizen may speak, write and publish freely, provided he be responsible for the abuse of this liberty, in the cases determined by law.

Article 12: A public force being necessary to give security to the rights of men and of citizens, that force is instituted for the benefit of the community, and not for the particular benefit of the person to whom it is entrusted.

Article 13: A common contribution being necessary for the support of the public force, and for defraying the other expenses of government, it should be divided equally among the members of the community, according to their abilities.

Article 14: Every citizen has a right, either of himself or his representative, to a free voice in determining the necessity of public contributions, the appropriation of them, and their amount, mode of assessment, and duration.

Article 15: The community has the right to demand of all its agents an account of their conduct.

Article 16: Every community in which a security of rights and a separation of powers is not provided for lacks a constitution.

Article 17: The right to property being inviolable and sacrosanct, no one shall be deprived of it, except in cases of evident public necessity, legally ascertained, and on condition of a previous just indemnity.

SELECT BIBLIOGRAPHY

This Select Bibliography includes, as well as the books and articles listed at the ends of the chapters, other works without restriction of language: standard works of reference, fundamental monographs, and also the more recent treatments of particular fields. Certain major collections, such as Migne's *Patrologia*, are now available on CD-ROM. We include all the principal works to which we have had recourse. We give a disproportionately large section on Scottish legal history both for the benefit of our own students and also for others interested in the history of Scots law for whom such information is not readily available. We are conscious of the extent of the specialized literature on the topics we have merely outlined; our debt is sometimes direct, at others it explains the shading of the picture. The extent of our obligation will be evident; we gratefully acknowledge it.

INDEX TO THE SELECT BIBLIOGRAPHY

A. (a) An indispensable bibliographical tool is:

Handbuch der Quellen und Literatur der Neueren Europäischen Privatrechtsgeschichte (Munich, 1973–), published by the Max-Planck-Institut für Europäische Rechtsgeschichte in Frankfurt-am-Main. The Institute also publishes *Ius Commune*, a journal of European legal history, with supplementary

Sonderhefte (which contain texts, monographs or collections of studies), and a special series on case law, *Rechtsprechung: Materialen und Studien*.

Among other major tools of research are:

Bibliography on Foreign and Comparative Law, ed C Szladits (USA, 1955–)
Introduction bibliographique à l'histoire du droit et à l'ethnologie juridique,
    ed J Gilissen (Brussels, 1963–)
Repertorium bibliographicum Institutorum et Sodalitatum iuris historiae
    (Leiden, 2nd edn, 1980)

Historical bibliographies also have entries on legal history and law.

A. (b) Among dictionaries, reports of congresses, and various series are:

Atti del convegno internazionale di Studi Accursiani, Bologna 1963, ed G Rossi
    (Milan, 1968)
*Atti del terzo congresso internazionale della Società Italiana di Storia del
    Diritto – La formazione storica del diritto moderno in Europa*
    (Florence, 1977)
Bartolo di Sassoferrato. Studi e Documenti per il VI centenario (Milan, 1962)
Bibliotheca Eruditorum, Internationale Bibliothelz der Wissenschaften, eds
    D Maffei and H Fuhrmann (Keip Verlag)
Comparative Studies on Continental and Anglo-American Legal History
Dictionnaire de droit canonique, ed R Naz (Paris, 1935–1965)
Forschungen zur neueren Privatrechtsgeschichte
Handwörterbuch zur Deutschen Rechtsgeschichte, eds A Erler and E Kaufmann
    (Berlin, 1964–)
Histoire du droit et des institutions de l'Église en occident, eds G le Bras and
    J Gaudemet (Paris, 1955–)
Ius Romanum Medii Aevi (= IRMAE) (Milan, 1961-81)
Monumenta iuris canonici include reports of international congresses
Quaderni Fiorentini per la storia del pensiero giuridico moderno
Recueils de la Société Jean Bodin pour l'histoire comparative des institutions
Schriften zur Europäischen Rechts-und Verfassungsgeschichte

A. (c) Up-to-date information is given in the relevant sections of indexes to legal literature, such as:

European Legal Journals Index (Hebden Bridge, 1993–)
Index to Foreign Legal Periodicals (London, 1960–)
Index to Legal Periodical Literature (USA, 1888–1924; 1933–)
Index to Legal Periodicals (USA, 1908–)
Legal Journals Index (Hebden Bridge, 1986–)

B. (a) See also the bibliographies, bibliographical notes and similar material in the relevant specialized periodicals themselves, such as:

American Journal of Legal History (AJLH)
Annali di Storia del Diritto (ASD)
Bulletin of Medieval Canon Law

Diritto Romano Attuale
Journal of Legal History (JLH)
Law and History Review (L & HR)
Orbis Iuris Romani (OIR)
Rechtshistorisches Journal (RHJ)
Revista de historia del derecho (RHD)
Revue d'Histoire des Facultés de Droit et de la Science Juridique
Revue historique de droit français et étranger (RHDFE)
Rivista di storia del diritto italiano (RSDI)
Rivista internazionale di diritto commune
Rivista italiana di storia del diritto (RISD)
Studia et documenta historiae iuris (SDHI)
Tijdschrift voor Rechtsgeschiedenis (TvR - or TR)
Zeitschrift für neuere Rechtsgeschichte
Zeitschrift der Savigny-Stiftung für Rechtsgeschichte – Germanistische,
       Kanonistische, Romanistische Abteilungen (ZSS or SZ (*Germ. Kan.*
       Rom.))[The context may make clear which series is meant]

B. (b) Other journals of interest to the legal historian, including those reflecting the growth of a European private law are:

Acta Juridica (AJ)
American Journal of Comparative Law (AJCompL)
Cambridge Law Journal (CLJ)
Edinburgh Law Review (EdLR)
European Review of Private Law
Harvard Law Review (HLR)
Index
Irish Jurist (new series) *(IJ)*
Juridical Review (JurRev)
Law Quarterly Review (LQR)
Michigan Law Review (MichLR)
Oxford Journal of Legal Studies (OJLSt)
Revue Internationale des Droits de l'Antiquité (RIDA)
Seminar
Speculum
Studi Senesi
Traditio
Transactions of the Royal Historical Society (TRHS)
Tulane Law Review (TulLR)
Virginia Law Review (VirgLR)
Zeitschrift für Europäisches Recht

C. (a) There are various wide-ranging treatments of European law and legal themes. A particularly helpful short guide to the philosophical background is:

Kelly, JM   *A Short History of Western Legal Theory* (Oxford, 1992)

The *Continental Legal History* series, of which some volumes have been mentioned in the Further Reading, had much the same aim as our present work, but it is based on the viewpoints and the researches essentially of the nineteenth century, and was compiled by persons of very varying expertise. Others of interest are:

Astuti, G   *Tradizione romanistica e civiltà giuridica europea* (Naples, 1984)
Bellomo, M, tr. L Cochrane   *The Common Legal Past of Europe, 1000-1800* (USA, 1995)
Caenegem, RC van   *Judges, Legislators and Professors: Chapters in European Legal History* (CUP, 1987)
        tr DEL Johnston, *An Historical Introduction to Private Law* (CUP, 1992)
Cairns JW & OF Robinson, eds   *Critical Studies in Ancient Law, Comparative Law and Legal History* (Richard Hart Publishing, Oxford, 2000)
Cannata, CA   *Histoire de la jurisprudence européene* (Turin, 1989)
Coing, H,   *Europäisches Privatrecht (1500-1800: Älteres Gemeines Recht)* (Munich, 1985)
        Europäisches Privatrecht (1800-1914: 19. Jahrhundert) (Munich, 1989)
Gilissen, J   *Introduction historique au droit* (Brussels, 1979)
Hattenhauer, H   *Europäische Rechtsgeschichte* (Heidelberg, 2nd edn 1996)
Jones, JW   *Historical Introduction to the Theory of Law* (Oxford, 1940)
Lawson, FH   *A Common Lawyer Looks at the Civil Law* (Ann Arbor, 1953)
        Selected Essays (New York & Oxford, 1977)
Lombardi, G   *Saggio sul diritto giurisprudenziale* (Milan, 1967)
Merryman, JH   *The Civil Law Tradition* (Stanford, 2nd edn, 1985)
Stein, P   *Legal Institutions* (London, 1984)
        The Character and Influence of the Roman Civil Law (London and Ronceverte, 1988)
        Roman Law in European History (CUP, 1999)
Thieme H   *Ideengeschichte und Rechtsgeschichte* (Cologne & Vienna, 1986)
Various European Authors   *A General Survey of Events, Sources, Persons and Movements in Continental Legal History* (Continental Legal History series, vol I, Boston, 1912)
Watson, A   *Legal Transplants* (Edinburgh, 1974)
        The Nature of Law (Edinburgh, 1977)
        The Evolution of Law (Baltimore, 1985)
        Roman Law and Comparative Law (Athens, Georgia, 1991)

There are some books which trace specifically Roman rules or institutions, and those of the *ius commune*, into the modern world; for example, in English are:

Buckland, WW & A MacNair   *Roman Law and Common Law* (rev'd FH Lawson, CUP, 1965)
Gordon, WM   *Studies in the Transfer of Property by Traditio* (Aberdeen, 1970)
Jolowicz, HF   *Roman Foundations of Modern Law* (Oxford, 1957)
Lawson, FH & BS Markesinis   *Tortious Liability for Unintentional Harm in the Common Law and the Civil Law* (CUP, 1982)
Stein, P   *Fault in the Formation of Contract in Roman law and Scots law* (Aberdeen UP, 1958)
        Regulae Iuris (Edinburgh, 1966)
Stein, P & J Shand   *Legal Values in Western Society* (Edinburgh, 1974)
Zimmermann, R   *The Law of Obligations: Roman Foundations of the Civilian Tradition* (Cape Town, 1990)

C. (b) Accounts of the legal history of individual European countries usually relate their history to its European background. Examples are:

Besta, E & P del Giudice *Storia del diritto italiano* (Milan, 1923–1927)

Blécourt, AS de *Kort Begrip van het oud-vaderlandsch Burgerlijk Recht* (Groningen, 7th edn (ed HFWD Fischer), 1959)

Brissaud, J *History of French Private Law* (Continental Legal History series, vol III, Boston, 1912)
  History of French Public Law (Continental Legal History series, vol IX, Boston, 1915)

Caenegem, RC van *An Historical Introduction to Private Law* (CUP, 1992) – primarily on Belgium and the Netherlands

Calisse, C *History of Italian Law* (Continental Legal History series, vol VIII, Boston, 1928)

Coing, H *Epochen der Rechtsgeschichte in Deutschland* (Munich, 2nd edn, 1971)

Garcia Gallo, A *Manual de Historia del Derecho Español* (Madrid, 8th edn, 1979)

Hahlo, HR & E Kahn *The South African Legal System and its Background* (Cape Town, 1968)

Hattenhauer, H, *Die geistesgeschichtlichen Grundlagen des deutschen Rechts* (Heidelberg, 4th edn 1996)

Hübner, R *History of Germanic Private Law* (Continental Legal History series, vol IV, Boston, 1918)

Holdsworth, WS *History of English Law* – 16 vols, various editions

Johnson, WS *Chapters in the History of French Law* (Montreal, 1957)

Lee, RW *An Introduction to Roman-Dutch Law* (Oxford, 5th edn, 1953)

Orfield, LB *The Growth of Scandinavian Law* (Philadelphia, 1953)

Ourliac, P & J de Malafosse *Histoire du droit privé* (Paris, 1968–1971)

Plucknett, TFT *A Concise History of the Common Law* (London, 5th edn, 1956)

Viollet, P *Histoire du droit civil français* (Paris, 3rd edn, 1905)

Wal, N van der & JHA Lokin *Historiae iuris graeco-romani delineatio. Les sources du droit byzantin de 300 à 1453* (Groningen, 1985)

Wesenberg, G *Neuere Deutsche Privatrechtsgeschichte* (Lahr, 4th edn (ed G Wesener), 1985) – this has a particularly good basic bibliography

Wieacker, F *Privatrechtsgeschichte der Neuzeit* (Göttingen, 2nd edn, 1967) tr. T Weir *A History of Private Law in Europe* (OUP, 1995)

D. (a) For the Roman period and the first millennium:

Bloch, M *Feudal Society* (London, 2nd edn, 1962)

Chadwick, H *The Early Church* (Penguin, 1967)

Chevrier, G 'L'évolution de l'acte à cause de mort en Dauphiné du 7e à la fin du 11e siècle' *Recueils Soc d'hist des anciens pays de droit écrit* 1 (1948) 9

Collins, R *Early Medieval Spain* (London, 1983)
  Early Medieval Europe 300–1000 (London, 2nd edn 1999)

Drew, KF *Law and Society in Early Medieval Europe* (London, 1988)

Ganshof, FL *Feudalism* (London, 3rd edn, 1964)

Gaudemet, J   'Survivances romaines dans le droit de la monarchie franque du 5e au 10e siècle' *TvR* 23 (1955) 149

Hadrill, JM Wallace   *The Barbarian West, 400-1000* (London, rev'd edn, 1985)

Herlihy, D   *The History of Feudalism* (New York, 1970)

James, E   *The Origins of France* (London, 1982)
         The Franks (Oxford, 1988)

Jonkers, EJ   'Pope Gelasius and the civil law' *TvR* 20 (1952) 335
         'The application of Roman law by councils in the sixth century' *TvR* 20 (1952) 340

Kern, F   *Kingship and Law* (tr SB Chrimes, Oxford, 1939)

King, PD   *Law and Society in the Visigothic Kingdom* (CUP, 1972)

Lawson, FH   *The Roman Law Reader* (New York, 1969)

Lemarignier, J-F   'Les actes de droit privé de Saint Bertin au haut moyen âge' *RIDA* 5 (1950) 35

Liebs, D   *Die Jurisprudenz im spätantiken Italien, 260–640 n Chr* (Berlin, 1987)

Livingstone, EA   *The Concise Oxford Dictionary of the Christian Church* (Oxford, 1977)

McKitterick, R   *The Carolingians and the Written Word* (CUP, 1989)

Nicholas, B   *Introduction to Roman Law* (Oxford, 1962)

Pocock, JGA   *The Ancient Constitution and the Feudal Law* (CUP, rev'd edn, 1987)

Pollock, F & FW Maitland   *The History of English Law before the time of Edward I* (CUP, 2nd edn, ed SFC Milsom, reissued 1968)

Radding, CM   *The Origins of Medieval Jurisprudence* (Yale UP, 1988)

Robinson, OF   *The Sources of Roman Law* (Routledge, 1997)

Southern, RW   *The Making of the Middle Ages* (London, 1953)
         Western Society and the Church in the Middle Ages (Penguin, 1970)

Tellegen-Couperus, O   *A Short History of Roman Law* (London, 1993)

Vinogradoff, P   'Customary Law' in *The Legacy of the Middle Ages* (eds CG Crump & EF Jacob, Oxford, 1926)

Watson, A   *Roman Law and Comparative Law* (Athens, Georgia, 1991)

Wickham, C   *Early Medieval Italy* (London, 1981)

Wolff, H-J   *Roman Law* (Oklahoma UP, 1951)

D. (b) For the medieval period generally:

Baldwin, JW   'The intellectual preparations for the canon of 1215 against ordeals' *Speculum* 36 (1961) 613

Bartlett, R   *Trial by Fire and Water* (Oxford, 1986)

Benson, RL & G Constable, eds   *Renaissance and Renewal in the Twelfth Century* (Oxford, 1982)

Berman, HJ   *Law and Revolution* (Harvard UP, 1983)

Caenegem, RC van   'Law in the Medieval World' *TvR* 49 (1981), 13
         'History of European Civil Procedure' in *International Encyclopedia of Comparative Law*, vol XVI (Tübingen etc)
         Legal History: a European Perspective (London, 1991)

Calasso, F   *Medio Evo del Diritto – Le Fonti* (Milan, 1954)

Chalmers, H   'The concurrence of criminal and civil actions in medieval law' *SDHI* 39 (1973) 385

Clanchy, MT   *From Memory to Written Record* (London, 1979)
Coing, H   'The Roman law as *ius commune* on the Continent' *LQR* 89 (1973), 505
Dawson, JP   *A History of Lay Judges* (Harvard UP, 1960)
    The Oracles of the Law (Ann Arbor, 1968)
Fawtier, R   *The Capetian Kings of France* (London, 1960)
Feenstra, R   *Philip of Leyden* (Murray Lecture, Glasgow, 1970)
    'Les origines du *dominium utile* chez les glossateurs' in *Flores Legum HJ Scheltema Oblati* (Groningen, 1971) 49
    Fata Iuris Romani (Leiden, 1974)
    Le droit savant au moyen âge et sa vulgarisation (London, 1986)
    'Roman law' in *The Legacy of Rome: a New Appraisal,* ed R Jenkyns (OUP, 1992)
Genzmer, E   'Die Justinianische Kodifikation und die Glossatoren' in *Atti Congresso internazionale di diritto romano* I (Bologna, 1934) 347
Giordanengo, G   *Féodalités et droits savants dans le Midi médiéval* (Aldershot, 1992)
Gouron, A   *La science du droit dans le Midi de la France au moyen âge* (London, 1984)
    Études sur la diffusion des doctrines juridiques médiévales (London, 1987)
Hallam, EM   *Capetian France* (London, 1980)
Haskins, CH   *The Renaissance of the Twelfth Century* (Harvard UP, 1927)
Hazeltine, HD   'Roman and canon law in mediaeval Europe' in *Cambridge Mediaeval History,* vol V (CUP 1927), ch xxi
Jolowicz, HF   'The stone that the builders rejected' *Seminar* 12 (1954) 34
Kantorowicz, H   *Rechtshistorische Studien* (eds H Coing & G Irnmal, Karlsruhe, 1970)
Kantorowicz, H & WW Buckland   *Studies in the Glossators of the Roman Law* (CUP, 1938, 2nd edn (ed P Weimar), 1969)
Kleffens, EN van   *Hispanic Law until the End of the Middle Ages* (Edinburgh, 1968)
Knowles, D   *The Evolution of Mediaeval Thought* (London, 1962)
Koschaker, P   *Europa und das römische Recht* (Munich, 4th edn, 1966)
Kunkel, W   'The reception of Roman law in Germany: an interpretation' in *Pre-Reformation Germany* ed G Strauss (London, 1972)
Lawson, FH   *The Roman Law Reader* (New York, 1969) ch vii
Levy, J-P   'La pénétration du droit savant dans les coûtumiers angevins et bretons au moyen âge' *TvR* 25 (1957) 1
MacKay, A   *Spain in the Middle Ages* (London, 1977)
Meijers, EM   *Études d'histoire du droit* (eds R Feenstra & HFWD Fischer, Leiden, 1956-73)
Meynial, E   'Roman Law' in *The Legacy of the Middle Ages* (eds CG Crump & EF Jacob, Oxford, 1926)
Paradisi, B   *Studi sul medievo giuridico* (Rome, 1987)
Reynolds, S   *Fiefs and Vassals. The Medieval Evidence Re-interpreted* (OUP, 1994)
    Kingdoms and Communities in Western Europe, 900–1300 (Oxford, 2nd edn, 1997)
Savigny, FC von   *Geschichte des römischen Rechts im Mittelalter* (Heidelberg, 2nd edn, 1834–51)

Schrage, EJH, ed   *Das römische Recht im Mittelalter* (Darmstadt, 1987)
        *Utrumque Ius. Eine Einführung in das Studium der Quellen des
        mittelalterlichen gelehrten Rechts* (Berlin, 1992)
Smith, JA Clarence   'Bartolo on the Conflict of Laws' *AJLH* 14 (1970) 157; 247
        Medieval Law Teachers and Writers (Ottawa, 1975)
Stein, P   'The mutual agency of partners' *TulLR* 33 (1959) 595
        'The influence of Roman law on the law of Scotland' *JurRev* (1963), 205
        The Teaching of Roman Law in England around 1200 (Selden Society
        supp. series 8, 1990)
        Roman Law in European History (CUP, 1999)
Tierney, B   *The Crisis of Church and State, 1050–1300* (Englewood Cliffs,
        New Jersey, 1964)
Turpin, CC   'The Reception of Roman law' *IJ* 3 (1968) 162
Ullmann, W   *The Mediaeval Idea of Law* (London, 1946)
        Mediaeval Political Thought (Penguin, 1965)
        Law and Politics in the Middle Ages (CUP, 1975)
        Jurisprudence in the Middle Ages (London, 1980)
Vinogradoff, P   *Roman Law in Mediaeval Europe* (Oxford, 2nd edn, 1929)
Yntema, H   'Equity in the Civil Law and the Common Law' *AJCompL* 15
        (1967) 60

D. (c) On canon law and ecclesiastical history:

Bowker, M, ed   *An Episcopal Court Book for the Diocese of Lincoln 1514–
        20* (Lincoln Record Society, 1967)
Bras, G le   'Canon law' in *The Legacy of the Middle Ages* (eds CG Crump &
        EF Jacob, Oxford, 1926)
        L'âge classique 1140–1378 (Paris, 1965)
Brundage, JA   Law, *Sex and Christian Society in Medieval Europe* (Chicago
        & London, 1987)
        Medieval Canon Law (London 1995)
Cheney, CR   *Episcopal Visitation of Monasteries in the Thirteenth Century*
        (Manchester, 2nd edn, 1983)
C Duggan   *Decretals and the Creation of the 'New Law' in the Twelfth
        Century: Judges, Judgements, Equity and Law* (Aldershot, 1998)
Ferguson, PC   *Medieval Papal Representatives in Scotland* (Stair Society
        vol.45, Edinburgh, 1997)
Gaudemet, J   *Le gouvernement de l'Église à l'Époque classique: le
        gouvernement local* (Paris, 1979)
        La formation du droit canonique médiéval (London, 1980)
        Église et société en Occident au Moyen Age (London, 1984)
Helmholz, RH   *Marriage Litigation in Medieval England* (CUP, 1974)
        'Excommunication as a legal sanction' *ZSS* (*Kan*) 68 (1982) 202
        Roman Canon Law in Reformation England (CUP, 1990)
        The Spirit of Classical Canon Law (University of Georgia Press, 1996)
Hill, RMT, ed   *The Rolls and Register of Bishop Oliver Sutton, 1280–99*
        (Lincoln Record Society, 1948–1969)
        History of Medieval Canon Law series (Catholic University of
        America Press, 1998–)
Jullien, A   *Juges et avocats des tribunaux de l'Église* (Paris, 1970)

Kuttner, S   *Harmony from Dissonance*, reprinted in *The History of Ideas and Doctrines of Canon Law in the Middle Ages* (Aldershot, rev'd edn, 1992)
Medieval Councils, Decretals and Collections of Canon Law (Aldershot, rev'd edn, 1992)
Gratian and the Schools of Law, 1140–1234 (London, 1983)
Studies in the History of Medieval Canon Law (Aldershot, 1991)
Ollivant, S   *The Court of the Official in pre-Reformation Scotland* (Stair Society vol 34, Edinburgh, 1982)
Robinson, OF   'Canon law and marriage' *JurRev* (1984) 22
'Canon law in theory and in practice' *Index* 22 (1994)
ed. *The Register of Walter Bronescombe, Bishop of Exeter 1258-80*, vols 1 & 2 (Canterbury and York Society vols 82 & 87, 1995 & 1999)
Russell, FH   *The Just War in the Middle Ages* (CUP, 1975)
Scanlan, JD   'The tribunal of the Sacred Roman Rota' *JurRev* (1969) 97
Schrage, E   '*Descendit ad inferos*: And Belial sued Jesus Christ for trespass' in *Critical Studies in Ancient Law, Comparative Law and Legal History* eds JW Cairns & OF Robinson (Richard Hart, 2000) ch 29
Southern, RW   *Western Society and the Church in the Middle Ages* (Penguin, 1970)
Sweeney, JR & S Chodorow, eds   *Popes, Teachers and Canon Law in the Middle Ages* (Cornell UP, 1989)
JAF Thomson   *The Western Church in the Middle Ages* (London, 1998)
Tierney, B   *The Crisis of Church and State, 1050–1300* (Englewood Cliffs, New Jersey, 1964)
Church Law and Constitutional Thought in the Middle Ages (London, 1979)
Tillman, H   *Pope Innocent III* (London, 1980)
Ullmann, W   *The Growth of Papal Government in the Middle Ages* (London, 3rd edn, 1970)
The Church and the Law (London, 1975)
Vetulani, A   *Institutions de l'Église et canonistes au moyen âge* (Aldershot, 1990)
Sur Gratien et les Décrétales (Aldershot, 1990)
Vodola, E   *Excommunication in the Middle Ages* (Berkeley, 1986)

D. (d) On the Law Merchant the basic monograph remains:

Goldschmidt, L   *Handbuch des Handelsrechts* (Stuttgart, various edns, 1868–91)

Also worth consultation are:

Baker, JH   'The Law Merchant and the Common Law before 1700' *CLJ* 38 (1979) 295
Bautier, RH   *The Economic Development of Mediaeval Europe* (London, 1971)
Gross, G,   ed *Select Cases concerning the Law Merchant, 1270–1638* (Selden Society, vol 23, 1908)
Holdsworth, WS   *A History of English Law*, vol V, 60–154; vol VIII, 99–300
Hyde, JK   *Society and Politics in Medieval Italy* (London, 1973)
Jackson, AM *Glasgow Dean of Guild Court: a History* (Glasgow, 1983)

Jados, SS, tr   *Consulate of the Sea and Related Documents* (Alabama, 1975)
Jenks, E   'The early history of negotiable instruments' *LQR* 9 (1893) 70
Lopez, RS   *The Commercial Revolution of the Middle Ages 950–1350* (CUP, 1976)
Lopez, RS & IW   Raymond *Medieval Trade in the Mediterranean World* (London–New York, 1955)
Mitchell, W   *Early History of the Law Merchant* (CUP, 1904)
Roover, R de   *Money, Banking and Credit in Medieval Bruges* (Cambridge, Mass, 1948)
   'The organization of trade' in *Cambridge Economic History* vol III (CUP, 1963)
   Business, Banking and Economic Thought (Chicago, 1974)
Roseveare, H ed   *Markets and Merchants of the late Seventeenth Century* (OUP, 1988)
Stein, P   'The mutual agency of partners' *TulLR* 33 (1959) 595
Usher, AP   *The Early History of Deposit Banking* (Cambridge, Mass, 1943)

On notaries:

Abbondanza, R, ed   *Il notariato a Perugia* (Rome, 1973)
Barraclough, G   *Public Notaries and the Papal Curia* (London, 1934)
Cheney, CR   *Notaries Public in England* (Oxford, 1972)
Costamagna, G   *Il notario a Genova tra prestigio e potere* (Rome, 1970)
Durkan, J   'The early Scottish notary' in *The Renaissance and Reformation in Scotland. Essays in honour of G Donaldson* (eds IB Cowan & D Shaw, Edinburgh, 1983)
   Gepasseerd: de rol en positie van notarissen in het verleden (Gerard Noodt Instituut, Nijmegen, 1987)
Petrucci, A   *Notarii: Documenti per la storia del notariato italiano* (Milan, 1958)
Stein, P & CW Brooks & RH Helmholz   *Notaries Public in England since the Reformation* (London, 1991) (Italian edition: *Notari in Inghilterra prima e dopo la Riforma* (Milan, 1991), which includes a translation of Cheney, in the series *Per una storia del notariato nella civiltà europea*)

D. (e) On English law:

Baker, JH   *The Order of Serjeants at Law* (London, 1984)
   The Legal Profession and the Common Law: Historical Essays (London, 1986)
   An Introduction to English Legal History (London, 3rd edn, 1990)
   'The third university of England: the inns of court and the common law tradition' (Selden Society Lecture 1990)
   The Common Law Tradition: Lawyers, Books and the Law (London, 1999)
Baker, JH & SFC Milsom   *Sources of English Legal History: Private Law to 1750* (London, 1986)
Barton, J   *Roman Law in England* (IRMAE V 13a, Milan, 1971)
Bush, JA & A Wijffels eds   *Learning the Law: Teaching and Transmission of English law 1150-1900* (London & Rio Grande, 1999)

Caenegem, RC van *Royal Writs in England from the Conquest to Glanvill* (Selden Society, vol 77, 1958–59)
    The Birth of the English Common Law (CUP, 2nd edn, 1988)
Clanchy, MT *England and its Rulers 1066–1272* (Fontana, 1983)
Coquillette, DR *The Civilian Writers of Doctors' Commons, England* (Berlin, 1988)
    The Anglo-American Legal Heritage. Introductory Materials (Durham NC, 2000)
Cornish, WR & G de N Clark *Law and Society in England 1750–1950* (London, 1989)
Fifoot, CHS *Lord Mansfield* (Oxford, 1936)
Harding, A *The Law Courts of Mediaeval England* (London, 1973)
Holdsworth, WS *History of English Law* – 16 vols, various editions
Ibbetson, DJ   *An Historical Introduction to the Law of Obligations* (OUP, 1999)
Lloyn, HR *The Governance of Anglo-Saxon England 500–1087* (London, 1984)
Manchester, AH *A Modern Legal History of England and Wales 1750–1950* (London, 1980)
    Sources of English Legal History. Law, History and Society in England and Wales 1750–1950 (London, 1984)
Milsom, SFC *Historical Foundations of the Common Law* (London, 2nd edn, 1981)
Oldham, J *The Mansfield Manuscripts and the Growth of English Law in the Eighteenth Century* (London, 1992)
Plucknett, TFT *A Concise History of the Common Law* (London, 5th edn, 1956)
Simpson, AWB *Legal Theory and Legal History. Essays in the Common Law* (London, 1987)
Squibb, GD *The High Court of Chivalry* (Oxford, 1959)
    Doctors' Commons (Oxford, 1977)
Whitelock, D *The Beginnings of English Society (The Anglo-Saxon Period)* (Penguin, 1952)
Wormald, P   *The Making of English Law*, vol 1: *King Alfred to the Twelfth Century* (Blackwell, 1999)

D. (f) On the fifteenth and sixteenth centuries:

Chadwick, O *The Reformation* (Penguin, 1972)
Coing, H 'Roman law as the *ius commune* of the continent' *LQR* 89 (1973) 505
Dawson, JP 'The codification of the French customs' *MichLR* 38 (1940) 765
    The Oracles of the Law (Ann Arbor, 1968)
Durkan, J 'Henry Scrimgeour, Renaissance bookman' *Edinburgh Bibliographical Society Transactions* 5 (1971–74) 1
Franklin, JH *Jean Bodin and the Sixteenth Century Revolution in the Methodology of Law and History* (New York & London, 1963)
Gilmore, MP *The World of Humanism* (New York, 1952)
    Humanists and Jurists (Harvard UP, 1963)
Hazeltine, HD 'The Renaissance and the laws of Europe' in *Cambridge Legal Essays* (CUP, 1926) 139
Helmholz, RH   *Canon Law in Protestant Lands* (Berlin, 1992)

Kelley, DR   *Foundations of Modern Historical Scholarship* (Columbia UP, 1970)
   History, Law and the Human Sciences (London, 1984)
Kisch, G   *Studien zur humanistischen Jurisprudenz* (Berlin, 1972)
Kunkel, W   'The reception of Roman law in Germany: an interpretation' in *Pre-Reformation Germany* (ed G Strauss, London, 1972)
Maclean, I   *Interpretation and Meaning in the Renaissance. The Case of Law* (CUP, 1992)
McNeil, DO   *Guillaume Budé and Humanism in the reign of Francis I* (Geneva, 1975)
Maffei, D   *Gli inizi dell'Umanesimo giuridico* (Milan, 1968)
Mortari, VP   *Diritto romano e diritto nazionale in Francia nel secolo xvi* (Milan, 1962)
Osler, DJ   'Graecum legitur' *RHJ* 2 (1983) 194
Prest, W, ed   *Lawyers in Early Modern Europe and America* (London, 1981)
Rodgers, CP   'Humanism, history and the Common Law' *JLH* 6 (1985) 129
Shennan, JH   *The Parlement of Paris* (London, 1968)
Stein, P   'Elegance in law' *LQR* 77 (1961) 242
Strauss, G   *Law, Resistance and the State. The Opposition to Roman Law in Reformation Germany* (Princeton UP, 1986)
Wacke, A   'The reception of Roman law in Germany' *Lesotho Law Journal* 1 (1985) 165
Zulueta, F de   *Don Antonio Agustín* (Murray Lecture, Glasgow, 1939)

D. (g) On the seventeenth and eighteenth centuries:

Arnaud, AJ   *Les origines doctrinales du Code Civil français* (Paris, 1969)
Barbour, V   *Capitalism in Seventeenth Century Amsterdam* (Baltimore, 1950)
Bergh, GCJJ van der   *The Life and Work of Gerard Noodt, 1647–1725* (Oxford, 1988)
Broadie, A ed   *The Scottish Enlightenment: an Anthology* (Canongate Classics vol 80, Edinburgh, 1997)
Brownlie, I   *Basic Documents on Human Rights* (Oxford, 1971)
Cairns, JW   'Blackstone, an English institutist: legal literature and the rise of the nation state' *OJLSt* 4 (1984) 318
Carey, JS   *Judicial Reform in France before the Revolution of 1789* (Harvard UP, 1981)
D'Entrèves, AP   *Natural Law* (London, 1951)
Feenstra R & CJD Waal   *Seventeenth Century Leyden Law Professors and their Influence on the Development of the Civil Law* (Amsterdam, 1975)
Finnis, J   *Natural Law and Natural Rights* (Oxford, 1980)
Gorla, G & L Moccia   'A "revisiting" of the comparison between "continental" law and English law' *JLH* 2 (1981) 143
Haakonssen, K   *Grotius, Pufendorf and Modern Natural Law* (Aldershot, 1999)
Jones, P & AS Skinner, eds   *Adam Smith Reviewed* (Edinburgh, 1992)
Kupiszewski, H & W Wolodkiewicz, eds   *Le droit romain et sa réception en Europe* (Warsaw, 1978)
Lloyd, Lord   *An Introduction to Jurisprudence* (London, 5th edn by Lord Lloyd & MDA Freeman, 1985)

Luig, K   'The institutes of national law in the seventeenth and eighteenth
centuries' *JurRev* (1972) 193
MacLean, AJ   'Jeremy Bentham and the Scottish legal system' *JurRev* (1979) 21
Maillet, J   'The historical significance of the French codifications' *TulLR* 44
(1970) 681
Peterson, C   *Peter the Great's Administrative and Judicial Reforms: Swedish
Antecedents and the Process of Reception* (Stockholm, 1979)
Seipp, D   'The structure of English Common Law in the seventeenth century'
in *Legal History in the Making* (eds WM Gordon & TD Fergus,
London, 1991)
Stein, P   'The attraction of the civil law in post-revolutionary America' *VirgLR*
52 (1966) 403
Legal Evolution (CUP, 1980)
Strakosch, H   *State Absolutism and the Rule of Law* (Sydney UP, 1967)
Thieme, H   *Das Naturrecht und die europäische Privatrechtsgeschichte*
(Basel, 2nd edn, 1954)
Turpin, CC   'The antecedents of Roman Dutch law' *AJ* (1963) 1
Vanderlinden, J   *Le concept de code en Europe occidentale* (Brussels, 1967)
Watson, A   *Legal Transplants* (Edinburgh, 1974)
The Making of the Civil Law (Harvard UP, 1981)
Wesener, G   'Kaspar Manz, a German jurist in the seventeenth century' in
Critical Studies in Ancient Law, Comparative Law and Legal History
ed JW Cairns & OF Robinson (Richard Hart, 2000) ch 33
Williams, D ed   *The Enlightenment* (CUP, 1999)
Zimmermann, R   'Roman-Dutch jurisprudence and its contribution to
European private law' *TulLR* 66 (1992) 1685
Zweigert, K & H Kötz (tr T Weir)   *An Introduction to Comparative Law*
(Amsterdam–Oxford, 3rd edn, 1998)

D. (h) On the nineteenth and twentieth centuries and thereafter:

Allen, CK   *Law in the Making* (Oxford, 7th edn, 1964)
Alvarez A et al,   *The Progress of Continental Law in the Nineteenth Century*
(Continental Legal History series, vol XI, Boston, 1918)
Atiyah, PS   *The Rise and Fall of Freedom of Contract* (Oxford, 1979)
Berger, M   'Codification' in *Perspectives in Jurisprudence* (ed EMM
Attwooll, Glasgow, 1977)
Blackie J & N Whitty   'Scots law and the new *ius commune*' in *Scots Law
into the Twenty-first Century* ed HL MacQueen
Cappelletti M et al, *The Italian Legal System: an Introduction* (Stanford UP, 1967)
Chalmers, D   *European Union Law* I-II (Aldershot, 1998)
Christie, J Roberton   'Joint-stock enterprise in Scotland before the Companies
Acts (1909–10)' *JurRev* 21 (1909–1910) 128
Coing, H & W Wilhelm, eds   *Wissenschaft und Kodifikation des Privatrechts
im 19ten Jahrhundert* (Frankfurt, 1974–)
Cornish, WR & G de N Clark   *Law and Society in England 1750–1950*
(London, 1989)
Dahn, F   'The new code for the German Empire' *JurRev* (1890) 15
David, R 'The international unification of private law' in *International
Encyclopedia of Comparative Law*, vol II, ch 5

David R & JEC Brierley   *Major Legal Systems in the World Today* (London, 2nd edn, 1978)

Dawson, JP   '*Negotiorum gestio*: the altruistic intermeddler' *HLR* 74 (1961) 817; 1073
  The Oracles of the Law (Ann Arbor, 1968)
  Gifts and Promises (Yale, 1980)

Dicey, AV   *Law and Public Opinion in England* (London, 2nd edn, 1914)

Edward, DAO   'A little cloud like a man's hand' *Journal of the Law Society of Scotland* 30 (1985) 10

Feenstra, R   'The Dutch *kantheros* case and the history of *error in substantia*' *Tul LR* 48 (1974) 846

Fergus, TD   'Women and the parliamentary franchise in Great Britain' in *The Legal Relevance of Gender*, ed S McLean & N Burrows (London, 1988)

Foster N, ed   *Blackstone's EEC Legislation* (London, 10th edn, 1999)

Friedmann, W   *Legal Theory* (London, 5th edn, 1967)

Gordon, WM   'Property and Succession Rights' in *The Legal Relevance of Gender*, ed S McLean & N Burrows (London, 1988)

Hahlo, HR   'Early progenitors of the modern company' *JurRev* (1982), 139

Hedemann, JW *Die Fortschritten des Zivilrechts im XIX Jahrhundert* (Berlin, 1910)

Horn, N & J Kocka, eds   *Law and the Formation of the Big Enterprises in the Nineteenth and early Twentieth Centuries* (Göttingen, 1979)

Hunt, BC   *The Development of the Business Corporation in England* (Cambridge, Mass, 1936)

Ibbetson DJ   'A reply to Professor Zimmermann' in *The Europeanisation of Law* ed TE Watkin

John, M   *Politics and the Law in Late Nineteenth Century Germany. The Origins of the Civil Code* (Oxford, 1989)

Joll, J   *Europe Since 1870* (Penguin, 4th edn, 1990)

Jones, PK jnr   'Roman law bases of suretyship in some modern civil codes' *Tul LR* 52 (1977–78) 129

Kantorowicz, H   'Savigny and the Historical School of law' *LQR* 53 (1937) 326

MacQueen, HL, ed   *Scots Law into the Twenty-first Century: Essays in Honour of WA Wilson* (Edinburgh, 1996)

Manchester, AH   *A Modern Legal History of England and Wales 1750–1950* (London, 1980)

Orth, JV   *Combination and Conspiracy: a Legal History of Trade Unionism* (Oxford, 1991)

Osler, D   'The myth of European legal history' *RHS* 16 (1997) 393

Paul, C and G de Burca   *The Evolution of European Union Law* (Oxford, 1999)

Payne, PL   *Entrepreneurship in the Nineteenth Century* (London, 1974)

Pelling, H   *A History of British Trade Unionism* (Penguin, 2nd edn, 1976)

Rodger, AF   'The codification of commercial law in Victorian Britain' *LQR* 108 (1992) 570

Rotondi, M, ed   *La science du droit au cours du dernier siècle* (Padua, 1976)

Rubin, GR & D Sugarman, eds   *Law, Economy and Society* (London, 1984)

Santuari, A   'The joint-stock company in nineteenth century England and France' *JLH* 14 (1993) 39

Schmidt, F 'The abstract approach of the BGB' *Scandinavian Studies in Law* 9 (1965) 131

Schulze, R & T Hoeren, eds *Dokumente zum Europäischen Recht I–II* (Berlin 1999)

Schwartz, B, ed *The Code Napoléon and the Common Law World* (New York, 1956)

Schwarz, AB *Rechtsgeschichte und Gegenwart* (eds H Thieme & F Wieacker, Karlsruhe, 1960)

Stein, P *Legal Evolution* (CUP, 1980)

Thomson D *Europe since Napoleon* (Penguin, 2nd edn, 1966)

Usher, JA, ed The State of the European Union: Structure, Enlargement and Economic Union (Longman, Harlow, 2000)

Villey, M *La formation de la pensée juridique moderne* (Paris, 1980)

Watkin, TG, ed *The Europeanisation of Law* (UKNCCL, 1998)

Whitman, JQ *The Legacy of Roman Law in the German Romantic Era* (Princeton UP, 1990)

Williams, I *The Sources of Law in the Swiss Civil Code* (Oxford, 1923)

Wyatt D & A Dashwood *European Community Law* (London, 3rd edn, 1993)

Zimmermann, R *The Law of Obligations: Roman Foundations of the Civilian Tradition* (Capetown, 1990)
    'Savigny's legacy – legal history, comparative law and the emergence of a European legal science' in *The Europeanisation of Law* ed TG Watkin

D. (i) On the history of Scots law we recommend:

Barrow, GWS *The Kingdom of the Scots* (London, 1973)
    The Anglo-Norman Era in Scottish History (Oxford, 1980)

Burleigh, JHS *A Church History of Scotland* (Oxford, 1960)

Cairns, JW 'Institutional writings in Scotland reconsidered' *JLH* 4 (1983) 76
    'Rhetoric, language and Roman law: legal education and improvement in eighteenth century Scotland' *LHR* 9 (1991) 31
    'John Spotswood, Professor of Law: a preliminary sketch' in *Miscellany III* (Stair Society vol 39, Edinburgh, 1992) 131
    'The origin of the Glasgow law school: the professors of the civil law' in *The Life of the Law* (ed PBH Birks, London, 1993)
    'The influence of the German Historical School in early nineteenth century Edinburgh', *Syracuse J of Int.Law & Commerce* 20 (1994) 191
    'The law, the advocates and the universities in late sixteenth century Scotland' *ScHR* 73 (1994) 171
    'From "speculative" to "practical" legal education: the decline of the Glasgow law school, 1801-30', *TR* 62 (1994) 331
    '"As famous as a school of law as Edinburgh for medicine": the Glasgow law school, 1761-1801' in *The Glasgow Enlightenment*, ed A Hook & R Sher (East Linton, 1995)
    'Scottish law, Scottish lawyers and the status of the Union' in *A Union for Empire. Political Thought and the British Union of 1707*, ed J Robertson (CUP, 1995) 243
    Introduction to Scotish Legal History (Blackstone Press, 2000)

Cairns, JW, TD Fergus & HL MacQueen   'Legal Humanism in Renaissance Scotland' *JLH* 11 (1990) 40

Carey Miller DL & R Zimmermann, eds   *The Civilian Tradition and Scots Law: Aberdeen Quincentenary Essays* (Berlin, 1997)

Cowan, IB   *The Scottish Reformation* (London, 1982)
ed. J Kirk, *The Mediaeval Church in Scotland* (Edinburgh, 1995)

Dickinson, W Croft   *The Sheriff Court Book of Fife 1515–22* (Sc Hist Soc vol 12, 1928)
The Court Book of the Barony of Carnwath (Sc Hist Soc, 1937)
Early Records of the Burgh of Aberdeen (Sc Hist Soc, 1957)
'The administration of justice in mediaeval Scotland' *Aberdeen University Review* 34 (1951–52) 338
Scotland from the Earliest Times to 1603 (Oxford, 3rd edn (rev'd by AAM Duncan), 1977)

Donaldson, G   *The Scottish Reformation* (CUP, 1960)
Scotland: James V to James VII (Edinburgh, 1971)

Duncan, AMM   '*Regiam Maiestatem* – a reconsideration', *JurRev* (1961) 199
Scotland: The Making of the Kingdom (Edinburgh, 1975)

Evans-Jones, R, ed   *The Civil Law Tradition in Scotland* (Stair Society supplementary vol 2, Edinburgh, 1995)

Ferguson, W   *Scotland: 1689 to the Present* (Edinburgh, 1968)

Galloway, BR & BP Levack   *The Jacobean Union. Six Tracts of 1604* (Sc Hist Soc, Edinburgh, 1985)

Gilbert, JM   *Hunting and Hunting Reserves in Medieval Scotland* (Edinburgh, 1979)

Gordon, WM   'Roman law in Scotland' in *The Civil Law Tradition in Scotland* ed R Evans-Jones (Stair Society, 1995)

Hannay, RK   *The College of Justice. Essays by RK Hannay* (Stair Society, supplementary series vol 1, ed HL MacQueen, Edinburgh, 1990)

Jackson, AM   *Glasgow Dean of Guild Court* (Glasgow, 1983)

Jones, C, ed   *The Scots and Parliament* (Edinburgh UP, 1996)

Levack, BP   'The proposed union of English and Scots law' *JurRev* (1975) 97

Levie, WE   'Celtic tribal law and custom in Scotland' *JurRev* 39 (1927) 191

Macfarlane, LJ   *William Elphinstone and the Kingdom of Scotland 1431–1514* (Aberdeen UP, 2nd edn, 1995)

McKechnie, H   *Judicial Process upon Brieves 1219–1532* (Murray Lecture, Glasgow, 1956)

MacLean, AJ   'The 1707 Union: Scots law and the House of Lords' *JLH* 4 (1983) 50

McNeill, PGB   'The passing of the Scottish Privy Council' *JurRev* (1965) 263

MacQueen, HL   'The brieve of right in Scots law' *JLH* 3 (1982) 52
'Scots law under Alexander III' in *Scotland in the Reign of Alexander III, 1248–86* (ed NH Reid, Edinburgh, 1990) 74
'The laws of Galloway: a preliminary study' in *Galloway. Land and Lordship* (eds G Stell & R Oram, Edinburgh, 1991) 131
Common Law and Feudal Society in Medieval Scotland (Edinburgh, 1993)
ed   *Scots Law into the Twenty-first Century: Essays in honour of WA Wilson* (Edinburgh, 1996)

MacQueen HL & WJ Windram   'Laws and courts in the burghs' in *The Scottish Medieval Town* (eds M Lynch et al, Edinburgh, 1988) 208

MacQueen, J, ed   *Humanism in Renaissance Scotland* (Edinburgh, 1990)

Nicholson, R   *Scotland: The Later Middle Ages* (Edinburgh, 1974)

Phillipson, NT   *The Scottish Whigs and the Court of Session 1785–1830* (Stair Society vol 37, Edinburgh, 1990)

Reid, KGC and R Zimmermann, eds   *History of the Private Law of Scotand* 2 vols (OUP, 2000)

Robertson, JJ   'The development of the law' in *Scottish Society in the Fifteenth Century* (ed J Brown, London, 1977)

Rodger, AF   'Scottish advocates in the ninetenth centruy: the German "connection"' *LQR* 110 (1994) 563

Sanderson, MHB   *Scottish Rural Society in the Sixteenth Century* (Edinburgh, 1982)

Sellar, WDH   'Celtic law and Scots law: survival and integration' *Scottish Studies* 29 (1989) 1
  'The common law of Scotland and the common law of England' in *The British Isles 1100–1500* (ed RR Davies, Edinburgh, 1988) 82
  'A historical perspective' in *The Scottish Legal Tradition* (ed SC Styles, Edinburgh, 1991)
  Introduction to Scottish Legal History (Butterworths, 2000)

Smith, TB   Scotland: *The Development of its Laws and Constitution* (London, 1962)
  Studies Critical and Comparative (Edinburgh, 1962)

Smith, TB et al, eds   *The Laws of Scotland: Stair Memorial Encyclopaedia*, vol 22, 'Sources of Law' (Edinburgh, 1987)

Stein, P   'The influence of Roman law on the law of Scotland' *JurRev* (1963) 205
  Roman Law in Scotland (IRMAE V 13b, Milan, 1968)
  'The source of the romano-canonical part of *Regiam Majestatem*' *Scottish Historical Review* 48 (1969) 107

Sutherland, R   *Lord Stair and the Law of Scotland* (Glasgow, 1981)

Tompson, RS   'James Greenshields and the House of Lords: a reappraisal' in *Legal History in the Making* (eds WM Gordon & TD Fergus, London, 1991) 109

Walker, DM   *Scottish Legal System* (Edinburgh, 7th edn, 1997)
  The Scottish Jurists (Edinburgh, 1985)
  A Legal History of Scotland (Greens, Edinburgh, 1988–) [This work assembles a huge quantity of material but is deficient in the analysis and independent assessment of these sources.]

Webster, B   *Scotland from the Eleventh Century to 1603* (CUP, 1975)

Whetstone, AE   *Scottish County Government in the Eighteenth and Nineteenth Century* (Edinburgh, 1981)

Wilson, WA   *Introductory Essays on Scots Law* (Edinburgh, 2nd edn, 1984)

Wormald, J, gen ed   *The New History of Scotland* (8 vols by various authors, London, 1981–1984; now Edinburgh)

and many articles from the *Juridical Review* (Edinburgh, 1888–) and *The Stair Memorial Encyclopaedia*

Scottish Texts and Calendars (eds D & WB Stevenson, Sc Hist Soc, Edinburgh, 1987) provides a guide to serial publications on Scottish history; these include many editions of legal texts. The Stair Society's publications are devoted to the history of Scots law; they include *Regiam Majestatem* and other sources, such as Balfour's *Practicks*, or Baron Hume's *Lectures*. Volume 1 (1936) surveys the sources and literature of Scots law; the bibliography is brought up to date by WJ Windram and HL McQueen 'The sources and literature of Scots law: a select critical bibliography, 1936-82' *JLH* 4 (1983), 1 (repr in *New Perspectives in Scottish Legal History* (eds A Kiralfy and HL McQueen, London, 1984)). An extremely useful bibliography of literature on the theme of Roman law and Scots law is by WM Gordon in *The Civil Law Tradition*, ed R Evans-Jones, 310. Also of particular use explicitly as an introduction to Scottish legal history is Stair Society vol 20 (1958).

INDEX

The Index is designed to be used in conjunction with the Contents. For example, French customs are given the fullest treatment in Chapter 12, but the paragraphs relevant to France in Chapters 7 and 15 should also be consulted.

There are too few cases and statutes for separate tables, and so both are listed in their alphabetical place, eg *Taff Vale* under T.

Rulers are listed before other persons in the order: Popes, Emperors, Kings and other rulers. (P = Pope, Byz E = Byzantine Emperor, HRE = Holy Roman Emperor, K = King, Q = Queen.) Like rulers, mediaeval men are normally to be found under their first names. Dates, especially mediaeval ones, may be approximate. Rulers' dates are normally of their rule.

Within a major heading it is the keywords which provide the alphabetical order.

canon law – *contd*
procedure. *See* procedure, canonical.
See also church courts
canonist defined 2.9.4. *See also*
Decretist, Decretalist
canons defined 1.4.2; 5.1.1
Canossa (1077) 1.13.3–4
Canterbury 1.14.6; 5.7.2; 8.2.2–3;
8.9.11. *See also* Arches, Court of
Canute (Cnut), K of Denmark &
England (1016–35) 8.2.6; 8.5.1
Capet, Hugh, K of France (987–96) &
Capetian dynasty 1.10.4; 2.8.3;
7.5.4
capitularies 1.9.4
feudal 2.2.1; 9.2.1–2
Forged 1.11.2
of Quierzy 2.4.4
Carmer, C von (1721–1801) 15.5.4
*Carolina = constitutio criminalis
Carolina* (1532) 11.4.1; 11.5.1–2;
13.4.3
Carolingian Franks 1.7.4; 1.8.6; 1.9;
1.10; 1.11.5–8; 2.1.3; 2.5.1; 2.5.3;
6.1.1
Carpzov, Benedikt (1595–1666) 7.3.9;
11.3.6; 11.4.4; 11.5.4; 14.2.2;
15.4.1
cartularies 1.14.5
Casale Monferrato 4.6.2
cases. *See* individual names
reports of. *See* reports
Cassation, Court de 16.5.2–2
Castile, New and Old 7.6; 13.2.5
Castile-León 7.6
castles 8.5.4. *See also* feudalism
casualties. *See* feudal obligations
casus 3.7.1; 3.7.4; 4.5.3
Catalonia 1.9.3; 1.10.1; 1.11.4; 7.6.1;
7.6.5
Catalan language 6.3.5
Cateau-Cambrésis, Treaty of (1559)
10.1.8
cathedral chapter 5.7.3
Catherine II, E of Russia (1762–96)
15.2.6
Catherine de Medici (1519–89), Q of
France 10.1.8
Catholic Church 5.1.1. *See also* canon
law; Orthodox
Roman 5.1.1; 10.1.7. *See also*
Protestantism
causa 5.3.6; 5.9.3–4
Celestine I, P (422–32) 1.4.2–3
Celtic peoples and customs 9.1; 9.2.1
Ceylon 13.4.4

Chalcedon, General Council of (451)
1.4.2–3; 1.6.1
chamberlain, king's (in Scotland)
9.2.4–5; 9.7.5
Chambres of the *Parlement* of Paris
7.5.10–11. *See also* Paris,
Parlement of
Champagne, fairs of 6.5.1–3
chancellor and chancery in England
6.5.5; 7.7.6; 8.2.6; 8.5.8; 8.6.9–10;
8.6.11; 8.8.1; 8.8.5; 8.9.2–7; 8.10.2–3
in Scotland 9.7.5; 9.7.8; 14.3.1
Charlemagne, K of the Franks (768–
814) & E (800–14) 1.8.6; 1.9.3–4;
1.11.2; 2.6.1; 2.9.1
Charles IV, HRE (1347–78) 11.1.2
Charles V, HRE (1519–58) = Charles I
of Spain 10.1.3; 10.8.2; 11.1.3;
11.5.1; 13.4.3
Charles V, K of France (1364–80) 7.5.6
Charles VII, K of France (1422–61)
7.5.6; 12.5.1
Charles IV, K of Spain (1788–1808)
7.6.6
Charles Albert of Piedmont (1831–49)
16.1.4
Charles of Anjou, K of Naples (1266–
85) 4.1.3; 4.2.3
Charles the Fat (881–87) 1.10.1
Charles Martel of the Franks (Mayor
719–41) 1.7.4; 1.9.1
Charles (Karolus) de Tocco (early 13c)
2.9.1; 3.8.4
charters, Merovingian and Carolingian
1.11.3–8. *See also* capitularies,
feudal
Châtelet 7.5.5; 15.7.1
children at work. *See* employment law
China 16.4.9
Chivalry, Court of 8.9.8
Christian V, K of Denmark (1670–99)
15.3.6
Christianity, introduction of 1.3.4; 5.1.3
survival in Britain 1.7.1; 8.2.2
Christina, Q of Sweden (1632–54)
13.2.7
Church 1.3.4; 1.4; 5 *passim*
courts 5.1.2; 7.4.3; 7.7.1–2; 8.1.1;
8.9.11; 10.8.2; 11.2.5; 13.4.2;
14.1.3–5; 14.5.1; 14.5.4
Doctors of the 1.4.1
Early 1.4; 1.6; 1.13.1
Roman Catholic as compared to
Reformed 10.8.2; 10.8.6
Cicero (106–43 BC) 1.1.1; 1.14.6;
10.5.1; 10.5.7; 13.2.2; 13.2.10

Windscheid, Bernhard (1817–92)
16.3.5; 16.4.4; 16.4.5
Windsor, Assize of (1179) 8.6.8
Wisby 6.3.5. *See also Waterrecht*
witan 8.2.6; 8.3.1; 8.4.4; 8.5.2; 8.3.4;
8.4.4; 8.5.2. *See also* Council, King's
Wolff, Christian (1679–1754) 13.2.11;
13.3.7; 15.4.2; 15.5.6; 15.5.7;
15.7.1; 16.2.1; 16.3.2
women, legal status of 8.4.4; 17.1.8;
18.1.3; 18.3.1–4; 18.10
World War I (1914–18) 17.1.2; 17.3.6–
8; 17.4.9; 18.0; 18.3.3; 18.5.1
II (1939–45) 18.0; 18.5.1–2
Worms 6.5.4; 11.5.3
Concordat of (1122) 1.13.4
Diet of (1521) 10.1.4
writers, Writers to the Signet 14.5.7; 14.5.8
writing, written law 1.5.1–3; 1.8.2–3;
2.2.1; 2.8.1; 2.9.6; 2.9.8; 3.1.2;
4.6.1; 6.6.9; 7.3.5; 7.6.2; 8.5.6;
9.6; 10.4.4; 11.1.5–6; 12.2.2–3

writs 8.5.6; 8.5.8; 8.6.3; 8.6.9–11;
8.7.2; 8.8.5; 8.8.6; 8.9.3. *See also*
brieves
writ of right 8.6.8; 8.6.11
Würtemburg 7.4.1

Year Books 8.7.2; 8.8.6; 8.8.8
York–Antwerp rules 17.5.1; 17.5.3
Yugoslavia 15.6.5

Zasius, Ulrich (1461–1536) 7.4.3;
10.3.4; 11.3.8; 11.4.2; 11.5.6
Zeeland 13.2.7; 13.4.3
Zeiller, Franz von (1753–1828) 15.6.2
*Zeitschrift für geschichtliche
Rechtswissenschaft* 16.2.4
ZGB (East German civil code) 18.4.5
ZGB = *Zivilgesetzbuch* (Swiss civil
code) 15.7.11; 16.6; 18.2.1
Zouche, Richard (1590–1661) 13.5.3
Zürich 10.1.5; 16.6.1
Zwingli, Ulrich (1484–1531) 10.1.5

Printed in Great Britain
by Amazon

59900778R00233